Homeland and National Security

UNDERSTANDING AMERICA'S PAST TO PROTECT THE FUTURE

Dr. Monique M. Chouraeshkenazi

Bassim Hamadeh, CEO and Publisher

Mary Jane Peluso, Senior Specialist Acquisitions Editor

Leah Sheets, Associate Editor

Christian Berk, Associate Production Editor

Jess Estrella, Senior Graphic Designer

Alexa Lucido, Licensing Associate

Don Kesner, Interior Designer

Natalie Piccotti, Senior Marketing Manager

Kassie Graves, Director of Acquisitions and Sales

Jamie Giganti, Senior Managing Editor

ISBN: 978-1-5165-1894-4 (pbk) / 978-1-5165-1895-1 (br)

Homeland and National Security

UNDERSTANDING AMERICA'S PAST TO PROTECT THE FUTURE

CONTENTS

Foreword..x

Endorsement..xii

Dr. Ash Carter Bio...xiv

Acknowledgements..xviii

Preface...xxii

About the Author..xxiv

List of Figures...xxvi

CHAPTER 1 The Evolution of American Policy: Timelines,
Events, & Conflicts..2

    Introduction..3

    French and Indian War...3

    American Revolutionary War..4

    The Aftermath of the American Revolution..5

    The French Revolution..10

    The Jefferson Era and Manifest Destiny..15

    American Civil War...19

    Spanish-American War...21

    Philippine-American War...23

    The Invasion of Panama (Operation Just Cause).....................................24

    The Mexican Revolution...25

    World War I..27

    World War II...29

    Cold War Era..32

    Post-Cold War Era..35

    Summary...36

    Chapter 1 Case Studies..37

    Chapter 1 Practice Problems..41

Chapter 2 Introduction to U.S. National Security..............................42

    Learning Objectives...42

    Key Terms..42

Introduction..43

National Values 43

National Interests...64

The Global Grid of Alliances and Adversaries.....................................68

The Universal Continuum of Conflict...71

American Federal Government, Politics, and Power.............................76

Summary..79

Chapter 2 Case Studies..79

Chapter 2 Practice Problems..83

Chapter 3 The Conceptualization of National Security............85

Learning Objectives...85

Key Terms..85

Introduction..86

The Institutionalization of National Security......................................88

Accountability of the President..89

The Goldwater-Nichols Act..90

National Security Act of 1947 and the National Security Council.....91

Evolution of the U.S. Military and Intelligence Communities...........94

Summary..128

Chapter 3 Case Studies..128

Chapter 3 Practice Problems..132

Chapter 4 National Security Methodologies and Policies.....135

Learning Objectives...135

Key Terms..135

Introduction..136

Policy Development and Decision Making..136

Military vs. Noncombatant Affairs...140

Summary..144

Chapter 4 Case Studies..145

Chapter 4 Practice Problems..148

Chapter 5 Introduction to Homeland Security: A Historical

Impression...149

Learning Objectives...149

Key Terms..149

Introduction: The Birth of Homeland Security..................................150

Homeland Security Act of 2002 and Department of Homeland Security........151

Leadership Roles and Chain of Command........153

DHS Agencies and Supporting Organizations........155

DHS Response Agency: FEMA and the Rise of Emergency Management in America........158

Emergency Services Sector........159

Local, State, and Federal Responsibilities........161

Civil Defense: America's Response........162

Summary........164

Chapter 5 Case Studies........165

Chapter 5 Practice Problems........169

Chapter 6 Historic Disasters: The Evolution of Homeland Security in the U.S.

........170

Learning Objectives........170

Key Terms........170

Introduction: Elijah Parish Lovejoy and American Terrorism........171

Attack on Pearl Harbor: 1948........174

United States Embassy Bombing: 1983........176

The First Attempt on the World Trade Center: 1993........178

The Oklahoma City Bombing and the Aftermath: 1995........180

Khobar Towers Bombing: 1996........182

USS Cole Bombing: 2000........183

9/11........185

Law Enforcement and Homeland Security........190

Summary........193

Chapter 6 Case Studies........194

Chapter 6 Practice Problems........197

Chapter 7 American Terrorism

........198

Learning Objectives........198

Key Terms........198

Introduction........199

Probing Modern Terrorism........206

Understanding Terrorism........207

International Terrorism........207

Domestic Extremism and Foreign Terrorist Organizations........215

World's Known Terrorists........239

Boston Marathon Bombing: 2013..248

San Bernardino Attacks: 2015..252

Orlando Nightclub Shooting: 2016..254

Agroterrorism..257

Cyberterrorism and Cybersecurity..258

Narcoterrorism..265

Summary..266

Chapter 7 Case Studies..267

Chapter 7 Practice Problems..270

Chapter 8 Homeland Security Statutes and Initiatives................271

Learning Objectives..271

Key Terms..271

Introduction..272

Nunn-Lugar Cooperative Threat Reduction Initiative..272

USA PATRIOT Act of 2001..273

USA FREEDOM ACT..275

Homeland Security
Act of 2002..276

Homeland Security Presidential Directive No. 5..278

The 9/11 Commission Report..280

Emergency Management Reform Act..282

DHS Legislation..283

Congressional Budgeting and Appropriations..285

Summary..290

Chapter 8 Case Studies..291

Chapter 8 Practice Problems..295

Chapter 9 Weapons of Mass Destruction and Preventative
Measures..296

Learning Objectives..296

Key Terms..296

Introduction..297

CBRNE Weapons..297

CBRNE Defense..306

Nuclear Warfare..308

Protective Methods and CDC Responsibilities..311

Summary..314

Chapter 9 Case Studies...315

Chapter 9 Practice Problems..319

Chapter 10 Intelligence and Security..................................320

Learning Objectives..320

Key Terms..320

Introduction..321

The Intelligence Community..321

U.S. Customs and Border Protection and Transportation Security
Administration...345

Critical Infrastructure, Industrial, and Utility Facilities...............................347

Railroad and Port Security..348

Emergency Operations: Government and Private Sector Planning..................351

Summary...353

Chapter 10 Case Studies..354

Chapter 10 Practice Problems..357

Chapter 11 Emergency Operating Procedures:
Preparedness and Mitigation...359

Learning Objectives..359

Key Terms..359

Introduction..360

CBRNE Preventative Measures..361

Radiological Dispersion Device (RDD) Events..367

Mitigation and Preparedness for Terrorist Acts...370

Civil-Government Relations and Exercise Planning......................................372

Summary...374

Chapter 11 Case Studies..374

Chapter 11 Practice Problems..378

Chapter 12 Communication, Response, Recovery,
and Technology..379

Learning Objectives..379

Key Terms..379

Crisis and Risk Management..380

Federal, State, and Local Response..381

National Incident Management System (NIMS)...382

Research and Development..384

Summary..385

Chapter 12 Case Studies...386

Chapter 12 Practice Problems..389

Chapter 13 Where National Security Meets Homeland
Security..391

Learning Objectives..391

Key Terms...391

Introduction...392

Congressional Roles and Involvement...392

National Security Advisor and Secretaries of Department and Homeland
Defense..394

Department of Defense (DoD) and Department of
Homeland Security (DHS)...398

Department of State (DoS) and Foreign Diplomacy..........................400

Homeland Security Strategy Goals...403

Summary..417

Chapter 13 Case Studies...418

Chapter 13 Practice Problems..419

Chapter 14 The Future of National and
Homeland Security...421

Learning Objectives..421

Key Terms...421

The Debate..422

Security Risks and Assessments...422

Top National Security Concerns...424

2015 National Security Strategy: President Barack Obama...............428

America's Internal War on Sustaining Global Roles
and Coalition Relations...454

Summary..458

Chapter 14 Case Studies...459

Chapter 14 Practice Problems..463

Glossary...464

References...476

Index..504

Foreword

From 2012 to 2013, Dr. Monique M. Chouraeshkenazi served as my enlisted military assistant when I was Deputy Secretary of Defense. Air Force Technical Sergeant Chouraeshkenazi served for thirteen years, including a combat tour in Afghanistan, growing to become a trusted aide, not just to me and my predecessor and successor as Deputy Secretary at the Pentagon but also to the Director of the Joint Improvised-threat Defeat Agency, the entity charged with our protecting our people from IEDs. Throughout it all, Monique was everything Americans want to see in our service members. She is bright, articulate, dedicated, and willing to go the extra mile for her country and those she served alongside.

As with everything Monique does, there was even more. While serving as my assistant, I learned Monique was putting herself through school and pursuing her doctorate in Public Policy and Administration. Her dissertation, on which I was proud to serve as an advisor, analyzed one of the Defense Department's most difficult acquisition (the F-35 Joint Strike Fighter program) challenges and provided real insights to policymakers and researchers alike. It is a commendable work, and one that I was proud to keep on the table in my office when I became Secretary of Defense.

To those of us who know Monique well, it is no surprise that with a doctorate in hand she has continued to serve the country and her community, now as a business owner and educator. Her firm has helped establish new standards in professional education and to raise the level of awareness for security threats at private and public sector institutions. Monique also continues to teach, whether in the classroom, on her podcast, or in her writing.

Monique continues her remarkable service in these pages. With *Understanding America's Past to Protect the Future,* Monique has made a lasting contribution. In this new, incisive, informative book, she helps undergraduate and graduate students understand how the nation's homeland security and defense are intertwined, and she provides readers with the framework to identify not just the challenges the nation faces but also to develop the innovative solutions required to continue to protect this country from threats of all kinds.

In *Understanding America's Past to Protect the Future*, Monique also demonstrates her uniquely strategic mind. She appreciates that defense of the United States is so vital that we, to whom it is entrusted, must ensure defense across the domains of armed conflict not just air and land and sea, but space, and cyberspace, across military services and government agencies, from presidential administration to presidential administration and from strategic era to strategic era. This book was written with that world and mission in mind.

In today's strategic era, the United States is confronting no fewer than five immediate, but distinct, and evolving challenges. We're countering the prospect of Russian aggression and coercion, especially in Europe. We are also managing historic change in the Asia-Pacific—the single most consequential region for America's future. We are strengthening our deterrent and defense forces in the face of North Korea's continued nuclear and missile provocations. We are checking Iranian aggression and malign influence in the Gulf, and helping defend our friends and allies in the Middle East. Finally, we are countering terrorism and accelerating the certain and lasting defeat of ISIL.

Of course, at the same time, the United States also must contend with an uncertain future—ensuring that our military and the country are ready for challenges we may not anticipate today. As we do, we're fortunate to have Dr. Chouraeshkenazi standing with us, providing us the advice, the education, and the support we will need in this era and beyond. I am so proud of Monique, so impressed with this book, and so thankful for her efforts to help defend this country and make a better world.

Dr. Ashton B. Carter
25th Secretary of Defense

Endorsement

This book covers a lot of complex subjects in a digestible, understandable way. Dr. Maldonado methodically reviews how the uniquely American concepts of national security and homeland security have evolved both before and after the birth of our Republic. She then develops and explains how the two concepts intersect and overlap, especially since the terrible tragedy of September 11, 2001. By so doing, she suggests ways by which we might better confront emerging 21st century threats to American security."

- Robert O. Work
32nd United States Deputy Secretary of Defense

Dr. Ash Carter Bio

Ash Carter served as the 25th Secretary of Defense for the United States.

For over thirty-five years inside government under presidents of both political parties as well as in the private sector, Ash Carter has leveraged his extraordinary experience in national security, technology, and innovation to defend the United States and make a better world.

Carter served as Defense Secretary from 2015 to 2017. Leading the largest organization in the world with more than three million civilian and military employees and an annual budget of more than half a trillion dollars, Carter became known for his savvy leadership and for ensuring the Pentagon thought "outside its five-sided box." At a time of global change and congressional gridlock, Carter transformed the way the Defense Department fought adversaries, stood with allies and partners, planned and budgeted, partnered with private enterprises, and managed its talent.

As Secretary, Carter advised President Obama and transformed the department's strategic thinking and operations on critical global challenges and across the domains of armed conflict—not just sea and air and land, but also in space and cyberspace. He changed the trajectory of the military campaign to deliver ISIL a lasting defeat, coordinating a global coalition of dozens of nations, simultaneously conducting operations in Iraq, Syria, Afghanistan, Libya, and beyond, and eliminating ISIL's leaders and plotters.

Carter also designed and executed the strategic pivot to the Asia-Pacific, established the Defense Department and NATO's new playbook for confronting Russia's aggression, and launched the Defense Department's latest cyber strategy.

At the same time Carter directed America's global operations, he also spearheaded revolutionary improvements to the Defense Department. To develop new technological and operational capabilities, he pushed investments in research and development to nearly $72 billion dollars in the fiscal year 2017 budget alone. Carter also launched six transformative "Force of the Future" initiatives to change the way the department recruits, trains, and retains quality people, and he also directed the opening of all military positions to women without exception. To make the department more innovative, Carter created the Defense Digital Service to bring tech experts into the Pentagon for a tour of duty. He also opened Pentagon outposts in Silicon Valley, Boston, Austin, and other tech hubs to reconnect the government and military with visionary private sector leaders and companies, and established the Department's first Defense Innovation Board, which attracted thought leaders such as Google Alphabet's Eric Schmidt, astrophysicist Neil Degrasse Tyson, LinkedIn's Reid Hoffman, and many more, as well as the Pentagon's Chief Innovation Officer position.

Before becoming Secretary of Defense, Carter served in the department's number two and number three jobs.

As Deputy Secretary and Chief Operating Officer from 2011 to 2013, he oversaw the department's management and personnel and steered strategy and budget through the turmoil of sequester.

Under Secretary of Defense for Acquisition, Technology, and Logistics (ATL) from 2009 to 2011, Carter led the department's procurement reform and innovation agenda, the successful completion of key procurements like the KC-46 tanker and the cancellation of unsuccessful programs like the presidential helicopter, rapid acquisitions (including the development of thousands of mine-resistant ambush-protected "MRAP" vehicles that saved countless service members' lives in Afghanistan and elsewhere), and global logistics for the largest enterprise on earth.

Earlier in his government career, Carter served as Assistant Secretary of Defense for International Security Policy from 1993 to 1996. He was responsible for the Nunn-Lugar program that removed and eliminated nuclear weapons in Russia, Ukraine, Kazakhstan, and Belarus, the military planning during the 1994 crisis over North Korea's nuclear weapons program, and the U.S. nuclear arsenal. In the Defense Department and on Capitol Hill during the Cold War, Carter was known for his work on missile defense and the then-Strategic Defense Initiative, as well as basing options for the MX Missile. Over the past three decades, Carter has also served on the Defense Policy Board, the Defense Science Board, and the Secretary of State's International Security Advisory Board.

In addition to his government service, Carter has taught at many of the world's outstanding academic institutions. He has been a distinguished visiting fellow at Stanford University's Hoover Institution and a lecturer at Stanford's Freeman Spogli Institute for International Studies. At Harvard's Kennedy School from 1996 to 2009, Carter was a Professor of Science and International Affairs and Chair of the International and Global Affairs faculty. He served as a physics instructor at Oxford University, a postdoctoral fellow at Rockefeller University and M.I.T., and an experimental research associate at Rookhaven and Fermilab National Laboratories. Secretary Carter is also author or coauthor of eleven books and more than 100 articles on physics, technology, national security, and management.

Outside of government and the university, Carter was a Senior Executive at the Markle Foundation's America-wide initiative to shape technology and trade strategies to enable all Americans to flourish in a networked global economy. Previously Carter was a Senior Partner of Global Technology Partners focused on advising major investment firms in technology and an advisor on global affairs to Goldman Sachs. Carter has also served on the boards of the MITRE Corporation, Mitretek Systems, and Lincoln Laboratories at the Massachusetts Institute of Technology (M.I.T.) and as a member of the Draper Laboratory Corporation. He was also elected a Fellow of the American Academy of Arts and Sciences and is a member of the Council on Foreign Relations and the Aspen Strategy Group.

For his government service, Secretary Carter has been awarded the Department of Defense Distinguished Service Medal, the department's highest civilian honor, on five separate occasions, and he twice received the Joint Distinguished Service Medal from the Chairman and Joint Chiefs of Staff.

Secretary Carter earned his bachelor's degrees in physics and in medieval history, summa cum laude, at Yale University, where he was also awarded Phi Beta Kappa, and he earned his doctorate in theoretical physics from Oxford University, where he was a Rhodes Scholar.

After serving as Secretary of Defense, Dr. Carter was appointed as Director of the Belfer Center for Science and International Affairs and Professor of Technology and Global Affairs at Harvard Kennedy School.

A native of Philadelphia, he is married to Stephanie Carter and has two grown children.

Acknowledgements

I would like to thank my mentor and friend, Dr. Ash Carter. Without your fantastic leadership and unwavering support, this dream would not have come true. From day one, you believed in me and have always made time to provide crucial feedback and guidance for my education and professional journey. I would not have made it this far without your support. Thank you very much! I would like to thank the Cognella Academic Publishing team for making this book happen. Without your support, guidance, training, and advisement, this achievement would not have come to fruition. You all have been wonderful to work with. Mary Jane Peluso, thank you for believing in me and my vision for this book. Since you read my proposal, you have been "Team Monique," and that is the support I needed to get through this challenging yet rewarding experience. Leah Sheets, thank you so much for working with me and making sure I have stayed on the timeline while producing a quality book. Your enthusiasm and energy are what I needed to get to the finish line! Natalie Piccotti, thank you so much for you and your team's eagerness and excitement over this product. You all formulated a fantastic advertising and marketing plan, and your commitment to *Understanding America's Past to Protect the Future* showed that you truly believe in my work. Thank you! Also, I would like to thank Christian Berk, Tim Serpico, and Ivey Preston. Thank you all so much for keeping me ahead of the timeline, working tirelessly to ensure the final product was to the utmost standards and ready to be advertised to the nation. Your assistance in this process is very much appreciated. I would like to thank Jennifer Ng for providing excellent testing mechanisms and case study curricula for this book. Your expertise in the intelligence and national/homeland security realms brought so much innovation and realism to this project! Jess Estrella: thank you very much for designing such a profound book cover to capture my vision of what this book stands for. It represents the self-lessness of the U.S. Armed Forces, the struggle of understanding the complexities of homeland/national defense objectives and initiatives as the soldiers look beyond terrains for hope and peace, and most importantly, the United States flag representing the greatest country in the world. A very special thank you to scholars: Dr. Michael Herbert, Dr. Kenneth Goldberg, Dr. Robert Cadigan, and Dr. George M. Frogge, who were reviewers through my writing process. I am honored that you all took the time and effort to review this textbook and give me constructive feedback to produce a quality resource for students in our field of academia. It is also an honor to have such distinguished educators who served as my professors and leadership

to be a part of this project. Again, thank you very much! Finally, I would like to thank the American Public University System, Southern New Hampshire, and Tiffin universities. I am proud to be an educator for each establishment, and I am thankful that each educational institution has provided me with succinct training, professional development, and teams that are responsibility for my educational growth as professor and student.

I dedicate this book to the men and women (my brothers and sisters) in uniform who continue to fight for this country's freedom, protect American citizens, and aid victims. Through turmoil, uncertainty, and apparent division, America can always depend on and be proud of the United States Armed Forces, emergency services personnel, fire fighters, law enforcement, and veterans. America's greatest servants. Thank you for your selfless service. We have the best military in the world.

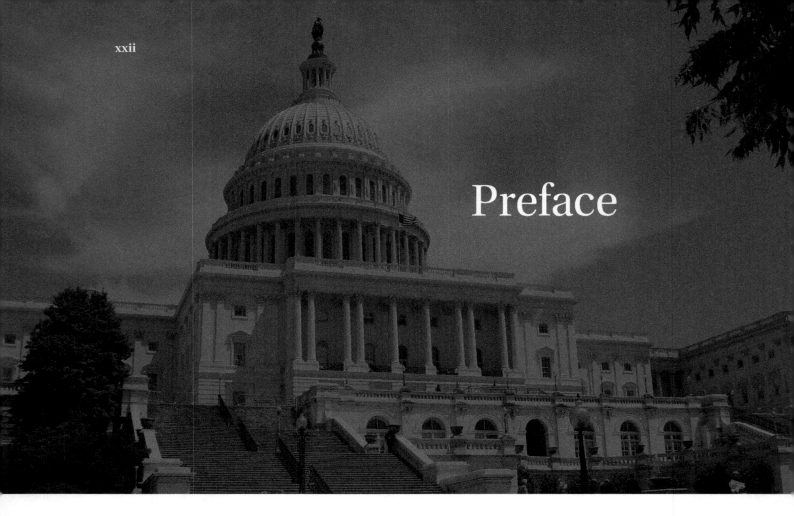

Preface

I was introduced to homeland and national security realms when I swore to defend the Constitution of the United States on August 16, 2001, in the world's greatest Air Force. I held various positions that directly and indirectly impacted American national security. Portions of this book contain content from my work as an expert with over fifteen years in homeland/national security, criminal justice, and research fields. Additionally, content in this book derives from my Ph.D. dissertation at Walden University in 2015, *A Qualitative Study on F-35 Production Delays Affecting National Security Guidance*, and from my August 2016 article in *Homeland Security News*, "America's Conflict Spectrum: How It Affects National Security." I trust this contribution of this textbook appropriately discusses the history of national security and significant events that have changed the way the United States government does business.

Homeland & National Security: Understanding America's Past to Protect the Future examines major events that unavoidably incited American national security policy dating to the Constitutional Convention of 1787, which officially identified a threat to national security. Many years of framing legislation led to the birth of the nation's largest federal government agency, the Department of Defense, mandating the need to "provide the military forces needed to deter war and to protect the security of our country." Furthermore, this book emphatically discusses the evolution of homeland security, as America faced the largest terrorist attack on its own soil. The September 11th attacks motivated the establishment of the United States' third largest Cabinet department, the Department of Homeland Security which is charged with "preventing terrorism and enhancing, managing our borders, administrating immigration laws, securing cyber-space, and ensuring disaster resilience."

Understanding America's Past to Protect the Future is predicated on the major conflicts such the Cold War, which influenced the extensive streamlining of the United States government's military and government agencies. The Cold War influenced the evolution of national security, and 9/11 persuaded American government to reevaluate security postures and how to protect national interests. This book also discusses the importance of understanding the United States' position on the conflict spectrum, strengthening alliance relationships, and recognizing the enemy because there are new actors and threats. The American landscape is constantly changing, making it a requirement to enforce American foreign policy, democratic governance, and continuing to train our military forces to maintain global dominance and protect national security.

Understanding America's Past to Protect the Future fast-forwards to modern terrorist attacks that happened on American soil: the September 11th attacks, the San Bernardino shooting, and the Orlando nightclub shooting. The execution of the deadliest attacks committed in U.S. history shows that American terrorism exists and it will take education, research, technological advancement, decision-making, policymaking, and competent leaders to deter the threat and destroy terrorism. This book also includes the aftermath and devastating effects of manmade and natural disasters that have traumatized the United States and the evolution of emergency management policies, which have shaped the way emergency management and first responders respond to future tragedies.

Though U.S. values and top security concerns have not dramatically changed, the threat and the enemy have. The United States, its allies, and security partners currently face innovative terrorism, unconventional and asymmetrical conflicts, economic instability, human trafficking, transnational drug trafficking, terrorist money laundering, and secret enemies. In addition, one of the greatest threats to America and its allies is nuclear warfare and the proliferation of nuclear weapons by terrorist organizations and rogue nations. To mitigate these matters, the United States must fortify legislative initiatives, bolster foreign policy and security, regenerate globalization, and promote democratic governance.

About the Author

D r. Monique M. Chouraeshkenazi is Associate Professor for the School of Security and Global Studies in Homeland Security Studies at the American Public University System. She has expertise in education, homeland/national security, and military matters. She currently educates in homeland security, national security studies, legal and ethical issues, research design and analysis, and public policy. Dr. Chouraeshkenazi is also the Lead Professor for the School of Graduate and Degree Completion Programs for Tiffin University's Master of Criminal Justice department. Finally, Dr. Chouraeshkenazi is a former Subject Matter Expert for Tiffin's national security, criminal justice, and research courses as well as a former Antiterrorism Instructor for the United States Air Force. In addition to teaching, Dr. Chouraeshkenazi served as a Technical Sergeant in the United States Air Force and was on active duty for over thirteen years in Cyber Security, Knowledge Operations Management, and Security Management. Earlier in her career, she had a dual role in Antiterrorism and Security positions. One of the most prominent positions Dr. Chouraeshkenazi has held in her military career was the Enlisted Military Assistant and Noncommissioned Officer in Charge to the Deputy Secretary of Defense for Secretaries Dr. Ashton Carter, Ms. Christine Fox, and Mr. Robert Work. She was also the Military Executive Assistant to the Joint Improvised-Threat Defeat Agency Director, LTG John Johnson (retired), as her last assignment on active duty. Dr. Chouraeshkenazi is a former certified Level II Antiterrorism Instructor and has various certifications in the information assurance, security, antiterrorism, and force protection fields. She has an A.A.S. in Information Resource Management from the Community College of the Air Force, B.A. in Homeland

Security from American Military University, Master of Criminal Justice from Boston University, and a career diploma in Private Investigation from Penn Foster College. Dr. Chouraeshkenazi earned a Ph.D. in Public Policy and Administration with a specialization in Terrorism, Mediation, and Peace from Walden University.

PHOTO BY SHELLRAY BOTHWELL, TPP OPERATIONS

Prestigious Positions and Titles Held

Associate Professor for the School of Security and Global Studies in Homeland Security

Founder and CEO, MD Educational Consulting Firm, LLC

Creator of Homeland and National Security Blog, *The Dr. Mo Show*

Contributor to *In Homeland Security News*

Military Executive Assistant to the Joint Improvised Explosive Device Defeat Organization Director

Enlisted Military Assistant to the Deputy Secretary of Defense

Assistant Noncommissioned Officer-in-Charge of the Office of the Deputy Secretary of Defense

Lead Professor for the School of Graduate and Degree Completion Programs in Criminal Justice

Chief Special Security Officer for 18th Wing

Writer/Columnist, *PA Times*

List of Figures

Chapter 1

1.1 American Revolutionary War 4

1.2 Continental Congress approves the
Declaration of Independence 5

1.3 American Civil War...................................... 19

Chapter 2

2.1 Founding Fathers sign the United States
Constitution.. 44

2.2 President Harry S. Truman.......................... 46

2.3 U.S. Army Helicopter Assault Companies at
170th & 189th at Polei Kleng 48

2.4 Nazi troops in Nuremberg, Germany on
November 9, 1935 48

2.5 President Truman signing the National
Security Act of 1947 49

2.6 James V. Forrestal, First United States
Secretary of Defense 50

2.7 The Pentagon.. 51

2.8 President John F. Kennedy discusses the
Cuban Missile Crisis 52

Chapter 3

3.1 Senator Barry Goldwater and Representative
William Flynt Nichols 90

3.2 General George Washington, Commander-in-
Chief of the Continental Army 102

Chapter 4

4.1 Conceptual Framework for State Analysis. 137

4.2 Naturalization Ceremony at the Smithsonian's
National Museum of American History on June
14, 2016... 141

Chapter 5

5.1 Department of Homeland Security Seal 148

5.2 DHS ICE Badge.. 148

5.3 Tom Ridge, First Secretary of Homeland Security 151

5.4 Michael Chertoff, Second Secretary of Homeland Security 151

5.5 Janet Napolitano, Third Secretary of Homeland of Security 152

5.6 Jeh Johnson, Fourth Secretary of Homeland of Security 152

5.7 John Kelly, Fifth Secretary of Homeland Security 152

5.8 Elaine Duke, Acting Secretary of Homeland Security 152

5.9 Emergency Management Continuum........ 158

Chapter 6

6.1 Battleship USS West Virginia engulfed in flames and smoke during the attack on Pearl Harbor on December 7, 1941 173

6.2 "The Day of Infamy" Speech by President Franklin D. Roosevelt on December 8, 1941 ... 174

6.3 Aftermath of the Beirut bombings on October 23, 1983... 175

6.4 Aftermath of the Oklahoma City Bombing, 1995.. 178

6.5 Aftermath of Khobar Towers Bombing, 1996.. 180

6.6 Aftermath of the USS Cole Bombing, 2000.. 182

6.7 Aftermath of the September 11th attacks, 2001.. 183

Chapter 7

7.1 Boots of the soldiers who died in the Fort Hood shootings 233

7.2 Aftermath of the Boston Marathon bombing, April 15, 2013... 249

7.3 Hooded Anonymous Dark Person 256

Chapter 8

8.1 Senators Sam Nunn and Richard Lugar with 25th Secretary of Defense Dr. Ashton B. Carter 270

8.2 The 9/11 Commission Report Cover......... 278

Chapter 9

9.1 CBRNE Weapons...................................... 295

9.2 Major Categories of Biological Agents with Probability to be Used as Bio-Weapons.......... 299

9.3 List of Chemical Weapons 301

9.4 CDC Preparedness and Response 312

Chapter 13

13.1 U.S. Capitol Hill Building 391

13.2 Flag of the Secretary of Defense 394

13.3 Unified Combatant Commands 395

13.4 Secretary of Homeland Security Flag 396

13.5 Department of State Seal 398

KEY TERMS

Abolitionism

Absolute monarchy

Articles of Confederation

Atomic bomb

Bill of Rights

Colonialism

Containment

Continental Army

Continental Congress

Declaration of Independence

Democracy

Emancipation Proclamation

Executive branch

Feudalism

Governance

Imperialism

Insurrection

Judicial branch

Legislative branch

Liberalism

Martial law

Policy of Attraction

Primogeniture laws

Representative government

Republicanism

Satellite states

Trench warfare

Western Civilization

CHAPTER 1

The Evolution of American Policy: Timelines, Events, & Conflicts

LEARNING OBJECTIVES

After reading this chapter, students will be able to:

- Analyze a comprehensive overview of historical battles that affected North America
- Discuss how past conflicts have shaped America's security initiatives
- Identify historical events that led to the evolution of American democracy
- Review timeline of events of how the United States responded to security responsibilities
- Define selected terms related to American policy

INTRODUCTION

The timeline of events which directly and indirectly affected the United States is an important concept in examining how the nation has responded to maintain global dominance and protect its borders. Each conflict has showed how the United States expanded its area of responsibilities with security initiatives and foreign policy to respond to adversarial threats and political aggression after its independence from Great Britain. The following topics are a brief chronological arrangement of key conflicts that led to notable policies which shaped American **democracy**, a system of government in which citizens elect members of state through elections. Some events will be discussed in-depth in different chapters.

FRENCH AND INDIAN WAR

Known as the Seven Years' War, the French and Indian War involved France's territorial expansion into the Ohio River valley, which was controlled by British colonies. Constant battles between the two countries eventually led to a declaration of war in 1756. Because British Prime Minister William Pitt gained financial support to fund Prussia in the war, the effort improved their strategic operations, and the British won battles at Louisburg, Fort Frontenac, and Quebec. Seven years later, the British expanded their rule and claimed France and Spain's territories in Canada, Florida, and the Mississippi Valley.

The effects of the French and Indian War had a magnificent impact on Great Britain, as it made way for the expansion of its territory through North America. However, the cost of the war caused significant debt for the country, and as a result, benefited the American colonists. Prior to the war, the thirteen colonies had increased tensions among each other, causing disagreements and cynicism. This single conflict caused American colonists to unite and strengthen forces together, gain power, and fight against their common enemy, which was Great Britain. The end of the war resulted with France leaving North America, offering a vast amount of land for colonization. The British would impose the Royal Proclamation to mitigate American colonists from settling in the available land. Further legislations such as the Sugar and Stamp Acts caused increased tensions between the Americans and the British. Continued disputes between Great Britain and American colonists eventually led to the American Revolutionary War, which ended in 1763 when both parties signed the Treaty of Paris. This negotiation awarded America independence and established foreign diplomatic policy when the British ceded from North America, which doubled the size of the country for the American colonization. Furthermore, the Americans established civil initiatives with its people by ending the persecution of loyalists and allowing them to restore their confiscated land. The expansion of the United States allowed American colonists to establish national and foreign policies while promoting imperialism, as they gained territory between the Allegheny Mountains and the Mississippi River. Additional information on the French and Indian War is discussed in Chapter Two.

Figure 1.1 American Revolutionary War

AMERICAN REVOLUTIONARY WAR

The American Revolution was one of the greatest victories in world history as Americans fought for and won U.S. independence against Great Britain, which was considered the most powerful country in the world during this period. The war derived from growing tensions between the colonial government and Great Britain's thirteen North American colonies. In April 1775, the Battles of Lexington and Concord began the official declaration of the American Revolution between British troops and colonial military forces, who were fervently fighting for their independence. Three years later, the French entered the war and joined forces with the **Continental Army** (a militia established by Second Continental Congress of volunteer soldiers from the original thirteen colonies), making the American Revolution an international war. With assistance from the French, the Americans claimed their independence when the British surrendered at the Battle of Yorktown in 1781. The war officially ended in 1783. The **Declaration of Independence** (declaration by the Second Continental Congress stating the thirteen American colonies were free from British rule) was signed on July 4, 1776. Additional information on the American Revolutionary War is discussed in Chapter Two.

THE AFTERMATH OF THE AMERICAN REVOLUTION

After the end of the American Revolution, the United States signed the Treaty of Paris, winning its independence from Great Britain and ending the war. **Continental Congress** (delegates from the thirteen original colonies that became the governing body during the American Revolutionary War) appointed five members of the commission to negotiate with Great Britain: John Adams, Benjamin Franklin, John Jay, Thomas Jefferson, and Henry Laurens. Because Laurens was captured by the British and held hostage at the Tower of London, and Jefferson was not in the United States at the time, Adams, Franklin, and Jay handled negotiations. The three members ensured democracy and liberty would be the utmost moral standards for United States independence.

Figure 1.2   Continental Congress gathered for the Declaration of Independence

The Declaration of Independence

When in the Course of human events, it becomes necessary for one people to dissolve the political bands which have connected them with another, and to assume among the powers of the earth, separate and equal station to which the Laws of Nature and of Nature's God entitle them, a decent respect to the opinions of mankind requires that they should declare the causes which impel them to the separation (Declaration of Independence: A transcription., n.d., para. 1).

The Declaration of Independence was a formal legal document that announced the thirteen original colonies' freedom from British control. The declaration entails the abuses inflicted upon the country by the British monarchy, and it was used as a mechanism to receive support from countries that were enemies of Great Britain. One of the most notable statements from the declaration reads:

We hold these truths to be self-evident, that all men are created equal: that they are endowed by their Creator with certain unalienable rights; that among these are life, liberty, and the pursuit of happiness (Declaration of Independence: A transcription., n.d., para. 2).

The Declaration of Independence was adopted by the Second Continental Congress, which represented American freedom and that the thirteen original colonies were no longer controlled by the British crown.

Human equality was the forefront for the Declaration of Independence, but there were still challenges to bring the concept to fruition. Slavery still existed within the United States, and women did not have equal rights. Thomas Jefferson, who was one of the primary authors of the Declaration, owned slaves, so the preamble seemed to be a contradictory message to Americans. Jefferson included a passage condemning slave trade with Europe, but the passage was deleted through a vote of members of the Continental Congress before the document was signed. Instead, the Declaration of Independence was written in the fashion of idealistic language:

... secure these rights, Governments are instituted among Men, deriving their just powers from the consent of the governed, That whenever any Form of Government becomes destructive of these ends, it is the Right of the People to alter or to abolish it, and to institute new Government, laying its foundation on such principles and organizing its powers in such form, as to them shall seem most likely to effect their Safety and Happiness (US, 1776).

The purpose of the passage was to identify the government's role in securing "people's rights" and the power of the government from those who governed (selected officials from the American people). If these laws were not adhered to, the American people had the right change or eliminate the government. Scholars interpreted this statement in radical form because the concept that citizens could reject a government was part of the revolutionary movement.

The American Revolution heavily influenced **liberalism** (the concept of having liberal views) throughout Europe, which caused challenges and brought success in the evolution of a new democracy. Such struggles led to the French Revolution among other revolutions in Spanish-American colonies. Independence provided hope for those who were slaves and resulted in the dawn of the abolitionist movement nearly a hundred years later. In England, land inheritance vanished, and the Anglican Church struggled because it was an important part of the British crown. **Republicanism** became an important concept among federations in the United States when Continental Congress members were drafting constitutions during the revolution. Republicanism represents a sociopolitical view in which citizens are under a republic where there is popular sovereignty. Such progressive changes in the aftermath of the war were precursors to the emergence of the political perspectives of the nineteenth century.

> *Republicanism is political dogma that opposes authoritarianism and is indicative of a political system established by the rule of law, citizens' rights, and sovereignty.*

Slavery

After the war for independence came new prospects for Americans that would have serious consequences in the future. As mentioned, slavery was a heavily debated topic in the nineteenth century, along with the fight for African American equality. Some political leaders openly advocated for equal rights within the United States because they felt the phrase "life, liberty, and the pursuit of happiness" should apply to all Americans. The world's first antislavery association was established in Philadelphia by the Quakers in 1775 (during the war). Thirteen years later, American colonies founded at least thirteen societies; some northern colonies entirely banned slavery, and some prepared for the gradual abolishment. Most slaves gained freedom during the Revolution and did not require formal **emancipation** (freedom from the control of slavery). U.S. independence had a global effect, and other countries mirrored democratic **governance** (the act of governing) as it represented equality and freedom. Because the British wanted to worsen the colonial economy, they freed many slaves who traveled south while northern slaves obtained their freedom if they agreed to fight in the war. Nonetheless, slavery lasted until the mid 1860s, but African American communities flourished because of the war.

Social Law

British law was no longer relevant, and Americans did not have to obey the British monarch or colonial charters. The United States adopted a new form of governance and had the legal right to eradicate or support laws deemed relevant. Authoritative control and government was not the only concern; instead, specific laws for land holdings were changed. British law mandated land be inherited from fathers to their oldest sons. Nearly 20 years after the war, **primogeniture laws** (the right of succession belonging to the first-born child, a common-law matter) were nonexistent, which caused tension because those who paid the royal monarch for the land were angered by the ramifications. Loyalists, who possessed land, were forced to divide their ownership into smaller sects, which affected those who lived in New England colonies. Furthermore, the Treaty of Paris gave the United States land that expanded to the Mississippi River and offered citizens a reason to move west and create establishments. However, new land laws benefited only rich land owners, stabilizing social status, and loyalists were forced to sell their land, creating a new social outlook.

Political Reverence

The new America needed rules to fully operate, and during the war, Continental Congress members began writing constitutions as the body of laws to follow. The republicanism ideology appealed to political leaders, and they created documents to adopt such ideals to fit progressivism and democratic principles. Therefore, leaders established thirteen republican offices and appointed representatives from the colonies to form the **Articles of Confederation** (an agreement among the thirteen colonies which was the original Constitution before it was replaced by the United States Constitution because of the Constitutional Convention, discussed in Chapter Two). Congress established states and selected governors to lead and ensure each sect did not obtain too much power, and checks and balances were enacted. Congress also created three branches of government: **executive**, **judicial**, and **legislative**. The executive branch is the federal branch of the United States government that is responsible for the employing and supporting laws and regulations established by the legislative and judicial branches. The judicial branch is a federal branch of United States government that is responsible for interpreting laws and overseeing justice. Finally, the legislative branch is a federal branch of the United States government that is responsible for writing and passing laws. Branches were elected methodically through the checks-and-balances process to ensure that politicians were held accountable for their actions. Also, some states approved the **Bill of Rights** (the first ten amendments of the United States Constitution) to protect personal liberties and to mitigate dictatorship.

The Bill of Rights is the first ten amendments of the United States Constitution.

Each state had its respective Bill of Rights and made changes for the betterment of its citizens. Wealthy leaders had many legislative seats but could not maintain their control in government. This was due to the transfer of state capitals from wealthy towns to the central cities. Per the Pennsylvania Capital Preservation Committee and Albany Institute, at least seven states adjusted their central governments like Pennsylvania, which moved its capital from Philadelphia to Harrisburg, and New York, which moved its capital from New York City to Albany (The history of Pennsylvania's early capitols, n.d., paras. 3 and 17). Massachusetts made the most notable changes which the United States adopted. The Massachusetts constitutional convention made changes to the state constitution and inspired Continental Congress members to use the same model to ratify the Articles of the Confederation.

Women's Movement

The revolution also influenced women's rights, a movement that would not only be national but global. Women, whose roles were to be the head of households while men worked, became more self-assured in their rights. John Adams's wife, Abigail Adams, was one of the first pioneers who advocated for women's rights. Puritans, primarily from Massachusetts, opposed the modernization of women's rights and preached the moral efficacy of men. During this time, progressive theorists believed a republican government would succeed only if its citizens were educated, which included women. Thus, if the new government were to succeed, women had to be educated, so they could teach their children. Female conservatories were established in the mid 1790s, and the movement was known as Republic Motherhood. Like the abolition of slavery, women's rights were not an overnight success, but the American Revolution enhanced the movement. With the establishment of women's universities, women became powerful pioneers.

The Declaration of Independence shaped American policy, and became the world's most important example of liberty and natural rights for all humans. In establishing rights and freedoms for all, the United States has not sacrificed security in exchange for promises or deals for civil liberties. This document destroyed past experiences of oppression and suffrage by Great Britain and established a solid foundation that all Americans had rights and that natural rights would no longer be violated. Additionally, the Declaration of Independence ensured the protection of the country and its people. As the third President of the United States, Thomas Jefferson, stated, "It is their right, it is their duty, to throw off such Government, and to provide new Guards for their future security" (University of Chicago, 1987, para. 1). This document was the first to identify American policy in terms of national freedom and security and to show the importance of government to control and sustain such concepts to protect liberties and securities. An excerpt from the Preamble to the Constitution states the very such thing to identify American standards:

> *Republic Motherhood was a movement in women's roles evolving after the American Revolution.*

> "Secure the Blessings of Liberty to ourselves and our Posterity." A threat to America's security is also a threat to Americans' liberties" (US, 1776).

Not only were security and freedoms an important part of the adoption of the Declaration, but the establishment of the branches of federal government ensured checks and balances, including the separation of powers, to mitigate conflict and sustain such rights.

The Evolution of War and Military Forces

Americans lost more battles than they won. Conflicts such as Bunker Hill, Saratoga, and Yorktown were notable victories, but the Revolutionary War brought a negative impact to the country. Next to the American Civil War, the Revolution had the highest casualty count, which caused difficult times for those who had to reestablish their lives. Scholars believed Americans did not assess the seriousness and major challenges of the war, and such interest in the concept caused many to join military forces. At the time, British forces were the most equipped and strongest in the world, and American forces were not experienced enough to fight them. Additional challenges arose because the Continental Congress could not obtain sufficient numbers to join the Continental Army because of the harsh standards and long-term obligations.

At the time, General George Washington was the leader of the Continental Army and needed a permanent force to have a chance for victory. The Continental Congress enforced stricter military standards to meet quota requirements to strengthen the forces. The House mandated that each state increase its quotas, adding attractive military service benefits, including signing bonuses and free land for those who returned to the military after their obligation was completed. With incentives to entice more to join the army, Congress still did not meet its quota of 75,000 because men were hesitant to join, believing doing so would jeopardize their freedom under the new government. Though patriots thought it was a positive concept to volunteer and do their part in battle to deter the enemy, there were still unavoidable challenges. The Continental Congress did not have the financing to buy supplies or pay the army, which forced troops to invade private residences and take food and personal property. Soldiers were outraged because they believed American citizens were unpatriotic and did not support the war nor the cause. Near the end of the war, soldiers protested about their poor living conditions and lack of payment. Army leadership agreed that they were not treated well during the war, but Congress believed that their actions were demeaning and that they should serve their country with dignity and sacrifice. Tensions between officers and Congress grew when officers were denied lifetime pensions after the Revolution, and they threatened to plot against the government. Washington intervened before the plan was executed. Nevertheless, the Continental Army won the battle against the British, and the war ended with much support from the French. At the end of the war, Congress was still had reservations about the army, as there were still suspicions, grudges, and animosity within the regiments.

THE FRENCH REVOLUTION

The French Revolution began in 1789 and ended in 1799, involving a series of battles for social and political change within France. Based on **Western civilization** (the societal, ethical, traditional, political, and belief and innovative schemes derived from the European nations), the Revolution overthrew the French kingdom, established a republican government (like the United States), and ended with the reign of Napoleon Bonaparte as dictator of France. The French Revolution was a notable part of history because liberalism and radical ideology enriched the evolution of modern history, which influenced the regression of **absolute monarchy** (type of government where the monarch has absolute authority of its citizens and country). The Revolution also caused conflicts between Caribbean islands and the Middle East.

Certain causes were responsible for the Revolution, following the Seven Years' War and the American Revolutionary War. The French government suffered significant debt due to taxation conspiracies, and years of economic distress triggered animosity towards those who were upper class. Furthermore, the country significantly invested in the American Revolution, which along with King Louis XVI and his predecessor's spending left the country heading toward impoverishment. Moreover, years of bad harvesting had exhausted citizens' resources, which left them desperate, poor, and angry. Such tensions caused demands for progressive standards, predominantly the conceptualization of citizens' rights and a sovereign nation. French statesman Charles Alexandre de Calonne suggested a financial reform to restore the country's economy, and the plan would include a comprehensive land tax that no one would be exempt from, including aristocracies. To mitigate a rebellion, King Louis established the Estates-General and immediately mandated a meeting on May 5, 1789, during which representatives from the three estates met to discuss their region's grievances.

By the late 1790s, France's population had changed considerably, as Third Estate members represented nearly 100% of the people but could still be overruled by the First and Second estates. Middle-class citizens wanted to establish equality by representation. The aristocrats did not like the idea of citizen representation and were not willing to sacrifice their privileges because they preferred the French monarchy system. Tensions in the voting process led to hostility between the three domains and overshadowed the initial intent of the Estates-General. By June 17, the Third Estate individually met with the General-Estates, as negotiations stalled with the other orders.

> *Estates-General was an assembly established by King Louis XVI, which represented clergy (First Estate), aristocrats (Second Estate), and middle-class (Third Estate) of France for the first time since in the 17th century.*

The new group took the name of National Assembly and pledged not to separate until France's constitution was completed (known as the Tennis Court Oath). After the National Assembly was established, the group continued to meet at Versailles even though the majority opposed it. Since the assembly represented the decline of royal power, citizens feared an overthrow of the French government. The first battle began when rebels invaded the Bastille fortress to secure gunpowder and weapons, which was considered the preamble to the French Revolution.

Following the Bastille fortress raid, battles erupted for years with laborers pillaging and burning homes of tax collectors, landlords, and landowners. The next notable battle, the Great Fear, was a series of riots among pillagers who responded to rumors of a conspiracy that the king and nobilities plotted to overthrow the Third Estate. The panic period influenced the National Constituent Assembly, which ended **feudalism** (a specific social system during the Middle Ages in which land was held for a fee between a lord and vassal) on August 4, 1789. Like America's Declaration of Independence, the National Assembly adopted the Declaration of the Rights of Man and of Citizens. The document asserted the National Assembly's obligation to supersede the French monarchy with a more progressive system of government, which included equal opportunity, citizens' rights, sovereignty, and a **representative government** (a government based on electoral representatives). With a modern government, challenges ensued as authors of the new declaration could not formulate essential inquiries on how to draft France's new political methodologies. Primarily due to questions about how much power the king would have over new government, the National Assembly wrestled with ideas that would establish a representative government as well as checks and balances. The draft of France first constitution proclaimed a constitutional monarchy where the king could mandate sanctions and appoint ministers. The majority opposed the constitution because they wanted a republican governance. Prominent figures such as Maximilien de Robespierre, Camille Desmoulins, and Georges Danton represented such ideals of a democratic administration and drew support from the majority.

By April 1792, the Legislative Assembly declared war on Austria and Prussia because they believed expatriates were establishing an insurgency against France. Also, rebellions heightened tensions when extremists (called the Jacobins) attacked the king's private residence and arrested him. The arrest provoked Parisians to slaughter hundreds of anarchists and resulted in the Legislative Assembly replacing the National Convention, eradicating the French monarchy. On January 21, 1793, King Louis XVI was sentenced to death for treason and numerous state crimes. After the execution, various battles between European powers created a complete division within the National Convention, escalating the French Revolution. By the following year, the Jacobins gained control of the National Convention and established a chain of radical events such as abolishing Christianity and formulating a new calendar. The Jacobins also began the Reign of Terror, in which revolutionaries fought to eliminate foreign invaders from France. Maximilien de Robespierre, a leader of the Committee of Public Safety, was responsible for the mass killings, executing orders until his slaying on July 28, 1792. His death was the preamble to the Thermidorian Reaction, which was the revolution against the radicals who caused the Reign of Terror.

On August 22, 1795, the National Convention approved a second constitution that established France's first bilateral government. Under the new constitution, the parliament appointed a five-member *Directory* as part of the executive branch. Traditionalists and Jacobins opposed the new administration, but the army (under Napoleon Bonaparte) enforced stabilization. The Directory lasted for approximately four years but was plagued by the same issues the government faced after the American Revolutionary War. The group was forced to heavily rely on military forces to maintain order within the country and gave a substantial amount of power to the generals. By 1799, Bonaparte executed a military coup which eliminated the Directory and established the French Consulate. The overthrow of the government culminated the French Revolution and the beginning of the Napoleon era, dominating most of Europe.

The Napoleonic era was the final stage of the French Revolution which lasted from 1799–1815, ending the Hundred Days and Napoleon's downfall at the Battle of Waterloo.

The French Revolution provoked many conflicts throughout Europe, therefore forcing the United States to establish impartial policies to avoid involvement. The result of the revolution influenced American politics, including supportive and non-supportive parties that stood to affect American domestic and foreign policy. The United States suggested democratic reforms to strengthen American-French relations to use as a republican coalition force against Great Britain. The foreign policy agreement would be the beginning of mandating social change standards while revolutionizing policies for political instability and security.

American and European Affairs: The Aftermath of the French Revolution

The French Revolution tremendously impacted the country and had a significant influence on Europe and Western civilization, particularly North and South America. The war was dubbed as one of the most important conflicts that affected the history of the world. Because the French Revolution increased political tensions, a significant number of immigrants feared for their lives and left the country, moving to other parts of Europe and the United States. After leaving the country, many French emigrants influenced different parts of the world with their cultures, policies, and traditions for over 100 years. French settlers heavily impacted foreign countries, bringing them closer together, epitomizing tolerance, and ending traditional laws and practices. However, new establishments created by the French were destroyed and counteractions from previous reigns reversed the French's progression and dissolved the reforms established.

In the aftermath of the Revolution, France sought an opportunity to induct legal equality and establish the reigning Catholic Church as an organization controlled by the government. Paris rose and became the primary city within country, strengthening its government and its military forces while establishing "left-wing" and "right-wing" positions of political supporters. French citizens earned independence and had a voice within governmental decisions, something that was not a consideration before the war. The most important changes were the King now ruled the country, the Catholic Church no longer had convents, the aristocrats lost much of their land, and the people elected officials such as clergy, judges, and government officials. In addition, the military belonged to the National Guard, which was established under the French reform. Impressions of the French Revolution left long-term effects, such as formulizing new policies, societies, and progression. Also, the country had a new sense of nationalism. Napoleon became an iconic figure for France, and such progression influenced countries within Europe, especially German states. Historian Alphonse Aulard states his perspective of the long-term impact of the war in his book *Modern France: A Companion to French Studies*:

> From the social point of view, the Revolution consisted in the suppression of what was called the feudal system, in the emancipation of the individual, in greater division of landed property, the abolition of the privileges of noble birth, the establishment of equality, the implication of life ... The French Revolution differed from other revolutions in being not merely national, for it aimed at benefiting all humanity (p. 115).

French philosopher Marquis Condorcet compared the French Revolution to the American Revolutionary War (as cited by Tobias George Smollet in *The Critical Review: Or, Annals of Literature*):

> It was more complete, more entire than the American Revolutionary War. It was attended with greater convolutions in the interior of the nation because the Americans were satisfied with the code of civil and criminal legislation which they had derived from England. They had no corrupt system of

finance to reform, no feudal tyrannies, no hereditary distinctions, no privileges of rich and powerful corporations, no system of religious intolerance to destroy. They had to direct their attention to the establishment of new powers, to be substituted in the place of those exercised over them by the British government (p. 539).

At its inception, the Revolution had full support from the United States until the king was assassinated, resulting in changes with American politics. After Napoleon's death, George Washington professed disinterest in the European wars, and this decision led to the *first party system*. By 1793, Thomas Jefferson established the *Democratic Societies*, and the party supported the French in the aftermath of the war and after the Napoleon's death. Alexander Hamilton formalized the *Federalist Party*, which derided the Democrat's moniker and idealistic motives. Washington criticized both parties as not showing republican characteristics, and both parties were dismantled. Later that year, a European war developed, and Washington maintained neutrality for the United States in the war. Even though the United States remained neutral through the wars, the government managed to purchase Louisiana from France in 1803.

> *The first party system developed when national parties within the United States competed for control in Congress. During the Revolutionary period, the Federalist Party (created by Alexander Hamilton) and Democratic-Republican Party (created by Thomas Jefferson) were the two major parties within Congress.*

American colonies contested the challenge of establishing international diplomacy and support to battle British forces. The success of the Revolution was the relationship the country forged with France. American and French government representatives signed the *Treaty of Alliance and Treaty of Amity* on February 6, 1778, which ensured mutual military support between the countries if France faced a war with British forces. The Treaty of Amity was simply a military alliance to guarantee either party would not agree to sign a peace agreement with Great Britain, and American independence would be the result in any future armistice agreement. These treaties also established international trade and commercial ties between the United States and France.

The United States depended on the French for financial assistance to defeat the British forces. The Continental Congress established the Secret Committee of Correspondence (discussed in Chapter Two) to advertise the United States' role in Europe. France was defeated by the British during the *Seven Years' War* and lost a significant amount of North American territory because of the *Treaty of Paris* agreement. The French saw an opportunity to take advantage of the British's predicaments in the war and obtain its North American colonies, gathering intelligence from secret agents. The Continental Congress worked with the French government on declaring independence and knew foreign alliances would be the key to defeating the British. They outlined the *Model Treaty* as the foundation for their secret operatives, and once independence was officially declared, a group of representatives was sent to negotiate with France. In addition, the French were very supportive of Founding Father Benjamin Franklin, which bolstered support for America's independence. In the aftermath of the Revolution, France faced continued conflict with Austria and Great Britain in its attempts to spread its progressive ideologies throughout Europe. By 1792, Austria and Prussia invaded France and were defeated at the *Battle of Valmy*. The United States and France's relationship after the French Revolution were products of liberty, progression, and republican ideologies. As a gift, France gave the United States the Statue of Liberty.

The Battle of Valmy was declared on September 20, 1792 when Austria and Prussia invaded France. This conflict followed the aftermath of the French Revolution and was France's first victory during this time.

THE JEFFERSON ERA AND MANIFEST DESTINY

The Jefferson Era was the establishment of the *Jeffersonian Republic Party*, which governed the United States from 1800–1840. After the French Revolution, there were still tensions in Europe, and neutrality in wars was not a sufficient standing anymore for the United States. Thomas Jefferson and his successor James Madison were forced to establish American initiatives.

Prior to the 1800 presidential election, Thomas Jefferson and Aaron Burr competed with John Adams and Charles Cotesworth for presidency. Jefferson and Burr believed they had an advantage since the Federalists had provoked increased taxes to fund a large American army, which was responsible for the *Whiskey Rebellion* and *Jay's Treaty*. Jefferson was nominated for president, and Burr was slated for vice president, and the two won. Both Jefferson and Burr received 73 electoral votes, which was unusual because the Constitution held that since it was a tie, Burr was eligible to be president as well. Because Burr was eligible as a presidential candidate, the House of Representatives (which was still controlled by Federalists) had the authority to decide. Most gave their support to Burr, but the House vote resulted in a deadlock, which forced American statesman and Founding Father Alexander Hamilton to influence the decision by stating Jefferson would be the better choice. Jefferson was elected, and Burr was the vice president. This incident ratified the *Twelfth Amendment*, separating votes for the president and vice president positions.

The presidential election in 1800 was an historic moment within the United States because it exemplified republican beliefs and showed that a governing process was possible without conflict, bewilderment, or violence. Furthermore, it is one of the most important elections because even though there was controversy, it was a peaceful process of transitioning powers from the Federalist to Republican Party. Moreover, Jefferson wanted to spread republican values throughout the entire government. In history, administrations did not have an election process and were not replaced with successors; instead, they replaced when leaders were killed or by an inherited successor. The election symbolized a diplomatic transition, accepting progression in the new century.

The Federalists easily lost to the Republicans due their internal disputes and division. Also, they neglected American opinion, and the division within the party caused some to support Hamilton and Adams separately. The most important factor in the transferring powers to the Republic Party was that the group would have to show it could govern the country effectively. Jefferson's first inaugural address emphatically expressed his political philosophy of governing the nation based on republican principles. The following is an excerpt from his address on March 4, 1801:

> Equal and exact justice to all men ... peace, commerce, and honest friendship, with all nations, entangling alliance with none; the support of the state governments in all their right; the preservation of the general government in its whole constitutional vigor, as the sheet anchor of our peace at home and safety abroad; a jealous care of the right of election by the people; absolute acquiescence in the decisions of the majority; a well-disciplined militia—our best reliance in peace and for the first moments of war, till regulars may relieve them; the supremacy of the civil over the agriculture, and of commerce as its handmaid; freedom of religion; freedom of the press; freedom of person under the protection of the habeas corpus; and trial by juries impartially selected (Harris and Bailey, 2014, p. 10).

Jefferson had an informal approach, which made his presidency different from his predecessors. His unconventional decisions identified Jefferson's liberalism and at the same time showed that he was a frugal leader. His approach of both liberalism and conservatism included elements that were openly expressed and supported by both political parties. He was a genuine liberal and emphasized the pursuit of happiness in freedom of religion, speech, and expanding republican philosophies with democratic values. However, he was supportive of a strong government. In a letter he wrote to James Madison, Jefferson stated, "I own I am not a friend to a very energetic government. It is always oppressive. It places governors indeed more at their ease, at the expense of the people" (edited by Mooy, 2003, p. 114). Even though he did not centralize his values on expanding the nation's military during his tenure, he was willing to go to war for freedom within the United States and was emphatic about how the government was managed in terms of focusing on the American people. He was considered one of the first supporters of education for all children because he believed that education was unquestionably the result of democratic institutions and mitigated oppression. He said, "Enlighten the people generally, and tyranny and oppressions of body and mind will vanish like evil spirits at the dawn of day" (Ford, p. 25).

Jefferson also had ideals of a minimal government, requesting to cut military spending and excise tax on whiskey. He focused on the county's large deficit, determining it was a threat to the republican government. To mitigate the deficit, he decreased federal expenses, primarily military spending, and decreased army manpower and forces. Those who were concerned about cutting military spending saw it as a need for American forces to defend the land. Federalists believed Jefferson's military ideals were borderline pacifistic and believed that not focusing on military forces would put the United States in a vulnerable and dangerous position. Less focus on the military power caused foreseeable wars ignited by European powers, and Jefferson was criticized for neglecting a solid military establishment. His unorthodox style was controversial, as Republicans wanted to hold majority of the political offices in government, but Jefferson only appointed those he saw as competent, no matter the political party. He did not fire

Federalists, but a significant number retired, and those who saw Jefferson's direction and vision switched parties and became Republicans.

As politics were new within the United States, such debates became personal among leaders. Jefferson's highly-publicized political (and personal) rival was Founding Father and American statesman Alexander Hamilton. Jefferson did not agree with Hamilton's monopolization in creating a national bank. Such tensions affected the warfighter in which Jefferson believed Hamilton influenced George Washington into following un-successful policies that cost wars and created exceptional division. Jefferson's era showed that the United States was a strong nation, and there was a governing system the American people trusted. Despite controversy over implementation and execution, Jefferson emphasized the transition of power was successful because it involved no war or death. The accomplishment was considered revolutionary. He stated:

> We are all Republicans, we are all Federalists. If there be any among us who would wish to dissolve this Union or to change its republican form, let them stand undisturbed as monuments of the safety with which error of opinion may be tolerated where reason is left to be free to combat it. I know, indeed, that some honest men fear that republican government cannot be strong, that this Government is not strong enough; but would be the honest patriot, in the full tide of successful, abandon a government which has so far kept us free and form on the theoretic and visionary fear that this Government, the world's best hope, may by possibility want ener-gy to preserve itself? I trust not. I believe this, on the contrary, the strongest Government on earth (First inaugural address, 2008, para. 2).

Through Jefferson's presidency, the Federalist party slowly diminished because it did not support major political initiatives. The party's reigning power was cut short because it did not support the War of 1812, comprised of innovative campaign initiatives and territorial expansion. However, the Federalist party had remarkable accomplishments such as creating the Constitution and implementing those provisions and establishing a financial system for the House to imitate. In addition, they settled diplomatic matters with England, France, and Spain, which deferred armed conflict until the United States became powerful. After the Federalists' party demise, the federal government became a one-party system. During this time, some republicans called themselves National Democrats but were still represented under the Republican system. The controversial, yet peaceful, transition still had controversy and divided the nation.

By 1824, political divisions were apparent when five presidential candidates emerged from the Republican party, and eventually John Quincy Adams became president. Considered another controversial election, this appointment was the last to be controlled by the House of Representatives. Four years later, the old *Democratic Republican* party re-emerged and were known as Democrats. Andrew Jackson, who would become the seventh President of the United States, served as the leader of the Democratic party and eventually beat Adams in the presidential election. Jackson's administration was not prepared for a political opposition, and the remainders of the old Federalist party (includ-ing Adams supporters and conservatives) called themselves National Republicans, but were not considered an official party.

Andrew Jackson's presidential election influenced the establishment of the anti-Jacksonians, which called themselves *Whigs*. The party was active until the late 1850s, and its demise was due to slavery matters. During this time, the Whig party had political power when its candidate, William Henry Harrison, defeated Jackson's successor, Martin Van Buren. The party divided with the Democrats and could have prospered, but there was too much controversy on slavery matters. In addition, the National Bank and protective tariff distracted the Jackson administration. By the 1840s, American government had changed significantly, adding president and vice president on a single slate for political parties, and voting privileges were granted to all adult white males. Many of the changes made were successful without international interference, which strengthened American powers. During this time, the United States flourished and expanded, but the undertones of slavery were the largest conflict responsible for dividing the nation, which affected the institution of domestic politics.

Manifest Destiny

Manifest Destiny was a notion that settlers within the United States were meant to expand democratic establishments across North America. The idea assisted the expansion of the western settlements within the United States from 1812 to 1860, removing Native Americans from the area and ending the war with Mexico. The lexicon "Manifest Destiny" derived from the early 1840s, and it was predicated on the mission of Anglo-Saxon Americans to extend their influence in establishing civilization and institutions from coast to coast. No legal document or formal policy supported this concept. Instead, it was a set of principles defining North America's new movement. This expansion caused territorial conflicts, but the progression of freedom and economic stability outweighed tensions within the United States. American columnist and editor John L. O'Sullivan coined the term, saying, "our manifest destiny is to overspread the continent allotted by Providence for the free development of our yearly multiplying millions" (Sullivan, 1845, pp. 5–6, 9–10). Sullivan's statement regarding America's seizure of California, Oregon, and Texas from Mexican territory first appeared in the *United States Magazine and Democratic Review*.

Historian William E. Weeks has argued that three key facets explain Manifest Destiny:

- The virtue of the American people and their institutions
- The mission to spread these institutions, thereby redeeming and remaking the world in the image of the United States
- The destiny under God to do this work (1996, p. 61).

Scholars have suggested that manifest destiny represented the values of expansionism and innovation. Many aspects and views of the term made it difficult to establish resolutions, and a formal policy did not come to fruition. While manifest destiny was considered a plan for North America to expand, some opposed the concept, believing that specific regions would not be included on national affairs, particularly those who settled on the east coast. Nonetheless, American settlers believed God gave them this land to expand the country and enabled growth for the new America. Because of ambiguity regarding cultural and racial superiority during the time, they believed the Puritan way of life would be the most beneficial for everyone.

The effects of Manifest Destiny influenced many countries such as Guam, the Philippines, and Puerto Rico. The Spaniards released these countries to the United States after the Spanish-American war. Afterwards, the United States expanded colonies rather than states, which sustained the growth of American **imperialism,** the practice of extending economic and political powers of a nation through territorial means. The result of the doctrine highly impacted U.S. foreign policy for both western expansion towards the Pacific and relationships with other nations. From an international standpoint, Manifest Destiny was an example of American growth and influence. Not only did the country significantly expand, the American Navy increased as well to smooth the transition of the new America, provoking the security of international trade and commercial shipments. The doctrine also put the United States in the position of a global power in the twentieth century.

Figure 1.3 American Civil War

AMERICAN CIVIL WAR

The *American Civil War* was the most detrimental internal conflict fought in the United States for four years in the nineteenth century (1861–1865). Abraham Lincoln won the presidency during the 1860 election and supported the abolition of slavery in all territorial grounds of the United States. Lincoln's support for abolishing slavery resulted in seven southern states seceding from the Union to form the *Confederate States of America*. Later, four more states joined during the Civil War, and the conflict included historic battles such as *Antietam*, *Bull Run*, *Chancellorsville*, *Gettysburg*, and *Vicksburg*. The internal conflict caused much tension between neighboring states, and by the culmination of the war, it was considered the costliest war fought on American soil with over 600,000 soldiers killed, shaking the Southern region and severely affecting the national economy.

In the mid-1800s, the United States had a period of growth and the first instance of economic influence in the northern and southern region. The northern region soared with the manufacturing industry, and a large-scale agricultural system developed in the south, which was heavily dependent upon African American slaves. Views of abolishing slavery were highly publicized in the north, and southerners feared that abolitionism (the civil rights movement to end slavery) would cause economic disaster. By 1854, Congress passed the *Kansas-Nebraska Act*, which afforded all new territories to establish slavery by entering a popular sovereignty rather than adhering to congressional laws. Those who opposed the law formulized the Republican Party, and their ideologies opposed the expansion of slavery in western territories. The United States Supreme Court finalized the bill to approve slavery in such territories, resulting in the *Battle at Harper's Ferry*.

> *Harper's Ferry was a raid instigated by abolitionist John Brown, which led to a slave revolt from October 16, 1859 to October 18, 1959. Brown's armed party was overpowered by U.S. Marines led by First Lieutenant Israel Greene.*

President Abraham Lincoln's election in 1860 was the last straw for southerners, and months later, South Carolina, Mississippi, Florida, Alabama, Georgia, Louisiana, and Texas seceded from the United States. When Lincoln took office the following year, Confederate forces threatened Fort Sumter and fired the first shots at the military installation, starting the Civil War. Fort Sumter's commander surrendered less than 48 hours after the war's inception, and Confederate leader Pierre G.T. Beauregard took over. Four more states (Arkansas, North Carolina, Tennessee, and Virginia) joined the Confederacy. The bordering states (Kentucky, Maryland, and Missouri) did not secede but were very sympathetic to the Confederate cause.

The *Confederates* maintained a strong military system. and they believed in preserving cultures and traditions, including slavery. The conflict led to the *First Battle of Bull Run*, which began on July 21, 1861, when 35,000 Confederate soldiers forced the Union army to withdraw and head toward Washington, D.C. In 1862, General George B. McClellan led the Union Army to the Potomac and captured Yorktown, but then he was forced to retreat by the combined forces of Andrew Jackson and Robert E. Lee. McClellan wanted to advance to Richmond, but Lincoln refused, and the army headed to Washington, D.C. During this time, Lee advanced the Confederate troops north, splitting the army in two units, and advancing to different regions. Jackson's unit met with General John Pope's army in Manassas and entered the *Second Battle of Bull Run*, while Lee's unit conducted a massive attack, forcing the Union army back to Washington, D.C. Following his victory, Lee initiated the first Confederate invasion in the north, but without confirmation from the president, McClellan restructured his army and attacked Lee's regiment. The attack forced Lee and his unit to withdraw to Antietam Creek. By September 17, the *Army of the Potomac* attacked Lee's unit, and this battle was considered the bloodiest day in American history, killing nearly 14,000 Confederates and over 12,000 Union soldiers. The Union Army's victory was significant, as its strategy forced the Confederates to leave Maryland and re-position to Virginia. However, President Lincoln removed McClellan from command, and he was replaced with Ambrose E. Burnside. Under his command, the Union Army fought Lee's unit near Fredericksburg, and the Confederates lost. Burnside was then replaced with Joseph "Fighting Joe" Hooker.

On January 1, 1863, after the Union Army's defeat, Lincoln introduced the **Emancipation Proclamation**, which freed all slaves in the Confederate states and was justified through a wartime operation. Interestingly, Lincoln did not free slaves in border states that had loyalty to the Union. The Emancipation Proclamation drastically affected the Confederates' labor force and influenced international public opinion to support the Union Army. In 1863, the Union was invaded in a surprise attack by Lee's forces on May 1, 1863, and General Joseph Hooker positioned his troops at Chancellorsville. In another costly battle, the Confederates lost 13,000 troops, and the Union had 17,000 casualties. On July 1, Lee executed another invasion on the Union Army, led by General George Meade in southern Pennsylvania near Gettysburg. Lee lost nearly sixty percent of his troops but escaped and fled to Virginia, which was the last area invaded by the Confederates in the northern region. The same month, Union forces, under the command of Ulysses S. Grant, seized Vicksburg. The Confederates won at Chickamauga Creek, but Lincoln expanded Grant's command, and the Union army claimed victory at Chattanooga in late fall.

After the victory, Lincoln named Grant the supreme commander of the Union army, and they positioned in Washington, D.C., to face Lee's army in northern Virginia. Lee developed a new strategy, putting Petersburg under fire for nine months. On March 25, 1864, after battling for so long, Lee's unit was exhausted but captured Fort Stedman, but in an instant counteroffensive, the Union army claimed victory. Lee's force rebased in Richmond, and for the next seven days, Ulysses Grant and George Meade fought Confederates along the Appomattox River. On April 9, Lee surrendered to Grant at the Appomattox Court House after no more possibilities of escape. On April 14, John Wilkes Booth assassinated President Abraham Lincoln at Ford's Theater in Washington, D.C. By April 26, Joseph Johnston surrendered to William Sherman at Durham Station, North Carolina, officially ending the American Civil War.

The result of the Civil War began with establishing diplomacy between the Confederate states of the United States along with other world powers. The United States was successful in sustaining neutrality among the global powers, and even though certain countries recognized the Confederacy, no one interfered in the American conflict. The end of the war caused the collapse of the Confederacy and the abolition of slavery, and over four million slaves were freed. American policy drastically changed as ending of the Civil War established civil rights to all slaves within in the country, solidifying the idea that all individuals in the United States were mandated freedom and rights.

SPANISH-AMERICAN WAR

On April 21, 1898, the *Spanish-American War*, a conflict between Spain and the United States, began. The war ended Spanish **colonialism** (political and economic control of a country) in North America, and the United States acquired Spanish acquisition territories in Latin America and the western Pacific. The Spanish-American War was predicated on Cuba's struggle for independence from Spanish reign, which the country had been under for over three years. Insurgencies had ensued within the country for many years, and the retaliation the Spaniards used in response to Cuba's actions caught America's attention. Cuba requested American assistance, and the United States intervened when the USS Maine was destroyed in the Havana Harbor, after being positioned there to protect American citizens and property. On April 9, Spain provided an armistice agreement, granting Cuba limited powers to self-govern, but the United States intervened and demanded that Cuba have full independence, and Spain withdraw its forces from the country.

In 1492, Spain was considered the first European country to sail to the Atlantic Ocean and colonize nations in the Western Hemisphere. Spain's success with colonization gained states in North America from Virginia to the southern tip of South America, westward to California and Alaska, and in the Pacific (such as the Philippines). Latin America gained its independence from Spain, but Cuba found difficulty with the concept. In the 1860s, Cuba initiated many insurgencies (the *Ten Years' War*) against Spain, seeking autonomy, but was unsuccessful. In the 1890s, the Cubans reignited their passion for independence and established the *Cuban Revolutionary Party* on January 5, 1892 within the United States. Before the contentions for independence, the United States sought interest in purchasing Cuba, realizing that there was significant amount of valuable land, particularly sugar cane and home-grown beet sugar. The United States invested nearly $50 million dollars into Cuba in the mid 1890s for the country's sugar (considered highly profitable) and annual trade. On June 12, 1895, President Grover Cleveland's proclamation to remain neutral from war was distributed, but conflict grew as General Valeriano Weyler enacted the *Reconcentration Policy* (a strategy used to move Cubans to central locations where they could be controlled by the Spanish army under **martial law)**. Martial law is the suspension of ordinary law through military government action. Cleveland overturned his decision and said the United States would intervene if Spain did not stop the crisis in Cuba (The World of 1898: The Spanish American War, 2011). Cleveland left office, and President William McKinley, the 25th president of the United States, supported his predecessor's policy on Spain. By February 15, a suspicious explosion destroyed the *USS Maine*, an American ship stationed at the Havana Harbor to protect U.S. citizens and property during the Cuban revolt. The explosion caused McKinley to pass a law to provide defense funding of more than $50 million toward building U.S. military forces. By April 21, President McKinley executed a blockade on Cuba, resulting in a declaration of war.

On April 24, 1898, Spain declared war on the United States for interference, and in return, the United States declared war on Spain the following day. The United States added an addendum to the declaration of war, the *Teller Amendment*, emphasizing that the country would not attempt to control Cuba. Spain did not have sufficient military or naval forces geographically located for the war, and the United States had the advantage. On May 1, 1898, Naval Commodore George Dewey headed the American naval unit in Manila Bay, Philippines which destroyed the Spanish fleet.

The Teller Amendment was an addendum created in April 1898 which declared the United States would not permanently control Cuba.

On May 1, the official war began at the *Battle of Manila Bay* in a misunderstanding of surrender and peace in the Philippines. The Spanish governor surrendered in Guam. (He did not know his country was at war with the United States at the time.) The armistice agreement was signed, unknown to Commodore Dewey and Major General Wesley Merritt, who were commanders of the U.S. Army, and they invaded Manila the following day. In June, the United States Marines Corps captured Guantanamo Bay, with less military strength than what the Spaniards presented. By July 1, the United States invaded San Juan Heights and forced Spanish troops to move within the country. About two weeks later, the Spanish agreed to surrender nearly 24,000 troops near San Juan Hill. Days later, United States General Nelson Miles traveled from Guantanamo Bay to Puerto Rico, and his forces migrated to Ponce, entering San Juan with a militant strategy. By December 10, 1898, representatives of the United States and Spain signed the *Treaty of Paris*, which resulted in Cuba's independence. In addition, Guam and Puerto Rico were relinquished to the United States, and the country also had purchasing power of the Philippine Islands.

The influence the Spanish-American War had on national security and foreign policy was detrimental, and policies established then are still in effect today. When both governments signed the Treaty of Paris, the agreement led to Cuban independence and relinquished Guam and Puerto Rico to the United States. Before President Obama left office on January 20, 2017, he worked aggressively to restore relations with Cuba by easing travel restrictions, lifting importing and exporting constraints, agreeing to prisoner swap, and most importantly removing Cuba from the nation's State Sponsors of Terrorism list, which was considered the most historic event between the United States and Cuba since the 1962 embargo. By 2015, Americans could travel to Cuba at leisure, and both countries increased flights to and from by the beginning of the following year. Finally, President Obama became the first sitting American president to visit the country in nearly 90 years. Guam and Puerto Rico are territories of the United States, which significantly influence the nation's economy and security as both countries host American bases in a strategic platform to protect the nation, its regions, and surrounding partners.

PHILIPPINE-AMERICAN WAR

After a devastating defeat by the United States, Spain surrendered control of the Philippine Islands to the United States by signing the Treaty of Paris. Filipinos opposed this decision and wanted total autonomy rather than a change of colonial leaders. On February 4, 1899, before the treaty was approved, a battle between American and Filipino forces erupted for Filipino independence. The war lasted three years, killing more than 4,000 American troops and over 20,000 Filipino forces. Furthermore, more than 200,000 Filipino civilians died from various diseases, famine, and aspects of the war.

The United States' decision to annex the Philippine Islands came with much controversy. Those who supported the capture of the Philippines believed the United States could benefit from commercial opportunities in Asia. Also, it was their belief the Filipinos could not self-govern, so obtaining the country would be very valuable. Furthermore, there was fear that flourishing European countries might try to seize the country if the United States did not take the opportunity. The opposition believed that it was morally wrong for the United States to invade and take over the country, something that the United States experienced when they won independence from Great Britain in 1763. Furthermore, those who opposed the annexation felt such actions supported by McKinley's administration were undertones of imperialism.

While American policymakers disputed the annexation, Filipino revolutionaries led by Emilio Aguinaldo captured most of the Philippines' main island, Luzon, and mandated Philippine independence. The United States was adamant on colonizing the island, which led to a large-scale war. Interestingly, Americans referred to the war as an **insurrection** (a violent rebellion against a government) rather than acknowledge they were foreign invaders. In two segments of the war Aguinaldo attempted to fight a conventional war against better equipped American forces. The first phase lasted from February to November 1899. The second phase was a series of guerilla warfare tactics which lasted until 1902. American forces had a significant advantage, as the military was highly trained and had consistent weapons supply. On the contrary, Filipino forces suffered with insufficient weapons supply and lack of operative training, which caused a significant casualty count. Aguinaldo was captured by American forces, and President Theodore Roosevelt declared the end of the war on July 4, 1902.

Minor conflicts would ensue against the American forces for the next few years, but the United States still established its colonial rule. Under President William Howard Taft, the American government formulated the *Policy of Attraction*, which was proposed to attract Filipino elitists and those who did not support Aguinaldo, offering a modest degree of self-governing, introduction to social reforms, and innovative plans for economic development (The Philippine-American War, 1899–1902, n.d., para. 7). The policy worked, and the United States won over a significant number of revolutionaries, winning the war. The Philippines finally declared its independence in 1946 under the United States' *Jones Act*.

The Philippine-American War influenced many aspects of national security within the United States. After the end of the war, Americans realized the importance of pacification and peacekeeping. This brought up challenges predicated on politics between the two countries. The Filipinos realized they lacked the resources, weaponry, training, leadership, and most importantly the competitive disadvantage in being "geographically challenged" to defeat American soldiers. Nonetheless, the bilateral agreement afforded the opportunity for both countries to establish peace and international cooperation. President William McKinley called for "benevolent assimilation" in his address to the people in December 1898 (The World of 1898: The Spanish-American War, n.d.). The Philippine military would work closely with the American Army after the war to ensure peacekeeping and stability within the region; in the twenty-first century, multilateral cooperation agreements still stand between the country and the United States to maintain security and mitigate transnational crime and terrorism within the region.

THE INVASION OF PANAMA (OPERATION JUST CAUSE)

On December 20, 1989, the United States Army executed a preemptive strike on the Panamanian Defense Forces (PDF) to reinstate Panama's democratic government with Guillermo Endara and remove Manual Antonio Noriega from office. Codename *Operation Just Cause*, the invasion was considered one of the most convoluted combat operatives since the United States involvement in the Vietnam War. Over 26,000 American troops deployed to Panama where they attacked twelve targeted locations within the country, exploiting a multifaceted range of tactical strategies such as Airborne, Air-Assault, Military Operations on Urbanized Terrain (MOUT), and Special Forces operations (Operation Just Cause: The Invasion of Panama, n.d., para. 1).

The American government developed a thorough strategic operative, which covered militant warfare procedures and political policies that would remove Noriega from the Panamanian government. Originally, the operation was planned to build up U.S. forces in Panama, and then it changed when Noriega coordinated attacks against the political candidates that did not support him. In addition, he threated American civilians and soldiers, and President George H.W. Bush sent nearly 2,000 additional troops to the country to increase protection measures (Operation Nimrod Dancer). Bush also selected General Maxwell Thurman as the U.S. Southern Command commander, and he was adamant in taking down the Panamanian army. The modified plan was to prevent Noriega from spreading his regime throughout the country, making it tougher to defeat.

The United States Army's intense training and preparation made the operation a success. The 193rd Infantry Brigade began training in early summer of 1989, practicing in improvised substructures. The 82nd Airborne Division and the 7th Infantry Division deployed units to Panama and enhanced training operatives. American forces used increased security measures to their advantage since real-world operations with securing American facilities was the exact training needed for their invasion. In the interim, American forces' operations went undetected by PDF. Though it was difficult, Operation Just Cause epitomized the example of expedient military operations and political goals to achieve a positive end result. The operation was very skilled in defeating dangerous forces without jeopardizing the Panamanian civilian population. The United States Army's succinct training prepared them for worst-case scenarios, and it took less than a week to successfully overthrow Noriega's regime. On January 3, 1990, Noriega surrendered and nearly two weeks later Operation Just Cause was completed.

THE MEXICAN REVOLUTION

The Mexican Revolution was based on increased tensions and a turbulent relationship between Mexico and the United States within a ten-year period (1910–1920). The actual battle would last only two years with an American victory. On February 2, 1848, the two countries signed the *Treaty of Guadalupe Hidalgo*, and Mexico resigned the American sovereignty of the state of Texas. The revolution concluded the authoritarianism in Mexico and established a constitutional republic and a new Mexican culture.

Mexican citizens (mostly middle-class) protested the dictatorship of Porfirio Diaz, who had reigned over the country for 35 years. Diaz was an Army officer who claimed power when his regime overthrew the government in 1876. Though he was in power for nearly 40 years, he was not able to sustain a stable government where politicians controlled elections, opposition, and public order. During his tenure, some wealthy families monopolized the economic system and had political power in other regions of the country. The economy soared because newfound money in the country's government system increased foreign trade and investments. Mexico established railways that traversed the entire country, and coal mining was a very profitable industry at the time. In addition, the agricultural business thrived, and the cities developed paved streets, electrical systems, trams, and critical infrastructures. Even though other Latin American countries were modernized, this development for Mexico was especially important because of innovative efforts produced under an authoritarian control.

Mexico benefited from Luis Terrazas, who had control of the northern region of the country. He had large livestock estates and coal mines and was involved in politics, which affected Diaz's control. Other oligarchy families invested in imported machinery and could produce items that benefited international markets. Such families were connected to each other, and they established a stable economic platform for Mexico. The families increased capital for the Mexican government and alleviated the national budget in the 1890s, and Mexico became quite an attractive country for conducting international business. With such a growing economy and market, the Mexican people thought they would see peace and prosperity from Diaz. Instead, he overthrew the government, and his contentious actions plagued the country for over a decade.

Before Diaz overthrew the government, Mexicans flourished from oligarchies within the region. The expansion of the country and the economy promoted growth and established professional leaders such as attorneys, doctors, educators, entrepreneurs, and political officials. Though the country benefits from oligarchies, some citizens did not approve of the small groups' monopolization of the country's economic standing as well as Diaz's autocracy. Mexican citizens feared that if Diaz stayed in office, the country would not have a favorable, representative government.

In 1908, Diaz initially claimed that he supported a democratic government when he planned to run for president in 1910. Francisco Madero, leader of the Antireeleccionistas, ran against Diaz for presidency, and tensions ensued. Diaz had Madero arrested and declared himself as the president of Mexico. When Madero was released, he established a revolt against Diaz which failed, but citizens did not give up. From the north, Mexican revolutionaries Pascual Orozco and Pancho Villa developed their armies and raided government quarters. In the south, Emiliano Zapata, leader of the Morelos, started a blood-stained campaign against Diaz's regime. In 1911, revolutionary forces seized Ciudad Juarez and forced Diaz to resign, and Madero was declared president.

Madero's presidency was not smooth after overthrowing Diaz. His failure to restore the Mexican government in an expedient fashion angered Zapata, and he turned against the president. Mexican Revolutionary leader, Pascual Orozco was also despondent of the president's hesitance in creating reforms for restoring land to exiled Native Americans and established a revolutionary movement in the north. Eventually, the United States stopped supporting the Mexican government because Diaz's pacifist behavior towards insurgent groups was dangerous to American business interests, and the U.S. believed a civil war would ensue. Felix Diaz, Porfirio Diaz's nephew, led rebel groups and established a revolt against the Mexican army in Mexico City, which was ordered by military officer Victoriano Huerta (who would be Mexico's 35th president). Huerta and Diaz signed the Pact of Embassy with U.S. Ambassador Henry Lane as witness. The pact stated that the two forces would work together to overthrew Madero and appoint Huerta as president. Huerta became president the next day, and Madero was assassinated days later.

It was not long until rebels wanted Huerta thrown out of office. Revolutionaries Alvaro Obregon, Venustiano Carranza, and Pancho Villa developed the *Plan de Guadalupe*, which requested Huerta's resignation. Rebel forces marched into Mexico City and forced Huerta into exile, and Carranza declared himself president, something that Villa did not want. Tensions grew until the parties were forced to elect Eulalio Gutierrez as interim president of Mexico. Zapata supported Gutierrez, and Villa supported Zapata, which caused increased tension. Both parties lost power, and Villa blamed President Woodrow Wilson for his support of Carranza. In retaliation, Villa killed 17 American citizens and then advanced to Columbus, New Mexico where he killed 17 more. President Wilson ordered General John J. Pershing and his unit to enter Mexico and counterattack. By 1917, Carranza took the presidential seat for the second time and wrote the Mexican constitution, which awarded dictatorship to the president, but citizens were granted equal rights, partial rights were given to the Catholic Church, and citizens had the right to seize land from wealthy proprietors. By 1920, he was killed, fleeing Mexico City, and Huerta was interim president until Obregon was elected in late fall. The Mexican constitution was considered the end of the revolution, even though revolts continued for nearly a decade.

WORLD WAR I

World War I, also known as the *First World War*, was an international conflict that began in Europe and lasted for four years (1914–1918). WWI was one of the world's largest wars in which over 70 million personnel were mobilized to fight in Europe. Over nine million soldiers and seven million civilians died, making WWI one of the deadliest wars in global history. The war involved *Allied Powers* totaling 25 nations, including Great Britain, France, Russia, Serbia, Montenegro, Belgium, Japan, Portugal, and Italy. The United States joined in 1917. The *Central Powers* included Germany, Austria-Hungary, the Ottoman Empire, and Bulgaria. WWI was an unprecedented conflict that encompassed massive levels of innovative weaponry, which was introduced in the twentieth century, the evolution of **trench warfare** (a type of military warfare where both parties create trenches as a defense), and more casualties that any war has seen. There were historical conflicts which led to WWI, but its inception began when Serbian nationalist Gavrilo Princip assassinated Archduke Franz Ferdinand and his wife in Sarajevo, Bosnia on June 28, 1914. Tensions grew and produced mobilization orders among European forces, and by August war began between the Allied Powers and the Central Powers.

The assassination instantly ignited revolt within Europe. Austria-Hungary held the Serbian government responsible for Ferdinand's and his wife's death and used the incident as rationalization for

Events Which Led to World War I
- *Triple Alliance, 1882*
- *Franco-Russian Alliance, 1914*
- *Anglo-German Naval Arms Race, 1898–1912*
- *Entente Cordiale, 1904*
- *First Moroccan Crisis, 1905–1906*
- *Anglo-Russian Entente, 1907*
- *Bosnian Crisis, 1908–1909*
- *Agadir Crisis, 1911*
- *Italo-Turkish War, 1911–1912*
- *Balkan Wars, 1912–1913*
- *Assassination of Franz Ferdinand, 1914*
- *July Crisis, 1914*

Slavic nationalism. Russia immediately supported Serbia, and as a precaution, Austria-Hungary waited for German support before they declared war, anticipating possible Russian intervention. On July 5, German leader Kaiser Wilhelm secretly gave his support to Austria-Hungary, and the country went to war. The Serbian government authorized its military forces to mobilize, and a few weeks later Austria-Hungary declared war on Serbia, which collapsed the European great powers. The same week, Belgium, France, Great Britain, Russia, and Serbia created the Allied Powers and targeted Germany.

Germany invaded France through Belgium (which was a neutral country at the time) in the west and antagonized Russia. By August, German soldiers had crossed the border into Belgium, which violated the country's neutrality terms. They conducted the first line of battle to attack and captured Liege, using their most innovative weaponry. They killed Belgian citizens, annihilated the city, and advanced to France where the *First Battle of the Marne* began on September 6 and ended three days later. French and British forces counterattacked the Germans, forcing them north of the Aisne River, and ended the Germans' plans for a rapid victory in the region. The war would continue for the next three years (*Battles of Verdun* and the *Somme*), killing millions of soldiers between the two battles.

In the east, the Soviet Union army invaded Prussia and Poland but was immediately stopped by the German and Austrian forces at the *Battle of Tannenberg*. Even though Germans won the victory, they were forced to move two units from the west to the eastern front to build forces. The Soviet Union had a strong military operative, and its allied reliance ensured a long-term and grueling war with the Germans. The Russian army's strategic plan built numerous incursions on the eastern region but was unsuccessful in infiltrating German forces. Russia's citizens were infuriated with how the war caused poverty and disease. In 1917, such discontent spawned the *Russian Revolution*, led by Vladimir Lenin and the Bolsheviks. Lenin's first order declared an end to Russia's alliance with Austria-Hungary and its withdrawal from the war. Lenin signed an armistice agreement with the Central Powers, removing military forces from the war, and Germans had full range to confront other enemies of Austria-Hungary.

By late 1914, Allied Powers advanced to the region where the Ottoman Empire was located and attempted to attack, but failed and were forced to launch a full-scale conquest of the Gallipoli Peninsula in the spring of 1915. Again, the invasion failed, and the Allied Powers were forced to retreat to the coast of the Peninsula, losing a quarter of a million casualties. Allied Powers, led by Great Britain, combated the Turkish in Egypt and Mesopotamia, and Austrian and Italian forces confronted them alongside the Isonzo River. The first battle along the Isonzo River took place in 1915, and roughly six months later, in the *Twelfth Battle of the Isonzo River* (*Battle of Caporetto*), the Allied Powers defeated the Austrian-Hungarian forces. After the victory, American, British, and French soldiers advanced to the region and confronted the Germans on Italy's territory.

In January 1915, the *Battle of Dogger Bank* (the battle at sea) began, and it took a year before the German navy decided to confront the British Royal navy, utilizing their U-boat submarine operatives. By the following year, the *Battle of Jutland* (considered the largest naval war during WWI) began, and the British Royal navy had a strong hold in which their blockade against the Germans was never infiltrated. In 1917, the United States joined the Allied Powers because the Germans failed to check submarine aggression, which affected shipping interests to Great Britain. Americans were angered that the British ocean liner, the Lusitania, was sunk and immediately turned against the

Germans. By February 1917, the American government passed an arms appropriations bill of $250 million to prepare the United States military for war. During this time, the Germans sunk four American merchant ships, and the 28th President of the United States Woodrow Wilson declared war against Germany before Congress.

It was difficult for the Allied Powers to stand up to German forces after the country built its military forces on the western front. Leader of the German troops Erich von Lundendorff propelled the last offensive attack and confronted the French, known as the *Second Battle of the Marne*. The Allied Powers counterattacked the Germans a few days later, forcing the Germans to end their offensive in the north, losing their anticipated victory. The battle turned the tables for the Allied Powers, and they quickly reinforced their military strength. By 1918, the Central Powers had lost their momentum and could not recover, devastating their economy and land. Even though they won at Gallipoli, they were forced to sign an armistice agreement by October 1918, and other agreements followed. Austria-Hungary signed an armistice agreement on November 4, 1918, and Germany signed a peace treaty on November 11, 1918.

In 1919, representatives from each country attended the peace conference in Paris where the Allied Powers requested to shape a global environment that would preserve such powers from future conflicts. Thus, on June 28, 1919, the *Versailles Treaty* was signed, but it did not include such a request. The Germans were angered and felt they were misled into signing the peace treaty and because they were denied as members into the *League of Nations*, their contentions towards the treaty agreement grew, essentially becoming the result of World War II.

WWI heavily affected American national security policy. The result of the war expanded the United States military establishment, which significantly impacted foreign policy reform and world politics. American involvement in one of the world's largest conflicts influenced class, racial, and other social systems while providing progressive frameworks and ideologies to strengthen economies and promote globalization. Most importantly, the United States promoted democratic governance and societies to mitigate repressiveness in Europe. The United States' attempt to foster democracy and remove authoritarianism somewhat undermined democratic government within the nation and resulted in the country changing to a more conservative model a few years after the war.

WORLD WAR II

Known as the *Second World War*, World War II (WWII) was an international conflict between the Allied and Axis Powers. WWII was larger than WWI, mobilizing over 100 million military forces from 30 countries. In addition, this conflict produced the most casualties, between 50–85 million, including the Holocaust, in which approximately six million Jews were killed and five million civilians. Moreover, over one million casualties derived from America's attack on Japan with the use of atomic bombs on Hiroshima and Nagasaki. WWII is considered the deadliest war in American history. The war featured the first use of nuclear weapons in global history, the spread of communism in Europe, and the international shift in powers to two superpowers: The Soviet Union and the

United States. These two countries would fight for supreme power at the culmination of WWII leading to the Cold War.

Because there were still remnants of animosity and hatred from WWI, the second war was inevitable, producing another international conflict approximately twenty years later. German leader and dictator Adolf Hitler and his National Socialist Party (Nazi Party) rose to power and immediately established alliances with Italy and Japan for this strategic plan of power. Hitler's idealistic principle behind the Nazi Party was global domination, and he started his plan by invading Poland in 1939. The invasion forced France and Great Britain to declare war on Germany, and WWII began.

Two decades before the invasion, the First World War resulted in the fall of the Austro-Hungarian, German, and Ottoman, and Russian empires. In addition, new countries were established in Europe and the Middle East. The Treaty of Versailles developed nine nations; Austria-Hungary dissolved and became separate nations; Czechoslovakia and Yugoslavia converted to independent nations from Austria-Hungary; Turkey separated from the Ottoman Empire; and Poland was re-established after years of division by Austria-Hungary, Germany, and Russia. In addition, Estonia, Finland, Latvia, and Lithuania were developed from Russia, and Austria-Hungary and Russia gave Romania its independence. The League of Nations diminished, and the United Nations was established to be a neutral ground for all countries and to promote global collaboration among its members. The inception of the Cold War would be during this time, and, most importantly, the world saw the rise of two superpowers: The Soviet Union and the United States.

Even though there were positive changes after WWI, the devastation and instability of Europe left unsettled matters, which opened doors for WWII. Predominantly, German economic and political implications in Germany were the main issues that fueled Hitler's campaign to attempt world domination. In 1933, Hitler was appointed Reich Chancellor and immediately named himself Fuhrer (supreme leader). He was obsessed with power and believed the only way he could expand (lebensraum) German culture and race (called Aryan) throughout the world was through war. His first move was secretly re-arming the German force, which violated the Treaty of Versailles agreement. In 1937, he advanced military forces to Austria and the following year to Czechoslovakia. Hitler's actions were unnoticed, as France and Great Britain did not have interest in another confrontation. The two countries suffered the most economic and political devastation from WWI. Furthermore, the Soviet Union and the United States were focused on domestic government matters, thus, Hitler moved in secret without accountability due to violation of international agreements.

By 1939, the German and Soviet prime ministers signed the *German-Soviet Nonaggression Pact* (also known as the *Ribbentrop-Molotov Pact*), which was a neutrality agreement between two countries for international trade. The agreement angered France and Great Britain because the new alliance meant that if Germany went to war, it would not have to fear the Soviet Union. Also, the two countries together could easily divide Poland. Hitler's intentions were to invade Poland, and if so, France and Great Britain had an alliance with the country to provide military support. On September 1, 1939, Nazi Germany invaded Poland, and two days later, France and Great Britain declared war on Germany, which was the inception of WWII. Two weeks later, Soviet Union forces invaded Poland; with Germany invading from the west and the Soviet Union from the east, Poland was immediately destroyed. By early 1940, Germany and the

Soviet Union divided Poland, and the Soviets quickly advanced to dominate the *Baltic Federations* (present-day Estonia, Latvia, and Lithuania). Stalin's quick advancement led to the defeat of Finland during the *Russo-Finnish War* on March 13, 1940.

On April 9, 1940, Germany concurrently invaded Norway and Denmark, and one month later invaded Belgium and the Netherlands, which was known as the blitzkrieg, or an immediate victory. A few days later, Hitler's regiment advanced to the Meuse River and attacked French forces at Sedan, a place fortified with barriers to withstand attack. The attack provoked the British Expeditionary Force to relinquish Dunkirk, as French forces greatly suffered. To the dismay of France, Italian Prime Minister Benito Mussolini activated the *Pact of Steel* (an alliance with the Soviet Union), and Italy declared war on France and Great Britain.

On June 14, German forces invaded Paris and divided France into two zones. Germany occupied one zone, and the French controlled the other under Marshal Philippe Petain's leadership. After Hitler divided France, he aimed for Great Britain with a strong offensive strategy. Because Germany and Great Britain were separated by the English Channel, Hitler planned to attack the country via airstrikes. The bombing commenced throughout the summer of 1940, causing large civilian casualties and structural damage. After the airstrikes, Hitler planned to invade Great Britain but suspended the operation after Great Britain defeated the German Air Force. In 1941, the United States sent aid to Great Britain under the *Lend-Lease Act*.

By 1941, German forces had invaded Yugoslavia and Greece, and Bulgaria, Hungary, and Romania joined the Axis Powers. Hitler had alternative plans that were unknown to the Soviet Union. He formed an alliance with the Soviet Union to ensure the country would not invade Germany. After he conquered the Baltic States, he planned to invade the Soviet Union because the country had large territorial grounds needed to expand the "pure" German race. His tertiary strategic objective was to exterminate all Jewish communities throughout Germany. His plan, called the *Final Solution*, killed over six million Jews in death camps. Hitler declared the invasion of the Soviet Union on June 22, 1941 under codename *Operation Barbarossa*. The Soviet's resources and weaponry outweighed Germany's, but their acquisitions were outdated, making it easier for Hitler's regiment to advance near Moscow. By November 1942, the Soviets conducted a counterattack against the Germans, ending with the Battle of Stalingrad, and the Germans surrendered on January 31, 1943.

> *The German-Soviet Nonaggression Pact agreed that Germany would create manufactured products in exchange for raw materials from the Soviet Union.*

> *The Lend-Lease Act provided military aid and resources to Great Britain and other foreign alliances during WWII.*

The United States entered the war on December 7, 1941 when the Japanese conducted a preemptive strike on Pearl Harbor, killing over 2,300 service members. The following day, the United States declared war on Japan, and the Axis Powers declared war on the United States. Initially, the Japanese won victories, but when the United States won the *Battle of Midway*, there was a major change in the direction of the war. Additionally, the defeat of the Japanese regiment in a six-month period in the Solomon

Islands increased the United States' strength in the Pacific. By summer of 1943, Allied naval forces conducted a counterattack on Japanese forces, using amphibious assault tactics on major Japanese islands. American forces were successful, which led to the goal of invading mainland Japan.

Also in 1943, the United States and Great Britain defeated the Italians and Germans in North Africa. The same year, Allied Powers invaded Sicily and destroyed the Italian government, fighting Italian and German forces by 1945. On June 6, 1944, Allied Powers conducted a counteroffensive invasion in Europe, mobilizing 156,000 American, British, and Canadian soldiers on the coast of Normandy. Hitler's offensive was to rebuild forces in west, affirming units would obtain victories in the east. Soviet Union regiments advanced into Czechoslovakia, Hungary, Poland, and Romania, and Hitler advanced his troops to confront American and British forces in the *Battle of the Bulge*, which was last offensive attack in the war. By April 30, 1945, Hitler committed suicide, and when Allied Powers invaded Germany with aerial weaponry, they forced the Germans to surrender on May 8, 1945. After the Germans surrendered, the Soviets gained much control over Germany.

After the official dissolution of WWII, President Harry S. Truman, Winston Churchill, and Joseph Stalin deliberated the continuing war with Japan and debated peace agreements with Germany during the Potsdam Conference. They decided Germany would be divided into four zones which were to be controlled by France, Great Britain, the Soviet Union, and the United States. Truman and Churchill did not want to make any agreements until the Soviet Union ensured its support in the fight against Japan. Because Japan was a deadly threat due to the casualties at Iwo Jima and Okinawa, and because there was anticipation of an extensive land invasion, Truman authorized American forces to use an innovative weapon (during the WWII era): the **atomic bomb** (a weapon of mass destruction and an explosive device that is created through fission, fusion, or both; a nuclear weapon). On August 6, 1945, atomic bombs were used to annihilate two Japanese cities, Hiroshima and Nagasaki, killing nearly 130,000 people. By August 10, the Japanese surrendered aboard the *USS Missouri* in Tokyo Bay, Japan, and accepted the terms of the *Potsdam Declaration*.

COLD WAR ERA

The *Cold War* was a military and political conflict between the United States and Russia directly after WWII which would last for over four decades. The tensions were between the *Western Bloc* (comprised of the United States and its allies) versus the *Eastern Bloc* (the Soviet Union and its **satellite states**). Satellite state countries were autonomous but were politically and economically controlled by the Soviet Union. The Cold War would last from the Truman era in 1947 until approximately 1991, when the Soviet Union dissolved. The conflict was called the Cold War because the United States and the Soviet Union did not have any direct conflict during this period but instead supported proxy conflicts that involved each other's opposition.

During WWII, the United States and the Soviet Union were coalition forces, fighting together as a part of the Allied Powers. However, the relationship between the two countries was very strained. For many years, the United States was very cautious of the Soviet Union's leader, Joseph Stalin, and his strict, authoritarian control of the communistic government. Because the United States were wary of the Soviets, it resulted in delays with the country entering both world wars, resulting in millions of Russian casualties. The aftermath brought criticism against the United States and portrayed distrust between the two countries. Additionally, after the war, the spread of Communism throughout Europe was a major concern for the United States, as it believed that Russia planned global domination. Furthermore, the Russians did not support American forms of foreign policy and military operatives, believing that the country's methods and interventionist approach were not appropriate.

After WWII, the American government emphasized that the best strategy to handle the Soviet Union was **containment**, a geopolitical strategy to mitigate expansion of the country. The strategy was also justification for the United States to strengthen its military forces, and the National Security Council supported President Truman's decision to increase military movement to mitigate the Soviet Union's expansionism within Europe. The American government also approved the development of atomic bombs, which were used against the Japanese in WWII. In 1949, the Soviets began testing atomic bombs, which provoked the American government to build a more lethal bomb: the hydrogen bomb or "H-bomb." The United States tested the first H-bomb in the Marshall Islands, and the results were devastating; the bomb created a 25-square-mile fireball and vaporized the island, blowing a large whole in the ocean floor. The catastrophic effects of the test were rumored to be able to annihilate half of Manhattan. Both countries tested their bombs at the same time, causing pollution and radioactive waste in the hemisphere. Testing nuclear weapons worried the American population, forcing them to build shelters and to prepare for the aftermath. They conducted exercise scenarios and worked with local emergency management teams for schools and public organizations.

Space Era

Space exploration was a very important movement during the Cold War, and the two countries battled for superiority in sending human life into the intergalactic world. On October 4, 1957, the Soviets launched the world's first missile into space. Russian for "traveler," the *Sputnik* was the first man-made piece of technology to be placed into the Earth's orbit. Russia's accomplishment was a setback for the Americans, as it should have been a triumph for the dominating superpower. Space exploration was the United States' next attempt to gain global superiority, and the Russians launching Sputnik showed that Americans needed to try harder for total dominance.

In 1958, the United States began the space race by launching its own satellite, *Explorer I*, designed under the direction of rocket scientist Wernher von Braun by the United States Army. Later that year, President Dwight Eisenhower signed a bill establishing the *National Aeronautics and Space Administration*, a federal organization dedicated to military and civilian space exploration. The United States still treaded behind the Soviets as the U.S. sent the first American into space in April 1961. On July 20, 1969, Neil Armstrong was the first man to land on the moon, defeating the Soviet Union in the space race.

Anticommunism

After the United States' accomplishment of landing on the moon, Americans were viewed as heroes and true dominators while the Russians were dubbed as "the bad guys" who worshipped the communist system. Such tensions grew as Americans made it evident that communism was not supported. The *House Un-American Activities Committee (HUAC)* was established and heavily affected the entertainment community within the United States. The committee forced those who had left-wing political beliefs to testify against each other, and nearly 1,000 people lost their jobs, and it was almost a decade before they could recover. HUAC also accused government employees, particularly in the state department, of subversive activities, and thousands were investigated, fired, and even victimized. During this period, those who were accused of entertaining communistic principles were reprimanded, shaking the whole nation.

In 1938, House Un-American Activities Committee (HUAC) was created to examine private and public sectors that were suspected to be involved in communism.

The War Abroad

The conflict abroad was the inception of the Cold War when North Korea invaded South Korea in 1950. The Soviet Union supported North Korea's actions while America believed this action was a strategy to start the country's plan for global domination. American policymakers mandated that the United States mobilize, and President Truman ordered military troops to enter Korea. The war lasted for three years and finally dissolved. Other international conflicts occurred during this time, such as the *Bay of Pigs Invasion* and the *Cuban Missile Crisis* (both of which will be further discussed in Chapter Two). Such conflicts made World War III between the United States and the Soviet Union seem inevitable. Additionally, the *Vietnam War* was a critical conflict when the French regime was annihilated, and there was division between northern leader Ngo Dinh Diem, an American and democratic supporter, and southern leader and communist Ho Chi Minh in the battle for dominance. The United States was forced to intervene and mitigate the spread of communism, a conflict that lasted nearly twenty years.

When President Richard Nixon assumed office, he wanted to establish a new strategy for handling international relations, particularly the Soviet Union. He believed it would be more effective to negotiate diplomacy rather than military actions, and the start of his campaign was for the United Nations to recognize China as a member. He flew to Beijing and established diplomatic relations with the country, and soon after, he met with Soviet premier Leonid Brezhnev, and both signed the *Strategic Arms Limitation Treaty*, known as *SALT I*.

The efforts to establish global peace would be interrupted soon after when Nixon left office and Ronald Reagan became president. Reagan believed communism was a threat everywhere, and, therefore, he worked directly with anticommunist countries, providing financial and military resources

The Strategic Arms Limitation Treaty (SALT I) was an armistice agreement between the United States and the Soviet Union that mitigated the assembly of nuclear weapons.

(known as the *Reagan Doctrine*). He worked hard to ensure communism would not consume the war, but at the same time, the Soviet Union was diminishing. The country faced severe economic and political difficulties, and the new premier, Mikhail Gorbachev, wanted to make changes. In 1985, he restructured the Soviet Union's global relationship by enacting economic reform and establishing political transparency. Such changes caused many governments to transfer to non-communistic governing principles. On November 9, 1989, the Cold War culminated with the historical event of the destruction of the *Berlin Wall*. By December 26, 1989, the Soviet Union had collapsed.

Like WWI, the Second World War significantly impacted American national security and foreign policy. Initially neutral to the conflict, the United States was heavily impacted economically once it entered as an Allied Power after the bombing on Pearl Harbor. Prior to the bombing, American politics was divided about interventionism and isolationism. In addition to maintaining global peace and stability, the United States was responsible for preventing communism from spreading throughout the world. Because countries such as the Soviet Union were communist supporters, the U.S. was responsible for ensuring it did not spread to other countries that were not influenced by it. Finally, Japan's failure to obliterate the United States in the attack on Pearl Harbor only caused the nation to show its economic strength (even though America was still recovering from WWI), and the country produced a powerful military operation that had not ever been seen before, resulting in the Allied Powers victory and the United States becoming the most powerful country in the world.

POST-COLD WAR ERA

Decades of tension between the United States and the Soviet Union defined the Cold War period as a symbol of global domination enabled by the evolution of technological advancement. During this time, foreign policy and international-relations ideologies entirely shifted, establishing the birth of a rising country and the fall of the Soviet Union and Japan. The collapse of the European imperial system allowed the superpowers to occupy and control, having territorial dominance. Once WWI ended, European countries established new states, which forced the two countries to fight for domination. Many conflicts throughout the twentieth century identified the struggle for power and dominance, but the Cold War directly identified Europe's decline and the two powers' competition to be a global force.

The aftermath of the Cold War brought critical shifts within the international system. In 1991, the *Chinese Communist Party* emerged, and China grew as a large, international trade market, dominating over Japan. The same year, the *Maastrict Treaty* was created, which was the evolution of the *European Union*. The United States became the leading country and produced a drastic change in coalition forces based on unconventional conflicts. It is clear three elements identified positions after the Cold War: American power, the rise of China, and re-development of the European nation.

The evolution for the Cold War developed two phases of the Post-Cold War era: the collapse of the Soviet Union until the attack on American soil (known as 9/11) and 9/11 to present. The first phase showed the United States was a dominant force in the aftermath of the Cold War and had strong political and military power. The phase focused on the three Great Powers: The United States, China, and Europe. The international shift changed the worldview in economics, governance, and politics. Also, the Post-Cold War era highlighted the rapid emergence of the Islamic world.

During this era, the United States became the most powerful country in the world and China, a relatively weak country, soared to rise as a second global power. With such a shift after the last three global efforts, the United States' national security objective has been to rebalance the Asian Pacific region by "remaining focused on efforts to strengthen relationships and modernize U.S. alliances in the Asia-Pacific region, which is a priority for the twenty-first century security interests and sustaining U.S. global leadership" (Obama, 2012, p. 2). In addition, Europe fought for economic dominance and succeeded, as for many years it was divided and controlled by dominating governments. Most importantly, the emergence of military globalization was an important political move for all global powers.

The fall of the Soviet Union was one of the most significant changes in the world. The country controlled a substantial amount of infrastructure, policies, and territory in the Eastern and Western Blocs, which was heavily predicated on capitalist and communist principles. However, the collapse certainly posed an existential threat for many governments, such as the United States. After the Berlin Wall was destroyed, socialist political parties' membership dropped due to the ideal of winning free market access. Some positive global changes included the abolishment of apartheid in South Africa. Apartheid was criticized because it was considered an anti-communistic system and was no longer supported by the West after the decline of the Cold War. Capitalism was a growing concept during this time, and it was supported by nationalistic and liberal parties. By the end of the Cold War era, nearly one-third of the global population was controlled by communism, and with the culmination of the conflict, economies seemed to instantly boost throughout the world.

SUMMARY

Chapter one briefly presents a timeline of historical events and conflicts that not has only shaped the United States but the entire world. From global dominance to technological advancement, many countries played the role of either an ally or an adversary in the fight for freedom, independence, peace, and power. This chapter prepares students to understand national security and homeland security initiatives that have shaped the nation since its independence from Great Britain. Dating back to the Articles of Confederation, when the Founding Fathers of the United States helped shaped the nation and declared independence for Americans, freedom often came at a price: national security. When North America declared its independence, policymakers knew it would not be the end. To maintain independence and freedom for all, the new America needed a national defense system. Outlining important events that have shaped national security in the United States is important to the understanding of future threats. Furthermore, examining the consistent tensions between superpowers reveals that a strong government and military force would be the ultimate weapon for total omnipotence. Additionally, the chapter not only identifies international conflicts the United States faced, but also highlights internal conflicts that almost destroyed the nation, as delineated in the history of the American

Civil War. However, the United States recovered through many styles and perspectives of presidency and foreign policy. Leaders also shaped America by living by the words of the U.S. Constitution, breaking barriers of slavery, inequality, and discrimination so that all Americans could lively freely and fight for the country as one. Eventually, the nation recovered, becoming a global power after the culmination of the Cold War.

CHAPTER 1 CASE STUDIES

Case Study 1
The American Revolution

America's independence from Britain is considered one of the most decisive turning points in world history. What started as a series of protests and skirmishes in the thirteen colonies eventually developed into a full-scale American Revolutionary War. The results of this war would give birth to one of the world's greatest superpowers and a new way of life.

The British colonies in North America were populated with various English settlers who had traveled to America to seek religious freedom, self-government, acquisition of land and wealth. While the British generally left the colonies to themselves, the French and Indian War fought on American soil had left the British purse empty. The British government decided that it was only fair that the colonies pay their share since the war was fought in their defense. They pushed through a series of taxation acts on various commodities imported into the colonies (Logan, 2001). The colonists, used to self-government, were upset by this interference of the government in Britain. Moreover, they were angry about being taxed without representation in Parliament. While representative government was not a new idea, the colonists were outraged that they were being denied the rights other English men and women had. Parliament had a right to impose tax and as far as the people were represented in Parliament, taxes were considered the "people's will." However, without the representation and consent of the people, the colonists considered it tyranny (Milestones: 1750–1775: French and Indian War, n.d.).

Coupled with the Taxation Acts, Parliament passed the Quartering Act, which required the colonists to feed and house British soldiers serving in America, and the Stamp Act, which required every paper document to bear a stamp purchased from royally appointed stamp agents. This was widely seen as an invasion of privacy, an insult to personal liberty, and an attack on personal rights. Fed up, the colonists bonded in opposition to the tyranny. They formed secret societies known as the Sons of Liberty and drafted a "Declaration of Rights and Grievances," which proclaimed that the colonists were entitled to all the rights of British subjects in the mainland and that taxation without representation was a violation of those rights (Milestones: 1750–1775: French and Indian War, n.d.). The British government took notice and finally repealed the Stamp Act and other tax duties, except for the tax on tea, which remained to maintain Parliament's authority to levy taxes on the colonists. This tea taxation would eventually lead to the famous Boston Tea Party, which inspired similar tea parties on the Eastern coast (American Revolution history, 2009).

As a punitive measure to restore order in the colonies post "Tea Party," the British Parliament passed the Coercive Acts, also known by the colonists as the Intolerable Acts. However, this law had the opposite effect the British had hoped for and led to the colonists convening the First Continental Congress where they declared the Intolerable Acts unconstitutional. Furthermore, the colonists claimed that Parliament's actions had violated their natural rights, an idea born from the Enlightenment and the principles of the British constitution. The appeal to natural rights was significant because it justified colonial opposition to the monarchy (Milestones: 1750–1775: Parliamentary taxation, n.d.). The convening of the First Continental Congress marked an important turning point in colonial relations with Britain as the decisions it made laid the foundations for rebellion. Following the Continental Congress, the colonists proposed an idea by which the colonies would govern themselves but still acknowledge the British monarchy as head of state. Parliament denied the colonist's proposal and declared the Massachusetts colony to be in rebellion (Milestones: 1776–1783: Continental Congress, n.d.). Tensions continued to escalate until the "shot heard round the world" at the Battle of Lexington and Concord, the battle that marked the start of the Revolutionary War. Rather than fight the British forces on open fields, the colonists used guerilla ambush tactics to outmaneuver the British troops as the Redcoats retreated to Boston (Battles of Lexington and Concord, 2009).

Shortly after the Battle of Lexington and Concord, the Second Continental Congress convened to decide how to handle the volatile situation. The gathering of representatives at the Second Continental Congress desired to avoid a full-on war and made a final attempt to halt the revolution by sending the Olive Branch Petition to Britain. Despite the colonists' plea to call off the British troops in Boston and restore peace, the British crown rejected the petition, and the Revolutionary War was in full swing (Milestones: 1776–1783: Declaration of Independence, n.d.).

When the Revolutionary War started, the British made a significant error in assuming that opposition to British policies came only from a core of dissenters. They believed that if they captured these rebel ringleaders, the revolt would collapse. What they failed to understand was that a large portion of the American population disliked British rule and desired their own rule. The colonists, who were already discontent with the British government, had developed a bond and identity among themselves, post French and Indian War (Wallace, 2017).

Elected to be Congress' principal author, Thomas Jefferson drafted the Declaration of Independence, proclaiming independence on behalf of all the American colonists. He drew inspiration from Enlightenment philosophies. From John Locke, he took the idea of separation of church and state and the idea of unalienable human rights. From Jean-Jacques Rousseau, he took the idea that society should be guided by the general will of the people. In addition, he took the idea of a three-branch government with checks and balances from Baron de Montesquieu and the idea of laissez-faire from Adam Smith (Toothman. 2010).

The Declaration also included a detailed account of the tyrannical abuses that the British crown had committed against the colonists, such as denying representative colonial legislature, illegally assuming judicial powers, and conspiring against the colonists with other nations. While the colonists had tried repeatedly to restore peace and relations, the British government continually ignored them; therefore, the colonists had no choice but to declare independence from the British and establish a government that would protect their rights. When the Declaration was finally completed, the justification was not only strong enough to convince other nations that the rebellion was necessary and justified, but to convince them to become allies of America (Wallace, 2017). The French, still smarting over their defeat in the French and Indian War, saw the revolution as an opportunity to get back at the British and supplied the Americans with money and arms. Soon after, the Spanish and Dutch also entered on the side of the French, again, to spite the growing British empire (Milestones: 1776–1783: Secret committee, n.d.).

For several years, the colonists, with the help of the French, Spanish, and Germans, fought Britain for independence. The war finally came to a head at the Battle of Yorktown, where the British general Lord Cornwallis surrendered the British forces and presented General George Washington, leader of the American Continental Army, his sword. This victory was rather momentous since one of the world's most powerful nations had to admit defeat at the hands of a nation that barely existed. However, it wasn't so much that the American colonists won the War as it was they defeated Britain's will to continue fighting (Milestones: 1776–1783: Secret committee, n.d.).

With independence achieved, the Founding Fathers of the nascent country were faced with the Herculean task of building a nation. This included creating laws without being tyrannical, representing the will of the majority without ignoring the rights of the minority, proclaiming liberty without falling prey to anarchy, and protecting the natural and unalienable rights of the people. Borrowing Enlightenment political philosophy, they drafted the Articles of Confederation, which served as a framework for the government. This later became the Constitution. More importantly, the Founding Fathers had to find a way to secure safety and survival for the new country. Through a series of negotiations, the Founding Fathers brokered additional territories west of the colonies and established the recognition of American independence on a global scale, allowing the country to take its place among other nations in the world.

Case Study 2
The Spanish-American War

In 1895, America went to war with Spain to free Cuba from Spanish domination. The conflict ended Spanish colonial rule in the Americas and resulted in the U.S. acquisition of territories in the western Pacific and Latin America. While the war included a few battles, it is not known for its military prestige. Rather, the war had major historical significance as it signaled the emergence of the United States as a great power on the global stage, demonstrating a move from isolationism to imperialism. This shift in policy was rather interesting for the United States since colonialization went against the very ideals that the nation was founded on. Imperialism challenged life, liberty, and the self-government identity the country held dear. This war demonstrated the United States' use of information colonialism and actual imperialism. The war also depicted a prevailing pattern of smaller nations not welcoming U.S. interference in world affairs.

The Spanish-American War began with the Cuban struggle for independence from Spain, and Spain's repressive measures to mitigate rebellion were reminiscent of the

United States' struggle with Great Britain. These infractions were sensationally reported by yellow journalism newspapers, causing American sympathy (Milestones: 1866–1898: Spanish American War, n.d.).

When the USS Maine, a warship berthed in the Port of Havana, exploded, it gave the United States a valid justification for war (The Maine explodes, n.d.). The Rough Riders handled many of the land battles, while the U.S. Navy faced the Spanish Navy. Many believed the United States would face difficult challenges since Spain's navy was a major force with the great Spanish Armada. In terms of the numbers of ships and resources and the fighting experience of their captains, Spain had an impressive naval unit. However, the country's navy was not as powerful as other nations believed. Though they had a significant number of ships, most were antiquated and inoperable. The ships were no match for the newer ships of the United States Navy with modernized assets, especially the steel warships (Spanish American War, 2010).

With the Treaty of Paris, Spain withdrew from Cuba, ceded Puerto Rico and Guam to the United States, and transferred sovereignty of the Philippines to the United States. Spain's defeat decisively turned the Spain's attention away from its overseas colonial excursions and inward to its domestic needs. The United States, on the other hand, emerged from the war not only as a reunited union but as a global power with newly acquired overseas possessions and a new stake in global politics that would lead the country to play a determining role in European affairs (Spanish American War, 2010).

Post-American Civil War, America concentrated on expanding west, settling the territories until the country spanned from sea to sea. During this time, European nations continued to amass far-flung empires throughout the rest of the world. If the United States wanted to be a "great power" like the European nations, the nation had to emulate the Great Powers and that meant being involved in colonial business. To the point of the Spanish-American war, the United States generally claimed to be against colonization and was an advocate of freedom, democracy, and self-government for all, which is why the annexation of the Philippines, Puerto Rico, Guam, and Hawaii was an anomaly (Milestones: 1866–1898: Spanish American War).

One of the reasons the United States annexed the Philippines was to "Christianize" the Filipinos. However, this made little sense since the Filipino population was primarily Catholic. Still, the United States persisted in this desire due to American ignorance and the "white man's" burden." This philosophy proposed the white man as the "racially superior nation" had a moral obligation to civilize the non-white people of the world by education, providing social and economic progress and government through colonialism (Gilson, 2003).

In addition to the "white man's burden," the United States used "informal colonial" influence to protect trade and influence. They promoted democracy to open markets for its manufacturers and sources of raw materials, like the economic relationship that European powers had with their colonies (Carlin, 2013). Not only did certain U.S. companies and shareholders have major investments in the sugar plantations and mines in Cuba, but having ownership of the Philippines provided an American coaling station and naval base to protect U.S. trade interests and maintain stability through Asian waters (Carlin, 2013).

Furthermore, the United States feared Spain would give up Cuba and Puerto Rico to another great nation such as Russia or China, resulting in such countries having access to America's backyard. Therefore, in declaring war on Spain for Cuban independence, the United States ensured its own national security. Cuba and the United States signed a series of treaties which prohibited the Cuban government from entering any international treaty that would compromise Cuban independence or allow foreign powers to use the island for military purposes (Carlin, 2013). Additionally, they passed the Platt Amendment, which allowed the United States to intervene unilaterally in Cuban affairs (Milestones: 1866–1898: Spanish American War).

The Spanish-American War, while not a particularly impressive military war, had significant ramifications on U.S. policy. It established the United States as a new global power as well as illustrated the country's first use of imperialism. Furthermore, the aftermath of the Spanish-American Treaty of Paris created anti-imperialist sentiments in the Philippines, which would lead to the Philippine-American War and later the Vietnam War.

CHAPTER 1 PRACTICE PROBLEMS

1. How did the involvement of the Native Americans affect the American Revolution?

2. Was the American War for Independence inevitable? Why or why not?

3. What are some of the key ideals of the Declaration of Independence? From where and whom did the writers of the Declaration of Independence draw their inspiration?

4. What was the significance of the 1800 U.S. Presidential Election?

5. Could the Civil War have been prevented? Why or why not? Please explain.

6. What effect did the Emancipation Proclamation have on the Civil War?

7. Why did U.S. Congress pass the Teller Amendment as an addendum to the Declaration of War?

8. Why did Spain, a nation with a more experienced naval force, lose to the United States, a fledgling nation?

9. What impact did the Mexican Revolution have on U.S.-Mexican relations?

10. Did the outcome of World War I lead to World War II? What was unfinished in WWI that influenced WWII? Explain your answer.

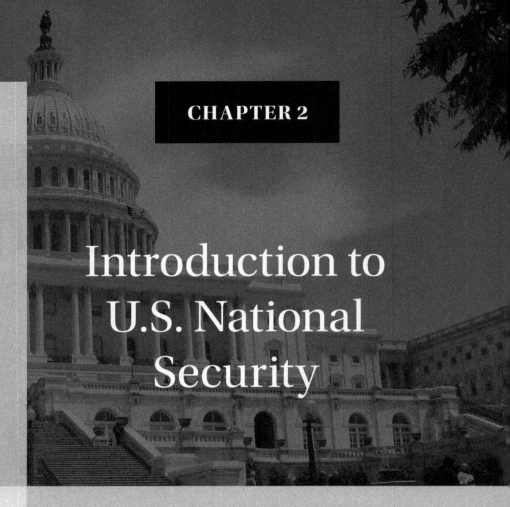

KEY TERMS

Biological weapons

Blockade

Chemical weapons

Capitalism

Coercive power

Communism

Conflict spectrum

Counterproliferation

Democracy

Expert power

Federalists

Global dominance

Globalization

House of Representatives

Legitimate power

National security

Nuclear weapons

Permissive Action Link

Referent power

Republican

Socialism

Reword power

Rogue nations

Unconventional warfare

Weapons of Mass Destruction

CHAPTER 2

Introduction to U.S. National Security

LEARNING OBJECTIVES

After reading this chapter, students will be able to:

- Analyze terminology to define national security objectives
- Discuss events that shaped American national security and foreign policy
- Evaluate the history of weapons of mass destruction and counterproliferation policies
- Summarize historical events and conflicts that shift the international spectrum

INTRODUCTION

This chapter introduces the evolution of the U.S. national security and how specific events shaped not only national security but foreign policy and international relations. The purpose of understanding national security objectives is to analyze and compare initiatives based on historical decision-making that influences existing policies today. Furthermore, the objective of this chapter is to bring awareness of chronological events, which has led to unmatched policies (i.e. National Security Act of 1947, Goldwater-Nichols Act, etc.) that are still relevant in the twenty-first century. Developing strategic guidelines to assist homeland and national experts, policymakers, and professionals is paramount in bringing awareness to identifying top concerns, strengthening international relations, maintaining global security and peace, and promoting globalization. Finally, this chapter summarizes the inception of national security, U.S. values, and the American political system. Understanding America's alliances and adversarial threats, which heavily affects the universal spectrum of peace and conflict, is key to maintaining global dominance. Discussing top threats to security, such as weapons of mass destruction, will be briefly covered in this chapter, but an in-depth reading can be found in Chapter 9. Consequently, all matters begin with the American federal government, politics, and power: how these concepts affect the overall success of the world's most progressive and technologically advanced nation. Understanding national security concerns and distinguishing them from homeland security yet understanding that both overlap is critical, as there is a common objective: protecting American citizens and the homeland.

NATIONAL VALUES

The term national security entered American bureaucratic rhetoric as early as the *Constitutional Convention of 1787*. The purpose of the convention was to reexamine the *Articles of Confederation*, but there was political discourse on the need for a new government. The Constitutional Convention resulted in the establishment of the *United States Constitution*, creating a stronger, federal government system by appointing a chief executive (president) and instituting Congress, national court systems, and taxing powers.

The new government system caused much debate, with concerns about how to split executive power, legal processes, and appointment protocol. In addition, **federalists** (individuals who support federalism and/or were members of the Federalist Party) were concerned about the protection of domestic land, resources, and people. One of the Founding Fathers of the Constitution and America's first Secretary of the Treasury, Alexander Hamilton, was concerned about the civilized infrastructure that controlled the military, which affected national defense. He was very vocal in his concern of civilian authority over the United States military. On January 10, 1788, Hamilton wrote to the people of New York in *The Federalists* (No. 29) about his concerns that "regulating the militia" would be the best defense to protecting the United States (para. 1): "If a well-regulated militia be the most natural defense of a free country, it ought certainly to be under the regulation and at the disposal of that body, which is constituted the guardian of the national security" (1788, para. 3).

Figure 2.1 Founding Fathers sign the United States Constitution

Defining National Security

Alexander Hamilton's statement in "Concerning the Militia" opened dialogue about the meaning of protecting national land over the past 200 years. It also brought much debate about how defining and understanding national security objectives was detrimental to protecting the United States. Such controversy provoked a myriad of terminology. For instance, one of the first instances of the term "national security" in an official government setting was when the United States' first Secretary of Defense, James Forrestal, testified during a Senate hearing in August 1945. His knowledge of national security initiatives and objectives were pivotal in the establishment of the *National Security Act of 1947*. His concepts of national security are centralized in one of the most prominent reorganizations in American history.

Scholars and authors Morton Berkowitz and P.G. Bock defined national security as something that "… can be fruitfully defined as the ability of a nation to protect its internal values from external threats" (1965, p. 1).

Authors and national security experts Ira S. Cohen and Andrew C. Tuttle definition said, "Security may be defined as a protective condition which statesmen's either try to acquire, or preserve, to guard the various components of their politics from external or internal threats" (1972, p. 1).

Robert H. Ullman, author of *Redefining Security*, describes national security this way:

> There is, in fact, no necessary conflict between the goal of maintaining a large and powerful military establishment and other goals such as developing independence from Persian Gulf oil, promoting self-sustaining

development in poor countries … and promoting greater public tranquility and a more healthful environment at home. All these objectives could be achieved if the American people choose to allocate the resources to do so (1983, p. 132).

Melvyn P. Leffler, author of "National Security" in the *Journal of American History* suggests national security is centralized on core values versus costs and security policy dimensions, stating, "… [national security] is a part of interests pursued notwithstanding the cost incurred" (1990, p. 145). David L. Boren, the primary author of the National Security Education Program legislation and founder of the Boren Awards organization, broadly defines national security as:

Recognizing the scope of national security has expanded to include not only the traditional concerns of protecting and promoting American well-being, but also the challenges of global society, including: sustainable development, environmental degradation, global disease and hunger, population growth and migration, and economic competitiveness (2016, para. 1).

Modern and historical terms for national security are now identified in mission statements and by agencies whose mission is to protect national defense, providing a more innovative and politically correct meaning to define and execute policies and initiatives. Today, agencies are more apt to describe how they protect the nation through their organizations' visions and missions. The *National Security Agency's* (NSA) website simply states the meaning of its role to protect national security as:

- Understanding the threat
- Securing networks and data
- Supporting the military
- Leading research (n.d., para. 2).

The Department of Defense (DoD) website states its mission is to: "… provide the military forces needed to deter war and to protect the security of our country" (n.d., para. 9).

The meaning of (and understanding of) national security has chaanged, but political debate continues due to the ambiguity of actual governmental responsibilities. Many Americans have a misconception of what national security relates to as well as the responsibilities to protect it. Author Maxwell D. Taylor expressed vividly in *The Sword of the Pen*:

Most Americans have been accustomed to regard national security as something having to do with the military defense of the country against a military enemy, and this as a responsibility primarily of the armed forces … To remove past ambiguities and recognize the widened spectrum of threats to our security, we should recognize that adequate protection in the future must embrace all important valuables, tangible or otherwise, in the form of assets, national interests, or sources of future strength ... An adequate national security policy must provide ample protection for the foregoing classes of valuables, wherever found, from dangers military and non-military, foreign and domestic, utilizing for the purpose all appropriate forms of national power. (Taylor, 1976, pp. 3–4).

Taylor's opinion of American ignorance on national security initiated a nationwide dispute centered on how continued ambiguities of the concept affected federal governance. National security experts and policymakers Morton Berkowitz and P.G. Bock had a solid definition in the twentieth century, but with judicious speculation comes debate and opposition. German professor and scholar Arnold Wolfers believed there was an instability and obvious ambiguity within most definitions and stated:

> when political formulas such as national interest or national security gain popularity they need to be scrutinized with particular ... they may not mean the same thing to different people ... they may not have any precise meaning at all (Wolfers, 1973, p. 42).

Nonetheless, Wolfers' perception of national security was clear and valid. The constant change of a nation is inevitable, and thus, fluid definitions of national security can mitigate the context and the conceptualization of application for policies and decision-making. If the term changes to benefit the current threat, theoretical frameworks will also change. Furthermore, Wolfers believed the term he established was not only accurate but relevant for the future interpretation and decision-making. He explains, "Security points to some degree of protection of values required" (1952, p. 44).

Figure 2.2 President Harry S. Truman

Truman Doctrine

U.S. national security policy played an unconventional role when the country became a mediator and supporter in international conflict. The United States joined the *United Nations* on July 28, 1945 and was one of five permanent members along with the Soviet Union, Great Britain, France, and China. As permanent members, these countries had the power to sanction certain actions, which was a major advantage over other countries. The United Nations enjoyed considerable success in brokering international cooperation agreements among the countries on economic stability, health, and education. However, the intergovernmental agency was less successful on military operations and nuclear warfare programs. It was prior history that the super powers had global tensions, and all were threats to other countries.

The United States' initial conflict with the Soviet Union derived from the Greek-Turkish relations that resonated between the armistice and hostility when Greece won its independence from Turkey (the *Ottoman Empire*) in 1832. Since the mid-1800s, Greece and Turkey battled in four wars: The *Greco-Turkish War* (1897), the *First Balkan War* (1912), *World War I* (1914), and the second *Greco-Turkish War* (1919). The Soviet Union tried to overthrow the government in both Greece and Turkey. The United States stepped in when Great Britain ceased assistance due to economic instability within its own country.

During the time of the conflict, President Harry Truman requested aid for both countries, mandating $400 million for governmental assistance in both countries, which resulted in the *Truman Doctrine*. He also requested to send American advisors to both countries to assist with government restoration. Three years later, Congress approved, sending more than $600 million to Greece and Turkey.

The Truman Doctrine "established political, military, and economic assistance to all democratic nations under threat from external or internal authoritarian forces" (The Truman Doctrine, n.d., para. 1). It also provided global assistance to allies and coalition forces and revolutionized American foreign strategies by enforcing an unconventional policy where the United States indirectly assisted and was not directly involved in conflict.

The Cold War

The Cold War was a term used to describe an unusual relationship between the United States and Soviet Union. Both countries were major powers, though other countries were involved. The two countries were not directly involved in conflict with each other, but there were dangerous tensions predicated on different ideologies: **capitalism** and **communism**. Throughout history, the two superpowers never trusted each other's policies and governance and exuded a dangerous tension for over forty years. The United States and the Soviet Union used their client states to fight battles on their behalf. For example, the United States assisted Afghanistan with weaponry when the Soviet Union invaded in 1979.

Based on the lack of trust, the United States and the Soviet Union inadvertently established a long-term conflict for dominance and superiority. According to the John F. Kennedy Presidential Library and Museum website, "The two superpowers continually antagonized each other through political maneuvering, military coalition, espionage, propaganda, arms buildup, economic aid, and proxy wars between other nations" (The Cold War, n.d., para. 1). Even though the countries were never allies, they had one enemy in common during this period: Nazi Germany.

On May 1945, the tensions between the two became highly apparent when Germany's government began to collapse and the top powers under the United Nations (the United States, Great Britain, France, and Russia) were left to resolve the country's matters. The Russians heavily populated one of Germany's major cities, Berlin, and the Western alliances were mostly in the western side of the country. The Soviets did not like the Western presence in the city and established a **blockade** (an action of blocking a location to prevent imports or exports from entering or leaving the premises) to remove them. The Westerners formed a larger alliance and formulated a massive airlift, providing food, supplies, and other support, known as the *Berlin Airlift*. Nearly a year later, the

Figure 2.3 U.S. Army Helicopter Assault Companies at 170th & 189th at Polei Kleng

Figure 2.4 Nazi Troops in Nuremberg, Germany on November 9, 1935

airlift and other conflicts throughout the Cold War period made it apparent that it would be difficult to repair Germany. Consequently, the Western powers established a new country, West Germany, and the Soviets created East Germany.

The Cold War infected other continents such as Africa, Asia, and Central America. By 1949, China, a pro-communist supporter, joined ranks with the Soviet Union. A year later, North Korea invaded South Korea. China intervened to support North Korea in the effort while the United States provided military support to South Korea. Not until 1953 when the Korea War ended and both parties signed the *Korean Armistice Agreement*, was there a concern that more global conflict would cause dangerous tensions.

National Security Act of 1947

The *National Security Act (NSA) of 1947* was a direct response to the aftermath of World War II (WWII) with significant ramifications for the Cold War. The NSA of 1947 was the United States' largest reorganization of government agencies and military service departments, which was an important legacy created during the Cold War legislation. This act alone became the foundation for U.S. foreign policy framework on military structure and how the nation would make decisions during the Cold War for the next four decades. The most prominent decision-making policies from the NSA established the following:

- The position of Secretary of Defense (SECDEF)
- The Department of Defense (DoD), initially named National Military Establishment (NME)
- Renamed the Department of the Army (was Department of War, which included Department of the Navy)
- Created the Department of Air Force (which was a part of the Army Air Corps)
- Merged all serviced department under DoD

Figure 2.5 President Truman Signing the National Security Act of 1947

- Crafted the Joint Chiefs of Staff (JCS)
- Shaped the National Security Council (NSC)
- Established the Central Intelligence Agency (CIA)

Secretary of Defense (SECDEF)

The Secretary of Defense is the "principal defense policy advisor to the *President of the United States* (POTUS)" (Defense Leaders, n.d., para. 2). He is the most senior executive official for the nation's largest federal government agency, the Department of Defense. The secretary is responsible for the world's largest military, totaling over 1.3 million military service members and nearly 750,000 federal government civilian personnel. This position is equivalent to Defense Ministers that exist in other countries. The position is appointed by the president with the approval of the *Senate*. The secretary is also a member of the President's Cabinet and an executive member of the *National Security Council.*

The secretary is directed to "exercise authority, direction, control over DoD" and exercise military authority and related matters. The mission of the secretary is to lead DoD

Figure 2.6   James V. Forrestal, First United States Secretary of Defense

and "provide military forces needed to deter and to protect the security of [our] country" (DoD, n.d., para. 9). *James V. Forrestal* was the first Secretary of Defense appointed as a direct result of the restructuring of government agencies within the NSA of 1947.

Department of Defense (DoD)

The Department of Defense is "America's oldest and largest government agency" (DoD, n.d., para. 2). Its headquarters, the Pentagon, is in Arlington, Virginia, and is one of the world's largest office buildings. Per the DoD website, the Pentagon is double the size of the Merchandize Mart in Chicago and had approximately three times the floor space existing within the Empire State Building in New York City. The DoD is the heart of America's national security policies and framework. The agency is responsible for keeping America safe by housing the world's strongest military forces and deploying them all over the world to enforce global peace, stability, trade, and security.

The Army, Navy, and Marine Corps were created in 1775 because of the American Revolution. The service departments were combined to create the *Department of War* nearly 15 years later. In 1790, the *United States Coast Guard* was established and was directed under the Navy during war, but reported under the policies of Homeland

Figure 2.7 The Pentagon

Security in garrison. When the *Department of the Navy* was created in 1798, the Coast Guard reported directly to the newly established agency under wartime operations.

When President Harry S. Truman signed the NSA of 1947, the *National Military Establishment* (NME) replaced the Department of War and formed three military branches: *Department of the Air Force*, *Department of the Army*, and the *Department of the Navy* (including the United States Marine Corps). The Department of the Air Force, which houses the United States Air Force, is charged with aerial warfare, domestically and abroad. The Department of the Air Force is headed by the *Secretary of the Air Force*, a senior executive civilian, and the Air Force's most senior uniformed officer, the Chief of the Staff of the Air Force. Both are principal advisers to the president on all military matters.

The Department of the Army is responsible for the United States' largest military branch, the United States Army. With over one million military personnel, the Army is accountable for all land-based operations within the United States and all permanent military installations and combat zones overseas. The *Secretary of the Army* oversees the department and the Chief of Staff of the Army is highest-ranking military official. Both are advisers to the president on all Army matters.

The nation's oldest military agency, the Department of the Navy, includes the United States Navy, the United States Marine Corps, and the United States Coast Guard (during times of war). The Navy, responsible for all naval warfare operations, is considered the most reliable and technologically advanced navy in the world, having the most naval ships, carriers, aircraft, and nuclear weapons in history. The Marine Corps' mission is encompassing all land, air, and sea task force operations, producing powerful protection for the Navy. Finally, the Coast Guard is a maritime service operator, with military and law enforcement missions, providing a distinctive operation among the other branches of service. Having federal law enforcement objectives, the Coast Guard has jurisdiction in both domestic and international waters. In peacetime missions, the Coast Guard reports to the Department of Homeland Security, and during wartime operations, the Department of the Navy has authority. All branches of the Navy report to the Secretary of Navy, who is the highest-ranking defense civilian, and the *Chief of Naval Operations*, the most senior naval military officer (except for the Chairman of the Joint Chiefs of Staff, if applicable). Both officials are advisors to the president on all naval warfare matters.

Joint Chiefs of Staff (JCS)

The *Joint Chiefs of Staff* is a group of senior military leaders within the DoD who advise the president, the *Secretary of Defense*, the *Homeland Security Council*, and the *National Security Council* on all military matters. All positions are appointed by the president and confirmed by the Senate. The JCS is comprised of:

- Chairman of the Joint Chiefs of Staff
- Director of the Joint Chiefs of Staff
- Vice Chairman of the Joint Chiefs of Staff

Figure 2.8 President John F. Kennedy discusses the Cuban Missile Crisis

- Military Service Chiefs
  - › Chief of Staff of the Air Force
  - › Chief of Staff of the Army
  - › Chief of Naval Operations
  - › Commandant of the Marine Corps
  - › Chief of the National Guard Bureau
  - › Commandant of the Coast Guard (operates under Department of Homeland Security during peacetime, falls under Department of the Navy during wartime operations)
- Service Secretaries
  - › Secretary of the Air Force
  - › Secretary of the Army
  - › Secretary of the Navy

In 1986, JCS was reorganized as a military organization by the *Goldwater-Nichols Act*, and responsibilities were given to senior military advisors who provided personnel readiness, policy, planning, and training initiatives directly to the president and the Secretary of Defense. Also, their responsibilities are to provide military advice to the *Unified Combatant Commands*, who are directly involved in the operational command of U.S. military personnel.

The *Chairman of the Joint Chief of Staff (CJCS)* is the highest-ranking senior military officer in the United States military. In addition, the CJCS is the chief military advisor to the president, the Secretary of Defense, the Homeland Security Council, and the National Security Council. CJCS receives assistance from the Vice Chairman of the Joint Chiefs of Staff, which is the second-highest ranking senior military officer in the United States Armed Forces. Both chairmen outrank all department chiefs within the DoD and are sworn in responsibilities under *Title 10 of the United States Code 153*. Additionally, both chairmen can serve up to two years and can be renewed at the discretion of the president, totaling six years. Under CJCS authority, a senior military officer can serve only two terms if he or she has served a term as the vice chairman. During wartime operations, there is no limit to how many terms a chairman serves.

National Security Council (NSC)

The National Security Council (NSC) is the "president's principal forum for considering national security and foreign policy matters with his senior national security advisor and cabinet officials" (National Security Council, n.d., para. 1). The NSC was established as a part of the NSA Act of 1947, and its fundamentals have been to advise and assist the president on all national security and foreign policy matters. The council is chaired by the president and consists of the following members:

- Vice President
- Secretary of State

- Secretary of Treasury
- Secretary of Defense
- Assistant to the President for National Security Affairs
- Chairman of the Joint Chiefs of Staff
- Director of National Intelligence
- Chief of Staff to the President
- Counsel to the President
- Assistant to the President for Economic Policy

Central Intelligence Agency (CIA)

The *Central Intelligence Agency (CIA)* is the largest foreign intelligence agency in the United States. Created through the NSA of 1947, the CIA does not have law enforcement capabilities. The CIA's sole responsibility is "research, development, and deployment of high-leverage technology for intelligence purposes" (About CIA, n.d., para. 5). Additional responsibilities include:

- Creating special, multidisciplinary centers to address high-priority issues such as nonproliferation, counterterrorism, counterintelligence, international organized crime and narcotics trafficking, environment, and arms control intelligence.
- Forging stronger partnerships between the several intelligence-collection disciplines and all-source analysis.
- Taking an active part in Intelligence Community (IC) analytical efforts and producing all-source analysis on the full range of topics that affect national security.
- Contributing to the effectiveness of the overall IC by managing services of common concern in imagery analysis and open-source collection and participating in partnerships with other intelligence agencies in the areas of research and development and technical collection (About CIA, n.d., para. 7).

The *Director of Central Intelligence (DCI)* serves as the "head of the United States Intelligence Community and acts as a principal adviser to the president for intelligence matters related to national security … and serves as the head of the Central Intelligence Agency" (About CIA, n.d., para. 1). DCI's responsibilities comprise:

- Collecting intelligence through human sources and by other appropriate means, except that he shall have no police, subpoena, or law enforcement powers or internal security functions;
- Correlating and evaluating intelligence related to the national security and providing appropriate dissemination of such intelligence;
- Providing overall direction for and coordination of the collection of national intelligence outside the United States through human sources by elements of the IC authorized to undertake such collection and, in coordination with other

departments, agencies, or elements of the United States government, which are authorized to undertake such collection, ensuring that the most effective use is made of resources and that appropriate account is taken of the risks to the United States and those involved in such collection; and

- Performing such other functions and duties related to intelligence affecting the national security as the president or the Director of National Intelligence may direct (About CIA, n.d., para. 3).

The Bay of Pigs Invasion

On January 1, 1959, *Fidel Castro* overthrew Cuba's president, General Fulgencio Batista, an ally of the United States, and took over the country. The American-trained Cubans were overpowered by Castro's insurgents, and the invasion ended after approximately 48 hours of battle. Even though Batista was considered a corrupt leader, he was pro-America and a major supporter of U.S. businesses. American entrepreneurs owned nearly 50 percent of Cuba's agricultural and mining systems, which Castro's regime opposed. In addition, Castro opposed American business initiatives in Cuba and wanted to take control. Immediately after taking position, Castro drastically reduced American presence and influence in Cuba. Per the United States Office of the Historian, Castro "quickly severed the country's formerly strong ties with the United States by expropriating U.S. economic assets in Cuba and developing close links with the Soviet Union" (The Bay of Pigs Invasion and its Aftermath, April 1961-October 1962 n.d., para. 1)

With Fidel Castro in control of Cuba, the United States expressed great concern due to drastic changes within a short period. Also, Cuba's proximity to the United States was deemed dangerous, as the country is only approximately 100 miles from domestic land. With Cuba's new relationship with the Soviet Union, the United States had to establish a ploy to overthrow Castro's regime. In 1960, during his administration, President Dwight D. Eisenhower devised a plan to use Cuban exiles to invade Cuba and overthrow Castro. In 1960, the CIA led a paramilitary troop invasion where nearly 1,500 Cubans attempted a military coup, but it was not successful.

The United States' first sanction against Cuba was prohibiting the importation of Cuban sugar. By 1961, the federal government dissolved diplomatic dealings with Cuba and continued to plan the invasion. Presidents from Eisenhower to John F. Kennedy had taken office, and Castro was still a threat to the United States because of the newfound relationship between the country and the Soviet Union. Not only was Castro's regime dangerous to the U.S., but to Latin America as well; therefore, Kennedy continued Eisenhower's plan to annihilate Castro's administration.

The failed attempted only strengthened Castro's regime and relationship with the Soviet Union. Also, Castro publicly announced the country's intent to adopt **socialism** (a system in which the government controls private property and natural resources, and what is manufactured is shared by those who contributed to its production) and ratify socialist policies. In the aftermath, the United States government had to reevaluate its policy and formulate a new strategy to get Fidel Castro out of command. *Operation MONGOOSE* was the second attempt to invade Cuba, and it was based on the "coordinated program of political, psychology, military, sabotage, and intelligence operations, proposing assassination attempts on key leaders, including Castro" (The Bay of Pigs Invasion and its Aftermath, April 1961-October 1962, n.d. para. 5).

Operation Mongoose was not considered successful, and it did not affect Castro's authority. Instead, it was a lesson learned and an important part of American foreign policy. Even though there was not a military invasion, the United States maintained intelligence and surveillance on Cuba, which provided cryptic information about the country's secret shipments from the Soviet Union. Through surveillance, the U.S. found reasonable evidence to speculate that the Soviet Union was possibly shipping live nuclear and ballistic missiles, which was a significant threat to the United States. This secret operation provoked the *Cuban Missile Crisis*.

The Cuban Missile Crisis

The Cuban Missile Crisis was one of the most dangerous conflicts the United States faced and was a direct confrontation with the Soviet Union, proving the Cold War was not over. After two failed attempts to overthrow Fidel Castro (The Bay of Pigs Invasion and Operation MONGOOSE), the Soviet Union's premier, *Nikita Khrushchev*, established a classified agreement with Castro's regime to give the country nuclear weapons (offensive missiles) in case the United States attempted another invasion. Through U.S. surveillance, information surfaced that Cuba was developing missile sites with assistance from the Soviet Union, which made the United States a primary target.

Historians Lawrence Chang and Peter Kornbluh edited documents on the Cuban Missile Crisis from the National Security Archives (NSA) and provided spirited conclusions as to why Nikita Khrushchev offered such an agreement for Fidel Castro. Per NSA documents, there were three potential reasons for the deal: "(1) increase Soviet Union striking power, which was inferior to the United States, (2) deter the United States from invading Cuba, and (3) the double standard by which the United States stationed missiles on the Soviet perimeter but denied the Soviets a reciprocal right" (Chang and Kornbluh, 1992, p. 351).

After speaking with his advisers, Khrushchev proposed the deployment deal to Castro (Garthoff, p. 1989, 13). There were concerns that the secret agreement could be detected by the United States, but Khrushchev convinced his Ambassador to Cuba, Aleksandr Alekseyev, and other hesitant advisers to secretly travel and discuss negotiation with Castro. After negotiations were finalized, Khrushchev certified "24 medium-range ballistic missile (MRBM) launchers, and each launcher was furnished with two missile and nuclear warheads" (National Security Agency, 1992, p. 351). In addition, the Soviet Union provided four elite combat regiments, 24 advanced SA-2 surface-to-air missile (SAM) batteries, 42 MiG, interceptors, 42 IL-28 bombers, 12 Komar class missile boats, and coastal defense cruise missiles (Garthoff, p. 1989, pp. 12–18).

Fidel Castro's decision to accept the Soviet's nuclear deployment was not only to deter the United States from a third possible invasion but to express his interest in shifting to socialism. After secret talks between Fidel Castro's brother Raul (the prime minister) and Soviet leadership in Russia, the plan was to finalize and implement a military strategy of how weapon systems would be shipped in order to be undetected by the United States. It was not until August 1962 that U.S. intelligence reports surfaced stating nuclear missiles from the Soviet Union were entering Cuba. CIA Director *John McCone* briefed President Kennedy there were reports that proved the Soviets were shipping MRBMs to Cuba. For weeks, McCone developed contingent data to prove the Soviets and Cuba were working together and building offensive missile installation sites, meaning Cuba was planning for an attack against either the United States or its Western allies. Secretary of State *Dean Rusk* and Secretary of Defense *Robert McNamara* believed McCone's statements were purely anecdotal and that Cuba was only building its defense. By the end of August 1962, President Kennedy addressed Director McCone's concerns of a possible Cuban attack. After the Chairman of the Joint Chiefs of Staff *Maxwell D. Taylor* suggested a "more aggressive" Operation MONGOOSE mission, knowing that the current strategy was not solid enough to overthrow Castro's regime, Kennedy approved a more aggressive plan but openly expressed there would not be a direct military conflict towards Cuba.

The NSC was called to dispute whether Cuba was planning an offensive attack against the United States or if the country was just building defensive forces. Rusk and McNamara were adamant that McCone did not have sufficient evidence about Cuba's intensions. Thus, President Kennedy directly tasked the NSC to institute a contingency plan that was approved in the *National Security Action Memorandum (NSAM) 181*.

In the NSAM, President Kennedy directed the following seven items be answered:

1. What action can be taken to get Jupiter missiles out of Turkey? (Action: DoD)
2. What information should be made available in the U.S. and abroad with respect to these new bloc activities in Cuba? (Action: Department of State, in consultation with USIA and CIA).
3. There should be an organized effort to bring home to governments of our NATO allies the meaning of this new evidence of Castro's subservience to the Soviets and the urgency of action on their part to limit their economic cooperation with Cuba. (Action: Department of State (DoS)
4. The line of activity projected for Operation MONGOOSE Plan B plus should be developed with all possible speed.
5. An analysis should be prepared of the probable military, political, and psychological impact of the establishment in Cuba of either surface-to-air missiles or surface-to-surface missiles which could reach the U.S. (Action: White House, in consultation with DoS, DoD, and CIA).
6. A study should be made of the advantages and disadvantages of making a statement that the U.S. would not tolerate the establishment of military forces (missile or air, or both?) which might launch a nuclear attack from Cuba against the U.S. (Action: DoS, in consultation with DoD with respect to study in item 7 below).
7. A study should be made of the various military alternatives which could be adopted in executing a decision to eliminate any installations in Cuba capable

McGeorge Bundy / U.S. Department of State, "National Security Action Memorandum No. 181." 1962.

of launching nuclear attack on the U.S. What would be the pros and cons, for example, of pinpoint attack, general counter-force attack, and outright invasion? (Action: DoD) (Bundy, 1962, pp. 1–2).

With no definitive information on whether U.S. intelligence reports were factual, President Kennedy remained clear that no action would be taken on Cuba. Tensions grew within the federal government, as there was direct evidence that Cuba could be planning an attack. State Department official Walt Reston recommended that Operation MONGOOSE enhance its forces, and as a result, Cuba infiltrate with no direct U.S. involvement. It was report Cuba was recreating SAM bases for surface-to-surface missiles, and after speaking with the Ambassador to the Soviet Union, *Anatoly Dobrynin,* there was assurance the Cuba would not be basing offensive missiles within the country.

On September 4, 1962, President Kennedy released a statement that the United States was aware of the increased military presence and SAMs systems in Cuba. He said,

> There is no evidence of any organized combat force in Cuba from any Soviet bloc country; of military bases provided to Russia; of a violation of the 1934 Treaty, relating to Guantanamo; of the presence of offensive ground-to-ground missiles; or of other significant offensive capability ... were it otherwise the gravest issues would arise (Wenger, 2000, p. 278).

In response to Kennedy's statement, Dobrynin reassured the Ambassador to the United Nations, Adlai Stevenson, "Only defensive weapons are being supplied to Cuba" (Garthoff, 1989, p. 29).

Finally, the Soviet Union's spokesperson released a statement denouncing the United States: "The arms and military equipment sent to Cuba are intended solely for the Soviet Union to set up in any other country—Cuba for instance—the weapons it should for repelling aggression, for a retaliatory blow" (Weldes, 1999, p. 29).

President Kennedy gave Cuba another warning on September 13, 1962:

> [If Cuba] ... should ever attempt to export its aggression by for force ... or become an offensive military base of significant capacity for the Soviet Union, then this country will do whatever must be done to protect its own security and that of its allies (Magee, 2013, p. 74).

After statements of warning and assurance, the United States still was not satisfied with Cuba or the Soviet Union. By mid-September 1962, the United States Intelligence Board had clear reports that two Soviet ships contained military cargo, and a further report identified a talkative drunken Cuban pilot as saying, "We will fight to the death, and perhaps we can win because we have everything, including atomic weapons" (Handel, 2003, p. 194). Also, there was evidence that the Cubans were building SA-2 air defense systems.

In response to these developing reports, the United States Senate passed a sanction on Cuba for the possible use of force:

The United States is determined to prevent the creation or use of an externally supported offensive military capability, endangering the security of the U.S. and to support the aspirations of the Cuban people for a return to self-determination (Wikenheiser, 1975, p. 15).

In addition to Senate response, the House of Representatives permitted three ratifications to the sanctions the United States would deny aid to any country that supported and provided military supplies to Cuba. The Soviet Union's Foreign Minister, Andrei Gromyko, blamed the United States for creating "hysteria" and emphatically voiced, "Any sober-minded man knows that Cuba is not building up her forces to such a degree that she can pose a threat to the United States or its allies … to any state in the Western Hemisphere" (Excerpt from State by Soviet Ambassador Valerian A. Zorin to U.N. Council, 1962, para. 19). Gromyko ended his statement by threatening that if the United States attacked Cuba or any Cuban shipment, it would mean war.

By October 1, 1962, U.S. intelligence sources had briefed Secretary McNamara that the Cubans had positioned MRBMs on the Province of Del Rio. McNamara directed the Navy to prepare a blockade and commanded the Air Force to preposition its forces for a potential airstrike contingency plan. Consequently, McNamara reported his plans to the Joint Chiefs of Staff and clearly informed both service departments of six circumstances in which military actions would be provoked:

1. Soviet action against Western rights in Berlin.
2. Evidence that the Castro regime was permitting the positioning of bloc offensive weapons on Cuban soil or in Cuban harbors.
3. An attack against the Guantanamo Naval Base or against U.S. planes or vessels outside Cuban territorial air space or waters.
4. A substantial popular uprising in Cuba, the leaders of which request assistance.
5. Cuban armed assistance to subversion in other parts of the Western Hemisphere.
6. A decision by the President that the affairs in Cuba have reached a point inconsistent with continuing U.S. national security (The naval quarantine of Cuba, 1962, 2015, para. 14).

On October 6, 1962, the *Commander-in-Chief, Atlantic Command (CINCLANT)*, ordered military units to escalate readiness capabilities and implement *Operation Plan (OPLAN) 312*, or *Status of Readiness for the Cuban Operation,* for an airstrike on Cuba. This plan ensured that the United States amplified its military forces, aircraft, naval vessels, and other assets needed to prepare for a full-scale invasion on Cuba. OPLANs 314 and 316 followed.

Cuban President Osvaldo Dorticos Torrado ardently pressed the United Nations to sanction U.S. trade embargos against Cuba. The State Department consulted with the Soviet Union about evidence collected that Cuba was harboring Soviet nuclear missiles; the Soviet Union denied this allegation.

The United States proved its theory of the Soviet Union's secret agreement with Cuba when the first American U-2 flew reconnaissance missions over Cuba on October 15,

1962. The successful mission was the first *Strategic Air Command (SAC)* operation after Secretary McNamara approved preparing military forces for a possible airstrike. U.S. Air Force U-2 pilot Major Rudolf Anderson, Jr., flew the first top-secret mission that not only confirmed missile sites in Cuba, but he would be the first and only one killed when Cubans fired Soviet SA-2 surface-to-air-missiles and shot him down, killing him instantly.

Analysis of the surveillance Major Anderson collected showed 23 SAM sites and the unpacking of IL-28 bombers in San Julian. Again, military forces and equipment were postured, concealing actual real-world operations with a prominent exercise plan called *PHIBRIGLEX-62* to engage "troops and equipment for deployment aimed at increasing military readiness for an airstrike on Cuba" (Kennedy Library observes fortieth anniversary of Missile Crisis, 1962, p. 359).

With advisement from the Executive Committee of the National Security Council (EXCOM) and personal advisors, President Kennedy formulated a strategy that included comprehensive military involvement and direct conflict with Cuba to remove missile sites. Because investigative photos did not show warheads, Kennedy ordered two U-2s to fly additional reconnaissance missions to gather additional information. As flying operations ensued, EXCOM devised a conceivable scenario for how to mitigate the Cuban crisis (Maga, 2003, p. 100). There were four possible strategies:

1. A single, surgical airstrike on the missile bases
2. An attack on various Cuban facilities
3. A comprehensive series of attacks and invasion
4. A blockade of Cuba (Maga, 2003, p. 100).

Each scenario was regarded as provoking a negative reaction from Cuba and the Soviet Union, causing either a full-scale invasion or a counteraction from the Soviet Union. The United States believed an invasion in Cuba would automatically involve the Soviet Union assisting Cuba and possibly establishing a blockade in Berlin, Germany. With much consultation, President Kennedy thought a blockade of Cuba would be the best strategy because it aligned more with American principles. Kennedy finalized the blockade, which was called the *Quarantine Plan,* on October 21, 1962. With the finalization of the Quarantine Plan, President Kennedy emphatically articulated to Air Force leadership to be prepared to carry out airstrikes the next day, if needed.

By October 22, 1962, over 300 aircraft were armed with nuclear weapons and prepared for nonstop air operations. Personal letters from President Kennedy were sent to world leaders and embassies to discuss the missile crisis in Cuba and the United States' decision to form a blockade, preventing shipments to Cuba from the Soviet Union. Most leaders supported the blockade and heightened their force protection measures as a sign to enhance security operations for American forces throughout the world. However, other leaders were concerned about the consequences of the blockade. For example, British Prime Minister Harold MacMillan was concerned that increasing force protection measures would weaken support for the United States since Great Britain's economy still suffered from the Cold War. MacMillan was also concerned the blockade would force the Soviets to counteract, resulting in retaliation from the United States. Per the Prime Minister, provoking the United States and possibly causing WWIII has always been a tactic of the Soviet Union.

Nonetheless, on October 22, 1962 at 7:00 p.m., President Kennedy addressed American citizens about the Cuban Missile Crisis and announced that the United States would take steps to "quarantine the problem" but would be prepared to deter any nuclear weapons launched from Cuba against any nation in the Western Hemisphere. He also addressed the Soviet Union in the televised message that if it became involved, the United States would retaliate. President Kennedy said:

> If at any time the Communist build-up in Cuba were to endanger or interfere with our security in any way, including our base at Guantanamo, our passage to the Panama Canal, our missile and space activities at Cape Canaveral, or the lives of American citizens in this country, or if Cuba should ever attempt to export its aggressive purposes by force or that threat of force against any nation in this hemisphere, or become an offensive military base of significant capacity for the Soviet Union, then this country will do whatever must be done to protect its own security and that of its allies (Magee, 2013, p. 74).

Fidel Castro took President Kennedy's message as aggression toward the country and mobilized his military units exponentially up to 270,000. Kennedy officially formalized the quarantine plan, Proclamation 3504, on October 23, 1962 and articulated to CINCLANT to enforce the blockade the next morning. Castro contested the blockade, stating that Cuba did not have offensive missiles. He was steadfast in mandating that the United States would not inspect any ships that were arriving to Cuba. The Soviet Union prepared its forces as well; "battle readiness and vigilance of all troops had been raised" (White, 1996, p. 190).

On October 24, 1962, the quarantine plan was officially in effect by the United States Navy. Tensions rose when U.S. leadership recognized that Soviet ships were not planning to obey the blockade. Even though President Kennedy did not want hostilities to ensue, the United States had prepared to intercept the ships and enforce courses of action. Premier Khrushchev informed President Kennedy that the blockade was an act of aggression and that he would not instruct Soviet ships to comply. With Khrushchev's response, it was obvious that United States would intensify its measures. President Kennedy directed that DoD formulate civil defense strategies to prepare for military involvement against Cuba. Two separate plans would cover the groundworks for conventional warfare and a possible nuclear attack.

As tensions grew, the United Nation's Secretary-General U Thant intervened and started negotiations between the United States and the Soviet Union. Thant proposed that the United States remove its Jupiter missiles from Turkey and that the Soviets remove its missiles from Cuba. President Kennedy was unyielding about ending the blockade nor did he have interest in removing assets from Turkey. He believed such action would give Cuba and the Soviet Union leverage to have their forces continue constructing their plan of assembling missiles that were already on site. Thant's second proposal requested that the United States and the Soviet Union refrain from direct conflict while the blockade existed.

CIA Director McCone announced on October 25, 1962 that Cuba had operational missiles. Later that day, President Kennedy authorized CIA sabotage teams to travel to Cuba and terminate missile site facilities. Realizing the blockade would not entirely halt shipping operations, the United States prepared for possible airstrikes by increasing low-altitude reconnaissance flights and collecting additional intelligence. As an invasion by the United States was imminent, KGB Station Chief (and later found to be a Soviet spy) *Aleksandr Fomin* proposed to State Department Correspondent John Scali that there should be an intervention to mitigate an invasion on Cuba. Fomin said, "Soviet bases would be dismantled under United Nations supervision, and Fidel Castro would pledge not to accept offensive weapons of any kind, ever, in return for a U.S. pledge to not invade Cuba" (Fursenko and Naftali, 1997, p. 265).

Fomin's proposition was not authorized by the Soviet Union, but this was not known to Scali at the time. However, Khrushchev wrote a private letter to the United States embassy in Moscow that if the United States did not invade Cuba, the Soviets would dismantle the missiles and remove their experts from Cuba. Lost in translation, Castro sent a message in Spanish that was translated into Russian, saying that a U.S. invasion was imminent and requesting that the Soviet Union execute a preemptive strike against American forces. Castro claimed the message was mistranslated, and his intent was to warn the Soviets that if the United States invaded Cuba, they needed to retaliate with nuclear weapons.

On October 26, 1962, Castro ordered antiaircraft units to open fire on U.S. aircraft flying over Cuba. The United States counteracted and developed an attack plan to increase airstrikes to mitigate Castro's open-fire strategy. Khrushchev publicly addressed his country and stated the Soviets would dismantle missiles in Cuba if the United States dismantled its Jupiter missiles in Turkey. Raymond Hare, the Ambassador to Turkey, deplored the public proposition and stated Turkish officials would "deeply resent" any deal that involved the country and Cuba. He believed that Turkey should not be a factor in the missile crisis and a worst-case scenario suggested that if the missiles were to be dismantled, it would have to be over a period. Khrushchev was obstinate that the United States comply because the Jupiter missiles were near his country. If the United States felt threatened with missiles in Cuba, then the Soviet Union was threatened by the missiles in Turkey.

Finally, on October 28, 1962, Nikita Khrushchev announced that the Soviet Union would terminate operations in Cuba, dismantle weapons, and return them back to the country. Fidel Castro was highly upset as he was not informed about Khrushchev's intentions prior to the public announcement. Accordingly, President Kennedy ceased reconnaissance operations during that period. Castro was not completely satisfied and demanded additional measures be completed by the United States, which he called the five points:

1. End the blockade against Cuba.
2. End subversive activities against Cuba.
3. Halt all attacks on Cuba from U.S. military bases in Puerto Rico.
4. Cease all aerial and naval reconnaissance flights in Cuban air space and waters.

5. Return Guantanamo Bay Naval Base back to Cuba (The Cuban Missile Crisis timeline, n.d., para. 14).

President Kennedy ordered minimal low-level sorties but halted all reconnaissance missions after Khrushchev officially notified Cuba that the missiles would be dismantled. Also, U.S. leadership revised OPLANS that incorporated innovative strategies in response to the Soviet's agreement. The United States blockade on Cuba officially ended on November 20, 1962, when President Kennedy believed most of the operations were completed and when Khrushchev assured him the IL-28 bombers would be shipped back to the Soviet Union within 30 days.

Americans sometimes have a difficult time discussing their values because they are not something contemplated until they can be possibly taken away. No one American is the same, and it would be unreasonable to try to classify all under one category. Most Americans, however, value and respect the liberties and values given them just by being U.S. citizens. L. Robert Kohls, executive director for the Washington International Center, wrote an article on what he considers 13 (this text covers 12) American values (with foreign visitor perspectives):

Personal control over the environment. Everyone has the right to believe he or she can do anything (within the confines of the law) and has the right to control the environment as he or she sees fit.

Change. The United States is the most resourceful and technologically advanced country in the world due to innovation, evolution, resiliency, and adaptability. Such change revolutionizes primitive thoughts of continuing to develop societal differences and preserving historical legacies and customs.

Time. One of the most important concepts is that time is valued. The philosophical theory behind time is that it enables productivity, creativity, success, wealth, patience, and so forth. Time gives individuals unlimited resources and opportunities to accomplish goals, meet timelines, and enjoy "timeless" events in life.

Egalitarianism. This single freedom is what makes the United States so desirable to other countries, and the opposition insulted. American have the right to not be discriminated against due to age, sex, race, color, origin, religious preference, and disability. The nation has revolutionized in the twenty-first century to allow same-sex marriages to be recognized across the country, epitomizing the term "equality."

Privacy. Americans have the right to privacy, which is not a privilege in many countries around the world. As Kohls stated, privacy is the "ultimate result of individualism" (Kohls, 1984, para. 3). Few countries allow such privacy rights, and that is why it is a value that is respected by Americans because the U.S. government enforces this right by law.

Self-Determination. Americans could be accepted for the work accomplished, and no one can claim right for their achievements. In addition, individuals are motivated by their upbringing to set any goals they choose, no matter their social class or background. Americans take pride in working and providing for their families, whatever the motivation may be.

Competition. Americans are competitive individuals, which is part of self-determination. Competition is a value that is appreciated because it gives the gift of productivity, inventions, and technological advancements that assist economic efforts in building a resilient country. A little competition does not hurt, and Americans find that bolstering competitiveness builds progression.

The Future. The future's worth is undervalued by Americans. Living in the past and present has always been a comfortable means for Americans, and not worrying about the future has become a lackadaisical concept that is not considered important until there is a crisis. The future has become important as the United States has suffered through the 9/11 attacks, the San Bernardino and Orlando shootings, and police brutality and unjustified killings. Such events make Americans worry about the future of the nation and the millennials who will greatly influence the direction of the United States.

Work. Americans are one of the most hardworking groups of individuals in the world. Even though there are different societal classes, all work hard to provide the future they want for their families. Labor is something that is expected, and if one does not work, he or she is considered lazy. Working is a part of the American culture, and it is something that is respected and appreciated.

Informality. Americans are exceptionally relaxed, and it is something that is valued since other countries are very strict, especially in work environments. Even in corporate offices, senior executives are more prone to be informal, preferring to be called by their first names. Informalities have been found to increase productivity and create a positive working environment.

Honesty. Americans are more likely to be direct and honest, especially when it comes to negative matters. The key to being honest and direct is that there is room for innuendo or miscommunication. Matters can be resolved when individuals are open and direct with one another. This is especially important in the workplace, as employees need to know their strengths and weakness to improve their productivity and complete the mission.

Efficiency. Americans are characterized as predominantly accurate and concrete but also meticulous and resourceful. Efficiency is an important quality to have in the United States military, as less efficient operations can detrimentally affect mission operations. Efficiency is a trait that is appreciated because it separates the most successful from those who are subpar or below standards.

It is safe to believe that over thirty years later, American values are basically the same today. Though such values may seem minuscule in the bigger picture of national security, each one is the right of Americans. When such values are threatened because of other countries' standards, it affects national interests. The U.S. Army outlined a methodical chart of the importance of values and interests, shown in Figure 1.25. National values that are the right of Americans influence U.S. national interests.

NATIONAL INTERESTS

Greatest Threats to U.S. National Interests by National Leaders

President Barack Obama

The single most important national security threat we face is nuclear weapons falling into the hands of terrorists (Schwartz, 2015, para. 3).

Former President George W. Bush

The biggest threat facing the country is weapons of mass destruction in the hands of a terrorist network (Perry, 2005, p. 1).

Former Secretary Ashton B. Carter

North Korea's nuclear and missile provocations underscore that a diverse and dynamic spectrum of nuclear threats still exists ... so our deterrence needs to be credible and extended to our allies in the region (Garamone, 2016, para. 11).

The Congressional Commission

It appears that we are at a tipping point in proliferation if Iran and North Korea proceed unchecked to build nuclear arsenal; there is a serious possibility of a cascade of proliferation following (Allison, 2010, p. 8).

United Nations

We are approaching a point at which the erosion of the non-proliferation regime could become irreversible and result in a cascade of proliferation (Chari, 2008, p. 56).

National security is the conception of political ideas that a government or assembly establishes to protect its people from state crises through many facets of power projections. To protect national security, governments should have specific interests that are the foundation of their country's ideologies and principles. Going through the Cold War and coming close to another global war with Cuba and the Soviet Union, the United States built national security frameworks that would not only be unique to the processes lacking within the country but also to implement policies based on lessons learned from past conflicts.

When the Cold War dissolved in 1991, the United States still faced tensions with the Soviet Union, even though its new leader, Mikhail S. Gorbachev, worked hard to mitigate pressures between the Eastern and Western Hemispheres. Even with pressures cooled down, the United States and the Soviet Union were two superpowers that would not stop to claim global superiority. Both countries would remain heavily armed with the world's most innovative weaponry, and that was a threat that client states feared most. With the Soviet Union denouncing universal democracy, the United States was steadfast in promoting global democratic governance for its allies and security partners.

The early 1990s proved that Soviet communism was diminishing when Russia and the Soviet Union turned against each other, giving the United States the upper hand to promote dominance, superiority, and a global power. When the Warsaw Pact crumbled in 1991, Russian Vice President Gennadi Yenayev lead a military coup to overthrow Gorbachev to "reinstate the communist dictatorship he had been systematically dismantling for over five years" (Snow, 1998, p.). The unsuccessful coup showed that communism was in jeopardy and that the Soviet Union was collapsing, and its internal allies were turning against each other.

As previously mentioned, World War II and the Cold War aftermath birthed national security frameworks that United States envisioned as a solid method that would represent safety, security, and protection. The National Security Act of 1947 was America's largest reform; with new organizations structured to better implement national security, this strategy seemed like an optimistic endeavor until the United States was confronted directly with its new enemy, terrorism. The terrorist attacks on the World Trade Center and the Pentagon on September 11, 2001 opened the eyes of America to a deadly, innovative threat in the twenty-first century.

President Barack Obama outlined America's national interests in the 2015 National Security Strategy. He stated the top priorities included

- The security of the United States, its citizens, U.S. allies and partners;
- A strong, innovative, and growing economy in an open international economic system that promotes opportunity and prosperity;
- Respect for universal values at home and around the world; and
- Rules-based international order advanced and opportunity through stronger cooperation to meet global challenges (Obama, 2015, p. 2).

Such keen interests rely on a considerable amount of risk. Based on current vulnerabilities, it is the federal government's responsibility to mitigate such risks toward national interests. Per the National Security Strategy, such risks that pose a threat to U.S. interests include

- catastrophic attack on U.S. homeland and critical infrastructures;
- threats or attacks against U.S. citizens abroad and our allies;
- global economic crisis or widespread economic slowdown;
- proliferation and/or use weapons of mass destruction;
- severe global infectious diseases outbreaks;
- climate change;
- major energy market disruptions; and
- significant securing consequences associated with weak or falling states (including mass atrocities, regional spillover, and transnational organized crime) (Obama, 2015, p. 2).

Identifying national interests is half the battle, but having the appropriate tools to mitigate risks is the key to protecting the homeland and global prosperity. To ensure protection of U.S. interests, policymakers must continue to formulate strategic prospects to form the economic platform to establish and bolster new relationships with developing countries that are devoted to democratic governance. To implement policies protecting national interests, President Obama stated that the United States will

- Lead with purpose
- Lead with strength
- Lead by example
- Lead with capable partners
- Lead with all instruments of U.S. power
- Lead with long-term perspectives (Obama, 2015, pp. 2–5).

As a global force, the United States has the responsibility of leading with purpose. With an international economy that is constantly adapting to an ever-changing environment, the national interests identified are the foundation of what the United States represents to promote a global governance of peace, stability, security, protection, and economic standing. Having a purpose means establishing a framework that ensures the United States has an effective and all-encompassing plan that addresses each national interest susceptible to threats in order of priority.

The United States has the largest most technologically advanced forces in the world. Even though the economy has drastically shifted post 9/11, the U.S. has been resilient in its recovery and remains the strongest economic platform in the world. America offers an example of improved employment and unmatched military structure and has managed to overcome the nastiest financial crisis since the *Great Depression*. In the last decade, the United States education system, healthcare, technological advancement, and research and development has improved exponentially.

It is critical that the United States upholds its national values and defends the law of democratic governance. The country's allies and security partners have formed positive relationships due to the civil liberties and justices emphasized in the nation's policies. Furthermore, to maintain transnational cooperation agreements and formulate relationships with emerging countries, it is important to preserve transparency and accountability by following the international standards. The world is watching, and while some dysfunction may exist between all forms of government and the private sector, it must be mitigated to show the United States is overall a unified entity that follows national priorities.

Having the most innovative assets to defend the United States is the most powerful resource the country must have to protect its borders and enforce global stability. President Obama stated, "Our influence is greatest when we combine all our strategic advantages" (2015, p. 4). With such advantages, United States will maintain diplomatic and military readiness to support and defend national interests. Furthermore, collaborating with allies and security partners enriches global prosperity and commitment to the international standards of conduct.

Authors Sarkesian, Williams, and Cimbala (2013) suggest three orders of national interests:

1. Vital interests
2. Critical interests
3. Serious interests (p. 6).

Vital interests are imminent events that affect the United States and may result in military mobilization. For example, the September 11th attacks were a clear vital interest where military deployment was executed to protect national security and interests. Also, the establishment of the Department of Homeland Security (discussed in Chapter Five) provoked innovative homeland defense methods to mitigate another terrorist attack on American soil. Such vulnerability to vital interests permits many government agencies to organize and establish counterterrorism and antiterrorism policies and initiatives.

Critical interest matters are considered not to have a direct effect on United States operatives. As stated by Sarkesian, Williams, and Cimbala (2013), threats or vulnerabilities may not be imminent but have the potential to be vital interests soon. Serious interests are matters that are not as imminent as vital and critical interests but should be monitored and kept on the radar. The authors provide a logical paradigm of how policymakers prioritize national security matters and interests to plan short-term and long-term strategic policies.

Irrefutably, vital interests take precedence and are "conditions that are strictly necessary to safeguard and enhance America's survival and well-being in a free and secure nation" (Allison, 2010, p. 1). The purpose of identifying national interests is to

- Prevent, deter, and reduce the threat of nuclear, biological, and chemical weapons attacks on the United States or its military forces abroad
- Ensure survival of U.S. allies and their active cooperation with the U.S. in shaping an international defense system
- Prevent the emergence of hostile major powers of failed states on U.S. borders
- Ensure the viability and stability of major global systems (i.e. trade, financial markets, supplies of energy, and the environment)
- Establish productive relations, consistent with American interests, with nations that could become strategic adversaries (Allison, 2010, p. 4).

Allison's perspective on the measurability of interests is undeniably like that of Sarkesian, Williams, and Cimbala in relation to importance (i.e. vital, critical, and serious). He argues that interests are measured as extremely important, important, and less important. American leadership is held accountable for determining the seriousness of interests to enhance military structure, intelligence capabilities, and promote healthy relationships between U.S. allies and security partners. One difference, Allison contends, is that while there are less important interests, all should have a level of importance. He points out that the less important interests on the U.S.'s agenda would include

- Balancing bilateral trade deficits
- Enlarging democracy for everyone
- Preserving the territorial integrity or political constitution of other states
- Enhancing exports as specific economic factors (Allison, 2010, p. 7).

THE GLOBAL GRID OF ALLIANCES AND ADVERSARIES

The United States has collective alliance agreements with many countries around the world. Each agreement has specific details regarding each country's relationship with the United States. Called the *Defense Pact*, the United States has formed contractual and military alliances with all countries who wish to practice democratic governance and restore peace, security, and economic growth around the world. Most importantly, each treaty was signed to support and defend each other in times of hostility from adversarial threats.

North Atlantic Treaty Organization (NATO)

The *NATO Treaty* was created by the United States and other countries within the *Western Hemisphere* to impose transnational security measures against the Soviet Union. Signed on April 4, 1949, the treaty became the "first peacetime military alliance the United States entered into outside of the Western Hemisphere" (North Atlantic Treaty Organization, 1949, para. 2). Europe failed to rebuild its economy and security standing after World War II, and since the United States was heavily involved in European matters, a plan was initiated to develop a strategic outlet from the Soviet Union. The NATO treaty essentially states that when any country is threatened, that is considered aggression against them all. The treaty is currently the largest peacetime military agreement in the world and since its inception has extended membership to some former Soviet states such as Estonia, Latvia, and Lithuania.

Alliances: Albania, Belgium, Bulgaria, Canada, Croatia, Czech Republic, Denmark, Estonia, France, Germany, Hungary, Iceland, Italy, Latvia, Lithuania, Luxemburg, Netherlands, Norway, Poland, Portugal, Romania, Slovak Republic, Slovenia, Spain, Turkey, United Kingdom, United States.

Australia, New Zealand, and United States (ANZUS) Treaty

A communal agreement between Australia, New Zealand, and the United States to co-operate on military matters in the Pacific Region, the *ANZUS Treaty* is one of multiple agreements signed in response to tensions with the Soviet Union and its communistic ideologies during the Cold War. The treaty was established on September 1, 1951 for all parties involved to "recognize that an armed attack in the Pacific Region on any of the parties would be dangerous to its own peace and safety and declares that it would act to meet the common danger in accordance with its constitutional processes" (U.S. Collective Defense Arrangements, n.d., para. 3).

Mutual Defense Bilateral Treaty

Signed between the United States and the Philippines, the bilateral agreement was imposed to deter external attacks against both countries. The treaty was signed on August 30, 1951 to prepare for any attack in the Pacific Region on either party. On August 28, 2014, the *Enhanced Defense Cooperation Agreement (EDCA)* was signed between the two countries to boost the relationship between the United States and the Philippines that was initially formed over sixty years ago. EDCA allows the United States to establish transient military installations in the Philippines as well as ground forces for possible deployment.

Southeast Asia Treaty Organization (SEATO)

SEATO is an agreement signed on September 8, 1954 between the United States, Australia, France, New Zealand, the Philippines, Thailand, and the United Kingdom to provide mutual security measures against communist powers that attempted to affect the Southeast Asian region. Due to loss of interest and many members withdrawing from the armistice, SEATO dissolved on June 30, 1977.

Treaty of Mutual Cooperation and Security Bilateral Agreement (Japanese) Treaty

The agreement between the United States and Japan ensured collective security relations between the two countries. It was amended in January 1960 to maintain peace in East Asia and defend Japanese conflicts. Now, the revised version states that the United States is to inform Japan of any military mobilization and that in the event of any attack against either country, both countries would respond together to deter aggression, resulting in permanent U.S. military installations in the country. Finally, the agreement promoted international cooperation and improved economic platforms.

Republic of South Korea Treaty

Signed on October 1, 1953, this agreement between the United States and South Korea provides mutual aid if either country faces aggression from adversarial threats. As with the Japanese treaty, the United States established permanent military bases in South Korea.

Inter-American Treaty of Reciprocal Assistance or Rio Treaty

The *Rio Treaty* is an agreement that was signed on September 2, 1947 by most of the countries in North and South America. If any country that signed the agreement faced aggression or threats from adversarial nations, that would be considered an attack against all under the Pan-American arrangement. Again, this was another international cooperation to mitigate communist powers that tried to infiltrate both American continents.

Alliances: Argentina, Bahamas, Bolivia, Brazil, Chile, Colombia, Costa Rica, Cuba, Dominican Republic, Ecuador, El Salvador, Guatemala, Haiti, Honduras, Nicaragua, Panama, Paraguay, Peru, Trinidad & Tobago, United States, Uruguay, Venezuela.

Post-Cold War era, the United States developed relationships with countries that practiced the same political, economic, and *globalization* (is the process of interacting with investments, trading, people, companies, cultures, and governments of different countries) philosophies. Such countries were classified into categories. The Department of State calls these classifications tiers. Per Donald M. Snow (1998), the first tier is a membership of the Organization of the Economic Cooperation and Development (OECD) that signifies the most technologically advanced countries in the world.

First-tier countries have comparable democratic political structures and depend on capitalistic methodologies to promote globalization. While some of these countries have different perspectives based on cultural diversity, they are not sufficient to detract from the similarities that make such countries flourish as a collective, international unit. Again, such stable countries are unlikely to pose a threat to each other, meaning they are less likely to go to war. First-tier countries work closely together to sustain international cooperation, and a significant amount of focus is centered on the movement of the second-tier countries.

Second-tier countries are considered 85% of the world's population. Also, called the *Third World*, such countries are economically deficient but run democratic governments. Per Snow, the difference between the first tier and the second tier is the second-tier countries lack commitment to political democracy or advanced market-based capitalism, defined as the entrance to high-technology revolution (p.12). While most second-tier countries are considered undeveloped, Middle Eastern countries with oil-based wealth are placed in the latter category due to non-democratic governments.

THE UNIVERSAL CONTINUUM OF CONFLICT

The United States has an ever-changing predicament that will indefinitely affect the direction of global security, peace, and economic stability. There will always be international conflict, and that is why it is imperative that the nation stays vigilant on the evolution of war and technological advancement. The U.S. military continuously transmutes its strategic platform to mitigate modern tactics and adversarial engagement against emerging enemies. This has become more evident in the twenty-first century, more currently, in terms of the *Islamic State and the Levant (ISIL)* and *Operation Inherent Resolve*. Staying cognizant of trends and cultures has been a predominant trait of U.S. military operatives. Such preparation has been detrimental to safeguarding military forces and maintaining perpetual readiness to combat current and emerging threats on the conflict spectrum.

The **conflict spectrum** (a range of military events to which experts refer when hypothesizing conflict by alliances and adversaries on the effectiveness, methods, forces, sophistication, level, and challenge/difficulty) is essentially the United States' awareness in terms of tracking the effectiveness and capability of international conflict. Understanding such concepts is a demand for comprehension of new and evolving wars. As former infantryman of the 75th Ranger Regiment in Iraq and Afghanistan Paul Scharre said, "Conflict has refined and expanded our understanding of war, and our lexicon must change as well" (p. 73). Scharre also emphasized how modern terminology has affected military strategies because what was once considered to be a low-intensity conflict has revolutionized into something of greater magnitude. Furthermore, a significant advantage for global foes that can detrimentally affect national security is "sophisticated nation-state adversaries [that] have expanded the spectrum of military operations by investing in advanced technologies designed to blunt U.S. power projection and thwart U.S. advantages," Scharre said.

The purpose of the conflict spectrum is to identify the classification and physiognomies of a specific threat and how the United States relates to it on a global scale. U.S. military strategy is a key functioning force in determining the measurability of future conflict. As authors Sam C. Sarkesian, John A. Williams, and Stephen J. Cimbala explain, the conflict spectrum "assesses U.S. capabilities and effectiveness." They also note that although the threat of war among states has allayed, the major concern is increased conflict between states within the country, which is high on the spectrum (see Namangan Dzuverovic's Peace Study on Intra State Conflict).

In addition, **unconventional warfare** (operations that are conducted by enemies through guerilla or insurgency tactics and/or subversion) poses a major threat to the United States, its allies, and security partners. For example, since its inception in 2006, ISIL has proven to the world that it is more than just a terrorist organization and instead is a global insurgent movement. Not only has the group taken over major cities in Iraq and Syria (which have been reclaimed and taken back), the group is currently on the verge of capturing Ar-Rutbah, a town in the Western Al Anbar province of Iraq, per Chris Tomson of *Al-Masdar News*. Moreover, to show its strength and sophistication, ISIL has influenced or been directly responsible for nearly 150 terrorist attacks in thirty countries around the world. Contributors Tim Lister, Ray Sanchez, Mark Bixler, Sean O'Key, Michael Hogenmiller, and Mohammed Tawfeeq of CNN News claim the group has "killed at least 2,043 people," and its strategy is difficult to detect because experts cannot seem to "divine the precise role that international terrorists play in this or that attack." Furthermore, having a net worth of $2 billion, ISIL is currently the richest terrorist organization in the world, setting precedents for wealth, sophistication, unconventional tactics, and deadly, covert attacks on enemies.

The United States' current National Security Strategy outlines such initiatives to mitigate the conflict and threats like ISIL and advises American leaders on national values, interests, conflicts, top concerns, and solutions on the international continuum. Understanding the conflict spectrum and having the ability to maintain dominance is indicative of military capabilities and protecting national security. Recognizing that conventional conflicts have declined and acknowledging the new emphasis on asymmetrical and unconventional warfare is the United States' leverage to maintaining global supremacy. Authors John Arquilla and David Ronfeldt in *A New Epoch and Spectrum of Conflict* claim, "no good old-fashioned war is in sight." American lexicon and new initiatives on national interests have progressed since the Cold War and even the *Gulf War* eras, and grasping these ideologies today is the key to achieving the goal: protecting national security. Again, comprehending the type of wars the United States will face is a major step and can be accomplished by responding with modern measures, such as counterinsurgency. Michael R. Melillo, author of "Outfitting a Big-War Military With Small-War Capabilities," notes that the best strategy "... includes peacekeeping, stability and support operations, nation-building, and humanitarian missions" (2006, p. 26). The scale of defeating and containing the enemy is predicated on the sophistication of the threat.

Weapons of Mass Destruction

The United States' ultimate security challenge is facing aggressive states and terrorists that have access to **weapons of mass destruction** (biological, chemical, nuclear, or radiological agents that are used to cause pervasive destruction and death). To mitigate a high-scale disaster, America, its allies, and security partners must have a comprehensive strategy that covers all facets of destruction. Having an effective policy to counter WMDs is one of the fundamental components of protecting America's national security. With innovative terrorism measures thriving, the United States faces unique challenges on how to protect the homeland. To maintain **global dominance** (a country or state dominating on an international level based on national power) and security, it is important to stay in sync with the evolution of technology and stay vigilant, increasing emphasis on intelligence collection and analysis as well as strengthening relations with federal and local law enforcement.

In addition, the United States needs to maintain focus on solidifying its alliances with security partners, including forming new relationships with developing countries and former adversaries. Securing relationships and staying vigilant are solutions to alleviating the use of WMDs by adversarial threats. WMDs could enable the enemy to inflict considerable destruction on the United States, its military forces, and international alliances.

There are non-states and **rogue nations** (states that are accused of breaking international law and pose a threat to other nation states) that not only support terrorism but have WMDs and are continually thinking of ways to increase their capabilities with advanced technology to instill coercion and intimidation. These countries do not see WMDs as a worst-case scenario but instead as a premeditated, conscious effort of action proposed to undermine the other nation's conventional methods and to dissuade with significant aggression and affliction against alliances and vital interests. Furthermore, terrorist organizations have an increased awareness in WMDs because their goals are to annihilate large populations without culpability or attrition.

WMDs can be categorized as biological, chemical, nuclear, or radiological weapons that can cause harm to a large populace, infrastructure, man-made constructions, or the environment. The inception of WMDs reverts to the mid-1700s when British military officers planned to conduct a biological attack and distribute smallpox as a ploy to kill their enemies. **Biological weapons** include bacteria, anthrax, smallpox, hepatitis, influenza, toxins, staff, and ricin. There are three ways biological weapons can infiltrate: through the skin, through the gastrointestinal system, and through the respiratory system. Biological weapons are very threatening and easier to access than other WMDs. With that said, a biological attack against the United States could cause catastrophic damage due to a large spread at a quick rate.

Arsenic smoke was used frequently during the world war eras. More recently, in the twentieth century, sarin was used by terrorist Aum Skinrikyo in the Tokyo subway attack that killed twelve people. Roger Von Bergendorff was arrested in 2008 for possessing ricin and paraphernalia used to make ricin at an Extended Stay America hotel in Las Vegas. **Chemical weapons** are not as dangerous as biological weapons due to ineffectiveness, based on the equation to the number of chemicals needed versus the amount produced that can cause the greatest number of casualties.

Nuclear weapons produce the greatest threat to the United States, especially if such weapons land in the hands of terrorist organizations or rogue nations. There are currently five nuclear weapons states under the terms of the *Treaty on the Non-Proliferation of Nuclear Weapons*: The United States, United Kingdom, France, China, and Russia. The non-proliferation treaty is an international agreement between the five countries to prevent the spread and execution of nuclear weapons and weapons technology as well as to promote cooperation in peaceful uses of nuclear energy and achieve disarmament. Some large countries are not a part of the treaty such as India, Pakistan, and North Korea, and Israel is the only such country assumed to have nuclear weapons. Israel's policy, the *Policy of Deliberate Ambiguity*, states a country can deliberately be ambiguous on specific aspects of foreign policy, particularly if a country has WMDs.

There are also weapons sharing agreements, such as NATO's nuclear weapon sharing program with Belgium, Germany, Italy, the Netherlands, and Turkey. The United States has provided the country's nuclear materials to collect and position. Because American nuclear weapons are protected by **Permissive Action Links** (security mechanisms to prevent unauthorized detonation of nuclear weapons), host states cannot arm bombs without authorization from DoD. Nuclear weapons are considered the most dangerous weapons in the world. These weapons have only been used twice in world history when the United States dropped bombs on Nagasaki and Hiroshima in 1945. Based on the number of state actors and non-NPTs, there are approximately 22,000 nuclear weapons in the world, and more than 2,000 nuclear tests have been performed.

The top goal for the United States is to assist with the global disarmament of nuclear weapon programs. Since its inception, the United Nations has fought to ban nuclear weapons. The first attempt was the *UN General Assembly Resolution*, which established a Commission to handle nuclear and atomic energy matters. Under the Commission, there was a proposal to eliminate global armament of nuclear and atomic weapons and other related weapons of mass destruction. Multiple bilateral and multilateral agreements have been established over the years with an emphasis on mitigating the proliferation and testing of nuclear weapons:

- Non-Proliferation Treaty
- Treaty on Banning Nuclear Weapon Tests in the Atmosphere
- Partial Test Ban Treaty
- Comprehensive Nuclear Ban Treaty
- Nuclear Supplies Group
- Missile Technology Control Regime
- Wassenaar Agreement
- Hague Code of Conduct Against Ballistic Missile Proliferation
- Nuclear Nonproliferation Treaty and International
- Atomic Energy Agency
- Fissile Material Cut-Off Treaty
- Organization for the Prohibition of Chemical Weapons
- International Code of Conduct Against Ballistic Missile Proliferation
- Nonproliferation and Threat Reduction Cooperation
- Nunn-Lugar Program

Because WMDs are the greatest threat to national security, the United States has established categories to the national security strategy:

- Counterproliferation
- Nonproliferation
- Consequence Management

Counterproliferation

It is a deadly reality that WMDs can lie in the hands of terrorists and rogue nations. Therefore, it is critical that the United States fully implement strategic initiatives that include **counterproliferation** (preventing the expansion and/or possession of nuclear weapons) measures to protect national security and homeland security postures. Active interdiction is a vital component of U.S. military strategy to combat WMD. It is necessary to innovate current capabilities that include military, intelligence, and law enforcement to prevent the movement of WMDs, materials, technology, and experts that benefit hostile states and terrorist organizations.

Some radical states and terrorist are aggressively pursuing WMDs to target the United States and its allies. Deterrence is another countermeasure that is an integral component in preventing WMD movement to adversarial threats. A modern initiative is needed for deterrence, posture, and a full range of political instruments to convert potential threats and to deny the use of WMDs. Deterrence mechanisms include bolstering military capabilities, intelligence, law enforcement, and interdiction. Combining all capabilities reduces the adversary's advantage of WMD use.

Deterrence alone can be an effective solution to preventing the use of WMDs, and thus, the United States needs to develop improved defense and mitigation policies. Such requirements are necessary to identify and terminate the enemy's WMDs. Moreover, the United States needs to implement vigorous active and passive military defenses as well as mitigation measures to accomplish distinctive operatives to prevents use of WMDs. Active defenses ensure the disruption, incapacitation, and annihilation of WMDs. Such high-tech capabilities include vigorous air and missile defenses. Passive defenses entail developing specific defenses that are unique to WMDs, while ensuring such operations do not affect deployed strengths. Protecting the nation is not just a responsibility for military forces. Law enforcement is a crucial component in assisting military forces in responding to potential use of WMDs against the homeland. Both working forces' key focus is to deter an imminent attack before it progresses and eradicate planned attacks. Merging deterrence and prevention strategies is very sensitive because to mitigate WMDs, an effective and rapid response with rapid attribution and forceful strike proficiency is necessary. Most importantly, vigorous responses in destroying WMDs will send a message to adversaries that powerful policies and operations are set in place to deter future use of WMDs.

Aside from tactical and operational strategies to defeat WMDs, there are political avenues. The United States is heavily involved in pursuing political approaches for consensual and multifaceted agreements in pursuit of nonproliferation goals. It is important that suppliers are dissuaded from providing supplies, which will essentially diminish proliferation plans and end WMD programs. Thus, countries that possess WMDs should be held accountable for complying with standards of nonproliferation policy. Because nonproliferation policies are non-threatening, it is important use alternative measures like counterproliferation, deterrence, mitigation, and prevention.

The United States must be responsible and act as the lead country for export control. There must be an understanding that the nation thrives from globalization and business with many countries. The nation should find solutions to reinforce export protocols to prevent the shipment of nuclear materials. Such standards invoke American legislation to enhance security controls that will satisfy both commercial interests and nonproliferation objectives. Furthermore, sanctions can be another additive to the deterrence of WMDs.

AMERICAN FEDERAL GOVERNMENT, POLITICS, AND POWER

The United States' political system is based on a federal nation, which operates under the executive powers of the president, Congress, and the court system, which is based on the Constitution. The federal government is categorized by the executive, legislative, and judicial branches, which share sovereignty with fifty contiguous states. The executive branch is led by the President of the United States and functions separately from the legislative and judiciary branches. The president has an administration, known as the Cabinet. Such officials include the vice president, Speaker of the House, and executive-level senior officials. The legislative branch contains Congress, which consists of two chambers: The Senate and the House of Representatives. The judicial branch holds the *United States Supreme Court* and lower courts, which are predicated on the Constitution, federal laws, and regulations.

Democratic and *Republican* are the two major powers within the United States government. The political system differs from most democracies. The Senate has a significant amount of power in the legislative branch. The Supreme Court has a greater range and wider spectrum in its processes, though there is a checks and balances methodology in place.

In the twenty-first century, the United States continuously faces innovative threats through international terrorism, unconventional attacks, domestic terrorism, nuclear pro-liferation, and contingencies of war. Furthermore, the nation is plagued with international concerns that significantly affect the modern platform of globalization. There is much concern over how the government's principles lack specific abilities as to maintaining democratic governance. Sarkesian, Williams, and Cimbala note, "democracies lack many of the qualities required to maintain an effective national security posture, and the nature of democracies works against developing and implementing the strategies required for long-rate success in the complicated security era of today and the future" (p. 15). With such controversy and debate on democratic principles, the United States sits on the necessary suggestions that democratic governance does not follow author-itarian viewpoints. Democratic government is fundamentally predicated on diverse and practical theologies.

Democratic governance is grounded on political tolerance that favors equality, peaceful changes, and self-determination. The validity of democratic governance is predicated on upholding the idealistic structures and enforcing such dogma with accountable leaders by ensuring all stay true to the Constitution. While the democratic system has obvious flaws, the positive qualities offer greater assets and advantages than any other political system in the world. French historian Alexis de Tocqueville stated in a passage from "Real Advantages of Democratic Government:

> Nothing is harder than the apprenticeship of liberty. This is not true of des-potism. Despotism often presents itself as the remedy for all ills suffered in the past. It is the upholder of justice, the champion of the oppressed, and the founder of order. Nations are lulled to sleep by the temporary prosperity to which it gives rise, and when they awake, they are miserable. Liberty, in contrast, is usually born in stormy times. It struggles to establish itself amid civil discord, and its benefits can be appreciated only when it is cold (Delogu, 2014).

The dissemination of power is a major feature of the United States political scheme, which institutionalizes the dispersal of political power. Disputes over policies can create power struggles within the national government, and this can cause major conflict with foreign policy and national security matters, affecting vital interests and values which are crucial components of the United States political system.

Power in national security and politics is the ability to utilize historical decisions and precedence to influence future resolutions. Additionally, power is a significant instrument that can be a positive or negative factor in decision making, depending on how it is used. Policymakers recognize we live in a modernized world, which encompasses innovative threats and adversarial attacks. Understanding the ability to make change by enforcing current policies and establishing new ones based on evolution is the key to protecting national security and maintaining a strong government. For administrations to remain steadfast on protecting national security, certain fundamentals must be followed that involve the dominance of power. In 1959, two American sociologists, John French and Bertram Raven published an article titled, "The Bases of Power." They emphasize five power sources that are critical within organizations:

- Coercive
- Expert
- Legitimate
- Referent
- Reward

Each factor is important to commitment, compliance, and resistance within the government. It would be uncouth to state policymakers and government officials to use force or threats to have decisions made within a government, but it is something that happens in corrupt countries. Using **coercive power** (the ability influence decision making by enforcing punishment or some type of action if an individual does not follow instructions) in government is common, and it is a technique used to influence the decision-making process. The concept comes in different forms, and its use depends on how policymakers enforce and how the public responds. For example, when President John F. Kennedy executed a blockade to prevent the Soviets from shipping missiles to Cuba, the use of coercive power was dangerous because three nation states (and governments) were involved, and if the blockade had been prolonged, it could have caused a large-scale war. The United States enforced this sanction to protect the homeland and its allies, as movement between Soviet and Cuban forces showed they were preparing for a possible attack. Even though not all forms of coercion are considered violent, usually some physical form of violence and aggression is threatened.

Expert power is the capability to influence based on experience and knowledge. When dealing with expert power within a government, a significant scale of influence is evident toward behaviors that are based on expertise in a specific area. The cliché "knowledge is power" is very true, and having expert power in government is an integral component to solving challenging problems, making complex decisions, and performing critical tasks that are imperative in national security. Policymakers' opinions and ideas are held in high regard because they are senior public servants, and they have the power to influence the American people with their decisions. Leaders with expertise have a robust power base, and they can manage confidently. For example, when an individual is running for President of the United States, the individual should have enough experience and knowledge on how to run a government so that the American public will feel confident in voting for the person as a leader. Management professor Gary A. Yukl says, "Expert power is more important than reward-based or coercive power in leading people effectively. If you have expert power, your team is likely to be more open to your efforts to guide them, and you will find it easier to motivate them to their full potential" (2012, p. 23).

Legitimate power is the ability to influence and obtain power through a position or office held at an authoritative level within an agency, especially within government. Because much power and influence is evident at the legitimate power level, those who fill this role have the power to make decisions based on the authority of being in such a position. For example, the Secretary of Defense is the highest senior executive level within the Department of Defense, responsible for over two million personnel. Because of his expertise, knowledge, and position, he has a certain authority to exercise control over other senior executive defense officials, the United States Armed Forces, civilians, and contractors due to the importance of the role. Legitimate power is an asset because the authority concept provides a distinct advantage over many levels and sources of authority that is predicated on policies, laws, and regulations within an organization.

Referent power is indicative of interpersonal relationships when individuals support others within an agency. Leaders who possess referent power likely have an ability or quality that subordinates identify (Mossholder, et al., 1998). It is common that if a government leader has qualities that are admired and respected by the public, his or her subordinates are more likely to imitate such characteristics in hopes of producing the same results of respect and appreciation. There is a commonality with referent and expert power in that the two possess charismatic qualities with expertise, which makes these leaders more credible to the people.

Finally, **reward power** is the capability to influence a person (or persons) by providing incentives within an organization. Such incentives can be promotions, positive evaluations, and awards. It is important that organizations have reward programs as an internal "morale booster" to motivate subordinates and show their worth. Subordinates are more inclined to stay with an organization that takes care of its people, and in return, this element increases productivity, produces positive relationships, and magnifies retention rates. It is common for employees within government to receive awards and promotions for supporting the nation's demands, which is important because employees in high-demand positions are needed to continue to provide their expertise in specialized fields (i.e. Senior Executive Service, political, or presidential appointee). All sources of power are based on commitment, compliance, and resistance.

SUMMARY

The objective of this chapter on is to apply knowledge in the development of strategic guidelines to assist national and homeland security experts, scholars, authors, students, and policymakers in bringing awareness to the evolution of innovative threats to the United States. This chapter draws on lessons learned over hundreds of years. The Founding Fathers realized the country had a need to protect national security during the formation of the United States Constitution. Historical events, such as World War I, World War II, the Cuban Missile Crisis, and the Cold War helped to introduce America's largest reorganization when the National Security Act of 1947 was established and better aligned the United States Armed Forces to create a superior force against global and domestic adversaries.

This discussion chapter begins with a summary of national values and interests, global alliances, adversaries, weapons of mass destruction, and the American political system. It also presents major events and policies considered in the development of national security strategies that are executed by the President of the United States to identify top national security concerns with long-term policies. Finally, chapter two presents a series of case studies of national security responses to catastrophic events and how United States policy protects the homeland and promotes international peace, security, and globalization.

CHAPTER 2 CASE STUDIES

Case Study 1
The Nuclear Arms Race

After World War II, the global scene once again shifted and set the stage for the Cold War, a time of tense diplomatic maneuvering and military posturing between the Soviet Union and the United States. Although countries in a cold war typically rely on threats, propaganda, and indirect conflict through support of satellite states, the U.S. and Soviet Union almost came into direct warfare during the nuclear arms race. During World War II, the U.S., alongside the Western Powers, had formed a fragile alliance with the Soviet Union against the Axis Powers. However, once Nazi Germany and its allies were defeated, this alliance quickly dissolved. In its wake, it left two superpowers with very different opposing ideologies and views on how to rebuild Europe.

At the time of the German surrender, the Allied Powers occupied different regions of German territory. While all four nations agreed that it was necessary to punish the Nazi leadership for their crimes, none of the powers wanted to give up control of its occupied territory. The Soviet Union, concerned about border security, intended to use its occupied territories as buffer states to provide extra insurance. This made the U.S. uneasy as it feared that the Soviet Union's ever-expanding communist agenda into Eastern Europe indicated a desire to rule the world (Milestones: 1945–1952: Berlin Airlift, n.d.). Taking a cue from the Monroe Doctrine, which cautioned the world against new attempts to colonize the Americas, the U.S., under the Truman Doctrine, warned the Soviet Union that the U.S. would act to halt the spread of communism wherever it threatened democracy. This strategy of containment would shape U.S. foreign policy for the next several years and would give rise to the Domino Theory, a policy that would later lead to the conflict in Southeast Asia.

With the growing threat of communism, the U.S. came to believe that containment was no longer enough. U.S. officials feared that if one country came under communist influence or control, its neighboring countries would soon follow in a domino effect. An additional factor in the Domino Theory was concern that many nations were simply incapable of resisting communism, especially if it were to take hold in their region.

Most nations were economically exhausted after World War II. Governments were poor and weak, and the people were starving. This made them easy targets for the communist revolution (Domino theory, 2009). To prevent the communist domino, the U.S. implemented the Marshall Plan, which was aimed at hunger, poverty, desperation, and chaos. Witnessing how quickly totalitarian regimes rushed to fill the void of postwar economic catastrophes, U.S. officials believed that economic well-being was the best ally of democracy. The country invested billions of dollars into the reconstruction of Europe while also supporting governments or rebel groups that opposed communism. This support of anti-communist groups would later lead the U.S. into conflicts such as the Vietnam War, the Korean War, and the War on Terror (Milestones: 1945–1952: The Marshall Plan, n.d.).

The containment strategy also provided the rationale for an unprecedented arms buildup in the U.S. To use military force to contain communist expansion, U.S. officials encouraged the development of atomic weapons like the ones used in Japan. In response, the Soviets tested their own atom bomb. Both countries continued competing against each other with the development of greater and more destructive weapons, amassing large stockpiles of nuclear weapons, thus beginning the "arms race" (Milestones: 1945–1952: Atomic diplomacy, n.d.).

Tensions escalated when the U.S. announced that any major Soviet attack would be met with a massive nuclear response. In October 1957, the world was introduced to the fear of a missile attack when Sputnik was launched. This was to lead to Intercontinental ballistic missiles (ICBMs) which could be launched from one continent to another, equipped with an internal guidance system while carrying a nuclear warhead. As a result, the U.S. built a defense missile early warning system around the Arctic. The Soviet Union invested heavily in producing more big missiles, regardless of quality, while the U.S. focused on building fewer but better quality missiles. By 1986, it was estimated that there were more than 40,000 nuclear warheads in the world (Trueman, C.N., 2015).

ICBMs changed the format of Cold War military strategy. With ICBMs, both countries now possessed the capability of decimating the other country in a matter of minutes, all with a press of a button. However, it was understood that if one country launched missiles, the other would retaliate by launching its own missiles, leaving both countries destroyed. This view, known as mutually assured destruction, became a deterrent to war since both countries would be less likely to launch missiles, knowing it would result in mass mutual destruction (Clark, 2008).

The nuclear arms race hit a critical point with the Cuban Missile Crisis in 1962, when the U.S. discovered that the Soviet Union was positioning missiles in Cuba, only miles from U.S. soil. Leaders in both the U.S. and Soviet Union were presented with a serious diplomatic challenge as officials on both sides advised a missile launch. While the crisis was eventually de-escalated due to skillful political negotiation, both sides learned that risking nuclear war in pursuit of political objectives outweighed the benefits. It was simply too dangerous, and this was the last time during the Cold War that either side would take that risk (Clark, 2008).

With the end of the Cold War, the U.S. and the Soviet Union cut down on nuclear weapon spending, using the money to repair environmental damages produced during the nuclear arms race. Although large inventories of nuclear weapons and facilities remain, there has been a significant effort made to reduce the number of missile stockpiles. Nuclear weapons are still used as a modern-day deterrent; however, with more nations possessing nuclear capability, the mutual assured destruction policy is even more prevalent when weighing the risk of war.

Case Study 2
The National Security Act of 1947

As political relations between the U.S. and the Soviet Union worsened, the possibility of war escalated. The U.S. needed a unified military structure to fight the Soviet Union in the event of an assault. However, government officials were wary of a unified militarized bureaucratic system, fearing that a stronger military would lead to a "Gestapo" situation in the U.S., much like what had happened in Germany. Despite this concern, the need for a more efficient and manageable foreign policy establishment outweighed the risk. This unified structure came in the form of the National Security Act, one of the most important pieces of legislation to come out of the Cold War. This act completely reorganized the War Department and gave birth to the National Security Council, the organization responsible for the coordination of U.S.'s foreign policy.

The National Security Act had three main parts. It first reorganized the War Department into one comprehensive structure, streamlining the nation's military by merging the Navy Department and War Department into the National Military Establishment. This organization later became the Department of Defense (DoD), which unified the armed forces into a federated system. (Prior to World War II, the U.S. never had a truly unified military structure.) The DoD was charged with coordinating and supervising all agencies and functions of the government concerned directly with national security and the United States Armed Forces (Milestones: 1945–1952: National Security Act, n.d.).

The NSA also recognized the Air Force as an independent service from the Army. Personnel of the Army Air Forces (AAF) were transferred from the Department of the Army (formerly the War Department) to the Department of the Air Force and established as the United States Air Force (USAF). The Air Force was charged to organize, train, and equip air forces for air operations, including joint operations; to gain and maintain general air superiority; to establish local air superiority where and as required; to develop a strategic air force and conduct strategic air reconnaissance operations; to provide airlift and support for airborne operations; to furnish air support to land and naval forces, including support of occupation forces; and to provide air transport for the armed forces except as provided by the Navy for its own use. As the U.S. came to rely upon a strategy of deterrence, the Air Force gave highest priority to its long-range atomic bombing force, using air refueling to lengthen its reach (The United States Air Force, n.d.).

Similarly, the NSA also protected the Marine Corps as an independent service (under the Department of the Navy) by prohibiting it from being absorbed by the Army. It reaffirmed the traditional and garrison duties of the Marine Corps as well as recognized the amphibious nature of Marine operations. Under the NSA, the Marine Corps was charged with being organized, trained, and equipped to provide Fleet Marine Forces of combined arms; providing Fleet Marine Force with combined arms and supporting air components for service with the United States Fleet in the seizure or defense of advanced naval bases and for the conducting of such land operations as may be essential to the execution of a naval campaign; developing, in coordination with the Army, Navy, and Air Force, the doctrine, tactics, techniques, and equipment employed by landing forces in amphibious operations; and providing detachments and organizations for service on armed vessels of the Navy and security detachments for the protection of naval property at naval stations and bases (Hittle, 1947).

Secondly, the NSA established the National Security Council (NSC), which serves as the coordinating agency for U.S. foreign policy. The council's job is to coordinate political and military questions and advise the President on issues of foreign and defense policy. It also ensures cooperation between the various military and intelligence agencies (Truman signs the National Security Act, 2009). Chaired by the Commander in Chief, who selects the personnel on the council, the council serves as the President's means of controlling and managing competing departments and agencies. As such, the NSC usually reflects the attitudes and needs of the current Commander in Chief. Key members of the council include the Secretary of State, the Secretary of Defense, and the National Security Adviser, as well as the Vice President, the Secretary of the Treasury, the Chairman of the Joint Chiefs of Staff, and the Director of Central Intelligence. The NSC is staffed by both civilian and military advisers and organized into regional, issue-focused, or functional directorates, each led by a Special Assistant to the President with the title of Senior Director. Each directorate has approximately two to ten advisers as staff members. While the President is head of the NSC, the NSC staff is led by the National Security Advisor and functionally managed by the Executive Secretary and Chief of Staff of the NSC (The Administration: The White House, n.d.).

Finally, the National Security Act set up the Central Intelligence Agency, which replaced the OSS. When President Truman signed the National Security Act, his goal was to modernize the outdated defense setup by unifying the armed services under one civilian chief. He also included a secondary goal of reforming intelligence. During World War II, the Office of Strategic Services supplied policy makers with essential facts and intelligence estimates, often playing a key role in directly aiding military campaigns. However, on a larger scale, intelligence was not coordinated between the Pacific and European theaters. Intelligence flowed from various sources, but officials didn't have the ability to properly coordinate it for the overall benefit of the military, nor did the OSS have complete jurisdiction over all foreign intelligence activities (A look back, 2008).

Under the NSA, the CIA became an independent agency under the supervision of the NSC, coordinating the intelligence of the rest of the government. The Agency was responsible for correlating, evaluating, and disseminating intelligence that affected national security as well as performing other such duties and functions related to intelligence that the NSC might direct. It also oversaw strategic analysis and coordinating clandestine activities abroad, but not as a controlling agency. This allowed for competition as the CIA and other agencies pursued common targets while fostering an exchange of perspectives and abilities. The act also drew a line between foreign and domestic intelligence, divvying out responsibilities between the CIA and FBI. While the CIA would have not policymaking role or law enforcement power, the Director of the CIA was charged with protecting intelligence sources and methods (A look back, 2008). The NSA remained the charter of U.S. intelligence and national security until the National Security Intelligence Reform and Terrorism Prevention Act of 2004, which created the Office of the Director of National Intelligence, the head of the U.S. intelligence community. Lauded as a major accomplishment, the NSA reorganized and modernized U.S. armed forces, foreign policy, and the Intelligence Community. The passing of the National Security Act of 1947 created many of the lasting institutions that U.S. presidents found useful when formulating and implementing foreign policy and is considered one of the most important pieces of legislation to come from the Cold War.

CHAPTER 2 PRACTICE PROBLEMS

1. What is national defense? Please be specific.

2. What was the significance of the Truman Doctrine?

3. What effect did satellite states have on U.S. national policy during the Cold War?

4. Which department does the Coast Guard fall under, and why is it not a permanent entity under the Department of Defense?

5. What is the greatest threat to U.S. national security and why?

6. What is the purpose of the National Security Council?

7. What are the differences between the Central Intelligence Agency, the Federal Bureau of Investigation, and the Department of Defense?

8. In your opinion, which country was responsible for the Cuban Missile Crisis? Please explain.

9. What was the significance of the Sputnik I launch in 1957?

10. The text lists 12 of the 13 American values proposed by Robert Kohls, the Executive Director for the Washington International Center. What do you think are the top American values?

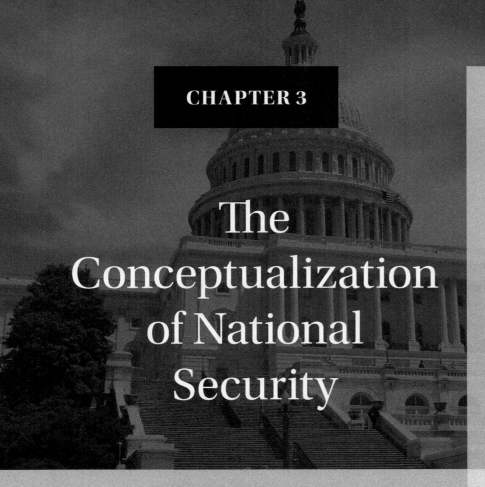

CHAPTER 3

The Conceptualization of National Security

KEY TERMS

Articles of War

Chain of command

Defense policy

Executive orders

Goldwater-Nichols Act

Loyalists

Presidential Accountability Act

Security

Status quo ante bellum

Unified Combatant Commands

LEARNING OBJECTIVES

After reading this chapter, students will be able to:

- Identify the relationship between the conceptualization and institutionalization of national security

- Analyze how economic, political, and social change shaped the United States and its national objectives

- Evaluate the American government's innovative methods of gathering intelligence that influenced the nation's U.S. military objectives.

INTRODUCTION

Understanding national security is to acknowledge the term as a concept. Donald Snow emphatically stated that Americans tend to think of national security incorrectly because "units of the international system are states" (1998, p. 21). Nonetheless, the term national security is used within the United States and is heavily regarded in the federal government, especially the Department of Defense.

The primary understanding in terms of national security is that whatever improves security within a country is favorable, and any deterrence from security (the mitigation of danger and/or threats) is considered a threat or vulnerability. Such perceptions are biased, and each state focuses on primary issues that influence or hinder national security (i.e., American national security strategy). Other issues address long- and short-term initiatives to formulate resolutions to mitigate national security concerns. If there are systematic processes in place to maintain a safe state with respect to the international system, then there is sustenance in maintaining a protected state. Where interests and modern threats evolve, interests in protecting the country must exist. National states must also understand how long- and short-term policies can positively or negatively affect the international system.

A key concept of national security is that more permanent strategies balance national and global security dilemmas. David A. Baldwin argues that he sees a failure to acknowledge concepts in security. He says, "neglect of security as a concept is reflected in various surveys of security affairs as an academic field" (1997, p. 8). His argument emphasizes the need to understand security as an idea.

In 1965, one study lamented thus far there have been very few attempts to define the concept of national security (Berkowitz, 1966, p. 124). In 1973, Klaus Knorr began a survey of the field by stating his intention to deliberately bypass the semantic and definitional problem generated by the term national security (Knorr, 1973, p. 5). In 1975, Richard Smoke observed that the field had paid quite inadequate attention to the range of meanings of security (Smoke, 1975, p. 259). In 1991, Buzan described security as an underdeveloped concept and noted the lack of conceptual literature on security prior to the 1980s (Buzan, n.d., pp. 3–4). Two studies of the security studies, for example, did not bother to define security (Walt, 1998, pp. 5–27). None of the eleven course syllabi described in security studies for the 1990s includes Wolfer's seminal article on the concept of national security (Schultz, Goodson, and Greenwood, 1992).

What Is Security?

Security can be defined as the state of being separated from endangerment or threats. In terms of national security, Oxford University Press defines security as the "safety of a state or organization against criminal activity such as terrorism, threat, or espionage" (Cottey, 2012, p. 7). D.M. Snow believes security has two aspects: the physical and psychological states. The physical state of security is the protecting of a country's borders from threats. This is the most essential physical form of security as it is important to protect the state and its resources. Even though this is an indispensable facet of security, the psychological state of national security is just as important. Snow's emphatic statement regarding the psychological fear of threats is "we are free from fear to the extent that we lack feeling of fear" (Snow, 1998, p. 24).

Such debate caused division regarding the scale of protection that would suit the American public. For example, in the 1990s, the United States' major concern was nuclear weapons and adversarial threats (which are still concerns today). Some believe state security was of importance back then because a large threat (the Soviet Union) affected a large population within the United States. Others believed individual security was more important than protecting the entire country since national security did not invest in individual lives. Additionally, those who opposed state security believed national security matters were a problem that caused friction on a large scale. National security concerns influence international security objectives. Some believed state security and government interference would cause international devastation.

What is considered contribution or detraction to national security objectives is discussed under national interest and national security strategy. It is very difficult to reshape security objectives. Policies and regulations often receive more emphasis than the actual concept of security. David A. Baldwin (1997) believes there is more focus on policies that centralizes efforts on "human rights, economics, the environment, drug trafficking, epidemics, crime, or social justice" (p. 5). With additional focus on issues that are agreeably of importance, security is often overlooked, without major threats and challenges to focus on. Baldwin also suggest three useful ways to identify common security concepts:

1. Ask basic questions in social science.
2. Promote rational analysis by facilitating comparison of one of type of security polity with another.
3. Facilitate scholarly communication by establishing common ground between disparate viewpoints (1977, pp. 4–5).

Simple processes are sometimes neglected because of the expectation for methods to be more convoluted or challenging. Conceptual analysis has been used in multiple research studies to identify the challenges within security frameworks. The element of breaking philosophical boundaries is often the justification for ambiguity regarding security is a concept and why it is a neglected matter. Such challenges can pose problems with understanding national security objectives.

Neglect of security as a concept can revert to Wolfer's 1952 article of conceptual analysis and various studies in the 1960s and 1970s. To understand security as a concept and challenge national security as the same, five possible explanations are offered:

1. It is difficult to comprehend as a concept.
2. It overlaps between security, power, and concepts.
3. People lack interest in security matters.
4. Scholars and researchers are focused on new advancements in technology and initiatives.
5. Policymakers believe ambiguity of security as a concept is useful.

Such explanations have been found to be less legitimate since emerging threats and global distress have required that the concept of security be considered. Experts have paradoxically neglected security issues based on its importance during a specific time. For example, the United States has been involved in many events in which security was of interest. The Cold War, the Cuban Missile Crisis, or anything that could gravely harm the United States' assets and artificial infrastructure forced experts and scholars to become interested in state security. When there is intermittence, security is pushed to the back burner until a threat to the United States emerges. Essentially, any major crisis threatening national security of the United States would be of interest to policymakers and experts, but when the threat is low, security is neglected. The 9/11 attacks are a great example of scholars' increased interest in security studies. Baldwin's stance on neglected security concepts referenced scholars' perception and interest:

> If military force was relevant to an issue, it was considered a security issue. If military force was not relevant, that issue was cosigned to the category of low politics (p. 1997, p. 9).

THE INSTITUTIONALIZATION OF NATIONAL SECURITY

Identifying security as a concept and understanding the physical and psychological aspects is not only warranted but required. Recognizing that this concept should be at the forefront of policymakers' minds is essential to protecting national interests. National security's existence dates to the Articles of Confederation when our Founding Fathers identified a need to protect our land. Implementing national security objectives essentially began when President Harry S. Truman signed the National Security Act of 1947. Prior to the NSA Act, there was a need for security, and Douglas T. Stuart noted this when he wrote "Creating the National State" in 2008. The need for security standards was apparent after World War I. Stuart wrote, "We were at war—but we foresaw a small possibility of military danger to this country."

Stuart noted this was the first time that security became an important matter during peacetime. Post WWI, Army Chief of Staff General George Marshall advised President Franklin D. Roosevelt to implement a plan to include security initiatives and foreign policy. He wanted Roosevelt to devise a plan to establish state-run mobilization to protect the United States. President Roosevelt was interested in a draft plan in which males would be required to complete one year of military service at 18 years of age. Marshall believed there should be a long-term plan to mitigate future attacks against the homeland.

Roosevelt's draft plan backfired because mandatory military time insinuated war, and this did not please the American public. During the time, former President Warren G. Harding's victory help reshaped America's stance on foreign policy. Roosevelt supported the new ideology and became neutral in crafting a mobilization plan to satisfy the American public. By the late 1930s, new threats emerged against the United States and Roosevelt realized a strategy to deter aggression was needed when the Japanese invaded China. The invasion heightened global and political awareness that blatant aggression against other countries should not be tolerated. As tensions progressed between the countries, President Roosevelt's stance on establishing formal policy became controversial. His policies were too ambiguous. However, the 28th President of the United States Woodrow Wilson argued that the United States needed alliances for global support to spread democracy.

ACCOUNTABILITY OF THE PRESIDENT

The president's responsibility in terms of national security relies on the guidance of the National Security Advisor and the Secretary of Defense. During periods when the president declares a national emergency (i.e. 9/11) or Congress declares war (i.e. Operation Iraqi Freedom), the president is mandated to maintain all Executive Orders (orders issued by the President of the United States that are announced to federal agencies within the American government for adherence and awareness) that are relevant to such emergencies. Also, the **Presidential Accountability Act** was enacted by Congress to ensure the president or vice president does not involve himself or herself or participate in any way that may affect his or her financial interests. In addition, the president follows these guidelines:

- Maintenance of file and index of presidential orders, rules, and regulations during national emergencies.
- Presidential orders, rules, regulations, and transmittals to Congress.
- Expenditures during national emergency must be reported to Congress (From Title 50—War and National Defense, n.d.).

> **Executive orders** established by the president should be reported to Congress when the president announces a national emergency or Congress declares war, and all orders must be reported to Congress within 90 days at the end of each six-month period after statements were initiated. Also, all expenditures should be reported to Congress on funding provided by the federal government.
>
> The president of the United States is responsible for establishing national security strategy. One of the primary documents POTUS uses to outline national security objectives is the National Security Strategy (NSS), which has Congressional input. The NSS outlines all major national security matters that are important to the federal government, in addition to how such issues will be resolved. The foundation of this policy is originated in the political standings of the Goldwater-Nicholas Act (Obama, 2015).

Figures 3.1a and 3.1b Senator Barry Goldwater and Representative William Flynt Nichols

THE GOLDWATER-NICHOLS ACT

The National Security Strategy (NSS) is a policy that is prepared by the executive branch and signed by the president and summarizes top national security concerns and on how the government will address those matters. The NSS is predicated on the **Goldwater-Nichols Act** (legislation passed to improve interoperability within the Department of Defense and military components, the largest military restructure since the NSA Act of 1947), named after Senator Barry Goldwater and Representative William Flynt Nichols, and other strategic doctrines such as the national defense strategy and national military strategy.

Known as the Goldwater-Nichols Department of Defense Reorganization Act of 1986, this policy is the most significant restructure to the Department of Defense since the National Security Act of 1997. Signed by President Ronald Reagan on October 1, 1986, the Goldwater-Nichols Act redesigned the United States Military, which gave decision-making authority to the Chairman of the Joint Chiefs of Staff. Additionally, the act restructured the **chain of command** (the order of authority within an organization) from the president to the Secretary of Defense directly to combatant commanders (combatant commanders do not receive orders from service chiefs or secretaries).

The act made significant changes with the military structure, and the first exercise under the new restructure was the *Invasion of Panama* in 1989 where Army General Maxwell Reid had full control to exercise operations over all service departments without having to go through individual service branches. Also under the act, the Chairman of the Joint Chiefs of Staff is the principal military adviser to the president, National Security Council, and Secretary of Defense. In addition, the Vice Chairman of the Joint Chiefs of

Staff was established to run the administrative and daily operations at the Department of Defense. Both positions must have general officers from different branches of the military. The CJCS had greater authority regarding the overall strategy for all forces as well as providing command authority to field commanders.

Because there was some conflict about how the service departments interacted, the combatant commanders had the authority to train, organize, and equip military units, and service chiefs were responsible for personnel and management matters within the respective branches. Also, service chiefs would have authority over unique functions such as special operations, strategic transportation, and the **Unified Combatant Commands** (nine combatant commands established to provide effective control of U.S. Armed Forces during peace and contingency operations). The Goldwater-Nichols Act also influenced the personnel management of military officers. Officers selected for joint-duty assignments attend DoD and joint military education for development and progression.

Since 1986, there have been some changes regarding the Goldwater-Nichols Act:

- On April 5, 2016 Secretary of Defense Ashton Carter addressed reform decisions during his speech at the Center for Strategic and International Studies.

- On November 10, 2015, Senator John McCain announced there would be an effort to revise the act.

- On October 24, 2002, former Secretary of Defense Donald Rumsfeld mandated functions and regional commanders to be addressed as combatant commanders instead of CINC because that was the president's abbreviation (Commander-in-Chief).

NATIONAL SECURITY ACT OF 1947 AND THE NATIONAL SECURITY COUNCIL

The National Security Act of 1947 was America's largest reorganization, which influenced military establishment and foreign policy within the federal government. The Act created the first Secretary of Defense position, along with establishing service departments, the Central Intelligence Agency (CIA), and the National Security Council (NSC). President Harry S. Truman signed the act into law on September 18, 1947, following World War II (WWII), and other provisions that related to the military establishment took effect.

James Forrestal was appointed and confirmed as the first Secretary of Defense (SECDEF) the day before the signing of the NSA act. His responsibilities were pivotal when the amendment to NSA was enacted within two years, creating the Department of Defense and giving him more power over the service departments. The service departments' names were changed to epitomize the act of military establishment. The Department of War was renamed the Department of the Army and the *National Military Establishment (NME)* (now called the Department of Defense). The Air Force seceded from the Army Air Force and became the Department of the Air Force. The Marine Corps remained its own entity but was a caveat of the Department of the Navy for direction on combat operations and naval warfare contingencies.

At the time of inception, service secretaries had their own leadership roles until the amendment to the NSA act was signed on August 10, 1949, which recognized SECDEF as the "CEO" of national defense and the Department of the Defense headquarters at the Pentagon. Services now reported to the SECDEF, the NME officially changed to Department of Defense, and three service departments were established as a federal configuration. Federal acknowledgement of the service departments was America's largest military reorganization. As previously mentioned, the act established the NSC and the CIA. The Joint Chiefs of Staff was established under Title II, Section 211 of the original act and was later structured under United States Code, Title 10, and Title 32 (the responsibilities of DoD, the service departments, CIA, and JCS can be found in Chapter 1).

The NSC is the primary committee, which advises the President on all national security and foreign policy matters. The NSC is comprised of Cabinet-level officials and senior national security advisors, which establishes the Executive Office of the President. Under President Truman's legislative order (NSA of 1947), the NSC was charged with advising the President on national security and foreign policy obligations. In addition to the inception of the NSC responsibilities, the committee serves as representatives for establishing policies and initiatives for implementing across respective governmental entities.

Prior to the NSC, the National Intelligence Authority (NIA) was the leading agency to handle national security matters. Established under President Truman's Executive Letter (signed on January 22, 1946), NIA's responsibility was to oversee the Central Intelligence Group (now known as the Central Intelligence Agency). The agency had fewer Cabinet-level officials than what it is today. The Secretary of State, Secretary of War, Secretary of the Navy, and the Chief of Staff to the Commander-in-Chief (now known as the Chairman of the Joint Chiefs of Staff).

Initially, the purpose of the NSC was the need for increased responsibility in hand Soviet Union matters. The tensions between the Soviet Union and the United States created a need for more oversight on American diplomatic matters, which was beyond the Department of State's adequacy at the time. The formalization of the NSC mandated transparent coordination between the service departments and the Intelligence Community under the new specification of the National Security Act.

The History

The evolution of American national security initiatives and foreign diplomacy has been a main priority for presidential administrations, especially in the twentieth century. The problem was each presidential administration-- there were deficiencies and limiting factors that needed to be resolved that influenced current administrations. Such issues heavily impacted coordination, management, and policymaking. Since the inception of the NSC, there were various changes to fit the ideological, sociopolitical, and needs of the President in office. For instance, President Truman's efforts to mitigate constant changes and stabilize a coordinated infrastructure on American diplomacy created within the NSC, including the Secretary of Defense and Secretary of State as the most members to represent national defense and foreign policy efforts. Having such vital, strategic insight from Cabinet-level officials were to advise the President.

In the early stages of the NSC, the committee was run by the Secretary of State and was instrumental in coordinating and implementing policies. The council's Executive Secretary became Assistant to the President. During the Kennedy administration, President John F. Kennedy wanted the Secretary of State to focus on foreign policy, dismantling the NSC and appointing the Special Assistant for National Security Affairs and his executive staff to take responsibility for the "NSC" role. Authors James Paquette and Chris Miller (2006) cited President Kennedy's "freewheeling style tended to erase the distinction between policymaking and operations that President Eisenhower's regimented staff system so carefully observed" (p. 6).

Having a similar management style as Kennedy, President Lyndon B. Johnson relied on his immediate staff and establish groups when needed. By the 1960s, President Johnson increased responsibilities to the Secretary of State to oversee interdepartmental operations abroad. It was not until Nixon and Ford administrations that the NSC role expanded. Henry Kissinger, the 56th Secretary of State and National Security Adviser, served both presidents and assisted with the effort, focusing on analytical date from governmental agencies to enhance the National Security Adviser's position to advise the President. Kissinger's strategy of giving the Secretary of State major, American diplomatic and some foreign matters while having the Secretary of Defense focus on weapons, acquisition, treasury, and international financing was aligned with President Nixon's vision. In the end, Kissinger essentially performed both roles as State Secretary and the President's adviser.

By the 1970s, President Carter re-established the NSC, making the National Security Adviser the principal official of all foreign affairs and changed the Secretary of State as an operational role. New roles caused tension due to the advisor's new responsibilities were more of a public advocate for the President's vision rather than a sheltered position. The reformation exacerbated already tense relationships between the State Department and other governmental agencies. President Reagan's administration focused on policymaking, downgrading the National Security Adviser's role, and increasing the Chief of Staff to the President's role within the White House. However, the changes were not well received, especially among the Cabinet officials, resulting in the party working separately within the NSC.

President George H.W. Bush's considerable background in government and politics (former Vice President of the United States and Director of Central Intelligence) was paramount in vision for restoring foreign policy and diplomacy within the NSC. He reformed the council and appointed a Principals Committee, Deputies Committee, and eight Policy Coordinating Committee (Hooker, 2016, p. 3). During his administration, the NSC coordination was instrumental in the fall of the Soviet Union, the unification of Germany, and the deployment of American troops in Iraq and Panama (Turner, 2005, p. 136).

By the 1990s, President Clinton's administration expounded on President Bush's stance on accentuating a shared approach on foreign policy and national security matters. In addition, Clinton expanded the number of Cabinet-level officials as member, including the Secretary of Treasury, U.S. Representative to the United Nations, Assistant to the President for Economic Policy (newly created position under his administration), Chief of Staff to the President, and the National Security Adviser (History of the National

Security Council, 1947–1997, n.d., para. 10). By the twenty-first century, President Barack Obama merged the White House supporting staff along with the Homeland and National Security Councils to form the National Security Staff. Both bodies continued to separate bodies due to legislative statutes. In 2014, the name changed back to the National Security Staff (Hayden, 2014, para. 1).

On January 29, 2017, the Trump administration revived the Principals Committee (initiated by President George H.W. Bush) which became a subset of the NSC. During this reformation, President Trump reduced the attendance of the Chairman of the Joint Chiefs of Staff and the Director National Intelligence in which they were not obligated to attend mandatory principal meetings. Though this did not mean the roles were eliminated from the NSC, National Security Presidential Memorandum 2, both should be included in the Principals Committee when matters are relevant to their offices (Presidential Memorandum Organization of the National Strategy Council and the Homeland Security Council, 2017). A few months later, National Security Presidential Memorandum 4 was established, highlighting the Chairman of the Joint Chiefs of Staff and Director National Intelligence participation in the Principals Committee meetings. The memorandum also added the Administrator of the United States Agency for International Development (USAID) as a regular member of the Deputies Committee (Lieu, 2017).

Since President Truman's establishment of the NSC, many presidential administrations have used their own style and prominence to embed their legacies within the committee. In the twentieth century, the evolution of the NSC to focus on national defense and foreign policy have been instrumental in protecting American interests.

EVOLUTION OF THE U.S. MILITARY AND INTELLIGENCE COMMUNITIES

It is important to understand how the United States Military has shaped America. The United States Armed Forces has been around for over 200 years beginning with one of the most prominent events in establishing a military movement, fighting Great Britain for American independence: The *American Revolutionary War*. From 1754 to 1783, American forces showed their strength against the British, who wanted to continue to control the land. Other historical events such as the *Seven Years' War* (1756–1763), the *French and Indian War* (1754–1763), the *American Civil War* (1861–1865) and *World War II* (1941–1945) represented the New America fighting for freedom and justice and protecting its allies. The United States advanced with Spanish and French forces, and with skilled precision showed that America is a superpower that remains a global force today. The inception of American military forces started as early as the Seven Years' War.

The French and Indian War

The French and Indian conflict was a battle between North America, Great Britain, and France in congruence with the conflicts happening in Europe. The battle began in 1754 due to increasing tensions over France and Great Britain persisting in extending their regional presence in North America. Prior to the war, the British controlled thirteen colonies along the Eastern coast line from New Hampshire to Florida in North America, and the French established colonies in Louisiana throughout the Mississippi River, nearing Canada. With such a close perimeter in ownership, the French and British debated over territories located near the Ohio River valley, and the French established forts to claim ownership. The British attempted to seize the area and were defeated by the French, which resulted in a preemptive strike declared by Prime Minister Thomas Pelham-Holles. Those who opposed the British Cabinet made the prime minister's clandestine operations public, and the French government was notified, which led to war.

The British Parliament appointed General Edward Braddock as commander-in-chief of the war and sent him to the thirteen colonies in North America, but his reluctance to cooperate with Native allies and American colonialists made British operations too difficult to execute. A year later, Braddock was killed during an ambush when he attempted to seize Fort Duquesne, which made operations in North America a little stagnant. For the next few years, the war remained low-key (except for the French's victory in seizing Minorca in the Mediterranean), and there was not any major conflict until 1757 when the British defeated the French in India and Canada.

The French attempted peace negotiations, but British Prime Minister William Pitt wanted the French to give up their rights to Canada. The French government did not want to conform, and negotiations failed between the two countries. Once negotiations failed, King Louis XV's cousin offered to aid the country and established the Family Compact on August 15, 1761. The requirements of the pact mandated that the Spanish would declare war on the British if the war did not end with the French before May 1, 1762. The provisions were to have the British conform to peace negotiations, and not only did the war continued with the French, Great Britain declared war on Spain on 1762. As the Office of the Historian notes, the British prevailed and captured French Caribbean islands, Cuba, and the Philippines (French and Indian/Seven Years' War, n.d.). A year later, the French and Spaniards opted to have peace negotiations with the British, resulting in the Treaty of Paris. This was a major victory for Great Britain, as the result ended in claiming territories within North America.

With the finalization of the French and Indian War, Great Britain was faced with economic hardships within its American colonies. The aftermath of the war caused financial stress and economic unrest, and thus, the British Parliament found a way to monopolize the American colonies. The British imposed a series of laws between 1763 and 1775 that regulated trade and taxes to suppress the instability of the war. American colonies were upset over the impositions, which caused tensions, as Great Britain's actions exemplified authoritative control in America.

Continental Congress

American military forces were established a few years prior to acknowledging the concept of national security. In 1775, the Continental Congress established the Continental Army. The Continental Congress was founded as a governing body to make political and strategic decisions about Great Britain's control over the United States. American colonists created governments, and they were the considered the liaison between the colonists and the British. The Continental Congress was pivotal in being the national government for the United States and ensured interests were balanced to reflect decisions on behalf of both parties. The inception of the Continental Congress birthed diplomacy and democracy within the United States and would create a total of three conventions from declaring war to adding the Articles of Confederation.

The Continental Army was born from the increasing tensions between American colonists and Great Britain. In the mid 1770s, the British Parliament introduced what colonists called the Intolerable Acts (or Coercive Acts). As tensions grew between Great Britain and its colonies, American catalysts informed the British about their distaste over the new tax laws. They believed that new legislative acts against them were illegal and unjust against the American settlements. After the Boston Tea Party, the British attempted to enforce the Intolerable Acts, but colonials defied such laws and continued to rebel. The British enacted additional provisions to reprimand colonies that did not comply with their demands.

American colonists responded with the *Suffolk Reserves*, rebuking British powers outside of Boston. The colonial government was determined to disregard the British taxation laws until the British government included American representation on decisions made that affected the colonies. In retaliation, Great Britain imposed more taxation laws that affected the thirteen colonies. After the Suffolk Reserves, colonial officials established Continental Congress, in which twelve of the thirteen original colonies were members, to provide direction, institute committees, and create other governing bodies to mitigate Great Britain's powers. During this period, Continental Congress would meet three times:

1. Convened to discuss response to Intolerable Acts, which resulted in reprimanding the Massachusetts Province.
2. Conducted deliberations about remaining under Great Britain's control.
3. Enacted the Congress of Federation (discussed later in the chapter).

The Second Continental Congress was pivotal as delegates deliberated about whether they wanted to remain under Great Britain's control. Initially, some of the colonial representatives resisted, but when committees convened on July 2, 1776 and signed into law the Resolution of Independence, no one opposed. This newly established independence from Great Britain formed the United States of America.

In June 1775, the British became the colonists' governing body and attempted to seize ammunition and weaponry, which led to British forces invading Boston. During this time, the Continental Congress appointed *George Washington* (who would be the first President of the United States) to lead military forces. The evolution of the colonial militia would be the Continental Army, and Washington would be promoted as commander-in-chief of the newly established regiment. Congress formally enacted the Resolution of Independence on July 4, 1776.

As commander-in-chief of the Continental Army, George Washington did not have much experience with large military units, but he did excel as a resilient leader during the American Revolution War. Washington earned mixed reviews in America because Great Britain's commander-in-chief, William Howe, could manipulate and defeat Washington in the early stages of the war. When Washington and his regiment captured Hessian forces (armed forces hired by the British), he took over New Jersey. His record of winning war victories was not high, but he was considered a brilliant strategist, which was apparent in the victories at the *Battles of Trenton and Yorktown*.

When Americans' faith was restored in Washington and the Continental Army, Howe formulated a new strategy to overpower them. He hired British military officer John Burgoyne to contain American forces in the New England colonies. Howe did not assist Burgoyne and traveled farther south to seize Philadelphia (initially the capital of the newfound America). With no assistance, Burgoyne and his troops ran out of supplies and were forced to surrender in 1777 during the *Battle of Saratoga*. Great Britain's loss at Saratoga caused major problems in their future conflict with the American Army.

France and Spain had clandestine operations with colonials, providing weaponry and other supplies to the Americans. After the Saratoga defeat, the French officially entered the American War in 1778 and became an ally of the United States for independence. Since Northern colonies proved to be difficult for British, their forces moved South to destroy Southern American colonies. Howe appointed *Charles Cornwallis* to lead the southern operation, and his team captured American forces in Charleston, South Carolina.

The following year, Spain entered the war, providing support to the French, and initiated *Pacte de Famille*. The British response was to declare war on the Dutch Republic. When Cornwallis and his regiments were consecutively defeated two times, they to travelled to Virginia to escape. The *Battle of Chesapeake* victory won by the French mitigated Cornwallis' plan to escape. The French Army formed an alliance with American forces under the leadership of Jean-Baptiste Donatien de Vimeur, comte de Rochambeau and George Washington, which lead to the *Battle of Yorktown* against the British. The Franco-American alliance forced Cornwallis to surrender and nearly 10,000 British soldiers were captured.

The British continued war with France and Spain and eventually defeated both countries during the *Great Siege of Gibraltar* when France and Spain attempted to capture the Iberian Peninsula from the British. On September 3, 1783, the Americans and the British signed the Treaty of Paris, which ended the American Revolutionary War. Under the circumstances of the treaty, Great Britain agreed to respect the sovereignty of the United States and gave up territories that are now Canada, Florida, and the Mississippi River.

Seven Years' War

The Seven Years' War received its name due to global conflicts spanning over seven years (1756–1763). The war included Europe and five other continents (i.e. the Americas, West Africa, and the Philippines) against Great Britain and its allies (i.e. Prussia, Portugal, Hanover, and German states) and France (i.e. Austria, Russia, Spain, and Sweden).

Additionally, the Indian Empire (Mughal) played a role and fought Great Britain over Bengal. The initial conflict began when the British attacked the French over disputed areas in North America. In 1754, the British seized hundreds of French merchants as a symbol to antagonize and increase turmoil. During this time, Prussia faced conflict with Austria, fighting for dominance over the Roman Empire. In 1756, both countries switched, with Austria leaving Great Britain to support France and Prussia entering an alliance with Great Britain (the Diplomatic Revolution).

As the conflicts ensued, Prussia attacked the state of the Roman Empire, which caused major turmoil in Europe. As Austria formed an alliance to reclaim Silesia (now modern-day regions of Poland, Czech Republic, and Germany), Prussia aided Great Britain. Austria gained more support from specific sects of the Roman Empire, while Great Britain-Prussian alliance gained smaller regions within Germany. Sweden fought Prussia prematurely due to fear that the country would attempt to expand in addition to protecting the *Swedish Pomerania* (which is now the Baltic coast of Germany and Poland). In 1762, Spain interceded to support France and invaded Portugal, which was embarrassingly unsuccessful. Russia teamed up with Prussia after initial concerns that the country would invade the *Polish-Lithuanian Commonwealth*. Small successions within Europe attempted to evade conflict; however, there were close calls such as Denmark-Norway and Russia. The Dutch, along with Naples, Sicily, and Savoy, remained impartial. The war caused financial hardship on Russia, which resulted in a peace agreement with Prussia.

The war resulted in Great Britain claiming much of France, Spanish Florida, portions of islands in the West Indies, Senegal, and French trading posts in India. The Native Americans were taken by the British, and they were exiled from their settlements. After an initial bad start for Prussia, the country gained momentum when King Frederick's strategic war plan resulted in obtaining the nation's existing structure. After the Seven Years' War, Prussia became a great power in Europe. Austria, Portugal, Spain, and Sweden redeemed **status quo ante bellum** (existing before the war). France suffered financial ruin; Spain lost Florida, but maintained control of Louisiana, Cuba, and the Philippines (which was captured by the British at the beginning of the war). The Seven Years' War could be debated as the first world war since World War I happened nearly 200 years later. The war caused a global revolution, which restricted the European political system and influenced future conflicts such as the *Pax Britannica* and the *French Revolution*.

American Civil War

The *American Civil War* was fought in the United States for four years in the nineteenth century (1861–1865). Abraham Lincoln was declared the president during the 1860 presidential election, and he supported the abolishment of slavery in all territorial grounds of the United States. Lincoln's support in abolishing slavery resulted in seven southern states seceding from the Union to form the *Confederate States of America*. Later, four more states joined during the Civil War, and the conflict included noted historical battles such as *Antietam*, *Bull Run*, *Chancellorsville*, *Gettysburg*, and *Vicksburg*. The internal conflict caused much tension with neighboring states, and by the culmination of the war, it was considered the costliest war fought on American soil with over 600,000 soldiers killed, shaking the Southern region and severely affecting the national economy.

In the mid-1800s, the United States had a period of economic growth in the northern and southern regions. The northern region soared with the manufacturing industry, and a large-scale agricultural system rose in the south, which was heavily dependent on African-American slaves. Views of abolishing slavery were highly-publicized in the north, and southerners feared that abolitionism (the civil rights movement to end slavery) would cause extinction of the economy. By 1854, Congress passed the *Kansas-Nebraska Act*, which afforded all-new territories to establish slavery by entering a popular sovereignty rather than adhering to congressional laws. Those who opposed the law formed the Republican Party, and their ideologies opposed the expansion of slavery in western territories. The United States Supreme Court finalized the bill to approve slavery in such territories, resulting in *Battle at Harper's Ferry*.

Abraham Lincoln's election in 1860 was the last straw for southerners, and months later, South Carolina, Mississippi, Florida, Alabama, Georgia, Louisiana, and Texas seceded from the United States. When Lincoln took office the following year, Confederate forces threatened Fort Sumter and fired the first shots at the military installation, starting the Civil War. Fort Sumter's commander surrendered less than 48 hours after the war's inception, and Confederate leader Pierre G.T. Beauregard took over. Four more states (Arkansas, North Carolina, Tennessee, and Virginia) joined the Confederacy. The bordering states (Kentucky, Maryland, and Missouri) did not secede, although they were very sympathetic to the Confederate cause.

The *Confederates* maintained a strong military system, and they believed in preserving cultures and traditions, including slavery. The conflict led to the *First Battle of Bull Run*, which convened on July 21, 1861, where 35,000 Confederate soldiers forced the Union army to withdraw and head toward Washington, D.C. In 1862, General George B. McClellan led the Union Army to the Potomac and captured Yorktown, but then he was forced to retreat by the combined forces of Andrew Jackson and Robert E. Lee. McClellan wanted to advance to Richmond, but Lincoln refused, and the army headed to Washington, D.C. During this time, Lee advanced the Confederate troops north, splitting the army into two units and advancing to different regions. Jackson's unit met with General John Pope's army in Manassas and entered the *Second Battle of Bull Run*, while Lee's unit conducted a massive attack, forcing Union troops back to Washington, D.C. Following his victory, Lee headed the first Confederate invasion in the north, and without confirmation from the president, McClellan restructured the Union army and attacked Lee's regiment. The attack forced Lee and his unit to withdraw to Antietam Creek. By September 17, the *Army of the Potomac* attacked Lee's unit in what was considered the bloodiest day in American history, killing nearly 14,000 Confederates and over 12,000 Union soldiers. The Union Army's victory was significant, as their strategy forced the Confederates to leave Maryland and reposition to Virginia. However, President Lincoln removed McClellan from command, and he was replaced by Ambrose E. Burnside. Under his command, the Union Army fought Lee's unit near Fredericksburg, and the Confederate suffered significant losses. Burnside was then replaced with Joseph "Fighting Joe" Hooker.

On January 1, 1863, Lincoln introduced the **Emancipation Proclamation**, which freed all slaves in the Confederate states and was justified through a wartime operation. Interestingly, Lincoln did not free slaves in border states, as they had loyalty to the Union. The Emancipation Proclamation drastically affected the Confederates' labor force and influenced international public opinion to support the Union Army. In 1863, the Union was invaded in a surprise attack by Lee's forces on May 1, 1863, and General Joseph Hooker positioned his troops at Chancellorsville. In another costly battle, the Confederates lost 13,000 troops, and the Union had 17,000 casualties. On July 1, Lee executed another invasion on the Union Army, led by General George Meade, in Southern Pennsylvania near Gettysburg. Lee lost nearly 60 percent of his army but escaped and fled to Virginia, which was the last state invaded by the Confederates in the northern region. The same month, Union forces under the command of Ulysses S. Grant seized Vicksburg. The Confederates won at Chickamauga Creek, but Lincoln expanded Grant's command, and the Union army claimed victory at Chattanooga in late fall.

After the victory, Lincoln named Ulysses Grant the supreme commander of the Union army, and they positioned in Washington, D.C. to face Lee's army in northern Virginia. On March 25, 1864, after battling for so long, Lee's unit was exhausted but captured Fort Stedman and in an instant counteroffensive, the Union army claimed victory. Lee's forced rebased in Richmond, and for the next seven days, Ulysses Grant and George Meade fought Confederates alongside the Appomattox River. On April 9, Lee surrendered to Grant at the Appomattox Court House after no more possibilities of escape. On April 14, John Wilkes Booth assassinated President Abraham Lincoln at Ford's Theater in Washington, D.C. By April 26, Joseph Johnston surrendered to William Sherman at Durham Station, North Carolina, officially ending the American Civil War.

The result of the Civil War began with establishing diplomacy between the Confederacy of the United States and the United States along with other world powers. The United States was successful in sustaining neutrality among the global powers, and even though certain countries recognized the Confederacy, no one interfered in the American conflict. The ending of the war caused the collapse of the Confederacy and the abolition of slavery, and over four million slaves were freed. American policy drastically changed as the ending of the Civil War established civil rights laws to all slaves within in the country, solidifying that all individuals in the United States were mandated freedom and rights.

World War II

Known as the *Second World War*, World War II (WWII) was an international conflict between the Allied and Axis Powers. WWII was larger than WWI, mobilizing over 100 million military forces from thirty countries. In addition, this conflict produced the most casualties, between 50–85 million, including the Holocaust in which approximately six million Jews and five million civilians were killed. Moreover, over one million casualties derived from America's attack on Japan with the use of atomic bombs on Hiroshima and Nagasaki. WWII is considered the deadliest war in American history. The war featured the first use of nuclear weapons in global history, the spread of communism in Europe, and the international shift in powers to two superpowers: The Soviet Union and the United States. These two countries would fight for supreme power at the culmination of WWII, leading to the Cold War.

Because there were still remnants of animosity and hatred from WWI, the second war was almost inevitable. German leader and dictator Adolf Hitler and his National Socialist (Nazi) Party rose to power and immediately established alliances with Italy and Japan for this strategic plan of power. Hitler's idealistic principles behind the Nazi Party intended global domination, and he started his plan by invading Poland in 1939. The invasion forced France and Great Britain to declare war on Germany, and WWII began.

Two decades before the invasion, the First World War resulted in the fall of the Austro-Hungarian, German, and Ottoman, and Russian empires. In addition, new countries were established in Europe and the Middle East. The Treaty of Versailles developed nine nations; Austria-Hungary dissolved and became separate nations; Czechoslovakia and Yugoslavia converted into independent nations from Austria-Hungary; Turkey separated from the Ottoman Empire; and Poland was re-established after years of division by Austria-Hungary, Germany, and Russia. In addition, Estonia, Finland, Latvia, and Lithuania were developed from Russia, and Austria-Hungary and Russia gave Romania its independence. The League of Nations diminished, and the United Nations was established to be a neutral ground for all countries and to promote global collaboration among its members. The inception of the Cold War would be during this time, and most importantly, the world saw the rise of two superpowers: The Soviet Union and the United States.

Even though there were positive changes after WWI, the devastation and instability of Europe left matters unsettled, which opened doors for WWII. Predominantly, German economic and political implications in Germany were the main issues that fueled Hitler's campaign to attempt world domination. In 1933, Hitler was appointed Reich Chancellor and immediately named himself, Fuhrer (supreme leader). He was obsessed with power and believed the only way he could expand German culture (lebensraum) and race (Aryan) throughout the world was through war. His first move was secretly rearming the German force, which violated the Treaty of Versailles agreement. In 1937, he advanced military forces to Austria and the following year to Czechoslovakia. Hitler's actions were unnoticed, as France and Great Britain did not have interest in another confrontation since the two countries suffered the most economic and political devastation from WWI. Furthermore, the Soviet Union and the United States were focused on domestic government matters, so Hitler moved in secret without accountability of violation of international agreements.

By 1939, the German and Soviet Union prime ministers signed the *German-Soviet Nonaggression Pact* (also known as the *Ribbentrop-Molotov Pact*), which was a neutrality agreement between two countries for international trade. The agreement angered France and Great Britain because the new alliance meant that if Germany went to war, they would not have to fear the Soviet Union. Also, the two countries together could easily divide Poland. Hitler's intentions were to invade Poland, and if so, France and Great Britain had an alliance with the country to provide military support. On September 1, 1939, Nazi Germany invaded Poland, and two days later, France and Great Britain declared war on Germany, which was the inception of WWII. Two weeks later, Soviet Union forces invaded Poland; with Germany invading from the west and the Soviet Union from the east, Poland was immediately destroyed. By early 1940, Germany and the Soviet Union divided Poland, and the Soviets quickly advanced to dominate the *Baltic Federations* (present-day Estonia, Latvia, and Lithuania). Stalin's quick advancement led to the defeat of Finland during the *Russo-Finnish War* on March 13, 1940.

On April 9, 1940, Germany concurrently invaded Norway and Denmark and one month later invaded Belgium and the Netherlands, which was known as the blitzkrieg or immediate victory. A few days later, Hitler's regiment advanced to the Meuse River and attacked French forces at Sedan, a place fortified with barriers to withstand attack. The attack provoked the British Expeditionary Force to relinquish from Dunkirk, as French forces greatly suffered. At the French's expense, prime minister of Italy Benito Mussolini activated the *Pact of Steel* (alliance with the Soviet Union) agreement, and Italy declared war on France and Great Britain.

On June 14, German forces invaded Paris and divided the country into two zones. The Germans occupied one zone, and the French controlled the other under Marshal Philippe Petain's leadership. After Hitler divided France, he aimed for Great Britain with a strong offensive strategy. Because Germany and Great Britain were separated by the English Channel, Hitler planned to attack the country via airstrikes. The bombing continued throughout the summer of 1940, causing large civilian casualties and structural damage. After the airstrikes, Hitler planned to invade Great Britain but suspended the operation after Great Britain defeated the German air force. In 1941, the United States sent aid to Great Britain under the *Lend-Lease Act*.

By 1941, German forces invaded Yugoslavia and Greece, and Bulgaria, Hungary, and Romania joined the Axis Powers. Hitler had alternative plans that were unknown to the Soviet Union. He formed an alliance with the Soviet Union to ensure the country would not invade Germany. After he conquered the Baltic States, he planned to invade the Soviet Union because the country had large territorial grounds needed to expand the "pure" German race. His tertiary strategic objective was to exterminate all Jewish communities throughout Germany. His plan, called the *Final Solution*, killed over six million Jews in death camps. Hitler declared the invasion of the Soviet Union on June 22, 1941 under codename *Operation Barbarossa*. The Soviet's resources and weaponry outweighed Germany's, but their acquisitions were outdated, making it easier for Hitler's regiment to advance near Moscow. By November 1942, the Soviets conducted a counterattack against the Germans, ending at the Battle of Stalingrad, and they surrendered on January 31, 1943.

The United States entered the war on December 7, 1941 when the Japanese conducted a preemptive strike on Pearl Harbor, killing over 2,300 service members. The following day, the United States declared war on Japan, and the Axis Powers declared war on the United States. Initially, the Japanese won victories, but when the United States won the *Battle of Midway*, there was a major change in the direction of the war. Additionally, the defeat against the Japanese regiment in a six-month period in the Solomon Islands increased

Figure 3.2 General George Washington, Commander-in-Chief of the Continental Army

the United States' strength in the Pacific. By summer of 1943, Allied naval forces conducted a counterattack on Japanese forces, using amphibious assault tactics on major Japanese islands. American forces were successful, which led to the goal of invading mainland Japan.

Also, in 1943, the United States and Great Britain defeated the Italians and Germans in North Africa. The same year, Allied Powers invaded Sicily and destroyed the Italian government, fighting Italian and German forces by 1945. On June 6, 1944, Allied Powers conducted a counteroffensive invasion in Europe, mobilizing 156,000 American, British, and Canadian soldiers on the coasts of Normandy. Hitler's offensive was to rebuild forces in west, affirming units would obtain victories in the east. Soviet Union regiments advanced into Czechoslovakia, Hungary, Poland, and Romania, and Hitler advanced his troops to confront American and British forces in the *Battle of the Bulge*, which was last offensive attack in the war. By April 30, 1945, Hitler committed suicide, and when Allied Powers invaded Germany with aerial weaponry, they forced the Germans to surrender on May 8, 1945. After the Germans surrendered, the Soviets gained much control over Germany.

After the official dissolution of WWII, President Harry S. Truman, Winston Churchill, and Joseph Stalin deliberated the continuing war with Japan and debated peace agreements with Germany during the Potsdam Conference. They decided Germany would be divided into four zones and were to be controlled by France, Great Britain, the Soviet Union, and the United States. Truman and Churchill did not want to make any agreements until the Soviet Union ensured its support in the fight against Japan. Because Japan was a deadly threat due to the casualties ensued at Iwo Jima and Okinawa, and there was anticipation of an expensive land invasion, Truman authorized American forces to use an innovative weapon: the **atomic bomb** (a weapon of mass destruction and explosive device that is created through fission, fusion, or both; a nuclear weapon). On August 6, 1945, atomic bombs were used to annihilate two Japanese cities, Hiroshima and Nagasaki, killing nearly 130,000 people. By August 10, the Japanese surrendered aboard the *USS Missouri* in Tokyo Bay, Japan, and they accepted the terms of the *Potsdam Declaration*.

Continental Army

Pre-National Security Act, the *Continental Army* was established by Continental Congress, formalizing a unique structure that was best suited for administrative and command operations during the American Revolutionary War. With seven regional departments (that were subject to change and were alternated during the war), the regiment was considered the largest part of the Continental Army's operations. At the time, the headquarters were regional departments that maintained multiple regiments. Authors Jesse Russell and Ronald Cohn note, "brigades, divisions, and field armies existed, but were only temporary units that were not assigned to any particular department" (n.d.).

The Continental Congress appointed and removed department commanders. Because George Washington was General and Commander-in-Chief during the time of the war, he had the same authority to make temporary decisions for leadership, pending congressional approval. Congress eventually approved most temporary units as official departments, making the army a more stabilized military. Working with the Continental Congress, the Continental Army and Navy were pivotal military organizations that represented civil control of military operations that were expressed in the Articles of Confederation and the United States Constitution.

As officials of America's new federal government, department commanders worked directly with state departments, and under this structure, departments were commanded by major generals. The seven departments were Canadian, Eastern, Highlands, Middle, Northern, Southern, and Western.

Canadian Department. The Continental Congress established the Canadian Department to appease the Canadians to join forces and institute reorganization. The Canadians were promised religious freedom and annex, which was a prominent aspect for Province of Quebec (Wright, 2006). The reorganization was deemed unsuccessful, and American forces attempted to seize the Montreal region. The coup was unsuccessful as well, and the American militia reestablished the department in Fort Ticonderoga, New York (the New York Department) on July 17, 1776.

Eastern Department. The Eastern Department was created on April 4, 1776 for military forces that were sent to assist in the Siege of Boston. According to Wright, the department existed before the inception of the Continental Army and continued to thrive after the Boston and Rhode Island wars. Changed to the New England Department, the military function encompassed Connecticut, Massachusetts, New Hampshire, and Rhode Island. The New England Department was considered the largest function during the initiation of the American Revolutionary War and was considered one of the primary armies during this time.

Highlands Department. The Highlands Department was considered the smallest of the seven. It was initially part of the Middle Department but due to its important function (and strategic location), it segregated into its own unit. The department was formed along the Hudson River, approximately 50 miles from New York City, intersecting the river and Appalachian Mountains. After the British seized New York City, the American defensive locations were critical to military strategy. Because the British maintained naval forces at the Hudson River and New York City, American forces strategy was critical in taking cover along the waterway. Thus, American troops built defenses at West Point and along the Hudson River, which stayed in position until the end of the war.

Middle Department. The Middle Department was formulated on February 27, 1776, and included Delaware, Maryland, New Jersey, New York, and Pennsylvania. As previously mentioned, New York moved to the Highlands Department. Wright explains that some of the most notable battles were fought through this department such as the Monmouth/New Jersey/New York/Philadelphia Campaigns and the Battles of Princeton and Trenton, as well as Valley Forge.

Northern Department. The Northern Department was initially the New York Department, but was reestablished after the British took over New York City. This department was the only one to remain active after the American Revolutionary War.

Southern Department. The Southern Department was created on February 27, 1776, and included Virginia, North Carolina, South Carolina, and Georgia plus present-day West Virginia, Kentucky, Tennessee, Alabama, and Mississippi. This department was considered more independent than the other six. The most prominent events were the Battle of Camden and the Surrender of Charleston. Other events included the Savannah and Charleston crises. The department closed toward the end of the war.

Western Department. The Western Department was responsible for parts of Virginia and Pennsylvania and present-day Ohio, Indiana, Illinois, Michigan, and Wisconsin. The department was responsible for the western frontier and had its most notable operation in the Illinois Campaign. The organization remained until after the war.

Continental Navy

The *Continental Navy* was established alongside the Continental Army during the American Revolutionary War. On June 12, 1775, the Rhode Island General Assembly passed a declaration to establish a navy within the state. The primary goal of the navy was to divert shipments of British products and disrupt their maritime operations. The British placed Boston under martial law, and the Continental Congress began the construction of warships to place a blockade on British maritime operations. At the time, General and Commander-in-Chief George Washington oversaw several ships with the same intentions.

The State Assembly passed a declaration on August 26, 1775 to establish initial movement for a naval strategy in Rhode Island. The declaration instructed Congress to introduce legislation in response to the infractions imposed on Rhode Island, stating:

> This assembly is persuaded that building and equipping an American fleet, as soon as possible, would greatly and essentially conduct to the preservation of the lives, liberty, and property of the good people of these colonies and therefore instruct their delegates to use their whole influence at the ensuing congress for building, at the continental expense, a fleet of sufficient force for the protection of these colonies and for employing them in such a manner and places as will most effectively annoy our enemies, and contribute to the common defense of these colonies (Bradford, 1985, para. 1).

The decision to initiate a naval plan against the British caused much disagreement since the block support from that was coming from the Continental Army. At any rate, the Continental Congress moved forward because the navy needed to establish a plan to mitigate distress from the British frigates. Because there were financial issues with funding the naval blockade, the Rhode Island Assembly passed another declaration on August 26, 1775 that the Continental Congress would fund the Continental Navy. Even George Washington paid for several ships with his personal funds. One of the prominent ships he paid for was commissioned on September 5, 1775. The Hannah was based at the port of Beverly, Massachusetts.

The official establishment of the Continental Navy convened on October 13, 1775 when Congress authorized the purchase of warships to defeat the British merchant ships (the Andrew Doria and Cabot). The first ship commissioned was the *USS Alfred*. The following month, Congress passed a declaration which enforced two marine battalions for the commissioned ships. John Adams, who would serve as the first vice president and second president of the United States, was one of the Founding Fathers who formulated regulations that Congress adopted, and they remained in effect until the conclusion of the war. Congress re-evaluated the Rhode Island declaration and passed it on December 13, 1775. This declaration authorized the construction of thirteen frigates that would harbor weapon systems. The thirteen frigates were named the *Washington, Effingham, Congress, Montgomery, Randolph, Raleigh, Boston, Trumbull, Providence, Delaware, Warren, Hancock,* and *Conqueror.*

The Continental Navy consisted of many African American sailors, loyalists (American patriots who were loyal to the British during the American Revolutionary War), and British from the capture of Royal Navy ships. After the establishment of the continental fleet, many conflicts ensued. The maritime missions were not always successful due to limited capabilities. The British proved to be unmatched, capturing or destroying most of the ships. There were some success stories between the Continental Navy and private ships that had nearly 1,700 letter of marques that were issued by Congress. During the war, American private ships seized approximately 2,200 British ships estimated at $66 million.

With more frigates destroyed and captured than in the control of the American navy, the Continental Navy did have some successful highlights in strengthening maritime operations. After the end of the Revolutionary War, the new America needed financial stability to build from the aftermath. Thus, the Continental Congress sold the final frigate to a private dealer. Like the Continental Army, the navy was the beginning establishment of what is today's United States Navy. More information about the United States Navy can be found in Chapter One.

U.S. Military

The Continental Army and Navy were the center stone for America's military forces, which led to the United States Armed Forces (or the U.S. Military). The Armed Forces was birthed from the Continental Army and Naval forces, which were structured before the Declaration of Independence. The Continental Amy was created on June 14, 1775 and the Navy followed on October 13, 1775. As previously mentioned, both forces fought various wars to protect American interests. Both military structures demobilized in 1784 after the Treaty of Paris was signed, establishing the United States' independence from Great Britain. On June 3, 1784, The Congress of the Confederation passed legislation and established the United States Army. Nearly ten years later, now called the United States Congress, formulized the United States Navy and followed with the United States Marine Corps on July 11, 1798. The United States Coast Guard was created on August 4, 1790 during the inception of the Revenue Cutter Service, and merged with the U.S. Life-Saving Service.

The nation's youngest military force, the U.S. Air Force was established on September 18,

On August 4, 1790, the U.S. Revenue Cutter Services was created through Congress to serve the nation as an armed customs enforcement entity under the U.S. Department of Treasury.

Established in 1878, the U.S. Life-Saving Service was charged with humanitarian efforts, particularly saving lives of those shipwrecked. On January 28, 1915, the U.S. Life-Saving Service merged with the U.S. Revenue Cutter Service to form the U.S. Coast Guard.

1947 when it seceded from the U.S. Army under the National Security Act of 1947. The Service branch was formed to focus on aerial and space warfare operations, including air support for land (Army) and naval (U.S. Marine Corps and U.S Navy) forces.

The National Command Authority consists of the President of the United States, the Vice President of the United States, the Secretary of Defense, and the Deputy Secretary of Defense and refers to having the ultimate discretion of all military orders.

Structure

The President of the United States is the Commander-in-Chief to the U.S. Armed Forces and is responsible for all military policy alongside the Department of Defense and the Department of Homeland Security. The U.S. Constitution created legislation for the Armed Forces and allows the establishment of executive Departments led by principal officers who advises the President (Gormley, 2016, p. 27). The legislative excerpt was responsible for the Department of Defense under the National Security Act of 1947 and the Department of Homeland Security under the Homeland Security Act of 2002. The Secretary is head of the Department of Defense and is the second in command over the U.S. Armed Force (excluding the U.S. Guard, which falls under the Secretary of Homeland Security area of responsibility). The Defense Secretary is the advisor to the President on all national security matters. Both the President and the Secretary of Defense form the National Command Authority, which is the ultimate law of military orders.

The President utilizes the National Security Council to coordinate military political and strategic operations. The Secretary of Defense and the Secretary of Homeland Security are responsible for the establishment and maintain civilian authority of the Armed Forces. In addition, the three service departments: U.S. Army, the U.S. Navy (includes the U.S. Marine Corps), and the U.S. Air Force have civilian authority:

- Secretary of the Army
- Secretary of the Navy
- Secretary of the Air Force

The U.S. Coast Guard falls under the Secretary of Homeland Security's purview. However, during war, the President or Congress can transfer authority to Secretary of the Navy.

The President and Secretary of Defense are advised by the Joint Chiefs of Staff, which is under the purview of the Chairman of the Joint Chiefs of Staff (CJCS). The CJCS is the highest-ranking officer in the U.S. Armed Forces and the Vice Chairman of the Joint Chiefs of Staff (VCJCS) is the second highest-ranking. The Joint Chiefs of Staff are comprised of:

- Chief of Staff of the Army
- Chief of Naval Operations

- Commandant of the Marine Corps
- Chief of Staff of the Air Force
- Chief of the National Guard Bureau

The Joint Chief of Staff is charged with advising the President, Secretary of Defense, the Homeland Security Council and the National Security Council on all military matters. Though, each officer is the most senior within their respective service departments, they do not have operational command authority, as the Goldwater-Nicholas Act only gives them advisory responsibilities. (More about the Goldwater-Nichols Act is at the beginning of this chapter).

On the hand, Combatant Commander has operational command authority overseeing the joint military effort (the Unified Combatant Commands), Combatant Commanders are senior commissioned (general officers) who have the authority to "command all forces, regardless of the branch of service within the geographical or functional command. Per 10 United States Code 164, the chain of command resides with the President to the Secretary of Defense to the Combatant Commanders and the Chairman of the Joint Chiefs of Staff can be a liaison between the Secretary and the Combatant Commanders.

Unified Combatant Commands

- United States Africa Command (USAFRICOM)
- United States Central Command (USCENTOM)
- United States European Command (USEUCOM)
- United States Northern Command (USNORTHCOM)
- United States Pacific Command (USPACOM)
- United States Southern Command (USSOUTHCOM)
- United States Special Operations Command (USSOCOM)
- United States Strategic Command (USSTRATCOM)
- United States Transportation Command (USTRANSCOM)

Intelligence Communities

The Federation of American Scientists (FAS) believed the concept of intelligence was a product of the Cold War (1996, para. 1). Evidence suggests that intelligence collecting dated back to the American Revolutionary War with the establishment of the Continental forces.

Like the evolution of the United States Armed Forces, intelligence communities existed due to the Revolutionary War. Paul Revere, an American patriot, was one of the first to provide intelligence when he warned the troops of British militants prior to the *Battles of Lexington* and *Concord*. His actions to mitigate American troops from being invaded were his personal responsibility, but nonetheless, he provided intelligence against British adversaries.

During the Revolutionary War, military leaders utilized spies as part of their search-and-hunt services. Such approaches gained the attention of George Washington, who assigned Joshua Meserau and John Honeyman as spies to work with organizations like the Knowlton Rangers. Intelligence collecting was an important tactic during the Revolutionary War. Intelligence was more than simply gathering information. It was a strategy to protect forces, land, and resources.

Again, the Continental Congress established intelligence operations to assist the Continental Army during the war. Congress established a secret committee for domestic and oversea intelligence services. In addition, there was a spy committee for tracking spies from the *Patriot Movement*.

Secret Committee

The *Secret Committee* was created on September 18, 1775 by the Second Continental Congress. As noted by the Office of the Historian, the Secret Committee was not an actual intelligence organization, but it served the purpose of a secret agency to obtain military equipment and supplies to sell to private dealers without adversaries' knowledge. The committee also negotiated deals with Congress for undisclosed contracts for weaponry, and once transactions were completed, records were destroyed. The committee commissioned secret agents abroad to support the committee of secret correspondence. The organization gathered intelligence to seize ammunition from Americans that supported the British. In addition, the committee gathered intelligence to confiscate British supplies and equipment in the southern colonies. They also purchased military stores and products through intermediaries to conceal that the federal government was the actual purchaser.

Committee of Secret Correspondence

Because Congress knew the need for foreign cooperation, the *Committee of Secret Correspondence* was established. Author of note for the Journal of Congress John Dunlap stated in response to the Committee of Secret of Correspondence:

> RESOLVED, that a committee of five would be appointed for the sole purpose of corresponding with our friends in Great Britain, and other parts of the world, and that they lay their correspondence before Congress when directed;
>
> RESOLVED, that this Congress will make provision to defray all such expenses us they may arise by carrying on such correspondence, and for the payment of such agents as the said committee may send on this service (1778, para. 1).

The Continental Congress appointed *Benjamin Franklin*, *Benjamin Harris*, *Thomas Jefferson*, and James Lovell. The four would be America's new foreign intelligence agency officers.

The Committee had many responsibilities such as covert operations, cryptograph systems, coding and decoding programs, human intelligence processes, advertising and marketing, foreign publications, distribution methods, and clandestine maritime capabilities (Milestones: 1776–1783: Secret Committee, n.d., para. 1). A few years later, the committee was renamed Committee on Foreign Affairs, yet still conducted intelligence operations. The *Committee on Foreign Affairs* handled foreign policy matters in conjunction with intelligence functions. In addition, the committee was established as the *Department of Foreign Affairs* (present-day Department of State), which was charged with obtaining the most information possible regarding foreign affairs matters. The Department of Foreign Affairs established a solid intelligence community and foreign diplomacy.

Spy Committee

The spy committee was formed on June 5, 1776 to establish policies for those who cooperated and gave intelligence to adversaries. Congress selected *Thomas Jefferson*, *Edward Rutledge*, *James Wilson*, and *Robert Livingston* to modify the *Articles of War* (frameworks established to regulate how a nation conducts its military operations) to include consequences of espionage against the United States Armed Forces. On November 7, 1775, the committee added the death penalty as a criminal action for espionage.

On August 21, 1776, the Continental Congress adopted the new law, which stated:

> RESOLVED, that all persons, not members of, nor owing allegiance to, any of the United States of America, as described in a resolution of the Congress of the 24th of June last, who shall be found lurking as spies in or about the fortification or encampments of the armies of the United States, or any of them, shall suffer death, per the law and usage of nations, by sentences of a court martial, or such other punishment as such court martial may direct (1975, p. 9).

On February 27, 1778, the espionage law was expanded to those who served as intelligence operatives to aid adversaries. This also applied to those who actions resulted in capturing or killing American forces.

Methods Which Shaped American Intelligence

The Committee of Secret Correspondence mandated that all facets of funding and training intelligence personnel be kept in house. Because of the sensitivity of intelligence operations, the committee approved a declaration that names of intelligence personal would be withheld and ensured that covers would not be blown by separating secret correspondence from "public" correspondence that foreign alliances had access to. As intelligence missions increased and the agency's area of responsibility expanded, the committee implemented its own oath of secrecy statement for intelligence personnel to understand the importance of their positions of potential employment.

Clandestine and Protective Operations

On November 9, 1775, the Continental Congress drafted a secrecy of operations oath for those who joined the intelligence organization (Dunlap, 1778):

> RESOLVED, that every member of this Congress considers himself under the ties of virtue, honor, and the love of his country, not to divulge, directly or indirectly, any matter or thing agitated or debated in Congress, before the same shall have been determined, without leave of the Congress, which is a majority of the Congress, shall order to be kept Secret. And that if he shall be expelled this Congress, and deemed an enemy to the liberties of America, and liable to be treated as such; and that every member signifies his consent to this agreement by signing the same (Dunlap, 1778).

After new employees were hired, Congress prepared secrecy requirements that were employed on June 12, 1776: "I do solemnly swear, that I will not directly or indirectly divulge any manner or thing which shall come to my knowledge as (sic) of the board of the war and ordnance for the United colonies … so help me, God" (Dunlap, 1778).

The Continental Congress had mandated a regulation for strict confidentially requirements. During this period, George Washington and his confidant *John Jay* had disputed about intelligence methods and resources. Jay was adamant with Washington that even though they had a high regard for one another, the issue of differences on intelligence and clandestine operations remained. Washington believed it would be beneficial to advertise intentions of intelligence operatives to gain support and boost public morale. He stated, "The release of information [intelligence] in an authentic and pointed manner would give a certain spring to our affairs in general" (Knott, 1996, p.35).

On the contrary, the President of the Continental Congress stated to Washington:

> The opinion that greater results from communicating important Events to the People, in an authentic manner, than by unauthorized Reports, is certainly just, though often neglected. The Intelligence alluded to is, unfortunately, of such a Nature, or rather so circumstanced, as to render secrecy necessary (Knott, 1996).

John Jay's adamancy towards clandestineness was appropriate and just. When his tenure ended as President of the Continental Congress, he was appointed to be minister to Spain. Nonetheless, his approach to secrecy and intelligence operations remained steadfast. Jay summarized his position on intelligence and secrecy to his friend Alexander McDougall: "The fewer Parties [involved] the better" (Knott, 1996, p. 35).

Covert Operations Using Cover

Covert operations were prevalent during the Revolutionary War. American Agent Robert Townsend posed as a merchant and worked for the Committee of Secret Correspondence, which was a very successful operation. Townsend worked in New York, which was controlled by the British during war. He was of the *Culper Ring* and had aliases such as Samuel Culper, Jr., Culper Junior, and 723, conducting clandestine missions for George Washington. Because Townsend was heavily involved in secrecy operations, his direct supervisor, Colonel *Benjamin Tallmadge*, wanted to disengage from this part of job to concentrate on intelligence gathering for the Committee of Secret Correspondence. George Washington denied the request because Townsend's excellent capabilities and embedment into the "intel world" was important in obtaining information on the British. At the time, Townsend was a silent partner in a coffee shop where many British militants gathered. According to the CIA, it was a great way to listen to British conversations that were pertinent to the war.

Townsend was a gold mine during the American war, and George Washington refused to lose his talent, stating:

> It is my opinion that Culper Junior should be was advised to give up his present employment. I would imagine that with a little industry he will be able to carry on his intelligence with greater security to himself and greater advantage to the United States. Under the cover of his usual business ... it prevents also those suspicions which would become natural should he throw himself out of the line of his present employment (From George Washington to Major Benjamin Tallmadge, 24 September 1779, 1779, para. 1).

As Townsend's operations increased, other agents joined clandestine missions posing as everyday workers. Major *John Clark*, who was responsible for all intelligence operations in Philadelphia, expanded agents within the area, and it was considered a successful strategy. Agents collected intelligence on British movements, preemptive attacks, critical infrastructures, and supplies. Another notable intelligence leader, *Enoch Crosby*, covered as a shoemaker and infiltrated loyalist cells in southern New York, and *John Honeyman* covered as a butcher to British agents to spy on British military movements in New Jersey. His operations were successful, and George Washington conducted a surprise attack on German contractors (*Hessians*) in Trenton.

Concealment

Disguises were common during the Revolutionary war and among the intelligence agency. One of the most prominent and successful disguises to collect intelligence on British military was *Nancy Morgan Hart*. According the National Women's History Museum, Nancy Morgan Hart was a "legendary hero of the American Revolution who made it her mission to rid the Georgia territory of British Loyalists (or Tories)" (n.d., para. 1). Even though she was responsible for political issues with the British government, she also served as a spy for the American. Six-feet tall, red-haired, and awkward, Nancy stood as a muscular, feminine figure, which was to her advantage. She would dress as a man, go to British encampments to gain information on their movements, and report it to the Americans. Her most notable act was capturing British soldiers. Some British soldiers killed her turkey and mandated that she cook it for them to eat. She developed a plan by sending her to daughter to get water and secretly gave her a horn to let Americans know the British were near. As she got them drunk on her corn liquor and food, she secretly stole their weapons. When they caught her stealing the weapons, she threatened to shoot. One soldier lunged at her, and she killed him, wounding one, and the rest surrendered.

Code Writing and Surreptitious Communications

During the war, George Washington had American spies use specific forms of coding to avoid detection when crossing in British territory. *Silas Deane,* an American spy, was known for using "heat-activated invisible ink" to write secret intelligence reports. His concoction consisted of cobalt chloride, glycerin and water, and was also used as a stain for secret military information sent from London to America. With invisible ink, clandestine writings were placed between the lines and spaces of the actual wording. This was a precautionary method to prevent adversaries from reviewing actual information in case messages were seized. Invisible ink messages could be revealed over an open flame or sodium carbonate. John Jay, who was a physician and the brother of Continental Congressman John Jay, used this stain to write clandestine reports and ended up furnishing the ink to George Washington and Silas Deane. Deane preferred the ink from Jay because it had an added layer of security, as it required a chemical to write the message and another one to develop it. George Washington approved of the ink and reported to his agents about Robert Townsend using it for his operations and stated: "Culper Junior [said] that the ink will not only render his communications less exposed to detection, but relieve the fears of such persons as may be entrusted in its conveyance" (FAS, n.d. para. 21).

Washington was a true supporter of code writing, using special ink, and believed it was best for transporting clandestine messages during the war. He suggested that the ink could be used for registers, publications, books, and pamphlets. He also mandated all agents camouflage their reports using the ink, especially for intelligence matters. The Central Intelligence Agency conveyed even though Americans had excellent ways to disguise their secret messages, the British could decipher more than half of them during the war. There were disadvantages to using the ink; if liquids touched the letter, the ink would smear, making it difficult to decipher. Also, intelligence letters were crucial documents used by American spies during the war. Such letters consisted of data concerning adversarial strategic military plans, movements, and spy operations.

Secret Coding

American forces appointed spies to use secret codes and cryptographic processes to hide their communications during the war. For spies to decipher secret messages, they had to have keys or word banks. In addition, they used *Benedict Arnold's* deciphering method, but when it was decoded by British forces a new scheme was developed by *Benjamin Tallmadge*.

Another secret coding method was to pose as merchants gathering information from the British. All messages were posed as documents to be a legitimate business transaction so that the technique would not be detected. According to the University of Michigan, anyone who read the secret messages would believe it was honest business data (n.d.). In addition, American spies used personal pocket dictionaries to encrypt messages. With this method, spies assembled words with numbers. Some spies allotted letters with corresponding numbers or even inverted letters within the alphabet. Cleverly, some agents altered major location names and if the key letters were added, their alliances would know the actual location.

Office of Strategic Services

The *Office of Strategic Services* (OSS) was a wartime intelligence agency that was established during World War II before the Central Intelligence Agency was brought to fruition. The OSS was comprised of criminals to fulfill requirements of intelligence collection, support for allies, and fighting the enemy during the war. Before the OSS, U.S. intelligence was conducted on case-by-case basis when intelligence officers were needed. There was not a structured American intelligence organization, and there still was not a solid structure during its inception. Multiple departments such as the Department of Navy, State, Treasury, and War were responsible for intelligence operations without any official or hierarchical chain of command with specific guidance. Additionally, unofficial offices were charged with dealing with intelligence and secret missions respective to their areas of responsibility (i.e. the Committee of Secret Correspondence). Each branch of service had its leadership, processes, missions, and code words during the war. All international operations were considered "loose" and were run by "ad-hoc" committees within each respective branch while the FBI was responsible for all domestic intelligence operations.

During World War II, President Roosevelt was concerned with the deficiencies, lack of coordination, and accountability within intelligence offices, and with senior leadership guidance from the British, prompted senior American intelligence officer William J. Donovan to create an intelligence agency that emulated the British's Secret Intelligence Service (MI6) and SOE. Donovan would eventually be the head of the nation's first intelligence agency: OSS. Donovan's critical responsibility incurred challenges, due to the lack of a central intelligence agency in the United States. As a result, he had to conduct research to determine the international military position. He published the *Memorandum of Establishment of Service of Strategic Information*, which led to his appointment as Coordinator of Information (COI), the leader of the new office on July 11, 1941. After its inception, Donovan did not have any authoritative power and a significant amount of intelligence was derived from the British.

Not until June 13, 1942 did President Roosevelt pass the presidential military order that led to the formulization of the OSS. The Joint Chiefs of Staff (JCS) were responsible for all OSS functions and coordinated espionage missions conducted by the United States Armed Forces. The direct mission of the OSS was to supervise and control espionage operatives during the Second World War. According to the National Park Service, William Donovan was at a football game when he was telephoned by the American government. He received notice that the Japanese bombed *Pearl Harbor*, and immediately Congress declared war. President Roosevelt established the OSS and named Donovan as the director. Donovan had a very impressive background as a decorated World War I veteran and businessman. Now as the director of the OSS, he was the first to succeed in establishing and maintaining a civilian-controlled agency during global wartime operations.

Roosevelt recognized that the service, state, and war departments worked independently on intelligence operations. Working separately posed great risks for the United States without any effective communications among the departments. He also knew increased tensions in Europe and Asia would eventually be dangerous for the United States. Donovan was tasked with evaluating global military positioning to determine American intelligence requirements. On July 11, 1941, Donovan developed the Memorandum of Establishment of Strategic Information, which formalized the *Coordination of Information (COI)*. The Americans coordinated with the British, and Donovan had responsibilities under the new office but did not secure an authoritative position. In addition, President Roosevelt wanted to implement modern ideas in reforming national intelligence plans, but political pressure prevented him from doing so. This arrangement made American patriots hesitant because British involvement was significant in the process such as intelligence agents training with the *British Security Coordination (BSC)* in Canada and various regions within the United States. Most intelligence was gathered from the United Kingdom, so it was easy for Donovan to develop a blueprint based on MI6 and SOE, which became the foundation for an amalgamated intelligence entity. The British were pivotal in providing equipment and supplies until American construction plans were established. On June 13, 1942, President Roosevelt executed a presidential military order for OSS to collect, gather, and analyze strategic information for conducting special operatives in congruence with JCS.

With British guidance and oversight, Donovan leased federally owned land and built critical infrastructures that were in proximity to Washington, DC. He acquired isolated areas, such as the *Chopawamsic Recreational Demonstration Area* (now *Prince William Forest Park*) and *Catoctin Mountain Park* to conduct training and mission operations. Quickly, individuals were recruited as OSS agents and were chosen based on proficiencies and experience after passing numerous psychological and mental tests. Recruits were sent to the new site locations and given supplies and equipment for training, which was confidential. They received false identification documents and their real identity was never disclosed.

During the war, the OSS managed numerous missions with specialized instruments. The equipment was unique to each mission to give the United States and its allies a competitive advantage. The organization's research and development department spent countless man-hours manufacturing weapons. Additionally, during WWII, OSS was responsible for conducting multiple intelligence operations, including espionage, sabotage, instigating war propaganda, and organizing anti-Nazi resistance forces.

The unit became increasingly successful in its operations and at the height of the agency's inception employed nearly 30,000. OSS's greatest accomplishment during WWII was infiltrating Nazi Germany. According to *Horrific Invasions* (published by Marshall Cavendish Corporation), OSS-trained German and Austrian personnel for military missions within Germany, which consisted of exiled communists, Socialist party members, labor activists, prisoners of war, and Jewish and German refugees (2011, p. 93).

Central Intelligence Agency

The *Central Intelligence Agency (CIA)* is the largest foreign intelligence agency in the United States. Created through the National Security Act of 1947, the CIA does not have law-enforcement capabilities. The CIA's sole responsibility is the "research, development, and deployment of high-leverage technology for intelligence purposes" (About CIA, n.d., para. 5). The CIA was created as establishment for foreign intelligence analysis in protection of national security objectives. Since the agency has evolved in the last 70 years, its main purpose is to collect, process, analyze, and distribute foreign intelligence for the President and the Cabinet. Though the CIA has limited domestic intelligence missions, the National Resources Division's sole purpose is handling domestic intelligence functions. The agency is considered one of the primary members of the Intelligence Community and is part of the five major intelligence entities. The agency's primary method of collection is human intelligence (HUMINT) and is considered the all-encompassing manager of coordinating HUMINT operation, even though it is not the sole agency that specializes in such activities for the Intelligence Community. However, it is the only agency that conduct clandestine operations at the President's request. Additional responsibilities include:

- Creating special, multidisciplinary centers to address such high-priority issues such as nonproliferation, counterterrorism, counterintelligence, international organized crime and narcotics trafficking, environment, and arms control intelligence.

- Forging stronger partnerships between the several intelligence collection disciplines and all-source analysis.

- Taking an active part in Intelligence Community (IC) analytical efforts and producing all-source analysis on the full range of topics that affect national security.

- Contributing to the effectiveness of the overall IC by managing services of common concern in imagery analysis and open-source collection and participating in partnerships with other intelligence agencies in the areas of research and development and technical collection ("CIA," n.d., para. 7).

The *Director of Central Intelligence (DCI)* serves as the "head of the United States Intelligence Community and acts as a principal adviser to the president for intelligence matters related to national security … and serves as the head of the Central Intelligence Agency" ("CIA," n.d., para. 1). Prior to the Intelligence Reform and Terrorism Prevention

Act of 2004, the Director of Central Intelligence had the purview of the Intelligence Community. Now the Director of National Intelligence heads all intelligence entities. DCI responsibilities comprise of:

- Collecting intelligence through human sources and by other appropriate means, except that he shall have no police, subpoena, or law enforcement powers or internal security functions;
- Correlating and evaluating intelligence related to national security and providing appropriate dissemination of such intelligence;
- Providing overall direction for and coordination of the collection of national intelligence outside the United States through human sources by elements of the IC authorized to undertake such collection and, in coordination with other departments, agencies, or elements of the United States government which are authorized to undertake such collection, ensuring that the most effective use is made of resources and that appropriate account is taken of the risks to the United States and those involved in such collection; and
- Performing such other functions and duties related to intelligence affecting the national security as the president or the Director of National Intelligence may direct (CIA, n.d., para. 3).

Because the CIA's responsibilities and personnel increased after the September 11 attacks, it currently has the largest congressional budget within the intelligence community. The agency has also increased its area of responsibility, such as conducting clandestine paramilitary operations. Also, the organization has increased its counterterrorism and cyberterrorism operations to stay concurrent to the ever-evolving threat to the United States.

After the dissolution of the OSS, the CIA's primary mission was to provide an area of responsibility for foreign intelligence and policy analysis. Today, the agency's mission is to collect, analyze, examine, distribute foreign intelligence, and conduct clandestine operations. Its strategic priorities have been identified by American policymakers as primary concerns for the Intelligence Community.

China

- Stability. The CIA sponsored an unclassified conference on prospects for China's stability over the next ten years during which intelligence analysts and other experts from academia and U.S. government agencies set out their views on unrest in the rural areas and the implications of economic reforms for social disturbances.
- Policy Support. The CIA provided analytic support to policymakers on a variety of issues affecting US-China relations.
- Human Rights Negotiation Support. A CIA team reviewed and translated materials on dissident activities in support of the 11–12 January 1999 State Department human rights negotiations with China.

U.S. Central Intelligence Agency, "Strategic Priorities," www.cia.gov. 2012.

Cuba

- List of Warning Indicators Developed. The CIA developed a capability to respond to crises in the Caribbean by developing a list of indicators to provide warning of rapid change in Cuba that is updated quarterly.

- Illegals Network. In May 1999, a 26-count superseding indictment was brought against the ten members of an illegals network in Miami, Florida, who were arrested on September 12, 1998. Most notably, this indictment included a count charging one of the subjects with conspiracy to commit murder in relation to the Cuban downing of two "Brothers to the Rescue" airplanes on February 24, 1996.

- Cuban Techniques. FBI investigations and operations have identified techniques used by Cuban intelligence officers in spotting and assessing U.S. persons for possible recruitment to include individuals working within the U.S. Government.

North Korea

- Ongoing Support. The CIA supported U.S. military commanders and policymakers by providing assessments of North Korean developments.

- Support to Deployed Forces Along the Korean DMZ. The National Ground Intelligence Center (NGIC) and NIMA produced a definitive baseline report of all North Korean border defense posts along the DMZ.

Russia

- All-Source Analytic Support. The CIA produced a large body of analysis focused on key Russian political, economic, and military issues.

- Internet Sources Exploited. In response to the explosion of Internet sources, the CIA initiated a daily Internet selection list based on material found on multiple Russian Internet sites which cover a broad range of topics from daily news to political, economic, military, and scientific information. The list has been well received by customers and has been used in analytic products (CIA, n.d., paras. 1–4).

Since September 11th, the CIA has expanded its office of responsibilities. Missions such as clandestine paramilitary, counterterrorism, and cyber operations have become prominent of the agency's objectives. Report from CIA's budget in 2013 stated the primary responsibilities of the agency are:

- Counterterrorism
- Nonproliferation of nuclear weapons and other weapons of mass destruction
- Keep American ambassadors and diplomacy of international events
- Counterintelligence
- Cyber intelligence

The agency has five directorates:

- The Directorate of Digital Analysis
- The Directorate of Analysis
- The Directorate of Operations
- The Directorate of Support
- The Directorate of Science and Technology

Collaboration with Other Agencies in the Intelligence Community

For domestic operations, the CIA works with the National Reconnaissance Office (with the U.S. Air Force) to maintain espionage satellites belong to the U.S. Armed Forces. In addition, the Special Collection is a collaborative effort of the CIA and that National Security Agency that conducts clandestine missions via electronic surveillance for global surveillance operations. As for foreign intelligence initiatives, the CIA works with the following agencies:

> *FIVE EYES is an intelligence alliance between Australia, Canada, New Zealand, the United Kingdom, and the United States. The countries share common intelligence methods, and because of this, all countries are part of the United Kingdom-United States Agreement, which is predicated on signals intelligence.*

- Australian Secret Intelligence Service (ASIS)
- Chinese Ministry of State Security (MSS)
- Egyptian General Intelligence Service
- French Secret Intelligence Service (Direction Generale de la Securite Exterieure—DGSE)
- Indian Research and Analysis Wing (RAW)
- Israeli Mossad
- Russian Foreign Intelligence Service (Sluzhba Vneshney Razvedi, SVR)
- United Kingdom Secret Intelligence Service (SIS or M16)

The United States' closest intelligence allies are: Australia, Canada, New Zealand, and the United States. Because these countries are closely related to the United States' intelligence methodologies, special communications can be shared (FIVE EYES).

Federal Bureau of Investigation

Created in 1908 as the Bureau of Investigation (BOI), the Federal Bureau of Investigation (named changed in 1935) is the United States' federal intelligence and law enforcement agency. The FBI is a subcomponent of the Department of Justice and a member of the nation's intelligence community, which concurrently reports to the Attorney General of the United States and the Director of National Intelligence. The FBI is the nation's leading agency specializing in counterintelligence, counterterrorism operations, and criminal investigations. Its primary mission is to support other federal agencies in protecting national security, with federal law enforcement authority.

The agency has over 400 offices across the United States, and it has sixty offices throughout the world, serving U.S. consulate and embassy offices to coordinate with foreign security entities. The FBI has the authority to conduct international intelligence and clandestine operations, though coordination is usually required between the United States and foreign governments. The FBI headquarters is in Washington, D.C. at the J. Edgar Hoover Building.

The FBI's mission is to "protect the American people and uphold the Constitution of the United States" by:

- Protecting civil rights
- Combating transnational/national criminal organizations and enterprises
- Combating major white-collar crime
- Combating significant violent crime (FBI's Mission, n.d., para. 2).

According to the Department of Justice, the FBI's priorities are to:

- Protect the United States from terrorist attacks
- Protect the United States against foreign intelligence operations and espionage
- Protect the United States against cyber-based attacks and high-technology crimes
- Combat public corruption at all levels
- Protect civil rights
- Combat transnational and national criminal organizations and enterprises
- Combat major white-collar crime
- Combat significant violent crime
- Support federal, state, county, municipal, and international partners
- Upgrade technology to successfully perform the FBI's mission (Organization, Mission, and Function Manual: Federal Bureau of Investigation, n.d., para. 3).

The major functions of the FBI are to:

- Conduct professional investigations and authorized intelligence collection to identify and counter the threats posed by domestic and international terrorists and their supporters within the United States, and to pursue extraterritorial criminal investigations to bring the perpetrators of terrorist acts to justice. In

U.S. Department of Justice, "Organization, Mission, and Function Manual: Federal Bureau of Investigation," Organization, Mission, and Function Manual. 2012.

furtherance of this function, the FBI designs, develops, and implements counterterrorism initiatives which enhance the FBI's ability to minimize the terrorist threat.

- Conduct counterintelligence activities and coordinate counterintelligence activities of other agencies in the intelligence community within the United States. (Executive Order 12333 includes international terrorist activities in its definition of counterintelligence.)

- Coordinate the efforts of U.S. government agencies and departments in protecting the nation's critical infrastructure by identifying and investigating criminal and terrorist group intrusions through physical and cyber-attacks.

- Investigate violations of the laws of the United States and collect evidence in cases in which the United States is or may be a party in interest, except in cases in which such responsibility is by statute or otherwise specifically assigned to another investigative agency.

- Locate and apprehend fugitives for violations of specified federal laws and, when so requested, state and local fugitives pursuant to federal statutory authority.

- Conduct professional investigations to identify, disrupt, and dismantle existing and emerging criminal enterprises whose activities affect the United States. Address international criminal organizations and terrorist groups which threaten the American people and their property through expanded international liaisons and through the conduct of extraterritorial investigations as mandated by laws and executive orders.

- Gather, analyze and assess information and intelligence of planned or committed criminal acts.

- Establish and implement quality outreach programs that will ensure FBI and community partnerships and sharing.

- Conduct personnel investigations requisite to the work of the Department of Justice and whenever required by statute or otherwise.

- Establish and conduct law enforcement training programs and conduct research to aid state and local law enforcement personnel. Participate in interagency law enforcement initiatives which address crime problems common to federal/state/local agencies.

- Develop new approaches, techniques, systems, equipment and devices to improve and strengthen law enforcement and assist in conducting state, local, and international law enforcement training programs.

- Provide timely and relevant criminal justice information and identification services concerning individuals, stolen property, criminal organizations and activities, crime statistics, and other law enforcement related data not only to the FBI but to qualified law enforcement, criminal justice, civilian, academic, employment, licensing, and firearms sales organizations.

- Operate the Federal Bureau of Investigation Laboratory not only to serve the FBI but also to provide, without cost, technical and scientific assistance, including expert testimony in federal or local courts, for all duly constituted law enforcement agencies, other organizational units of the Department of Justice, and other federal agencies, and to provide identification assistance in mass disasters and for other humanitarian purposes.

- Review and assess operations and work performance to ensure compliance with laws, rules, and regulations and to ensure efficiency, effectiveness, and economy of operations.

- Effectively and appropriately communicate and disclose information on the FBI mission, accomplishments, operations, and values to Congress, the media, and the public (Organization, Mission, and Function Manual: Federal Bureau of Investigation, n.d., para. 3).

Prior to the FBI, the *National Bureau of Criminal Identification* was established in 1896, which was a national agency charged with establishing a massive database to identify criminals. With the assassination of President William McKinley in 1901, President Theodore Roosevelt feared the United States would be viewed as anarchist and mandated additional authority to monitor them. When the Oregon land fraud scandal happened, President Roosevelt reiterated his demands to form an investigative service which would have its own special agents. At the president's request, Attorney General Charles Bonaparte organized the Bureau of Investigation.

On July 26, 1908, the Bureau of Investigation was created using Department of Justice expeditionary funds. According to Tim Weiner, author of *Enemies: A History of the FBI,* Attorney General Charles Bonaparte used the Department of Justice expense fund to hire 34 personnel to work for BOI (2012, p. 11). Stanley Finch was hired as BOI's first director. The new investigative agency's first task was enforcing the *Mann Act*, to mitigate prostitution within the United States. By 1932, the agency was renamed to the United States Bureau of Investigation and the following year, the Division of Investigation. By 1935, the investigation was recognized as a separate entity of the Department of Justice and was named the Federal Bureau of Investigation.

The FBI's most prestigious director was J. Edgar Hoover, who served a total of 45 years with BOI, DOI, and FBI. Over the years, his roles expanded with increased authority, as he was responsible for establishing the Scientific Crime Detection Laboratory (known as the FBI Laboratory). During his tenure, agents began investigating homicide and mitigating the violence of white supremacy and Neo-Nazi groups. Hoover was involved in high-profile and major investigations during his career, and with his longevity with the bureau, it was known that he made some controversial decisions. After his tenure and death, Congress passed legislation that FBI Directors would serve no more than ten years.

By the 1930s, the FBI was involved in wiretapping in attempts to capture bootleggers. Due to the conflict of wiretapping as a violation of the Fourth Amendment, Congress passed the *Communications Act of 1934,* which banned the FBI from wiretapping without approval, but bugging was considered legal. However, after *Nardone vs. United States*, Congress decided the evidence the FBI received through phone tapping was considered unacceptable. By 1967, Congress passed another act, *Omnibus Crime Control Act,* giving law enforcement the authority to receive warrants first and then tap phones during open investigations.

By the 1940s, national security became a crucial addition to the FBI's mission. Counter-espionage operations became a clandestine mission for the agency when it was evident that foreign spies were infiltrating and gathering information against the

United States and its coalition forces. In the next two decades, the FBI would be heavily involved in investigating civil rights violations and organized crime, conducting counter-intelligence operations to disrupt rebellious and extremist groups within the United States. Hoover would have increasing tensions with civil rights leader and activist Martin Luther King, Jr., who would accuse the director of giving special treatment to white supremacy groups. Hoover publicly denied these claims.

In the 1980s, the FBI established special teams such as hostage rescue teams (HRT), Special Weapons and Tactics (SWAT), and the Computer Analysis and Response Team (CART) to respond to terrorist acts and violent crimes. Toward the end of the Cold War, over 300 special agents were reassigned because the threat of terrorism was mitigated, and they began more domestic missions, such as aiding with developing DNA testing and fingerprinting procedures. By the mid-1990s, the counterterrorism effort was increased again due to the substantial terrorist threats and attacks against the United States by domestic and international terrorists (i.e. 1993 World Trade Center bombing, the Oklahoma City bombing, and the Unabomber).

Not until the twenty-first century did the FBI significantly increase its counterterrorism tactics after the September 11 attacks. Robert Mueller was sworn in as the director of the FBI just weeks before the attacks and mandated a reorganization of all FBI critical infrastructure and operations. Director Mueller's leadership was pivotal as he made all federal crimes a top priority (FBI, 2015). Though Director Mueller's efforts were positive, the 9/11 Commission Report identified the CIA and FBI as responsible for the lack of intelligence reports and information sharing that could have potentially mitigated the attacks.

Intelligence Community

- Air Force Intelligence
- Army Intelligence
- Central Intelligence Agency
- Coast Guard Intelligence
- Defense Intelligence Agency
- Department of Energy
- Department of Homeland Security
- Department of State
- Department of Treasury
- Drug Enforcement Administration
- Federal Bureau of Investigation
- Marine Corps Intelligence
- National Geospatial Intelligence Agency
- National Reconnaissance Office
- National Security Agency
- Navy Intelligence (Members of the IC, n.d.).

Modernizing Defense Policy

Defense policy is a facet of initiatives predicated on international security and military strategies. Such policies are implemented to ensure national development and restore nation states that suffered from adversarial actions and aggression. The president of the United States, Chairman of the Joint Chiefs of Staff, and the Secretary of Defense are the policymakers for national military policy. Defense policies identify current and future threats against nation states, and a significant amount of intelligence analysis is the primary source for the decision-making process. Intelligence analysis delineates the military scope of alliances and security partners, combat readiness, military departments, national security, and technological advancement. Developing defense policies are technical and complex because many components are involved in both short- and long-term objectives. Defense policy methodologies include identifying priorities such as budget, research and development, personnel, technology, and complete national development. Military policy processes are administrative, managerial, and political responsibilities to complete and execute military operatives and objectives. The United States have three national policies: *national defense strategy*, *national military strategy*, and *national security strategy*. Each policy not only outlines objectives based on national security concerns, but each one is revised to meet the current threat. There are also other factors such as capability management, diplomacy, economy, private sector companies, and small arms proliferation.

National Defense Strategy

The National Defense Strategy (NDS) is a militarized plan established to construct business practices, critical infrastructure, force structure, funding, manpower, and modernization. The NDS is pivotal to identifying military capabilities that are mandated in the National Security Strategy (NSS). The strategy is part of the *Planning, Programming, Budget, and Execution (PPBE)* process, a long-term strategic policy that coincides with NMS and NSS. Additionally, the NDS is a strategic platform for specific objectives outlined in the *Quadrennial Defense Review (QDR)* such as deployment campaigns, contingency preparations, force development, and intelligence analysis.

The defense strategy is critical to the United States objectives on deterring the threat, supporting allies, and security partners, and ensuring adversaries do not use weapons of mass destruction. The NDS's main national interests and objectives are derived from the NSS:

1. Counterterrorism and irregular warfare
2. Deter and defeat aggression
3. Project power despite anti-access/area denial challenges
4. Counter weapons of mass destruction
5. Operate effectively in cyberspace and space
6. Maintain a safe, secure, and effective nuclear deterrent
7. Defense the homeland and provide support to civil authorities

8. Provide a stabilizing presence
9. Conduct stability and counterinsurgency operations
10. Conduct humanitarian, disaster relief, and other operations

The NDS is an important document that is conglomerated with various strategic initiatives to make a logical assessment of the "current and future strategic environment" (p. 23). Identifying concerns, listing them in terms of priority, and understanding the risks are crucial to successfully accomplishing America's goals. Also, understanding such initiatives cannot be completed alone; it is important that America strengthens its relations with alliances and security partners. Former Secretary of Defense Robert M. Gates stated in the NDS:

> Tackling our common challenges requires a clear assessment of the strategic environment and the tools available to construct a durable, flexible, and dynamic strategy. This National Defense Strategy outlines how we will contribute to achieving the National Security Strategy objectives and secure a safer, more prosperous world for the benefit of all. This strategy builds on lessons learned and insights from previous operations and strategic reviews, including 2006 Quadrennial Defense Review. It represents the distillation of valuable experience across the spectrum of conflict and within the strategic environment. It emphasizes the critical role our partners play—both within the U.S. Government and internationally—in achieving our common goals ... the complex issues the United States faces still remain. This strategy is a blueprint to succeed in the years to come (p. 5).

National Military Strategy

The *National Military Strategy (NMS)* is a plan established by the Chairman of the Joint Chief of Staff (CJCS) for the Secretary of Defense that gives an in-depth overview of strategic policies for the United States Armed Forces. Like the NDS, the NMS primary structure is derived from the National Security Strategy.

The CJCS coordinates with the Joint Chiefs of Staff (JCS), the Joint Staff, the Office of the Secretary of Defense, and Unified Combatant Commanders (UCC) to establish the NMS under the Title 10 United States Code Section 153, Chairman Functions. Under *Title 10 U.S.C 153*, such requirements required that the Chairman submit a modified national military policy every two years to the *Senate Committee on Armed Services* and the *House Committee on Armed Forces*. The plan must align with the current standards of the NSS and QDR and must be submitted to Congress from the Chairman and the Secretary of Defense. Unlike the NDS, the NMS must report in-depth information about challenges, national interests, national security, and strategic environment within the United States. Like the NSS, the NMS is mandated to report significant threats, such as terrorism, to the United States, its allies, security partners, and resources. According to the NMS, military capabilities are employed in the evolution of national power such as diplomacy, economic status, funding, information, intelligence analysis, legal, and force structure.

The NMS should report risk assessments and the difficulty of executing mission operatives. Such risks should be thoroughly explained, including how it affects force readiness and combative operations. The chairman must outline such information to the Secretary of Defense, who reviews the NMS and determines solutions to risk assessments before submitting it to Congress for review. General Joseph Dunford, Chairman of the Joint Chiefs of Staff, discussed the dangers and unpredictability of global and adversarial threats:

> Today's global security environment is the most unpredictable I have seen in forty years of service. Since the last National Military Strategy was published in 2011, global disorder has significantly increased while some of our comparative military advantage has begun to erode. We now face multiple simultaneous security challenges from traditional state actors and transregional networks of sub-state groups—all taking advantage of rapid technological change. Future conflicts will come more rapidly, last longer, and take place on a much more technically challenging battlefield. They have increasing implications to the U.S. homeland. The National Military Strategy describes how we will employ our military forces to protect and advance our national interests. We can rapidly adapt to new threats while maintaining comparative over traditional ones. Success will increasingly depend on how well our military instrument can support the other instruments of power and enable our networks of allies and partners. The 2015 NMS continues to call for great agility, innovation, and integration. It reinforces the need for the U.S. military to remain globally engaged to shape the security environment and to preserve our network of alliances (p.3).

National Security Strategy and Strengthening National Security Initiatives

The *National Security Strategy (NSS)* is a policy that is prepared by the executive branch and signed by the president that summarizes top national security concerns and how the government will address those matters. The NSS is predicated on the *Goldwater-Nichols Act* (named after *Senator Barry Goldwater* and Representative *William Flynt Nichols*) and other strategic doctrines such as the National Defense Strategy and National Military Strategy.

The NSS is established by the executive branch and approved by the president of the United States and submitted to Congress, outlining American interests and concerns while formulating solutions to handle them. As mentioned, the NDS and NMS use the NSS as a basis for policies and initiatives. The Goldwater-Nichols Act was instrumental in establishing guidelines for the report because such legislation was needed to mitigate

Selection from General Joseph Dunford, "Chairman's Foreword," *The National Military Strategy of the United States of America*, p. i. 2015.
Selection from President Barack Obama, National Security Strategy, pp. 7-28. 2015.

political discourse and address current and future national security concerns. The Act informed congressional and executive parties on the importance of understanding the strategic environment and how policymakers should outline initiatives to protect the homeland, domestically and abroad. President Obama made this statement on the National Security Strategy:

> The challenges we face require strategic patience and persistence. They require us to take our responsibilities seriously and make the smart investments in the foundations of our national power. Therefore, I will continue to pursue a comprehensive agenda that draws on all elements of our national strength that is attuned to the strategic risks and opportunities we face and that is guided by the principles and priorities set out in this strategy. Moreover, I will continue to insist on budgets that safeguard our strength and work with the Congress to end sequestration, which undercuts our national security. This is an ambitious agenda, and not everything will be completed during my presidency, but I believe this is an achievable agenda, especially if we proceed with confidence and if we restore the bipartisan center that has been a pillar of strength for American foreign policy in decades past. As Americans, we will always have our differences, but what unites us is the national consensus that American global leadership remains indispensable. We embrace our exceptional role and responsibilities at a time when our unique contributions and capabilities are needed most, and when the choices we make today can mean greater security and prosperity for our nation for decades to come (Obama, 2015, p. 1).

The executive department has established initiatives of promoting diversity and inclusion in the national security workforce. On October 5, 2016, President Barack Obama signed a memorandum expressing the need for diversity and inclusion in the national security field. He stated:

> Our greatest asset in protecting the homeland and advancing our interests abroad is the talent and diversity of our national security workforce. Under my administration, we have made important progress toward harnessing the extraordinary range of backgrounds, cultures, perspectives, skills, and experiences of the United States population toward keeping our country safe and strong. As the United States becomes more diverse and the challenges we face more complex, we must continue to invest in policies and recruit, train, and develop the best and brightest from all segments of our population. Research has shown that diverse groups are more effective at problem solving than homogenous groups, and policies that promote diversity and inclusion will enhance our ability to draw from the broadest possible pool of talent, solve our toughest challenges, maximize employee engagement and innovation, and lead by example by setting a

Selection from President Barack Obama, Presidential Memorandum—Promoting Diversity and Inclusion in the National Security Workforce. 2016.

high standard for providing access to opportunity to all segments of our society (Obama, 2015, p. 1).

SUMMARY

Great Britain's rule over the American colonies, monopolization of trade, and enforced taxation laws caused one of the greatest revolutions in history. The Seven Years' War, along with multiple battles, caused American patriots to rebel and establish an independence that continues to this day. The Continental Congress (present-day United States Senate) was established, representing the thirteen original colonies to set precedents and became a governing body during the American Revolutionary War. From 1774 to 1789, the Congress met in three capacities to institute federal laws to regulate, construct, and form the new America. The Founding Fathers signed the Declaration of Independence on July 4, 1776 after defeating the British and forming newfound independence.

North America's independence was a great victory for the nation but also brought conflicts for decades. The Cold War, Bay of Pigs Invasion, and the Cuban Missile Crisis are a few global conflicts in which the United States faced potentially global retaliation from "luke-warm" adversaries. Lessons learned from such conflicts showed the need for the United States to protect its homeland, domestically and abroad. Ad hoc agencies such as the Secret Committee of Correspondence and the Coordination of Information were deemed successful, but the need for a permanent platform was apparent post-Cold War. When President Truman signed the Truman Doctrine and implemented the National Security of 1947, the United States became a cornerstone for strength, dominance, and strategy.

CHAPTER 3 CASE STUDIES

Case Study 1
The Office for Strategic Services

During World War II, President Roosevelt created the Office of Strategic Services (OSS) to consolidate U.S. foreign intelligence gathering into a single organization and to coordinate collection effort. Prior to 1942, U.S. intelligence collection was widely disorganized and uncoordinated. There was no civilian intelligence agency responsible for the collection of secret information for policy makers. Each agency was more concerned with protecting their "turf" rather than sharing the information. However, the attack on Pearl Harbor changed that. The obvious lack of effective American intelligence network forced the president to improve U.S. intelligence capabilities. Under the Joint Chiefs of Staff, the OSS was established. The organization became responsible for building the collection structure and for improving its ability to perform economic, political, and strategic intelligence analysis for senior policy makers. It was also responsible for running special operations outside the other branches of the U.S. military. The OSS soon grew into a major agency, operating in many of the theaters of war.

President Roosevelt appointed William "Wild Bill" Donovan, a former Wall Street lawyer, World War I Medal of Honor winner, and former Coordinator of Intelligence, as the director of the newly established OSS. Donavan wanted to expand the role of the OSS to meet the new war conditions of World War II (William J. Donovan, 2017). Pursuant to the executive order, the head of the OSS could not be a civilian and would not report directly to the president but rather the Joint Chiefs of Staff. Under the JCS, the OSS was used for espionage, counterespionage, sabotage, and covert action. They worked behind enemy lines working to undermine enemy morale and resources. The OSS was split into eleven branches, most notably the X-2 Counterespionage Division, Special Operations Division, and the Morale Operations Division. The X-2 Division maintained operational security measures for the OSS and prevented infiltration of enemy intelligence services as well as providing guidance on selecting counterintelligence targets, distributing counterintelligence information and protecting sources. The Special Operations Division of the OSS was responsible for sending agents, saboteurs, and guerilla forces behind enemy lines, while the Morale Operations Division was charged with propaganda functions (Office of Strategic Services, n.d., *Dictionary of American History*).

Donovan also established two training school for his agents. The first camp, Camp X, was located thirty miles outside of Toronto, Canada while the second school was set up in Maryland in an area now known as Camp David. The purpose of these schools was to train agents to become operatives who would later be dropped behind enemy lines. With the underlying philosophy that "smart people could get things done, regardless of class, gender, ethnicity, or formal schooling," the OSS recruited a wide variety of men and women from a range of ranks, backgrounds, education, and skill sets (OSS primer—operational groups, n.d.). Despite that, it became a standing joke that OSS stood for "Oh So Social," referring to the fact that the OSS Director tended to recruit men and women from the wealthiest class of Americans as his operatives. This included David Bruce and Paul Mellon, millionaires and heirs. He also recruited renowned cook Julia Child, who helped to develop a shark repellent. Former Brooklyn Dodgers and Chicago White Sox catcher Moe Berg was also recruited to lead missions in Italy and Switzerland to interview Werner Heisenberg, the head of Nazi nuclear research and jet technology (Stanchak, 2007).

With America's historic ties to Great Britain and Director Donovan's ties to the British Secret Intelligence Service, it was no surprise that the OSS worked closely with the British Special Operations Executive (SOE) in supporting resistance and anti-German factions, known as Jedburghs, in Europe. The Jedburgh operated in teams that ranged in size from small groups up to 200 or more guerilla members operating throughout Europe, working with resistance units in those countries, and providing tactical intelligence to advancing Allied troops to include detailed maps, engineering information, troop strengths, biographies of enemy commanders, and geographical nuances (Jedburgs, n.d.).

The OSS also supported anti-German factions and armed partisans in Yugoslavia, France, Holland, Italy, and Germany. Occupied sections of Europe, specifically Germany, proved to be a little more difficult for operations. Recruiting sources and help proved to be a challenge since the Geneva Convention prohibited the recruitment of Prisoners of War. Furthermore, Americans soldiers fluent in German could not pass themselves off as German civilians since all healthy young German men were in the German military (Jedburgs, n.d.).

In addition to conducting covert operations in enemy territory, agents established an OSS branch in Switzerland. Under the supervision of Allen Dulles, a lawyer and OSS operative, the Swiss branch of the OSS collected information from a wide array of sources, tapping into Switzerland's American community, including executives from National City Bank and Standard Oil. These sources provided details on the German atomic bomb project and key details about German rockets and facilities. Working with the Swiss bank, the OSS discovered the German's plans of transferring gold units to revive the Nazi movement if they were defeated in Germany. The OSS kept detailed notes on the transactions that passed through the Swiss bank to foreign nations, ensuring the money would not be utilized for its intended purpose (Office of Strategic Services, n.d.).

The OSS also played a role in the Pacific theater, although its role was significantly smaller. This was largely because both the Navy and the Army refused to cooperate with the OSS. They had their own sources of intelligence in this area, relying on Army G2 and Office of Naval Intelligence for information. Furthermore, the ethnicity of OSS agents made it harder for them to blend with the native populace. As a result, their role was usually confined to training guerilla armies. OSS agents and cooperating British intelligence men set up native spy circuits of Asian guerilla fighters and taught them code, espionage, and radio skills (Office of Strategic Services, n.d.).

Despite its success in the field, the OSS was not without its faults. Complaints of frivolousness, mismanagement and lack of accountability rumbled through military and political leaders alike. Fearful that it was in danger of becoming the next Gestapo, the OSS was disbanded shortly after the Japanese surrender in 1945. While it was the official end of the OSS, its legacy carried on (Stanchak, 2007). The OSS provided a generation of leaders who would influence U.S. intelligence operations over the next forty years, as well as providing lessons learned on strategy, tactics, and operational security. Furthermore, the necessity of having a centralized office for intelligence was recognized. This would later come to fruition as the Central Intelligence Agency.

Case Study 2
The Spies of the American Revolution

The American War of Independence gave birth to a country that would later become one of the strongest global powers in the world, yet the outcome might have unfolded differently had it not been for the intelligence networks and the daring patriots who risked their lives to collect critical information. At the start of the Revolution, the Americans were a fledgling force, a rag-tag group of farmers, soldiers, and merchants who rebelled against the British Empire. Barely even a formal military, they did not have a reliable intelligence network until George Washington stepped in. The Commander of the American Continental Army quickly recognized the need for an organized approach to espionage and worked to develop group of trusted patriots to gather intelligence on the British (Spying and espionage, 2017). The most successful and best-known operations of the period was the Culper Ring.

Charged by Washington to establish a spy network to operate behind enemy lines, Major Benjamin Tallmadge, head of the Continental Army's Secret Service, established what become known as the Culper Spy Ring. Mindful of the consequences of being caught, Tallmadge was extremely cautious. He recruited only those whom he could absolutely trust, a small group of six civilians from his hometown in Long Island (The Culper spy ring, 2010). The identities of these individuals were known only to him — he wouldn't even tell Washington.

To avoid being caught, the core ring of six performed an elaborate dance to pass the information from New York City to Washington in upstate New York. Robert Townsend, code name Samuel Culper Junior, was a society reporter for a New York City loyalist newspaper and dry goods shop owner. The newspaper gave him access to social functions all over town, where he could talk to British soldiers without raising suspicion. The dry goods store gave him access to people in and outside the city (The Culper gang, n.d.). Austin Roe, code number 724, a tavern keeper in Long Island, acted as a courier for the Culper Ring. With the excuse of buying supplies for his business, he would travel to Manhattan and visit Townsend's shop, leaving a set of inquiries from John Bolton, Tallmadge's code name. Townsend would write a report that answered the questions, which would then be smuggled out hidden in the goods Roe took home.

Once Roe returned home, he would place the letter in a pre-arranged dead drop in a pasture where he tended his cattle for the next agent to pick up (The Culper gang, n.d.). Aaron Woodhull, code name Culper Senior, was a childhood friend of Tallmadge and initially ran the group's day-to-day operations on Long Island. He traveled back and forth to New York collecting information and observing naval operations in the area (The Culper spy ring, 2010). Since his house was conveniently next to Roe's pasture, he would pick up the letter after Roe had left, and add his own information and details to the message. Anna Strong, his neighbor across the bay, used her laundry on her clothesline to signal that the courier, Caleb Brewster, code number 725, was available to carry the message between Long Island and Connecticut. She would hang out a black petticoat to signal that Brewster's boat was in. The number of handkerchiefs on the clothesline would tell Woodhull by which bay or dock Brewster could be found or which cove he was in along the shore. Under cover of darkness, Woodhull would sneak to the cove and give the courier the encoded message (The Culper gang, n.d.). Brewster would row back across the bay and give Major Tallmadge the letter, and he would then pass the message to Washington.

This arrangement worked well most of the time, but there were still dangers of letters being intercepted. After a surprise raid in Connecticut, Tallmadge added several security measures to the letter. Noting that invisible inks designed to respond to fire or acids were used, Washington sought the help of James Jay to develop an ink that would reveal itself through a chemical reaction. In addition to the use of invisible ink, they used codes and ciphers to conceal messages. Due to the frequency of message interceptions, codes and ciphers were constantly reinvented. However, communicating the changes wasn't easy. To change a code, the author would have to set a network into motion to send a letter describing the new code. As an added security measure, the codes were only given to Woodhull, Townsend, Tallmadge, and Washington as they were the only ones who needed to decode the information (Spying and espionage, 2017).

While Tallmadge, Townsend, Brewster, Strong, Woodhull, and Roe were the main members of the Culper Ring, other subagents helped the group gather information. This included Hercules Mulligan, who was an active member of the Sons of Liberty, and his accomplice, Cato. Mulligan owned a clothing business near Townsend's dry goods shop and could get access to British officers who would talk to him about military matters. Cato would then take messages from Mulligan to Alexander Hamilton who was Washington's aide at the time. Although Mulligan was arrested once on suspicion of espionage, there was no substantiating evidence, and he was subsequently released. He continued to spy on the British, working with Townsend when he was unable to communicate with Hamilton directly. The information collected by Mulligan and Cato helped prevent several attempts on American leaders by the British.

The Culper Ring also had a hand in uncovering the American traitor Benedict Arnold and the involvement of Major John Andre, a British spy under General Henry Clinton, commander of the British forces in New York. Andre was in correspondence with Benedict Arnold, an American general who was disgruntled that he had been passed over for promotion and accused of profiteering. Arnold worked as a double agent, playing his role as an American military office, while secretly passing information to the British. Using secret codes, the two communicated though letters, and Joseph Stanbury, a loyalist, relayed plans back to the British Army. Together, they conspired to give the British control over the West Point Army Fort. Andre was captured in 1779 and hung as a spy the following year. Arnold openly defected to the British and was appointed as a general in the British Army. He led a few attacks on behalf of the British but never accomplished much militarily. He eventually went back to Britain where he died in 1801 (Arnold, 2009).

During its tenure, the Culper Ring collected information on key British troop movements, fortifications, and operations in New York and surrounding areas. Their biggest success was in discovering the British's plan to ambush the French in Rhode Island. Shortly after the Culper Ring had been suspended, a large French naval force, under the command of Count de Rochambeau had arrived in Newport, Rhode Island (Tyler, 2014). At the same time, British reinforcements began to arrive in New York, which posed a threat to the Americans. The Culper Ring was quickly reactivated to help decipher the intent of the British. The information collected revealed that the British intended to attack the French naval force before the French could fully recover and set up defenses after their sea journey to America. Washington used that piece of intelligence to create a diversion to prevent the British navy from sailing to Newport. Fortunately, the plan worked, and the British ships were called back to New York, which allowed the French to disembark without opposition and secure an alliance that would pave the way towards American independence (Tyler, 2014).

Without the use of spies and the Culper Ring, the outcome of the Revolutionary War might have been completely different. The war for independence was not just a physical battle, but it was one of intelligence. Although the Americans were faced with a formidable adversary with better equipment, training, and military, the Americans could out-spy the British which was enough to win the war.

CHAPTER 3 PRACTICE PROBLEMS

1. What is the relationship between national security and foreign policy?
2. What is the president's role when it comes to matters of national security?

3. Why does the U.S. have a separate national defense strategy, national military strategy, and national security strategy?

4. How did Great Britain's national security concerns during the French and Indian War lead to the American Revolution?

5. How did the Continental Congress address U.S. national security focus and concern during its nascence?

6. What were some of the lessons learned regarding intelligence collection during the American Revolution?

7. What was the significance of the Goldwater-Nichols Act and the National Security Act of 1947?

8. Why was President Roosevelt's plan to establish state-run mobilization to protect the U.S. by using a draft unpopular?

9. What role did the OSS have within U.S. national security?

10. The Executive Department has established initiatives of promoting diversity and inclusion in the national security workforce to strengthen national security initiatives. What are other initiatives you would recommend for strengthening national security?

CHAPTER 4

National Security Methodologies and Policies

KEY TERMS

KEY TERMS

Aggression

American Diaspora

Combatants

Expatriates

Foreign diplomacy

Foreign policy analysis

Force structure

Just war theory

Noncombatants

Noncombatant immunity

Non-state actors

Power projection

Policymakers

Public policy

LEARNING OBJECTIVES

After reading this chapter, students will be able to:

- Understand the American government system and unique process to develop national security methodologies
- Analyze American public policy development and decision-making processes
- Examine how the Geneva Convention affects combatant and noncombatant legalities during global and domestic armed conflict
- Summarize citizen rights and responsibilities of the American public

INTRODUCTION

A ccountability, command and control, or organization cannot exist without policy development and decision making within the federal government. This chapter discusses the American government system and how it has a unique and progressive approach to improve homeland and national security methodologies. Also, this chapters show distinction between being the most dominant country in the world or falling from its reign and succumbing to vulnerabilities and threats. The key to maintaining a strong and unwavering government is formulating appropriate policies that are relevant to the principles the government epitomizes, knowing its global and military position, recognizing threats (domestic and international), strengthening international relations, and understanding globalization to promote security and peace. Establishing legislative laws that idealize democratic governance is the first step to protecting America's borders, its citizens, and its resources. Secondly, identifying the respective agencies that are responsible for policymaking and decision making is crucial to American interests, values, and top national security concerns. This chapter also explains the roles of military and noncombatants and their responsibilities during conflict. American governmental policy and foreign relations dictate the specific directives that explain how the U.S. Armed Forces will operate during wartime missions. Finally, the American public is the heart of the United States of America. With the many different cultures, ethnicities, and backgrounds that make the United States "the melting pot" of the world, understanding freedom is the most important value of the country. American citizens depend on the federal government to make the right decisions in the best interest to ensure that the nation is protected for many generations to come.

POLICY DEVELOPMENT AND DECISION MAKING

The objective of national security policy is to analyze historical initiatives and current methodologies to define the decision-making process. It is also important to understand contemporary and emerging threats the United States faces to deter and defeat domestic and global **aggression** (hostile and/or violent behavior). Furthermore, national security policies play an important role in handling global threats, so it is imperative to work with allies and security partners to affect the plan of maintaining peace, stabilization, and globalization. Policymakers should be senior executive military or civilian officials or politicians, who are experienced in dealing with high-risk political and government issues and can make effective and complex decisions, especially in government. Despite the unpredictability of emerging concerns, policymakers are charged with offering reasonable solutions with acceptable levels of risk and making decisions that protect the American public, its borders, resources, allies, and security partners. Policy and decision making are predicated on six factors:

- The governing body and responsibilities
- National security concepts

- American values and interests
- Policy framework
- Defense budget
- Foreign diplomacy/relations
- Implementation

Scholars and former government officials Whittaker, Brown, Smith, and McKune suggest that the national security process is dependent upon various guidelines and how each are "developed, coordinated, articulated, and implemented is important" to protecting the homeland (2011, p. 5). Experts say the process begins internally with federal organizations responsible for national security and usually results in the president finalizing such plans (Whittaker, et.al., 2011). For a well-developed policy process, the president and his administration should follow a clearly defined approached utilizing the National Security Council (NSC) and its cooperating intergovernmental agencies. Processes should be in the best interest of the nation and must not conflict with federal laws and international agreements.

As previously discussed in chapters two and three, the NSC is the primary agency to establish policies on security matters for the United States. One of the president's executive organizations and the primary governing body for national security policy, the NSC also is the foundation for foreign policy and works directly with the Department of State to develop a structured platform for foreign diplomacy. Furthermore, the NSC is a prime advisor to the president and other federal agencies on coordination of all foreign national security and foreign policy matters with the newly established Homeland Security Council (discussed in chapter five).

As discussed in chapter two on the conceptualization of national security, such concepts emphasize that a government should protect the country against threats, aggression, and natural disasters. The concept provides various methodologies including diplomacy, economic power, military **force structure** (ensuring military organizations are prepared through combat-readiness planning by determining how military personnel, resources, weapons, operations, and doctrine are relevant during conflict), and political power. Considerable leverage in developing concepts is centered on intelligence to analyze, collect, evaluate, and interpret capabilities and movements of adversaries. Such information given to the national security organization is used to construct strategies (i.e. National Defense Strategy, National Military Strategy, and National Security Strategy). Additionally, these strategies are deemed powerful instruments for security analysis and how it affects the country's processes for protecting its borders, people, and resources. Furthermore, the unit of analysis (i.e. adversaries, aggressors, non-state actors, etc.) is a vital element in **power projection** (the capability of a country to apply elements of national power, which include economic, political, and military elements, and how such factors can be effectively executed to respond to and deter crises as well as improve regional stability and security). The unit of analysis is another mechanism utilized to maintain national interests and values, which can involve significant costs. Security models are very often used as a basis for implementing national concepts, and complex knowledge fields are needed to produce system paradigms and scientific computations to conceptualize security matters of interest. National security policies are based on historical precedence and events that warrant regulation in security matters. For the United States, national interests and values are primary elements in classifying and determining objectives.

Various national security terms were defined in chapter one to explain how the nomenclature has evolved and how scholars, policymakers, and professionals believe terminology affects public understanding of American national security objectives. Establishing national security policies involves the same concept of evolution and progression. Modern concepts were established during the Cold War era, but Walter Lippmann, Pulitzer Prize winner and political commentator, unambiguously defined national security.

Post-Cold War frameworks established the foundation of national security as behaviorism and systems analysis became primary factors of emerging security concerns. Distinguished professor and author Morton Kaplan (1957) correlated societal behavior to all facets of actions, which compose a singular behavioral system. To connect national security interests to societal behavior is a matter of organizational structure.

The development of American national security systems is based on administrative and political changes the United States faced in the aftermath of World War II. Again, major global conflicts suggested that the United States had deficiencies in terms of handling its adversaries rising technological advancement. Understanding that some countries (including adversaries) possess nuclear weapons was enough to establish a need for specific policies and international initiatives to ensure that nation states will not attempt to use weapons of mass destruction. Furthermore, such concerns initiated force structure, military strategies, and political and economic considerations among the United States, its allies, and its security partners. When President Truman signed the National Security Act of 1947, the policy was to establish organizational structure, integrate policies, and execute governmental functions relating to national security.

Policy development is focused on public policy initiatives at the local, state, and federal government levels. **Public policy** (courses of action, financial processes, regulatory concerns, and system of laws to implement government policies that affect a population) is how a government addresses and implements the needs of citizens through a federal framework. For the United States, public policy is how all governments formulate policies that support citizens based on the U.S. Constitution. The term is very broad because it deals with a series of laws, policies, and regulations, and it is established through a political process.

Policy development is achieved through research, analysis, and consultations to establish suggestions for action that are in the best interest of the servicing agency. The development process also evaluates current and future policies to determine changes in congruence with the evolution of government needs and responsibilities. Defense budgeting is a critical component to developing policy frameworks and enforcing implementation. The *Congressional Budget Office (CBO)* says that approximately seventeen percent of federal spending is set aside for national defense. The CBO is also responsible for assessing high levels of budgetary legislation to produce cost-effective reports for current and future defense programs. The Department of Defense is the largest federal agency within the United States and accounts for nearly all the nation's defense spending. Because the DoD is a large agency, with over two million employees (including the United States Armed Forces, civilians, and contractors), most of the budget funds daily and contingency operations. One of the largest challenges is the unpredictability of the annual budget needed to fund all military and government operations to secure and complete national defense operatives. To sustain funding, the budgeting agency analyzes and anticipates possible reductions, so the DoD can adjust

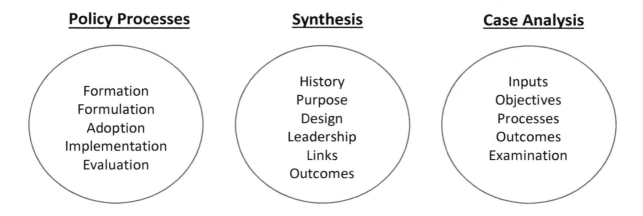

Figure 4.1 Conceptual Framework for State Analysis

acquisition, budgeting, and military force structure strategies. More information about budgeting concerns is discussed in Chapter 13.

Foreign diplomacy (the concept of maintaining positive relationships between foreign governments) is a nation's specific strategies to defend national interests by working with other countries. Having international allies and security partners is indicative of protecting global affairs such as peace, security, trade, and globalization. It is important to know that **non-state actors** (individuals and/or groups that are politically involved but are not considered a coalition force or ally to any country or nation state) are an integral part of the process and play a key role in governance because they have enough authority to influence change but do not have an official single system of government. The federal government and Secretary of State are responsible for foreign policy initiatives and objectives. Additional information on Department of State and foreign policy is discussed in chapter 13.

Finally, implementation is the most important and powerful part of the policy-development and decision-making process. Without implementation, policy frameworks are useless. Policy implementation is predicated on communication from the office of responsibility to the governing body that has the authority to execute such initiatives. For defense policies, national security agencies are responsible for producing policies and implementation, which can be derived by defense secretaries (i.e. Secretary of Defense and Secretary of Homeland Security) or the higher governing body, Congress.

Policies should be clearly addressed so there is not any misinterpretation between the office of responsibility and the governing body. Furthermore, lack of direction for policy implementation can obfuscate processes for agencies that are responsible for review and consultation with governing bodies. Knowing that policy formulation is not only a governmental but a political method and understanding that the process levies a significant level of ambiguity and caution make communication imperative. That is why communication is a primary factor in effective execution, as ambiguity can lead to judiciary involvement and possible denial of potential implemented policies. Besides, political disgraces and incompetence to establish sound national defense policies will slow down the implementation process. Finally, having sufficient resources for policy implementation is important to ensure integrated processes are conducted without interference or conflict. The moral confliction of policy development, policymakers' failure to complete initiatives, and the long-term process of implementation, can make it difficult for policies to come to fruition.

MILITARY VS. NONCOMBATANT AFFAIRS

The perception of history is the primary source for understanding the modernization of military noncombatant roles. Prior to the Revolutionary era, the conception of war strategies depicted those who were not involved in direct combat or a part of any military force structure as the enemy (including women and children). It was not until warfare atrocities increased that militant presence and **noncombatants** (civilians and/ or military personnel who are not considered combatants or are engaged in conflict) were segregated from direct conflict. Understanding innocent lives were sacrificed and were not considered part of warfare movements instituted the development of military organizations. War was considered aggression with nation states and not targeted at citizens. The earliest policy to enact the modern concept was the United States in 1863. Lester Nurick, author of *The Distinction Between Combatant and Noncombatant in the Law of War*, notes that the Department of War issued General Order 100 that pertains to combatants in combatant zones and stated:

> As civilization has advanced during the last centuries, so has steadily advanced, especially in war on land, the distinction between the private individual belonging to a hostile country and the hostile country itself, with its mean in arms ... the principle has been more and more acknowledged that the unarmed citizen is to be spared in person property, and honored as much as the exigencies of war will permit (p. 681).

The issue of **combatants** (individuals, especially military personnel, who are actively engaged in combat during a war) and the civilian population is a complex and controversial matter since fundamental ideologies of international law are a great challenge for nation states. Such challenges require factual evidence and theoretical frameworks to express military necessity, and they have become an ostensible component of military and noncombatant affairs. In some historical events (i.e. the Gulf War), belligerents failed to recognize standards for military and noncombatant roles, thus establishing groundwork to expand combative objectives to include elements of civil populations for engagement. In the past, combatants and noncombatants were interlinked to increased presence and strengthen military forces. It was uncommon to believe in the philosophical and theoretical notions of humanity in the eye of war, and if so, support was scarce during wartime.

According to Joshua E. Keating, author of "What's the Difference Between Combat and Noncombat Troops?" published in *Foreign Policy,* the difference between combatant and noncombatant is more political than military. As previously mentioned, combatants are directly involved in conflict during war, and noncombatants are not. They merely operate in a support role during times of conflict, even though some operations and responsibilities can still have combat capabilities and requirements. Combatant and noncombatant roles can be visualized from two perspectives. For example, Operation Iraqi Freedom and Operation Enduring Freedom were the largest combat operations in response to the 9/11 attacks and in initiating the global war on terrorism. The National Academies Press stated, "Since the beginning of the war in Afghanistan and Iraq, over 1.9 million U.S. military personnel have been deployed in 3 million tours of duty lasting more than thirty days as part of Operation Enduring Freedom and Operation Iraqi Freedom" (Returning from Iraq and Afghanistan, 2010, p. 17). Although all military personnel are deployed to a combat zone, only a certain percentage serve in combat units and are directly in conflict, serving combative locations. The second perspective is combat armed forces that transition to noncombatant roles, most commonly when conflict has ceased and troops are withdrawn from the combat zone. For instance, when President Obama announced American troops would be withdrawn from Iraq by the end of 2011, one of the first steps was ending combat operations, which ceased August 31 of the year. However, 50,000 troops remained in Iraq until 2012 to conduct "training and advise Iraqi Security Forces, conduct partnered and targeted counterterrorism operations, and protect ongoing U.S. civilian and military efforts" (Keating, 2010, para. 2). Understanding the differences between both roles is critical because it is not only a military tactic to mitigate combat responsibilities and bring troops home safely, but also it is a political and security stratagem to ensure regional stability, peace, and transition from conflict to restoration of a society.

Noncombatants and Immunity

Noncombatants are civilians who are not directly involved in hostilities pertaining to war. Individuals, such as medics and chaplains, are members of the armed forces but are protected due to their professional status. Such provisions are found in the *Protocol 1 of the Geneva Convention of 1977*. Combatants are military members involved in armed conflict and are directly in combat or serve in neutral positions as recognized under the *Geneva Convention of 1864*. Noncombatants do not have the same right as combatants, thus making it a thin line on what they can do during contingencies operations of armed conflict. Non-fighters do not have the authority to kill adversaries, or they will be considered criminals. Because of their special professions, they have the right to care if they are victims of war-related attacks and should not be directly targeted, as stated in the fourth Geneva Convention, article three:

In the case of armed conflict not of an international character occurring in the territory of one of the High Contracting Parties, each Party to the conflict shall be bound to apply, as a minimum, the following provisions:

1. Persons taking no active part in the hostilities, including members of armed forces who have laid down their arms and those placed *hors de combat* by sickness, wounds, detention, or any other cause, shall in all circumstances be treated humanely, without any adverse distinction founded on race, color, religion, or faith, sex, birth, or wealth, or any other similar criteria. To this end the following acts are and shall remain prohibited at any time and in any place whatsoever with respect to the above-mentioned persons: (a) violence to life and person, in particular murder of all kinds, mutilation, cruel treatment and torture; (b) taking of hostages; (c) outrages upon personal dignity, in particular humiliating and degrading treatment; (d) the passing of sentences and the carrying out of executions without previous judgment pronounced by a regularly constituted court, affording all the judicial guarantees which are recognized as indispensable by civilized peoples.

2. The wounded and sick shall be collected and cared for (Elder, 1979, pp. 57–58).

Research and theory on the concept of noncombatants and immunity were predicated on the just-war theory.

A just war is a war against aggression or the serious intentional threat of military aggression or a war of intervention to protection fundamental human rights … a just war must also satisfy a proportionality norm: the reasonably expected moral gains of commencing and sustaining military intervention must exceed the reasonably expected moral costs (Arneson, 2006, p. 66).

Just-war theory (the explanation of how and why wars are fought) created the ideology of separateness for justice and wartime operations. Such notions established **noncombatant immunity**, meaning civilians or even service members who were not engaged in armed conflict were immune from combative operations. Individuals who actively engage in war effort are forbidden from directly attacking noncombatants.

The Geneva Conventions

The Geneva Conventions are a series of protocols comprised of fours treaties that are the groundwork for international laws on how individuals should be treated during wartime and armed conflict. The first Geneva Convention was established in 1864 and three more followed in the twentieth century (1906, 1929, and 1949). The final convention updated all treaties in the aftermath of World War II. The Geneva Conventions are comprehensive policies that outline the protection of civilians during direct or indirect conflict, protections for the wounded and ill, combatant and noncombatant procedures, and the rights of wartime prisoners. The final ratification of such policies was approved by nearly 200 countries. Because the Geneva Conventions do not discuss warfare methodologies and the use of weapons, *The Hague Conventions* discuss warfare techniques. Protocol 1 highlights important articles for combatant and noncombatant provisions during armed conflict. Furthermore, it discusses the targeting of civilian objects and prohibitions against directly attacking civilians.

- *Article 3* pertains to the provisions of noncombatants during armed conflict.

- *Article 42* says that pilots and crewmembers are considered combatants until they are parachuting from aircraft due to distress and then cannot be attacked, regardless of territorial grounds. If such combatants land on enemy grounds, they must have the opportunity to surrender, unless they attempt to evade or start hostile acts. There are not any exceptions for airborne forces. They are not protected and may be attacked unless they are incapable of serving in war.

- *Article 50* outlines provisions for civilians who are not privileged combatants, and they do not receive protection. Only privileged civilians are protected under Article 51.

The three protocols of the Geneva Convention cover international conflict, non-international conflicts, and additional distinctive emblems.

Figure 4.2 Naturalization Ceremony at Smithsonian's National Museum of American History on June 14, 2016

The American Public

The United States more than likely has the most patriotic citizens in the world. America is derived of many different national origins, and citizenship is based on allegiance to the nation, not necessarily one's own nationality or ethnicity. Comprised of dual citizens, **expatriates** (individuals who do not live in their native country), and non-citizen residents, the United States makes a unique distinction between citizens and residents who have the right to claim American identity. The term "American" is derived from the original thirteen American colonies, and it was used to distinguish inhabitants of the colonies from British subjects from England.

Native Americans were the original inhabitants of America as well as the people of Guam, Hawaii, Puerto Rico, and the Philippines who became American through the expansions of the United States early in the nineteenth century (American Samoa, the Northern Mariana Islands, and the United States Virgin Islands expanded within the twentieth century.) Because the United States is a multi-ethnic structure, it is considered a Westernized culture, centered on customs and traditions from Northern and Western European colonies. In the early nineteenth century, U.S. cultures consisted of American, Creole, Cajun, and Hispanics from the southern border with Mexico. It was not until the late nineteenth and early twentieth centuries that immigration was prevalent from Asia, Africa, Eastern and Southern Europe, and Latin America. Many Americans (and their ancestors) immigrated to the United States as slaves. Considered the "melting pot" of the world, the United States is an amalgamation of people of many generations who have distinctive cultural characteristics and freely celebrate their heritage. Americans also live all over the world. According to the State Department, the **American Diaspora** (U.S. citizens who live outside of the United States) is about eight million all over the globe.

SUMMARY

Understanding the American government system and having specific processes to develop national security methodologies and polices is key to maintaining a strong government. Policy development and decision making is the first step in establishing governing laws for protecting national security, America's borders, and resources. In addition to current policies, lawmakers are responsible for ensuring such initiatives are relevant to the nation's affairs. The National Security Council sets directives for protecting national security, and the agency works closely with the Department of Defense, the Department of Homeland Security, and its subordinate agencies to ensure that policies coincide with national values, interests, and top national security concerns.

This chapter discussed the differences between military and noncombatants during wartime operations and armed conflict. Specific directives dictate how military and noncombatants are to act and conduct themselves, and the guidelines are outlined in the Geneva Conventions established in the early nineteenth century. The Geneva Conventions are a series of laws regarding how military service members are required to conduct operations in combat-mission operatives. It also discusses the importance of noncombatant roles in which personnel (and citizens) are protected from hostilities.

Finally, the American public includes citizens from many different cultures, ethnicities, and backgrounds. American citizens are what makes the nation. Adopting other traditions and promoting Western culture is why natives and immigrants from all continents choose to settle in the land where speech, freedom, and the right to be who one wants to be is accepted and valued.

CHAPTER 4 CASE STUDIES

Case Study 1
The Timeline of Combatant Deployments during Operation Enduring Freedom

Operation Enduring Freedom (OEF) was one of the world's longest running conflicts since the Vietnam War. Led by American-led coalition forces, OEF was the lexicon given to identify the war in Afghanistan, which was declared during President George W. Bush's administration in response to the September 11 attacks. The conflict was declared on October 7, 2001 when the United States conducted multifaceted operations such as airstrikes and naval warfare operations in conjunction with the United Kingdom. The purpose of OEF was for the United States and its coalition forces to apprehend al-Qaeda leadership, end terrorist operations, and obliterate terrorist training camps and critical infrastructures in Afghanistan. President Bush emphasized such goals in his statement to the American public and the world in his address to the Joint Session of Congress on September 20, 2001. In the address, President Bush also acknowledged Osama bin Laden was responsible for the 9/11 attacks and gave the Taliban an ultimatum or a declaration of war would ensue:

1. Relinquish all al-Qaeda leaders to the United States
2. Release all foreign nationals who were imprisoned
3. Surrender all terrorists and their sympathizers to the American authorities
4. United States will inspect all terrorist training camps
5. Close all terrorist training camps (Williamson, 2009, p. 166).

American and British combatants were deployed to Afghanistan after the Taliban refused to consent to the demands as well as release Osama bin Laden without evidence that the terrorist leader was responsible for the 9/11 attacks. By November 2001, the United States doubled its military strength while Australia, Canada, France, Germany, Italy, the Netherlands, Poland, and the United Kingdom deployed combatants to Afghanistan to support the U.S. efforts. The following month, the United Nations authorized the International Security Assistance Force to provide security support to the Afghans, a British-led effort. While deployed to support the Afghans and annihilate terrorism in the regional area, the coalition forces were supportive of Afghanistan's milestone election of its first egalitarian president, Hamid Karzai, the first sign of democratic governance in Afghan history. The country also held its first parliamentary and provincial elections that had not been conducted in over thirty years.

In 2007, President Bush asked NATO to increase combatant forces when Taliban insurgents executed a suicide bombing targeted at former Vice President Dick Cheney. By early 2009, newly elected President Barack Obama approved 17,000 troops to deploy to Afghanistan, increasing American forces to over 45,000 (Returning from Iraq and Afghanistan, 2010). Toward the end of the year, President Obama sanctioned another deployment surge to Afghanistan, approving 30,000 additional troops, totaling almost 100,000 American troops within the region (Operation Enduring Freedom fast facts, 2016). During the increase of troops, policymakers and coalition forces worked feverishly to ensure the Afghan government could practice democratic governance (despite many scandals and fraud allegations), instill order, and strengthen/train the Afghan National Security Forces.

One of the greatest accomplishments during OEF was the capture and death of Osama bin Laden. On May 2, 2011 American forces, including Navy Seals, raided a compound where intelligence found bin Laden was hiding in Abbottabad, Pakistan. Top military leader and commander Mullah Dadullah was killed, and the Taliban's leader, Mullah Mohibullah, was killed on August 10, 2011. After bin Laden's death, President Obama announced the 30,000 additional troops that were deployed would be going home in 2012 and that all American combat operations in Afghanistan would officially end in 2014 (Operation Enduring Freedom fast facts, 2016). By 2012, former Secretary of Defense Leon Panetta announced combat forces would cease by 2013, and the remaining troops would serve in a "noncombatant role," providing supporting and training until the country was able to operate without coalition presence (Keating, 2010). Coalition forces did the same and began removing combatants from the war zone while noncombatants remained for continuity purposes.

OEF was not only a contingency in Afghanistan, but Georgia, Kyrgyzstan, the Philippines, the Sahara, and Somalia. In 2002, over 1,000 Special Operations personnel were deployed to the Philippines where groups such as al-Qaeda, Abu Sayyaf Group, Jemaah Islamiyah, and the Taliban expanded terrorist operations within the country. Special Operations Command Pacific forces were deployed to mitigate terrorist activity and support the Armed Forces of the Philippines. Toward the end of the year, the Combined Task Force 150 and the United States Special Forces were deployed to Camp Lemonnier in Djibouti to provide humanitarian aid within the Horn of Africa to mitigate terrorist operations within the province.

On June 18, 2013, the Afghan National Security Forces officially took over all combat operations, and on December 28, 2014, the United States and NATO ended all combat operations in Afghanistan. For thirteen years, the United States sacrificed its military service members, fighting a war from a significant distance to battle terrorism. According to Rand Corporation, "never before in modern times had the United States fought a war from land bases and aircraft carriers positioned so far away from a combat zone" (Operation Enduring Freedom, 2005, p. 2). Because OEF was one of the largest conflicts in world history, some inadequacies influenced how military strategies and decision making affected combatant operations. With eight time zones and two headquarters responsible for all executions of the war, such disadvantages affected how the war was conducted, influencing the rules of engagement. Is it possible that global disadvantages and geographical locations impacted the constant surge of American troops? If war operations and executions were geographically sound, could it be possible that the U.S. would not have sacrificed over 4,000 lives in OEF? Can such hypotheses help the country prepare for future potential conflicts? Why or why not?

Case Study 2
The American Diaspora: How Does It Affect the Country?

Chapter 4 discussed the American Diaspora, U.S. citizens who live outside of the United States, but with growing global tensions and tainted relationships with allies and security partners, is it safe for American citizens to live abroad? No solid statistical data indicates how many Americans are living abroad. As mentioned in Chapter 4, "The American Public," approximately eight million American citizens live throughout the world (International Diaspora Engagement Alliance, n.d.; Russo, n.d.). What are the reasons for living abroad? According to Amanda Klekowski von Koppenfels, author of *Americans Abroad: A Disillusioned Diaspora,* "Diaspora engagement has reached a new height as governments around the world increasingly seek to achieve tighter bonds with their citizens abroad, encouraging them to become more engaged with their country of birth" (2015, para. 1). Though this is a positive aspect for citizens, living abroad can cause some challenges and conflicts with current citizenship. For example, living in diaspora can create benefits for other countries such as economic growth, contributing to the development of societies, and the financial benefit from expatriates.

Expatirates face some challenges of "cultural clashing" while integrating into foreign societies and becoming a successful and positive influence on their communities. Nonetheless, Americans choose to live abroad for many reasons. Klekowski von Koppenfels stated Americans leave the United States to seek financial freedom from what is considered extreme government policies such as high taxes and medical insurance expenses. The diaspora is not just American citizens leaving, but the country's businesses as well. Joe Russo, author of *The American Diaspora,* reported American business are moving their businesses to foreign countries for financial benefit and tax relief. He says, "Employee salaries/benefits, production costs, overhead expenses, and taxation are less expensive in other countries, making it very attractive for many U.S. firms to emigrate" (Russo, n.d., para. 1). In the twenty-first century, Americans are moving overseas more than ever for a better and comfortable lifestyle that may not seem affordable in the United States.

With millions of Americans living around the world, should there be a concern for the United States? As of 2017, immigration is a top political and national security matter for the United States, but migration is not a concern for the nation. Lyman Stone, author of "Why Americans Are Going Abroad: When Citizenships Globalizes, Governance Changes," wrote in his article that the United States "doesn't talk about diasporas" (2015, para. 4). Because diaspora is not a term used for American citizens living abroad (instead "expatriates" is the term used), the migration heavily affects national culture. Stone said that the increase of American diaspora will significantly affect "American culture, economic vitality, and political influence" (2015, para. 5). The spread of innovative ideas and technically advancement from American citizens can significantly benefit foreign countries. Should the United States be concerned about the increased migration of its citizens? Should the nation strengthen its diaspora policies or implement progressive frameworks to prevent citizens from leaving? The United States will inevitably feel the effects of the American diaspora as migration increases.

CHAPTER 4 PRACTICE PROBLEMS

1. Why is it important to have a defense budget? What are the dangers of not having one?

2. List several characteristics that a competent policymaker should have. Analyze a current policymaker and compare him or her with your list.

3. In what ways does the foreign policymaking process resemble the domestic policymaking process?

4. What makes a good foreign policy?

5. What are the national interests and values of the United States? Does U.S. policy currently support those interests and values?

6. Why were the Geneva Conventions created?

7. How do the Geneva Conventions differ from The Hague Convention?

8. What role does the theory of "just war" have regarding national security?

9. What does it mean to be an American citizen? Who has a right to claim the "American identity" and why?

10. The United States is considered a "melting pot" of people and cultures. Name several cultural characteristics that the United States has adopted from its immigrants.

CHAPTER 5

Introduction to Homeland Security: A Historical Impression

KEY TERMS

Civil defense

Consequence management

Contingency planning

Crisis management

Emergency management

Emergency responders

First responders

Fusion centers

Homeland security

Situational reports

State of emergency

LEARNING OBJECTIVES

After reading this chapter, students will be able to:

- Understand the inception of homeland security's ideological principles and how it compares to national security concepts
- Analyze homeland security initiatives and policies following the Cold War era
- Examine the evolution of emergency management readiness programs and first responders in the twenty first century
- Summarize the history of civil defense and how it affects homeland security operations and governance

Figure 5.1 Department of Homeland Security Seal

Figure 5.2 DHS ICE Badge

INTRODUCTION: THE BIRTH OF HOMELAND SECURITY

The concept of **homeland security** (the concept of protecting the American land by coordinating emergency management efforts to detect, respond, prepare, investigate, and mitigate terrorist attacks and other large-scale disasters) originated during the Articles of Confederation period when national security was a concept connected to the constant battles of American patriots fighting for rights and independence. Protecting and defending the homeland was a critical component for American patriots before the Revolutionary War, and because adversaries were an international and internal threat, national security was a centralized ideology that provoked wars, conflicts, justice, and American governance. Americans were adamant against the British controlling the nation's land, resources, and people. Initiatives, guidelines, laws, and critical infrastructures were established based on the conceptualization of national security. The more formal incarnation of homeland security was developed in response to the September 11, 2001 attacks. Less than two weeks after the terrorist attacks President George W. Bush established the Department of Homeland Security and appointed former Pennsylvania Governor Tom Ridge as the Director of the Office of Homeland Security. On October 8, 2011, Ridge was charged with coordinating all homeland security efforts, which was addressed in the official announcement (cited from Yale University on October 8, 2001):

> The mission of the office will be to develop and coordinate the implementation of a comprehensive national strategy to secure the United States from terrorist threats or attack. The office will coordinate the executive branch's

efforts to detect, prepared for, prevent, protect against, respond to, and recover from attacks within the United States.

HOMELAND SECURITY ACT OF 2002 AND DEPARTMENT OF HOMELAND SECURITY

President George W. Bush enacted the *Homeland Security Act of 2002* in the aftermath of the September 11 attacks. Nearly 120 Congressional members supported the act, and it was signed into law on November 25, 2002. HSA's execution established the *Department of Homeland Security*, which was considered the largest reform since the Cold War and the largest federal reorganization since the Department of Defense came to fruition under the National Security Act of 1947. The HSA also established the Cabinet level position of *Secretary of Homeland Security*. Under HSA, Tom Ridge's titled changed from Director of the Office of the Homeland Security to Secretary of Homeland Security, making him an executive-level Cabinet office as part of the president's administration.

DHS superseded the Office of Homeland Security and continued to run operations in an advisory function. The agency also adopted major departments such as the *U.S. Coast Guard*, *U.S. Immigration and Customs Enforcement* (includes Homeland Security Investigations), *U.S. Customs Service* (includes Border Patrol), the *Federal Emergency Management Agency*, *U.S. Federal Protective Service*, and the *U.S. Secret Service* to protect the contiguous states and territories. The *Homeland Security Appropriations Act 2004* was a crucial provision to provide funding for DHS and ensure that border and national security functions were a primary responsibility for the new department's mission. HSA is another post-Cold War act, which was enacted to reorganize and centralize federal agencies as well as provide security to meet evolving threats and challenges. On March 1, 2003, DHS assumed responsibility for the *Immigration and Naturalization Service (INS)* and established two agencies, Immigration and Customs Enforcement, and Citizenship and Immigration Services (as previously mentioned). INS also established the *U.S. Border Patrol*, the *U.S. Customs Service*, and the *Animal and Plant Health Inspection Service*. Finally, the *Federal Protective Services* is subordinate to the National Programs and Program Directorate. DHS also created the *Homeland Security Investigations* team to ensure both agencies had proper investigation and intelligence units. The act states that the Department of Homeland Security is charged with the primary responsibility of preventing and deterring terrorists within the United States and its territories. Because terrorism is a federal issue, the Federal Bureau of Investigations is the actual charging authority while DHS supports in an analytical and advisory role with intelligence undertakings.

The Homeland Security Act of 2002 is not only the foundation for the Department of the Homeland Security, but for the following:

- Critical Infrastructure Information Act of 2002
- Cyber Security Enhancement of Act of 2002
- Directorate for Information Analysis and Infrastructure Protection

In addition, with being charged as the primary responsibility of preventing terrorism on America, DHS is accountable for the *Emergency Preparedness and Response Directorate*. The directorate is the foundational policy that ensures DHS protects American citizens, resources, and interests. Finally, the directorate oversees federal government national response and recovery strategies and is responsible for the development of treatment programs for potential biological weapon attacks.

The cabinet department is accountable for public security, and its mission involves providing antiterrorism and cybersecurity programs, border security, immigration and customs, and disaster prevention and management. With 240,000 employees, DHS's mission is to "secure the nation from the many threats we [America] face, and the vision of homeland security is to ensure a homeland that is safe, secure, and resilient against terrorism and other hazards" (DHS, n.d.). It is the third largest federal agency after the Department of Veterans Affairs, and all policies are directly coordinated with the White House through the *Homeland Security Council*. There is much speculation if DHS is a part of DoD because of the similarities of the missions, initiatives, and objectives. DoD is responsible for U.S. Armed Forces movements, particularly abroad, and DHS is based on working with civilians to protect the United States within its borders and territories to prevent and respond to domestic emergencies.

Provisions

The Homeland Security Act of 2002 includes numerous provisions that identify specific responsibilities under the Emergency Preparedness and Response Directorate (EPR). According to the HSA of 2002, the EPR Directorate's summary states:

> The Homeland Security Act of 2002 (P.L. 107–296) requires the Emergency Preparedness and Response Directorate (EPR) of the Department of Homeland Security (DHS) to coordinate federal emergency management activities. The law consolidates federal emergency authorities and resources into EPR—but not terrorism preparedness activities, which are administered by the Border and Transportation Security Directorate within DHS. This report provides summaries of and references to the entities that constitute EPR, as well as brief statements of issues that may come before the 108th Congress (Bea, et al., 2003, para. 1).

EPR has specific priorities that are the responsibility of DHS to understand the evolution of threats and enhance response capabilities to those threats. The following are overview provisions:

- Promote the effectiveness of emergency responders
- Support the Nuclear Incident Response Team through standards, training, exercises, and provision of funds to named federal agencies
- Provide the federal response by managing, directing, overseeing, and coordinating specified federal resources
- Aid recovery

- Build an intergovernmental national incident management system to guide responses
- Consolidate existing federal response plans
- Develop programs for interoperate communications for emergency responders

LEADERSHIP ROLES AND CHAIN OF COMMAND

The Secretary of Homeland Security is the principal leader for the Department of Homeland Security and is charged with protecting American borders, its citizens, and resources. The position is also a Cabinet-level entity based on its role in the Homeland Security Council. President Bush signed the law on March 9, 2006 to amend the President Succession Act of 1947 and incorporate the Secretary of Homeland Security position in the line of succession to presidency after the Secretary of Veterans Affairs. Congress elected to have the Secretary of Homeland Security position in line of succession after the Attorney General, but the law has since then expired and has not been reviewed. Because the department is relatively new, only five secretaries (Figures 5.3–5.7) have been nominated by the President and confirmed by the Senate to run the Department of Homeland Security. [Editor's note: A sixth secretary, Kirstjen Nielsen, was sworn in prior to the publication of this book. Her photo was not available for this edition.]

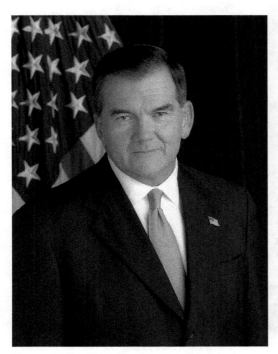

Figure 5.3 Tom Ridge, First Secretary of Homeland Security (January 24, 2003—February 1, 2005)

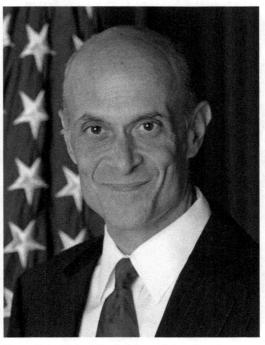

Figure 5.4 Michael Chertoff, Second Secretary of Homeland Security (February 15, 2005—January 21, 2009)

Figure 5.5 Janet Napolitano, Third Secretary of Homeland of Security (January 21, 2009—September 6, 2013)

Figure 5.6 Jeh Johnson, Fourth Secretary of Homeland of Security (December 23, 2013—January 20, 2017)

Figure 5.7 John Kelly, Fifth Secretary of Homeland Security (January 20, 2017—July 31, 2017)

Figure 5.8 Elaine Duke, Sixth (Acting) Secretary of Homeland Security (July 31—December 6, 2017)

DHS AGENCIES AND SUPPORTING ORGANIZATIONS

DHS is now an integrated department that ensures maximum effectiveness between the agencies that were established under the Homeland Security Act of 2002 and federal agencies that joined the largest reorganization since the Department of Defense. The following agencies are under DHS:

- Citizenship and Immigration Services Ombudsman
- Office of Civil Rights and Civil Liberties
- Domestic Nuclear Detection Office
- Federal Law Enforcement Training Center
- Office of Intelligence and Analysis
- Office of the General Counsel
- Office of Health Affairs
- Office of the Inspector General
- Office of Legislative Affairs
- Office of Public Affairs
- Office of Partnership and Engagement
- Office of Operations Coordination
- Office of Policy
- Privacy Office
- Science and Technology Directorate
- Management Directorate
- U.S. Customs and Border Protection
- Federal Emergency Management Agency
- U.S. Immigration and Customs Enforcement
- National Protection and Programs Directorate
- Transportation Security Administration
- U.S. Citizenship and Immigration Services
- U.S. Secret Service
- U.S. Coast Guard

There have been multiple revisions to the guidance established under the Homeland Security Act of 2002 that have had a direct effect on the supporting agencies. On February 15, 2005, Secretary Michael Chertoff enacted the *Second Stage Review (2SR)* to examine DHS's methodologies and processes to ensure all policies were congruent with modern threats and homeland security matters. For example, a 2SR was conducted on July 13, 2005, which resulted in a major reorganization of the department (the *Department Six-point Agenda*), as there was a concern for not having specific facets of knowledge on technological advancement of adversarial strategies and modern threats.

The Department Six-point Agenda was established from the 2005 S2R, which addresses six elements that can best protect the United States from current and future threats:

- Increase overall preparedness
- Create better transportation security systems to move people and cargo more securely and efficiently
- Strengthen border security and interior enforcement and reform immigration processes
- Enhance information sharing with our partners
- Improve DHS financial management, human resource development, procurement and information technology
- Realign the DHS organization to maximize mission performance (Department Six-point Agent, n.d., para. 2).

This agenda established the Office of Policy, Office Intelligence and Analysis, Director of Operations Coordination, and the Directorate for Preparedness. The Office of Policy was a catalyst for the department to have a more formalized process of establishing policies and was keen on enforcing a regulatory system for short and long-term strategic planning. Such coordination includes the offices of Internal Affairs, Private Sector Liaison, Homeland Security Advisory Council, Immigration Statistics, and the Senior Asylum Officer.

The Office of Intelligence and Analysis ensures the intelligence community has the most modern resources to complete pertinent mission operatives, conduct advanced analysis, and work with policymakers to make decisions on the betterment of DHS. Such information is distributed to local, private sector, state, and federal stakeholders. The Chief Intelligence Officer works closes with the Secretary of DHS to ensure the department has the most experienced intelligence analysts work with other intelligence constituents to intensify intelligence operations. The Director of Operations Coordination was formulated to manage joint operations with supporting agencies and synchronize incident management actions. The office is responsible for working with Intelligence and Analysis to interpret intelligence policies and initiatives for instant decision making.

The Directorate of Preparedness works with other emergency management agencies to coordinate readiness procedures. This office is responsible for assisting with grants and administering readiness policies to support national first responders, public awareness, public health, critical infrastructure, and cyber security training. The Chief Medical Officer is charged with ensuring national training is conducted and executing policies regulated by DHS. Also, the Chief Medical Officer works closely with the Under Secretary to establish grants for training and the emergency management exercises.

On October 13, 2006, Congress passed the *Security Accountability for Every Port Act (SAFE Port Act) of 2006* (Public Law 109–347). The SAFE Act was enacted to include port security and online gambling. Port security guidelines were in response to the Dubai Ports World Controversy, which prevented foreign owners from controlling primary U.S. ports and can be found in the *Exon-Florio Amendment*. This act was responsible for establishing numerous programs to strengthen U.S. ports:

- Additional maritime facility requirements
- Establishment of the Transportation Worker Identification Credential
- Customs Trade Partnership Against Terrorism
- Formulation of Interagency Operations Centers for port security
- Port Security Grant Program
- Container Security Initiative
- Foreign port assessments (n.d., para. 2).

The SAFE Act also authorized the *Domestic Nuclear Detection Office (DNDO)* and restructured FEMA, integrating the *Radiological Preparedness Program* and the *Chemical Stockpile Emergency Preparedness Program* into the agency.

Another reorganization provision was the Implementing Recommendation of the 9/11 Commission Act of 2007, Public Law 110–53, which was authorized on August 7, 2007. Congress passed the Implementation act to execute recommendations based on the 9/11 Commission, which includes all inspections on air and sea cargo entering the United States. The act also certified the creation of **fusion centers** (information sharing centers between two or more agencies, primarily military, intelligence, and law enforcement, to detect, prevent, examine, and respond to criminal and terrorist events) and provided an avenue for reallocating federal funding for antiterrorism operations. An abundance of homeland security initiatives is supported by the *9/11 Commission Report* recommendations. The 9/11 Commission Act is predicated on policies and guidelines from the *Post-Katrina Emergency Management Reform Act of 2006* and is responsible for introducing the Assistant Secretary for Intelligence and Analysis and Under Secretary level positions.

The transfer of *Federal Protective Service (FDS)* to *National Protection and Programs Directorate* was an important reorganization as federal law enforcement was not a subsidiary of DHS. On October 29, 2009, Secretary Janet Napolitano announced this reformation that FDS would be transferred from U.S. Immigration and Customs Enforcement (ICE) to the National Protection and Programs Directorate (NPPD). The change was designed to streamline decision-making processes and to include protecting federal buildings as a part of DHS's critical infrastructure-protection responsibilities. Under the announcement, Napolitano emphasized:

> Securing government facilities is a vital aspect of DHS' critical infrastructure protection mission. Transferring FDS to NPPD will enhance oversight and efficiency while maximizing the Department's overall effectiveness in protecting federal buildings across the country (NPPD-Critical Infrastructure Activities, 2015).

Having FDS under NPPD is an advantage to focus efforts on the primary mission, which is safeguarding all federal buildings owned by the General Services Administration and employing all suitable countermeasures. Finally, Janet Napolitano was responsible for creating the *Quadrennial Homeland Security Review (QHSR),* a document that established "a strategic framework for homeland security missions and goals" (Quadrennial Homeland Security Review Report: A Strategic Framework for a Secure Homeland, 2010, p.3). Like the Quadrennial Defense Review, the QHSR outlines

DHS's objectives and is published every four years. Initially, the department managed a *Bottom-Up Review (BUR)* to ensure mission requirements and organizational structures aligned with DHS's policies and initiatives. The review was pivotal in establishing the QHSR to epitomize the utmost comprehensive assessments and department analysis methodologies.

DHS RESPONSE AGENCY: FEMA AND THE RISE OF EMERGENCY MANAGEMENT IN AMERICA

FEMA is the primary emergency management agency within the United States and falls under DHS realm. Before FEMA was transferred to DHS, it was created on April 1, 1979 under the *Presidential Reorganization Plan No. 3 of 1978*. President Jimmy Carter signed this executive order that established the largest emergency management organization within the United States. Originally, the agency was charged with coordinating the response to natural disasters that have occurred within the United States and its territories, but it has expanded local, tribal, state, and federal government roles and responsibilities. FEMA dates to the *Congressional Act of 1803*, which was the first crisis legislation in the United States. President Carter also signed *Executive Order 12127*, which was designed to outline the responsibilities of FEMA.

During the early 1800s, several disasters ensued throughout the country, and there was not a permanent organization for crises. Not until the 1930s did federal governance become a primary key to establishing the *Reconstruction Finance Corporation* to approve loans for disaster events and to provide supplies and reconstruct infrastructures in the aftermath. Under federal procedures, each state governor has the authority to declare a **state of emergency** (when a government suspends normal daily and working operations in the event of a natural disaster or emergency) and must formally request that the president of the United States provide FEMA and federal government assistance (i.e. Hurricane Katrina and Hurricane Sandy). There are specific procedures when natural disasters or attacks occur on federal grounds. FEMA provides local and state governments with funding and provides supplies to rebuild in the aftermath of an emergency. The agency also provides funding for training and exercises to ensure emergency and readiness personnel are prepared at a moment's notice.

It was not until the 1980s that a solidified system was enacted, which involved a presidential election. *The Robert T. Stafford Disaster Relief and Emergency Assistance Act (Public Law 100–707)* was signed on November 23, 1988 to supersede the *Disaster Relief Act of 1974*. The emergency act was established to improve disaster readiness procedures and enhance intergovernmental relationships in the event of crisis or disaster. This act authorizes a presidential declaration to utilize financial assistance and supplies from FEMA and is responsible for coordinating national government relief efforts. In addition, it is aimed at constructing systematic policies for all levels of government to complete responsibilities for crisis and disaster victims. Finally, the assistance act has been the foundational constitution for numerous FEMA legislations (i.e. the Homeland Security Act, Post Katrina Emergency Management Reform Act,

Sandy Recovery Improvement Act of 2013, and FEMA Implementation of the Sandy Recovery Improvement Act).

The Mission

FEMA's mission is to support American citizens and **first responders** to ensure that as a nation we work together to build, sustain, and improve our capability to prepare for, protect against, respond to, recover from, and mitigate all hazards.

Regional Divisions

FEMA has nearly 15,000 employees and has ten regional offices throughout the United States that assist communities based on geographical locations.

- Region 1 spans over Connecticut, Maine, Massachusetts, New Hampshire, Rhode Island, and Vermont.
- Region 2 supports New Jersey, New York, Puerto Rico, and the Virgin Islands.
- Region 3 covers Delaware, the District of Columbia, Maryland, Pennsylvania, Virginia, and West Virginia.
- Region 4 is responsible for Alabama, Florida, Georgia, Kentucky, Mississippi, North Carolina, South Carolina, and Tennessee.
- Region 5 includes Illinois, Indiana, Michigan, Minnesota, Ohio, and Wisconsin.
- Region 6 is accountable for Arkansas, Louisiana, New Mexico, Oklahoma, and Texas.
- Region 7 is comprised of Iowa, Kansas, Missouri, and Nebraska.
- Region 8 involves Colorado, Montana, North Dakota, South Dakota, Utah, and Wyoming.
- Region 9 contains Arizona, California, Hawaii, Nevada, America Samoa, Guam, the Commonwealth of the Northern Mariana Islands, the Republic of the Marshall Islands, and the Federal States of Micronesia.
- Region 10 covers Alaska, Idaho, Oregon, and Washington.

EMERGENCY SERVICES SECTOR

The *Emergency Services Sector (ESS)* is comprised of highly trained personnel that are responsible for prevention, preparedness, response, and recovery services for emergency readiness purposes. **Emergency responders** (firefighters, military, paramedics, law enforcement, transportation and logistics, and other emergency management professionals who respond to emergencies) are located throughout the United States in geographically separated locations and are equipped through local, state, and federal levels of government as paid employees and/or volunteers to work in crisis facilities.

In addition, emergency management personnel work closely with private sector and emergency medical services to complete mission operatives.

The mission of ESS is to "save lives, protect properly and the environment, assist communities impacted by disasters, and aid recovery during emergencies" (2016, para. 1). The sector has five responsibilities to ensure multifaceted functions and procedures:

1. Law enforcement
2. Fire and emergency services
3. Emergency medical services
4. Emergency management
5. Public works

The ESS is derived from the *Emergency Services Sector-Specific Plan*, which outlines how the *National Infrastructure Protection Plan (NIPP)* will be implemented for national risk-management plans.

Emergency Management Continuum

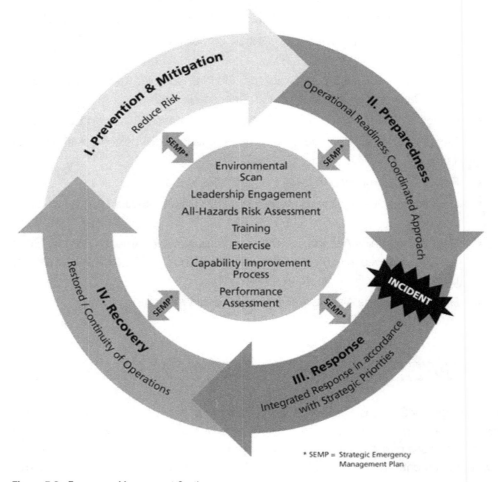

Figure 5.9 Emergency Management Continuum

Figure 5.9, the Emergency Management Continuum under the Canadian Strategic Emergency Plan is a prime example of how the emergency management process works and is like the nation's disaster and emergency management policies. The continuum chart shows the four major steps in emergency management:
1. Prevention & mitigation
2. Preparedness
3. Response
4. Recovery

LOCAL, STATE, AND FEDERAL RESPONSIBILITIES

Local

Most disasters occur at the local level and local governments are responsible for emergency management services. Citizens of the local area are those who suffer in the aftermath, and their local governments are responsible for assistance. Local governments are accountable for funding, response and recovery efforts, and for requesting assistance from state and federal governments. Also, local governments are responsible for providing first responders for emergency response services. They establish policies such as the Emergency Operations Center and *Comprehensive Emergency Management Plans* as guidelines for national emergency readiness procedures. Emergency management professionals are charged with coordinating response objectives with citizens, private-sector companies, and medical service providers. In times of imminent crisis and disasters, the local government (typically the state governor) notifies the *State Emergency Agency* on such situations and actively submit **situational reports** (SITREPs) on emerging threats or aftermath events.

Local government involvement in emergency policies is vital to activating mutual aid compacts and multilateral cooperation agreements. Local governments also work with intergovernmental agencies, state, and federal departments to formulate response agreements. Such initiatives assert emergency plans for governments to authorize and utilize resources, including disbursing funds and bypassing traditional bidding courses for good and services. Finally, local governments (state governors) can request state of emergency management to provide state and/or federal assistance.

State

Local governments can escalate requests to the state level when resources are inadequate. The challenge is that the state many have numerous local governments requesting aid simultaneously, causing delays or possible lack of assistance. State governments are the registered agents when local jurisdictions need federal assistance. State governments are responsible for monitoring local jurisdiction situations. They also review and evaluate local government situational reports, response procedures, and assistance requests. State governments may activate a *State Emergency Operation Center* to determine state assistance availability and to regulate if local emergency matters are beyond the scope of state and federal assistance. State governments also declare state of emergency addresses to initiate *State Disaster Preparedness Plans* and to provide state assistance and resources, and initiate the process for requesting federal assistance. Requesting federal assistance includes an emergency declaration under the *Robert T. Stafford Disaster Relief and Emergency Resistance Act* and a specialized request for federal agencies for their own emergency management programs.

Federal

The federal government is the highest level of authority within the United States, and when crises are so severe that local and state governments together cannot find a means to aid, the request is escalated. FEMA is the federal organization that organizes the execution and implementation of the federal plan so that states can work together to support local and tribal governments. Local governments do not work directly with the federal government. Instead, state governments are the liaison for assistance from the federal level. The federal government is responsible for conducting joint Preliminary Damage Assessments (PDAs) with local and state governments to investigate damage to agricultural facilities, critical infrastructures, and private-sector companies, and to initiate specific activities before and after disasters.

The federal government approves and denies requests, which are specific processes. If federal requests are approved, the government appoints a *Federal Coordinating Officer (FCO)* to lead the *Emergency Response Team (ERT)* and is responsible for establishing the *Disaster Field Office (DCO)* to organize response and recovery efforts. The FCO works closely with the *State Coordinating Officer (SCO)* to address response and recovery procedures and activates *Federal Response Plans (FRP)* to assess federal resources. The federal government also establishes an *Emergency Support Team (EST)* to monitor and observe mission operations and identify *Emergency Support Functions* (ESF) from Washington, DC.

CIVIL DEFENSE: AMERICA'S RESPONSE

Civil defense is the concept of non-combatants protecting citizens from military effects or natural disasters. Civil protection is a vital element of emergency management services, and its principles are based on the prevention, mitigation, preparation, response, emergency evacuation, or recovery during the aftermath. The ideological principle of civil defense dates to the 1920s and formal policies were implemented during the 1930s, as nuclear weapons attacks became an international threat during this time.

The United States federal civil defense program existed under *Public Law 920*. The federal program was reformed in 1993 by Public Law 103–160 and a major reformation was implemented the following year. There are now sections located in *Title VI of the*

Robert T. Stafford Disaster Relief and *Emergency Assistance Act, Public Law 100–107*. Since the inception of the Cold War, civil defense has become a prominent focus due to the modern concepts of **consequence management**, **contingency planning**, **crisis management**, **emergency management**, emergency services, and civil protection. Civil defense became a global matter, but ideological principles, functions, policies, and implementation were different among Western countries. The United States established the *Office of Civil Defense* in May 1941 to organize civil defense efforts. The office was a subsidiary of the Department of the Army and existed until the *Civil Air Patrol (CAP)* was organized on December 1, 1941. CAP's primary mission was search and rescue during wartime contingencies until it was banned from combat duties through Public Law 79–476. Today, CAP's mission is search and rescue for downed aircraft, pilots, and aircrew. When the Department of the Air Force was created, CAP became an auxiliary component. CAP also has a subsidiary, the *Coast Guard Auxiliary*, which has a similar responsibility.

Civil defense was a primary agency during the 1950s and 1960s when a nuclear weapons attack was imminent. The United States and other NATO countries executed exercises during the period, as civil defense practices and missions were needed more than ever. As for the United States, nuclear weapons threats were at their height, and an imminent attack produced a larger response for civil protection. Not until the Cold War era did civil defense become controversial. In 1950, the *National Security Resources Board* created a document called the Blue Book, which was the prototype for civil defense legislation.

For civil defense, some of the most noted efforts included the establishment of shelters. President John F. Kennedy was motivated to construct shelters throughout the United States. Such shelters would deter the radiological efforts of a nuclear war but would not mitigate blast impacts and medical needs. In 1951, the *Control of Electromagnetic Radiation* was formed where primary stations would alert other stations throughout the network. A prominent study predicted that approximately 27 million citizens would be saved through civil defense awareness and education training when the United States Armed Forces performed a military exercise during the Cold War era. Again, controversy arose, as policymakers believed a ballistic missile defense weapons system program would be more beneficial than creating a full-scale civil defense platform. Research believed the cost-benefit analysis conducted at the time proved this theory because of inconsistent civil defense preparations with other NATO countries. Also, theorists believed a ballistic missile program was more cost-effective since a civil defense program was deemed too expensive. The lack of consistent civil defense efforts was because Western countries did not believe the Soviet Union's nuclear wear threats were imminent. However, the USSR had master plans of minimizing nuclear weapons striking on its own territory. Thus, the country considerably strengthened its civil defense tactics and was better prepared and more effective than the United States.

The decline of civil defense preparations was inevitable because most Western countries were conflicted with the concept of *Mutual Assured Destruction (MAD)*. Because of the issues with funding a large program that was based on the unpredictability of adversarial threats and natural disasters, Western countries believed that a full-scale defense program was too expensive. Also, some countries believed that a civil defense program would be largely ineffective program for a powerful nuclear weapon attack. As interest in civil defense programs waned, the program did not seem to be an important asset for emergency management programs. The United States ad-hoc civil defense programs (i.e. CAP) existed until such responsibilities were outlined when FEMA was established in 1979. In 2002, FEMA became a part of the Department of Homeland Security. There is where specific civil defense preparations on nuclear weapons transferred to all hazards outlined in the *Comprehensive Emergency Management*. After the September 11 attacks, the United States ideology of civil defense has been discussed under the realm of homeland security. Natural disasters and the development of modern threats have centralized focus on new forms of civil protection versus traditional civil defense methodologies.

SUMMARY

The birth of homeland security can be considered an ideological principle conceived within the conceptualization of natural security, but it is evident that responsiveness was not emphasized until the aftermath of the September 11 terrorist attacks. On September 11, 2001, hijackers created the most devastating act on U.S. soil in American history. President George W. Bush responded by signing the Homeland Security Act of 2002 and other legislation, creating the Department of Homeland Security, the largest reorganization since the National Security Act of 1947, creating the Department of Defense, and reestablishing military departments. The Act also formalized a new position, the Secretary of the Department of Homeland Security, charged with protecting the United States and its territories. Not only did 9/11 prompt a new federal establishment, the reorganization of existing agencies was a primary factor to ensuring America's borders and territories are protected. FEMA, FPS, Secret Service, U.S. Coast Guard, U.S. Customs and Border Protection, and U.S. Immigration Customs Enforcement are among the 22 agencies now embedded under the Department of Homeland Security to align with the organization's new policies and initiatives.

The evolution of emergency management readiness and first responders was critical, as the 9/11 aftermath showed that military and law enforcement could not provide all assistance during crisis and disasters. First responders and emergency management professionals became the forerunners for responding to emergencies, providing national assistance for victims, rebuilding critical infrastructures, and obtaining resources during times of crisis. FEMA is the federal government's largest emergency management agency, and policymakers have been focused on outlining modern readiness practices to ensure that America is ready to respond at a moment's notice. With a new mission, the emergence of the Department of Homeland Security became the prominent in protecting America's national borders from modern threats and natural disasters of the twenty-first century.

CHAPTER 5 CASE STUDIES

Case Study 1
Katrina vs. Sandy

Hurricane Katrina caused an estimated $108 billion in damage, making it the largest, costliest, and most destructive natural disaster in U.S. history. Several years later, another catastrophic storm, Hurricane Sandy ripped through and caused $65 billion in damage (Currie, C., 2015). While both these hurricanes undeniably left mass devastation in their wake, the severity of these disasters vastly differed, largely due to the Federal Emergency Management Agency's (FEMA) efforts in handling the situation.

President Jimmy Carter created FEMA by executive order in 1979 to lead the nation in preparing for and mitigating domestic disasters. FEMA took on a wide range of responsibilities, including all possible disasters and civil defense plans in the case of war. This encompassed both natural disasters, such as hurricanes and earthquakes, as well as other man-made disasters, such as hazardous substance spills and bombings (Grabianowski. E., 2005). Since its inception, FEMA has put a great deal of effort into disaster preparation such as hurricane-proofing homes and helping to make cities safer in the event of an earthquake, but the onset of Hurricane Katrina and Hurricane Sandy sorely tested those preparations.

When Hurricane Katrina hit, it was the fifth hurricane of the 2005 Atlantic hurricane season. Considered one of the five deadliest hurricanes in U.S. history, it brought severe destruction along the Gulf Coast from central Florida to central Texas, but the effects of the storm were mostly felt in New Orleans, a city with an average elevation six feet below sea level and surrounded completely by water. The U.S. Army Corps of Engineers (USACE) had previously constructed a system of levees and seawalls to help prevent flooding in the city, but over time, the levees became unstable. Officials expected some short-term flooding, but they did not anticipate complete failure of the levee system (Hurricane Katrina, (2009). When the storm surged, it overwhelmed the city's levees and drainage canals, causing the water to seep through the soil underneath the levees and sweep others away. Eventually, eighty percent of the city was under water (Hurricane Katrina, 2009).

While the storm itself did a lot of damage, the aftermath was truly catastrophic. The rescue and recovery efforts following Katrina became highly politicized, with federal, state and local officials pointing fingers at one another. Critics blamed an aging and neglected federal levee system since it was found that the failures of the levees and seawalls were the result of system design and construction flaws (Robertson, 2015). Per the Flood Controls Act of 1965, the USACE was charged with the conception, design, and construction of the region's flood control system. However, incorrect calculations and assumptions led to reduced structural integrity while the straight design and lack of outward flow enabled salt water to enter fresh water areas, damaging the cypress forests and wetlands that had previously protected the city from storms (Freudenburg, Gramling, et al., 2009).

In addition to the USACE and the failed levees, critics blamed slow state and local response following the disaster for the high loss of life and damage (The response to

Hurricane Katrina, 2012). Authorities had received multiple warnings regarding the threat of Katrina, but they ignored the warnings and treated Katrina as if it was a normal storm. The Mayor of New Orleans didn't issue an emergency evacuation order until less than a day before the storm struck. By the time the storm struck, it was too late to evacuate, and many people remained stranded in the city (The response to Hurricane Katrina, 2012).

The dispersed nature of authority in the U.S. bureaucracy further weakened response, as federal responders failed to recognize the need to more actively engage (Hurricane Katrina, 2009). There were basic problems in coordination with the involved organizations and disagreements about what to do and who was going to do it, spurring a free-for-all for responders with little to no coordination with local, state, federal agencies. Part of the failure to establish a unified command center was caused by confusion over new policies in the National Response Plan, which set forth rules for how responders were supposed to coordinate in the event of an emergency (The response to Hurricane Katrina, 2012). Furthermore, while the Louisiana Office of Homeland Security and Emergency Preparedness (LOSHEP) was responsible for setting up an Emergency Operations Center to channel state and federal response, it did not have enough people to man the center. They had to call in the National Guard; however, it took several days for the National Guard to arrive since many of the National Guard from the local area were deployed in Iraq. Furthermore, because National Guardsmen are state assets, active duty and National Guard operations were directed by two separate chains of command, even though the two departments were doing the same things.

This coordination issue also affected non-government organizations, such as the Red Cross, which struggled with FEMA's failure to provide reliable information or follow through on promised logistical needs (The response to Hurricane Katrina, 2012). Firefighters and ambulance crew members weren't allowed to enter the city without first being mobilized by local and state authorities. This intensely hindered the emergency response to the disaster. When they were finally brought in, they were utilized inappropriately. Furthermore, as international donors tried to provide aid, due to bureaucratic entanglements, their aid shipments were hindered or even refused in the case of Venezuela because the U.S. government did not approve of the Venezuelan leader (Shah, 2005).

In addition to preventing foreign aid, bureaucracy heavily crippled FEMA, which had a direct correlation with the Agency's failure during Katrina. Under the Bush administration and because of 9/11, FEMA lost many of its resources to the U.S. counterterrorism mission. People with little emergency experience were put in key leadership positions. They downsized the importance of FEMA, believing that it had become an "oversized entitlement program" (Senate Report, 2006: 14–2). As FEMA declined, senior managers left, taking with them years of experience and relationships with state responders. The agency had a fifteen to twenty percent vacancy rate, causing specific functions to go unmanned. FEMA was forced to rely heavily on temporary employees who lacked the right training, equipment, and experience to be effective (Senate Report, 2006: 14–2). Had these issues been mitigated, the unified command center for the Katrina response network could have stood a chance.

While the response to the Hurricane Katrina disaster is widely considered reactive, comparatively, the initial response to Hurricane Sandy was proactive. Superstorm Sandy was the most destructive hurricane of the 2012 Atlantic hurricane season and the second costliest in U.S. history. It affected the entire eastern seaboard from Maine to Florida and even across to Michigan and Wisconsin. It hit particularly hard in New Jersey and New York, flooding streets, tunnels, and subway lines, cutting power throughout New York City (Overview of response to Hurricane Sandy-Nor'Easter and recommendations for improvement, 2013).

Using lessons learned from Hurricane Katrina, FEMA, in coordination with other federal departments, pre-positioned staff and resources in predicted impact areas before the storm hit. President Obama signed emergency declarations for affected states, which allowed FEMA to transfer resources directly to state and local organizations for preparation arrangements prior to the storm. Furthermore, with the president's guidance of minimizing red tape, government agencies at all levels worked to remove barriers to response and restoration, aiding movement of crews and equipment across the country (Overview of response to Hurricane Sandy-Nor'Easter and recommendations for improvement, 2013). States also anticipated response relief and long-term recovery requirements, leveraging their relationships with private and public sectors to call in aid and relief workers. The Sheltering and Temporary Essential Power Program helped New York City, Nassau, and Suffolk Counties pay contractors to do emergency repairs, turning people's homes into shelter-in-place locations and allowing 10,000 families to return home (Byrne, 2013).

FEMA also benefited from having an agency leader who, coming from a fire- and first-responder background, was highly knowledgeable in the science of disaster and familiar with disaster research (Naylor, 2012). Similarly, relief efforts were better primed to respond since local and state governments as well as first responders understood the complexity of the impending disaster and had implemented an Incident Command Structure, which enabled Operations to manage the disaster and the FEMA workforce support to local governments (Byrne, 2013). Governors also appointed dual-status commanders who had both state and federal authority. The new command structure preserved the separate chains of command of the National Guard and Active Duty, while streamlining coordination efforts, operations, and information gathering (Insinna, 2012).

However, as with the case of Hurricane Katrina, evacuation orders for New York City came late (Bucci, et al. 2013). While government agencies and some New York City hospitals evacuated 6,300 patients from 37 healthcare facilities, there weren't major hospital evacuations. Widespread power outages forced hospitals to rely on backup generators, which eventually failed because of the flooding. Underground transformers were rendered dysfunctional, as they were flooded by the corrosive sea water.

Additionally, despite the increased coordination, there was still a lack of information and understanding of where resources were located, which hindered the government's abilities to prioritize restoration efforts to areas that could have received help. In a post assessment, data showed that fewer than half of those affected who requested disaster recovery assistance had received any, and a total of 30,000 residents of New York and New Jersey remained displaced (McGeehan, 2013).

To make matters worse, thousands of people were denied flood insurance claims for homes destroyed by Hurricane Sandy based upon fraudulent engineers' reports (The storm after the storm, 2015). The changed reports were used to justify a significantly reduced insurance payout. Hundreds of Hurricane Sandy victims are now suing insurance companies and engineering firms, who are part of the FEMA-backed flood program.

The insurance companies are overseen by FEMA's National Flood Insurance Program, a fund that is currently $23 billion in debt to the U.S. Treasury (FEMA: Evidence of fraud in Hurricane Sandy reports, 2015). Due to the lawsuit and the necessity to re-review all claims, it took homeowners over two years to get paid out.

While FEMA response to Hurricane Sandy was better than it had been for Hurricane Katrina, the agency still faced challenges. To be better prepared, the organization needs to focus on improving its ability in national preparedness, disaster response and recovery, and agency management (Currie, 2015).

Case Study 2
How the Department of Homeland Security Changed American Security

In the wake of the terrorist attacks on September 11, 2001 and the Anthrax attack, the government implemented the Homeland Security Act of 2002, which established the Department of Homeland Security (DHS) and created the new cabinet-level position of the Secretary of Homeland Security. It also unified 22 formerly dispersed nonmilitary government agencies that were responsible for many functions related to the nation's security into one department, making this the largest federal reorganization since the National Security Act of 1947. While the Department of Defense (DOD) is responsible for military actions and operations, the DHS works in the civilian realm, protecting the U.S. within, at, and outside its borders. The department is charged with overall public security and with preventing terrorist attacks within the U.S., reducing the vulnerability of the country to terrorism and minimizing damages from potential attacks and/or natural disasters. DHS responsibilities also include border security, immigration and customs, cyber security, and disaster management.

The DHS is the third-largest department of the government with a workforce of 229,000 employees and 22 components including TSA, Customs and Border Protection, Immigration and Customs Enforcement, U.S. Citizenship and Immigration Services, FEMA, the Coast Guard, and the Secret Service. Under the Secretary of Homeland Defense's leadership, DHS is responsible for counterterrorism, cybersecurity, aviation security, border security, port security, maritime security, administration and enforcement of immigration laws, protection of national leaders, protection of critical infrastructure, detection of and protection against chemical, biological and nuclear threats to the homeland, and response to disasters.

As part of the creation of DHS, offices and agencies reorganized to better support the DHS's mission sets. The Coast Guard, Customs Service, INS and Border Patrol, Animal and Plant Health Inspection Service (APHIS) of the Department of Agriculture, and the Transportation Security Administration grouped together to protect America's borders, territorial waters, and transportation systems by centralizing information sharing and databases that track and monitor all aspects of border control and America's transportation systems. To meet the Emergency Preparedness and Response mission, FEMA, the FBI's National Domestic Preparedness Office, and multiple Health and Human Services Offices collaborated to create one emergency response plan to be used at all levels of government. It also established FEMA as the federal government's lead agency in emergency preparedness, giving it the responsibility to ensure that first responders from the federal government level down to local levels receive proper training and equipment.

The Department of Homeland Security should be in the business of preventing terrorist attacks. This is about prevention rather than cure. The U.S. military is, for the most part, restricted from operations inside the United States. It is armed to deal with foreign military powers rather than terrorists who act more like criminals than military organizations. DHS was established to handle protecting the American land by coordinating emergency management efforts to detect, respond to, prepare for, investigate, and mitigate terrorist attacks and other large-scale disasters.

CHAPTER 5 PRACTICE PROBLEMS

1. What is the difference between the Department of Defense and the Department of Homeland Security?

2. What are the responsibilities of the Emergency and Response Directorate?

3. A large hurricane has hit the coast of Florida. The local government is completely overwhelmed and does not have enough resources to handle the situation. What should it do? Explain the roles and responsibilities of local, state, and federal governments in this situation.

4. The SAFE Act established many programs and authorized restructuring of several offices. What was the most important aspect of the SAFE Act and why?

5. What is the role of a fusion center in homeland security?

6. Why does the U.S. Coast Guard fall under the Department of Homeland Security?

7. What is the difference between Immigration and Customs Enforcement and Customs Service?

8. What was the most notable achievement of the Implementing recommendations of the 9/11 Commission Act of 2007?

9. What are the primary concerns of Homeland Security policy makers, and what challenges do they face?

10. What is the biggest threat to homeland security in today's world?

KEY TERMS

Abolitionist

Continuity of government

Domestic terrorism

Fatwa

International terrorism

Jihad

Majuhideen

Terrorism

CHAPTER 6

Historic Disasters: The Evolution of Homeland Security in the U.S.

LEARNING OBJECTIVES

After reading this chapter, students will be able to:

- Discuss historical disasters against the United States which have shaped American policy

- Analyze international relationships between the United States and its coalition forces in the aftermath of terrorist incidents

- Compare historical case studies on terrorist attacks on the United States within the twentieth and twenty-first centuries

- Summarize terrorist incidents to understand the evolution of domestic homeland protections and innovative American policymaking

INTRODUCTION: ELIJAH PARISH LOVEJOY AND AMERICAN TERRORISM

Terrorist attacks on American soil were documented as early as the 1800s when American **abolitionist** (opposes slavery) Elijah Parish Lovejoy was killed by a pro-slavery gang in Alton, Illinois. Lovejoy's perseverance and resilience was evident, as he opened four printing presses after they all had been vandalized by racists. After the third destruction of his printing firm, Lovejoy moved to Alton and established the *Alton Observer*, an abolitionist newspaper. On November 7, 1837, a group of thugs vandalized the warehouse where Lovejoy's printing press was located. They exchanged gunfire, and he was ultimately killed in the attack. His murder was attributed to an ideological stance on inequality and abolitionism. His death was not in vain, as he was praised for not fearing terrorism and racism. He died protecting his legacy as an abolitionist to end slavery within the United States.

Lovejoy's death was considered a terrorist incident as abolitionism was a controversial political issue in the nineteenth century. Terrorism has evolved over the past two centuries. Scholars and federal agencies have offered their own classifications and characteristics of terrorism. The FBI has three definitions of terrorism, and each term is predicated on three elements.

This chapter will discuss the elements of terrorism derived from historical events in which the United States and its citizens were targeted domestically and abroad. The historical events selected offer a clear depiction of the evolution of policies and initiatives implemented in response to attacks executed to destroy the United States. In addition, this chapter will examine global conflicts which targeted the United States to reduce the country's position as a superpower, based on American foreign policy, governance, and Western principles.

Terrorism Terms

Federal Bureau of Investigation:

- **International terrorism is:**
  › violent or dangerous acts toward human life that violate federal or state law.
  › intended to coerce or intimidate civilian population or government.
  › occur outside the United States and it territories.

- **Domestic terrorism is:**
  › violent or dangerous acts toward human life that violate federal or state law.
  › intended to coerce or intimidate civilian population or government.
  › occur primarily within the United States and its territories.

- **18 U.S.C. § 2332b defines "federal crime of terrorism" as an offense that:**

> › is calculated to influence or affect the conduct of government by intimidation or coercion, or to retaliate against government conduct; and

> › is a violation of one of several listed statutes, including § 930(c) (relating to killing or attempted killing during an attack on a federal facility with a dangerous weapon) and § 1114 (relating to killing or attempted killing of officers and employees of the U.S.) (n.d., paras.1–3).

Central Intelligence Agency (in accordance with Title 22 of the United States Code, Section 2656f(d):

- The term "terrorism" means premeditated, politically motivated violence perpetrated against noncombatant targets by subnational groups or clandestine agents.
- The term "international terrorism" means terrorism involving the territory or the citizens of more than one country.
- The term "terrorist group" means any group that practices, or has significant subgroups that practice, international terrorism (n.d., para. 1).

Department of Defense:

The unlawful use of violence or threat of violence to instill fear and coerce governments or societies (para. 1).

Department of Homeland Security (in accordance with the Section 2 of the Homeland Security Act 2002):

The term "terrorism" means any activity that (A) involves an act that (i) is dangerous to human life or potentially destructive of critical infrastructure or key resources and (ii) is a violation of the criminal laws of the United States or of any State or other subdivision of the United States; and (B) appears to be intended (i) to intimidate or coerce a civilian population, (ii) to influence the policy of a government by intimidation or coercion, or (iii) to affect the conduct of a government by mass destruction, assassination, or kidnapping.

Department of State (in accordance with Title 22 of the United States Code, Section 2656f(d)(2):

- the term "international terrorism" means terrorism involving citizens or the territory of more than one country;
- the term "terrorism" means premeditated, politically motivated violence perpetrated against non-combatant targets by subnational groups or clandestine agents; and
- the term "terrorist group" means any group practicing, or which has significant subgroups which practice, international terrorism (n.d., para. 1).

National Counterterrorism Center (in accordance with Title 22 of the United States Code, Section 2656f(d)(2), as described by the National Counterterrorism Center Country Reports on Terrorism 2005 Statistical Annex:

Premeditated, politically motivated violence perpetrated against noncombatant targets by subnational groups or clandestine agents (2005, para. 3).

North Atlantic Treaty Organization (NATO):

The unlawful use or threatened use of force or violence, instilling fear and terror, against individuals or property in an attempt to coerce or intimidate governments or societies, or to gain control over a population, to achieve political, religious or ideological objectives (NATO's Military Concept for Defence against Terrorism, 2016, para. 3).

International terrorism is acts that are dangerous and violent in nature against the United States, its citizens, and resources by a foreign individual(s) and/or terrorist organizations. Understanding terrorism and the evolution of its meaning is important, as the world continues to see new tactics from technologically advanced adversaries. Several federal agencies have recognized the same meaning of terrorism by adopting Title 22 of United States Code's definition of terrorism and how it should be recognized. Scholars have similar definitions.
Brian Michael Jenkins (expert on terrorism and transportation security):

The use or threatened use of force designed to bring about political change (Whittaker, 2003, p. 3).

Bruce Hoffman (Director of the Center for Security Studies and Direct of the Security Studies Program at Georgetown University):

Terrorism is thus violence—or equally important, threat of violence—used and directed in pursuit of, or in service of, a political aim (Hoffman, 2006, p. 3).

Alex P. Schmid (scholar in terrorism studies and former Officer-in-Charge of the Terrorism Prevention Branch of the United Nations):

Terrorism is an anxiety-inspiring method of repeated violent action, employed by semi-clandestine individual, group or state actors, for idiosyncratic, criminal or political reasons, whereby—in contrast to assassination—the direct targets of violence are not the main targets. The immediate human victims of violence are generally chosen randomly (targets of opportunity) or selectively (representative or symbolic targets) from a target population and serve as message generators. Threat- and violence-based communication processes between terrorist (organization), (imperiled) victims, and main targets are used to manipulate the main target (audiences), turning it into a target of terror, a target of demands, or a target of attention, depending on whether intimidation, coercion, propaganda is primarily sought (Schmid and Jongman, 2005, p. 28).

The variety of definitions portray both similar and different characteristics, as national and homeland security matters have evolved over past two centuries. Nonetheless, some key elements should be addressed, as the United States continues to face threats. Terrorism is the blatant intent to sabotage a nation's government or its citizens through use of force, intimidation, or fear to promote political propaganda, religious views, radical and extremist epithets, or philosophical ideologies to either entice voluntary recruitment or force conversion for a specific cause. To date, the evolution of terrorism with technological advancement is not only used as a resource, but as a weapon.

In addition to terrorist acts within the United States, catastrophic natural disasters have not only devastated the economy but changed the lives of over 330,000 million American citizens. The United States' most notable natural disaster was the 1900 Galveston Hurricane when a tropical cyclone hit Galveston, Texas on September 8, 1900. The hurricane allegedly started from a distinctive trough in West Africa, which seriously affected the weather in the Caribbean. Thus, the hurricane materialized through the Florida channels as a tropical storm a few days before it hit Galveston. The stormed reportedly rushed through the city, which was approximately eight feet above sea level, and destroyed nearly 4,000 homes. The hurricane still claims to be the deadliest tragedy in American history, killing up to 12,000 residents. Although not all terrorist acts and natural disasters within the United States are discussed in this book, chapter 6 will cover prominent tragedies that have shaped the nation on American soil or in alliance nations where Americans represented our government in the twentieth and twenty first centuries.

ATTACK ON PEARL HARBOR: 1948

On December 7, 1941, the Imperial Japanese Navy Air Service conducted a preemptive military strike on the United States naval base located at Pearl Harbor, Hawaii. The attack was to prevent the United States from interfering in military operations the Japanese were conducting in Southeast Asia. The attack initiated the United States' official entrance into World War II. The battle was a victory for the Japanese and was one of the deadliest attacks on American soil.

By the early 1920s, tensions were obvious between Japan and the U.S., and both prepared for military contingencies. Not until Japan invaded China in 1931 (the *Japanese invasion of Manchuria*) did tensions increase, as Japan fought to expand through China for resource independence. After nearly a decade of fighting, the invasion caused the *Second Sino-Japanese War* in 1937. Through the end of 1937, numerous incidents, including the Japanese attack on the *USS Panay*, the assault of United States Ambassador John Moore Allison (the *Allison Incident*), and the *Nanking Massacre*, strained relations between the two countries.

In 1940, Japan invaded French Indochina to prevent supplies from reaching China, and the United States terminated shipments of supplies, aircraft, and gasoline to Japan. Because of Japan's continued conflicts, President Franklin D. Roosevelt ordered the Pacific Fleet to move from San Diego to Hawaii and increased American forces in the Philippines. The Japanese planned a preemptive military strike on the United States to prevent intrusion since their intentions were to invade the United Kingdom's Southeast Asian colonies. An attack on the colonies guaranteed U.S. involvement. By 1941, President Roosevelt terminated oil exports to Japan due to the new domestic oil consumption restrictions. Therefore, Japan attacked the Dutch East Indies to obtain oil supplies. Moreover, Roosevelt warned Japan that the United States was prepared to react if Japan continued to attack neighboring

Figure 6.1 Battleship *USS West Virginia* engulfed in flames and smoke during the attack on Pearl Harbor on December 7, 1941

countries. The ultimatum left Japan with two options: withdraw from China and Indochina or continue to attack and seize new resources from Southeast Asian colonies.

The proposition resulted with the two countries attempting negotiations to improve relations. Japan opted to withdraw from significant parts of China and Indochina if it could negotiate with the Nationalist government. Also, the country wanted to adopt sovereignty of the *Tripartite Pact* and to ensure there were equal laws and opportunities for trade. Because the American government denied the proposition, Japanese Prime Minister Fumimaro Konoe asked to meet with President Franklin Roosevelt, but the request was denied. Joseph Grew, U.S. Ambassador to Japan, feverishly advised the president to accept the meeting to mitigate further tensions with Japan, but the request remained negated.

On November 20, 1941, Japan gave the United States its final proposition to withdraw their forces from Indochina and not attack Southeast Asia if the United States would lift sanctions and if the Netherlands and the United Kingdom ceased support to China. On November 26 (which was November 27 in Japan), the American government counteroffered Japan to remove all its forces from China and resolve non-aggression agreements within the Pacific without stipulation. The United States was not aware that the Japanese attack fleet was already headed for Pearl Harbor on November 26.

Figure 6.2 "The Day of Infamy" Speech by President Franklin D. Roosevelt on December 8, 1941

The morning of November 26, 1941, the Japanese attacked Pearl Harbor without any declaration of war. The intent was to send a message to the United States that negotiations were concluded and attack 30 minutes after it was conveyed. However, by the time the note reached the Japanese Embassy in Washington, DC, it was too late. At 7:48 a.m., Hawaii-Aleutian Time, the Japanese attacked Pearl Harbor's naval base, using 353 Imperial Japanese fighter aircraft, bombers, and torpedoes. The aircraft was launched from six aircraft carriers in two compositions, damaging 188 American aircraft, all U.S. naval battleships, three cruisers, three destroyers, one minelayer, and an anti-aircraft training ship. The attack took the lives of 2,403 Americans, and 1,178 were wounded. The surprise military attack shocked the nation, as there was not an official declaration of war. Japan had a history of surprise military action; nonetheless, the terroristic act was not expected since negotiations were not formally concluded. President Franklin's speech to the American public the day after marked one of the most famous quotes of American history. Figure 6.2 shows the official typewritten "Day of Infamy" Speech where President Franklin proclaims "December 7, 1941, a date which will live in infamy, the United States of America was suddenly and deliberately attacked by naval and air forces of the Empire of Japan" (National Archives, 1941, p. 1). The following day, the United States officially declared war on Japan, and the United States entered World War II.

UNITED STATES EMBASSY BOMBING: 1983

The Beirut barracks bombings occurred on October 23, 1983 when a suicide bomber used two trucks to bomb buildings utilized by the United States, the *Multinational Force in Lebanon (MNF)*, and French service members. The *Islamic Jihad Organization (IJO)*, a Shia Islamist militia heavily involved in the *Lebanese Civil War* at the time, claimed responsibility for the attack. The terrorist plot was executed to remove the MNF, which was a peacekeeping force to resolve conflicts with Lebanon and Syria, from Lebanon. The Beirut bombings were considered the deadliest attack on American diplomacy during the 1980s and served as a symbolic opening salvo of Islamic extremist attacks on the United States.

Israel's invasion of Lebanon (the *Lebanon War*) on June 6, 1982, began the timeline of events which led to the Beirut bombings. Under the name *Operation Peace for Galilee*, the *Israeli Defense Forces (IDF)* invaded the southern portion of Lebanon because of repeated attacks and counter-attacks between the group and the *Palestine Liberation Organization (PLO)*. IDF provoked the attack when a gunman from *Abu Nidal Organization (ANO)* attempted to assassinate Israel's ambassador to the United Kingdom Shlomo Argov. Israeli Prime Minister, Menachem Begin accused the PLO of the assassination attempt and used that

Figure 6.3 Aftermath of the Beirut bombings on October 23, 1983

as basis to invade Lebanon. After the invasion, Bachir Gemayel was elected as Lebanon's president on August 23, 1982, but he did not take office because he was assassinated nearly a month later when Habib Tanious Shartouni detonated a bomb at the Phalange headquarters. Shartouni claimed that Gemayel was a traitor and had sold Lebanon to Israel. It was reported that Bachir was a partisan Maronite Christian and a clandestine associate of Israel. The FBI held the *Syrian Social National Party* liable for the assassination since Shartouni had ties to the nationalist political party.

By August 25, 1982, MNF deployed to Beirut to become a peacekeeping force and to manage the evacuation of PLO insurgents. A month later, MNF moved PLO members from Beirut for their protection and subsequently President Gemayel was assassinated (during this time, President Ronald Reagan ordered the 32nd Marine Amphibious Unit to leave Beirut). In response to the Gamayel's assassination, the Christian Lebanese right-wing political party *Phalange* killed approximately 3,500 civilians in what is known as the Sabra and Shatila massacre. According to reports, those killed were primarily Palestinians and Lebanese Shiites in the Sabra neighborhood and Shatila refugee camp in Beirut. An ally of IDF, the Phalange was instructed to remove PLO insurgents from the neighborhood as a strategic method for IDF to expand in Western Beirut.

In the wake of the Bachir Gemayel's assassination, his brother, Amine Gemayel, was elected president of Lebanon on September 21, 1982. A week later, the 32nd MAU redeployed to Beirut to join MNF, and a month later, the unit was relieved by the 22nd MAU to fulfill duties and responsibilities. Units continued to redeploy to reinstate order and central government authority in Lebanon during the third phase of the Lebanese Civil War. Dissenters and extremists warned that if United States and other coalition forces did not withdraw from Lebanon, attacks would ensue.

On April 18, 1983, a suicide bomber crashed a truck into the front entrance of the embassy building, detonating nearly 2,000 pounds of explosives. The explosion was so catastrophic that buildings miles away were affected in the aftermath. Sixty-three individuals perished, including 32 Lebanese government employees, seventeen Americans, and fourteen civilians. Of the Americans killed, eight were CIA agents, working as Middle East analysts and country directors in the embassy. In a telephone interview immediately after the attack, IJO claimed responsibility for the attack. According to Terry A. Anderson, a reporter for the *Syracuse Herald Journal*, the anonymous caller stated, "This is part of the Iranian revolution's campaign against imperialist targets throughout the world. We shall keep striking at any crusader presence in Lebanon, including international forces" (Anderson, 1983, p. 1).

The American government responded, condemning the terrorist group for the attack. The House of Foreign Affairs Committee approved $250 million, providing financial and military assistance to the Lebanese government. An amendment mandated formal approval if the United States chose to expand its role within the country to assist the country in counterinsurgency and antiterrorism operations. The Senate Foreign Relations Committee approved the same legislation, and the American government provided restitution to the families of victims killed in the attacks.

Following the attacks, the U.S. Embassy moved to a more secure location in eastern Beirut. The location was not deemed safe, as another extremist bombed the new location's front annex, killing twenty Lebanese government employees and two U.S. soldiers. More suicide attacks ensued after the first terrorist bombing in the region, targeting the American and French embassies and the U.S. Marine and French paratrooper barracks. The U.S. State Department reassessed American protocol on security measures abroad by establishing the Inman Report, which provoked the formulation of the U.S. Bureau of Diplomatic Security and the Diplomatic Security Service.

THE FIRST ATTEMPT ON THE WORLD TRADE CENTER: 1993

On February 29, 1993, the United States faced the first terrorist attack attempt on the *World Trade Center (WTC)* in New York City. A truck bomb, carrying over 1,300 pounds of explosives, detonated on the northern side of the tower, killing six people and injuring over a thousand. Even though the attack killed and injured many, the plan was considered a failure because the explosion did not have sufficient velocity to crash the North Tower into the South Tower. The five extremists responsible wanted the maximum amount of damage to obtain a larger death count.

The WTC was built in 1973 and was ranked the second-tallest building in the world behind the *Willis Tower* (*Chicago Sears Tower*), which was constructed in 1970. The building held more than 50,000 employees, and thousands visited the historical building each year. Two years after its creation was the first sign emergency management policies and procedures were needed when a disgruntled employee started a fire within the tower, causing millions of dollars in damages. The isolated incident provoked security consultants to conduct assessments for better emergency operation plans for possible terrorist attacks. Concerns about non-employees parking in the WTC's parking garage also presented a significant threat since it was not guarded. However, nothing was brought to fruition, and the company that owned the towers did not adhere to any security recommendations.

According to sources, on September 1, 1992, Ramzi Ahmed Yousef, the engineer behind the bombing, illegally entered the United States with Ahmed Ajaj to plan the attack. Yousef attempted to enter the United States with a false Iraqi passport and claimed political asylum, thus entering the country for a court date. When Ajaj attempted to use a false Swedish passport, he was detained for a secondary investigation, and when TSA officers found materials on how to construct bombs, he was immediately arrested. Yousef settled in New Jersey and would frequent New York City, receiving assistance from Sheikh Omar Abdel Rahman, who provided him accomplices (United States Court of Appeals for the Second Circuit, 2003, pp. 1–2).

On February 26, 1993, Yousef and one of his accomplices, Eyad Ismoil, drove a moving van into the underground parking garage located near the North Tower. Yousef ignited the fuse to the urea nitrate-hydrogen gas-enhanced mechanism and fled the scene. Approximately twelve minutes later, the bomb exploded, shutting down the main electrical and emergency systems and destroying the underground garage. The explosion also shut down the building's elevators, emergency commander center, public address system, and sprinklers.

Investigators on the scene found the VIN of the van in the rubble and linked it to Mohammad Salameh, who rented the van the day before the attack. He was arrested when he reported to the rental company to request his deposit for the vehicle. Salameh's arrest led to Abdul Rahman Yasin, who had been released after questioning. When authorities attempt to arrest him again, he fled to Jordan and was placed on the FBI Most Wanted Terrorists list. Nidal Ayyad, Mahmoud Abouhalima, and Ahmad Ajaj were later arrested in connection to the terrorist attack. Five employees, including a pregnant woman and a businessman, were killed because of the attacks. A memorial fountain created in honor of the five individuals was destroyed in the second terrorist attack on the WTC in 2001.

In the aftermath of the bombing, an FBI informant warned the agency of a plan to bomb the WTC in early 1992, which helped in speeding up the investigation. Ramzi Yousef, Mahmoud Abouhalima, Mohammad Salameh, Nidal Ayyad, Abdul Rahmah, and Ahmed Ajaj were arrested for the execution of the WTC bombing. By 1994, they were sentenced to life without the possibility of parole.

The government agency responsible for the World Trade Center restored the building's infrastructure and repaired all electrical and emergency systems. Because of the bombing, numerous security policies were implemented, and emergency procedures were modified to include antiterrorism protocols and provide enhanced evacuation procedures. *The New York Port Authority* was given authority over the WTC's security and critical infrastructure matters. Furthermore, WTC changed its official mail package procedures and added checkpoint stations to scan packages before they entered the building. Finally, free access to the rooftops immediately ended after the attack.

Figure 6.4 Aftermath of the Oklahoma City Bombing, 1995

THE OKLAHOMA CITY BOMBING AND THE AFTERMATH: 1995

The attack on the *Alfred P. Murrah Federal Building* (dubbed the *Oklahoma City Bombing*) occurred on April 19, 1995 in Oklahoma City, Oklahoma. *Timothy McVeigh* and *Terry Nichols* were the two perpetrators responsible for the attacks that killed 168 people and injured nearly 700. Later, it was found the two had accomplices (Michael and Lori Fortier) who had knowledge of the bomb plot and failed to contact local authorities or the federal government. The Oklahoma City Bombing was considered the deadliest domestic terrorist attack in American history next to the September 11 attacks.

In 1988, Timothy McVeigh and Terry Nicholas met in Army basic training (at the time Michael Fortier was McVeigh's roommate in the barracks). The three had radical political beliefs and interests against the American government. They publicly expressed their re-sentment toward government, especially federal law enforcement, and condemned them for specific actions. They were outwardly upset about how the FBI handled the *Ruby Ridge Standoff* and the *Waco Siege*. During this time, McVeigh developed a plan to bomb a federal building in response to both incidents.

Because McVeigh wanted his message received, he planned a large-scale attack that would kill a significant number of federal agents. He chose the Alfred P. Murrah building because it had a large law enforcement population, and he assumed there would be fewer civilian casualties. Also, he knew the building consisted of DEA and ATF agents (involved in both incidents) and military recruiting offices. McVeigh was interested in the infrastructure and how it would cause the most damage because the front was made entirely of glass, which would result in a greater blast impact. Finally, he was concerned about mitigating civilian casualties, so he thought that a federal building with a spacious parking lot would prevent the glass from hitting nearby residents and buildings.

Timothy McVeigh chose to execute his plan on April 19, 1995 because it was the two-year anniversary of the Waco Siege and the 200th anniversary of the Battles of Lexington and Concord (discussed in Chapter Two). He devised a plan to rent a moving van and park it in dropping zone and flee to the getaway vehicle before anyone could observe suspicious activity. Approximately four minutes later, the bomb was detonated. McVeigh's assumption about mitigating casualties was miscalculated because the blast destroyed 33 percent of the Alfred P. Murrah Federal building and damaged approximately 325 buildings within a sixteen-block radius. The attack affected more than just federal employees as hundreds of citizens were homeless, and many buildings within in the area were destroyed. The explosion cost the city nearly $700 million in damage.

McVeigh was pulled over about ninety minutes after the attack for not having license plates on his getaway vehicle. The officer arrested him for having a concealed weapon in his possession. Later, it was found that the VIN from the moving van used in the bombing was associated to a rental company in Kansas, which implicated McVeigh. Eventually, Terry Nichols turned himself into authorities, and Michael and Lori Fortier were identified as accomplices. McVeigh contradicted his words on not harming civilians by giving the following statement:

> I didn't define the rules of engagement in this conflict. The rules, if not written down, are defined by the aggressor. It was brutal, no holds barred. Women and kids were killed at Waco and Ruby Ridge. You put back in [law enforcement] face exactly what they're giving out (Michael and Herbeck, 2002, p. 234).

Timothy McVeigh was found guilty on eleven counts of murder and conspiracy and was sentenced to death. He was executed via lethal injection on June 11, 2001. Terry Nichols was found guilty of conspiring to build a weapon of mass destruction and eight counts of manslaughter of federal officers. He was sentenced to life in prison without the possibility of parole on June 4, 1998. Two years later, the State of Oklahoma charged Terry Nichols with 161 counts of first-degree murder. On May 26, 2004, he was found guilty on all charges, but the jury was deadlocked on the death penalty. Federal Judge Steven W. Taylor sentenced Nicholas to life without the possibility of parole. Michael and Lori Fortier were changed as accomplices with foreknowledge of the terrorist attack. Michael Fortier accepted a plea deal of twelve years in prison in exchange for his testimony against Timothy McVeigh and Nichols. Lori Fortier was granted immunity. On January 20, 2006, Michael Fortier was released from prison after completing ten years of his sentence, and he entered the witness protection program.

The aftermath of the Oklahoma City Bombing brought numerous pieces of legislation on antiterrorism and counterterrorism objectives. The federal government initiated the Antiterrorism and Effective *Death Penalty Act of 1996* and the *Victim Allocution Clarification Act of 1997*. In addition, the government mandated all federal buildings in major cities to utilize Jersey barriers to prevent related attacks in the future. This was a short-term mechanism until the government implemented permanent security infrastructures. Furthermore, new federal buildings were required to construct truck-resistant barriers with an impeding obstacle in proximity to surrounding streets to minimize vulnerabilities. The bombing led to improved engineering standards of federal building to withstand tremendous forces. In June 1995, the Department of Justice disseminated the vulnerability assessments of federal facilities, which resulted in a thorough evaluation of security at all federal buildings and a system for classifying risk at over 1,300 federal facilities owned or leased by the federal government.

KHOBAR TOWERS BOMBING: 1996

The *Khobar Towers Bombing* was a terrorist attack that destroyed portions of housing utilized by U.S. Armed Forces and coalition forces in Saudi Arabia. Coalition forces were assigned to the location during *Operation Southern Watch*. Nineteen U.S. servicemen and a Saudi citizen were killed during the attack. Hezabollah Al-Hejaz was found responsible for the Khobar Tower massacre. The attack was the result of the bombing in Riyadh on November 13, 1995. Radicals warned of a series of attacks if American forces did not leave Saudi Arabia. Extremists even claimed they would target Khobar Towers as the next atrocity if their demands were not met. During the time, the United States Air Force Security Forces team was aware of the threat, but the Saudi government did not give American forces authority to control operations outside the installation perimeter.

Figure 6.5 Aftermath of the Khobar Towers Bombing, 1996

It was reported the perpetrators smuggled explosives into Saudi Arabia from Lebanon in 1996. They spent approximately two hours surveying their target. On June 25, 1996, the extremists attempted to gain access through the main gate of the installation and were denied. Using their alternate plan, they drove the bomb with the truck, a secondary vehicle, and a getaway car to a parking lot that bordered the Khobar Towers. The parking lot was roughly 75 feet from the towers, near the fence line. After signaling the bomb was ready for detonation, they left the bomb truck near the fence, discarded the secondary vehicle, and left in the getaway car. The bomb detonated about four minutes later. U.S. Air Force Staff Sergeant Alfred R. Guerrero observed suspicious activity in the same location and immediately evacuated personnel out the building, as he believed the abandoned vehicles posed a threat. He was responsible for saving more than ten lives and was awarded the Airmen's medal for his bravery.

The bombing was one of the first incidents in which suspicious activity was noticed and military personnel were cognizant in saving lives within the Middle Eastern area. Also, it was reported that Jersey barriers were responsible for minimizing damage. The barriers deflected the blast energy upward, mitigating impact on the lower floors, which could have prevented the building from collapsing. The bombing claimed the lives of nineteen U.S. Air Force servicemen. The American government found Hezbollah Al-Hejaz responsible for the attacks, and Ahmed Ibrahim Al-Mughassil, Abdelkarim Hussein Mohammed Al-Nasser, Ali Saed al-El Hoorie, Ibrahim Salih Mohammed al-Yacoub, and Hani al-Sayegh were named as the conspirators. The CIA, DSS, FBI, and the Office of Special Investigations (Air Force) conducted a full-scale risk assessment to evaluate security vulnerabilities around all installations within Saudi Arabia. The risk assessment identified poor preparedness and intelligence procedures. The intelligence community and American forces received much criticism for lack of preparedness and foreknowledge of the plot, which was considered a major failure. Such vulnerabilities increased the threat of force against U.S. Armed Forces. The Clinton Administration did admit there was intelligence suggesting threats against American forces in Saudi Arabia. There were reportedly ten incidents two months prior to the bombing, but the government failed to sufficiently prepare and notify forces abroad. Senator Arlen Specter argued during a *Senate Intelligence Committee* meeting that intelligence was not an issue. More than 100 intelligence reports referenced a very probable threat concerning the Khobar Towers, and the issue was a matter of lack of communication and execution.

Because of high vulnerabilities and threats of future bombings, U.S. Armed Forces and coalition forces transferred to Prince Sultan Air Base. The location was considered highly secure and remote near the Royal Saudi Air Force. All military operations continued there until 2003 when the United States and British forces repositioned to Al Udeid Air Base in Qatar. The Saudi Arabian government refused to extradite terrorists to the United States. To date, the Saudi government has not publicly announced the charges, convictions, or whereabouts of the criminals.

USS COLE BOMBING: 2000

The *USS Cole Bombing* was the deadliest terrorist attack on a U.S. naval vessel since the *USS Stark* incident. The attack occurred while the vessel was being refueled at the Yemen Arden harbor. While the vessel was completing standard refueling maintenance, a small fiberglass boat maneuvered its way near the *USS Cole*. The boat contained two suicide bombers with explosives, which were detonated, destroying the side of the vessel. According to the United States Navy journal, the explosion (approximately 799 pounds of explosives) left a 40-by-60 feet gouge on the port side of the ship (p. 6). The force of the blast entered the mechanical location of the ship, killing personnel who were near the area in a waiting line to eat lunch. Seventeen servicemen were killed and thirty-nine were injured.

Al Qaeda claimed responsibility for the asymmetrical warfare attack. Videos surfaced of Osama bin Laden praising the attack, and he ensured that there would be more against U.S. forces. The American government sent CIA and FBI agents to Yemen to investigate the aftermath. Tensions rose over the federal law enforcement presence within the country, which made the investigation challenging, dangerous, and time-consuming. U.S. Federal Judge Robert G. Doumar found the Sudanese government accountable

Figure 6.6 Aftermath of the USS Cole Bombing, 2000

for the bombing and ruled that al-Qaeda was associated with the government, providing financial and logistic support. Judge Doumar said, "There is substantial evidence in the case presented by the expert testimony that the government of Sudan induced the particular bombing of the USS Cole by virtue of prior actions of the government of Sudan" (Conroy, 2007, para. 1).

The judge also mandated the government pay $8 million to the families of the seventeen servicemen killed. Conspirators responsible for the planning and execution of the attack were Abu Ali al-Harithi, Jamal Ahmad al Badawl, Fahd Mohammed Ahmed al-Quso, and Abd al-Rahim al-Nishin.

The rules of engagement significantly changed after the terrorist attack. The Department of the Navy re-evaluated its antiterrorism and force protection methods. The agency also improved its *Random Antiterrorism Measures*, a program designed to utilize force protection methods to enhance physical security awareness throughout a military installation (Holmes, n.d., para. 1). In November 2001, the Department of the Navy established the *Anti-Terrorism and Force Protection Warfare Center* at the Naval Amphibious Base at Little Creek in Virginia Beach, Virginia. In October 2004, the Navy consolidated anti-terrorism and force protection initiatives and established the *Maritime Force Protection Command* to "oversee the administration and training of expeditionary units the Navy deploys overseas to protect ships, aircraft, and bases from terrorist attacks" ("Commander, Fleet Forces Command Public Affairs," 2004, para. 2). The command has three subsidiaries: *Naval Coastal Warfare*, *Explosive Ordnance Disposal*, and *Expeditionary Mobile Diving and Salvage Forces*.

9/11

On September 11, 2001, nineteen hijackers conducted a series of four calculated terror-ist attacks against the World Trade Center and the Pentagon, killing nearly 3,000 people and injuring over 6,000. Dubbed as *9/11*, the incident is known as the deadliest and largest tragedy in American history on U.S. soil. September 11 is also considered the deadliest incident for emergency management, firefighters, and law enforcement offi-cers in United States history, killing approximately 415 personnel performing emergency management operations. The annihilation of the WTC and surrounding infrastructures significantly affected the United States economy and international markets. The terrorist attacks cost the American government over $3 trillion dollars in damages, including the operations in Iraq and Afghanistan.

Four U.S. airliners (American and United Airlines) were hijacked by nineteen terrorists in different locations within the United States. Reports stated all flights derived from the northeastern region of the United States, headed for California when the attack ensued. *American Airlines Flight 11* and *United Airlines Flight 175* crashed into the North and South Towers of the World Trade Center in New York City. In less than two hours, both towers collapsed, damaging the buildings adjacent to the trade center site and

Figure 6.7 Aftermath of the September 11th attacks, 2001

other surrounding infrastructures. *American Airlines Flight 77* purposely crashed into the Pentagon, the headquarters for the Department of Defense in Arlington, Virginia. Initially, the last plane, United Airlines Flight 93, was targeted to either crash into the White House or the United States Capitol, but instead crashed into a field in Stonycreek Township near Shanksville, Pennsylvania. Passengers on the plane attempted to distress the hijackers, forcing the extremists to miss the intended target.

Osama bin Laden and al-Qaeda

Tensions between the United States and al-Qaeda can be traced to the 1970s when the Soviet Union invaded Afghanistan. Bin Laden traveled to Afghanistan to help establish Arab **mujahideen** (ones engaged in jihad) with Soviet Union resistance. At the time, Afghani insurgents received military aid and financial assistance from the Chinese and Pakistani governments, which was ultimately funded by the United States and other Arab empires. Bin Laden worked closely with *Ayman al-Zawahiri* (the current leader of al-Qaeda), and he developed extreme radical ideologies. Between the period of the *Soviet-Afghan War* and the early 1990s, bin Laden turned against the United States, issuing his first **fatwa** (religious decision of Islamic law made by one of Islamic authority), demanding that American forces should not remain in Saudi Arabia. Khalid Sheikh Mohammed talked to Osama bin Laden about attacking the United States as early as 1996. Al-Qaeda experienced a major transition in moving from Sudan to Afghanistan, and when the African Embassy Bombings happened in 1998, bin Laden was adamant about attacking the United States. By 1998, bin Laden issued a second fatwa, voicing his stance on American foreign policy and its support of the State of Israel and emphasis that American forces remain in Saudi Arabia. He ordered Islamic extremists to attack Americans until the United States conformed to his demands.

Planning the Attack

Bin Laden gave Mohammed permission to plan that attack and a series of meetings would follow with the two and bin Laden's deputy commander, Mohammed Atef. Atef provided operational support, and bin Laden was the mastermind and financial backer of the plan. He selected Mohamed Atta, Marwan al-Shehhi, Ziad Jarrah, and Ramzi bin al-Shibh because they were quite educated, spoked English, and had experience with Western civilization. Eventually, al-Qaeda leaders would find a supporter that had a pilot's license and he joined the terrorist operative.

They were trained for months on how to assimilate into American culture from going to school, taking flying lessons, and attending social functions to eating at restaurants. The initial crew arrived in the United States at the end of the 2000 and began working under the leadership of bin Laden. In 2001, the rest of the recruits chosen for attack arrived in the United States and began coordinating plots and making final decisions on targets.

Intelligence

In 1999, the National Security Agency intercepted a phone call between Khalid Sheikh Mohammed and Khalid al-Mihdhar but decided not to act upon it. Additionally, Saudi intelligence warned the CIA that Mohammed and al-Mihdhar were al-Qaeda members and to investigate their backgrounds. The CIA searched al-Mihdhar and found he had a U.S. visa but did not report it to the FBI, which was tracking terrorist movements. Mohammed, Mihdhar, and another al-Qaeda recruit, Nawaf al-Hazmi, were found to be traveling together, but this was not reported to respective agencies. Eventually, when the CIA was notified about the three, even though they were known to be terrorists, they were not added to the FBI Most Wanted Terrorists list because the agency believed it was not in their realm of responsibility. By the summer, CIA director George Tenet believed a high probability of terrorist activity against the United States was imminent but thought it would be overseas rather than on American soil. In July, Tenet put federal agencies on alert and contacted the State Department and the FBI to notify embassies and police departments to implement force-protection measures. Finally, FBI analyst Margarette Gillespie became aware of Mohammed and Mihdhar's presence in the United States when the CIA gave her surveillance photographs. She reported to the Immigration and Naturalization Service (INS), the State Department, and U.S. Customs Service to put the three on their watch lists. Some agencies could not do this at the time, thwarting efforts to investigate the terrorists.

FBI agents forewarned the primary agency responsible for tracking bin Laden that it was highly likely that he had subordinates entering the United States to train. The same month, Jordanian authorities warned the American government that it would be attacked under a codename "The Big Wedding," and it involved aircraft. By August, the CIA presented a briefing to President Bush that Osama bin Laden planned to attack the United States. Federals agencies mandated that all flight schools identify Arab students and immediately a Minnesota flight school notified the FBI that it had a student who was suspicious. They reported the student asked skeptical questions, and the FBI found he was an extremist who traveled to Pakistan, and he was arrested for staying in the United States with an expired French visa.

September 11 showed serious communication breakdowns and lack of intelligence-sharing between federal agencies, which could have prevented the largest attack the United States has ever seen. Additionally, there was unwillingness to move forward with critical data that incriminated known terrorists linked to Osama bin Laden.

Responsibility for the Attacks

Al-Qaeda claimed responsibility for the 9/11 attacks, which led to the *Global War on Terror (GWOT)* and the American invasion of Iraq of Afghanistan, executing *Operation Iraqi Freedom* and *Operation Enduring Freedom*. Initially, Osama bin Laden denied that he was involved in the attacks, but later publicly claimed responsibility, stating that he condemned the presence of troops in Saudi Arabia, sanctions and embargos against Iraq, and the country's support of Israel. On September 16, 2001, Al Jazeera broadcasted a statement from bin Laden in which he stated, "I stress that I have not carried out this act, which appears to have been carried out by individuals with their own motivation" (Fox News, 2001, para. 5). Two months later, American forces recovered a video that proved bin Laden had knowledge of the attacks. In December, he made another video and stated to the public:

> It has become clear that the West in general and America in particular have an unspeakable hatred for Islam ... it is hatred of crusaders. Terrorism against America deserves to be praised because it was a response to injustice, aimed at forcing American to stop its support for Israel, which kills our people ... we say that the end of the United States is imminent, whether bin Laden or his followers are dead or alive, for the awakening of the Muslim umma (nation) has occurred (BBC News, 2001, para. 2).

Even though bin Laden did not directly claim responsibility in the statement, it would take three years before he incriminated himself. In a taped statement, he said:

> Your security is not in the hands of Kerry, Bush, or al-Qaeda. Your security is in your own hands. Each state that does not mess with our security has naturally guaranteed its own security. We are free ... and want to regain our freedom for our nation. As you undermine our security. we undermine yours. To the U.S. people, my talk is to you about the best way to avoid another disaster ... I tell you: security is an important element of human life, and free people do not give up their security. While I was looking at these destroyed towers in Lebanon, it sparked in my mind that the tyrant should be punished with the same and that we should destroy towers in America so that it tastes what we taste and would be deterred from killing our children and women. God knows that it had not occurred to our mind to attack the towers, but after our patience ran out, and we saw injustice and inflexibility of the American-Israeli alliance toward our people in Palestine and Lebanon, this came to my mind (Michael, 2004, paras. 3, 10, 12, 15).

Experts determined there were additional motives for the 9/11 attacks. The radical Muslim world who supported bin Laden believed the United States threatened security of countries in the Middle East. In bin Laden's 2002 letter to the United States he stated the following matters were why the nation was attacked:

- The United States alliance with the State of Israel
- Support of Russia's conflict with Muslims in Chechnya
- Support of Israel's aggression against Muslims in Lebanon
- Backing the Philippines conflict with Muslims in the Moro crisis
- Support of attacks on Muslims in Somalia
- Support by pro-American governments in the Middle East
- U.S. Forces remain in Saudi Arabia
- Sanctions against Iraq
- Support of aggression against Muslims in Kashmir

The Aftermath

As mentioned, the twin towers were destroyed, including four of the seven world trade center sites. In addition, the Saint Nicholas Greek Orthodox Church and the Marriott Hotel were damaged. The U.S. Customs House, World Financial Center, and the Deutsche Bank Building were severely damaged. Borough of Manhattan Community College was condemned, and the Millennium Hilton, One Liberty Plaza, and 90 Church Street were restored in the aftermath. The cleanup of the WTC took approximately a year to complete as well as the reconstruction of the Pentagon's western wing. In 2006, the construction of the One World Trade Center began, and it was officially opened eight years later. Additionally, memorials such as the National September 11 Memorial and Museum, the Pentagon Memorial, and the Flight 93 National Memorials were built to honor those who perished. Also, organizations established national relief funds to aid the victims and their families, and President Bush enacted a bill to provide victims compensation.

The September 11 attacks provoked immediate response from the United States, declaring war on Afghanistan and initiating the Global War on Terrorism. Furthermore, hate crimes, international responses, and public opinion ensued as the world watched America's reaction to the most heinous crime the country ever faced. President Bush immediately addressed the American people in a joint, national session with Congress about the attacks and his intent for recovery and rescue efforts. Innovative emergency management policies were needed immediately, and policymakers were motivated to establish contingency plans for the **continuity of government** (procedures permitting a government to continue vital operations in the wake of a disastrous event) as well as provide migration procedures for senior officials.

Most importantly, September 11 established the largest reorganization in modern history since the National Security Act of 1947. President Bush passed the Homeland Security Act of 2002, forming the Department of Homeland Security. In addition, Congress enacted the Uniting and Strengthening America by Providing Appropriate Tools Required to Intercept and Obstruct Terrorism Act of 2001, known as the *USA PATRIOT Act*. The act was established to detect and prosecute those involved in terrorist acts and breaking other federal laws. Bush broadened the responsibilities of the *National Security Agency (NSA)* to effectively anticipate and combat future terrorist acts and launched warrantless surveillance of telecommunications. Furthermore, the federal government expanded the *United States Foreign Intelligence Surveillance Court's* authority to obtain and share intelligence on U.S. and non-U.S. citizens internationally.

LAW ENFORCEMENT AND HOMELAND SECURITY

Since 9/11, there have been various changes on how the federal government protects the United States. President George W. Bush and Congress

Global War on Terror (GWOT) is a term coined by President George W. Bush to reference the international military campaign regarding the September 11 attacks.

were instrumental in passing various legislative acts to improve the efficiency of communication and information sharing in response to the September 11th attacks. Despite the steadfast initiatives to improving processes between agencies, there are still some challenges. Research shows that concepts of information sharing and preparedness between entities are "at times conflicting" and the "government's effort to create a trusted partnership and culture of information sharing among federal, state, and local agencies faces significant challenges" (Bean, 2009). Not only were operations an important factor in mitigating another terrorist attack on American soil, but the aftermath identified lessons learned, highlighting failed communications and information sharing processes. Congress emphasized such limiting factors on lack of continuity and communication between relevant agencies during 9/11. The Joint Inquiry of the House and Senate Intelligence Committee, which was responsible for the investigation of the attacks "discovered significant problems in how intelligence agencies shared information among themselves and with entities that need information to protect the national against terrorist" (Joint Inquiry into Intelligence Community Activities Before and After the Terrorist Attacks of September 11, 2001, 2002, p. 355). Additionally, the committee emphasized "one of the most significant problems examined during the open hearings was the lack of information sharing between agencies," referencing the multi-level security capability (Joint Inquiry into Intelligence Community Activities Before and After the Terrorist Attacks of September 11, 2001, 2002, p. 7). Even the 9/11 Commission, responsible for the 9/11 Commission Report, concluded its investigation stating the "biggest impediment to all-source analysis to a greater likelihood of connecting the dots, is the human or systemic resistance to information sharing" (The National Commission on Terrorist Attacks Upon the United States, 2004, p. 592). Many of the deficiencies found in the investigations after the attacks were the inspiration for the Intelligence Reform and Terrorism Prevention Act of 2004.

Before the inception of DHS, the Department of Defense's primary role was to protect the United States from foreign adversaries, handling most tasks from overseas. There were agencies such as customs and border patrol to protect the nation within the nation's natural boundaries, but September 11th showed America much more was needed to protect and defend the land: none other than our law enforcement. The Homeland Security Information Network—Law Enforcement organization was established to provide "law enforcement officials at every level of government with a means to collaborate security with partners across the geographic and jurisdictional boundaries" (Homeland Security Information Network—Law Enforcement, n.d., para. 1). The law enforcement network works diligently with DHS to deter weapons smuggling, narcotics trafficking, gang operations, and other criminal activities that threaten homeland security. The network's most important element of responsibilities is information sharing between homeland security agencies to improve its collaborative efforts, communication methods, and to mitigate potential threats. According to the Department of Homeland Security, the law enforcement network provides increased situational awareness to law enforcement via:

- DHS Situational Awareness Tool
- Real-Time collaboration and instant messaging

- A document library with daily and periodic reporting from federal, state, and local law enforcement sources

- User and "train-the-trainer" instruction (Homeland Security Information Network—Law Enforcement, n.d., para. 5).

In addition to the law enforcement network, DHS has unique partnerships with law enforcement at each level governance to protect the United States. Because these partnerships are vital to protecting homeland and national security, DHS and law enforcement have been charged as the first line of defense to carry out missions throughout the United States. Nearly, 90 percent of DHS employees are dispersed throughout the nation, alongside law enforcement to fulfill this unique mission.

The Office for State and Local Law Enforcement is another collaborative effort between law enforcement and homeland security agencies. Congress established the office in response to the 9/11 Commission committee's recommendation for law enforcement continuity on homeland security mission and objectives. The Commission's purpose for the office was to:

- Lead the coordination of DHS-wide policies related to state, local, tribal, and territorial law enforcement's role in preventing, preparing for, protecting against, and responding to natural disasters, acts of terrorism, and other man-made disaster within the United States

- Serve as the primary liaison between DHS and non-Federal law enforcement agencies across the country (The Office for State and Local Law Enforcement, n.d., para. 2–3).

The office's responsibilities are:

- Serve as the primary Department liaison to state, local, tribal, and territorial law enforcement;

- Advise the Secretary on the issues, concerns, and recommendations of state, local, tribal, and territorial law enforcement;

- Keep the law enforcement community up-to-date on Department-wide activities and initiatives such as "If You See Something, Say Something™", the Blue Campaign, Nationwide Suspicious Activity Reporting (SAR) Initiative (NSI), and the Department's efforts in Countering Violent Extremism;

- Identify and respond to law enforcement challenges that affect homeland security;

- Coordinate with the Office of Intelligence and Analysis to ensure the timely coordination and distribution of intelligence and strategic information to state, local, tribal, and territorial law enforcement; and

- Work with the Federal Emergency Management Agency to ensure that law enforcement and terrorism-focused grants to state, local, tribal, and territorial law enforcement agencies are appropriately focused on terrorism prevention activities (Philpott, 2015, p. 279).

As previously mentioned, information sharing is a critical factor with law enforcement's relationship with the Department of Homeland Security. Post 9/11, fusion centers were established to increase communication efforts between DHS, first responders, military, intelligence, and emergency management professionals. Fusion centers operate as state and major urban area focal points for the receipt, analysis, gathering, and sharing of threat-related information between federal, state, and local, tribal, territorial, and private sector partners (State and Major Urban Area Fusion Centers, n.d., para. 1). Such fusion centers have been categorized into field of specialty:

- Fusion Centers and Joint Task Forces
- Fusion Centers and FBI Field Intelligence Groups
- Fusion Centers and High Intensity Drug Trafficking Areas
- Fusion Centers and Regional Information Sharing System (RISS) Centers
- Fusion Centers and Emergency Operations Centers
- Tribal Participation in Fusion Centers
- Deployed Intelligence Officers and Protective Security Advisors
- Private Sector Engagement with Fusion Centers

Community-Oriented Policing has become a prominent element within the homeland security arena, as law enforcement have narrowed their efforts on working closely with its local communities. Though there have been doubts on whether COP would be a continuing initiative with unjustified killings, policy brutality, and the use of excessive force that has increase post-9/11, there has been newfound hope that this strategy is the key to safeguarding communities at large. For example, the proven success rate of COP was highlighted at the Texas Regional Community Policing Institute where the agency sponsored training established by the Wichita State Regional Community Policing Institute on the criticality of how policing plays a huge role in safeguarding communities. The training was predicated on improving situational awareness on what happens within communities and the importance for vigilance. The program also focused on the need for community members and local businesses to work closely with law enforcement to mitigate criminal activity and potential terroristic acts. However, there is still the negative stigma in some communities where law enforcement is not welcomed or trusted. Robert D. Putnam, author of *Bowling Alone: The Collapse and Revival of American Community*, is evident that there are still some internal conflict between communities and law enforcement. According to Sam Houston State University, Putnam's book is based on a "specific observation that captures the essence of our loss of connectedness ... observed that roughly the same percentage of Americans go bowling now as did in the 1950s ... the difference is that the activity is far less likely to occur in the context of teams or leagues; contemporary Americans are much more likely to go bowling alone" (The Role of State and Local Law Enforcement Agencies in Homeland Security: Revisiting Community-Oriented Policy, n.d., pp. 1–2).

Nearly 20 years since foreign adversaries committed the largest terrorist attack on U.S. soil in American history and the federal government has sifted through challenges and limiting factors to coordinate vital partnerships between law enforcement and homeland security agencies to protect and defend the United States. It is still in work progress and requires discipline between agencies to ensure the ability to share information to improve preparedness and mitigate terrorism. To have the ability, coordinating agencies must remain consistent and reliable with their efforts by enforcing accountability through system performance methods. Leading authorities must assess such standards through constant enforcement of implemented policies to examine the effectiveness of information sharing processes.

SUMMARY

The catastrophic events killed thousands of Americans and left damage that will never be forgotten: the memory of the destruction that took the lives of loved ones and those who sacrificed their lives for American freedom. Domestic terrorism is a prevalent weapon that will be used against the United States if we do not continue to revolutionize policies and initiatives to correlate to modern threats. International terrorism is another threat that is even more unpredictable with innovation and technological advancement. This chapter identifies that American intelligence and counter-terrorism activities are essential to ensure that U.S. service members and their families are protected abroad. Natural disasters are nature's beasts in terms of permanently destroying critical infrastructures, resources, and physical land.

In the past twelve years, the nation has suffered through catastrophic disasters against American citizens, its military service members, and the homeland that have displaced millions of citizens, drastically shifted the economy, destroyed cities, contaminated natural resources, and most importantly, claimed lives. Lessons learned and research showed a lack of cohesive communication among intergovernmental agencies. Proper preparation was lacking, and necessary resources failed to provide effective recovery responses. Understanding the deficiencies and insufficient resources that made America susceptible to domestic extremism and terrorist acts provides hope that America can recover with resilience and preserve human life and critical resources.

CHAPTER 6 CASE STUDIES

Case Study 1
The Attack on Pearl Harbor

December 7, 1941, is a "date which will live in infamy." The Japanese attack on Pearl Harbor was one of the deadliest attacks on U.S. soil, leaving 2,403 dead, with 188 destroyed planes and a crippled Pacific fleet that included eight damaged or destroyed battleships (Attack at Pearl Harbor, 1941, 1997). The attack commenced just before 8 a.m. on a Sunday morning, the time chosen specifically by the Japanese for maximum surprise. Many servicemen were on leave for the weekend, leaving only a minimal contingent of soldiers on duty at the time (Pearl Harbor attack, n.d.). The attack came in two waves, each wave containing hundreds of Japanese fighter planes carrying bombs and torpedoes. The Japanese aircraft concentrated on taking out the Pacific fleet vessels, including battleships and cruisers, anchored in the harbor. They also went after U.S. aircraft at Hickam, Wheeler, and Bellows airfields to prevent U.S. fighters from reaching the Japanese aircraft carriers. U.S. planes were parked wingtip to wingtip to protect them from potential sabotage, which made them easy targets for the Japanese, allowing the eastern nation to quickly achieve air superiority. The surprise attack lasted about two hours. By 1:00 p.m., the Japanese carriers that launched the planes from 274 miles off the coast of Hawaii were headed back to Japan (Attack at Pearl Harbor, 1941, 1997).

While the attack on Pearl Harbor was a surprise, tensions between the U.S. and Japan had increased over several decades due to Japan's expansionism operations. In 1937, the Japanese had successfully invaded China and Manchuria to gather needed resources to solve its economic and demographic problems. However, the U.S. refused to acknowledge Japan's authority in occupied China. This, along with the United States' own occupation of the Philippines during the Spanish American-War, fueled Japanese resentment. Japan's sphere of influence in the far western Pacific was being threatened by U.S incursions into the Pacific at a time when Japan was also vying for dominance in the region (Pearl Harbor attack, n.d.). U.S. officials responded to this aggression with an array of economic sanctions and trade embargoes, believing that without access to goods and essential supplies like oil, Japan would have to rein in its expansionism. Instead, these sanctions made the Japanese more determined to stand their ground.

The extent of the disaster and the unpreparedness of the U.S. military incited considerable criticism from the public, especially when it was later discovered that the incoming Japanese attack planes had been detected by the radar and reported but were mistaken for an incoming group of B-17 bombers from the mainland that morning (Pearl Harbor attack, n.d.). The failure to warn the Army and Navy command of the impending attack was not a failure of technology but rather a failure of organization and training. Effective cryptography and successful cryptanalysis were in its infancy. Under-funded, under-manned and under-equipped, cryptanalysts had been ordered to concentrate on Japanese diplomatic traffic, rather than naval messages (Pearl Harbor attack, n.d.).

Furthermore, War Plan Orange, a series of U.S. war plans for dealing with a possible war with Japan, demonstrated that U.S. officials had been aware that an attack by Japan was probable, but they had no knowledge of the time or place at which it would occur (Pearl Harbor attack, February 23, 2017). War Plan Orange explored the likelihood of a surprise attack by Japan, but the plan anticipated a surprise attack in the Philippines or elsewhere in the western Pacific in one of the nearby European colonies, including the Dutch East Indies, Singapore, or Indochina. No one believed that the Japanese would start a war with an attack on U.S. soil (Pearl Harbor, 2009).

Additionally, U.S. war planners failed to consider how technological advances in submarines and naval aviation had made previous naval doctrine obsolete. Specifically, they did not understand that aircraft could effectively sink battleships or that the Japanese might put the U.S. battleship force out of action in a single stroke (Miller, 2007). At the time, the U.S. Navy considered Pearl Harbor relatively safe from attack as it was too shallow, with an average depth of 45 feet, for an attack by torpedoes dropped from airplanes, which usually required about 75 feet of depth. However, learning from the 1940 British low-level nighttime torpedo attack against the Italian fleet at the harbor in Taranto, Italy, the Japanese had developed a shallow running torpedo that would skim the surface of the water in the harbor after being dropped from a low-flying aircraft (Pearl Harbor attack, 2017).

In March 1941, the commanders of the Army and Navy air fleets in Hawaii issued a memo describing a plan for the joint defense of Oahu in the event of Japanese attack. The memo, later known as the Martin-Bellinger report, warned of the likelihood of a surprise air attack on Pearl Harbor and predicted the attack with great accuracy. To prevent a surprise attack, the report recommended daily 360-degree air patrols as far out to sea as possible. However, patrols were limited to times when intelligence indicated a surface raid was probable because of aircraft and personnel shortages (Hart, 1941).

While the Japanese attack on Pearl Harbor severely crippled U.S. naval and air strength in the Pacific, it failed to incapacitate the Pacific fleet, specifically the aircraft carriers attached to the Pacific fleet. The aircraft carriers Enterprise and Lexington had previously been dispatched to Wake and Midway islands and were not at Pearl Harbor at the time, escaping the attack (Pearl Harbor attack (Airfield Development and Activities Behind the Lines, n.d). Additionally, the Japanese attack had failed to take out the base's most vital onshore facilities–oil storage depots, repair shops, shipyards, and submarine docks. As a result, the U.S. Navy could recover relatively quickly from the attack. Rallying around the attack, the U.S. entered World War II the next day.

Case Study 2
The 9/11 Terrorist Attack

On September 11, 2001, the U.S. became a nation transformed. Nineteen militants associated with the Islamic extremist group al-Qaeda hijacked four airliners and carried out suicide attacks against targets in the U.S. Two planes were flown into the twin towers of the World Trade Center in New York City, while a third plane hit the Pentagon just outside Washington, D.C., followed by the fourth crashing in a field in Pennsylvania. The terrorist attack that took place on that fateful day is considered the deadliest attack on U.S. soil, resulting in mass death and destruction, subsequently triggering major U.S. initiatives to combat terrorism (9/11 attacks, 2010).

The perpetrators were Islamic terrorists from Saudi Arabia and several other Arab nations, acting on the orders of al-Qaeda leader Osama Bin Laden in retaliation for U.S. support of Israel, its involvement in the Persian Gulf War, and its continued military presence in the Middle East (Bergen, 2017). The key operational planner of the 9/11 attacks was Khalid Sheikh Mohammed (KSM) who became active in the Muslim Brotherhood, the oldest political Islamist group in the Arab world, at age 16. As an adult, he traveled to Pakistan and then Afghanistan to wage **jihad** (the spiritual struggle against enemies of Islam) against the Soviet Union, which had launched an invasion against Afghanistan in 1979. Nine years later, Mohammed met bin Laden in Tora Bora, Afghanistan where Mohammed presented a proposal for plane operations, a plan that would involve training pilots who would fly the aircraft into buildings in the U.S. (Bergen, 2017). Bin Laden provided Mohammed with four initial operatives for suicide plane hijackings within the U.S., and in the fall of 1999, training for the attacks began (The 9/11 Commission Report, 2014). Al-Qaeda provided the recruits, money, and logistical support to execute the operation, while bin Laden wove the attacks on New York and D.C. into a larger strategic framework of attacking the "far enemy" to bring about regime change across the Middle East (Bergen, 2017). The terrorists established themselves in the U.S., many well in advance of the attacks. Some of the hijackers had lived in the U.S. for more than a year and had taken flying lessons at U.S. commercial flight schools. Others had slipped into the country in the months before September 11 and acted as the "muscle" in the operation (9/11 attacks, 2010).

On September 11, 2001, nineteen terrorists boarded four domestic aircraft bound for California at three East Coast airports, easily smuggling box cutters and knives through security. The planes were chosen because they were loaded with fuel for the long transcontinental journey and would create the most damage. Soon after takeoff, the terrorists disabled the crews, some of whom were stabbed with box cutters the hijackers had smuggled in, commandeered the four planes and transformed the jets into deadly projectiles (9/11 attacks, 2010). At 8:46 a.m., the first plane, American Airlines Flight 11, flew into the north tower of the World Trade Center. Seventeen minutes later, another plane, United 175, struck the south tower, removing any doubt that the U.S. was under attack. At 9:37 a.m., a third plane, American Airlines 77, crashed into the southwest side of the Pentagon, setting the immediate area on fire. Less than thirty minutes later, the final plane, United 93 crashed into a field near Shanksville, Pennsylvania.

Rescue operations began almost immediately as the country and the world sought to come to grips with the enormity of the losses (Bergen, 2017). At the World Trade Center site in Lower Manhattan, 2,753 people were killed when the hijacked planes were intentionally crashed into the north and south towers or because of the crashes. Of those who died in the initial attacks and the subsequent collapses of the towers, 343 were New York City firefighters, 23 were New York City police officers, and 37 were officers at the Port Authority. At the Pentagon in Washington, 184 people were killed when hijacked American Airlines Flight 77 crashed into the building. Near Shanksville, Pennsylvania, forty passengers and crew members aboard United Airlines Flight 93 died when the plane crashed into a field (September 11, 2001: Background and timeline of the attacks, 2016).

The 9/11 terrorist attack demonstrated that al-Qaeda was an organization of global reach, with planning meetings in Malaysia, operatives taking flight lessons in the U.S., coordination by terrorist leaders based in Hamburg, Germany, money transfers from Dubai, and recruitment of suicide operatives from countries around the Middle East. These activities were ultimately overseen by al-Qaeda's top leaders in Afghanistan (Bergen, 2017). Less than a month after 9/11, as part of the larger Global War on Terrorism (GWOT), the U.S. military invaded Afghanistan to remove the Taliban government harboring al-Qaeda. The war in Afghanistan became the longest-running war in U.S. history. Although formal U.S. combat operations ended in late 2014, more than 8,000 U.S. troops remain to help stem the ongoing Taliban insurgency. Similarly, U.S. troops invaded Iraq as part of the GWOT initiative and the suspicion of weapons of mass destruction production. When the U.S. pulled out of Iraq in 2011, it left the nation in an unstable state, creating conditions for another Islamic extremist group, ISIS, to rise to power (Green, 2016).

Because of the 9/11 attack, the U.S. government passed the Homeland Security Act of 2002, which created the Department of Homeland Security. The Act combined twenty-two agencies into one department. Airport security under the Transportation Security Administration received a series of upgraded responsibilities, including instituting new security procedures and managing screenings at every commercial airport checkpoint in the country (Green, 2016). Furthermore, intelligence surveillance operations grew with the passing of the PATRIOT Act and modification of the FISA Act, which temporarily expanded the search and surveillance powers of the Federal Bureau of Investigation (FBI) and other law-enforcement agencies at the expense of civil liberties (Bergen, 2017). These changes continue to have ripple effects across the globe today.

CHAPTER 6 PRACTICE PROBLEMS

1. You've read each of the different definitions of terrorism. What is your definition of terrorism?

2. Some consider the Japanese bombing of Pearl Harbor a terrorist act, while others claim that it was a preemptive attack of war. Based on your definition of terrorism, do you consider the bombing of Pearl Harbor to be an act of terrorism or an act of war? Why or why not?

3. Why didn't the U.S. anticipate the Japanese attack on Pearl Harbor?

4. What additional security measures and procedures did the U.S. put in place because of the attack on the U.S. Embassy in Beirut and the attack on the Khobar Towers?

5. Do you think that the previous bombing attempts on the World Trade Center influenced government actions leading up to the 9/11 attack?

6. How has the 9/11 attack affected U.S. homeland defense considerations?

7. What was Timothy McVeigh's objective when he set out to bomb the Alfred P. Murrah building?

8. Why are natural disasters considered a homeland defense threat?

9. What are some of the challenges first responders face when arriving on scene?

10. Attacks against the homeland are constantly evolving and getting more creative, making it more difficult to anticipate and prevent future incidents. What are some ways we can improve our homeland security posture and address these new challenges?

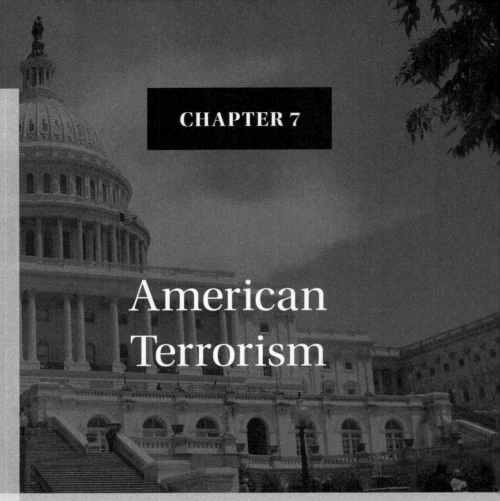

KEY TERMS

Abortion extremism

Agroterrorism

Anarchist extremism

Anti-immigration extremists

Anti-Semitism

Common laws

Communism

Covert operations

Cybersecurity

Cyberterrorism

Direct action

Domestic extremism

Homegrown terrorism

Ideologies

Infiltration

Insurgency

Islamic extremism

Left-wing extremism

Lone wolves

Militia extremism

Narcoterrorism

Nationalism

Nation state

Non-nation state

Political asylum

Political interference

Radicalism

Redemption movement

Right-wing extremism

Sovereign citizen extremism

Special interest terrorism

State terrorism

Terrorism

Threat modeling

Warfare

Western civilization

White nationalism

White supremacy

CHAPTER 7

American Terrorism

LEARNING OBJECTIVES

After reading this chapter, students will be able to:

- Analyze the multiple facets of terrorism and radical organizations in the twenty-first century
- Discuss heightened domestic extremism within the United States
- Evaluate the evolution of the largest terrorist attacks on U.S. soil
- Assess the future of American terrorism from the perspective of U.S. leaders and policymakers

INTRODUCTION

Terrorism has significantly influenced all governments, cultures, political, and economic circumstances. The history of terrorism is predicated on violence or instilling fear over a population of human beings. Terrorism can be traced to the first century between the conflict of the zealots and the Roman Empire, but historically and socially terrorism has been a term used to discuss conflicts between foreign entities or even internal war within countries in the seventeenth and eighteenth centuries. This chapter discusses American terrorism and how it derived from the historical background of global terrorism, which heavily influenced the nation's foreign policy, democratic governance, and national and homeland security objectives. Chapter seven also discusses the inception of American terrorism within the United States, details terroristic acts conducted on American soil and abroad, and offers a brief glimpse at the some of the world's notorious terrorist leaders. Finally, this chapter discusses the importance of understanding and mitigating "innovative terrorism" from becoming a concern for the homeland. Terrorist acts such as agroterrorism and bioterrorism are highlighted as significant concerns for the United States which could impact the future of America's national and homeland security.

Defining Terrorism

There has been debate among scholars on defining terrorism due to the physiognomies which delineates the actual meaning. For example, some academicians believe violent crimes and/or conflicts can be considered acts of terrorism, while others believe there should be some additional elements, such political interference or government involvement, for terrorism to be a sound definition to describe such encounters. The next section of this chapter will discuss the history of terrorism and how the term was adopted, which dates to the First century. This section will also discuss the evolution of terrorism and how each century was influenced by political ideologies, national figures, and historical events to shape the definition over time. The important notion on this debate is there is not a right or wrong way to define terrorism, but failure to come to a partial consensus could possibly pose vulnerable repercussions on how to mitigate it. The interesting perspective is researching the history of the concept to discuss various definitions, in addition to addressing issues on the understanding of terrorism. Andrew Silke (2004) have addressed that are multiple problems among scholars and experts when it comes to defining terrorism. Such debates were not successful in reaching an agreement on the commonality of key characteristics (Jenkins, 1980). Nonetheless, there are many definition to research that have many commonalities, which have been adopted from scholars, universities, and agencies focused on terrorism.

Various characteristics might not seem to be a concern when defining terrorism, yet, it is, especially when it deals with domestic and international warfare. Some experts who believe there is a contingent difference between on the definition of terrorism between nation and non-nation states. For instance, American historian and political commentator, Walter Laqueur emphatically stated there are basic differences in motives, function and effect between oppression by the state (society or religion) and political terrorism. Including state terrorism in the study of terrorism would have made the study of terrorism impossible, for it would have included not only U.S. foreign policy, but also Hitler and Stalin (Laqueur, 1986; 2003). As Ruth Blakeley (2012) stated, Laqueur's position was predicated on actor based, not action based, representing more than just an action of a criminal or insurgent. Laqueur closely followed and conceptualized the analysis of terrorism, understanding its characteristics are more than just "verb" but it is also political, strategic and thought-provoking. His position on terrorism expressed that terrorism is not predicated on state violence because nation and non-nation states are the example of the manipulation of power. Bruce Hoffman expressed comparable assertions on defining terrorism. He proclaimed:

> Failing to differentiate between state and non-state violence, and equating the innocents killed by states and non-state actors would ignore the fact that, even while national armed forces have been responsible for far more death and destruction than terrorists might ever aspire to bring about, there nonetheless is a fundamental qualitative difference between the two types of violence. This is based upon the historical emergence of rules and accepted norms of behavior that prohibit the use of certain types of weapons and proscribe various tactics and outlaw attacks on specific categories of targets ... terrorists have by contrast violated all these rules (Hoffman, 1998, p. 34).

Hoffman's position on terrorism is predicated on the idea that nation states do not infringe on the regulations outlined in the Geneva Conventions, but it is difficult to support the claim because they do. Not all nation states obey international laws and multilateral agreements, which makes it problematic and difficult to discount state terrorism from defining terrorism in terms of discussing violence and instilling fear. Additionally, nation states may have a right to use violence or aggression on other states to protect its national security standards and protects its citizens (i.e. the United States declaring on Iraq and Afghanistan in response to the September 11th attacks). Such acts are a form of terrorism even though the intent is not to cause purposely fear and violence, instead, respond to acts of violence.

Though there are different interpretation of terrorism, there common traits that define it. Terrorism expert, Paul Wilkinson believed there were five characteristics of terrorism, which are:

1. premeditated and aims to create a climate of extreme fear or terror.
2. is directed at a wider audience or target than the immediate victims of violence
3. inherently involves attacks on random and symbolic targets, including civilians
4. acts of literal sense that they breach the social norms, thus causing a sense of outrage
5. used to try to influence political behavior in some way (Wilkinson, 1992, pp. 228–229).

His definition emphasizes that terrorism is not solely based on harming one individual or a target, instead, the concept is an excuse to instill fear and harm others in the process. Wilkinson's definition is centralized on the action of the definition rather than who is responsible or commits the act. More scholars, such as Christopher Mitchell, David Carleton, George Lopez, and Michael Stohl agreed with the characteristics of Wilkinson's definition and incorporated elements of definition in their own. They defined terrorism as:

> Involves state or non-state actors, the deliberate coercion and violence, or the threat thereof directed at some victim, with the intention of inducing extreme fear in some target observers who identify with that victim in such a way that they perceive themselves as potential future victims. In this way, they are forced to consider altering their behavior in some manner desired by the actor (Mitchell, Carleton, Lopez, & Stohl, 1985, p. 5).

Bruce Hoffman defines terrorism as:

> [Terrorism] is thus violence—or equally important, the threat of violence— used and directed in pursuit of, or in service of, political aim (2006, pp. 2–3).

Does there need to be a single definition of terrorism? Ideally, yes, but there are many contributing factors and characteristics that describe terrorism and it could be completely different based on perspectives and viewpoints. For instance, political scientist Louise Richardson states, "like pornography, we know terrorism when we see it" (Richardson, 2006, para. 1). With that said, there are many terroristic definitions throughout the United States and the world, but there still is not a universal definition approved by the United Nations. There is a provisional definition in the UN's General Assembly Resolution 49/60, which was adopted on December 9, 1994, *Measures to Eliminate International Terrorism*. It states:

> Criminal acts intended or calculated to provoke a state of terror in the general public, a group of persons or particular for political purposes are in any circumstance unjustifiable, whatever the considerations of a political, philosophical, ideological, radical, ethic, religious, or any other nature that may be invoked to justify them (Measures to Eliminate Terrorism, 1994, para. 23).

I believe if there was a fundamental term that includes key factors in what defines terrorism, it would be suitable for clear understanding and finding ways to mitigate it. The opposition may argue, if you know it when you see it, why does it need to be defined? There needs to be a clear, universal understanding of terrorism that way those who condone it, support it, and are responsible for it are held accountable. If one is going to hold accountability, then the alleged need to know what they are answering to. Also, it is understanding and defining terrorism is for all humanity. All people throughout the world need to be protected from terrorism, which results to clearly define it. Ben Saul stated:

> Terrorism currently lacks the precision, objectivity and certainly demanded by legal discourse. Criminal law strives to avoid emotive terms to prevent prejudice to an accused, and shuns ambiguous or subjective terms as

incompatible with the principle of non-retroactivity. If the law is to admit the term, advance definition is essential on the grounds of fairness, and it is not sufficient to leave definition to the unilateral interpretations of States. Legal definition could plausibly retrieve terrorism from the ideological quagmire ... ultimately it must do so without criminalizing legitimate violent resistance to oppressive regimes—and becoming complicit in that oppression (Saul, 2008, p. 11).

Saul believes for justice to be pursued, predicated on a criminal act, an advanced definition of terrorism should be required. An advanced definition would be comparable to scholars, Alex P. Schmid and Albert J. Jongman definition of terrorism:

> ... an anxiety-inspiring method of repeated violent action employed by [semi-] clandestine individual, group or state actors, for idiosyncratic, criminal or political reasons, whereby—in contrast assassination—the direct targets of violence are not the main targets. The immediate human victims of violence are generally chosen randomly (targets of opportunity) or selectively (representative or symbolic targets) from a target population, and serve as message generators. Threat—and violence-based communication processes between terrorist (organization), (imperiled) victims, and main targets are used to manipulate the main target (audiences), turning it into a target of terror, a target of demands, or a target of attention, depending on whether intimidation, coercion, or propaganda is primarily sought (Schmid & Jongman, 1988, p. 28).

All the while, it is interesting to view the many definitions, established by nation states and international organization. The following will show commonalities and distinctions, which concludes there is agreeance on characteristics to certain extent.

Department of Defense (United States):

> The unlawful use of violence or threat of violence, often motivated by religious, political, or other ideological beliefs, to instill fear and coerce governments or societies in pursuit of goals that are usually political (Terrorism, 2017, p. 232).

Federal Bureau of Investigation (United States):

> The unlawful use of force and violence against persons or property to intimidate or coerce a government, the civilian population, or any segment thereof, in furtherance of political or social objectives (Terrorism 2002/2005, 2002, para. 9).

UN Security Council Resolution 1566:

> Criminal acts, including against civilians, committed with the intent to cause death or serious bodily injury, or taking hostages, with the purpose

to provoke a state of terror in the general public or in a group of persons or particular persons, intimidate a population or compel a government or an international organization to do or to abstain from doing any act (Security Council Acts Unanimously to Adopt Resolution Strongly Condemning Terrorism as one of Most Serious Threats to Peace, 2004, para. 2).

European Union:

As part of the Framework Decision on Combating Terrorism, given their nature or context, may seriously damage a country or an international organization where committed with the aim of: seriously intimidating a population; or unduly compelling a government or international organization to perform or abstain from performing any act; or seriously destabilizing or destroying the fundamental political, constitutional, economic or social structures of a country or an international organization (Directive (EU) 2017/541 of the European Parliament and of the Council, article 1, 2017, para. 1).

United Kingdom:

Under the Terrorism Act of 2000, an act designed to seriously interfere with or seriously disrupt electronic systems (Terrorism Act 2000, 2000, para. 1).

United States:
Under Title 18 of the United States Code (113B):

(A) involve violent acts or acts dangerous to human life that are a violation of the criminal laws of the United States or of any State, or that would be a criminal violation if committed within the jurisdiction of the United States or of any State;
(B) appear to be intended —
(i) to intimidate or coerce a civilian population;
(ii) to influence the policy of a government by intimidation or coercion; or
(iii) to affect the conduct of a government by mass destruction, assassination, or kidnapping; and
(C) occur primarily outside the territorial jurisdiction of the United States, or transcend national boundaries in terms of the means by which they are accomplished, the persons they appear intended to intimidate or coerce, or the locale in which their perpetrators operate or seek asylum (18 U.S. Code Chapter 113B–Terrorism, 2010, p. 2331).

Overall, terrorism is a disputed conceptualization of violence, political rhetoric, religious undertones, and most importantly instilling fear within a population. Because a simple concept is so complex in encompassing a universal understanding, there will more than likely not be a comprehensive definition of the term. The commonality between experts and scholars is the term within itself is biased and derogatory, but moving forward to establish a lexicon that meets criteria for the international community is found to be challenging, not to say, that it should not be accomplished. I believe this is an important component among terrorism scholars to develop a universal term because it will provide a clear understanding of what terrorism is under not only international law, but universal laws for human rights.

I believe Noam Chomsky's definition is best fitted for streamlining an international definition, *the calculated use of violence to attain goals that are political, religious, or ideological in nature … through intimidation, coercion, or instilling fear* (Booth & Dunne, 2002, p. 128). It is basic and gives all actors a starting point of how of conceptualizing the term will benefit the global environment. It is how I visualize terrorism to be understood, but know additional characteristics should be incorporated to be precise. Terrorism is:

> The premeditated and deliberate use of extreme violence to pursue a specific goal that is predicated on a self-belief system of ideological, religious, and/or sociopolitical principles by a nation state(s), non-nation state(s), or radical extremists to instill fear within an assembly, which practices governance over a large population (Chouraeshkenazi, 2017).

I believe it is paramount the international community understands terrorism can be committed by a **nation** or **non-nation state** in addition to insurgents and terrorist organizations. Reviewing the terms in this section, many fail to acknowledge the importance of nation states' participation in terroristic acts, known as **state terrorism**. State terrorism is terroristic acts committed by a state against a foreign entity or against its own natives. The French Revolution is considered one of the first dated examples of state terrorism predicated on the country's violence and heinous acts towards its aristocratic and foreign conspiracies. There is a plethora of examples that epitomize state terrorism and exists today because there will be states that commit atrocities against its own citizens to establish or alter political order. State terrorism also influences coercion and black for those to join the state's movement or be a victim of terrorism.

Nation state is a state which associates it political objectives along with culture of a nation to ultimately establish political rightfulness as a sovereign realm.

Non-nation state is a nation that is not its own state and/or does not possess sovereignty.

The History of Terrorism

The earliest signs of terrorism traces to the Zealots of Judea during the first century. Also, known as Sicariis by the Romans, Zealots were responsible for many violent crimes and the assassination of Roman forces around 66 CE. Zealots were those who opposed the Roman Empire and wanted all supporters and leadership to be exiled from the Holy Land of Judea (modern-day Southern part of Israel). Zealots believed the Romans would take over the Holy Land and extricate all Jews that lived within the area. Their belief was predicated on remaining faithful to religious, traditional, and cultural ideologies of Judaism while being under the rule of the Roman Empire.

Zealots were political adversaries to the Roman Empire and were emphatic on protecting their religious septum from the imposition of Roman influence. They also wanted to eradicate the Gentile rule (non-Jews) over the Jewish community. They initiated the revolt against the Romans, known as the First Jewish-Roman War or the "Great Revolt," which was cited as one of the three wars by the Jewish people against the Roman Empire (Aberbach & Aberbach, 2000). Such actions demonstrated violent acts against a regime to instill fear, enforce political, and religious standards, conceptualizing the birth of terrorism. The Great Revolt began in 66 CE, which derived from tensions between the Jews and the Roman Empire. Aggression between the two factions intensified due to attacks on the Romans and the influx of anti-taxation protests, which resulted in an adversarial response. Roman Empire governor, Gessius FLorus, declared retaliation by destroying the Second Temple and imprisoning Jewish leaders. Because the rebellion was more than what the Romans could handle, the Syrian Army infiltrated the country to end the uprising and restore order. Eventually the Syrian Army would be defeated by the Jews. Later that year, the Zealots attempted to control the city and was not successful, resulting in the execution of Sicarii leader Menahem ben Yenuda and banishment of the remaining Zealots.

The birth of the Assassins would be the next example of early terrorism. The Assassins were an Islamic group established in Iran and Syria that were responsible for overthrowing the Sunni order to proliferate their own ideologies. Bernard Lewis, author of the Assassins stated the group was "the first systematic use of murder as a political weapon" (1967, p. 169). The rise of the Assassins was much later after the Great Revolt, beginning in the 11th and 12th centuries. The group instilled fear within the Sunni community, killing Islamic leaders and supporters of the movement. Also, called the Nazari Ismalis, the Assassins terrorized with their consistent stratagem only killing leaders to leave a major platform of strength, superior, and dominance over it minions. The tactic was proven to be successful, as it prevented adversaries from direct combat because of their manpower deficiency. Additionally, the strategy established the "lone wolf" concept because their surprise attacks were conducted by individuals and not a large group. Because lone assassins killed many leaders, the attacks left damaging effects on the Sunnis. The Zealots and Assassins are traditional examples of historic terrorism, but are still relevant today, as they are the forerunners for the conceptualization of modern terrorism. Furthermore, their strategies, goals, and motivation are predicated on deep, psychological impacts, which have affected global security in the twenty-first century.

> *Zealots were those apart of the political movement in the first century that provoked the people of Judea to revolt against the Roman Empire and exile them from the Holy Land (known as the First Jewish-Roman War).*

> *Sicarii were groups of Zealots who heavily opposed the Roman Empire and struggled to exile them and their supporters out Judea.*

From the late 1200's, after the reign of the Assassins until the 16th century, terrorism was a primary tactic in conflicts and warfare, but it was not enough to successfully win battles. Rosa Ehrenreich Brooks (2005) states that it was not until the Treaty of Westphalia when modern terrorism rose that terrorism became a principal authority and

> *Jacobins were members of the Jacobin club, a democratic party established in Paris in 1789. They were considered a radical organization with extremist views during the inception of the French Revolution.*

increased existence, which lead in the 19th century. In ancient times, communication and implementation were insufficient, a disadvantage that was considered reasoning for the inception of terrorism and led conflict with organizations, internal, and other countries. Moreover, monarchies became nations and terrorism was a primary purpose enforced its authority.

The French Revolution, which lasted for 10 years is another revolt that implicated acts of terrorism leading into the 19th century. Myra Williams (2009) expressed the first term of terrorism was coined during the French Revolution (Reign of Terror) when the Jacobins chose to instill fear by executing violence against its enemies. Rumki Basu (2012) suggested the revolution "provided the first use of the word "terrorist" and "terrorism" (p. 385). Basu also stated the term "terrorism" began in 1795, referencing the Revolutionary government's instigation of the Reign of Terror (2012, p. 385). Those who were members of the Committee of Public Safety and the National Convention that enforced the policies of the conflict were referred to as "terrorists" (2012, p. 385). Monique M. Maldonado (2018) explained the term would be used throughout the 19th century during the inception of anarchism within Europe and the United States. The French Revolution identified oppression of future nation states and provoked Revolutionary leadership to increase authority of its subordinates to employ terroristic plots and tactics.

PROBING MODERN TERRORISM

Extreme political theories entered the nineteenth century, as there became centralized concerns of technological advancement by those who successfully defeated nation states during and after the French Revolution. Anarchism rose during this period and propaganda of ideological and sociopolitical viewpoints expanded from Europe and North America and was deemed successful until the birth of communism in the mid-1800's and became the principal ideological basis for political terrorism, which was significant in the 1900's. Nationalism also became prominent within the political system for citizens who pledged allegiance to their countries. According to Adebayo E. Adeyami (2015), when states emphasized national identities who were conquered or colonized, chose to assimilate and expanded within the 20th century.

Within the United States, modern terrorism became apparent prior to the American Civil War, when abolitionist, John Brown fought for the prohibition of slavery (found in chapter one). Brown's advocacy led to multiple revolts (1856–1859), including the well-known battle at Harper's Ferry. Eventually, Brown was defeated, captured, and executed for treason. His legacy continued, as his fight against slavery was a revolutionary event to reshaping the nation's political direction. Otto Scott stated Brown's purpose was "to force the nation into a new political pattern creating terror" (1979, p. 3).

UNDERSTANDING TERRORISM

In American history, terrorism was thought to be identified through the inception of the Klu Klux Klan (KKK). Anti-slavery icon John Brown led several attacks in the mid 1800s, but he is best known for the Battle of Harpers Ferry where he and his men attacked the armory. Biographer Scott Otto claimed John Brown's intention was to "force the nation into a new political pattern by creating terror" (Otto, 1983, p. 3). His attack was one of the significant events that led to the American Civil War to settle the issue of slavery and states' rights. The dissolution of the Civil War abolished slavery, protected American assets, and birthed the *Reconstruction Era*. Some Confederate veterans were not satisfied. Seven months after the war, on December 24, 1865, six former Confederates established the KKK. The KKK used extreme violent tactics (i.e. intimidation, lynching, and murder) against African Americans. As the group increased, it adopted an internal form of government by addressing specific ideologies: anti-African American, anti-Catholicism, anti-Semitism, nativism, racism, and white supremacism.

In the twentieth century, World War II established the definition of terrorism as specialized tactics (i.e. guerrilla warfare and resistant movements). After the war, resistance groups impacted failing European territories, resulting in such groups establishing anti-colonial ideologies. For instance, the Middle East resistance forces committed terrorist acts against the British colonized in Egypt. Additionally, the National Liberation Front launched guerilla attacks in the French-controlled region of Algeria. During this era, the United States dealt with many international conflicts which were terrorist acts, but when terrorism was identified within its own borders by American citizens, national security significantly increased (i.e. the Oklahoma City bombing, the September 11 attacks, the San Bernardino shooting, the Orlando shooting). Such terrorist events will be discussed later in the chapter.

INTERNATIONAL TERRORISM

International terrorism is the elemental concept of terroristic acts occurring outside the United States. Terrorists from countries outside the United States are likely to commit terroristic acts beyond their scope to target populations and/or geographical locations for a specific purpose. In the mid-1940s, international terrorism emerged, but it was not until the inception of Sunni Islamist terrorist organization, al Qaeda, that highly profiled attacks in the media was international terrorism was of much concern in the 1990s. Al Qaeda's massive involvement in terrorist attacks within the Middle East is what correlated such heinous crimes with Islamist terrorism. Al-Qaeda's ideological viewpoints and propaganda have significantly influenced the Islamic faith. According to the Constitutional Rights Foundation, al-Qaeda has used a "political form of 'Islamism' to justify an unholy war of terrorism (n.d., para. 1).

In 1988, Osama bin Laden founded al-Qaeda, and by the early 1990's, the group was committing attacks against American and African embassies in the name of its religious philosophies. On August 7, 1988, al-Qaeda concurrently detonated bombs the U.S. Embassy in Kenya and the East African Embassy in Tanzania. The bombs killed

12 Americans and approximately 250 Africans. More than 4,500 people were wounded from the incident (East African Embassy bombings, n.d., para. 1). Al-Qaeda gained American attention for the first time as result of the attacks, placing its leader, Osama bin Laden, on the Federal Bureau of Investigation's ten most most-fugitives lists. Intelligence gathered from the bombings linked al-Qaeda and members of the Egyptian Islamic Jihad (EIJ), an Egyptian terrorist organization whose primary goal was to overthrow the Egyptian government and establish an Islamic State. It was known that al-Qaeda and EIJ were linked and the bombings were believed to be retaliation for U.S. involvement in alleged torture and extradition of EIJ members, who were arrested in Albania for various murders of Egyptian citizens just months before the incident (Egyptian Islamic Jihad: Narrative Summary, n.d., para. 1). Al-Qaeda was responsible for the first terrorist plot against the United States in 1993. On February 26, 1993, members of the group detonated a truck bomb below the North Tower of the World Trade Center. Six people were killed over 1,000 were wounded. Five members of al-Qaeda: Ramzi Yousef (the mastermind behind the attack), Mahmud Abouhalima, Mohammad Salameh, Nidal Ayyad, and Eyad Ismoil were responsible for the attack and were charged by the United States for their involvement in the planning and execution. The motive for the bombing against the United States was group's ideological dominance of Islamic fundamentalism and American diplomatic support and alliance with Israel (more about the 1993 WTC bombing is discussed in chapter seven). The group's most prominent attack against the United States was the second attempt on the World Trade Center and the Pentagon on September 11, 2001. The bombing killed nearly 3,000 people and it still the largest terrorist attacked that happened in the American history (more about 9/11 is discussed in chapter seven). U.S. Forces found a videotape made by Osama bin Laden, which included information about his knowledge of the attacks. The provocation was apparent in the videotape. Bin Laden stated:

> It has become clear that the West in general and America in particular have been an unspeakable hatred for Islam. Terrorism against America deserves to be praised because it was response to injustice, aimed at forcing America to stop its support for Israel, which kills our people. We say that the end of the United States is imminent, whether bin Laden or his followers are alive or dead, for the following awakening of the Muslim umma (nation) has occurred (Bergen, 2006, p. 370).

It was not until a taped statement was found that Osama bin Laden claimed responsibility for 9/11.

> We are free ... and want to regain freedom for our nation. As you undermine our security, we undermine yours. Peace will come to those who do not threaten Muslims (Dionisi, 2006, p. 65).

Foreign terrorist groups have not just claimed responsibility for attacks against the United States, but its allies and security partners in the same. Al-Qaeda has been linked to London bombing in 2005, which killed 56 people and the Mumbai bombings in 2008 that killed over 160 people.

Al-Qaeda's rise of terrorism within the Middle East and throughout Arab nations exacerbated the proliferation of other extremist groups to fulfill its ideological philosophies through crime, violence, and terroristic acts. In the twenty-first century, ISIS is deemed and the richest and most dangerous terrorist group in the world that has committed many terrorist attacks since its inception in 2006. Known as the Islamic State in Iraq and the Levant (ISIL) and the Islamic State (ISIS), the group was

> *Islamic State is a distinctive type of government predicated on Shari'a law (Islamic law) to maintain justice and order within the Muslim community.*

initially formed as a "splinter" organization with its mission to create an Islamic State caliphate across Iraq, Syria, and other countries to spread its anti-Western and Islamic fundamentalism propaganda. Rooted from al-Qaeda, ISIS ideological stance like al-Qaeda is enforcing Shari'a Law, which epitomized the Ancient society sentiments. The difference is ISIS's protuberant position to enforce a direct Islamic caliphate, which is not an immediate concern for al-Qaeda. Significant differences to their reign is how they plan and execute attacks. Natasha Betrand (2015) argues that al-Qaeda has always "portrayed itself more of a militant group comprised of highly trained operational mastermind whose successful attacks on America and Europe would ultimately gain them enough key members to form a global movement of Muslims and the onslaught of the West" (para. 4). ISIS is known for killing groups of people at a time and carrying out heinous public executions, particularly beheadings. The group also uses modern weaponry and social media is a significant strategy in its propaganda and recruitment. Additionally, the group is reckless, destroying holy sites and valuable antiquities that should be remained preserved, as its leadership emphasize and important to return to ancient Islam. ISIS's wealth is astounding, as the extremist group is dubbed the wealthiest in the world. Its source of funding derives from oil production, smuggling of illegal products and drugs, taxes, kidnapping ransoms, and stolen valuables.

Al-Qaeda and ISIS are the most well-known and prominent terrorist groups in the world, but there are many groups on the rise that has been publicized in the media. The U.S. State Department maintains a list of foreign terrorist organizations and the dates designated, which remain a threat to the United States, its allies, and security partners. Notable terrorist groups on the list are:

- Abu Sayyaf (the Philippines)
- Al-Nursa Front (a subsidiary of al-Qaeda in Syria)
- Al-Shabaab (East Africa, operations in Yemen)
- Armed Islamic Group (Algeria)
- Boko Haram (Nigeria)
- Hamas (Palestine)
- Hezbollah (Lebanon)
- Islamic Jihad (Egypt)
- Islamic Jihad (Palestine)
- Islamic Movement (Uzbekistan)

- ISIL/ISIS (Syria and Iraq)
- Jaish-e-Muhammad (Pakistan)
- Kurdistan Workers' Party (Turkey)
- Lashkar-e-Taiba (Pakistan)
- The Taliban (Pakistan)

Except for al-Qaeda and ISIS, most of the groups mentioned have not executed international attacks. Instead, they use terrorism a ploy to overthrow governments within their countries.

ISIL/ISIS

Before the name ISIL/ISIS, the group was known as Jama'at al-Tawhid wal-Jihad when it was founded in 1999. The group pledged allegiance to al-Qaeda and participated in the Iraqi insurgency, which followed the invasion of Iraq by American forces in 2003. As previously mentioned, ISIS is an extremist group who spreads its Islamic fundamentalism to establish an Islamic State and caliphate. Controlling parts of Iraqi and Western Syria, the organization is known for its brutal and deadly tactics to enforce Shari'a Law throughout the region they control. Abu Bakr al-Baghdadi (discussed further in this chapter) is the group's founder and current leader is known for his inhumane acts and totalitarian style of leadership. ISIS's tactics and style of operations are so barbaric that al-Qaeda has condemned its actions. Before Osama bin Laden death, he dissolved relations with the group due to its "extreme brutality," negatively impacting al-Qaeda's reputation (Ostrovsky, n.d., para. 3). Even Hezbollah leader, Hassan Nasrallah called ISIS "a monster" (Ostovsky, n.d., para. 3). ISIS's strong jihadist presence within the Middle East should be praised, as it is emerging jihadism in places that had little influence, but its "extremist" schemes have disgusted other terrorist leaders, who choose not to associate with the group. Al-Qaeda's leader, Ayman al-Zawahiri (ruler since Osama bin Laden's death) have shown isolation towards the group and when al-Baghdadi rejected al-Qaeda's authority for a declared caliphate, he permanently severed ties with ISIS (Byman, 2015). ISIS recruits individuals from all over the world and is believed to have nearly 100,000 fighters is Iraq and Syria. The groups ideological vision is to support all styles of terrorism targeting Western civilizations, capturing territories that meet its standards, and accepting allegiance from anymore supports their organization. Their allegiance and recruitment are heavily promoted through social media, forcing the United States, Germany, the United Kingdom, and other alliances to infiltration their organization through deterrence and mitigation.

Al-Qaeda

Osama bin Laden, Abdullah Azzam, and several other extremists created al-Qaeda in 1988 when they fought against the Soviet Union in the invasion of Afghanistan. The group is considered a Wahhabi organization whose ideological goal is to join all Muslims together from around the world in a global jihad using punitive interpretations of the Shari'a Law. The group's network consists of Islamic extremist and Salafist jihadists.

As previously mentioned, the group was responsible for targeting the United States in the American Embassy bombings in Kenya and 9/11. In retaliation to the 9/11 attacks, the United States declared the Global War on Terror. They also claimed responsibility for the Bali bombings in 2002. Since the attack on the United States, Osama bin Laden became the number most-wanted terrorist. On May 2, 2011, United States Navy Seals of the U.S. Naval Special Warfare Development Group (Seal Team Six) killed bin Laden in his compound in Abbottabad, Pakistan. The CIA-led operative (*code-named Operation Neptune Spear*) alongside the Joint Special Operations Command included special units such as the 160th Special Operations Aviation Regiment and the Special Activities Division and ended the 10-year manhunt. Since Osama bin Laden's death, the group is still considered one of the most dangerous terrorist organizations in the world. They have changed their operatives from multiple, small units to the "lone wolf" system to execute terrorist attacks, which includes suicide bombings and bombing targeted locations. Their overall vision is to mitigate foreign influence from Muslim countries and create a new caliphate to take over the world with Muslim influence.

The Taliban

The Taliban was established in 1994 as a Sunni Islamic fundamentalist political movement in Afghanistan. In the late 1990s to the early twenty-first century, the group controlled approximately three-quarters of Afghanistan and mandated its strict interpretation of the Shari'a Law within the region. The Taliban was a prominent extremist group during the Afghan Civil War and remained in control until the invasion of Afghanistan by U.S.-led forces in 2001, overthrowing its regime. After the invasion, the Taliban restructured its strategic movement and began conducting insurgency operations to fight the Karzai administration and the International Security Assistance Force (ISAF). Mullah Mohammed Omar was the group's supreme commander and spiritual leader and was known for his shyness demeanor and lack of association with other leaders. He was not in the public eye and not much information was known about him during his reign of the Taliban. Omar died in 2013 of tuberculosis and Mullah Akhtar Mansour became the Taliban's leader. The group generates it revenue through illicit activities like drug smuggling/trafficking, extortion, and human trafficking. In addition to al-Qaeda's involvement of the 9/11 attacks, the Taliban was also responsible, contradicting its relationship with the United States. In the 1980s, the group was trained by Inter-Service Intelligence (ISI) and the United States to fight the Soviet Union during the invasion of Afghanistan. Another dangerous group within the world, the Taliban is known for its barbaric tactics and human violation rights against women and children.

Boko Haram

Formerly known as Jama'at Ahl as-Sunnah lid Da'wah wa'l-Jihad, Boko Haram (named changed in 2015), is a Jihadist militant movement in Nigeria. In 2002, the group was founded by Mohammed Yusuf, who was killed in 2009 amid the 2009 Boko Haram uprising when was captured by Nigerian military forces and executed. Since Yusuf's death, Abubakar Shekau has been the group's commander. According to the Global

Terrorism Report in 2015, the uprising was the deadliest terrorist events in the world with thousands of citizens killed and approximately 2.3 million emigrated from their communities (Measuring and Understanding the Impact of Terrorism, n.d., p. 1). The Global Terrorism Index report also stated Boko Haram "overtakes ISIL to become the most deadly terrorist group in the world" (Measuring and Understanding the Impact of Terrorism, 2015, p. 4). The group is extremely vocal in their stance against Western education and was known in the media for the kidnapping of 250 girls from Nigerian schools. Under Shekau's command, the group has killed nearly 10,000 people in pursuit of their causes. Also, they also responsible for the bombing of the United Nations building in Abuja, Nigeria. The bombing killed 21 and wounded at least 60 people. Boko Haram has been connected to ISIS, sharing the same support for the Sunni Islamic group and advocating for intolerant Shari'a laws. They objective is to overthrow the Nigerian government because of its "Westernized" influence.

Lashkar-e-Taiba

Lashkar-e-Taiba is considered the most active terrorist group within South Asia. The group was founded in 1987 by Hafiz Saeed, Abdullah Azzam, and Zafar Iqbal in Afghanistan and financially supported by Osama bin Laden. Lashkar-e-Taiba gained public attention for its involvement of the Parliament attack in 2001, the bombings in Delhi in 2005, and the Mumbai attacks in 2008. The group's objective is to establish an Islamic State in South Asia and "liberate Muslims residing in Indian Kashir," as its sole purpose is to free all Muslims from the region (Raza, 2009, p. 28). The terrorist is known for using young children to exploit their propaganda and terrorist activities.

Hezbollah

Hezbollah is a Shi'a Islamist political movement and paramilitary (Jihad Council) located in Lebanon. The extremist group was established by Muslim cleric (headed by Ayatollah Khomeini) and has a political party, the Loyalty to the Resistance Bloc, in the Lebanese parliament. When co-founder and Secretary General, Abbas al-Musawi was killed by the Israeli Defense Forces in 1992, Secretary General of the Lebanese political and paramilitary parties, Hassan Nasrallah has been the group's leader. Hezbollah has been identified a terrorist group by the Arab League, Canada, the Gulf Cooperation Council, Israel, and the United States. In 1982, the Israelis invaded Lebanon to support the Free Lebanon State and resulted in Israel's sieged of the South Lebanon strip, which was controlled by the South Lebanon Army. The group was established to amass the amount of Shi'a groups in the same region and serving as support for Iran in the Iran-Israeli conflict. Additionally, Hezbollah was founded to target the Israeli population and its objectives were to remove the Americans, the French, and their allies from Lebanon. Its manifesto stated the group was "ending any colonialist entity in their land, submission of Phalangists to just power and bring them to justice for the crimes they have perpetrated against Muslims and Christians and permitting all the sons of their people to choose the form of government they want, while calling on them to pick the option of Islamic government" (Bennett, 2017, p. 23). Hezbollah is sponsored by Syria and receives its monetary resources and training from Iran. They are responsible for the 10-year hostage crisis in Lebanon, the 1983 bombing of the U.S. Embassy in Lebanon, and the1994 Israeli Embassy bombing.

Al-Shabaab

A relatively young extremist, Salafist jihadist group, al-Shabaab was founded in 2006 in East Africa and led by Ahmed abdi Godane. In 2012, the group pledged allegiance to al Qaeda, and soon after, the two groups were in contentions over the partnership, resulting in al-Shabaab's setback. Al-Shabaab is a faction of the Islamic Courts Union and split into smaller units once the organization was defeated by Somalia's Transnational Federal Government and Ethiopian military allies. In 2015, the terrorist organization committed its deadliest attack when two armed members of its unit infiltrated the University of Northern Kenya, killing 147 people, wounding dozens, and holding hostage for a 15-hour standoff (Terror Attack Over, 147 Dead at Kenya University, 2015, para. 1). Its objective is to fight in the name of jihad against those who are enemies of Islam and deterring the military operations of Somalian forces has been designated as a terrorist group by Australia, Canada, the United Arab Emirates, the United Kingdom, and the United States. As of 2012, the U.S. State Department has open bounties on several of the group's senior commander (Mohr, Fear, & Sinclair, 2015, p. 159).

Hamas

Hamas or Harakat Al-Muqawama Al-Islamia is a Palestinian sociopolitical terrorist organization. Established in 1987, the group formed the Egyptian Muslim Brotherhood and has a social service called *Dawah* as well as a militant group, the Izz ad Din al-Qassam Brigades. The group's objective is carrying out jihad against Israel and procuring Palestine's freedom from Israeli occupation. In addition, Hamas strives to establish an Islamic State in Israel, particularly the West Bank and the Gaza Strip. The group has fought various wars with Israel in hopes of winning Palestine's freedom. Its military wing has launched numerous attacks against Israelis as retaliatory efforts, primarily assassination of Hamas' key leaders. The group has an alliance with Hezbollah in which the group funds Hamas' operations.

Kurdistan Worker's Party

The Kurdistan Worker's Party (PKK) is a Turkish group that is in Turkey, Iraq, Syria, and Iran. PKK has been known for its engagement is armed conflict with the Turkish and its objective is to have equal rights and Kurdish autonomy in Turkey. In 1978, the group was established by leader, Abdullah Ocalan and a group of Kurdish students. It sociopolitical objectives are predicated on revolutionary socialism and Kurdish nationalism, wanting its independence (known as Kurdistan) to be recognized by the Turkish state due to the oppression of Kurds within the region. The use of Kurdish language, dress, folklore, and names were banned in Kurdish-inhabitant areas. Also, the words, "Kurds," "Kurdistan," and "Kurdish," were officially banned by the Turkish government (Raw, 2011, p. 301). For those who violated Turkey's law were arrested and imprisoned and PKK was established in response to the oppression of the Kurdish people. The PKK have been engagement in full scale insurgencies with the Turkish state and its first uprising was on August 15, 1984. Though the group was considered a terrorist organization, it has changed its sociopolitical views from Marxism-Leninism to a democracy confederalism while stopping its propaganda for autonomy within the country. The PKK has been working with American lobbyist in Washington, D.C. to improve their positive image as advocacy organization for the support of Kurdish people.

Al-Nusra Front

On January 23, 2012, Al-Nusra Front was established and is a Salafist jihadist group that is known for fighting the Syrian government in the Syrian Civil War. Abu Mohammad al-Julani is the leader of Al-Nusra Front and his vision for the organization is to overthrow Bashar al-Assad's administration. The group received weapons from the United States because it opposes the Assad and the Islamic State (Fisher, 2016). The group was a subsidiary of al-Qaeda until the two organizations split in 2016. After the group's succession from al-Qaeda, they changed their name to Jabhat Fateh al-Sham. Their objective is to establish an Islamic State within Syria under Shari'a law. In 2015, Al Nusra Front became a highlighted terrorist group during the jihadist movement, the *Army of Conquest*, which siege large portions of Northwestern Syria. They have been dubbed as the most successful arm rebel forces (Ignatius, 2012, para. 2).

The United States, it allies, and security partners remain a high priority target against international terrorism. The global front to establish an Islamic State (eventually a world-wide caliphate) and/or other idealistic goals to dismantle Western civilization, is the main primary for most of the foreign terrorist organizations discussed in this chapter. Such groups pose a significant threat to homeland and national security as well as to our citizens living broad, jeopardizing the nation's global interests. Though the threat of terrorism originates from major parts of Middle Eastern cultures, ideologies, and religious sects, it is also deepened in Africa and Southeast Asia sociopolitical and idealist views. Not to mention terrorists who live in parts of the world such as the United States and Europe have committed attacks from these locales in support of and/or allegiance to foreign terrorist organizations within the geographical locations discussed. Modern terrorism has provided technological advancement of weaponry, terrorist cells, Internet capabilities, enhanced communication abilities, and social media to organize planned attacks from outside the scope of their headquartered locations and/or location of operations across the world. With the sustenance of illegal activities, support from respectable charities/organizations, the continued proliferation of weapons, and drug smuggling/trafficking, terrorists have significantly increased their operations, aggregating the number attacks as well as extremism, radicalism, and recruitment. The United States has endured major changes post September 11th to fight the Global War on Terrorism. Establishing fusion centers for increased information sharing and communication capabilities and working with federal law enforcement at all levels to coordinate efforts to deter the proliferation of terrorism (international domestic) has some significant elements in protecting the homeland. Establishing federal statutes to enforce responsibilities and regulations to protect the United States, strengthening American diplomacy and foreign affairs with our allies and security partners has been one of the primary responsibilities, yet challenging mission to protect the world from global violence, heinous crimes, and hatred. Finally, holding federal agencies accountable for preparedness and response methodologies to catastrophic disasters (natural or manmade) are the superior initiatives to protecting the homeland and its citizens.

DOMESTIC EXTREMISM AND FOREIGN TERRORIST ORGANIZATIONS

Because of the ambiguity of the term, domestic extremism has no official or legal definition. If domestic extremism cannot be defined, how can it be defended against? Defining the term is a critical attribute to preventing domestic terrorist attacks within the United States. **Domestic extremism** can be defined as a broad term to categorize and identify extremists, whether individuals or groups, who commit violent acts to terrorize or instill fear within the American government system and its citizens based on extreme views of governmental, idealistic, political, and religious interests.

Domestic extremists have different **ideologies** (system of beliefs and principles) and viewpoints, and their actions may result in violence, large-scale attacks, or possibly death. Such extremism is predicated on violent and radical ideologies. According to the Federal Bureau of Investigation, that the following have been identified as extremist groups:

- **Abortion extremism**
- **Anarchist extremism**
- **Animal rights and environmental extremism**
- **Militia extremism**
- **Sovereign-citizen extremism**
- **White supremacy extremism**

Also, it is appropriate to include homegrown terrorists and lone wolves, as such terrorists who have been known to conduct heinous attacks within the United States.

Abortion Extremists

Abortion extremists are individuals and/or groups who oppose abortion and vilify those who support it. Anti-abortionists, who have extreme views on abortion, have been identified as a domestic terrorist threat by the United States Department of Justice. Anti-abortion extremists are known to have committed acts of arson, attempted murder, assassination, assault, bombing, kidnapping, premeditated murder, and stalking. The first documented murder of an abortion doctor was in 1993. Michael Griffin claimed his intentions were to prevent Dr. David Gunn from performing abortions. Griffin was sentenced to life in prison. According to the Department of Justice, there is reportedly one exclusive anti-abortion extremist group in the United States, **The Army of God (AOG)**. AOG is a Christian terrorist group that has committed violence in response to anti-abortion laws, policies, and initiatives. The group was established in 1982, which was the year of its earliest documented attack. AOG is linked to numerous arsons, bombings, and murders. The group's website consists of numerous scriptures from the Bible that reference their mission on preserving life. The opening statement says:

> … He that hath no sword, let him sell his garment and buy one. Luke 22:26 Anyone who supports abortion has the blood of babies on their hands (n.d., para. 1).

Below are known members and associates of AOG:

- Michael Bray—minister and domestic terrorist, served 46 months for conspiracy and possession of explosives.
- Paul Jennings Hill—killed Dr. John Britton and James Barrett, executed by lethal injection on September 3, 2003.
- James Charles Kopp—domestic terrorist, killed Dr. Barnett Slepian, serving 25 years to life imprisonment.
- David Leach—anti-abortion activist.
- Scott Roeder—killed Dr. George Tiller, serving life in prison with possibility of parole in 50 years.
- Eric Robert Rudolph—domestic terrorist, known as Olympic Park Bomber, serving life in prison without possibility of parole.
- Shelly Shannon—shot Dr. George Tiller, wounding him in both arms, arson of abortion clinics, will be released in 2018.
- Donald Spitz—anti-abortion activist, spokesperson and webmaster for Army of God website.
- Fritz Springmeier—conspiracy theorist.
- Clayton Waagner—domestic terrorist, sentenced to nineteen years in prison.
- Robert Weiler, Jr.—arrested for planning to bomb Maryland abortion clinic, served five years in prison.

Such incidents included the kidnapping of Dr. Hector Zevallos, an abortion professional, and his wife. They were held hostage for eight days by three men claiming to be a part of AOG. They were released unharmed. In 1985, three men, including Michael Bray, planted bombs near seven abortion clinics in Maryland, Virginia, and Washington D.C.

The **Phineas Priesthood** consists of self-provoked vigilantes, who in addition to opposing abortion, dispute interracial relationships and marriages, mixing of races, and homosexuality. Phineas Priesthood is not considered an organization because there is not a governing body or a group of members of a hierarchical platform. An individual can simply become a Phineas Priest by adopting the beliefs derived from the book, *Vigilantes of Christendom: The Story of the Phineas Priesthood*. The movement was found to be involved in numerous clinic bombings that occurred in 1996.

Animal Rights and Environmental Extremists

For the past twenty years, radical movements in the defense of animal rights and environmentalism have caused more than $200 million in damages in the United States. Extremist incidents have increased with radicals establishing secret eco-terrorist cells within United States and abroad. Because such extremists are concerned with animal and environmental protections, they have targeted car dealerships, housing developments, medical research laboratories, restaurants, and other businesses that are responsible for polluting the environment, harmful testing, and death of animals.

Such extremists have been prevalent since the 1970s. Many groups supported animal and environmental rights, demanding strict protection laws to their liking. Some became so impatient with the legislative process that they began conducting violent attacks to make an ideological statement. Multiple violent acts eventually led to the establishment of terrorist organizations and clandestine cells within the county. Also known as eco-terrorists, radical crusaders operate in autonomous cells which are very difficult to detect and infiltrate. Well-known eco-terrorist organizations that have been acknowledged by the FBI are:

- Animal Liberation Front (ALF)
- Earth Liberation Front (ELF)
- Greenpeace
- Sea Shepherd Conservation Society
- People for Ethical Treatment of Animals (PETA)
- Earth First!
- The Coalition to Save the Preserves
- Hardesty Avengers

Animal Liberation Front (ALF)

Early traces of **Animal Liberation Front** formed in Great Britain when British journalist John Prestige watched hunters chase and kill pregnant deer during a Devon and Somerset Staghound event in England. Prestige condemned the actions and established the **Hunt Saboteurs Association**, and a subcomponent of it was named the **Band of Mercy**. By 1976, Clifford Goodman and Ronald Lee were arrested for raiding the Oxford Laboratory Animal Colonies in Oxfordshire, England, and sentenced to three years in prison. After serving twelve months, they were released and immediately recruited supporters, changing the name from Band of Mercy to the **Animal Liberation** Front to antagonize and plague those who abused animals.

ALF is an international extremist movement, operating in forty countries, and it is known to conduct illegal, **covert operations** (a concealed operation to mask the identity of those involved and the responsibilities) in pursuit of animal rights. Its supporters consider themselves modern-day vigilantes, taking animals from farms and laboratories to eradicate such infrastructures and prevent lab testing, slaughtering, and ill-treatment of animals. Because ALF groups are relatively small and embedded all over the world, it is difficult to trace and infiltrate their operations. On the ALF website, press officer for the movement Robin Webb said "That is why the ALF cannot smashed, it cannot be effectively infiltrated, it cannot be stopped. You, each and every one of you: You are ALF" (2007, para. 3). Overall, ALF activists claim to be low-threat and non-violent in terms of harming people. There is not a hierarchical system or membership process for ALF; thus, anyone who simply commits an attack or an act in support of ending abuse and exploitation of animals is automatically a part of the extremist movement. It is called **direct action**, which is "criminal activity designed to cause economic loss or to destroy victims' company operations or property" (Lewis, 2007, para. 5). ALF has escalated to coercion, intimidation, harassment, and threats of violence against testing laboratories where animals are held.

ALF became more prevalent within the United States in the late 1970s. Activists Freeman Wicklund and Kim Stallwood argued that operatives of ALF acted on American soil on May 29, 1977 when researchers Ken LeVasseur and Steve Lipman released two dolphins from the University of Hawaii Marine Mammal Laboratory. Two years later, activists related to the ALF movement raided the New York Medical Center and took a cat and couple of guinea pigs and dogs. A high-profile raid publicized in the media involved activists removing seventeen monkeys from the Silver Spring Laboratory due to suspected violations of animal cruelty for which the researcher was arrested. The monkeys disappeared and then returned once they were needed as evidence in the researcher's court case. Even though ALF is linked to arson and terrorist tactics, the organization has not hurt or killed anyone to date. John E. Lewis, Deputy Assistant Director of FBI, spoke before the Senate Judiciary Committee in Washington and said, "ALF has been linked to more than 1,100 criminal acts in the United States since 1976, resulting in damages conservatively estimated at approximately $110 million" (n.d., para. 4).

Earth Liberation Front (ELF)

The **Earth Liberation Front** is an extremist group that uses guerilla warfare tactics to mitigate the exploitation and destruction of the environment. Like ALF, ELF is an international crusade which does not have a hierarchical system, and it was founded in the United Kingdom around 1992. The movement allegedly has supporters and autonomous cells throughout seventeen countries and works closely with ALF because of similar interests and idealistic values. These groups have formed bilateral cooperation agreements to show support. Because of ELF's extreme violence, the FBI has classified it as one of the top domestic terror threats in 2001. ELF was labeled as a domestic terrorist group, and vigilantes were called "eco-terrorists." ELF's first act in the United States was the vandalism of McDonald's, a petrol station, and public relations office in Oregon on October 12, 1996. As noted in Steven Best and Anthony J. Nocella's book, *Igniting a Revolution: Voices in Defense of the Earth,* the vigilantes glued the locks and spray painted on the walls "504 YEARS OF GENOCIDE and ELF" on the buildings in Eugene (2006, p. 55). On December 25, 1996, ELF broke into a fur farm and removed about 150 minks in the Great Lakes area.

Greenpeace

Greenpeace is non-government organization which specializes in the protection of the global environment. The organization supports and has offices in over forty countries with a headquarters located in Amsterdam, Netherlands. According to the organization's website:

> Greenpeace is an "independent, campaigning organization which uses non-violent, creative confrontation to expose global environmental problems and to force the solutions which are essential to a green and peaceful future. Greenpeace's goal is to ensure the ability of the Earth to nurture life in all its diversity (2009, para. 20).

The organization is known as one of the most visible environmental organizations in the world. Even though its stated mission is to handle environmental affairs in a peaceful, non-violent manner, the organization has received criticism for some of its activities, including legal actions against Greenpeace activists and a highly-publicized event in which activists allegedly were responsible for destroying a genetically modified wheat laboratory. Greenpeace was established in the United States in 1975, and it is considered one of the largest environmental groups within the country. Greenpeace has not been reported to have committed any terrorist acts within the United States, but one incident involved Greenpeace activists damaging the Nazca Lines, which are in the southern region of Peru. In December 2014, crusaders reportedly entered a prohibited area and wrote in yellow letters, "Time for Change; the future is renewable." It was also reported there were strict compliance regulations, and government officials were not allowed within the area, and if so, must wear special shoes since the Nazca Lines are fragile, and footprints embedded can last for hundreds of years. The act was to demand increased governmental support for renewable-energy sources to mitigate climate change.

Sea Shepherd Conservation Society (SSCS)

The **Sea Shepherd Conservation Society** is a non-profit marine conservation located on San Juan Island, Washington. Like ALF, ELF, and Greenpeace, SSCS uses direct action strategies to safeguard marine life. Paul Watson, a former member of Greenpeace, established SSCS in 1977 when he left because he thought the organization did not use sufficient aggression for the cause. He immersed SSCS in public relations and media to spread its message, mission, and goals. In 2008, the organization received much publicity after it was a part of Animal Planet's series *Whale Wars*, showcasing its encounters with the Japanese whale fleet in the Southern Ocean (known as the **Antarctic Ocean**). Part of SSCS's direct action tactics involves interfering with fishing, whaling, and seal hunting. Such actions have been condemned by Greenpeace and by Australian and European governments, which labeled the group's actions as "terroristic activities." Even the Japanese government considers SSCS eco-terrorists, and U.S.

federal courts prohibited American SSCS members and Paul Watson from harassing Japanese whalers.

SSCS has been named in terrorist operations, in addition to the incident with the Japanese government and the whaling program. In 2002, the United States Congressional Committee received testimony (**The Threat of Eco-Terrorism**) from an FBI official that SSCS is the first organization to attack commercial fishing operations. There were also Canadian government intelligence reports suggesting that Paul Watson and other activists were involved in militant actions against whaling, drift net fishing, and seal hunting. They were accused of interrupting logging operatives and committing terroristic acts by preventing seal hunting operations and cutting drift nets.

Earth First!

In 1980, founders Dave Foreman, Mike Roselle, Howie Wolke, and Bart Koehler established **Earth First!** Created in the United States, the organization is considered a radical environmentalist organization and has offices in Europe, Central America, Africa, and Asia. Its ideologies are motivated by Edward Abbey's book *The Monkey Wrench Gang* and Rachael Carson's *Silent Spring.* All founders had a background in forestry, held environmental positions, and believed in the vital need to protect the environment. Their ideologies were imminent when the four decided to protect Mother Earth and that would be their campaign while traveling to a major biosphere reserve in Mexico. Leaders of Earth First! believed there should be a revolutionary movement to obtain a substantial amount of land within the United States for ecological preserves. The members believed this plan would modernize scientific concepts of conservation biology, which is a concept they believed conventional environmental groups were not working toward at the time.

Initially, Earth First! had a reasonable form of activism, such as forming marching protests and contacting politicians. By the 1990s, the organization adopted an anarchist political philosophy, which increased to extremism in many regions throughout the world. Founders believed that the organization would receive more attention if it established a mainstream leadership structure. ELF was created during the period of the Earth First! Movement, and the two groups worked closely together, especially during protests. Earth First! began protest movements during the time where trees were destroyed for timber sales in forests throughout the United States. Supporters chained themselves to trees, machinery, and inside offices to halt operations. In 1988, Mark Davis destroyed property at the Fairfield Snowbowl Ski Resort in Flagstaff, Arizona. According to Dean Kuipers, author of *Arizona: Earth's Last Roundup,* Davis used a torch to destroy the top pylon of one of the primary ski lifts at the resort, and he was arrested (1989). He was charged with conspiring to destroy the Diablo Canyon Nuclear Generating Facility, the Pablo Verde Nuclear Generating Station, and the Rocky Flats Nuclear Weapons Plant. He was sentenced to six years in federal prison. On August 10, 1991, Earth First! vandalized the Telluride Resort in Colorado, and operators were forced to close it due to the significant amount of damage received immediately after its opening that year. Perpetrators used chemicals to write messages on the golf course greens. Reports stated that messages such as "Earth First!," "Hayduke lives," and "Ron you pig," were written on eleven greens and some tee boxes on the resort's golf course. Hayduke was an eco-terrorist from Abbey's book, and authorities assumed that Ron Allred, the president and owner of Telluride Ski Report, was the group's target. Earth First! members were angered that the resort was built on wetlands as part of the mountainous development. In 1997, Earth First! members chained themselves to a redwood tree stump during the Head Waters Redwood protest, which was to protect the existing redwood trees from being logged by the Pacific Lumber Company.

The following decade, the organization was involved in many protests, primarily in the protection of forestry and environment destruction. Because their direct actions were physically manipulating companies and destroying infrastructure, they constantly faced law enforcement retribution. In addition to tree sitting, activists conducted street blockades, protests involving civil unrest, and sabotage of companies. Members became martyrs for their cause. For example, Earth First! member David Chain entered an unsafe part of the California forest to protest the cutting down of one of the state's oldest forestry sites. He died when a Pacific Lumber employee cut down a redwood tree, and it fell on him. One of the most highly publicized cases involved Earth First! activist Judi Bari. A bomb exploded while Bari and another member, Darryl Cherney, were inside a car. After the incident, the FBI arrested Bari and Cherney for transporting the bomb, which accidentally exploded. Bari argued that she did not have anything to do with the bomb; instead, extremists, who opposed her views, were responsible. The case was dropped due to lack of evidence, and Bari and Cherney sued the FBI, and they were awarded $4.4 million in damages in 2002. Bari would not live to see her lawsuit victory, as she died of breast cancer in 1997. The case remains unsolved. Even though the organization is known for **radicalism** (extreme beliefs or ideologies of those who through political, religious, or societal reform) in their actions to protect the environment, the group is not currently identified as a terrorist organization by the United States. However, its opponents have labeled the group as such.

The Coalition to Save the Preserves

Though under the radar, the **Coalition to Save the Preserves** is allegedly a group of mountain bikers that formed the organization in the early 2000s. The group's mission was (according to the Terrorism Research and Analysis Consortium, the group is currently inactive) to prevent housing developments in natural preserves in Arizona. Mark Sands, a former marketing and public relations executive, allegedly burned down a house that was being built in a Phoenix suburb. Sands made statements to news reporters that his initial intent was to conduct a small protest because the house would affect a jogging trail he frequently used. When Sands realized the owner had plans to rebuild, he started sending threatening messages to halt the construction. According to James Hibberd of the *New York Times*, Sands vandalized a construction site sign and wrote "'U Build–We Build Agin,' using the word 'we' and misspelling again" to have law enforcement believe it was children behind the arson and the message (2002, para. 10). He increased the number of arsons within the area, instilling fear in the public that an eco-terrorist was on the loose. Sands need for publicity and news coverage intensified because exposing his work through media chains was the ultimate power for his radical views. He gained notoriety for setting fires at construction sites for over a year, and he would write letters naming the Coalition to Save the Preserves accountable for the terrorist acts.

Local law enforcement requested assistance from the FBI, and surrounding communities raised reward money for anyone who had information on the terrorist activities.

Domestic Terrorism Section Chief, Counterterrorism Division of the FBI, James F. Jarboe testified before the Houses Resources Committee, Subcommittee on Forests and Forest Health, stating:

> The name of a group called the Coalition to Save the Preserves (CSP) surfaced in relation to a series of arsons that occurred in the Phoenix, Arizona area. These arsons targeted several new homes under construction near the North Phoenix Mountain Preserves. No direct connection was established between the CSP and ALF/ELF. However, the stated goal of CSP to stop development of previously undeveloped lands is similar to that of the ELF. The property damage associated with the arsons has been estimated to be in excess of $5 million (2002, para. 13).

According to Sands, the motives behind destroying housing and construction sites were to protect public land and prevent companies from destroying the preserves. The immediate attention his worked received gave him increased fuel to conduct more terrorist acts. He continued to hold Coalition to Save the Preserves responsible, stating the group was comprised of four mountain bikers to make the attacks more thrilling and increase publicity. He also vandalized construction sites by damaging company signs on site where he was caught and arrested. Mark Sands was dubbed as a **lone wolf** and lied to make the community believe it was an actual group of activists fighting to protect the preserves. He was sentenced to eighteen years in federal prison.

Anarchist Extremists

According to the FBI, **anarchist extremism** is a "belief that society should not have a government, laws, police, or any other authority" (2010, para. 2). Anarchism does not have set policies or a governing body of doctrine-related responsibilities. Because anarchist extremists do not believe in a governing body or ruling societies, their viewpoints are indicative of philosophical traditions. Considered a radical left-wing ideology, most lawful philosophical positions are comparable to anti-authoritarianism, anarchist communism, anarcho-syndicalism, collectivist anarchism, and mutualism. Their beliefs are legal and protected under the First Amendment and are usually low-threat and advocate through non-violence. However, some groups believe violence and excessive use of force is the key to promoting their views and beliefs. One of the first anarchist movements dates to 1919 when the FBI investigated numerous bombings within the United States. The following are anarchist extremist organizations that are active today:

- Anarchist Black Cross Federation
- Anarchist People of Color
- Bash Back!
- Capital Terminus Collective
- Common Struggle
- CrimetheInc

- Curious George Brigade
- Direct Action Anti-Authoritarians Collective
- Institute for Anarchist Studies
- Libertarian League
- Libertarian Workers' Group
- Love and Rage Revolutionary Anarchist Federation
- North Eastern Federation of Anarchist Communists
- RNC Welcoming Committee
- Unconventional Action
- The Vanguard Group
- Workers Solidarity Alliance

Currently, the FBI is concerned with anarchist extremist progression. According to the agency's website, multiple philosophical ideologies include "anti-capitalism, anti-global-ism, and anti-urbanization" (2010, para. 4). Also, the groups are known to be linked to eco-terrorist organizations known as "green anarchy" (Franks and Wilson, 2010, p. 162). Green anarchy is the sociopolitical concept of anarchism based on environmental matters. Like environmentalist terrorist organizations, anarchist extremists are not as sophisticated as structured terrorist groups and do not have a hierarchical leadership system. They are predicated on participating in protests involving large-scale environmental projects and political meetings. Anarchist extremists are known to oppose **Western civilization** (the study and modern culture of Europe and North America) and strategically target financial institutions, governments, law enforcement agencies, and multinational corporations. Such extremists have been involved in arson, bombings, riots, and vandalism. Modern threats of concern are the usage of Improvised Explosive Devices or IEDs.

Militia Extremists

Militia extremists are a faction of radicals who conduct military operations. Their radical actions include violence, such as military coups in attempts to overthrow the government. Militia extremists label themselves as "patriots" and believe governments are corrupt, so they believe they are conducting operations to protect the country, and they believe policymakers violate constitutional authority (n.d., para. 1). Because their radical idealism is based on the idea of a corrupt government or that the federal system fails to protect the country from international conflict and threats, they target those they believe are responsible, particularly judiciaries, police officers, public servants, and other law enforcement professionals. Many of these militia extremist organizations believe they are legitimate entities, sanctioned under federal laws and that others envision their causes as appropriate because they have the authority to rebel against governments they consider corrupt or incompetent. Extremists have built private organizations based on paramilitary operatives, and the earliest groups date to the early 1980s. In the 1990s, **Posee Comitatus** became a well-known group, having numerous conflicts with the American government. They rose to prominence, gaining recruits within all 50 states, and increased their membership to roughly 60,000 in the mid-1990s.

Considered a far-right crusade, militia extremists have been ostracized throughout history because modernized efforts expanded the conceptualization of liberal-type principles. Timothy McVeigh's plan for the Oklahoma City bombing was considered a militia movement due to his hatred toward the U.S. government due to its involvement in the Waco and Ruby Ridge Sieges. Despite the lack of a significant number of cases in the United States on militia extremism, the Department of Justice conducted an analysis of the likelihood of potential threats in the twenty-first century. They found no serious threat of recrudescence or retaliation among the nearly 900 militia groups at the time. There were a few conflicts during the 1990s, but attempts began to decline in the early 2000s. When the United States was heavily affected by the aftermath of 9/11 (the global financial crisis) and President Obama was re-elected, militia extremists re-emerged. For example, guerilla groups were responsible for the high-profile cases of the **2014 Bundy Standoff** and the **2016 Occupation of the Malheur National Wildlife Refuge**.

Table 7.1 Active Militia Extremist Organizations

3 Percenters	Arizona Border Recon
Huratee	Idaho Light Foot Militia
Michigan Militia	Militia of Montana
Missouri Militia	Ohio Defense Force
Pennsylvania Military Reserve	Texas Light Foot Militia

Radicalism

Radicalism is derived from the "radical movement," which was based on a lax political alliance by the British and Irish, who epitomized radical ideologies and assisted with the transformation of Whigs into the Liberal Party in the nineteenth century. The United Kingdom was responsible for radicalism when it mandated a system to use extreme methods for reforming the electoral system to expand the right to vote during this time. The idea of radicalism became acceptable and influenced the development of political liberalism, which later expanded throughout Europe. In the mid-nineteenth century, radicalism was introduced into American colonies when the country had tensions with the British to mandate better-quality governmental representation.

The word radicalism suggests a strong focus on a specific principle or ideology which surpasses traditional societal and governmental acceptances due to complex and extreme actions and/or movements. The concept is entirely assimilative and comprehensive to those who are predicated on such principles, and the intent is to spread a progressive form of human existence, beliefs, and innovation. The negative aspects of radicalism are intended to threaten universal laws and human existence based on extreme beliefs. Both perspectives of radicalism involve certain levels of violence and threats to specific targets, affirming results of truth through intense expression from euphoric divination to scientific research and scholarly debates. At any rate, the purpose of radicalism is to declare the sovereignty of a specific ideology or political fit and ensure it is consistent with the interpretation of an individual or group's human existence in the world.

The idea of radicalistic views may be misinterpreted based on the differences between radicalism and fanaticism. In terms of ideology, politics, and religion, fanaticism or zealotry has been identified as a form of permanent deference to a structure of radical ideals in pursuit of a systematic hierarchy of emotional and psychological platforms. The concept is committed to extreme causes (that can be viewed as radical) and is deeply rooted by emotional impressions, which is responsible for the attitudes and motives of zealots. Though zealotry is predicated on emotions, its form of expression is not indicative of the emotional compulsiveness seen in radicalism, which is blindsided by rational discipline. Cognitive thinking of radical concepts precedes the existence of three elements: 1) the expressive sentiment of radical thought is a methodical and moral decision, which is based on conjecture, 2) it is a facade to cover up the intent of true radicalistic themes, and 3) it is an insentient necessity for people or groups to form a peculiar form of action and expression.

The ideology of radicalism has derived from different factions of socially dysfunctional societies. Researchers believe there are other reasons for radicalism, but the displacement of societal structures was especially important because it enables the social structure of radicalism. Additionally, it is important to associate radicalism to the human mind because it is a psychological and emotional impression that is responsible for the actions (i.e. movements and violence) that have sometimes threatened the world. The Second President of the United States John Adams wrote in a letter to Thomas Jefferson on 1814 on "Radical Ideology and Human Imperfection":

> I never could understand the doctrine of the perfectibility of the human mind. Despotism, or unlimited sovereignty, or absolute power is the same in a majority of a popular assembly, an aristocratical council, an oligarchical junto, and a single emperor. Equally arbitrary, cruel, bloody, and in every respect diabolical. No man is more sensible than I am of the service to science...and liberty that would have been rendered by the [French] encyclopedists and economists by Voltaire, D'Alembert, Buffon, Diderot, Rousseau, La Lande, Frederic, and Catherine if they had possessed common sense. But they were all totally destitute of it. They seemed to believe that whole nations and continents had been changed in their principles, opinions, habits, and feelings by the sovereign grace of their almighty philosophy. They had not considered the force of early education on the minds of millions (Viereck, 2006, p. 117–118).

Radicalistic views were based on the perceptions of a mythical past and historical doctrine based on specific events that influenced the male population during the golden ages. Both viewpoints were considered controversial, but understanding one's mindset to visualize the principles of what is considered radicalism provoked an unspoken truth in what was considered a compelling need for profound doctrine. Such doctrine was motivated by frictions of systemized internal standards correlated with human experiences. Drastic beliefs and negative life experiences provoked displeasure with what was considered the "societal norm" and what was driven by man to formulate a doctrine based on radicalism and personal interest rather than a structure that would benefit all. Radicals' need to separate from society was very important, but it was very difficult as they were a small population of a large society, and as a result, they capitulated under sophisticated pressures to assimilate to the majority.

Some radicals relinquished their authoritarian standards, resulting in the positivity of philosophical evolution. On the other hand, those who maintained the ideals of radicalism needed innovative methods to bring awareness and action such as establishing movements. Such movements required supporters to shun societal norms and structured doctrine. As a result, these movements transformed into extremist organizations (extreme radical movements) and influenced major parts of society. Radicals established:

- Camaraderie among their organizations where faith and ideologies could be expressed freely
- Radical doctrine, separating its policies from universal law and societal frameworks
- Authoritative discipline to ascertain conduct, order to understand martyrdom, and suffrage, which were important aspects of the movement.

Modern Radicalism

Modernized radicalism originated from the constant attack on traditional attributes of the radicalism movement in terms of the hierarchical structure of corporate power that affected the liberal and political ideals of democracy. As early as the 1600s, during the Puritan Revolution, the fight for political and religious freedom in the Western Hemisphere coincided with the birth of modern democratic radicalism, causing major controversy. Later, religious radicalism would be secular during the Reformation period (Talmon, 1952). The new perspective of radicalism championed sovereignty among individuals and their rights. The democratic radical doctrine proclaimed that each person had the right to make decisions regarding his or her own life and other affairs (individual liberty). Political governance became another part of the doctrine and became an innovative part of the movement.

The Americans and French were among the first to show signs of modernized radicalism after the revolutions. Both countries did not show all sentiments of radicalism nor concentrate on extreme ideologies. According to Hackett Lewis (1992), author of *The European Dream of Progress and Enlightenment,* after the revolutions, there was a concentration on the ideals of enlightenment, which eventually developed into modern radicalism. Modern radicalism was based on five movements:

- Anarchism
- German idealism
- Jacobinism
- Philosophical radicalism
- Populism

Anarchism is based on theoretical assumptions that governments and laws are not necessary and supported societies based on voluntary cooperation from individuals and/or groups in a geographic location. William Godwin was responsible for the existence of philosophical anarchism (Stanford University, 2000), considered to be one of the most radical movements. His political stance emphasized that corrupt governments made society heavily dependent. He argued, "government is a corrupting force in society, perpetuating dependence and ignorance, but it will be rendered increasingly unnecessary and powerless by the gradual spread of knowledge and the expansion of the human understanding" (Stanford University, 2000, para. 1). Anarchism adopted economic reforms and as a result refused to participate in any governmental affairs.

German idealism was a German philosophical movement that began in the late 1700s to the early 1800s based on the ideologies of Immanuel Kant, Johann Fichte, Georg Hegel, and Friedrich Schelling. This philosophical movement was based on Kant's theory from *Critique of Pure Reason* which was closely associated with Romanticism and the Enlightenment eras. German idealism was predicated on aesthetics, epistemology, philosophy, metaphysics, morality, and political philosophy. Kant believed that these concepts would be an important asset to the general philosophical system, but Fichte, Hegel, and Schelling were more radical in thought. However, the four struggled to close the gap between empiricism and rationalism, and their efforts influenced the evolution of modern philosophy.

Jacobins (also known as Jacobinism era) were members of the Jacobin Club, which was a major influence of the revolutionary political movement during the French revolution. The club was known for its left-wing politics and had a significant involvement with the National Convention, eventually resulting in revolutionary dictatorship (the Committee of Public Safety and Committee of General Security). The movement also created a robust government where complex matters could be resolved. The Jacobins supported property rights and economic policies based on concepts that were more liberal in tone.

Philosophical radicalism was predicated on the philosophical minds of English political radicals during the eighteenth century. Members of the group included Jeremy Bentham, Charles Buller, George Grote, James Mill, John Mill, William Molesworth, Joseph Parkes, Francis Place, John Roebuck, and Edward Trelawny. Some of the members became radical members of Parliament and tried to exploit British publications to express their opinions. They did not support any philosophical aspects that included naturalism and were primarily interested in utilitarianism.

Populism is a form of political communication that is predicated on supporting the lives of ordinary people. This concept is very popular in democratic countries and is predicated on a political doctrine that supports those who are not considered part of the elite population. Populists are those who are members of any political party that represents the common people of a nation.

Sovereign Citizen Extremists

Known as the sovereign citizen movement, **sovereign citizen extremists** are primarily American critics, financial conspirators, and government conspirators. They do not believe in their government systems and only abide **common laws** (English customs and laws adopted by the United States) and do not consider themselves punishable under any court system, law, or governance. In addition, such extremists do not believe in the American dollar as well as subjection to legal limits. The Southern Poverty Law Center referenced sovereign citizens as follows: "Self-described sovereign citizens take the position that they are answerable to the natural law and are not subject to any statues or proceedings at the federal, state, or municipal levels, or that they do not recognize U.S. currency and that they are free of legal constraints" (n.d., para. 3).

Like militia extremists, sovereign extremists' ideologies and political stances evolved from the Posse Comitatus movement with teachings derived from William Gale, a Christian identity minister. He argued that the *Fourteenth Amendment* was created to transform sovereign citizens into federal citizens by offering assistances on behalf of the government. The citizens' stances on taxation conspiracies came from the **Christian Patriot** movement, a group of individuals who congregate in the belief of seeking God and influencing other advocates. Denouncing American currency and believing the government sacrifices its citizens as indemnity against foreign deficits is part of the **redemption movement**.

Because sovereign extremists recognize neither American government nor the criminal justice system, they have strong objections to taxation laws. They do not pay taxes. They generate their own currency, checks, and establish their own businesses, financial institutions, and government agencies. Researchers have argued that sovereign citizen extremists' movement guidelines and ideologies are comparable to the freeman on the land movement, which is very is common in Canada and the United Kingdom. According to the Law Society of British Columbia, sovereign citizens, "believe that all statute law is contractual and that law only governs them if they choose or consented to be governed" (n.d., para. 1). Because most sovereign citizens refuse to recognize American government as legitimate, their activists and public figures are highly criticized for their outspoken beliefs and emphatic rhetoric.

The FBI classifies some sovereign citizen extremists as domestic terrorists. The Southern Poverty Law Center estimates about 100,000 die-hard believers that have the capacity to become radical. According to the State of New Jersey's Office of Homeland and Preparedness, sovereign extremists have committed many violent acts with seventy percent of them targeting law enforcement. They are known to assault and murder government officials and have threatened judicial officials and law enforcement personnel. In 2015, surveys showed American law enforcement ranked sovereign citizen extremists more threatening than **Islamic extremism** (radical form of Islam that opposes democracy and Western civilization, and the universal law of mutual equality and respect for different faith and ideologies). The FBI considers sovereign extremists the third-largest threat within the United States.

White Supremacy Extremists

White supremacy extremists seek national dominance and believe they are the superior race. They are racists whose ideological postures are predicated on the belief that white people are superior in every aspect of characteristics, features, and traits to individuals of other cultural and racial backgrounds. Because they believe themselves to be superior, white people should have economic, political, and social control over all races. "White supremacy" is used in many academic studies to describe epithets of racial powers and to denote classification of structural and sociopolitical racism. White supremacy lexicon is indicative of historical, industrial, political, and social structures from the ideological viewpoint of white domination.

Various categories of white supremacism date to the seventeenth century. There are even determinations who is considered white and what races are not, particularly anyone who is not white and Jews. Such racial profiling influenced the anthropological disparities that shaped global and national relations toward the end of the ***Age of Enlightenment***. White supremacy dominated the United States in the nineteenth century and was responsible for restricting millions of non-whites during the slavery period. White dominance became the reason for state successions and the formulation of the ***Confederate States of America***.

Because white supremacy was prevalent in the United States in the early nineteenth century, it was common for non-whites to be barred from government office positions. The ***Naturalization Act of 1790*** ensured non-whites would not have privilege or acceptance because it barred them from U.S. citizenship, which an individual would need to hold government or political offices. The continuance of social and political injustice led to the ***Civil Rights Movement*** in the mid-1950s. In conjunction with the movement, sociologists were vocal on the stance of adamant division and segregation. For instance, demographics expert, professor, and sociologist Stephen Klineberg emphatically defended the social injustices in America by stating, "Northern Europeans are a superior subspecies of the white race," referencing U.S. Immigration laws and policies (Ludden, 2006, para. 3). The moment American history changed was when the Immigration and Nationality Act of 1965 legislation passed, giving entry to immigrants who were not of Northern Europe and German descent. This bill changed the demographic and cultures within the United States. With such a historical accomplishment, white supremacy still affected the lives of immigrants in North America. Interracial marriage was banned through anti-miscegenation laws in the late 1960s would be abolished through the United States Supreme Court in the case of ***Loving v. Virginia***. Interestingly, Native Americans were the first inhabitants of North America and had rights to the land before any immigrants arrived, but white supremacists believed Native Americans were obstacles to economic and political progression because of their claims and rights to U.S. land.

Most sociopolitical movements derived before the nineteenth century were based on ***Nordicism***, which is the ideology of the racial omnipotence of the Nordic culture. The dogma of racial separatism increased entering the nineteenth century, spreading throughout Europe, particularly Germany, where it concentrated on the division of white people. For example, author Madison Grant contends in his book *The Passing of the Great Race,* "Europeans who are not of Germanic origin but have Nordic characteristics such as blonde or red hair and blue, gray, green eyes, were a Nordic mixture and suitable for Nazism" (1916, p. 239). Nazi Germany propagated white supremacy based on the conceptual system of the *Aryan race* or *master race* for Germans, and was a term used to categorize racial alignment among other groups in the late nineteenth century.

Klu Klux Klan

The most prominent group to be associated with the white supremacist movement is the ***Klu Klux Klan***. The group is based on three idiosyncratic movements and is predominately Christian. In addition to Christianity, the group's ideals are centered on Nordicism, and they are against Catholic and Jewish (*anti-Semitic*) religions and cultures. The group is racially dependent on the color of a person's skin, and their ideological stances, such as racial segregation, are not necessarily based on religious viewpoints. The organization is known as a terrorist group because they use terrorism against those they oppose.

The first Klan was established in the late 1860s in Pulaski, Tennessee by military officers of the Confederate army. Initially formed as a social club, the group's initiatives and influence were derived from **Son of Malta**, from which the initiation process was adopted. The movement began as a small group and quickly expanded within the South, assuming the Klan name and using the same methods as other established groups before them. The name was derived from a combination of the Greek word *kyklos*, the idea of governments within a political progression, and Klan. It was considered a secret oath society, using extreme violence and acts of aggression to impose radical views. As the Klan expanded, so did its ideologies. The group quickly turned into an insurgent movement, encouraging defiance and white supremacy during the early to late 1870s. It became a clandestine vigilante group and targeted armies connected to and supporting emancipated slaves, using threats and violence. The Klan was known to kill African Americans and white Republicans, which led to the **Enforcement Acts** where the federal government prosecuted and suppressed Klan crimes. Some of the Klan's noted actions included driving African Americans out of politics and voting through terrorist threats, dominating political and government positions. In 1868, the KKK was responsible for injuring and murdering over 2,000 African Americans to subdue their voting rights in Louisiana. The Klan also established other chapters in the South, the *White League* and the *Red Shirts*, increasing white supremacy and designing their groups like insurgent guerrilla units.

The KKK established a national headquarters to be responsible for subsidiaries of the group. Since most of the members with the Klan were veterans, the organization used a military hierarchy and organized chapters in the Southern states. Even though it was austerely organized, all chapters were independent of another. Confederate General George Gordon was responsible for the creating the *Prescript*, a document that supported the white supremacy ideology. For members to be involved in the movement, everyone had to swear under oath the requirement outlined in the Prescript, and they would not be able to vote, which was referenced from the **Ironclad Oath**. Another general, Nathan Bedford Forrest, became **Grand Wizard** and declared himself the KKK's national leader. They wore full face masks and robes, hiding their identities and instilling fear through violent crusades against their opposition. Because their attacks were primarily committed at night, they called themselves the KKK night riders, asserting to be ghosts of Confederate soldiers.

In 1915, the second Klan movement formulized in Atlanta, Georgia, and a few years later established an innovative and systematized organization. The group adopted a business concept to generate a fraternal society, generate funding, and recruit members. The rise in white supremacy businesses quickly expanded throughout the states. Also, the second Klan was more vocal about ideological stances on refining American politics, condemning Catholic churches, expressing anti-Semitism, and demanding better accountability of prohibition. The organization outwardly conveyed its opposition to African Americans, Catholics, Jews, and Italians, threatening violence to those who disapproved their sociopolitical views. The second Klan proved better than the first, making national headlines and increasing its population. Near the 1930s, the society had roughly 4.5 million members. Corruption and criminal behavior caused tension in the group, and membership declined. By the early 1940s the second Klan diminished.

The third movement was established in the 1950s, and the name Klu Klux Klan became prominent. This evolution of the group generated new relationships and connections within law enforcement agencies and political offices. According to author Lorenzo Currie, the group formed alliances with police departments in Alabama and in government offices (2013, p. 60). Threats of violence and terrorism ensued to actual assassinations when members of the KKK were convicted of bombing children of the Baptist Church in Birmingham, Alabama in 1963. In addition, they were guilty of murdering civil rights personnel the following year. Even though the third Klan has been the most active, its membership is significantly lower than the first and second movements. Martin D. Nathan, et al. of Anti-Defamation League claims there are over 150 chapters with up to 5,000 members throughout the United States, and the group is prevalent in the Southern region and Midwest (2016, p. 1).

> *The Civil Rights Movement was an African American posture to end racial and social-political segregation and discrimination.*

> *Loving v. Virginia was a civil rights decision by the United States Supreme Court which overturned laws disallowing interracial marriages.*

Homegrown Terrorists

Known as domestic terrorism, **homegrown terrorism** refers to terrorist acts committed by citizens or permanent residents of a country without influence from international terrorist organizations with the goal of instilling fear in the population or government to express ideological, political, or religious objectives. Under the PATRIOT ACT, homegrown terrorism is defined as:

> Activities that (a) involve acts dangerous to human life that are a violation of the criminal laws of the United States or of any state; (b) appear to be intended (i) to intimidate or coerce a civilian population; (ii) to influence the policy of a government by intimidation or coercion; or (iii) to affect the conduct of a government by mass destruction, assassination, or kidnapping; and (c) occur primarily within the territorial jurisdiction of the United States (Cornell University, n.d., para. 1).

The concept is comparable to international terrorism and terrorism terminologies, but because the acts are committed on American soil or abroad against citizens, domestic terrorism clearly identifies the distinction. Additionally, because the attacks are homegrown, these terrorists imitate military and government ideologies, but the groups lack a hierarchical structure and operate independently. According to Laron K. Williams of the University of Missouri and Michael T. Koch and Jason M. Smith, as presented in *The Political Consequences of Terrorism: Terror Events, Casualties, and Government Duration,* homegrown terrorism has economic and political consequences, which is a narrower scope and area of responsibility than international terrorism operatives (2012, p. 1). The concept emerges from individuals attempting to overthrow the government or speaking to specific matters such as environmental dilapidation, racial and religious supremacy, political matter, or social justice. Additionally, homegrown terrorism is normally handled by law enforcement, falls under the advisement of the state or federal police, and requires little or no international involvement.

Referencing the United States, scholars and researchers have suggested home-grown terrorism has been around since the post-Cold War era. It was common for military conflicts to provoke non-state actors to conduct asymmetrical warfare operations after the war. Because American intelligence and law enforcement is highly competent, agencies could often uncover domestic terrorist plots before they were executed, but these incidents also served as a reminder that international adversaries were not the only enemy. Homegrown terrorism became heavily prevalent in the early 2000s after 9/11 when thousands of terrorist websites were established and drew supporters. As more websites were created on American network systems, it became apparent the United States has citizens who support terrorist operatives. Also, domestic terrorism became not just an individual effort, but Americans were found to be linked to international terrorist groups to accomplish their missions. Also, homegrown extremism such as eco- and agro-terrorists emerged during this time, posing an even more dangerous threat, as true intentions of destruction were not apparent. There are three categories of homegrown terrorism: **right-wing extremism**, **left-wing extremism**, and **special-interest terrorism**.

Right-wing Extremism

As previously stated, right-wing extremists' ideologies are predicated on racial supremacy and are anti-government, anti-regulatory, anti-Catholic, and anti-Semitic sentiment. Such extremists congregate in relatively small groups and use constitutional protections to voice their viewpoints. Their need to commit murders, violence, and destruction to advertise their radical viewpoints surpasses freedom of speech and assembly, forcing law enforcement intervention. However, some national extremist groups, including the Aryan Nation, the National Alliance, and the World Church of the Creator, pose a significant threat to national security. Faculty members of Liberty University Stephen R. Bowers and Stephen M. Parke state in their publication *Identification of Transnational Threats* that although efforts were made to reduce the role of racial supremacy within their political rhetoric, "racial-based hatred remains an integral component of these groups' core orientations" (2009, p. 9).

Left-wing Extremism

Next, left-wing extremists pose the same national security threat but have significant differences in sociopolitical views than right-wing extremists. For example, left-wing extremists are focused on revolutionary socialism and protecting citizens from capitalism and imperialism, and they believe they can accomplish such goals by involving themselves in the American government and political system. Because their beliefs were radicalized within the United States, they posed a domestic threat during the early 1960s. Their movement did not last too long as law enforcement disassembled such groups and the fall of communism in Eastern Europe heavily affected American values, diminishing political establishments and support.

Special-Interest Terrorism

Special-interest terrorism is more focused on political change and structure. The violence and emphatic movements of these groups are predicated on politically motivated acts that affect the American public, animals, the environment, society, and national conflict. Unlike right-wing and left-wing extremists, special interest terrorists are focused on a single issue rather than multiple ideological viewpoints. In addition, such groups commit acts to force society to change to its standards and ideologies, leading to extremist behavior. Most special interest terrorists are focused on abortion laws, environment, and nuclear technology, which have led to assassinations and bombings within the United States.

Testimony from Dale Watson, former Executive Assistant Director of the FBI over counterterrorism and counterintelligence, suggests that homegrown terrorism intensified after the September 11 attacks. He stated, "the terrorist attack of September 11, 2001, marked a dramatic escalation in a trend of more destructive terrorist attacks, which began in the 1980s" (2002, para. 2). He also gave damning statements in his testimony to the Senate Select Committee about how homegrown terrorism was very prevalent and indicated a threat to U.S. national security. He said, "... the United States faces significant challenges from domestic terrorists. In fact, between 1980 and 2000, the FBI recorded 335 incidents or suspected incidents of terrorism in this country" (2002, para. 5). An increase in domestic and international terrorism incarnated the realization the United States would continue to face significant national security concerns, and modernized adversarial efforts will only intensify the threat.

International Interests, Radicalism, and Training

Homegrown terrorists have more advantages than international groups due to logistical and geographical locations. Domestic extremists have inside knowledge and access to area that others would not. There are fewer issues with targeting certain cities, states, and infrastructures, and they have familiarity with customs, populations, and traditions. Having such advantage makes them valuable assets to international groups. For example, al-Qaeda and ISIS are aware of homegrown terrorists' knowledge and have recruited individuals or offered to form alliances to get those individuals to commit acts against their native land. This strategy is primarily indicative of American-Muslim influence and participation to establish single cells within the United States. Because terrorist operations are considered economical, the United States will always be a significant target for international terrorists.

No systematic road to extremism and radical ideologies exists among homegrown terrorists. They have diverse backgrounds from uneducated individuals to some of the most intelligent and affluent human beings. Author Cynthia Estella Quintero's argument in *A Typology of Homegrown Terrorist* says that homegrown terrorists are "individuals who act against their home nation, both through domestic and foreign criminal terrorist behavior" (2014, p. 3). She also notes that researchers have not been able to devise a demographic profile of homegrown terrorists nor provide an irrefutable set of factors to foresee radicalization (2014, p. 5). Socioeconomic factors such as upbringing, culture, traditions, financial status, education, and other influences are thought to be elements linked to radicalization. Profilers have developed common traits and behaviors to establish demographic attributes and can be considered pre-destined elements of radicalization, which law enforcement and military forces can use to detect, monitor, and prevent terrorist attacks. Furthermore, former CIA Operations officer Marc Sageman contends in his book *Leaderless Jihadi Terror Networks in the Twenty-First Century* that radicalization into terrorism is not necessarily a product of poverty, brainwashing, delinquency, illiteracy, educational deficiency, unemployment, lack of social responsibility, criminality, or mental illnesses (2008). An increase in homegrown terrorist recruitment is due to the Internet, news outlets, and social media. Internet and social media is deemed a primary factor in homegrown terrorism. International terrorist groups realize social networks and blog sites exacerbate radical beliefs, and they are considered crucial elements in the radicalization process.

The Internet has significantly increased radicalization objectives. According to scholar Daniel Koehler, author of *The Radical Online: Individualization Processes and the Role of the Internet,* the Internet is a major driving factor to establish and foster the development of radical contrast societies transmitting violent ideologies and translating them into political activism (2015, p. 116). Additionally, the Internet provides a platform for ideological development and training, individual radicalism, and information exchange. Finally, the Internet provides an environment for anonymous individuals to discuss radical and extremist views throughout virtual networks, to share information, to develop plans, and to establish targets. Training is an important component to radicalization. Homegrown terrorists who are connected to international terrorist groups go overseas to complete training, especially to countries such as Afghanistan, Iraq, or Syria, where extremism is prevalent. Homegrown terrorists will travel alone, as lone wolves, to achieve terrorist objectives rather than in groups, mitigating suspicion.

Lone Wolves

Lone wolves are individuals who commit terrorist acts and other forms of violence to accomplish economic, political, or religious goals. Such radicals are not connected to an organization or command structure and do not receive assistance from any terrorist group. However, lone wolves can be influenced by terrorist groups and believe in a group's ideological values or commit acts in support of terrorist leader or group. Lone wolves are considered unconventional terrorists, but they have significantly increased since the September 11 attacks. The terminology "lone wolf" was derived from white supremacists Alex Curtis and Tom Metzger. In the 1990s, they promoted and supported individual terrorist attacks and plots. Moreover, federal, state, and local law enforcement use the term to identify individuals who commit terrorist acts without assistance from terrorist organizations.

Because lone wolves work individually, it is difficult to counterattack their offensive. They do not affiliate with other individuals or groups, and they establish their own methods and tactics. Thus, intelligence and law enforcement find it difficult to gather data because lone wolves do not associate with or are not linked to organizations that are routinely surveillanced in counterterrorism measures. Lone wolves are a significant threat to the United States and have become a common form of terrorism. They have intelligently executed operations without adequate financial systems or training. Statistical data and academic information are lacking because of many discrepancies, but one thing many countries have in common are that lone wolves are on the rise. One of the most publicized lone wolf terrorist attacks was the 2009 Fort Hood Shooting.

2009 Fort Hood Shooting: Nidal Malik Hasan

On November 5, 2009, Nidal Malik Hasan, a U.S. Army major and military psychiatrist killed thirteen and injured thirty-two people. His actions were considered the deadliest lone-wolf attack on a U.S. military base in American history. Hasan's attack was committed through access, opportunity, and preparation, as he was a military officer and knew how to obtain resources and identify targets without detection.

Figure 7.1 Boots of the soldiers who died in the Fort Hood Shootings

Four months prior to the shootings, Hasan bought an FN five-seven semi-automatic pistol that he used in the shootings. According to Scott Huddleston of *My San Antonio*, Army Specialist William Gilbert said Hasan entered the store and requested "the most technologically advanced weapon on the market and the one with the highest standard magazine capacity" (2010, para. 1). The store manager and employee recommended the FN five-seven pistol. The following day, Hasan brought the gun, and a week later he purchased over 3,000 ammunition rounds and extra magazines.

The day of shooting, Hasan entered the **Soldier Readiness Processing Center (SRPC)**, a department where Army soldiers receive routine medical treatment prior to and upon return from deployment. He was expected to deploy with his unit and had been in the processing center numerous times to identify the building as his target. When Hasan entered SRPC, he asked to see Major Parrish, a military officer who had been assisting Hasan with his deployment preparations. As a soldier went down the hall to get Parrish, Hasan ran behind a desk and shouted, "Allahu Akbar (God is great)," and opened fire in the building. Army Captain John Gaffney and physician assistant Michael Cahill tried to stop Hasan, but they were shot and killed. Also, Army Reserve Specialist Logan Burnett attempted to stop him as well and was shot but lived. While Hasan walked through the building, an Army Specialist broke a window, and he and Major Parrish escaped through the back to the parking lot.

Hasan skipped over civilians and targeted uniformed soldiers throughout the building. Once he exited the SRPC, he encountered Sergeant Kimberly Munley, a civilian installation police officer. He shot at her, and she returned fire, getting hit by shrapnel when the bullet Hasan fired ricochet from a rain gutter. He shot at Munley two more times, knocking her to the ground. He removed her gun from her possession to prevent her from using the weapon. While Hasan was outside, soldiers secured the building to aid the shooting victims. Hasan continued to fire, wounding victims outside the building when another civilian installation police officer, Sergeant Mark Todd, engaged him, demanding he surrender. As Todd commanded him to drop his weapon, Hasan fired shots until he ran out of ammunition. Once Hasan ran out of bullets, he reached in his pocket for another magazine, and Todd shot him five times and handcuffed him once he fell to the ground. At the time he was handcuffed, Hasan fell unconscious. Hasan was paralyzed from his injuries.

Nidal Malik Hasan

Nidal Malik Hasan was born on September 8, 1970 in Arlington, Virginia to Palestinian parents who emigrated from al-Bireh in the West Bank of Israel to the United States in the early 1980s. He was raised a devout Muslim and was considered very faithful to his religion. He attended Wakefield High School in Arlington before his parents moved to Roanoke where he attended William Fleming High School. His family opened a Palestinian restaurant in Roanoke, and Hasan worked there with his brothers.

In 1988, Hasan joined the United States Army and after serving eight years as an enlisted soldier, he commissioned when he graduated from Virginia Tech in 1997. He was accepted into the Uniformed Services University of the Health Sciences (USUHS) program and earned a medical degree in 2003. He completed his medical internship and residency in psychiatry at Walter Reed Army Medical Hospital in Bethesda, Maryland. In 2009, after completing his internship, he went back to USUHS and earned a Master of Public Health and completed a two-year fellowship in Disaster and Preventative Psychiatry at the Center for Traumatic Stress. During this time, he was promoted from Captain to Major and was transferred to Fort Hood in the summer of 2009.

In hindsight, some negative issues that were considered warning signs about Hasan's behavior seemed to have been overlooked. After 9/11, he became increasing disturbed and had many confrontations with soldiers because of his opposition toward Operation Iraq Freedom and Operation Enduring Freedom contigencies. Before he transferred to Fort Hood, he received a poor performance evaluation. During his residency at Walter Reed Army Medical Center, he conducted a presentation that was considered controversial. Titled, *The Quranic World View as it Relates to Muslim in the U.S. Military*, Hasan emphatically expressed that the Department of Defense "should allow Muslim soldiers the option of being released as conscientious objectors to increase troop morale and decrease adverse events" (Jones, 2012, p. 359). Furthermore, the murders of two recruiters in Little Rock, Arkansas heavily affected Hasan. Former co-worker and retired Colonel Terry Lee mentioned that Hasan made peculiar statements because he did not support American presence in Afghanistan and Iraq. According to author Valerie Plaza in *American Mass Murders,* Hasan said, "Muslims should stand up and fight against the aggressor [the United States]" (2015, p. 206).

Hasan's family portrayed him as a loving and quiet man, who feared deploying because of the dreadful stories fellow soldiers told him as he treated them for therapy. He did not want to deploy and was often harassed by soldiers for expressing his views. Because he is Muslim, he did not want to deploy and face violence and possible death. At one point, he hired an attorney to devise a plan to separate from the Army and repay the government money spent for his enlistment, commission, and training provided. He also felt he was targeted because of his devout Islamic faith, but there was not any evidence to support such accusations. Those close to him did not know he expressed any extremist or radical Islamic views but knew he was very dedicated to his faith, even after his parents died. He was known to attend a mosque in Silver Spring, Maryland and sometimes frequented a mosque in Falls Church, Virginia. The imam in Silver Spring said Hasan was a committed solider and Muslim who yearned for a wife but was dedicated to his work. He was connected to the late Anwar al-Awalaki, who was imam of the Dar al-Hijrah mosque in Falls Church. Hasan had much contact with al-Awalaki, and after the shootings, his email interaction will the imam was investigated, but law enforcement officials found the communication was legitimate information for Hasan's research. Because of al-Awalaki's major influence on international, radical jihadis, Hasan's emails were intercepted by the FBI. In the aftermath, al-Awalaki was interviewed and denied having any connection or coerced Hasan to commit the shootings.

The Underwear Bomber: Umar Farouk Abdulmutallab

On December 25, 2009, Umar Farouk Abdulmutallab attempted to detonate an explosive, hiding the bomb in his underwear. After the incident, Abdulmutuallab confessed to the terrorist attack attempt, and it was found that **al-Qaeda in the Arabian Peninsula (AQAP)** was responsible for the plot. The group claimed to have trained him for the plot and provided the bomb he used in the airport. He was convicted of eight criminal counts, which included attempted murder of nearly 300 people and the attempted use of weapons of mass destruction. He was sentenced to four life terms plus fifty years without the possibility of parole.

Abdulmutallab came from a large, affluent family in Nigeria, as his father was a Chairman of the First Bank of Nigeria and the Nigerian Federal Commissioner for Economic Development. The youngest of sixteen children, Abdulmutallab was a gifted student and attended some of the most prestigious schools in Kaduna and Nairobi, Kenya. After he graduated high school, he attended University College London in 2005, seeking a degree in engineering and business finance. While attending the university, Abdulmutallab was president of the school's Islamic Society, an organization that was predicated on peaceful demonstrations against the United States Global War on Terrorism campaign. In 2007, he established "War on Terror Week" where attorneys, politicians, and motivational speakers attended to discuss jihadism and terrorism. Abdulmutallab would be the fourth president of the Islamic Society that would be arrested for terrorist acts over a three-year period.

In 2008, he earned a degree in mechanical engineering. Abdulmutallab was a devout Muslim and often detached himself from his friends and family. While he was in college, he also attended school at the San'a Institute for the Arabic Language in San'a, Yemen and often attended lectures at Iman University. Family members of Abdulmutallab stated his dedication to Islam conflicted with his family's business. According to Adam Nossiter of *The New York Times,* he did not support his father's professional career because he believed banking was "immoral" and "un-Islamic" for charging interest on customer and company accounts (2010, para. 2).

During Abdualmutallab's college years he became a person of interest to international intelligence agencies. He became a suspect by the United Kingdom's Military Intelligence, Section 5, known as **MI5**. The agency found that Abdulmutallab had suspected connections to Islamic extremists. In 2008, he received a multiple-entry visa from the American embassy in London, which was valid for two years and traveled to Houston, Texas for a couple of weeks in August. In 2009, Abdulmutallab was denied a visa to enter the United Kingdom because he was updated on the security watch list.

He attempted to enter the country to attend a program, which was later found to be fabricated. Later that year, it was discovered Anwar al-Awalaki, an AQAP member, was responsible for sending Abdulmutallab to al-Qaeda training in Yemen, and his cover story was that he was going back to attend San'a Institute for the Arabic Language. He did attend the Institute for a month before leaving but remained in Yemen where he attended lectures at Iman University.

Abdulmutallab's family became concerned when he decided not to finish his MBA program in Dubai and wanted to study *sharia* and Arabic in Yemen. His father did not approve and threatened to cut off his financial support, but Abdulmutallab was not interested since he was receiving assistance. According to authors Dominic Janes and Alex Houen in *Martyrdom and Terrorism: Pre-Modern to Contemporary Perspectives*, his final contact would be in October 2009 when he texted his father the following message:

> I've found a new religion, the real Islam; you should forget about me, I'm never coming back; please forgive me. I will no longer be in touch with you; and forgive me for any wrongdoing, I am no longer your child (2014, p. 233).

After he officially left the Institute, he met with a member of the AQAP to train in the Shabwah Province. There were videos found of Abdulmutallab training in the desert with other members prior to leaving Yemen. Officials stated Abdulmutallab's visa was two months past expired when he left Yemen for Ethiopia and then Ghana in December 2009. Ghanaian law enforcement stated that Abdulmutuallab was in the country from December 9 to December 24, one day before the attempted terrorist attack.

On December 25, 2009, Abdulmutallab left Ghana to Amsterdam where he boarded Northwest Airlines Flight 253, heading to Detroit, Michigan. He had a Nigerian passport with a U.S. tourist visa but attempted to pose as a Sudanese refugee. Officials stated Abdulmutallab went to the bathroom and stayed for roughly twenty minutes and then covered himself with a blanket when he returned to his seat. Witnesses stated they heard popping noises, and they realized Abdulmutallab's pants were on fire. Scott Shane and Eric Lipton of *The New York Times* said that Jasper Schuringa, a Dutch film director seated in the adjacent row on the opposite side of the aircraft jumped and subdued Abdulmutallab, attempted to put out the fire, and restrained him (2009, para. 5). Once flight attendants became aware of the incident, they used fire extinguishers to put out the fire. He was taken to the front of the aircraft until the culmination of the flight. It was found that he had an explosive device and was arrested at the Detroit Metropolitan Airport by U.S. Customs and Border Protection officers where he was turned over to the FBI.

After he went to the hospital for the burns he sustained, Abdulmutallab told FBI authorities he attempted to detonate an explosive device aboard the aircraft with direction from al-Qaeda. AQAP claimed responsibility for the attack. The motive was to retaliate against the United States for having American military presence in the opposition against al-Qaeda in Yemen. After questioning, he was sent to the **Federal Correctional Institution, Milan**, an American federal prison in York Charter Township, Michigan. On February 16, 2012, Abdulmutallab was sentenced to four life terms plus fifty years without the possibility of parole. He is currently held at the **United States**

Penitentiary, Administrative Maximum Facility
near Florence, Colorado.

In response to the "Underwear Bomber" attack, President Barack Obama made a public statement noting that those responsible for the attempted terrorist attack would be held accountable and demanded a review of detection and watch list procedures for suspected terrorists and groups. Also, restrictions were imposed on American travelers. Much criticism focused on how Abdulmutallab was not detected by security and how TSA agents failed to impose stricter security procedures that would have prevented him from boarding the flight.

This section includes the world's most dangerous terrorist leaders and organizations in addition to domestic groups that have committed crimes on American soil.

WORLD'S KNOWN TERRORISTS

Leader of the National Socialist German Workers Party—Adolf Hitler

Adolf Hitler was the Chancellor of Germany and leader of Nazi Germany from 1934 to 1945. His dictatorship and fascist ideologies lead to World War II, when he declared the Invasion of Poland in 1939. He was also responsible for the Holocaust in which six million Jews were killed. Hitler was born in Austria but moved to Germany when he was 24 years old and joined the German Army, participating in WWI. In 1919, he joined the German Workers' Party, which would later be transformed to the Nazi Party, and he would be leader by 1921. His first conflict as leader was the failed coup attempt in Munich to control the territory in 1923. He was captured and imprisoned for a year. After his release, he attacked the Treaty of Versailles, in which he gained popular support from Germany. His ideologies converted into anti-communism, anti-Semitism, Pan-Germanism, and Nazi propaganda. He was emphatic about his disapproval of international capitalism.

By 1933, the Nazi Party was the largest legislative body within the German government, and Hitler was elected as Chancellor. The Reichstag (the parliament) passed the *Enabling Act,* which gave Hitler the authority to pass laws without its involvement. Eventually, the Nazi Party became a one-party dictatorship predicated on the autocratic and totalitarian principles of National Socialism (Nazism). Hitler established a *New Order* (conquering areas in Europe and guaranteeing the supremacy of an Aryan-Nordic master race and the genocide of Jews). The New Order was in response to the injustices he believed happened after WWI by France and Great Britain. Though his terrorist ideas were apparent, he was successful in the expedient recovery of Germany from the Great Depression, annexation of large territories that belonged to the Germans, and catapulted restrictions imposed on Germany post-WWI, which gained him increased support from German citizens.

Fascism is an extreme form of authoritarianism government predicated on one-party dictatorship by an aggressive leader (i.e. anti-democracy).

The Holocaust was the genocide of six million Jews under Adolf Hitler's Nazi Party. The murder of the Jews took about two-thirds of the Jewish population within Europe. Millions of others were killed, totaling nearly eleven million that the Nazis believed to be "unworthy of life" (lebensunwertes Leben).

Hitler had imperialistic goals of expansion throughout Eastern Europe for the German people. His antagonistic views and strict foreign policy measures were the main reason for WWII, as his first order of business was to invade Poland. On September 1, 1939, Nazi Germany invaded Poland, which provoked France and Great Britain to declare war on Germany. Two years later, Hitler launched the invasion on the Soviet Union, and by the end of the year he declared war on the United States, as German military forces and its *Axis powers* had conquered most of North Africa and Europe. The Germans could not defeat the Soviet Union and the United States, and they suffered multiple defeats. On April 29, 1945, during the *Battle of Berlin*, Hitler married Eva Braun. The following day, both Hitler and Braun committed suicide to avoid capture by the *Soviet Red Army.*

Adolf Hitler epitomized the example of a terrorist, as his aggressive leadership and racially charged beliefs led to the murder of over six million Jews and over five million people that were considered "unworthy of life" (University of Michigan, n.d.). Overall, Hitler and the Nazi Party were responsible for nearly twenty million deaths during his reign. Approximately, thirty million soldiers and civilians died because of WWII, which is still the largest conflict and human death rate in world history today.

Premier and General Secretary of the Communist Party of the Soviet Union Joseph Stalin

Joseph Stalin was the dictator of the Soviet Union from 1929 to 1953. During this time, he would be Premier of the Soviet Union and General Secretary of the Central Committee of the Communist Party of the Soviet Union. Stalin's ideological background was predicated on Marxism and Leninism, which would eventually lead to "Stalinism." Stalin was born within the Russian Empire where he was influenced by Marxism. As a teenager, he joined the *Marxist Russian Social Democratic Labour Party*, where he was a devout member, editing the organization's newspaper and raising funds for the Bolsheviks. During his youth, he was arrested multiple times, causing him to flee. In 1917, the Bolsheviks gained authoritative power during the *October Revolution* (an insurgency that led to the Russian Revolution) and created a one-party state. After the revolution, Stalin became a member of the *Politburo* (administrative committee for Communist organizations) and assisted in formulizing the Soviet Union.

Stalin's decision to consolidate and become a one-party state increased his power throughout the Soviet Union. He was praised for establishing a "Marxism-Leninism" government through Lenin's *Communist International* faction (organization created to promote global communism) and heavily supported anti-fascist movements throughout Europe. However, the terrorist violence began when Stalin signed an agreement with Nazi German and assisted in the invasion of Poland. By 1945, the Soviet Union conquered Berlin, which was one of the victories that ended WWII. Post WWII, the Soviet Union and the United States became the superpowers of the world, and tensions ensued. The Soviet Union seized Estonia, Latvia, and Lithuania (the *Baltic States*) and promoted Soviet Marxist governments throughout China, Eastern Europe (the land Hitler wanted to control), North Korea, and North Vietnam. Meanwhile, tensions between the Soviet Union and the United States increased over the *Eastern Bloc* and the *Western Bloc* at the start of the Cold War.

Stalin was instrumental in leading the Soviet Union Reconstruction era, re-developing the country after the war. He was also responsible for the inception of the country's nuclear weapons programs. He was considered a very influential leader during his time, as he was accountable for spreading his ideological and political ideas throughout the world and fighting socialism within the working class. Today, he is considered one of the greatest wartime leaders of his time, and he helped the Soviet Union became a superpower. However, he was criticized for the deaths of millions through deprivation, labor camps, and repression. Stalin was directly responsible for the deaths of nearly twenty million during his reign as General Secretary, approximately 73 percent of the death toll from starvation. About one million were killed for political offenses and about ten million were deported or imprisoned.

President of Iraq— Saddam Hussein

Marxism is a set of ideologies derived from political theorist Karl Marx. Marxism simply suggests an economic and social system where production is not owned by an aristocratic system but instead by the producers themselves who have a means of production (i.e. anti-capitalism). It involved two class systems, those who have the means and those who do not, which provoked the struggle between those who do not have production rights vs. those who profit from it.

Leninism involved principles originated from Marxism and exploited by Bolshevik leader Vladimir Lenin. Leninism or Marxism-Leninism is an ideological system which promotes the vanguard party to formulate a workers' state to develop a socialist environment. Theoretically, this concept would eventually establish an ideal communist society.

The Eastern Bloc was considered the Eastern and Central parts of Europe and countries that were part of the Warsaw Pact were considered socialist states.

Saddam Hussein was the fifth President of Iraq for twenty-four years and was a senior member of the *Arab Socialist Ba'ath Party,* the *Baghdad-based Ba'ath Party,* and the *Iraqi Ba'ath Party*. He was born in Al-Awaja, Iraq, and his family were shepherds. His

The Western Bloc consisted of countries that supported NATO and were enemies of the Soviet Union and its coalition forces.

The Iraqi Interim Government was a provisional legislative body established by the United States and its coalition forces until Iraq established its new constitution and held its first National Assembly, which convened in 2005.

father left his family before his mother gave birth to him. His mother remarried and suffered abuse from his stepfather, forcing Saddam to flee his family and live with his uncle in Baghdad when he was ten years old. With the advice of his family, Hussein attended a nationalistic high school, and when he graduated, he attended law school. After three years of college, he left to join the pan-Arab Ba'ath Party and became a school teacher. The year after Hussein joined, the party participated in the Faisal II of Iraq coup, which he was responsible for orchestrating.

Initially, Hussein was the Vice President to General Ahmed Hassan al-Bakr and established a security forces regime, which was responsible for controlling tensions between the government and the military. He was also responsible for nationalizing oil industries to make a significant profit for the country. However, when state-owned banks were under his control, most of them bankrupted due to the various wars (i.e. Iran-Iraq and the Gulf War), not to mention United Nation sanctions. In the 1970s, Hussein's reigned as the oil industry heavily profited Iraq, boosting the economy precipitously. During this time, Sunni Muslims had significant power within the government, even though they were a small population within the country. He oppressed the Shia and Kurdish, as he believed the groups threatened to overthrow the government or obtain autonomy. As a result, he was heavily criticized for his aggressive dictatorship. Under Saddam Hussein's leadership, over 250,000 Iraqi citizens succumbed to genocide at the hands of the government's security services.

In 2003, the United States invaded Iraq to overthrow Saddam Hussein due to incorrect intelligence that the country had weapons of mass destruction and was supportive of al-Qaeda, the group responsible for the September 11 attacks. On December 13, 2003, Hussein was captured, arrested, and sent to trial through Iraq's Interim Government. On November 5, 2005, Hussein was found guilty of "crimes against humanity related to the killing of 148 Iraqi Shi'ites and was sentenced to death by hanging" (Semple, 2006, para. 1). He was executed on December 30, 2006.

Founder of al-Qaeda, Osama bin Laden

Osama bin Laden was the founder and leader of al-Qaeda and one of the deadliest terrorists in the world. He was responsible for the September 11 attacks against the United States. Born in 1957, bin Laden came from a wealthy Saudi Arabian family, as his father, Mohammed bin Awad bin Laden was a multi-billionaire and founder of the Saudi Binladin Group. He was raised a strict Sunni Muslim but studied at secular schools when he was younger. He was in the college and was very interested in studying religion when he joined the Mujahideen forces in Pakistan fighting against the Soviet Union in 1979. By 1988, he established al-Qaeda, and when the group was identified as a terrorist organization, he was permanently banished from Saudi Arabia. In 1996, he established his organization base in Sudan, but the United States forced his operations out the country. He would then move al-Qaeda to Afghanistan and declare war on the United States through numerous bombings. Bin Laden and his advisor and physician Ayman al-Zawahiri were identified for their involvement in the 1998 U.S. embassy bombings and were placed on the FBI's Ten Most Wanted Fugitives and Most Wanted Terrorists lists (FBI, 2008).

Bin Laden's ideological views were based on the theory that jihadists had a right to kill anyone who was a member of an enemy country. He had a hatred for the United States because he felt the nation's foreign policy "oppressed, killed, and harmed Muslims in the Middle East … they hate us for what we do, not who we are" (Roychoudhury, 2013, p. 101). He condemned the United States' Western philosophies and secular form of government. He even emphatically spoke that the Islamic world was facing catastrophe and the only way to resolve it was the complete restoration of Sharia law. He supported violent jihadism against the United States, as the nation was responsible for the oppression of the global Muslim community. He desired the annihilation of the Israeli state (he was heavily anti-Semitic) and demanded that the United States withdraw forces from the Middle East and every Islamic country in the world. After the September 11 attacks, Osama bin Laden was wanted by the United States because he was a prominent figure in the War on Terror. He was placed on the FBI bounty list, and a $25 million bounty was placed on him (Rooney, 2011). On May 2, 2011, Osama bin Laden was killed inside a Pakistani compound in Abbottabad in clandestine operations by the United States Naval Special Warfare Development Group and the CIA, ordered by President Barack Obama.

Leader of al-Qaeda—Ayman al-Zawahiri

Ayman al-Zawahiri is the current leader of al-Qaeda and has been the leader since the death of Osama bin Laden. Zawahiri was born in Cairo, Egypt in 1951 to an affluent and prestigious family. He was considered a distinguished, intelligent, and shy individual who excelled in school and was a fan of poetry. He was an activist and very political as a teenager, studying politics under his uncle Mahfouz Assam. By 14 years of age, al-Zawahiri became a member of the Muslim Brotherhood, listening to sermons of Islamic theorist and leading member of the Muslim Brotherhood Sayyid Qutb discussing the restoration of Islam. The following year, Qutb was executed by the Egyptian government for conspiracy. Al-Zawahiri and some friends formulated an underground cell to overthrow the government and create an Islamic state. He began the mission to carry out Qutb's ideological views, and he would eventually merge his cell to establish *Egyptian Islamic Jihad*.

In 1974, he went to medical school at Cairo University, and when he graduated, he became a surgeon for the Egyptian Army for three years. Once he transitioned from the army, he opened his own practice in Maadi, Egypt. In 1978, he earned another medical degree in surgery, and seven years later, he moved to Saudi Arabia to practice medicine for a year, where he would meet Osama bin Laden. His organization, Egyptian Islamic Jihad, merged with al-Qaeda, and al-Zawahiri became Osama bin Laden's advisor and physician. Al-Zawahiri's organization would be responsible for, implicated in, or involved in many terrorist attacks in Egypt (*assassination of President Anwar Sadat, suicide bombing and attempted assassination of Egyptian Interior Minister Hasan al-Alfi, and assassination attempt of Egyptian Prime Minister Atef Sidqi*), Pakistan (*1995 attack on Egyptian embassy in Islamabad, Pakistan, Operation Silence, assassination of Prime Minister Benazir Bhutto*), Sudan (*execution of senior leader of Jabhat Fateh al-Sham's sons*), and the United States (*1998 U.S. embassy bombings and USS Cole bombing*). The State Department has established a $25 million-dollar reward for intelligence or capture of al-Zawahiri since 2011. He is currently under worldwide sanctions by the al-Qaida Sanctions Committee (United Nations [UN], n.d.).

Leader of al-Nursa Front—Abu Mohammad al-Julani

Abu Mohammad al-Julani is the leader of the Syrian Islamic extremist group al-Nursa Front, also known as Jabhat al-Nursa. This group is a Syrian subsidiary of al-Qaeda. Born Ahmad Hussain al-Sharaa, al-Julani grew up in Al-Rafid, Syria in Golan Heights before moving to Damascus in his later years. His father was heavily involved in the oil industry and eventually moved to Saudi Arabia to expand his profession. He moved back to Syria and opened a business in Damascus. Abu Mohammad al-Julani attended the University of Damascus, studying media, but then the Iraqi conflict interrupted his education, and as a result, he left school and joined the insurgency in Iraq (*Middle East Journal*, 2017, para. 2).

When al-Julani left to fight in the invasion of Iraq (U.S.-led), he rapidly rose through the ranks of al-Qaeda. In 2006, the leader of al-Qaeda, Abu Musab al-Zarqawi, was killed by an American airstrike, which forced al-Julani to leave Iraq and go back to Lebanon. There, he provided support to the militant group Jund al-Sham and then returned to Iraq where he was arrested by American forces and detained at Camp Bucca. He was released in 2008 and rejoined his insurgent work with leader of ISIL (then Islamic State of Iraq) Abu Bakr al-Baghdadi. He would then be appointed as leader of ISI operations. After leading ISI operations, al-Julani was heavily involved in the Syrian uprising against Bashar al-Assad, planning logistics and operational missions. He formed a subdivision within Syria called Jabhat al-Nursa to play the supporting role for ISI forces located back in Iraq. Al-Baghdadi supported all Jabhat al-Nursa's operations, and al-Julani was appointed the leader of Jabhat al-Nursa. By the end of 2012, the State Department designated Jabhat al-Nursa as a terrorist group.

Tensions grew between al-Baghdadi and al-Julani because the leader of al-Qaeda would no longer identify al-Nursa as a subdivision of ISI (now ISIL), removing all local sovereignty of its leaders, logistics, and political decisions. This meant that al-Julani would lose some of his leadership power and al-Baghdadi would have sole control of Jabhat al-Nursa. To prevent this from happening, al-Julani pledged allegiance to Ayman al-Zawahiri, leader of al-Qaeda, to be an independent organization. Al-Baghdadi rejected al-Julani's allegiance and mandated the consolidation of both groups, which resulted in a fight for controlling regions in Syria. The organization has increased its operations in Syria and became a prominent figure within the country, as it mostly comprised of Syrian insurgents fighting for the cause.

Leader of Hezbollah, Hassan Nasrallah

Hassan Nasrallah is the Secretary General of the terrorist organization Hezbollah, which is geographically located in Lebanon. In 1960, Nasrallah was born into a *Shia* family in an eastern suburb of Beirut, Lebanon. Hassan grew up with a significant interest in theological studies, though his parents were not religious. In 1975, during the *Lebanese Civil War*, Nasrallah and his family were forced to move to Bazourieh, where he attended secondary school. There he became interested in politics and joined the *Amal Movement*, which was a Lebanese Shia political organization. Extending his theological interest, Hassan studied at the Shia seminary in Baalbek, Lebanon and Islamic studies at the Shiite seminary in Iraq. During his study in Iraq, he was forced to move back to Lebanon, as Sadaam Hussein banished Shias in the late 1970s. When he returned to Lebanon, he went back to school and taught politics for the Amal Movement organization. Amal's leader, Abbas al-Musawi, later appointed him as a political delegate, and he became the first member to hold a central office for the organization.

In 1982, Nasrallah joined Hezbollah after the Israeli invasion of Lebanon and quickly became significant within the group for his emphatic sermons. After joining the group, Nasrallah would travel throughout Iran to further his theology studies. In 1992, when co-founder, leader, and Secretary General of Hezbollah Abbas Moussawi was killed in an Israeli missile attack, Nasrallah became the new leader. During his reign in the early 1990s, Nasrallah acquired long-range missiles to attack the northern region of Israel, even though Israel occupied southern regions of Lebanon. In 1993, Israel executed *Operation Accountability,* which was a seven-day attack on Lebanon, targeting Hezbollah to mitigate their mission of using southern Lebanon as a striking base. In the aftermath, a significant portion of Lebanon's infrastructure was obliterated. Hezbollah requested an agreement with the Israeli government to end the attacks, resulting in Hezbollah ceasing fire in northern Israel. By 1996, Israel launched another attack, *Operation Grapes of Wrath*, in response to Hezbollah's continued attacks in northern Israel. As a result, the Israelis blocked significant harbor cities and bombed a Syrian base. When the operation ended sixteen days later, both parties signed the *Israeli-Lebanese Ceasefire Understanding.*

By 2000, Israel removed its forces from Lebanon, and Hassan was highly praised for culminating Israel's occupation of southern Lebanon, which greatly increased the group's political standing within the Lebanese government (Al Jazeera, 2006). He is also responsible for the prisoner exchange arrangement between Israel and Hezbollah in 2004. Hezbollah was responsible for the Lebanon War when it ambushed regions of Israel, killing three soldiers and kidnapping two. Nasrallah was condemned by Arab countries and some of the population in Lebanon for the unexpected attack on Israel, and they were emphatic they did not support Hezbollah's terrorist actions. Also, the group joined the Syrian Civil War stating it would wage war "against Islamic extremists and pledged Hezbollah would not allow Syrian militants to control areas that border Lebanon" (Mroue, 2013, para. 2).

Shia is a major subdivision of Islam where it is interpreted that the Islamic prophet Muhammad appointed Ali inb Abi Talib as his successor, who is the first Imam.

Leader of ISIS, Abu Bakr al-Baghdadi

Abu Bakr al-Baghdadi is currently the leader of the Islamic State of Iraq and the Levant (ISIL), a Sunni Salafi jihadi extremist terrorist organization. In 2014, al-Baghdadi was elected to be *caliph* (chief religious ruler, successor to Muhammad) of the Islamic State (McCants, 2015). Under this self-proclaimed title, al-Baghdadi believes he is a worldwide caliphate and claims military, political, and religious authority over all Muslims throughout the world. In 1971, al-Baghdadi was born Ibrahim Awwad Ibrahim Ali Muhammad al-Badri al-Samarrai in Iraq. Growing up, he was considered very intelligent, introverted, quiet, and most importantly, nonviolent. He earned B.A., MA., and Ph.D. degrees in Islamic studies from the University of Baghdad and used his religious intelligence to his advantage.

Al-Baghdadi was prominent during the reign of Saddam Hussein, and when the United States invaded Iraq in 2003, al-Baghdadi formed the group *Jamaat Jaysh Ahl A-Sunnah wa-l-Jamaah* (JJASJ), a militant group charged with fighting American troops. The following year, U.S. forces arrested al-Baghdadi and sent him to Abu Ghraib and Camp Bucca. By the end of 2004, he was released as mandated by the Combined Review and Release Board, as he was not considered a threat at the time (Zelin, 2014). By 2006, he joined and served on the Mujhideen Shura Council as a shari committee member. Later that year, the committee's name would be transformed to the Islamic State of Iraq (ISI), and al-Baghdadi became a senior member of the consultative council. ISI was a regional division of al-Qaeda.

On May 16, 2010, al-Baghdadi was appointed as the leader of ISI when its leader, Abu Omar al-Baghdadi, was killed in a joint American-Iraqi operation a month prior. Under his leadership, ISIS was responsible for 23 terrorist attacks in Baghdad in one year, including the 2011 suicide bombing at the Umm al-Qura Mosque. One month later, Osama bin Laden would be killed by U.S. Special Forces in Abbottabad, Pakistan, resulting in al-Baghdadi retaliation against the United States.

In 2013, ISI expanded into Syria and al-Baghdadi remained its leader, but appropriately for its new territory, the group was renamed the Islamic State of Iraq and the Levant (ISIL), or the Islamic State in Iraq and Syria (ISIS). Al-Baghdadi made this announcement of the new merge as well as al-Nursa Front's (also known as Jabhat al-Nursa) merge with the terrorist group. Al-Nursa Front's leader, Abu Mohammad al-Julani detested the merge, resulting in al-Qaeda's current leader, Ayman al-Zawahri, requesting al-Baghdadi should disappear and that ISI should maintain its control in Iraq. Al-Baghdadi ignored al-Zawahiri's request and took over eighty percent of al-Nursa Front's soldiers (Stanford University, 2017). By 2014, ISIL banished al-Nursa Front from Raqqa, Syria and al-Qaeda cut all ties with ISIL. ISIL captured Iraqi cities Fallujah, Hit, and Mosul, controlling most of the Anbar Province. The group also annexed Algeria, Libya, Egypt, North Caucasus, Pakistan, Saudi Arabia, and Yemen (DoS, 2015).

Al-Baghdadi is responsible for the enslavement, kidnapping, and rape of American Kayla Mueller. She was eventually killed by ISIS in early 2015, while the terrorist group claimed she was killed in a Jordanian airstrike against Syria. The group currently controls several countries and was identified as a terrorist organization by the European Union, NATO, and the United States. In 2011, the State Department identified al-Baghdadi as a terrorist and added him to the Specially Designated Nationals Lists and offered ten million dollars for his capture (Roggio, 2017). Five year later the reward was increased to $25 million (Ansari, 2016).

Leader of Boko Haram, Abukar Shekau

Abukar Shekau is the leader of Boko Haram, an Islamic extremist terrorist group based in Nigeria. Established in 2002, Mohammed Yusuf founded the terrorist organization based on Salafism and Islamic fundamentalism. When Yusuf was killed in the Boko Haram uprising in 2009, Shekau, who was then the deputy leader to Yusuf, became the new leader. In March 2015, Shekau pledged alliance to ISIS leader Abu Bakr al-Baghdadi. For the past seven years, there have been on-and-off again rumors about Shekau's death and alleged body doubles. In 2009, Nigerian law enforcement believed Shekau was killed during a battle between Nigerian security forces and Boko Haram. However, in the summer 2010, a video surfaced with Shekau maintaining his leadership within the terrorist group. Since their largest insurgency in 2009, Boko Haram is responsible for the murder of 20,000 people and diaspora of over two million. As of 2015, the Global Terrorism Index has dubbed Boko Haram as the "most deadly terrorist group in the world" (p. 2).

Shekau is known to be an intellectual who speaks four languages, including English, and has a sense of indestructability. He has spent several years provoking propaganda of his radical beliefs and taunting the public about how he will never be stopped. In 2013, Shekau made a video threatening the United States after he discussed the mosque attack which killed forty-four Nigerians (CNN, 2013). The year prior, the State Department identified Abukar Shekau as a terrorist and froze his assets in the United States (BBC News, 2012). In 2014, Shekau's most notable terrorist attack was the kidnapping of over 200 girls from the Government Secondary School in Chibok, Nigeria (Abubakar, 2017). Since 2013, the State Department has a $7 million reward for anyone who has information on the whereabouts of Abukar Shekau (DoS, 2013). In 2016, ISIS appointed Mohommed Yusuf's son Abu Musab al-Barnawi as the leader of Boko Haram to replace Shekau.

> *Salafism jihadism is a multinational religious ideology predicated on the objective perception of jihadism and the Salafi movement.*

Foreign Terrorist Organizations

Table 7.2 World's Dangerous Terrorist Organizations

Abu Nidal Organization (ANO)	Ansar al-Islam (AAI)
Abu Sayyaf Group (ASG)	Continuity Irish Republican Army (CIRCA)
Aum Shinrikyo (AUM)	Islamic State of Iraq and the Levant
Basque Fatherland and Liberty (ETA)	Islamic Jihad Union (IJU)
Gama'a al-Islamiyya (IG)	Harakat ul-Jihad-i-Islami/Bangladesh (HUJI-B)
HAMAS	Al-Shabab
Harakat ul-Mujahidin (HUM)	Revolutionary Struggle (RS)
Hezbollah	Kata'ib Hizbollah (KH)
Kahane Chai (Kach)	Al-Qaida in the Arabian Peninsula (AQAP)
Kurdistan Workers Party (PKK)	Harakat ul-Jihad-i-Islami (HUJI)

(Continued)

Liberation Tigers of Tamil Eelam (LTTE)	Tehrik-e Taliban Pakistan (TTP)
National Liberation Party (ELN)	Jundallah
Palestine Liberation Front (PLF)	Army of Islam (AOI)
Palestinian Islamic Jihad (PIJ)	Indian Mujahedeen (IM)
Popular Front for the Liberation of Palestine (PFLF)	Jemaah Anshorut Tauhid (JAT)
PFLP-General Command (PFLP-GC)	Abdallah Azzam Brigades (AAB)
Revolutionary Armed Forces of Columbia (FARC)	Haqqani Network (HQN)
Revolutionary People's Liberation Party/Front (DHKP/C)	Ansar al-Dine (AAD)
Shining Path (SL)	Boko Haram
Al-Qaeda	Ansaru
Islamic Movement of Uzbekistan (IMU)	Al-Mulathamun Battalion
Real Irish Republican Army (RIRA)	Ansar al-Shari'a in Benghazi
Jaish-e-Mohammed (JEM)	Ansar al-Shari'a in Darnah
Lashkar-e Tayyiba (LeT)	Ansar al-Shari'a in Tunisia
Al-Aqsa Martyrs Brigade (AAMB)	ISIL Sinai Province
Asbat al-Ansar (AAA)	Al-Nursah Front
Al-Aqida in the Islamic Maghreb (AQIM)	Mujahidin Shura Council in the Environs of Jerusalem (MSC)
Communist Party of the Philippines/New People's Army (CPP/NPA)	Jaysh Rijal al-Tariq al Naqshabandi (JRTN)
Jamaah Islamiya (JI)	ISIL-Khorasan (ISIL-K)
Islamic State of Iraq and the Levent's Branch in Libya	al-Qaida in the Indian Subcontinent

BOSTON MARATHON BOMBING: 2013

The 117th annual Boston Marathon convened on April 15, 2013 (**Patriots' Day in Massachusetts**). About 23,000 marathoners participated in one of the largest events in Massachusetts. Around 2:50 p.m., two bombs detonated near the finish line (with over 5,500 runners still in the race), killing three and injuring more than 260 people. The FBI was the leading agency on the case and received assistance from the CIA, DEA, and the Bureau of the Alcohol, Tobacco, Firearms, and Explosives. The agencies named two suspects who were responsible for the bombing: Tamerlan and Dzhokhar Tsarnaev. Authorities learned that the two suspects, who were originally from the Soviet Republic of Kyrgyzstan, had moved to the United States approximately ten years before the bombing. They were responsible for the planning and execution of the terrorist plot based on their own personal ideological values. They claimed to have not been connected to any terrorist organization, though their planning materials and influence were based on well-known groups such as al-Qaeda. According to the federal government, no intelligence reported a possible attack prior to the bombing, but leading officials stated that there had been meetings one week with no information on possible terrorist attacks. Boston and the surrounding cities where officially on lockdown while federal and local authorities actively searched for the suspects.

Tamerlan Tsarnaev

Tamerlan Anzorovich Tsarnaev was born on October 21, 1986 in the Kalmyk Autonomous Soviet Socialist Republic, which was a part of the Soviet Union. He was of Chechen and Avar descent and was raised as Muslim by his parents. He has one brother (terrorist Dzhokhar Tsarnaev) and two sisters. Before moving to the United States in 2004, Tamerlan and his family lived in Kyrgyzstan and Dagestan, Russian Federation. By the spring of 2002, Tsarnaev's parents, Anzor and Zubeidat, went to the United States on a three-month tourist visa, where Anzor applied for **political asylum** (protections granted by a country to a foreigner who has left his/her native land as a political refugee) because he feared his family was in danger for having ties to Chechnya. His parents received asylum, and Tsarnaev and his siblings moved to the United States two years later. The family moved to Cambridge, Massachusetts, where they were constantly transitioning, as they could not find stable work. Anzor was a mechanic and Zubeidat was a cosmetologist. They all received permanent residency in the United States in 2007.

Tamerlan attended high school at Cambridge Rindge and Latin School. After graduating high school, he applied to the University of Massachusetts and was rejected, so he attended Bunker Hill Community College where he studied accounting. He ultimately wanted to be an engineer, but dropped out to work on a boxing career. Tamerlan was a strict Muslim and did not have relationships with those who did not practice Islam. By 2008, he was a radical extremist and consumed himself with attending religious services at the Islamic Society of Boston. Even though he became an extremist, he was still involved in boxing and trained at the Wai Kru Mixed Martial Arts Center, and the following year, he won the New England Golden Gloves heavyweight championship. Tamerlan was known for having an abusive temperament. He assaulted his brother-in-law for allegedly abusing his sister and was arrested for aggravated domestic assault and battery against his live-in girlfriend. Tamerlan's uncle was concerned about his increasing radicalism and believed he was influenced by a converted Muslim.

Tamerlan wanted to obtain U.S. citizenship, so he could compete for the Olympic boxing team. However, his radicalism distracted him, as he believed Americans did not have any values and could not control themselves, delaying his process. By 2010, he had a new girlfriend, Katherine Russell, who dropped out of college when she became pregnant with their first child. After the two began dating, Russell converted to Islam and adopted the Muslim name Karima. They married on June 21, 2010. It was not until the end of 2010 that Tamerlan came under the security radar when he was detained by Dagestan authorities. A few months later, the Russian Federal Security Service told the FBI that Tamerlan was a radical extremist, and he planned to leave the United States for Russia to join unknown groups. The FBI interviewed Tamerlan and his family members and did not find any links to terrorist group or activities.

Despite the warning to the FBI, Tamerlan traveled to Russia for six months before returning to the United States. During his time in Russia, his father claimed Tamerlan only visited relatives, but homeland security officials believed that he completed training and thus became radical. Also, Russian authorities conducted surveillance and found that he was meeting with individuals who were linked to Islamic militants and terrorist groups, particularly al-Qaeda and the Caucasus Emirate. It was reported that Tamerlan attempted to join an Islamic insurgency but when his associates were killed, he returned to the United States. Tamerlan stated his reason for returning to Russia was to obtain a new Russian passport, so authorities were suspicious when he tried to leave without waiting for it. Tamerlan returned to the United States on July 17, 2012 and applied for citizenship on September 5, 2012, but the application was delayed because of the 2011 FBI interview.

Dzhokhar Tsarnaev

Dzhokhar Anzorovich Tsarnaev was born on July 22, 1993 in Tokmok, Krgyzstan. Shortly after his birth, the Tsarnaevs emigrated to Russia and then moved to the United States under political asylum when he was eight years old. Though his brother was not officially a U.S. citizen by the time of the bombings, Dzhokhar received his U.S. citizenship on September 11, 2012. He also attended high school at Cambridge Rindge and Latin School and was a wrestler. He was an all-star for the Greater Boston League and a lifeguard at Harvard University. Unlike Tamerlan, Dzhokhar was accepted at the University of Massachusetts, Dartmouth, and majored in marine biology. He seemed to have a different personality from his older brother, as he was not political, seemed to be sociable, and liked secular music. His peers described him as popular and could not comprehend that he was on one of the terrorists in the Boston Marathon bombings.

Dzhokhar's social media seemed rather "normal," as he posted everyday information that other teenagers would. Though he did post his Islamic views on a Russian website, it was reported that his views were not as radical as his brother's. He did express his opinions on independence for Chechnya and discussed the Syrian Civil War on his social media account. He did not show any radical extremism like his brother, but he did struggle in college, failing a few classes, and he owed thousands of dollars of student debt. Students stated that he was known to sell marijuana to pay his bills. A year before the bombings authorities found a radical Quran verse on his Twitter feed.

The Aftermath

Authorities found remnants of the bombs in the aftermath of the attacks. There were pieces of a pressure cooker bomb loaded with shrapnel and other explosive materials which were left in one of the backpacks. The suspects left the backpacks in the crowd, and both detonated within seconds of each other. After the bombs exploded, over 1,000 law enforcement authorities were activated to respond. After the attack, FBI analysts identified the Tsarnaev brothers through photographs, security cameras, and videos. Initially, the brothers' names were not known, so the FBI released images to the media, asking for public assistance on identifying them. When the brothers were identified, they forced law enforcement on a four-day exhaustive and high-threat search. During the interim of the chase, the brothers attempted to steal police officer Sean Collier's weapon and killed him. Authorities later linked them to the officer's murder, and it led to a hostage crisis. The oldest brother, Tamerlan, carjacked an individual driving an SUV and forced

Figure 7.2 Aftermath of the Boston Marathon Bombing, April 15, 2013

him to withdraw money from an ATM to flee to New York City. The brothers planned on detonating a bomb in Times Square. During this time, younger brother Dzhokhar followed them in a Honda Civic. The hostage escaped and notified law enforcement when the brothers stopped at a gas station in Cambridge. An important tip the hostage gave authorities was that his cell phone was still in the SUV, and it could be tracked. Hours later, authorities found both vehicles and a shootout ensued between them and the brothers. Police officers captured Tamerlan, who was fatally shot, but Dzhokhar took the SUV, driving towards the officers, accidentally running over his brother. He fled the scene, and Tamerlan was pronounced dead at the hospital. On April 19, 2013, Boston and surrounding cities were on lockdown until Dzhokhar was captured. Later that evening a Watertown resident found Dzhokhar seriously wounded in his docked boat and immediately notified law enforcement. He was arrested without incident. While hiding in the boat, the younger brother wrote a note that said the Boston Marathon bombings were in response the American wars in Muslim countries. On April 22, 2013, Dzhokhar was charged with using and conspiring to use a weapon of mass destruction, resulting in death and the destruction of critical infrastructures. Overall, Tsarnaev had thirty charges against him. On April 13, 2015, he was found guilty on all charges and a month later was sentenced to death by lethal injection.

SAN BERNARDINO ATTACKS: 2015

On December 2, 2015, terrorists Syed Rizwan Farook and his wife Tashfeen Malik attacked the San Bernardino County Department of Public Health training event and Christmas party, killing fourteen people and injuring twenty-two others. Farook was an American-Pakistni, who worked at the department as a health inspector, and his wife was a Pakistani-born permanent resident of the United States. Farook and Malik were prime examples of homegrown violent extremists and were heavily influenced by foreign terrorist organizations such as al-Qaeda. News outlets reported the couple became radicalized years before the attacks and were angered by Western civilization and the evolution of the Internet, which they considered "poison." They constantly expressed their jihadism and martyrdom to each other in private messages, and such communication formulated their plan to make a statement on behalf of their idealistic viewpoints. The San Bernardino Shooting was the deadliest attack since the Sandy Hook Elementary School shootings and the deadliest terrorist attack since 9/11 until the 2016 Orlando Nightclub shooting.

The day of the attacks, the couple left their six-month-old daughter with Farook's mother, stating they were going to a doctor's appointment. They traveled to the San Bernardino County Department of Public Health where Farook's office was holding a training event followed by a Christmas party. According to employee witnesses, the shooting began when the training session was transitioning to the party. Approximately eighty employees and their guests attended. Additional reports showed Farook attended the events around 8:30 a.m. and stayed a couple of hours before he left, leaving a laptop on the table. Before 11:00 a.m., there was an unplanned break due to technical difficulties, and that is when Farook and Malik began shooting outside the building, killing two people. Armed with semi-automatic weapons, face masks, and militant gear, the couple immediately entered the building and fired more than one hundred shots before leaving the scene. During the shooting, people escaped to other parts of the building, but one of the bullets hit a fire sprinkler, making it difficult for victims to see. Before Farook fled the scene, he left three explosive devices, which were pipe bombs assembled with Christmas lights and a remote-control car. All explosives failed to detonate, which saved many lives.

Police officers responded a little over three minutes after the shooting to the first emergency call. Four San Bernardino officers arrived to clear the building of the suspects. Four officers from the San Bernardino and Fontana Police Departments arrived minutes later to assist with clearing the building. Finally, the FBI's **Special Weapon and Tactics (SWAT)** team arrived nearly ten minutes after the emergency call, as they were conducting field training nearby. Officers established temporary triage centers to treat victims before sending them to the hospital. In total, over 300 law enforcement officers from neighboring counties were called to assist. During the chaos, an FBI SWAT team officer found the three explosives and had them detonated by a bomb squad later that evening.

While victims were treated and law officers completed their investigations, the Department of Homeland Security sent a surveillance aircraft to search for the terrorists. Victims told authorities they heard Farook's voice as one of the shooters and claimed he was assisted by a female, who authorities assumed to be his wife. They also learned Farook rented a black SUV days before for the shooting. Detectives went to Farook and Malik's residence for surveillance, and ten minutes later they were seen leaving the residence, which provoked a high-speed chase pursuit. During the chase, one of the perpetrators, thought to be Malik, threw what assumed to be a pipe bomb at officers on the highway. Farook exited the highway onto North Tippecanoe Avenue and stopped to put on gear and weapons. As an observing officer noticed the activity, the vehicle was seen turning on East San Bernardino Avenue, when Malik, who was in the back seat, started shooting at police. Decisively, Malik opened the door and shot at the first stopped police vehicle. Farook followed suit, exited out the driver's side of the vehicle, and fired shots at the police. As both terrorists fired shots, officers continued to reposition themselves to avoid direct hits. Finally, one police officer shot Farook, hitting him in the right side. He fell to the ground, shot in the legs and upper body. As he lay on the ground, he continued to shoot, injuring a police officer. He was shot several times before he died. After Farook's dead body was handcuffed, police officers continued to fire at Malik, who returned fire, injuring another police officer. Authorities used a police vehicle as a shield to rescue the second wounded officer. Malik was killed a few minutes later. Overall, the shootout lasted approximately five minutes; two police officers were wounded, and both terrorists were killed. Farook suffered twenty-six gunshot wounds, and Malik died from fifteen.

Farook and Malik were inspired by Islamic extremism and terrorist organizations. Reports showed both emphatically expressed their views of jihadism and martyrdom to each other in private messages. Their intentions were premeditated as intelligence reports showed that the two had been planning the attack for about a year. Former FBI Director James B. Comey stated Farook and Malik were radicalized and influenced by terrorist groups, but there was not any evidence that suggested that they were linked to any cell or specific organization.

Syed Rizwan Farook

Syed Rizwan Farook was born on June 14, 1987 in Chicago, Illinois and his parents were Pakistani immigrants. According to news reports, Farook grew up in an abusive household, as his father was violent toward his mother. Due to the violence, he had a troubled childhood but managed to have a decent life after the family moved to California. He graduated from La Sierra High School and attended California State University San Bernardino where he earned a bachelor's degree in environmental health. He was hired as a food inspector for the San Bernardino County Department of Public Health and had been there for five years. For some time, he was a temporary employee, but he was eventually hired permanently as an environmental health specialist and health inspector. He was considered nice, polite, and did not have a suspicious or awkward demeanor. Farook was a devout Muslim and often traveled to Saudi Arabia to complete *hajj*. He attended prayer services twice a day at the Islamic Center of Riverside. It was reported that after he married Malik, he stopped attending services. Farook's father was interviewed after the shootings and said that his son was obsessed with Israel and that he adopted al-Baghdadi's stance on establishing an Islamic state.

Tashfeen Malik

Tashfeen Malik was born on July 13, 1986 in Karor Lal Esan, Pakistan, but grew up in Saudi Arabia. She came from an affluent family who had political ties in her birth town. Malik attended Bahauddin Zakariya University in Multan, Pakistan, and graduated with a degree in pharmacology in 2012. In the aftermath of the San Bernardino shootings, Saudi Arabian official denied that Malik lived there and claimed that she only visited the country. While studying in Multan, Malik attended the **Al-Huda International Seminary**. She enrolled in the center's 18-month course, but left after a little more than a year to marry Farook. Experts stated that al-Huda courses were for educated, affluent women, teaching them a conservative form of Islam. It is said that such academics in the courses makes women who attend very judgmental and opinionated about those around them. Al-Huda teaches anti-Western views and borderline practices that could have them condemn non-believers. Administrators of the course stated that they do not condone violence or terrorist acts.

Supposedly, Malik met Farook over the Internet, and they married about a month after Farook traveled to Saudi Arabia in 2014. According to public record, Malik and Farook married on August 16, 2014 in Riverside, California. Malik entered the United States on a K-1 visa with a Pakistani passport. Farook completed Malik's permanent residency application in September 2014, which was issued in July 2015. For Malik to prove a legitimate marriage, she went through extensive criminal and national security background screenings. She had to complete two interviews with the consular in Pakistan and an immigration officer in the United States when she applied for a green card. During this process, there were not any indications of terrorist connections or political and religious extremism (even thought it was speculated that she had links to radical **Red Mosque**). She also was a devout Muslim; estranged family members stated that she grew up in a liberal and progressive Muslim movement, but she became radicalized when she moved to Saudi Arabia.

ORLANDO NIGHTCLUB SHOOTING: 2016

Considered the deadliest terrorist attack since 9/11, the Orlando Nightclub shooting claimed the lives of forty-nine people and wounded fifty-three others. The attack was also identified as a hate crime, as the terrorist targeted Pulse, a gay nightclub. Federal authorities stated the terrorist attack/hate crime was the deadliest mass shooting by a single individual in American history. On June 11, 2016, Pulse was hosting Latin night, which convened every Saturday, and the population is primarily Hispanic. The night of the massacre, it was reported over three hundred people were inside the club and bartenders were serving last call drinks around 2:00 a.m. Authorities said shooter Omar Mateen drove a van to the club and walked in the club, bypassing an off-duty Orlando police officer who worked there as a part-time security guard. Once Mateen entered the club, he began shooting individuals. Two police officers were inside and approached Mateen, which provoked a hostage situation.

Omar Mir Seddique Mateen

Omar Mir Seddique Mateen was born on November 16, 1986 in New Hyde Park, New York. His parents emigrated to the United States from Afghanistan in the 1980s. A few years after his birth, the family moved to Port St. Lucie, Florida. He grew up in a traditional Muslim household, and his family denounced radical views and acts of terrorism. Mateen showed signs of violence at an early age. According to reports, he was verbally abusive, aggressive, hyperactive, and rude in elementary school. One of his third-grade teachers stated Mateen talked about sex and violence and did not seem to get along with his peers. By the time Mateen was in junior high, he was transferred to different classes to avoid conflicts with his classmates. Because of his behavioral problems, he did not excel in his academics. He was known as a bully and disrespected female classmates. Some students said Mateen was bullied because of his Afghan heritage and weight. Teachers sent letters to parents, discussing Mateen's uncontrollable behavior, but his parents were unconcerned about their son's transgressions and did little control his behavior. Furthermore, teachers said that Seddique Mateen, Omar's father, was disrespectful to female teachers and argued about the complaints they had against his son.

By high school, Mateen was expelled from school for fighting in his math class. He was arrested for his actions, but the charges were subsequently dropped. According to Holbrook Mohr and Mitch Weiss of the Associated Press, Former Dean of Martin County High School Dan Alley made statements that the school "tried to counsel him and show him the error of his ways, but they never had the effect that we were hoping for." The Dean also stated that Mr. Mateen "would not back up the school and would always take his son's side." Due to his expulsion from Martin County High School, he was transferred to Spectrum, an alternative school for students with behavioral issues. Reports said that Mateen attended Spectrum during 9/11. He praised the terrorists for the attacks against the United States. Mateen claimed Osama bin Laden was his uncle and that bin Laden taught him how to shoot an AK-47 before it was made public bin Laden was the mastermind behind the attacks. He was suspended for five days for the incident, and his punishment was a slap in the face by his father. He was also expelled from St. Lucie West Centennial High School for fighting. Between junior high and high school, he transferred to various schools due to his expulsions and suspensions. By the time Mateen graduated from the Stuart Adult Vocation School in Martin County, he had been suspended forty-eight days from various school for fighting and injuring other students. In 2006, Mateen graduated from Indian Rivers State College with an associate degree in criminal justice. The same year, he was hired as a recruit for the Martin Correctional Institution through the Florida Department of Corrections.

In recruit training, there were red flags about Mateen's behavior as an adolescent. He admitted to experimenting with marijuana and explained why he was arrested at Martin County High School. While he was in training, the Virginia Tech shooting was highly publicized in the media and was a topic for discussion in class. Mateen admitted that he would bring a gun to class, and such statements made officers suspicious. Nearly two weeks after his comment about the shootings, Mateen was involuntarily dismissed from the program and did not become a licensed correctional officer. By the end of the 2007, he was hired to work for G4S Secure Solution as an armed security guard. The company stated Mateen's background screenings did not raise any red flags. However, after he was hired by G4S, he was removed from an assignment for threatening one of his co-workers. He supposedly threatened a deputy and said that he would have al-Qaeda kill his family. Mateen claimed he made the statement in anger because his co-workers were making racist comments towards him. Despite the incident, the company kept him, and he was transferred to a different assignment at a gated community in Palm Beach County. Excluding Mateen's past, he qualified for a concealed weapon carry permit, armed guard security license, and passed a medical clearance. He passed all background investigations and did not have an adult criminal record.

In 2009, Mateen married Sitora Yusufiy, an Uzbekistan woman he met on the Myspace social media account. After four months of marriage, they separated and divorced in 2011. The same year, he married his second wife, Noor Salman, whom he met on an online dating website. Of Palestinian Arab descent, Salman grew up in Rodeo, California. She moved to Florida with Mateen in 2012, and by 2015, they separated, and she moved back to Rodeo with her family. They have a son together.

There was speculation that Mateen may have been gay or bisexual. A former friend mentioned that the two hung out and that Mateen discussed dating. They would even frequent gay clubs together, and he was seen dancing with a man. Mateen was known to visit Pulse prior to the shootings and would sit by himself and drink. Another witness stated he had seen Mateen outside of the club an hour before the shootings and that he was texting him on a gay application called *Jack'd*. Sources stated his first ex-wife witnessed Mateen's father calling him gay and stated to her former fiancé that he had "gay tendencies." Nonetheless, FBI authorities have yet to find evidence proving such statements are valid.

Over one hundred police officers from the Orlando Police Department and Orange County Sheriff's office plus about eighty emergency medical services and fire personnel from the Orlando Fire Department were called to assist. Because Mateen created a hostage incident, victims were barricaded inside, including those who were wounded. It was difficult to maneuver about the club with the lack of light and loud music. A bouncer, who was a Marine veteran, opened a latched door allowing about seventy people to escape. Approximately sixteen people were hiding in the bathroom, and Mateen fired shots through the closed door, killing two people and wounding several others. He went inside another bathroom and opened fired, injuring additional patrons. When Mateen's rifle jammed, he switched to a handgun and continued to fire in the club.

Mateen barricaded himself in the bathroom. There was initial fire between Mateen, a security guard, and six police officers. Mateen stuck his head out the window, and officers shot at him. After the incident, Mateen did not fire any more shots, so officers were ordered to stand down, and the FBI SWAT team took over. Orlando Police Chief John Mina stated Mateen went from being an active shooter to a barricaded gunman with hostages. He also stated if Mateen continued to fire at officers, they would have entered the premises. Hostage negotiators spoke with Mateen three times, and he told authorities had strapped explosives to four victims, and they were strategically placed within the club. Fifteen minutes later, officers ended negotiations with Mateen. After 5:00 a.m., Mateen entered a women's bathroom and started shooting, killing a man who used his body as a shield to protect the women behind him. Minutes later, the SWAT team breached the infrastructure and drove a *BearCat* armored vehicle through the wall, shooting Mateen. By 5:14 a.m., police officers shot Mateen eight times, and he died. At 5:53 a.m., the Orlando Police department posted on Twitter, "Pulse Shooting: The shooter inside the club is dead."

Link to Terrorist Groups

While working at G4S Secure Solutions, Mateen told co-workers that his family had ties to al-Qaeda and that he pledged allegiance to **Hezbollah**. Allegedly, he also pledged allegiance to the **Islamic State of Iraq and the Levent (ISIL)** during the shootings. Furthermore, there were claims that he supported a suicide bomber who represented **al-Nursa Front**, a subsidiary of al-Qaeda in Syria, which is an enemy of ISIL. Reports indicated many contradictions as to which terrorist organizations he supported, and when the FBI interviewed him, he stated he made such claims because his co-workers were teasing him. During the ongoing investigation, he was placed on the FBI's terror watch list. Throughout the investigation, authorities could not determine how involved Mateen was with ISIL or al-Nursa Front. Nearly a year later, his investigation was closed, and he was not considered a threat. In 2014, Mateen became a subject of interest again when he was connected to Moner Mohammad Abu Salha, a Palestinian-Italian American who traveled to Syria and committed a suicide bombing in the name of al-Nursa Front. Abu Salha was the first known American suicide bomber to die in Syria. Mateen and Abu Salha attended the same mosque and were acquaintances.

Motive

Mateen claimed he was inspired by the Moner Mohammad Abu Salha suicide bombing attack in honor of al-Nursa Front. He called News 13 in Orlando and said, "I'm the shooter. It's me. I'm the shooter." He also stated the shooting was in the name of ISIL, and his actions were in response to the American-led air strike that killed ISIL commander Abu Wahib.

AGROTERRORISM

Agro-terrorism is the attempt to interrupt or devastate an agricultural industry and/or food supply distribution. Agro-terrorism is the "deliberate introduction of an animal or plant disease for generating fear, causing economic losses, or undermining social stability" (Monke, 2004, para. 1). Such actions are an attempt to affect a population by deliberately causing disease and destruction with animal or plant pathogens. Agroterrorism is closely related to biological and entomological warfare, but such terroristic acts are usually committed by domestic terrorists and extremists. Agroterrorism is a relatively a new concept within the United States, and with more research, it is closely parallel with bioterrorism as a terroristic act that involves the intentional release or distribution of biological agents.

Americans spend about eleven percent of their income on food compared to the global average of twenty to thirty percent (U.S. Bureau of Statistics, 2004, p. 234). These numbers were reported to the U.S. Bureau of Statistics less than three years after 9/11, and ten years later, the United States Department of Agriculture reported "U.S. consumers, businesses, and government agencies spent $1.46 trillion on food and beverages in grocery stores" (2004, para. 1). In 2006, the United States' agricultural industry is indicative of the economic stability of the nation, accounting for one of six jobs in a trillion-dollar empire. Agricultural products and similar resources entail of approximately ten percent of U.S. exports, equaling around $70 billion (U.S. Department of Agricultural, 2006). Because America's agricultural system is such a large domain of wealth with a massive food production chain, targeting it is an attractive concept to terrorists. Extremists know there is a lack of security processes for the agricultural industry, and it is the most vulnerable and the least protected asset within the United States. For example, American coalition forces found training materials on targeting agricultural sites when they invaded al-Qaeda's shelters in Afghanistan in 2002. There is little information on agoterrorism because modern threats of attacks are the frontrunner issues among countries today. Even though agro-terrorism is not highly publicized, it is not a new concept. Such terrorism dates to World War I when German agents within the United States infected horses and cattle that were in transit from the East Coast to France.

CYBERTERRORISM AND CYBERSECURITY

The FBI defines **cyberterrorism** as any "premeditated politically motivated attack against computer programs computer systems, data, and information, which results in violence against noncombatants targets by subnational groups or clandestine agents" (Singer, 2012, para. 3). The ideological and political stances of cyberterrorism include deliberate large-scale computer attacks through use of computer viruses and hacking operations. Cyberterrorism is also considered a deliberate attempt to to instill fear and threaten loss of life or violence for political or ideological gains using the Internet.

Figure 7.3 Hooded Anonymous Dark Person

History

Cyberterrorism dates to the 1980s with evidence of potential attacks on the Internet and large networks. According to researchers Joel G. Ogreen and James R. Langevin in their thesis, "Responding to the Threat of Cyberterrorism Through Information Assurance," Barry C. Collin was the first use of the term (1999, p. 5). A senior fellow at the Institute for Security in California, Collins described the term as the "convergence of cyberspace and terrorism" and more recently he stated cyberterrorism as the "intersection of the physical and virtual worlds that forms the vehicle of cyberterrorism, the new weapon that we face" (Bidgoli, 2004, p. 361). As the twenty-first century approached, there was much concern that the "millennial concept" would affect all technology, including computer networks, and electricity, and so forth. In addition, there was heightened concern for potential cyber-attacks based on increased vulnerabilities.

The millennial crisis was not associated with cyberterrorism, but it was a catalyst for terrorists to take advantage and launch a large-scale cyber-attack. Authors John Arquilla and Winn Schwartau had significant success publishing books on possible scenarios that could be reality in the realm of cyberterrorism. One of Arquilla's last published pieces titled *Last War Standing* claimed, "preemption is the only thing that can keep America safe" (2013, para. 1). Computer security expert Winn Schwartau authored *Information Warfare: Chaos on the Electronic Super Highway,* which introduced the concept of cyberterrorism in the late 1990s.

Controversy of the terminology of cyberterrorism makes it difficult to effectively maintain innovative policies and initiatives to mitigate the threat. Scholars and experts have broadly or narrowly defined the term based on specific network attacks to identify cybercrimes and "cyber terms," which are separate concepts. For instance, William L. Tafoya, Ph.D., author of the FBI's article *Cyber Terror,* emphatically states that cyberterrorism is a "component of information warfare, but information warfare is not cyberterrorism" (2011, para. 2). Jonathan Matusitz, author of *American Foreign Policy Interests* article "Cyberterrorism" says that cyberterrorism can be defined as the "international use of computer, networks, and public Internet to cause destruction and harm for personal objectives" (2005, p. 137). Because of the increase of cyber-attacks within the United States, there is a significant amount of concern about possible damage that can be caused by cyberterrorism.

Such concerns have increased responsibilities for the CIA and the FBI to prevent cyber-attacks and cyberterrorism. However, the controversy of understanding the conceptualization of cyberterrorism has produced more initiatives. The primary concern with defining cyberterrorism is determining motivation, such as targets, methods, modes of access, and specific use. The concept overlaps with cybercrime, cyberwar, and terrorism, blurring lines.

Specialist in National Security Policy and Information Operations Catherine A. Theohary and Specialist in Terrorism John W. Rollins expressed in the Congress Research Service article "Cyberwarfare and Cyberterrorism: In Brief" that cyberwar is typically "conceptualized as state-on-state action equivalent to armed attack or use of force in cyberspace that may trigger a military response with a proportional kinetic use of force" (2015, p. 1). Cyberterrorism can be considered an unconventional method of attack that can be conducted by non-state actors, which can be unpredictable, and future attacks are unknown. However, dissenters believe cyberterrorism is not a concept. Instead, it is more akin to hacking or information warfare, and they do not believe terrorism is a sociopolitical concept because the chances of instilling fear, causing bodily harm, or targeting a population via the Internet are significantly mitigated.

Capabilities

Dr. M.N. Sirohi in *Cyberterrorism and Information Warfare* notes three levels of cyber terror outlined by the Monterey Group:

- **Simple Unstructured**: The capability to conduct basic hacks against individual system using tools created by someone else. The organization possess little target analysis, command and control, or learning capability.

- **Advanced Structured**: The capability to conduct more sophisticated attacks against multiple systems or networks and possibly to modify or create basic hacking tools. The organization possesses an elementary analysis, command and control, and learning capability.

- **Complex Coordinated**: The capability for a coordinated attack capable of causing mass-disruption against integrated, heterogeneous defenses (including cryptography). Also, it is the ability to create sophisticated hacking tools and is highly capable of target analysis, command and control, and learning capability (2015, p. 7).

- Cyberterrorism will increase as the Internet becomes an omnipresent mechanism within the world. Hackers, groups, and terrorists can use cyber threats to affect communities, countries, and international conflict because cyberterrorism does not cause a physical threat, bodily harm, or death. The fact cyberterrorism is virtually anonymous increases the chances of large-scale attacks.

Concerns

Cyberterrorism is a stealth-like form of terrorism, and execution of an attack is unpredictable. Such attacks can affect a country's economy, leading to large-scale disasters such as the Great Depression. The United States has the highest threat of cyberterrorism. On November 14, 2013, FBI Director James Comey testified before the Senate Homeland Security Committee hearing to discuss Threats on the Homeland on Capitol Hill in Washington, D.C. He said, "cyber-attacks are increasingly becoming the primary threat to the United States." He also said, "while the threat of traditional terrorist strikes inside the United States is lower than it was before 2001, the potential threat from cyber-attacks continues to rise (FBI: Cyber-attack Surpassing Terrorism as Major Domestic Threats, 2013, para. 1).

Natural disasters like Hurricanes Katrina and Sandy have proven to be top national security threats, devastating American communities and critical infrastructures. The challenge is that nothing that can be done to prevent a natural disaster from occurring. First responders, law enforcement, military, and emergency management professionals can only properly prepare for such events with innovative, up-to-date, efficient and effective emergency management readiness protocols. However, expectations have increased for policymakers to formalize and implement preventative measures to mitigate possible cyber terrorist attacks.

As the Internet continues to innovate and expand, terrorism becomes a more serious threat. Dr. Sirohi notes that cyberterrorism "may become a more serious threat and is possibly one of the top ten events to the human race" (2015, p. 8). The author's statement acknowledges that humans depend heavily on the Internet, which gives terrorists an advantage to inflict a large-scale attack. Such advantage threatens a country's economic standing and national security objectives. Additionally, cyber-attacks have a prevalent advantage over physical terrorist plots, and terrorists understand it is inexpensive, can be executed remotely and anonymously, and most importantly does not require a significant amount of personnel, explosives, or weapons. It is hypothesized by scholars and theorists that future cyber-attacks will occur in the form of denial of service attacks, malware, and innovative methods that easily tracked or envisioned. Author Randall L. Schweller in *Maxwell's Demon and the Golden Apple: Global Discord in the New York Millennial* cited James A. Lewis, a computer security expert at the Center for Strategic and International Studies in Washington, D.C. about how cyberterrorism ranks in comparison to conventional warfare, comparing Iran and North Korea's cyber capabilities to nuclear weapons. Lewis said, "these countries are pursuing cyber weapons the way they are pursuing nuclear weapons ... it's primitive; it's not top of the line, but it's good enough, and they are committed to getting it (Perlroth and Sanger, 2013, para. 14).

Military Actions Against Cyberterrorism

The United States Strategic Command (USSTRATCOM), a subsidiary of the DoD, is responsible for combating terrorism. USSTRATCOM established the Joint-Task Force-Global Network Operations, which is the operational component of USSTRATCOM in support of DoD's Global Information Grid (GIG). Such operations are executed by integrating Global Network Operation capabilities through DoD computers, networks, and systems used by DoD combatant commands, services, and agencies.

The United States' first Air Force Cyber Command (AFCC), Major Command (MAJCOM) was established on November 2, 2016, and is responsible for all operations of monitoring and providing national defense in cyberspace. On August 18, 2009, the Twenty-Fourth Air Force was created and replaced AFCC. Twenty-Fourth Air Force houses prominent units such as:

- 67th Cyberspace Wing (Lackland Air Force Base, Texas)
- 624th Operations Center (Lackland Air Force Base, Texas)
- 688th Cyberspace Wing (Lackland Air Force Base, Texas)
- 689th Combat Communications Wing (Robins Air Force Base, Georgia)

On December 22, 2009, President Barack Obama created the Cybersecurity Coordinator position, a high-level position within the Executive Office of the president, who heads all computer security realms to coordinate American government, intelligence, and military to prevent hackers and deter cyberterrorism. Additionally, President Obama established the Executive Order Blocking the Property of Certain Persons Engaging in Significant Malicious Cyber-Enabled Activities, which gives the United States the authority to impose sanctions on individuals or organizations that are suspected to be involved in related crimes.

Cybersecurity

Cybersecurity is the protection against theft, damage, or sabotage to computer or hardware programs and the disruption of system networks. Computer security also includes controlling physical access to hardware systems and protecting such apparatus against belligerent harm executed via code injection, data access, and network access. This also includes malpractice through human operations whether accidental or intentional through deceptive procedures.

According to the Department of Homeland Security, cybersecurity is predicated on the national cyberspace realms that are vulnerable to cyber and physical threats. Such threats are conducted by sophisticated national and non-states using cyber expertise to manipulate susceptibilities by "stealing information, money, and developing capabilities to destroy, disrupt, or threaten the delivery of essential services" (DHS, 2016, para. 1). Cyberspace is defined as:

> Intangible place between computers where information momentarily exists on its route from one end of the global network to the other. Cyberspace is the ethereal reality, an infinity of electrons speeding down copper or glass fibers at the speed of light from one point to another. It also includes airwaves vibrating with cellular, microwaves, and satellite (Schwartau, 1994, p. 49).

These elements of cyber-attack and cyberterrorism threats require cybersecurity legislation and initiatives:

- **Backdoor**—a virus which compromises computer files and steals confidential information stored in the attacked computer.
- **Clickjacking**—also known as a *UI redress attack,* is a malicious technique to provoke a user to click on a web page different from what the user perceives to be clicked, resulting in capturing confidential information or taking control of the computer after the fraudulent page is clicked.
- **Denial of service corruption**—a malicious attempt by a hacker to deny a legitimate user from accessing information or services on the network.
- **Eavesdropping**—in computer and network security, it is a hacker's unauthorized attempt to intercept private communication via networks, secure lines, and telephones.
- **Phishing**—sending fraudulent emails to users in attempt to persuade them to reveal personal information, particularly sensitive information such as bank information, credit cards, and passwords.
- **Social engineering**—the act of provoking people to reveal confidential information.
- **Spoofing**—a malicious scam in which hackers attempt to gain unauthorized access with a fraudulent sender address with intent to obtain or gain access to confidential information.
- **Tampering**—making unauthorized alterations or destroying computer systems and networks.
- **Vulnerabilities**—circumstances that allow hackers to mitigate a system's information assurance protocols.

Cybersecurity efforts are crucial to protecting critical infrastructure within the United States. Sensitive systems should be taken into consideration because a large-scale attack could potentially annihilate what Americans entirely depend on in the twenty-first century, as critical infrastructures are based on technological advancement. The following are considered sensitive systems:

- Aviation
- Consumer devices
- Financial systems
- Government
- Industrial equipment
- Internet and physical vulnerabilities
- Large corporations
- Medical systems
- Utilities

Ardit Ferizi

A hacker known as Th3Dir3ctory, Ardit Ferizi was responsible for hacking into government and military websites in support of ISIS. A Kosovo citizen, Ferizi was the first terrorist hacker to be convicted of cybercrimes within the United States. He was charged with providing ISIS with what was considered a "hit list" that contained personal and sensitive information of approximately 1,300 military service members and government employees. He admitted to the federal government that he hacked a company's network and acquired personally identifiable information of thousands of its customers. Subsequently, he deconstructed records, separating military and government email accounts and gave information to ISIS recruiter Junaid Hussain. Hussain oversaw ISIS's cyber operations and previously published a similar hit list, containing the names and addresses of at least one hundred American military personnel, according to the Department of Justice (2016). Hussain used the information and released it online with the pre-existing list comprised of military and government officials. He died two weeks later in an American airstrike (Blake, 2016, para. 4). Hussain tweeted a few days before the incident, "we are extracting confidential data and passing on your personal information to the soldiers of the khilafah, who soon with the permission of Allah will strike at your necks in your own lands!" (Department of Justice, 2016, para. 8).

After the incident, Ferizi was identified by law enforcement as the culprit and was arrested in September 2015. U.S. Attorney Dana J. Boente said, "Cyberterrorism has become an increasingly prevalent and serious threat here in American both to individuals and businesses. However, cyber terrorists are no different from other terrorists: no matter where they hide, we will track them down and seek to bring them to the United States" (DOJ, 2016, para. 4). On September 16, 2016, Ferizi was sentenced to twenty years in prison for "providing material support to ISIS and a maximum sentence of five years for accessing a protected computer without authorization and obtaining information" (DOJ, 2016, para. 9).

Terrorist Motivation

There are many reasons as why hackers and terrorists are motivated to infiltrate computer and network systems. Some common hackers commit criminal attacks for financial gain, while some are motivated to destroy a company. Others may attempt a large-scale attack to catastrophically ruin a country's economy or send a political message. State-sponsored terrorists are more common in the twenty-first century, and it is important that governments understand the seriousness and develop **threat modeling** processes to identify the motivations behind system and network attacks.

Government Legislation, Role and Response

The federal government is charged with enforcing regulations and statutes to ensure corporations and organizations protect critical infrastructure and computer system networks. Policies such as information assurance are standardized to safeguard from cyber-attacks and destruction of the national power grid. The debate over government intervention through cyberspace directives is a realistic concern, as the American public wonders if the government is the best organization to solve cybercrimes. Some experts believe the government can best enforce cyber statutes since private sectors have not successfully tackled the problem. Others believe both the government and private sectors have not accomplished enforcing such important standards. Researcher Eric A. Kaijankoski published his thesis on "Cybersecurity Information Sharing between Public-Private Sector Agencies" and notes the transparency of government and private sectors "lacked capabilities against threats" (2015, p. v). Former National Coordinator for Security, Infrastructure Protection and Counterterrorism for the United States Richard A. Blake expressed concerns during the RSA Security Conference in San Francisco, claiming that the "industry only responds when threatened by regulations. If industry doesn't respond, you have to follow through" (Conyers, 2015, p. 54).

Although government interventions seem to be the best solution to the war on cybercrimes, the public believes such interference will hinder its abilities to modernize companies. The earliest legislation was passed by Congress in 1986, United States Code 1030, the Computer Fraud and Abuse Act, which prohibits unauthorized access or destruction to protected computers and networks. In 2009, President Obama established the International Cybercrime Reporting and Cooperation Act, which requires the government to report information and communication advancement of foreign countries and to establish statutes to assist coalition forces and security partners in mitigating cybercrimes and cyberterrorism. The following year, President Obama formulized the Protecting Cyberspace as a National Asset Act of 2010, an initiative enacted to increase security in cyberspace and mitigate virtual attacks which could immobilize critical infrastructure and disrupt the American economy.

NARCOTERRORISM

In 1983, the term "**narcoterrorism**" was coined by former Peruvian president Fernando Belaunde Terry in response to terrorist acts against the country's anti-narcotics law enforcement task force. Narcoterrorism was defined as the concept to identify belligerents who use terrorist tactics to hinder anti-narcotic operations. During the time, Colombian drug lord Pablo Escobar heavily influenced drug trafficking and corruption within the Colombian government and was considered the epitome of narcoterrorism. His drug operations supplied nearly eighty percent of the illegal shipment of cocaine entering the United States. He is considered the wealthiest criminal in the world, accruing over $21 billion annually in his prime. Narcoterrorism has been controversial since the 1980s. Today, the terminology presents different meanings. For instance, Brian Dodd, former Chief of Drug Enforcement Administration's Counter-Narcoterrorism Operations Center, presented in his seminar "The Nexus between Drugs and Terrorism" the definition of narcoterrorism as "drug trafficking organizations that use terrorist tactics (high-profile violence and intimidation) to advance or protect their drug trafficking activities" (n.d., para. 3).

On March 13, 2002, former DEA Administrator and current Governor of Arkansas Asa Hutchinson testified before the Senate Judiciary Committee Subcommittee on Technology, Terrorism, and Government Information that DEA defines cyberterrorism as:

> A subset of terrorism, in which terrorist groups, or associated individuals, participate directly or indirectly in the cultivation, manufacture, transportation, or distribution of controlled substances and the monies derived from these activities ... it is characterized by the participation of groups or associated individuals in taxing, providing security for, or otherwise aiding or abetting drug trafficking endeavors in an effort to further, or fund, terrorist activities (Department of State, 2002, para. 7).

Narcoterroristic acts include credit card fraud, counterfeiting, drug trafficking, extortion, human trafficking, illegal arms racketeering/trafficking, pirating, tax scams, and unlawful oil trade. Billions of dollars are invested into international illegal operations, and some is used to weaken political systems with bribery and corruption. The U.S. Department of State's International Narcotics Strategy Reports found "a direct connection between traditional Colombian drug trafficking and money laundering organizations and Middle Eastern money launderers tied to Hezbollah" (Ghosh, 2016, p. 361).

Because terrorist groups like Revolutionary Armed Forces of Colombia People's Army, Fuerzas Armadas Revolucionas de Colombia (FARC), National Liberation Front, Ejercito Liberacio Nacional (ELN), United Self-Defense of Colombia, Autodefensas Unidas de Colombia (AUC), Communists Party of Peru, Shining Path, Partido Comunista, Hamas, and the Taliban are known to be involved in drug operations alongside drug cartels, the term is heavily used. The growing concerns for drug trafficking and corruption in Colombia caused President George W. Bush to enact the Plan of Colombia to mitigate narcoterrorism among drug cartels and extremist groups in Colombia, primarily FARC and AUC.

In addition to Colombia's heavy presence of international criminal organization and narcoterrorists, many other countries are or have been involved in narcoterrorism. Other countries in Latin America are prevalent in the expansion of cocaine and heroin. Mexico's cartels have leaked into American soil and have caused many concerns, initiating the War on Drugs. As early as the 1980s, narcoterrorism became a concern when former Chairman of the Select Committee on Narcotics Abuse and Control Charles Rangel (Democrat-New York) cautioned the Senate, "We have never fought the war on drugs like we have fought other legitimate wars—with all the forces at our command" (1988, para. 2).

Furthermore, many international criminal and drug trafficking organizations cooperate with or are supported by terrorist groups such as al Qaeda, Hamas, Hezbollah, ISIS, and the Taliban. Additionally, some narcoterrorist groups are strictly anti-American and work with terrorist organizations to eliminate U.S. drug interdiction initiatives. According to the Majority Report completed by United States House Committee on Homeland Security Subcommittee on Oversight, Investigations, and Management, such groups formed alliances with Venezuela because former President Hugo Chavez stopped supporting U.S. drug sanctions within the country in 2005. Representative Michael T. McCaul said "for rogue leaders like Venezuelan President Hugo Chavez, who see embargoes and sanctions as just another manifestation of American oppression and imperialism, Iran has become their champion and welcome ally" (2012, p. 11). During this time, Chavez provided Venezuela as an asylum and conducted money-laundering operations between terrorist groups in Iran, Lebanon, and Syria.

In 2012, the United States and global partners gathered for the U.N. Commission on Narcotic Drugs to discuss the concerns of the heightened drug trafficking in the twenty-first century. During the session, there were discussions of failure to effectively mitigate such large-scale operations which resulted in no resolution to the issue. Officials believed the increased drug movement also heightened drug usage and addiction, which violated human rights. The United Nation's High Commissioner for Human Rights said, "all too often, drug users suffer discrimination, are forced to accept treatment, are marginalized and often harmed by approaches that over-emphasize criminalization and punishment while under-emphasizing harm reduction and respect for human rights" (United Nations, 2009, para. 3). Drug trafficking encourages terrorist organizations to build and expand. According to the International Narcotics Control Board, the Taliban resurrected its presence in Afghanistan, forcing over 50,000 U.S. troops to deploy. Their resurrection was predicated on the half-billion-dollar empire the group created from drug trading. Nonetheless, narcoterrorism heavily affects a global population of nearly 210 million drugs users with international revenue of over $320 billion annually. As a result, drug trafficking destroys communities while developing innovative methods for criminals to continue to threaten nations. Linking with terrorist groups for support and cooperation eventually leads to terrorism.

SUMMARY

Terrorism is a dangerous and unpredictable situation for the United States in the twenty-first century. Not only does the nation have concerns about global threats, but American terrorism literally hits close to home. Some American terrorists do not support the federal government, oppose laws, and do not recognize law enforcement.

Additionally, suppressed lone wolves and homegrown terrorists are secretly radicalized and use their extremist views to harm Americans because Western civilization is globally accepted. There are many facets to instilling fear in a country and its citizens and committing violent acts for an extremist's ideological, radical, or religious purpose. Highly publicized acts of terrorism have occurred in the late twentieth and twenty-first centuries, including agroterrorism, cyberterrorism, and narcoterrorism. Americans worry about the possible contamination of the nation's agricultural infrastructure with biological and chemical weapon systems. Furthermore, cyberterrorism has escalated over the past fifteen years and will increase as the Internet becomes an omnipresent mechanism within the world. Hackers, groups, and terrorists create cyber threats, affecting communities and countries and creating international conflict. Finally, narcoterrorism and international criminal organizations threaten American national security beyond illegal drug trade. Narcoterrorism is intricately associated with government corruption, money laundering, and politics. All facets of terrorism are critical concerns to protecting America's national security objectives, and it is incumbent upon government leaders and policymakers to strengthen relationships with coalition forces and security partners to ensure that all countries are protected. Benjamin Kuipers, author of *How to Defeat Terrorism*, said, "When terrorists are isolated criminals, viewed with suspicion by the clear majority of the public and reported to the authorities when they turn violent, then the war on terrorism has been won" (2004, para. 27). Kuipers simply stated response to ending terrorism is the epitome of global standards of succinct development, intelligence, integration, and multilateral cooperation between the United States and other countries against terrorism.

CHAPTER 7 CASE STUDIES

Case Study 1
Pablo Escobar, the Original Narcoterrorist

The illicit drug trade is one of the most lucrative businesses in the world, second only to the weapons sector, attracting many criminal organizations, including terrorists and extremist groups because of the high profit, which can then be used to fund nefarious activities. The growing relationship between crime groups and terrorists is a threat to national security as the drug war empowers and enriches non-state actors who do not operate within the law and seek to do the nation harm. The cartels not only put a strain on the U.S. criminal justice system and law enforcement resources, but they also threaten to jeopardize U.S. trade, compromise the integrity of financial systems and destabilize the already-weak border. Furthermore, this threat harms the U.S.' soft power credibility, diminishing its negotiating position, influence, and world standing (Wyler, 2011). If counterterrorism efforts are to be successful, funding for terrorism that comes from the illicit drug trade cannot be ignored (Higgins, 2017).

Narcoterrorism, a term first used by Peru's president Belaunde Terry in 1983 to characterize attacks by cocaine traffickers against the police, describes the nexus between drug trafficking and terrorism. There are four primary types of narcoterrorism:

drug traffickers who engage in terrorist activities to protect their business, terrorists who sell narcotics to fund terrorist activities, criminals who have an equal interest in both terrorism and drug trafficking, and the symbiotic relationship where each stay in their respective lanes, but mutually support each other (Higgins, 2017).

Pablo Escobar was a Colombian drug lord and narcoterrorist categorized under the first type of narcoterrorism. His ruthlessness was legendary. He used intimidation methods on anyone who opposed him, including judges, prosecutors, and police, with the goal of furthering his cartel business and extracting political concessions from the government (Zalman, 2014). Violence ran rampant, but he didn't care how many people were killed. Known as the "King of Cocaine," Escobar worked with a small group to form the infamous Medellin Cartel. By the mid-1980s, he controlled more than eighty percent of the cocaine smuggled into the United States (Escobar, 2016). *Forbes* magazine listed him as the seventh-richest man in the world with his personal wealth reported at $24 billion. His wealth and ruthlessness made it almost impossible for Colombian authorities to bring him to justice.

Escobar tried to influence Colombian politics toward a no-extradition clause and to grant amnesty to drug kingpins in exchange for giving up the trade. Knowing that his group was wanted in the U.S., he and his associates feared getting caught and sent to prison there. His group adopted the name "the Extraditables" as they set out to end extradition. Their motto became "Better a tomb in Colombia than a prison cell in the United States" (Farah, 1993). Escobar used terror tactics, notably "plato o plomo" (silver or lead) to deal with adversaries. If someone presented a challenge to his goal, he first attempted to bribe them. If that did not work, he would have them, and sometimes their families, neutralized (Zalman, 2014). His terror campaign resulted in the killings of thousands of people, including politicians, civil servants, journalists, and ordinary citizens. He even ordered the assassination of Colombian presidential candidates and was rumored to be behind the 1985 attack on the Supreme Court, in which several Supreme Court Justices were killed. On November 27, 1989, he was implicated in the bombing of Avianca flight 203, killing 110 people, including two U.S. citizens (Escobar, 2016).

With increasing pressure from the U.S. to extradite the drug lord, the Colombian government and Escobar's lawyers came up with an arrangement where the narcoterrorist would turn himself in and serve a five-year jail term but would be allowed to build his own prison and not be expedited to the U.S. When it came out that Escobar was still running his operations from prison, the Colombian government decided to move him to a normal prison. Fearing extradition, he escaped and went into hiding (Zalman, 2014). The Search Bloc, a special, U.S.-trained Colombian task force, organized a massive manhunt to track the narcoterrorist down. In 1986, President Reagan officially added drug trafficking to the list of threats to national security as part of his directive number 221, which authorized the U.S. military to intervene abroad to fight against drug production (Corti & Swain, 2009). With the help of the U.S., the Search Bloc found the drug lord holed up in a home in Medellin. During the attempt to bring Escobar in, a shootout eventually ended with the death of the notorious King of Cocaine (Zalman, 2014). Escobar's death led to the downfall of the Medellin Cartel, which was soon replaced by the rival Cali Cartel. Two decades after his death, he is still remembered as the powerful, ruthless drug lord, the original narcoterrorist.

Case Study 2
Agroterrorism

The U.S. agricultural industry contributes about thirteen percent of the nation's gross annual domestic product. As many as one in six jobs are linked to agriculture, a trillion-dollar industry (Monke, 2007). Terrorists trying to cripple the U.S. economy are provided with easy targets if they focus on the nation's agricultural industry for "soft" targets. Farms, ranches, and access to feedlots are open and generally unprotected. Agroterrorists can choose from a large variety of bio-agents, including pathogens such as botulism, E. coli, and salmonella, most of which are environmentally hardy and can be easily smuggled into the country. The food and supply chains offer an easy method for achieving mass death. Furthermore, many animal pathogens cannot be transmitted to humans, which makes them easier for terrorists to work with. There are also no weaponization issues since livestock are the primary vector for pathogenic transmission (Agroterrorism, 2003).

A subset of bioterrorism, *agroterrorism* is defined as "the deliberate introduction of an animal or plant disease for generating fear, causing economic losses, or undermining social stability (Monke, 2007). The goal of agroterrorism is not to kill cows or plants but rather to cause economic damage, social unrest, and loss of confidence in government. Terrorist leaders understand that U.S. strength comes largely from its economic vitality, which is why they are developing strategies that focuses on weakening the nation's economic strength. In addition to U.S. food supply being among the most vulnerable and least protected of all potential targets of attack, agroterrorists also realize that that a successful agroterrorism incident will threaten U.S. economic welfare and its standing as a leading exporter of agricultural products to the world (Agroterrorism, 2012). The subsequent effect of a deliberate act of sabotage would be felt through other sectors of the economy (Agroterrorism, 2003).

While agriculture may not have the "shock factor" of more traditional terrorist targets, such as bombings or murders, terrorism analysts consider it a likely viable secondary target. In 2002, evidence containing agricultural documents and manuals describing ways to make animal and plant poisons was found in al Qaeda hideouts in Afghanistan, suggesting that the terrorist group was looking at the agricultural industry as a target. However, it is important to not to focus solely on al Qaeda or other Middle-East terror groups as many of the terrorist attacks on U.S. soil have been carried out by American citizens. Homegrown terrorists may perpetrate an attack for a variety of reasons. Economic opportunists seeking financial gain because of a change in market prices may also pose a threat as well. Similarly, militant animal rights or environmental activists such as the Animal Liberation Front and the Earth Liberation Front are also a threat as they believe the use of animals for food is immoral (Agroterrorism, 2012).

If terrorists seek mass human casualties as their objective, the food supply, production and distribution chain provides a cheap and unsophisticated, yet effective means to disseminate toxins and bacteria. Furthermore, the agricultural industry has several characteristics that make it inherently vulnerable to potential terrorist attacks. One characteristic is that farms are geographically disbursed in unsecured environments. While some livestock are housed in facilities that can be locked, for the most part, agriculture generally requires large swaths of land that are more difficult to secure. Another issue is the practice of livestock being concentrated in confined locations, and transported or commingled with other herds, which allows diseases to move more quickly. Additionally, the number of lethal and contagious biological agents is greater for plants and animals than for humans. Many of these agricultural diseases can be obtained, handled, and distributed easily (Monke, 2007). It is also assessed that fruit- and vegetable-packing plants are among the most vulnerable venues for food-borne attacks since many represent small-scale manufacturers that specialize in ready-to-eat meats or aggregated foodstuffs, and they do not practice uniform biosecurity methods. Furthermore, they do not use heat, an effective front-end barrier against pathogens, in food processing, which offers a viable portal to introduce pathogens (Agroterrorism, 2012).

Despite the ease and consequences of a successful attack, agroterrorism is unlikely to be a primary form of terrorist aggression because it lacks a single, highly visible point of focus for the media, which is a primary consideration in any terrorist attack. However, terrorists may consider disrupting the agricultural industry as a follow up to a primary, conventional terrorist attack to further destabilize an already disoriented society. Being able to use cheap and unsophisticated means to undermine a nation's economic base makes this an attractive means of attack for terrorists, especially if those groups are faced with overcoming significant power inequities (Agroterrorism, 2003). Protecting the nation's agricultural industry will take combined efforts of the agriculture industry, government, law enforcement, and academic and scientific communities working in tandem to minimize both the likelihood of an attack and mitigate the severity of its impact (Schmitt, 2007).

CHAPTER 7 PRACTICE PROBLEMS

1. What is the impact of drug trafficking and other crimes on national security?
2. Compare U.S.-Mexico and U.S.-Colombian counter-narcotics efforts and assess the success of their operations.
3. Are extremism and terrorism interchangeable? Why or why not?
4. How sustainable is anarchy for society?
5. Analyze a homegrown terrorist scenario and identify different places in the timeline leading up to the attack where something could have been done to prevent the tragedy.
6. What characteristics set homegrown terrorists apart from other terrorists and terrorists groups?
7. The agricultural industry is one of the least protected assets within the U.S., making it an attractive target for terrorist groups. What are some actions that can be taken to mitigate the security vulnerabilities?
8. When does a cyberattack by another nation cross the line and become an official act of war? What actions can a nation take to address either scenario?
9. Can cyberterrorism be prevented? How?
10. How would terrorists compromise infrastructure in the U.S. in a cyberattack? What preventative measures does the U.S. have in place to mitigate the effects of a cyberattack on infrastructure?

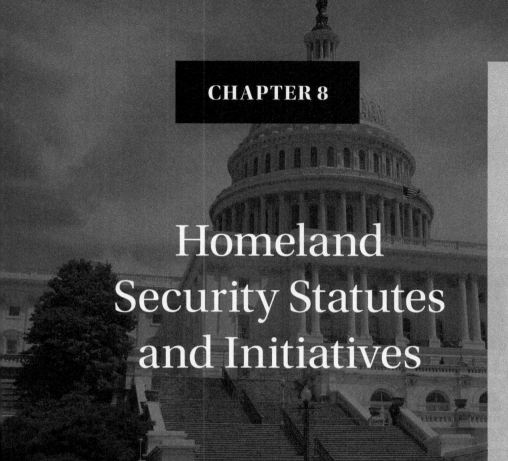

CHAPTER 8

Homeland Security Statutes and Initiatives

KEY TERMS

Allocations

Appropriations

Budget resolution

Conference report

Continuing resolution

Mandatory spending

Nuclear warfare

Nuclear weapons

President's budget

Proliferation

LEARNING OBJECTIVES

After reading this chapter, students will be able to:

- Discuss homeland security initiatives that have been established by congressional policymakers and the Department of Homeland Security
- Understand the congressional budget process and how it affects national security policies, methodologies, and stratagies
- Evaluate controversial frameworks predicated on civil liberties and privacy matters that protect national security objectives
- Examine key legislation that influenced the evolution of homeland and national defense operations

INTRODUCTION

I t is important to understand how homeland security initiatives have transpired based on the evolution of technological advancement, cultural diversity, progressive governments and societies, and terrorism/crimes/violence matters within the United States. The establishment of the Department of Homeland Security is dependent upon various legislation that has been enacted since the 9/11 attacks, and continuous threats of attacks against the United States has made such actions more paramount than ever. Since the attack on the homeland, the country has faced continued threats, terrorist acts, and violence against Americans, critical infrastructures, and resources both domestically and abroad. Understanding the inevitable and continuous threat against the world's superpower, policymakers realize progressive legislation that acknowledges the current threat is significant in formulating counterterrorism measures and stratagies to identify domestic and global threats.

Producing legislation that recognizes the threat, in addition to preserving institutional cultures that influence congressional decision making has never been more relevant than in post-9/11 responsibilities. The purpose of this chapter is to discuss top legislative acts and influential statutes from presidential directives to congressional rulings to identify the authoritative and infrastructural efforts that have been introduced to the American federal government regarding how to counter terrorism and protect the homeland. Such legislation has been enacted as a major reorganization within the federal government to fix gaps in administrative policies and establish innovative ways to formulate and implement national terrorism prevention measures. This chapter provides a brief synopsis of the most important and highly publicized legislative statutes that occurred in response to the September 11 attacks and revolutionized homeland and national security policy objectives.

NUNN-LUGAR COOPERATIVE THREAT REDUCTION INITIATIVE

Figure 8.1 Secretary of Defense Ash Carter poses with Senator Sam Nunn and Senator Richard Lugar

Known as the Nunn-Lugar Act, the *Nunn-Lugar Cooperative Threat Reduction* initiative is a policy established under the *Defense Threat Reduction Agency (DTRA)*, which outlines plans indicative of the *Soviet Nuclear Threat Reduction Act of 1991*. Co-created by Senator Sam Nunn (Democrat-Georgia) and Senator Richard Lugar (Republican-Indiana), the *Cooperative Threat Reduction (CTR)* program "supports national security strategy by pursuing objectives to prevent the **proliferation** (a rapid increase in numbers, particularly referring to nuclear weapons) of weapons of mass destruction and related materials, technologies and expertise from former Soviet Union states" (Defense Threat

Reduction Agency, n.d., para. 2). Additionally, the ingenuity of the CTR program was to assist the former Soviet Union to meet its arms control treaty requirements that mitigated nuclear proliferation risks. The objectives of the CTR program were to disassemble the former Soviet Union's weapons of mass destruction program, along with supporting elements, preventing proliferation of biological and nuclear weapons, and create transparency and higher standards of conduct within the country.

The CTR program offers specific capabilities and funding for former Soviet Union states to withdraw all biological, chemical, and **nuclear weapons** by reducing the proliferation of all weapons outlined in the Strategic Arms Reduction Treaty. Furthermore, funding set aside by the CTR program enhanced the protection and security of physical facilities which held biological weapons. Once all nuclear weapons were removed from the former Soviet Union's possession, the Nunn-Lugar initiative provided equipment and resources to demolish the missile warheads and the silos in which the weapons were stored. The program spanned its operations by establishing maritime border security and developing land resources in the former Soviet Union. Since the program's inception, the Nunn-Lugar Act has disabled more than 7,500 nuclear warheads, chemical weapons, mitigated biological weapons, and revamped weapons facilities to include stricter safety measures.

The Nunn-Lugar initiative is considered a success story, as the United States completed the final removal of highly enriched uranium from the former Soviet Union warheads in 2013. The mitigation of the nuclear weapons proliferation was "an unprecedented reverse with the denuclearization of former republics and the consolidation of nuclear weapons and fissile material inside Russia" (The National Security Archive, 2016, para. 2). This initiative was predicated on crucial decisions made in the post-Cold War era and with the dissolution of the Soviet Union, and as a result, Senators Nunn and Lugar were responsible for the Cooperative Threat Reduction Program as a collaborative effort between the United States and Russia. The initiative did not receive much recognition until Russia withdrew from the agreement in 2012, but the two countries still worked together on future efforts that would involve the annihilation of chemical weapons in Syria.

USA PATRIOT ACT OF 2001

Officially titled, "Uniting and Strengthening America by Providing Appropriate Tools Required to Intercept and Obstruct Terrorism," the USA PATRIOT Act of 2001 was enacted by President George W. Bush to enhance counterterrorism methods within the United States. President Bush anticipated this bilateral legislation would allow intelligence agencies and law enforcement to establish innovative methods and operations to deter future terrorist acts within the United States. *The Washington Post* cited President Bush's remarks at the signing for the USA PATRIOT Act of 2001, stating, "The new legislation greatly enhances the penalties that will fall on terrorists or anyone who helps them" (2001, para. 25). The act gave the U.S. Department of Justice and the National Security Agency additional powers concerning domestic and international surveillance electronic communications. In addition, the legislation augmented intelligence agencies' responsibilities and authority, which reduced restrictions on communications surveillance and provided multiple avenues to share information with civil law enforcement. Law enforcement responsibilities increased as well, broadening the spectrum of their responsibilities to include financial counterfeiting, smuggling and trafficking, and money-laundering systems that supported terrorist organizations. Finally, the act gave the FBI the authority to access financial and medical records of those who are linked to terrorist organizations and causes. According to the Department of Justice, the PATRIOT Act was established to:

- Allow investigators to use the tools that were readily available to investigate organized crime and drug trafficking.
- Facilitate information sharing and cooperation among government agencies so that they can better connect the dots.
- Update the law to reflect new technologies and new threats.
- Increase the penalties for those who commit terrorist crimes (n.d., paras. 1–4).

The Patriot Act outlines ten elements, including:

- Title I: Enhancing domestic security against terrorism
- Title II: Enhanced surveillance procedures
- Title III: Anti-money laundering to prevent terrorism
- Title IV: Border security
- Title V: Removing obstacles to investigating terrorism
- Title VI: Victims and families of victims of terrorism
- VII: Increased information sharing of critical infrastructure protection
- VIII: Terrorism criminal law
- Title IX: Improved Intelligence
- Title X: Miscellaneous

President Bush renewed the act in March 2006 and approved four revisions between 2005 and 2011, removing some congressional changes and reviewing specific portions that would expire.

Controversy

The act received much criticism because American citizens did not believe it would be the "end all" to preventing terrorism. Others (primarily civil rights activists) felt the Patriot Act would infringe on American civil liberties, violating privacy acts laws and giving the federal government too much power to examine Americans through clandestine operations. With such concerns, the act faced much scrutiny, and legal matters with civil liberty organizations like the *American Civil Liberties Union (ACLU)*, a nonpartisan, non-profit organization, centralized on protecting individual rights and liberties to American citizens. The group stated on its website:

> The Patriot Act was the first of many changes to surveillance laws that made it easier for the government to spy on ordinary Americans by expanding the authority to monitor phone and email communications, collect bank and

credit reporting records, and track the activity of innocent Americans on the Internet. While most Americans think it was created to catch terrorists, the Patriot Act actually turns regular citizens into suspects (2017, para. 1).

Furthermore, some members of Congress and other policymakers, who were once supportive, became weary of the act, as there was not a clear interpretation of how it would be implemented. Concerns exacerbated when former NSA employee Edward Snowden released sensitive information to the public showing federal agencies used the Patriot Act to justify data collected concerning phone calls among American citizens. After the incident, NSA ensured Section 215 of the act was intended to identify and track potential terrorist suspects. The *Foreign Intelligence Surveillance Court* (also called *FISA Court*) approved various surveillance operations, but nonetheless, those operations were considered privacy violations, and the U.S. Court of Appeals for the Second Circuit in New York ruled so in a lawsuit filed by the ACLU.

American citizens and civil liberties groups also find Title II under Section 215 to be one of the most controversial provisions under the act. The ability to intercept messages, legally tap telephone lines, and initiate surveillance are considered justified acts in ongoing investigations, but some consider it a privacy act violation. The Department of Justice states the Patriot Act:

- Expanded the types of entities that can be compelled to disclose information. Under the old provision, the FBI could obtain records only from a common carrier, public accommodation faculty, physical storage facility or vehicle rental facility. The new provision contains no such restrictions.
- It expanded the types of items that can be requested. Under the old authority, the FBI could only seek records. Now the FBI can seek any tangible things (including books, records, papers, documents, and other items) (n.d., Section 2015, paras. 16–17).

Also, opponents of the act under Section 215 under Title II believed the "any tangible things" provision was a lower standard and was concerned businesses could provide the federal government with private information. They also believed this concept along with wiretap operations were considered sunset provisions that would not be permanent unless reauthorized. Such provisions were reauthorized four times between 2005 and 2011, and on May 26, 2011, President Barack Obama passed an extension of the act, the *PATRIOT Sunsets Extension Act of 2011*, which was a four-year extension for three vital elements: roving wiretaps, searches of business records, and conducting surveillance of lone wolves (the *Intelligence Reform and Terrorism Prevention Act of 2004*).

USA FREEDOM ACT

On June 1, 2015, the sunset extension expired, as Congress did not come to an agreement on a revised extension. By June 2, 2015, President Obama signed the *Uniting and Strengthening America by Fulfilling Rights and Ending Eavesdropping,*

Dragnet-Collection and Online Monitoring Act (known as the *USA Freedom Act*), a bill that modified the provisions under the Patriot Act, which expired the previous day. The Freedom Act requires FISA court to release narrative interpretations of the legislation presented, making common law initiatives legal objectives for successive cases. Also, the new legislation sets precedence for providing guidance to allow or restrict surveillance operatives. The new act also included certain restrictions regarding how American intelligence agencies collected telecommunication metadata. New processes emphasized telephone companies would maintain phone records, and the NSA was required to make requests for information. The new act did reinstate the sanction of roving wiretaps and investigating lone wolves. Finally, the Freedom Act sanctioned financial institutions to report and track suspicious activity to the U.S. Department of Treasury to prevent money-laundering operatives.

HOMELAND SECURITY ACT OF 2002

President George W. Bush enacted the *Homeland Security Act of 2002* in the aftermath of the September 11 attacks. Nearly 120 Congressional members supported the act, and it was signed into law on November 25, 2002. HSA's execution established the *Department of Homeland Security*, which was considered the largest reform since the Cold War and the largest federal reorganization since the Department of Defense came to fruition under the National Security Act of 1947. The HSA also established the Cabinet-level position of *Secretary of Homeland Security*. Under HSA, Tom Ridge's titled changed from Director of the Office of the Homeland Security to Secretary of Homeland Security, making him an executive-level Cabinet office as part of the president's administration.

DHS superseded the Office of Homeland Security and continued to run operations in an advisory function. The agency also adopted major departments such as the *U.S. Coast Guard*, *U.S. Immigration and Customs Enforcement* (includes Homeland Security Investigations), *U.S. Customs Service* (includes Border Patrol), the *Federal Emergency Management Agency*, *U.S. Federal Protective Service*, and the *U.S. Secret Service* to protect the contiguous states and territories. The *Homeland Security Appropriations Act 2004* was a crucial provision to provide funding for DHS and ensure that border and national security functions were primary responsibilities for the new department's mission. HSA is another post-Cold War act enacted to reorganize and centralize federal agencies as well as provide security to meet evolving threats and challenges. On March 1, 2003, DHS assumed responsibility for the *Immigration and Naturalization Service (INS)* and established two agencies, Immigration and Customs Enforcement and Citizenship and Immigration Services (as previously mentioned). INS also established the *U.S. Border Patrol*, the *U.S. Customs Service*, and the *Animal and Plant Health Inspection Service*. Finally, the *Federal Protective Services* is subordinate to the National Programs and Program Directorate. DHS also created the *Homeland Security Investigations* team to ensure both agencies had proper investigation and intelligence units. The act states the Department of Homeland Security is charged with its primary responsibility of preventing and deterring terrorists within the United States and its territories. Because terrorism is a federal issue, the Federal Bureau of Investigation is the actual charging authority while DHS supports in an analytical and advisory with intelligence undertakings.

The Homeland Security Act of 2002 is not only the foundation for the Department of the Homeland Security but includes the following:

- Critical Infrastructure Information Act of 2002
- Cyber Security Enhancement of Act of 2002
- Directorate for Information Analysis and Infrastructure Protection

In addition, with being charged as the primary responsibility of preventing terrorism on America, DHS is accountable for the *Emergency Preparedness and Response Directorate*. The directorate is the foundational policy that ensures DHS protects American citizens, resources, and interests. Finally, the directorate oversees federal government national response and recovery strategies and is responsible for the development of treatment programs for potential biological weapon attacks.

The cabinet department is accountable for public security, and its mission involves providing antiterrorism and cybersecurity programs, border security, immigration and customs, and disaster prevention and management. With 240,000 employees, DHS's mission is to "secure the nation from the many threats we [America] face and the vision of homeland security is to ensure a homeland that is safe, secure, and resilient against terrorism and other hazards" (DHS, n.d.). It is the third largest federal agency after the Department of Veterans Affairs, and all policies are directly coordinated with the White House through the *Homeland Security Council*. There is much speculation if DHS is a part of DoD because of the similarities of the missions, initiatives, and objectives. DoD is responsible for U.S. Armed Forces movements, particularly abroad, and DHS is based on working with civilians to protect the United States within its borders and territories to prevent and respond to domestic emergencies.

Provisions

The Homeland Security Act of 2002 includes numerous provisions that identify specific responsibilities under the Emergency Preparedness and Response Directorate (EPR). According to the HSA of 2002, the EPR Directorate's summary states:

> The Homeland Security Act of 2002 (P.L. 107–296) requires the Emergency Preparedness and Response Directorate (EPR) of the Department of Homeland Security (DHS) to coordinate federal emergency management activities. The law consolidates federal emergency authorities and resources into EPR—but not terrorism preparedness activities, which are administered by the Border and Transportation Security Directorate within DHS. This report provides summaries of and references to the entities that constitute EPR, as well as brief statements of issues that may come before the 108th Congress (Bea, et al., 2003, para. 1).

EPR has specific priorities that are the responsibility of DHS to understand the evolution of threats and enhance response capabilities to those threats. The following are overview provisions:

- Promote the effectiveness of emergency responders
- Support the Nuclear Incident Response Team through standards, training, exercises, and provision of funds to named federal agencies
- Provide the federal response by managing, directing, overseeing, and coordinating specified federal resources
- Aid recovery
- Build an intergovernmental national incident management system to guide responses
- Consolidate existing federal response plans
- Develop programs for interoperate communications for emergency responders

HOMELAND SECURITY PRESIDENTIAL DIRECTIVE NO. 5

On February 28, 2003, *Homeland Security Presidential Directive No. 5 (NSPD 5)* was enacted to "enhance the ability of the United States to manage domestic incidents by establishing a single, comprehensive national incident management system (NIMS)" (Department of Homeland Security, para. 1). The policy states in the HSPD 5 that to

> Prevent, prepare, respond, and recover from terrorist attacks, major disasters, and other emergencies, the United States government shall establish a single, comprehensive approach to domestic incident management. The objective of the United States Government is to ensure that all levels of government across the Nation have the capability to work efficiently and effectively together, using a national approach to domestic incident management. In these efforts, with regard to domestic incidents, the United States government treats crisis management and consequence management as a single, integrated function, rather than as two separate functions (HSPD 5, 2003, p. 1).

The HSPD 5 outlines policies, departmental missions, and responsibilities of the Secretary of the Department of Homeland Security. The policy also covers Technical and Conforming Amendments to National Security Presidential Directives, which are directives used to publicize presidential decisions on national security matters.

National Incident Management System (NIMS)

The Department of Homeland Security developed NIMS as a systematic method of incident management. President George W. Bush established NIMS in 2004. NIMS was derived from HSPD 5 and was proposed to facilitate coordination among all responding agencies, including government, nongovernment organizations, public, and private sectors. The incident management system is based on three core systems:

- The Incident Command System (ICS) includes the operation characteristics, interactive management components, and the structure of incident management and emergency response organizations engaged throughout the life cycle of an incident.

- The Multiagency Coordination defines the operating characteristics, interactive management components, and organizational structure of supporting incident-management entities engaged at the federal, state, local, tribal, and regional levels through mutual aid agreements and other assistance arrangements.

- Public Information Systems refers to the processes, procedures, and systems for communicating timely and accurate information to the public during crisis or emergency situations (n.d., para. 1).

The purpose of NIMS is to offer national structure and methods to enable government agencies at all levels, nongovernmental organizations, and private-sector companies to communicate and share information in the event of an emergency. For instance, the incident management system provides resources for all organizations to prepare for, recover from, respond to, and prevent effects of national incidents. Having a structured management system provides groundwork to establish efficient and effective communications on a national level among all organizations, promoting faster response times. According to FEMA, organizations that utilize NIMS as part of the planning and preparation processes can locate an incident with little notice, understand incident-management policies and provide the correct resources and personnel to assist.

There are five components to NIMS:

- Preparedness
- Communication and Information Management
- Resource Management
- Command and Management
- Ongoing Management and Maintenance (FEMA, n.d., p. 1).

The five elements revert to the NIMs and the National Response Framework (NRF)

THE
9/11
COMMISSION
REPORT

FINAL REPORT OF THE NATIONAL COMMISSION ON
TERRORIST ATTACKS UPON THE UNITED STATES

Figure 8.2 The 9/11 Commission Report Cover

THE 9/11 COMMISSION REPORT

Known as the *Final Report of the National Commission on Terrorist Attacks Upon the United States,* the 9/11 Report is an account of events which led up to the terrorist attacks that were executed on September 11, 2001. The report requested by President George W. Bush was organized by the National Commission on Terrorist Attacks Upon the United States. President Bush established the commission on November 27, 2002, and the final report was given to the president on July 22, 2004. The 9/11 Commission Report stated, "long-term success demands the use of all the elements of national powers: diplomacy, intelligence, covert action, law enforcement, economic policy, foreign aid, public diplomacy, and homeland defense" (2004, p. 363).

Report Findings

In less than two years, the 9/11 Commission interviewed over 1,200 people within ten countries, reviewing over two million documents to formulate a report that showcased the vulnerabilities that led to the attacks. A significant number of the documents were classified; however, the committee focused on the FBI's operative investigation to gather evidence. The FBI's investigation, codename PENTTBOM (Pentagon/Twin Towers), was considered the largest criminal inquiry in the agency's history, utilizing over three thousand professional employees and over four thousand special agents.

After the findings of the commission report, Presidents Bill Clinton and George W. Bush were criticized by the CIA and the FBI due to major intelligence failures that were responsible for the attacks. The report identified that in addition to lack of intelligence and information sharing, there were security breaches at the airports. Evidence was provided to the committee, including recordings of the terrorists and passengers last moments to speak with their families before they died. The committee noted that over half (15) of the hijackers were from Saudi Arabia but concluded that the Saudi government did not have any connection or involvement in the planning of the attacks. The leader of the attacks, Mohamed Atta, was from Egypt, two hijackers were from the United Arab Emirates, and one was from Lebanon. All hijackers were al-Qaeda operatives led by Osama bin Laden.

The 9/11 Commission Report identified information regarding a connection between Iran and al-Qaeda due to intelligence that found that some of the hijackers traveled through Iran, but their passports were stamped upon entry. However, the committee

Selections from the U.S. Government Accountability Office, *9/11 COMMISSION REPORT: Reorganization, Transformation, and Information Sharing*, pp. 2-4. 2004.

could not find information that the Iranian government was involved in the planning or execution of the attacks. Significant information showed the military was not notified by the Federal Aviation Administration, even though its leadership testified that everyone who needed to be notified was contacted for emergency response purposes. There were also mandates for the government to improve regulations and policies to prevent another terrorist attack from happening on American soil. The Government Accountability Office's Comptroller General, the Honorable David M. Walker, testified before the Committee on Government Reform and the House of Representatives regarding recommendations that should be considered to deter terrorist acts on American soil.

Recommendations from the Government Accountability Office

The 9/11 Commission recommended several transformational changes, such as the establishment of a National Counterterrorism Center (NCTC) for joint operational planning and joint intelligence and replacing the current Director of Central Intelligence with a National Intelligence Director (NID) to oversee national intelligence centers across the federal government. The NID would manage the national intelligence program and oversee agencies that contribute to it. On August 2, 2004, the president asked Congress to create a NID position to be the principal intelligence advisor, appointed by the president, with the advice and consent of the Senate and serving at the pleasure of the president. Unlike the 9/11 Commission, the president did not propose that the NID be within the Executive Office of the president. He also announced that he would establish a NCTC whose Director would report to the NID, and that this center would build upon the analytic work of the existing Terrorist Threat Integration Center. He suggested that a separate center may be necessary for issues of weapons of mass destruction. Finally, he endorsed the 9/11 Commission's call for reorganization of congressional oversight structure. The President's proposal and the Commission's recommendations had several substantive differences. While praising the work of the 9/11 Commission and endorsing several of its major recommendations in concept, the president differed with the Commission on certain issues. These differences reflect that reasoned and reasonable individuals may differ and that several methods may exist to effectuate the transformational changes recommended. However, certain common principles and factors outlined in this statement today should help guide the debate ahead. Although the creation of a NID and a NCTC would be major changes for the intelligence community, other structural and management changes have occurred and are continuing to occur in government that provide lessons for the intelligence community transformation. While the intelligence community has historically been addressed separately from the remainder of the federal government and while it undoubtedly performs some unique missions that present unique issues, its major transformational challenges in large measure are the same as those that face most government agencies. As a result, GAO's findings, recommendations, and experience in reshaping the federal government to meet twenty-first century challenges will be directly relevant to the intelligence community and the recommendations proposed by the 9/11 Commission. The goal of improving information sharing and analysis with a focus upon the needs of the consumers of such improved information for specific types of threats can provide one of the powerful guiding principles necessary for successful transformation. This testimony covers four major points. First, it describes the rationale for improving effective information sharing and analysis and suggests some ways to achieve positive results. Second, it provides some overview perspectives on reorganization approaches to improve performance and notes necessary cautions. Third, it illustrates that strategic human capital management must be the centerpiece of any serious change-management initiative or any effort to transform the cultures of government agencies, including that of the intelligence community. Finally, it emphasizes the importance of results-oriented strategic planning and implementation for the intelligence arena, focusing management attention on outcomes, not outputs, and the need for effective accountability and oversight to maintain focus upon improving performance. It concludes by applying these concepts and principles to the challenges of reform in the intelligence community (Government Accountability Office [GAO], 2004, p. 1).

EMERGENCY MANAGEMENT REFORM ACT

Officially titled the *Post-Katrina Emergency Management Reform Act of 2006,* the Emergency Management Reform Act was established in response to nation's largest natural disaster, Hurricane Katrina. Hurricane Katrina was the largest natural disaster in American history, a catastrophe for which the country was not adequately prepared. Nearly two thousand people died from the effects and aftermath of the hurricane, and it affected multiple states (Alabama, the Bahamas, Cuba, Florida, Mississippi, Louisiana, and eastern parts of the United States). Hurricane Katrina caused nearly $110 billion in damage, and the everlasting on the effects on the communities and the victims has become unfathomable. Because there were many discrepancies, vulnerabilities, and an inadequate response to the natural disaster, the *Post-Katrina Emergency Management Reform Act* was established. The legislation significantly reorganized operations and responsibilities of the Federal Emergency Management Agency and increased emergency management processes to ensure that the country is prepared for future disasters. The new responsibilities included the following:

- Establishes a Disability Coordinator and develops guidelines to accommodate individuals with disabilities.
- Establishes the National Emergency Family Registry and Locator System to reunify separated family members.
- Coordinates and supports precautionary evacuations and recovery efforts.
- Provides transportation assistance for relocating and returning individuals displaced from their residences in a major disaster.
- Provides case management assistance to identify and address unmet needs of survivors of major disasters (FEMA, n.d., para. 2).

The legislation amended the Homeland Security Act of 2002 under Title I of the National Preparedness and Response initiative, which made significant changes to the emergency management provisions while leaving the agency under the Department of Homeland Security. Additionally, hierarchical changes were made to ensure accountability and continuity.

In response to the 9/11 and the enactment of the Homeland Security Act of 2002, Congress has passed numerous law on homeland security initiatives. Called the *Laws with DHS Impacts,* Congress has legislated in the defense of protecting the homeland and its citizens. Following are some statutes that have been passed that influences DHS and its mission operatives:

- DHS Implementation of Executive Order 13563
- The DHS Final Plan
- International Child Abduction Prevention and Return Act
- Accuracy for Adoptees Act
- Intelligence Reform and Terrorism Prevention Act of 2004
- Implementing Recommendations of the 9–11 Commission Act of 2007

DHS LEGISLATION

DHS Implementation of Executive Order 13563

Executive Order 13563, *Improving Regulation and Regulatory Review* was passed on January 18, 2011 consists of the "principles and requirements designed to promote public participation, improve integration and innovation, increase flexibility, ensure scientific integrity, and increase retrospective analysis of existing rules" (DHS Implementation of Executive Order 13563, n.d., para. 1).

The DHS Final Plan

The DHS Final Plan is a document crafted to uniquely identify unnecessary and obsolete regulations that are relevant to the mission and standards of DHS. The department's review process was implemented to "facilitate the identification of the rules that warrant repeal, modification, strengthening, complementing, or modernizing, where necessary or appropriate" (DHS Implementation of Executive Order 13563, n.d., para. 8).

International Child Abduction Prevention and Return Act

The Sean and David Goldman International Child Abduction Prevention and Return Act of 2014 (Pub. L. No. 113–150) reconstitutes the Homeland Security Act of 2002, in which the Secretary of Homeland Security, the Secretary of State, the U.S. Attorney General, and the Director of the FBI formulizes a sound program through U.S. Customs and Border Protection to thwart children from leaving the United States if a parent presents an order from a servicing a court with jurisdiction to ban their remove to a Customs and Border Patrol officer (2014 Laws with DHS Impacts, n.d., para. 1).

Accuracy for Adoptees Act

The Immigration and Nationality Act (INA) mandates that a Certificate of Citizenship or other federal document issued to be amended under section 320 of the INA reflect a child's name and date of birth, which is legally annotated on a birth certificate, certificate of foreign birth, certificate of birth abroad, or any other state and/or federal vital statistical record documentation issued by the minor's state of residence after the child has been adopted or readopted in that state (2014 Laws with DHS Impacts, n.d., para. 2). In addition to child matters, the INA also outlines DHS's responsibility to mandate provisions on the admission of aliens, the removal of aliens, grants of asylum, and the investigation of human trafficking (General DHS Laws, n.d., para. 6).

General DHS Laws

Intelligence Reform and Terrorism Prevention Act of 2004

Signed by President George W. Bush on December 17, 2004, the Intelligence Reform and Terrorism Prevention Act was created in response to the 9/11 attacks. This legislative act created the Director of National Intelligence position as well as the National Counterterrorism Center, and the Privacy and Civil Liberties Oversight Board. This act mandates DHS full authority of flight information of all airline passengers on international and domestic flights. In addition, TSA implemented a Secure Flight program to enforcement the regulations of the act. The intelligence form act has eight categories:

- Reform of the intelligence community
- Federal Bureau of Investigation
- Security clearances
- Transportation security
- Border protection, immigration, and visa matters
- Terrorism prevention
- Implementation of 9/11 Commission recommendations
- Other matters (Intelligence Reform and Terrorism Prevention Act of 2004, 2004).

Implementing Recommendations of the 9–11 Commission Act of 2007

Formally known as *The Implementing Recommendations of the 9–11 Commission Act of 2007*, this legislative piece outlines DHS's mission, cargo security, critical infrastructure protection, grant administration, intelligence and information sharing, privacy, and transportation security (General DHS Laws, n.d., para. 3).

Maritime Legislation & Transportation Security

The following are responsible for the security of the nation's waterways, ports, and maritime issues such as shipping, navigation, and natural disasters within the waters. It also includes legislation, which established TSA and was enforces Federal Aviation Administration and other security measures dealing with nation's transportation system:

- Maritime Transportation Security Act of 2002 (Public Law 107–295)
- Coast Guard and Maritime Transportation Act of 2006 (Public Law 109–241)
- Security and Accountability for Every Port Act of 2006 (SAFE Port Act) (Public Law 109–347)
- Coast Guard Authorization Act of 2010 (Public Law 111–281)
- Aviation and Transportation Security Act (Public Law 107–71)

CONGRESSIONAL BUDGETING AND APPROPRIATIONS

The United States budget process is predicated on the congressional framework used by the president of the United States to establish the nation's federal budget. The Budgeting and Accounting Act of 1921 and the Congressional Budget and Impoundment Control Act of 1974 created the budgeting process. The need for a federal budget was apparent when President Richard Nixon refused to spend funding allocated by Congress, causing the Senate to develop a formal process to ensure such matters were mitigated. As a result, additional budgeting legislation was developed, like the Congressional Budget Act of 1974, which created the *Congressional Budget Office (CBO),* gaining more insight and control of the budget, limiting presidential powers of the *Office of Management and Budget.*

Congressional Budget Office

The Congressional Budget Office (CBO) is a federal organization with the United States legislative branch and is responsible for all budgeting and economic information, which is reported to Congress. CBO was established as a nonpartisan department under Title II of the Congressional Budget and Impoundment Control Act of 1974 and was signed by President Richard Nixon on July 12, 1974. CBO was formulated to settle disputes between President Nixon and Congress, which was controlled by the Democratic Party at the time. According to Neal Q. Herrick in After Patrick Henry: A Second American Revolution, Congress wanted to protect the power of the purse from Nixon (2009, p. 27).

Since the inception of CBO, the organization has superseded OMB as the "authoritative source of information on the budget and economy" (Joyce, 2015, p. 1). The organization's mission is to "produce independent analyses of budgetary and economic issues to support the congressional budget process" (n.d., para. 1). In addition, CBO is responsible for the following:

- Helping Congress formulate a budget plan;
- Helping Congress stay within that plan; and,
- Helping Congress consider policy issues related to the budget and the economy (Reischauer, 1993, p. 3).

Annually, the organization releases reports and cost estimates for proposed bills without disseminating policy recommendations. CBO serves as a mechanism to align with the Joint Committee on Taxation for estimating revenue for Congress along with the U.S. Department of Treasury for estimating revenues for the executive branch. This also includes financial projections of the national deficit and cost estimates for proposed bills.

Under the Budget Act, CBO is required to submit periodic reports on fiscal policy to the House and Senate budget committees to provide baseline projections of the federal government budget. The *Economic and Budget Outlook* is currently the annual document that is prepared for such reports, and the *Analysis of the President's Budgetary Proposals* is based on the following fiscal year, which is mandated by the Senate Committee on Appropriations. Finally, CBO is subcategorized into eight classifications:

- Budget Analysis
- Financial Analysis
- Health, Retirement, and Long-Term Analysis
- Macroeconomic Analysis
- Management, Business, and Information Services
- Microeconomic Studies
- National Security
- Tax Analysis (n.d., para. 1).

The House and Senate Budget Committees provide recommendations to the Speaker of the House of Representatives and the president pro tempore of the Senate, who ultimately appoints the CBO Director. The CBO Director serves a four-year term with no limit on the number of terms one may serve. Directors can fill positions until his or her successor is appointed and can be removed from office by Congress by declaration.

Office of Management and Budget

The Office of Management and Budget (OMB) is the largest office within the Executive branch of the president of the United States. The organization's mission is to "assist the president in meeting his policy, budget, management and regulatory objectives and to fulfill the agency's statutory responsibilities" (n.d., para. 1). OMB's primary responsibility is to manage the president's budget, but the organization also assesses the worth of other federal agencies, policies, and procedures to determine if each complies with the president's policies and initiatives. OMB is headed by the OMB Director, who is appointed by and reports to the president, vice president, and the White House Chief of Staff.

Initially created as the Bureau of the Budget, OMB was established in 1921 as a subsidiary of the U.S. Department of Treasury under the Budget and Accounting Act of 1921, signed by President Warren G. Harding. In 1939, OMB was moved under the Executive Office of the President and reorganized in 1970 under the leadership of the Nixon administration. By the 1990s, OMB was once again restructured to identify the distinction between the management and budgetary staff that have dual roles within resource management offices. The purpose of OMB is to prepare the president's annual proposed budget to Congress and manage the administration of the executive branch organizations. In addition, the agency assesses the effectiveness of federal programs, policies, and procedures to ensure funding priorities are met. Finally, OMB ensures reports, rules, testimony, and proposed laws are coherent with executive administration policies and the president's budget.

OMB is charged with the coordination of executive branch's financial management, information, procurement, and regulatory policies. In all areas, the organization is responsible for improving administrative management procedures, coordinating mechanisms, developing performance measures, and mitigating unwarranted burdening on American citizens. OMB is comprised of presidential appointed and Senate-approved positions:

- Director
- Deputy Director
- Deputy Direct of Management
- Office of Information and Regulatory Affairs
- Office of Federal Procurement Policy
- Office of Federal Financial Management

The Federal Budgeting Cycle

The United States budgeting process commences when the president of the United States submits a budget request to Congress, which is between the first Monday in January and the first Monday in February of each year. At times the president's budget has been delayed due to unforeseen circumstances, but the timeframe is usually in the beginning of each year. President Warren G. Harding was responsible for the execution of the Budget and Accounting Act of 1921, which required presidents to submit an annual budget to Congress and created the Bureau of the Budget (now known as the Office of Management and Budget). During President Harding's era, the Bureau of the Budget was strategically under the U.S. Department of Treasury, but in 1939, the office moved to the Executive Office of the President. The Office of Management and Budget, the largest office within the Executive Office of the President, aids with the president's budget and a plan is devised over a few months to identify funding requests for all federal executive departments and independent agencies. During the formulation process, historical and supporting documents are used to determine the President's budget request by aligning such information with Congress's policy initiatives, proposals, and other revenue and spending propositions. The importance of the president's budget request is that the proposal is predicated on mandatory spending plans for the following fiscal year and includes a plethora of supporting details to motivate Congress to consider budget provisions. Furthermore, other executive and independent federal agencies provide their budget requests, which are considered during this time.

The United States congressional budgeting system is subcategorized as budget functions. Such functions include all spending for federal agencies and are predicated on budget resolutions by the president and Congress. The following are twenty classifications of major budget functions of the federal budget that are predicated on the purposes of the president and Congress.

Budget Determinations

After the formulation of the budget, the proposal is referred to the House and Senate Budget Committees and then to the CBO with all federal agency budget requests. Each March, CBO publishes an analysis of the president's budget proposals, the report, and other publications to its website. In addition, the CBO calculates the current-law baseline budget projects, which is intended to assess federal spending and revenues in absence of new legislation for the current fiscal year and up to the following ten years. Furthermore, during the month of March, the budget committee considers the president's budget proposals, predicated on the CBO budget report, and each committee submits a budget resolution to its respective house by April 1 of each year. The House and Senate ruminate the budget resolutions and make final decisions (with possible amendments) by April 15 of each year. A budget resolution is not a law and does not need the president's signature nor House or Senate approval to pass such a legislation. Instead, such resolutions are an outline for the appropriation (the sum of money allocated for a specific purpose) process. Budget resolutions are not always passed each year, and if this is the case, the previous year's resolution remains in effect until a new one is enacted.

After the budget resolution is passed, specific Representatives and Senators are selected to negotiate a **conference report** (the final legislation that is negotiated between the House of Representatives and the Senate from the conference committee) to reconcile differences between the House and Senate accounts. For the conference report to be approved, the House and Senate must both agree to the terms.

Appropriations

Appropriations are simply sums of money set aside for specific purposes. In terms of the Congressional budget, appropriations must be authorized through legislation by the committee charged with providing funding for federal government programs. Congress then authorizes the budget through the Appropriations Committee of the House. In theory, committees with precedence authorize specific programs and policy decisions, and the Appropriation Committees determine funding levels. The budget resolutions stipulate funding levels for the House and Senate Appropriations Committee, and the twelve subcommittees establish allocations (the process of distributing), budget sums, entitlements, and reconciliation instructions. Next, the appropriations committees begin allocations for the budget resolution and draft appropriations bills that are sent to the House and Senate for consideration after May 15. When the budget is finalized, the spending becomes available to the appropriations committee for the following fiscal year and is provided in a joint explanatory statement, which is included in the conference report. Finally, the appropriations committees allocate the approved allocations to the twelve subcommittees, and each is responsible for the control of the funding for programs under its authority.

During the appropriations process, a conference committee is required to resolve disputes between the House and Senate appropriations bills. When the conference bill is passed through Congress, it is sent to the president, who has the option sign or veto the bill. If the president signs the bill, it becomes law, and if not, Congress must pass another bill to avoid a shutdown of the federal government. There have been cases when Congress did not pass appropriations bills before the beginning of a fiscal year, causing **continuing resolutions** (an appropriation bill that allocates money for specific federal government agencies and programs) to suffice for temporary funding of government operations. Continuing resolutions is an appropriations legislation that provides funding for certain federal government agencies and programs when an appropriations bill is not passed by end of the fiscal year. Failure to appropriate funds as scheduled results in a situation such as the 2013 federal government shutdown. There are flaws within the Congressional appropriations and allocations processes, resulting in a modest number of programs lapsing due to lack of authorizations, and some programs do not receive funding at all.

Discretionary Spending

Discretionary spending is the process of government spending through an appropriations bill. The spending process is established by the House and Senate Appropriations Committees and the twelve subcommittees. Congress is responsible for discretionary spending, which is fixed for approximately a year, but some appropriations are for longer periods. For example, there are multi-year appropriations for housing and military procurement programs. As of 2017, twelve appropriations bills are required to be passed each fiscal year to sustain discretionary spending. The appropriation bills are as follows:

- Agriculture, Food and Drug Administration, Rural Development, and Related Agencies
- Commerce, Justice, Science, and Related Agencies
- Defense
- Energy and Water Development and Related Agencies
- Financial Services and General Government
- Full Committee
- Homeland Security
- Interior, Environment, and Related Agencies
- Labor, Health, and Human Services, Education, and Related Agencies

- Legislative Branch
- Military Construction, Veterans Affairs, and Related Agencies
- State, Foreign Operations, and Related Programs
- Transportation, Housing and Urban Development, and Related Agencies ("The U.S. House of Representatives Committee on Appropriations, n.d., para. 1).
- In some instances, multiple bills are combined to formulate one entire legislation, like the *Omnibus Appropriations Act of 2009*, which President Obama signed to fund Cabinet departments, except for the Department of Defense, Homeland Security, and Veterans Affairs.

Mandatory Spending

Mandatory spending is mandatory legislation enacted by the federal government to set aside funding for specific programs dictated by the government authority. Also, known as direct spending, mandatory spending is not dependent upon an appropriations bill and entails budgeting acquisitions for Medicare, Medicaid, and Social Security benefits, which are significantly large programs in the federal government's mandatory spending endeavors. The CBO is responsible for estimating costs for mandatory spending and determines the budget on a frequent basis. Even though the CBO is responsible for mandatory spending assessments, Congress can affect mandatory spending by altering eligibility requirements or the structure of programs. These are considered appropriated entitlements, which are specific programs authorized under appropriation bills (i.e. Medicaid, Medicaid, and Social Security benefits).

SUMMARY

The Nunn-Lugar Cooperative Threat Reduction is considered one of the most successful polices in American history, due to anticipated, global concerns about nuclear programs in the post-Cold War era along with the demise of the Soviet Union. Establishing the Cooperative Threat Reduction Program ensured the disarming and dismantling of weapons of mass destruction, particularly in former Soviet Union states, and has been an effective enterprise in the twenty first century. This historic initiative was honor on the 25th anniversary of the Nunn-Lugar Cooperative Threat Reduction legislation when the 25th Secretary of Defense, Dr. Ash Carter, presented former Senators Sam Nunn and Richard Lugar with Trailblazer Awards and a dedicated key to the Pentágon. Corresponding policies have led to further legislation enacted by American presidents and implemented after the 9/11 attacks.

The federal budget process is one of the most multifaceted and complex practices in the world. The president is responsible for the United States federal budget, which is predicated on the established congressional framework (primarily the Budget and Accounting Act of 1921 and the Congressional Budget and Impoundment Control Act of 1974). The president's budget is what begins the annual process, determining Congress' action on concurrent budget resolutions, the national deficit, revenue, and total spending for at least the following five years. In addition, Congress considers annual appropriation bills needed to fund discretionary programs along with specific legislation to fund mandatory spending and tax programs. The congressional budget is not perfect and has not been an effective mechanism over recent years (for example, the 2013 government shutdown and sequestration); however, it is America's system for funding and regulating federal programs.

CHAPTER 8 CASE STUDIES

Case Study 1
Conspiracies of the 9/11 Commission Report

The 9/11 Commission Report, formally named the Final Report of the National Commission on Terrorist Attacks Upon the United States, is the official report of the events leading up to the terrorist attacks against the U.S. on September 11, 2001. It was prepared by an independent, bipartisan commission created by congressional legislation, the National Commission on Terrorist Attacks Upon the U.S., at the request of President George W. Bush. Charged with preparing a complete report of the circumstances surrounding the terrorist attacks of September 11, 2001, including U.S. preparedness and immediate response, the Commission identified pre-and post-attack intelligence failures and made recommendations for improvements to prevent a future similar attack (9/11 Commission, 2011).

The 9/11 Commission began its first hearings in the spring of 2003, interviewing over 1,200 people in ten countries and reviewing over two million pages of documents. It presented its findings in a public report that was released in July 2004 (9/11 Commission, 2011). Upon its release, many were quick to criticize the report, pointing out that the 9/11 Commission was not truly independent and that it suffered from conflicts of interest due to connections between some of its members and key figures in the administration (9/11 Commission, 2011).

The President initially named Henry Kissinger, former Secretary of State, to lead the Commission. Kissinger had previously served as national security advisor to President Nixon and Secretary of State under President Ford. However, his appointment was criticized not only because of his ties to powerful national and international figures but because he had been accused of being involved in past cover-ups in Latin America (Roberts, 2002). Although Kissinger resigned from the position after two weeks, reports continued claiming that the White House was still attempting to control any information released with officials agreeing to testify only under certain conditions that included joint testifying, no requirement to take the oath, and no recorded testimonies (Solomon, 2006).

Furthermore, White House political director Karl Rove worried that a Commission report blaming President Bush for 9/11 would jeopardize the president's re-election. As a result, White House leaders attempted to derail the investigation from the onset, pressuring those on the Commission to withhold any reports that would make the president or his staff seem incompetent (Ex-9/11 panel chief denies secret White House ties, 2008). Executive Director of the Commission Philip Zelikow attempted to suggest a greater tie between al-Qaeda and Iraq (which the Bush administration had cited to justify the war) by altering a report to depict repeated communication between the terrorist network and Saddam Hussein's government (Yen, 2006).

Commission chairmen Lee Hamilton and Thomas Kean believed that there was an agreement at some level of the government to not tell the truth about what happened, deliberately obstructing the Commission's investigation. They accused the Central Intelligence Agency (CIA) of purposefully withholding and destroying interrogation tapes of two al-Qaeda operatives, despite repeated and detailed requests from the Commission to provide any documents or information about the interrogation (Mazzetti, 2007). Furthermore, in December 2003, the Commission had requested permission to interview the two detainees, but it was instead instructed to give the questions to CIA interrogators who would ask the prisoners. It was later discovered that much of the information reported about the planning and execution of the terror attacks on the U.S. was the product of "enhanced interrogation techniques," which may have affected their credibility. This was especially problematic since at least twenty-five percent of the footnotes used in the 9/11 investigation referred to information obtained during the controversial interrogations (Windrem and Limjoco, 2008). When questioned, Zelikow said, "We were not aware, but we guessed that things like that were going on.... We were wary... We tried to find different sources to enhance our credibility" (Windrem and Limjoco, 2008). In the end, the Commission chose to publicly release its understanding of what took place, regardless that, as a matter of law, evidence derived from torture is not reliable, in part because of the possibility of false confession (Windrem and Limjoco, 2008).

Like the CIA, officials at the North American Aerospace Defense Command (NORAD) and the Federal Aviation Administration (FAA) had provided inaccurate information regarding responses to the hijackings. Officials initially suggested that air defenses had reacted quickly and that jets had been scrambled and were prepared to shoot down United Airlines Flight 93 if it threatened the nation's capital. However, upon forcing NORAD and the FAA to release evidence under a subpoena, the audiotapes later showed this to be false. Between the reluctance to release the tape and the erroneous public statements and other evidence, the Commission believed that officials from both NORAD and the FAA sought to mislead the investigation and the public about what had happened on 9/11 (Eggen, 2006).

In addition to sections of the government impeding the Commission's investigation, many people also criticize the Commission's claim that there was no prior knowledge of the terrorist cell and its plan to attack the U.S. until the day of the attack. Former FBI Director Louis Freeh argues that the Commission's credibility is questionable at best since it refused to acknowledge testimony of the many pre–September 11 warnings given to the FBI and U.S. intelligence agencies and ignored key evidence from Able Danger, a data-mining project which had identified the alleged leaders of the hijackers and two of the three terrorist cells responsible for 9/11 (Goodwin, 2005). Furthermore, a federal report issued two years before the attacks warned that al-Qaeda might hijack an airliner and dive bomb it into specific government buildings as a reprisal for the U.S. airstrikes against the terrorist camps in Afghanistan. An FBI agent in Arizona also speculated in his notes about using planes as weapons, specifically noting that Zacarias Moussaoui was the type of person who would be capable of suicide hijacking. Moussaoui was later detained in Minnesota after raising suspicions at his flight school, where he wanted to learn to fly but not land or take off. However, the FBI failed to make a connection between the agent's warning and the incident in Minnesota (Brush, 2002). Additionally, the CIA had continuously warned policymakers throughout the summer before September 11 that the al-Qaeda cell might try to harm U.S. interests and discussed a range of possibilities that included hijackings (Brush, 2002).

Although the Commission was charged with preparing a complete report of the circumstances surrounding the terrorist attacks of September 11, 2001, they focused little on pre-9/11 attacks. Part of this stemmed from the White House "recommendation" that the Commission focus on analyzing enemy tactics and next moves rather than failures in the government. Even if the Commission had focused on pre- and post- 9/11 attack responses, the continuing resistance to the work of the Commission by many politicians; the deception of the Commission by various key government agencies, including the Department of Defense, CIA, NORAD and the FAA; and the denial of access by various agencies made it a difficult feat. Even the Commission chairmen themselves believed that they were set up for failure.

Case Study 2
Sequestration of 2013

In 2013, the U.S. federal government entered a shutdown from October 1 to October 16, ceasing all routine operations. The sixteen-day shutdown was the first shutdown since 1996 and the third-longest government shutdown in U.S. history. The failure of Congress to come to an agreement on the twelve appropriation bills to fund as well as spending priorities left the government without a budget to keep the government financed. Sequestration played a significant role leading up to the shutdown as the House and Senate argued where those mandatory cuts would take place.

Sequestration is a series of automatic cuts to federal spending to government agencies. It was originally passed as part of the Budget Control Act of 2011 (BCA), otherwise known as the debt ceiling compromise, which intended to serve as incentive for the Joint Select Committee on Deficit Reduction to cut $1.5 trillion over ten years (Matthews, 2013). The cuts would be split 50–50 between defense and domestic discretionary spending, with more than $500 billion being cut from the Department of Defense (DOD) and other national security agencies, with the rest on the domestic side (Smith, 2013). The Budget Control Act originally proposed that the cuts would take effect at the beginning of 2013; however, with the expiration of the Bush tax cuts and payroll tax cuts, it would have caused a fiscal cliff, throwing the U.S. back into another recession. Reluctant to see a recession, a deal was made that delayed sequestration to March 1 by the American Taxpayer Relief Act of 2012 (Matthews, 2013). Yet even with the delay, the House and Senate failed to come to an agreement on what to fund, with the Affordable Care Act funding being the primary matter of contention. Republicans staunchly refused to accept any plan that raised discretionary spending above $988 billion while Democrats pushed for funding closer to pre-sequestration levels at $1.058 trillion (Plummer, 2013). By midnight October 1, with no budget in place to keep the federal government financed, the government officially shut down.

The shutdown left 850,000 federal employees furloughed for a combined total of 6.6 million days, costing the federal government two billion dollars due to the lost productivity of furloughed workers and other costs because of the shutdown, including paying additional interest on payments that were late because of the shutdown. It also required another 1.3 million essential federal employees to report to work without known payment dates. Furthermore, the shutdown followed a three-year pay freeze for federal employees and cuts in training and support which made it harder for the government to attract and retain the skilled and driven workforce that the government needs (Burwell, 2013).

Despite the shutdown, under the Antideficiency Act, several key government functions specifically related to national security, public safety, or programs written into permanent law continued to operate. Under the public safety statute, air traffic control, all emergency medical care, border patrol, federal prisons, most law enforcement, emergency and disaster assistance, and operations overseeing the banking system, operating the power grid, and guarding federal property stayed open (Plummer, 2013). While the Federal Bureau of Investigation (FBI) and law enforcement continued to carry out operations, they were still impacted by the shutdown. The FBI released a compiled feedback report from field agents describing the impact on their operations, including being unable to pay informants and closing active cases due to lack of investigative personnel, leading to potential loss of highly sensitive classified information (Nathanson, 2013).

As a matter of national security, the president signed a last-minute Pay Our Military Act, which exempted the military from furloughs, stating, "If you're serving in harm's way, we're going to make sure you have what you need to succeed in your missions" (Michaels, 2013). Leading up to October 1, 2013, the Department of Defense, under the guidance of Deputy Secretary of Defense Ashton B. Carter, issued a contingency plan to continue essential activities if the budget lapsed. These activities included not only the war in Afghanistan but also other military operations and embassies abroad, and "many other operations necessary for safety of human life and protection of property, including operations essential for the security of our Nation" (Belasco, 2013). However, even with the Pay Our Military Act, the shutdown still affected the DOD as civilian workers who provided a range of services on military bases, including maintenance on buildings and barracks, and family counseling and survivor outreach, were furloughed (Michaels, 2013).

While the Defense Intelligence Agency and the National Security Agency weren't impacted as much as other agencies due to their military population, the Central Intelligence Agency furloughed 12,500 of its civilian workforce. Shawn Turner, former chief spokesman for the Director of National Intelligence, expressed concern that the Intelligence Community's ability to identify threats and provide information would be diminished, forcing them to assume greater risks and only focus on the most critical security needs (Hosenball, 2013). Additionally, troop movements and training were limited if not directly related to contingency operations overseas. The Air Force's Air Combat Command grounded several aircraft squadrons that were not set to deploy until after January, including the 366th Fighter Wing at Mountain Home Air Force Base. Because of the reduction in training hours, the 126th Air National Guard Refueling Wing at Scott Air Force Base had to ground eight of its KC-135 tankers (Reed and Lubold, 2013). Furthermore, reservists were not allowed to perform inactive duty training unless the training directly supported an excepted activity, and they weren't able to be ordered to active duty for annual training (Belasco, 2013). The private-sector defense industry, which relies heavily on U.S. government contracts, was forced to furlough employees as well. Defense contractors experienced disruptions as the shutdown prevented those companies from delivering goods, disrupting supply chains as well as receiving payments for work already done (Lazar, 2013).

After sixteen days of political fighting, Congress passed the Continuing Appropriations Act 2014, finally ending the government shutdown. However, the Act was only a temporary fix as spending levels were authorized only until January 15, 2014. Until the debt ceiling is reduced, sequestration and the approval of the Appropriations Act will continue to be an issue of contention for Congress, with the federal government anxiously awaiting the dawn of the upcoming fiscal year.

CHAPTER 8 PRACTICE PROBLEMS

1. What is the significance of the Nunn-Lugar initiative?
2. What were some of the criticisms of the USA PATRIOT Act of 2001? Do you think it violated the civil liberties of the American people?
3. How can the intelligence community and government better alleviate fears of civil liberties violation?
4. Why was NIMS established, and did it fulfill its purpose?
5. The 9/11 Commission failed to directly address Islamic extremism within the Middle East. If you were part of the 9/11 Commission, what would you do to address the problem?
6. Why did the Bush administration fail to reach minimum standards of implementation of the recommendations from the 9/11 Commission?
7. How did FEMA change under the Post Katrina Emergency Management Reform Act?
8. What are the immediate, short- and long-term effects if a budget resolution is not passed?
9. How are appropriations determined?
10. What are the drawbacks of a Continuing Resolution?

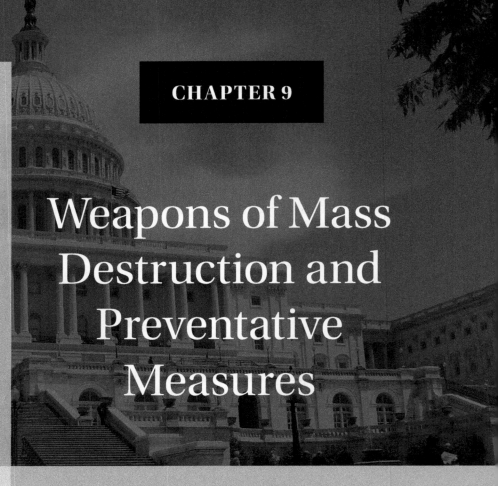

KEY TERMS

Acquiescence

Atomic bomb

Biological weapons

Bioterrorism

Capitulation

CBRNE defense

CBRNE weapons

Chemical weapons

Clandestine operations

Conventional weapons

Denial weapons

Fallout

Germ theory

Mass Assured Destruction (MAD)

Nuclear warfare

Nuclear weapons

Preemptive strike

Rules of Engagement (RoE)

Unconventional warfare

Unconventional weapons

Yield

CHAPTER 9

Weapons of Mass Destruction and Preventative Measures

LEARNING OBJECTIVES

After reading this chapter, students will be able to:

- Analyze all facets of chemical, biological, radiological, nuclear, or explosive (CBRNE) and modern weapons that are a threat to the United States and countries around the world

- Examine past and present CBRNE warfare frameworks, including American defense against and mitigation of weapons of mass destruction

- Explain the role of emergency management and first responders to natural and manmade disasters in the twenty-first century

- Understand the importance of reforming emergency management preparedness and readiness procedures to relate to adverse threats

INTRODUCTION

Ever since the attack on the nation's soil on September 11, 2001, officials have had concerns of another large-scale terrorist attack, primarily a concern if the United States will face a chemical, biological, radiological, nuclear, or explosive (CBRNE) attack. Because of the many threats against the world's dominant country, CBRNE hazards should be considered a prominent means of destroying the United States, damaging the economy, annihilating critical infrastructure, and most importantly, killing millions of Americans. After the world saw America drop bombs on Hiroshima and Nagasaki in 1945, tensions increased (which provoked the Cold-War era) about whether the two superpowers, the United States and the Soviet Union, would engage in the world's second nuclear conflict.

Not only must the United States be concerned with a possible CBRNE attack, the nation also must keep mind that traditional threats still exist such as natural and manmade disasters, which can be overshadowed by new and emerging dangers. Because of technological advancement and progressive research, the U.S. has some advantage in early detection in observing and tracking specific disastrous occurrences. While research continues, advancements continue, especially in the emergency management realm of producing highly trained and equipped professionals to implement preparedness and readiness doctrine to deter the threat or properly handle inevitable emergencies. This chapter will discuss how terrorism has increased the threat and/or risk of other large-scale hazards that could potentially target the United States. It will also discuss the differences between new and traditional threats and how tailored organizations such as the Centers for Disease Control and Prevention handle roles and responsibilities to ensure the United States is equipped to handle any potential threats that affect the nation's existence.

CBRNE WEAPONS

CBRNE is the abbreviation for chemical, biological, radiological, nuclear, and other explosives. Adversaries and terrorists have access to a wide range of CBRNE weapons, from simple weaponry to the most complex systems due to research, development, funding, and technological advancement. Most weapons can be detected with knowledge, preparation, and training by professionals such as emergency/first responders and military personnel. Such weapons are commonly divided into four classifications:

- Biological Weapons
- Chemical Weapons
- Conventional Weapons
- Unconventional Weapons

Figure 9.1 CBRNE Weapons

Rogue nations and non-state actors that have access to and/or can produce weapons of mass destruction pose a serious threat to the United States, its territories, allies, and security partners. In addition, CBRNE materials can catastrophically affect American military operations, and that is why joint commanders of the Unified Combatant Commands have considered these dangers to mitigate the spread of WMDs by providing innovative training and preparedness methods to deter possible execution by domestic and global adversaries.

Because the prevention of the use of CBRNE weapons is a predominant concern of the U.S. military, combatant commanders have formulated key regulations targeted towards the destruction and handling of WMDs:

- Joint Publication 3–27, Homeland Defense
- Joint Publication 3–28, Defense Support for Civil Authorities
- Joint Publication 3–41, Chemical, Biological, Radiological, and Nuclear Consequence Management

Joint Publication 3–11, Operations in Chemical, Biological, Radiological, and Nuclear Environments states CBRN weapons are:

a. Threats, which include the intent and capability to employ weapons or improvised devices to produce CBRN hazards.

b. Hazards, which include CBRN material created from accidental or deliberate releases, toxic industrial materials, chemical and biological agents, biological pathogens, radioactive material, and those hazards resulting from the use of WMDs, or encountered by the Armed Forces of the U.S. during the execution of military operations.

c. A CBRN incident is any occurrence involving the emergence of CBRN hazards resulting from the use of CBRN weapons or devices, the emergence of secondary hazards due to counterforce targeting, or the release of toxic industrial materials into the environment.

d. Refers to the employment of tactical capabilities that counter the entire range of CBRN threat and hazards (2013, p. 1).

Biological Weapons

Biological weapons (bio-weapons) are biological toxins or infectious agents used with the intention to kill humans and animals and destroy agriculture during conflict. Bio weapons are living organisms that can replicate and reproduce in host victims and can be generated various ways to obtain a strategic or tactical position over the enemy. Bio weapons can be used as **denial weapons**, which are "non-lethal, directed-energy, counter-personal systems with an extended range greater than currently fielded non-lethal weapons" (Department of Defense, n.d., para. 1). As a denial weapon, bio agents can target single individuals up to a large population with little detection or distraction. Because bio weapons can be developed or maintained by nation states and rogue nations, the distribution and use of them are illegal. Doing so is considered an act of **bioterrorism**. Bio weapons are controlled under the provisions of the *Biological*

GROUPS	DISEASES	AGENTS
A	Anthrax	Bacillus anthracis
	Botulism	Clostridium bomlinum toxin
	Plague	Fersinia pestis
	Smallpox	Variola major
	Tularemia	Francisella tularensis
	Viral hemonhagic fevers	Filoviruses and Arenaviruses
B	Brucellosis	Brucella spp.
	Epsilon toxin	Clostridium perfringens
	Food safety threats	Salmonella spp., E.coliO157·H7,Shigella
	Glanders	Burkholderia mallei
	Melioidosis	Burkholderia pseudomallei
	Psittacosis	Chlamydia psittaci
	Q fever	Coxiella burnetIld
	Ricin toxin	Ricinus communis
	Staphylococcal enterotoxin B	Staphdcoccus spp.
	Typhus fever	Rickerrsia prarxazehi
	Viral encephalitis	Allphaxiruses
	Water safety threats	Vibrio cholerae, Cryptosporidiumparxum
C	Emerging infectious diseases	Nipah virus and Hantavirus

Figure 9.2 Major Categories of Biological Agents with Probability to be Used as Bio-Weapons

Weapons Convention (BWC) and *Chemical Weapons Convention (CWC)*. In addition to the illegality of the bio weapons, they are prohibited under universal humanitarian law and international treaties.

The primitive existence of biological weapons dates to the sixth century when the Assyrians poisoned adversaries' wells with a specific fungus that resulted in a state of confusion and delirium if ingested. In the late 1300s, Mongol warriors died of the plague, and their bodies were thrown over the wall of Crimea, a city in Kaffa (Russia/Ukraine). The plagued bodies were considered responsible for the *Black Death* in Europe (though this is debated by experts and researchers). In the early 1760s, the British Army used smallpox as a biological weapon against Native Americans during the *Siege of Fort Pitt*, when Native Americans attempted to remove the British from Ohio and the Alleghany Plateau after Great Britain did not fulfill its agreement to establish treaties and voluntarily leave the area. The following year, at least 100 Native Americans were killed due to the smallpox outbreak.

By the twentieth century, **germ theory** (the concept of germs being produced by microorganisms) became a prominent concern within the United States, and bacteriology was the new complexity behind innovative methods for exploiting biological weapons. Signs of bio-agent attacks were prevalent during World War I when the Imperial German government was responsible for anthrax and glanders outbreaks. Considered one of the most heinous crimes during conflict, the Imperial Japanese Army Unit 731 conducted research and testing on human prisoners and produced biological weapons for war, killing nearly half a million people (this includes when the Japanese military bombed a city in China with the bubonic plague). As a result, the *Geneva Protocol of 1925* prohibited the use of biological and chemical weapons during conflict. During World

War II, the United Kingdom developed biological agents, and the research was initiated at *Porton Down* under the Ministry of Supply. Former British Prime Minister Winston Churchill supported the research, and bio agents were labeled as weapons of mass destruction. The United Kingdom did not use the agents as weapons but was credited as the first country to develop various pathogens and include them as a part of their manufacturing industry and processes.

By the 1950s, the United States Army Biological Warfare Laboratories had developed biological agents such as anthrax, brucellosis, coxiella burnetti, plague, and tularemia. Nearly two decades later, the United Kingdom and the Warsaw Pact requested the United Nations sanction biological weapons, which resulted in the United States terminating its biological weapons programs, permitting research for defensive operations. In 1972, the United Nations approved the *Biological and Toxins Weapons Convention* signed by the United States, the United Kingdom, the Soviet Union, and 137 other countries to prohibit the "development, production, and stockpiling of microbes or their poisonous products except in amount necessary for protective and peaceful research" (Joshi, 2007, p. 200).

As mentioned, the earliest prohibition of bio weapons dates to the 1972 BWC, which was the first multilateral disarmament treaty banning the development, production, and stockpiling of weapons of mass destruction (United Nations Office for Disarmament Affairs [UNODA], 2017, para. 1). The BWC was established to mitigate biological attacks or execution of bio agents which could result in mass casualties or destruction of economic and societal infrastructure. Despite the many prohibitions against biological weapons, according to the BWC, some countries continue to conduct research on bio agents to find ways to prevent attacks. During this time, France and Japan were establishing biological weapons programs. When the United States entered World War II, both the Americans and British had established solid research programs to study biological agents in Maryland. Both countries produced and tested biological and chemical agents at the Dugway Proving Grounds in Utah. Regardless of the initiative to sanction biological weapons, the Soviet Union continued to produce large quantities of biological weapons under the clandestine operation *Biopreparat*, preparing for offensive operations. According to the United Nations Office at Geneva, 178 countries and six signatory states have signed the Biological Weapons Convention initiative (n.d., para. 1). Adversaries use such biological weapons intentionally to harm others for various reasons (i.e. ideological, religious, sociopolitical, etc.), known as **bioterrorism**.

There are three categories of bioterrorism:

A—anthrax, botulism, plague, smallpox, tularemia, and viral hemorrhagic fevers
B—glanders, Q fever, ricin, salmonella, and typhus
C—hantavirus and tuberculosis (Eastern Kentucky University, n.d.).

Preventing bioterrorism can be extremely challenging as adversaries can distribute biological agents through covert operations. Additionally, such agents are difficult to detect, taking hours, days, or even weeks. This is especially true for bacteria and viruses, making it very important for trained professionals to sustain public health monitoring procedures and quickly identifying diagnoses. Another challenging predicament is the detection of exposure. If those who are exposed are not aware, this increases the chances of spreading the agent to other individuals and geographical locations at a rapid rate. Biological weapons can be exposed through skin contact or through the air, which exponentially increases the chances of spreading. In addition to infecting a large population, adversaries are known to execute attacks to disrupt economic and industrial elements of a community. For example, one of the largest bioterrorism attacks happened in 2001 when terrorist Bruce Edwards Ivins was responsible for mailing letters that contained anthrax spores to two U.S. Senators and news media offices, killing five people and infecting nearly twenty individuals. Agroterrorism is another form of terrorism that involves the intentional destruction of animals and agriculture. A large-scale attack could catastrophically ruin a geographical area, eliminating animals, crops, and human beings.

Chemical Weapons

Chemical weapons are specialized munitions, weapons of mass of destruction, which use chemicals to cause destruction and kill a large population. Such agents utilized during conflict are more lethal because they can be dispersed through gas, liquid, and solid forms that are easier to inflict on targets, and chemicals like nerve gas, pepper spray, and tear gas are three common forms of weapons. The use of chemical weapons dates to World War I (WWI) when countries used gas to cause suffering and death during combat. Mixed in ammunitions, artillery casings, and grenades, chemical weapons were also used as choking agents, and mustard gas was deployed to affect breathing and cause horrid skin damage. The use of chemical weapons during WWI caused approximately 100,000 deaths. There are four classifications of chemical weapons:

- Blister agents (persistent)
- Blood agents (nonpersisent)
- Choking agents (nonpersisent)
- Nerve agents (nonpersisent and persistent)

Exposure to chemical weapons is a serious threat to the United States and its military forces, producing hazards that could permanently destroy critical infrastructures and cause catastrophic death. Chemical agents are labeled persistent and nonpersistent to identify how long the chemical lingers within an environment. According to military emergency management professionals, persistent chemical agents can continue to affect a contaminated location for more than 24 hours up to several weeks. Nonpersistent agents lose strength and do not linger within a location for a long period of time, but they are more lethal and can kill a larger population in a shorter amount of time. It is important for emergency management professionals to know the type of chemicals exposed to the environment because contamination can be unpredictable. Adversaries understand that producing the most effective results from dispersing chemical agents is dependent upon weather conditions. Although it is possible they may not wait for favorable conditions, weather elements such as air stability, temperature, humidity, precipitation, and wind play critical roles in whether the attack will be successful.

RADIOACTIVE MATERIALS THAT MAY BE A THREAT				
AMERICIUM (heavy metal poison)	Nuclear fallout Smoke detectors	Inhalation Skin wounds Minimal GI	Renal and hepatic systems	DTPA EDTA chelation
CESIUM	Radiological dispersal services Medical radiothera-py devices	Inhalation (lung) Skin contact Gastrointestinal	Renal system	Prussian Blue
COBALT	Medical radiothera-py devices Commercial food Irradiators	Inhalation (lung) Some GI tract	Renal system	Chelation with Penicillamine
DEPLETED URANIUM (heavy metal poison)	Specialized armor, aircraft and munitions.	Shrapnel wounds Inhaled during tank fires	Renal system	Removal of any fragments in the skin NaHCO, Tubular diuretic
IODINE (RAI)	Normal fission product in reactor fuel rods	Ingestion Inhalation Contact with mucous membranes	Renal system, saliva, milk, sweat, bile	Prevention of thyroid uptake: NaI (sodium iodide) or KI. Propylthiouracil or methimazole
PHOSPHOROUS (32P)	Tracer used in hospitals and laboratories			Aluminum hydroxide Oral phos-phates
PLUTONIUM (239Pu. 238Pu) Usually contaminat-ed with americium	Lic Uranium reactors Predominant radioactive nuclear weapon	Inhalation (lungs) Gastrointestinal	Renal system Also excreted in stool	Nebulized or IV pentetate CaDTPA ZnDTPA
RADIUM (226Ra)	Nuclear weapon	Ingestion		Ammonium chloride
STRONTIUM (90Sr)	Direct fission product of uranium	Bone, respiratory and GI tract absorption	Renal system	Calcium Aluminum phosphate Stable strontium
TRITIUM (3H)	Nuclear weapon Gunfights, muzzle-velocity indicators		Renal system	Increase of oral fluid intake
URANIUM (238,235,239u)	Depleted uranium Natural uranium Fuel rods Weapons-grade material Fuel reprocessing plants or melted reactor cores	Inhaled	Renal system	NaHCO, Tubular diuretic

Figure 9.3 List of Chemical Weapons

The prohibition of chemical agents existed somewhat earlier than that of biological agents, beginning in 1899 under The Hague Convention. Under Article 23 of the Regulations Respecting the Laws and Customs of War on Land of The Hague Convention, it is especially prohibited:

> (a) To employ poison or poisoned arms; (b) to kill or wound treacherously individuals belonging to the hostile nation or army; (c) to kill or wound an enemy who, having laid down arms, or having no longer means of defence, has surrendered at discretion; (d) to declare that no quarter will be given; (e) to employ arms, projectiles, or material of a nature to cause superfluous injury (f) to make improper use of a flag of truce, the national flag, or military ensigns and the enemy's uniform, as well as the distinctive badges of the Geneva Convention; (g) to destroy or seize the enemy's property, unless such destruction or seizure be imperatively demanded by the necessities of war (n.d., para. 23).

In addition, there are frameworks such as *Washington Naval Treaty* and *Geneva Protocol*, which banned chemical weapons in the early 1920s. Today's modern laws against chemical weapons include the *Chemical Weapons Convention*, the *Convention on the Prohibition of the Development, Production, Stockpiling and Use of Chemical Weapons on Their Destruction*, and the *Organisation for the Prohibition of Chemical Weapons*.

Chemical weapons can be executed through various means such as gas, liquid, or solid. Such weapons can also be implemented through weapons systems. However, chemicals also can be mixed with other resources, including food supplies and water. Finally, chemical weapons can be transferred through skin contact. Unlike biological agents, chemical weapons can be immediately detected, through there are challenges of determining whether an attack occurred before initial testing. Also, weapons can linger in an affected environment for a long time or can dissipate within minutes of the attack.

The execution of chemical weapons is a rapid and severe experience, and the primary challenge is identifying the specific agent directly after the attack by first responders as well as training medical personnel to handle attacks. Without adequate training and equipment, there are limiting factors and restrictions to what can be accomplished in the aftermath. Therefore, first responders and hospital staff are restricted in their abilities to assist.

Conventional, Nuclear, and Unconventional Weapons

Conventional weapons are considered historical and traditional weapons used in conflict. Such weapons are not considered weapons of mass destruction and are generally:

- Ammunition and artillery

- Bombs
- Combat aircraft and vehicles
- Landmines
- Light weapons
- Missiles
- Munitions
- Rockets
- Sea mines
- Shells
- Small arms
- Warships

Conventional weapons use explosive materials that are predicated on chemical energy to detonate. Because these weapons are widely used during times of conflict, there are **Rules of Engagement (ROE)** that regulate how nation states can use weaponry. The *Arms Trade Treaty*, *Convention on Cluster Munitions*, *Geneva Conventions*, the *Ottawa Treaty*, and the *United Nations Convention on Certain Conventional Weapons* are doctrine that mandate acceptable use of conventional weapons during international conflicts. **Unconventional weapons** are asymmetrical weaponry that are not considered weapons of mass destruction or any ordnance that is classified as conventional weapons. Even though this is a simple statement on unconventional weaponry, the focus is on **unconventional warfare**, which includes combat operations that are conducted by enemies through guerilla (or insurgency) tactics and/or subversion. The United States Special Operations Command is one of the nation's largest units tasked with countering operations to handle unconventional weapons and attacks.

With conventional weapons, the explosive material used are contaminates that can goes through a chemical reaction, which releases a significant amount of energy, causing large paroxysms. In earlier centuries, gunpowder was considered one of the first explosives under conventional weaponry and now trinitrotoluene (TNT) and RDX (nitramide, which is an organic compound formula), along with innovative methods belligerents use is most common today. The difference between conventional and **nuclear weapons** (also known as an **atomic bomb**) is that the latter is dependent upon a nuclear reaction, which produces significantly greater energy. Conventional weapons are predicated on chemical reactions that are less powerful, so the type is based on the degree of energy released in the explosion, which causes the **yield** of a weapon. Additionally, nuclear weapons produce radioactive materials, resulting in deadly rays of nuclear radiation (called **fallout**), a capability that conventional weapons do not have. Where nuclear radiation can kill a population instantly, there are some differences in how conventional weapons kill and destruct.

According to Bullock, Haddow, Coppola, and Yeletayski, there are three ways radiation can be used in an attack:

- Detonation of a nuclear bomb
- Dispersal of radioactive material

- Attack on a facility housing nuclear material (2009, p. 185).

The most catastrophic nuclear and radiological weapons are difficult to acquire or develop, taking years to successfully test once completed. Because a significant amount of research, development, funding, and testing is required, the likelihood of a nuclear attack is considered significantly lower than biological and chemical attacks. Nuclear weapons can be executed through two manners: blast and radiation. According to "Ready," a government website, the blast of a nuclear weapon is an explosion with intense light and heat, a damaging pressure wave, and widespread radioactive material that can contaminate the air, water, and ground surfaces for miles around (n.d., para. 1). A significant amount of energy is released, causing an explosion that cannot be controlled. The shock wave causes a heat wave, heating to the point of detonation.

Radiation is considered the most dangerous near the detonation location. High concentrations of radiation can cause immediate casualties, but radiation particles can rise into the atmosphere, reaching hundreds of miles and lingering for years after the explosion. Radiological dispersion devices (RDD) are explosive devices that spread radiological materials upon detonation, without an actual nuclear explosion. Known as "dirty bombs" such devices are used more to spread terror within a population.

Types of nuclear weapons include:

- *Boosted Fission*—weapons that include fission but can be significant increased by incorporating materials that can endure fusion. The fission reaction is produced, and once it reaches specific temperatures and densities, the fusion reaction takes place.
- *Enhanced Radiation*—smaller thermonuclear weapons that are devised to produce substantial amounts of nuclear radiation, also called neutron bombs.
- *Pure Fission*—weapons that have a fission reaction (i.e. Hiroshima and Nagasaki)
- *Pure Fusion*—weapons that do not need fission to be activated for explosion.
- Salted Nuclear—thermonuclear weapons that are devised to produce substantial amount of radioactive fallout, also known as cobalt bombs.
- *Thermonuclear*—a weapon that obtains most of its yield from the fusion reaction, also known as hydrogen bombs.

There are also varying degrees and wide ranges of conventional weapons such as aircraft, ammunition, armored vehicles, artillery, mines, small arms, warships, and other light weapons. The definition derives from the concept that conventional weapons are the most common used weaponry in the world during conflict. An important concern is inadequate guidance and international policies on regulating the illegal trade of conventional arms. Post 9/11, there has been an increase in illegal conventional arms trade, especially to foreign terrorist and transnational crime organizations. The United Nations has addressed concerns of insufficient initiatives on arms transfer and what is considered appropriate through multilateral agreements. The organization has formalized coalition agreements such as the *Register of Conventional Arms* and the *Arms Trade Treaty* to address such concerns and "build confidence and minimize the risk of conflict by encouraging states to make the quantity and type of arms they transfer more transparent" (United Nations, n.d., p. 3). U.N. involvement shows the importance of establishing regulations for nations who do not follow universal laws on protecting human rights and existence through irresponsible arms transfer procedures. According to The United Nations Regional Center for Peace and Disarmament in Asia and the Pacific, the Arms Trade Treaty:

> Seeks to prohibit irresponsible arms transfers and prevent the shipment of arms to conflict zones where they are likely to exacerbate violence and contribute to repressions and human rights abuses, which includes:
> Convention on Prohibitions or Restrictions on the Use of Certain Conventional Weapons Which May be Deemed to be Excessively Injurious or Have Indiscriminate Effects;
> Convention on the Prohibition of the Use, Stockpiling, Production, and Transfer of Anti-Personnel Mines and on their Destruction (Mine Ban Treaty); Convention on Cluster Munitions (2017, para. 1–2).

Understanding conventional weapons is important because some rouge nations and non-state actors who are not involved in collaborative efforts of global peace and stability will attempt to threaten and destroy nations with unconventional methods. Even though the goal is not to use any form of weaponry, it is understood that conflict is inevitable. However, there are regulations as to what forms of weaponry can be used that are considered humane in conflict. Conventional weapons are the most common form of weapon used in conflict, and when nations fail to adhere to the standards, it becomes a matter of international concern. The United Nations holds annual conferences and conventions to ensure that nations stay within the regulations of the treaties established to prevent unconventional conflicts and attacks. For instance, the organization hosts the *Convention on Certain Conventional Weapons* (CCW) to "ban or restrict the use of specific types of weapons that are considered to cause unnecessary or unjustifiable suffering to combatants or to affect civilians indiscriminately" (n.d., para. 1). Unconventional weapons are not conventional weapons of mass destruction and are illegal to use in armed conflict. CBRNE weapons are a prime example of unconventional weapons.

CBRNE DEFENSE

Chemical, biological, radiological, and nuclear (CBRNE) defense involves protective methods to combat such threats. Shielding measures are combined with contamination avoidance, defense mitigation, and passive protection concepts. CBRNE attacks are intentional, malicious, and are meant to destroy a large population. The evolution of CBRNE dates from the early 1950s when the global threat already included atomic, biological, and chemical (ABC) attacks, and radiological agents became a new threat.

CBRNE defense depends on strategic warfare concepts, including deterring weapons of mass destruction and military methods to complete combat missions in such environments. In an operational environment, geographic and unified combat commands plan missions at the strategic level by analyzing geographic location and political environment. Additional CBRNE defense measures that impact strategic decision making include enforcing international lawmaking and customs, establishing multilateral agreements and treaties, and recognizing existing frameworks with the nation's allies, coalition forces, and security partners. CBRNE defense planning is a combination of all decision-making processes established at the strategic and operational levels.

In addition to CBRNE defense planning, CBRNE-related protection is needed to ensure that contaminated environments do not affect personnel, critical infrastructures, and resources. Methodologies also include defense regulations regarding weapons of mass destruction, which require similar input to deter the proliferation and execution of such weaponry. Assessments must be completed to ensure that all CBRNE defense processes are updated and relevant to the threat. The prime elements that should be observed are:

- CBRNE environments and their conditions/climates
- CBRNE resource allocations/appropriations
- Changes to CBRNE force vulnerabilities
- Changes to CBRNE threats and hazards
- Changes to unit capabilities
- Commander and staff assessments
- Increased risk and vulnerabilities
- Supporting efforts
- Validity of assumptions as they pertain to CBRN defense (Goldfein, 2013, p. 13).

The Department of Defense is the primary agency for CBRNE defense planning and policymaking, including the responsibility to determine how American military forces operate in contaminated environments. Furthermore, policymaking is conducted in a joint military environment because "joint protection function focuses on the preservation of effectiveness and survivability of mission-related military and nonmilitary personnel, facilities, information, and infrastructure against all threats" (Goldfein, 2013, p. 6). CBRNE defense mechanisms require "enabling support of unified actions for friendly forces to operate in a CBRNE environment and recover from CBRNE incidents, known as sustainment" (Goldfein, 2013, p. 7).

Because CBRNE defense involves numerous possible agents, multiple methods must be used to avoid such agents or infected animals or crops. One of the primary methods of preventing exposure to or the spread of CBRNE weapons is to shelter-in-place. Preventative measures can be found on all emergency management and other federal government agency websites related to CBRNE awareness and mitigation. Early detection is the key to the mitigation of CBRNE agents. The primary defense against the use of CBRNE weapons is awareness and proper training of emergency management professionals, first responders, and public health officials. See the following websites for more information on awareness and mitigation:

- Biological Weapons Convention, https://www.state.gov/t/isn/bw/
- Chemical Weapons Convention, https://www.state.gov/t/avc/trty/127917.htm
- Center for Disease Control and Prevention, https://www.cdc.gov

- Department of Homeland Security: Nuclear Security, https://www.dhs.gov/topic/nuclear-security
- Department of Energy, https://energy.gov
- Environmental Protection Agency, https://www.epa.gov
- Federal Emergency Management Agency, https://www.fema.gov
- Federal Energy Regulatory Commission, https://www.ferc.gov
- National Nuclear Security Administration, https://nnsa.energy.gov/aboutus/ourprograms/defenseprograms
- Office of Chemical and Biological Weapons: Chemical Weapons Convention, https://www.state.gov/t/avc/c51325.htm
- Ready, https://www.ready.gov
- U.S. Department of Defense: Nuclear Posture Review, https://www.defense.gov/News/Special-Reports/NPR/
- U.S. Department of State: Nuclear Nonproliferation Treaty, https://www.state.gov/t/isn/npt/
- U.S. Energy Information Administration, https://www.eia.gov
- U.S. Chemical Weapons Convention, http://www.cwc.gov

NUCLEAR WARFARE

Nuclear defense refers to military or political stratagem used to mitigate the use of nuclear weapons. The primary concern is the intentions of adversarial and non-state actors with nuclear weaponry and the unpredictability of possible use of these weapons. Compared to conventional warfare, nuclear weapons are technologically advanced systems that can inflict catastrophic damage rapidly and leave long-lasting radiological effects that can affect large populations and geographic locations. In addition, the aftermath of a nuclear weapons attack can leave dangerous fallout remnants and have negative global climatic effects that can last many years beyond the incident.

In world history, the United States is the only country to use nuclear weapons in combat when it dropped atomic bombs on Hiroshima and Nagasaki, two Japanese cities in 1945. The two bombs, "Little Boy" and "Fat Man," killed nearly 130,000 people during the final stages of World War II. The aftermath (nuclear effects) some four months after the bombing killed approximately 226,000 people. The effects included burns, radiation sickness, and other related injuries.

After World War II, other countries began developing nuclear weapons, which caused significant tensions that eventually led to the Cold War era. The Soviet Union was the first to establish a nuclear weapons program in the 1944, followed by France in 1960, and China in 1964. In 1974, India developed nuclear weapons after increasing tensions with Pakistan, which established its own problem in 1998. Israel, North Korea, and South Africa are known to have nuclear weapons, but it is not clear as to how many since they have not agreed on multilateral agreements on the proliferation of nuclear weapons. South Africa was the first country to destroy its inventory of nuclear weapons and has not been known to develop anymore. When the Soviet Union collapsed in 1991, which was the primary event ending the Cold War, it was thought that the threat of nuclear weapons would be mitigated, but increasing tension between nation and non-nation states has increased nuclear proliferation and the possibility of execution of nuclear weapons. According to Geoff Wilson and Will Saetren, authors of *The National Interest,* there are two categories of nuclear weapons during conflict: limited nuclear and full-scale war (2016). A limited nuclear war is a small-scale conflict with the use of nuclear weapons by two or more belligerents. Such war includes options of conducting a preemptive strike to prevent the enemy's attempt to attack, considered a defensive measure strategy. A full-scale nuclear war is a larger nuclear weapons conflict intended to attack a country with massive casualties. This type of war would cause catastrophic damage to a country's economic, military infrastructure, and social platform.

In the twenty-first century, there is a major concern for the future of nuclear warfare and the proliferation of nuclear weapons. With technological advancement and progressive research, a nuclear attack today could kill millions of people in a short period of time. Alexander Bolonkin, author of *Cheap Method for Shielding a City from Rock and Nuclear Warhead Impacts,* says, "pessimistic predictions argue that a full-scale nuclear war would bring about the extinction of the human race or its near extinction with a handful of survivors, mainly in remote areas, reduced to a pre-medieval quality of life and life expectancy for centuries after and cause permanent damage to most complex life on the planet, Earth's ecosystems, and the global climate" (2008, p. 7). In addition, studies conducted by the American Geophysical Union show that even a small-scale nuclear war could kill as many people as WWII, entirely changing the global climate and permanently damaging the world's ecosystem.

In hindsight, researchers and experts knew the execution of a nuclear weapon would forever change the world and how military operations would be handled in terms of conflict and resolution. American theoretical physicist and Manhattan Project lead manager Julius Robert Oppenheimer stated after the first nuclear detonation test:

> We knew the world would not be the same. A few people laughed, a few people cried, and most people were silent. I remembered the line from the Hindu scripture the *Bhagavad Gita*. Vishnu is trying to persuade the prince that he should do his duty and to impress him takes on his multi-armed form and says, "Now, I am become Death, the destroyer of worlds." I suppose we all thought that one way or another (Realexpo, 2011).

After the bombings on the Japanese cities, there was ambiguity about the future of nuclear weapon programs. The United States faced a dilemma as to whether a nuclear attack was necessary, as tensions continued to increase with the Soviet Union. The strategy was probable as a method of annihilating the Soviet Union's massive ground forces in Europe. The threat of bombing the country could influence Joseph Stalin (the Soviet Union leader at the time) into making dispensations to mitigate the "Cold War" conflicts. At the same time, the Soviet Union established its own nuclear weapon program through espionage on American operations and scientific research.

In 1946, the United States Atomic Energy Commission was established, and as a result, the nation's authority to develop and produce nuclear weaponry was transferred to the new agency. Despite uncertainty about the nuclear program, it was evident that the United States' program, at the time, was a lethal force and would prevent any attack against the nation. By 1949, the Soviet Union had tested its first nuclear weapons in Kazakhstan, which was something that American scientists feared. At the same time, the United States did not know the expedient completion of the nuclear weapon was due to espionage, primarily through Klaus Fuchs, who was an ally assisting with the Manhattan Project. The Soviet Union's bomb was allegedly a replica of the "Fat Man" atomic bomb that was dropped on Nagasaki. Following the Soviet Union was the United Kingdom, which tested its first nuclear weapon in 1952, France, and China respectively (as mentioned previously).

By the 1960s, the United States developed the first Single Integrated Operational Plan. During this time, the nation also established the Missile Defense Alarm System which featured twelve satellites tracking the Soviet Union's intercontinental ballistic missile launches, followed by the formulization of the Ballistic Missile Early Warning System in the mid 1960s. The next nuclear weapon attack was the Cuban Missile Attack (outlined in Chapter 1). By end of the 1960s, a significant number of Intercontinental Ballistic Missiles (missiles that have a range of approximately 3,400 miles, primarily used for nuclear weapons delivery) had been developed between the two superpowers that it was likely that a conflict would obliterate each country.

By the 1970s, Israel was considering a possible nuclear attack in response to the Arabs during the Yom Kippur War. The country developed thirteen nuclear weapons because of covert operations when Syrian tanks conducted surveillance through Golan Heights. Israeli Prime Minister Golda Meir authorized Minister of Defense Moshe Dayan to activate the nuclear weapons and deliver them to Israeli air force units in case they were faced with direct conflict. The Israelis were prepared to strike if faced with an attack from Egypt and Syria. If this were to happen, there was a significant chance the Soviet Union would retaliate against Israel, provoking the United States to intervene as the country's ally, resulting in a nuclear war. Fortunately, the United States and the Soviet Union were theoretically bound to **mutual assured destruction** (military doctrine and national security frameworks detailing a full-scale nuclear weapons attack by two or more entities would obliterate both the attacker and defender), and neither country provoked the other. During the same decade, India successfully conducted its first nuclear weapon test, and again the fear of a nuclear weapons attack surfaced. The United States and the United Nations were concerned that Soviet convoys in Europe would devastate NATO conventional warfare programs, resulting in potential nuclear attack.

President Ronald Reagan recommitted the defense program to increasing its military and resource strength by increasing spending on American military programs, focused on funding conventional and nuclear weaponry. During this decade, the United States enhanced the Navy's submarine-launched, nuclear-armed, ballistic missile (SLBM) capabilities. Such weaponry was a progressive advancement for the nation, since the chances of a nuclear war would be mitigated because the missile's stealth capability meant that it could be launched from anywhere in world without detection. This asset gave the United States a secondary form of nuclear destruction because not only could it not be detected, it decreased the amount of warning time from approximately thirty minutes to three.

After the Cold War era, tensions decreased between the United States and the Soviet Union, but both were still vigilant, as both countries continued to build substantial numbers of nuclear weapons. The new challenge was that both superpowers were concerned about additional countries developing nuclear weapons programs; this provoked the United States to create a program titled *Essentials of Post-Cold War Deterrence* to discuss the future strategic initiatives on nuclear weapons maintained by the United States and other countries.

PROTECTIVE METHODS AND CDC RESPONSIBILITIES

After the September 11 attacks, the United States recognized the need for emergency procedures in the event of a WMD attack due to increased concerns over a nuclear or radioactive attack. The following is information produced by the Centers for Disease Control and Prevention regarding how the organization would "assist state, local, and territorial authorities in protecting people's health and offer advice on steps that people can take to reduce their exposures to radiation" (CDC, n.d., para. 1). CDC prepared the following fact sheet to help people understand the roles and responsibilities of CDC during such an incident.

Because of the terrorist events of 2001, people have expressed concern about the possibility of a terrorist attack involving radioactive materials. During and after such an incident, the Centers for Disease Control and Prevention (CDC) would assist state, local, and territorial authorities in protecting people's health and offer advice on steps that people can take to reduce their exposures to radiation. CDC has prepared this fact sheet to help people understand the roles and responsibilities of CDC during such an incident.

Government Structure

CDC is a part of the Department of Health and Human Services (HHS), which includes the National Institutes for Health (NIH), the Food and Drug Administration (FDA), and several other health and family services agencies. As part of HHS, CDC is recognized as the federal agency that protects the health and safety of people. CDC's overall goal is to improve the health of the people of the United States. CDC reaches this goal through disease control and prevention, environmental health, and health promotion and education activities.

U.S. Centers for Disease Control and Prevention, "CDC's Roles and Responsibilities in the Event of a Nuclear or Radiological Terrorist Attack." 2016.

National Response Framework

In January of 2005, the National Response Framework (NRF) was initiated. This plan is designed to provide a unified joint response from all federal agencies to any type of incident, from natural disasters, such as earthquakes and hurricanes, to terrorist attacks, such as the explosion of a "dirty bomb" or the release of anthrax. This plan outlines the tasks that various government agencies will fulfill during a national emergency. The NRF includes several Annexes, which are designed to address the federal response to a variety of specific incidents. The Nuclear/Radiological Incident Annex describes how the various federal agencies will work together to help state, local, and territorial governments respond to a large-scale nuclear or radiological incident.

Under the NRF and the Nuclear/Radiological Annex, HHS has the major role in protecting people's health through:

- Monitoring, assessing, and following up on people's health
- Ensuring the safety of workers involved in and responding to the incident
- Ensuring that the food supply is safe
- Providing medical and public health advice

CDC's Roles

As part of HHS, CDC would be the chief public health entity to respond to a radiological incident, whether accidental or intentional. As the chief public health entity, CDC's specific roles and responsibilities would include:

- Assessing the health of people affected by the incident
- Assessing the medical effects of radiological exposures on people in the community, emergency responders and other workers, and high-risk populations (such as children, pregnant women, and those with immune deficiencies)
- Advising state and local health departments on how to protect people, animals, and food and water supplies from contamination by radioactive materials
- Providing technical assistance and consultation to state and local health departments on medical treatment, follow-up, and decontamination of victims exposed to radioactive materials
- Establishing and maintaining a registry of people exposed to or contaminated by radioactive materials

CDC's Partners

To carry out its roles, CDC would work with many other agencies to ensure that people's health is protected. These agencies may include:

- State and Local Health Departments
- Department of Homeland Security (DHS)
- Department of Defense (DoD)

- Department of Energy (DOE)
- Department of Transportation (DOT)
- HHS
- Food and Drug Administration (FDA)
- Agency for Toxic Substances and Disease Registry (ATSDR)
- Office of Emergency Response (OER)
- Health Resources and Services Administration (HRSA)
- Substance Abuse and Mental Health Services Administration (SAMHSA)
- Environmental Protection Agency (EPA)
- Federal Bureau of Investigation (FBI)
- Federal Emergency Management Agency (FEMA)
- Nuclear Regulatory Commission (NRC)
- Department of Agriculture (USDA)

CDC's Actions

In the hours and days following a radiological incident, CDC would assist and advise the state and local health departments on recommendations that the community would need to:

- Protect people from radioactive fallout
- Protect people from radioactive contamination in the area
- Safely use food and water supplies from the area
- Assess and explain the dangers around the incident
- Monitor people for contamination with radioactive materials and exposure to radiation

    CDC also will have representatives on the Advisory Team for Environment, Food, and Health (sometimes referred to as the A-Team), a collection of experts from a variety of federal agencies that advise state, local, and territorial governments on ways to protect people and the environment following a radiological incident.

    If necessary, CDC would also deploy the Strategic National Stockpile, a federal store of drugs and medical supplies set aside for emergency situations.

    In addition, CDC would give workers in the area information on:

- The amount of time they can safely work in an area contaminated with radioactive materials
- Equipment needed to protect themselves from radiation and radioactive materials
- Types of respiratory devices needed to work in the contaminated area
- How to use radiation monitoring devices

Radiation Exposure Registry

Following an incident involving radioactive materials, CDC/ATSDR might establish an exposure registry. The purpose of this registry would be to monitor people's exposure to radiation and perform dose reconstructions to determine the exact amount of radiation to which people were exposed. This registry would help CDC determine the necessary long-term medical follow-up for those who were affected by the incident.

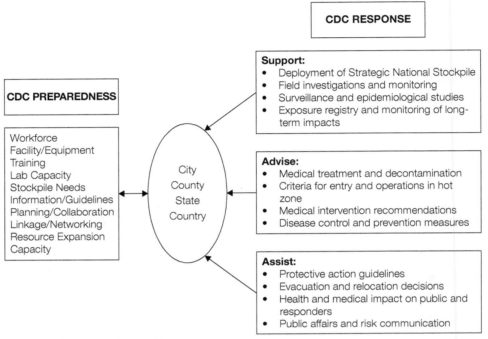

Figure 9.4 CDC Preparedness and Response

The Centers for Disease Control and Prevention (CDC) protects people's health and safety by preventing and controlling diseases and injuries; enhances health decisions by providing credible information on critical health issues; and promotes healthy living through strong partnerships with local, national, and international organizations.

SUMMARY

Terrorism is currently the primary threat against the United States, as some adversaries may want to destroy the nation and become the next superpower in the world. With the United States being the dominant country in the world since the Post-Cold era, new hazards have been introduced into the country's area of responsibility, and now there is a valid concern about how to deter aggression, threats, compromise of the nation's secrets, and protect American citizens and the country's resources. Such innovative threats have caused the nation to heavily invest in education and training for the U.S. military, local communities, emergency management professionals, and first responders to better anticipate the threat. Training has become a necessity rather than an optional luxury, as preparedness and readiness has become two critical objectives in protecting critical infrastructure and saving lives. Modern threats have created the necessity of establishing information-sharing organizations and intergovernmental cooperation to ensure that emergency management professionals, the military, federal government agencies, and local communities have necessary training.

Public health has a become a pivotal objective in the event of a disaster, and assistance is readily available to prevent the spread of CRBNE hazards as recovery efforts in the aftermath of an attack. Many public health initiatives have become a part of planning efforts and increased participation among government and private sectors entities to enhance communication and ensure financial platforms. This chapter discussed CRBNE weapons, defense, and warfare programs to bring awareness of the historical background of each and explain how new hazards can enhance traditional methods of destruction. The chapter also covered the roles and responsibilities of the CDC regarding how to respond to threats that the United States may face.

Finally, this chapter discusses the importance of understanding CBRNE weapons and how catastrophic the effects can be in the wrong hands. All CBRNE weapons are dangerous; the key to preventative measures includes ensuring emergency management, first responders, and public health officials are properly trained and educated. Early detection is also a primary factor in ensuring preparation and readiness standards. The American government has responded to this threat by enacting vital emergency management policies, reforms, and international treaties to ensure standards are modernized with the ever-evolving threat. Understanding the criticality of each agent can give policymakers a clear picture of what warfare provisions are necessary to mitigate or provide a rapid response to CBRNE weapons. Furthermore, the government has developed and published various sites for preventative measures that are essential for educational awareness and training. Finally, the government needs assistance from the American public. Civilian participation in preventative measures has been significantly low, and coordination and cooperation between local communities and their local emergency management organizations is needed. Risk perception and reduction should be recognized and considered a high priority in the war against the proliferation and execution of CBRNE weapons.

CHAPTER 9 CASE STUDIES

Case Study 1
How the Atomic Bomb Changed Security

When Japan made the decision to enter World War II, the country understood that it was an all-or-nothing gamble. Believing in honor in death, the island nation was fully committed to finishing the war, regardless of whether it stood a chance of winning. Near the end of the war, even after the Allied powers had subdued the Axis powers in Europe, the Japanese held fast to their promise. They inflicted Allied casualties totaling nearly half those suffered in three full years of war in the Pacific (The bombing of Hiroshima and Nagasaki, 2009). After Japan rejected the Potsdam declaration, which demanded an unconditional Japanese surrender, the Allied powers promised total destruction without prejudice (The bombing of Hiroshima and Nagasaki, 2009). Understanding that conventional bombing of Japan would result in up to one million casualties, the U.S. government opted for something that was more decisive and would end the war sooner (The bombing of Hiroshima and Nagasaki, 2009). President Truman's Secretary of State James Brynes had just the thing—the newly developed atomic bomb. During World War II, the U.S., Great Britain, Germany, and the U.S.S.R had embarked on a race to develop an atomic bomb. However, by 1945, only the U.S. had succeeded in that endeavor (Milestones 1945–1952: Atomic diplomacy, n.d.).

Under President Roosevelt, Byrnes had helped oversee the Manhattan Project and had met frequently with top scientists on the project to coordinate nuclear policy during the war, ensuring that the project had access to the necessary materials and financial resources. As a member of the secret interim committee that advised President Truman on the use of the bomb, it's no surprise he recommended the atomic bomb. However, that wasn't the only reason he suggested the bomb. Byrnes was also concerned about the U.S.S.R.'s influence in Asia. A proponent of "atomic diplomacy," he believed that not only would the bomb end the war faster, but it would also demonstrate U.S. military strength, which in turn would give the U.S. leverage in the postwar world scene (James F. Byrnes, 2017).

On August 6, 1945, the U.S. dropped its first atomic bomb on the Japanese city of Hiroshima, 500 miles from Tokyo. The 9,000-pound uranium bomb known as "Little Boy" was loaded onto a modified B-29 bomber, the Enola Gay, and exploded 2,000 feet above Hiroshima, destroying five square miles of the city (The bombing of Hiroshima and Nagasaki, 2009). Despite the devastation, it was not enough to make the Japanese surrender. A few days later, on August 9, another atomic bomb, "Fat Man," was dropped on Nagasaki. This bomb, weighing 10,000 pounds, was even more powerful than the one used at Hiroshima. The Japanese surrender came almost a week later in a radio broadcast from Emperor Hirohito. The war was over (The bombing of Hiroshima and Nagasaki, 2009).

Yet, the U.S.S.R did not react in the manner policymakers expected. Joseph Stalin, the leader of the Soviet Union, saw the U.S. actions as an anti-Soviet effort disruptive to the balance of power, making the U.S.S.R more anxious to protect its borders and interests. While the U.S. monopoly on nuclear technology didn't quite have the effect on the U.S.S.R. that Byrne had hoped for, it did have larger ramifications for global security. The atomic bomb became a tool of diplomatic leverage rather than a military tool to end wars (Yagami, 2009). Once the U.S. demonstrated its capability and willingness to use atomic bombs to defend itself, Western Europe relied on them to guarantee its security, rather than seek a supplemental agreement with the U.S.S.R. If they were protected by the U.S.'s nuclear umbrella, they were safe even without nuclear weapons of their own. With the advent of the B-29 bomber, it didn't matter that the U.S. did not maintain large contingents of troops in Europe because those planes could deliver a nuclear payload and could be deployed anywhere (The bombing of Hiroshima and Nagasaki, 2009). For the first time in history, armies and navies were no longer the main fighters in war. Whole cities could be obliterated while armies remained untouched (Hagen and Skinner, n.d.). It did not matter if a person was at the front line of battle, in the trenches, or at a supermarket in suburbia—nuclear weapons killed indiscriminately.

This first use of nuclear weapons also started the world down a path that led to the Arms Race between the U.S. and the U.S.S.R. just a few years later. Feeling compelled to develop its own nuclear weapons, in 1949 the U.S.S.R successfully detonated an atomic bomb, ending the American nuclear monopoly several years earlier than anticipated. Additionally, the U.S.S.R.'s launch of the Sputnik satellite paved the way for Intercontinental Ballistic Missiles (ICBMs), nuclear-capable missiles that could be launched from one continent to another. With little defense against a nuclear missile, both the U.S. and U.S.S.R stockpiled as many nuclear weapons as possible to retaliate for an attack. Implementing control over nuclear power and restraint as tensions escalated was crucial. Nuclear strategies and deterrents led to the creation of a "mutually assured destruction (MAD)" policy that tempered the use of ICBMs and nuclear weapons. However, MAD alone was not enough. The U.S. developed the Strategic Air Command (SAC) to serve as a major part of the deterrent against the U.S.S.R. SAC controlled most of the U.S. nuclear weapons as well as the bombers and missiles capable of delivering those payloads (Strategic Air Command, 2014).

These atomic weapons gave countries a strategic tool that could be used as diplomatic leverage rather than just a means to an end. It also changed the dynamic of international relations as a nation did not need to possess atomic bombs in its arsenal if a strong ally possessed one. Nuclear weapons, with their terrible power and penchant for devastation, transformed the way conventional wars were fought, for better or worse.

Case Study 2
2001 Anthrax Attack

The attack came only a week after the terrorist attack on September 11, 2001, but this time, it was in the form of a biological agent. Anonymous letters containing deadly anthrax spores were mailed to media offices and several politicians, resulting in the death of five people and infecting seventeen more. It was the worst biological attack in U.S. history. After the bioterrorist attacks were identified, the Federal Bureau of Investigation (FBI) and the United States Postal Inspection Service (USPIS) formed a task force known as the Amerithrax Task Force to investigate the crime.

The use of biological agents, germs that can sicken or kill people, livestock, or crops, is not a new concept. It has been used repeatedly through history, including the practice of deliberate contamination of food and water with poisonous material, using biological toxins or infected animals to incapacitate a population, and using biologically inoculated materials against the more susceptible. Anthrax, *bacillus anthracis,* is one of the more popular agents because its spores are easily found in nature, and it is persistent in the environment (Anthrax, 2014). It can be released quietly and can be placed in powders, sprays, food, or water without anyone's knowledge since the microscopic spores are odorless and tasteless. Furthermore, it only takes a small amount to infect many people. Anthrax is also a Tier 1 agent, which means that it presents the greatest risk of deliberate misuse with significant potential for mass casualties or devastating effect to the economy, critical infrastructure, or public confidence, and poses a severe threat to public health and safety (Anthrax, 2014).

In the 2001 anthrax attacks, the infections began within a week of exposure. People began showing signs of fevers, chills, chest heaviness, and cough. As the spores produced toxins that damaged the lungs and poisoned the bloodstream, several people succumbed to organ failure, which led to death (Greenemeier, 2008). Robert Stevens, a photo editor for American Media, Inc. based out of Florida, was the first to die. It's believed that an anthrax-laced letter was mailed to the *National Enquirer's* old mailing address and forwarded to its new offices at American Media, Inc. in Boca Raton, Florida where spores entered Stevens' skin or lungs as the envelope was handled. Though he was nitially diagnosed with pneumonia, his physician noticed that Stevens displayed symptoms of anthrax inhalation, but it was dismissed as an isolated case. As more patients trickled in complaining of chest pains, headaches, and unusual patterns of illness, doctors realized that something larger was at play (Weicker, 2011).

By mid-October, more anthrax-laced envelopes from Trenton, New Jersey, had been discovered. The letters, initially disguised as being sent from a fourth-grade class, contained sinister messages indicating that the perpetrators were Islamic terrorists. However, the mailing and deception of the anthrax letters displayed a degree of media and cultural acuity that would be unusual for foreign terrorists since the person who sent the letters knew which media outlets and newspapers would have the greatest influence on the public (Pate, 2004). They also found hoax letters mailed from St. Petersburg, Florida, claiming to contain anthrax. However, those letters contained a harmless substance that resembled talcum powder, but due to fears of contamination, buildings throughout Washington, D.C., including the Hart Senate Office Building, were shut down. Upon testing thirty-six postal facilities, including the Brentwood postal facility where the two postal employees died, the FBI found fifteen of those facilities positive for anthrax (Greenemeier, 2008).

Worried that al-Qaeda or another sympathetic terrorist group was involved, the Department of Justice (DOJ) ordered a series of tests to determine if the spores had been altered to make them deadlier. Initial assessments reported that the silica, a substance used to prevent spores from clustering, making for easier aerosol dispersal, was found. This led to the belief that the biological agent had been weaponized, making it 500 times more lethal than anthrax alone. However, upon further analysis, researchers found that the silica had formed on the spores naturally and there had been no weaponization of the agent (Greenemeier, 2008).

The Amerithrax Task Force expended thousands of investigative work hours on the anthrax case, interviewing ten thousand witnesses across six different continents, executing eight searches, and recovering more than six thousand items of potential evidence during the investigation (Justice Department and FBI, 2010). The investigation lasted seven years, but in August 2008, the DOJ and FBI officials announced a breakthrough in the case. Analysis of the anthrax spores from the letters revealed that they were all from the same strain. That strain, known as the Ames strain, originally came from a single cow that had died in Texas in 1981 and was first researched at the U.S. Army Medical Research Institute of Infectious Diseases (USAMRIID) in Frederick, Maryland, a federal biodefense research laboratory. The FBI pursued several suspects who worked at the research laboratory, finally narrowing down the suspect pool to Dr. Bruce Ivins. Ivins joined the USAMRIID in 1980 and worked on developing anthrax vaccines. The Amerithrax investigation found that the late Dr. Bruce Ivins acted alone in planning and executing these attacks. However, two months before he could be charged with the crime, Ivins overdosed on prescription drugs.

Ivins' misuse of anthrax is the worst biological attack in U.S. history, killing five people and infecting seventeen more. While the case is officially closed without charges, the

92-page investigative summary and attachments regarding victims of the attack, relatives of the victims, and appropriate committees of Congress have been released for public consumption and are posted on the Department of Justice's website under the Freedom of Information Act.

CHAPTER 9 PRACTICE PROBLEMS

1. Why would a biological agent be favored over a chemical agent?
2. How are biological weapons transferred?
3. What makes "dirty bombs" dangerous?
4. What is an example of an unconventional weapon and how would it be used?
5. What is the primary purpose of a chemical agent?
6. What are the early indicators of a possible chemical attack?
7. When is it best to use a conventional weapon?
8. Why is there a lower likelihood of a nuclear attack than other terrorist weapons?
9. What would an agroterrorism attack look like?
10. Why were Native Americans so susceptible to the smallpox the British gave them?

KEY TERMS

Continuity planning

Critical infrastructure

Government planning

Intelligence

Just-in-time distribution model

Maritime system

Port security

Public/private sector planning

Strategic planning

CHAPTER 10

Intelligence and Security

LEARNING OBJECTIVES

After reading this chapter, students will be able to:

- Study the inception of the Intelligence Community and how the United States collects information to protect the soldiers

- Analyze America's critical infrastructures and how risk and security vulnerabilities affect national security objectives

- Examine the challenges within the railroad and port security systems and how deficiencies pose a threat

- Understand the interdepartmental relationships between government, private, and public sector planning

INTRODUCTION

T he aftermath of the September 11 attacks changed how the nation operates through the federal government, state, and local communities. Ensuring the safety of America's citizens, resources, and critical infrastructure became a top priority, particularly providing better protection for the country's borders and enhanced security initiatives. In direct response to the attacks, President George W. Bush established the Office of Homeland Security to better align homeland security objectives and increase accountability. Understanding the threat was the largest it has been in global history, President Bush formalized the Department of Homeland Security to handle security matters at a Cabinet level and expanded the scope of responsibility to ensure not only that the United States would remain a powerful nation, but also that another 9/11-like attack will never happen on the homeland again. He appointed Tom Ridge (who was head of the Office of Homeland Security) as the nation's first Secretary of Homeland Security to the lead the "third largest Department of the U.S. government to be responsible for counter-terrorism, cybersecurity, aviation security, border security, port security, maritime security, administration and enforcement of our [the nation's] immigration laws, protection of our national leaders, protection of critical infrastructure, detection of and protection against chemical, biological and nuclear threats to the homeland, and response to disasters" (Johnson, 2015, para. 1–2).

The creation of DHS was one of the largest reorganizations since the National Security Act of 1947, and its primary responsibility was consolidating federal agencies that are directly responsible for homeland security initiatives and to increase executive leadership accountability to ensure such operations are successfully completed to protect the homeland. This chapter discusses the U.S. federal government's largest intelligence agencies and the responsibilities for ensuring safety and security measures under the Office of the Director of National Intelligence. The chapter also discusses how the intelligence agencies work with the nation's transportation and security organizations through innovative information sharing centers to deter further terrorist acts on U.S. soil.

THE INTELLIGENCE COMMUNITY

Intelligence is a strategic concept, primarily established under the National Security Act of 1947 when the federal government restructured military service departments and intelligence communities. On December 4, 1981, President Ronald Reagan enacted *Executive Order 12333, United States Intelligence Activities*, which established the United States Intelligence Community (IC) to extend authority and responsibilities to American intelligence organizations. The IC is comprised of sixteen federal government departments that are responsible for intelligence operations predicated on the foreign relations and American national security. Such agencies consist of executive departments within the presidential cabinet and civilian and military (i.e. Military and National Intelligence Programs) intelligence units in which managers are charged with leading American federal agencies to collaborate with the Central Intelligence Agency. The IC is solely responsible for collecting and producing domestic and foreign intelligence used to detect espionage and is a critical part of America's policymaking process. The

Director of National Intelligence (DNI) is responsible for the executive management and operations of the IC and reports directly to the President of the United States regarding these organizations:

- Defense Intelligence Agency
- National Geospatial-Intelligence Agency
- National Reconnaissance Office
- National Security Agency
- Military Intelligence Corps
- Office of Naval Intelligence
- Twenty-Fifth Air Force
- Marine Corps Intelligence
- Coast Guard Intelligence
- Office of Intelligence and Analysis
- Central Intelligence Agency
- Bureau of Intelligence and Research
- Office of Terrorism and Financial Intelligence
- Office of National Security Intelligence
- Intelligence Branch
- Office of Intelligence and Counterintelligence

The term "**intelligence**" relates to information collected from specific agencies that is collected, analyzed, produced, and distributed based on government requirements and responsibilities. An early definition of intelligence is taken from the *Dictionary of the United States Military Terms for Joint Usage*, which was revised in 1957:

> Intelligence is the product resulting from the collection, evaluation, analysis, integration, and interpretation of all available information which concerns one or more aspects of foreign nations or of areas of operations and which is immediately or potentially significant to planning (Central Intelligence Agency, 1995, para. 5).

The evolution of the term has been recognized by the Department of Defense and *Defense Technical Information Center* as:

> (1) The product resulting from the collection, processing, integration, evaluation, analysis, and interpretation of available information concerning foreign nations, hostile or potentially hostile forces or elements, or areas of actual or potential operations. (2) The activities that result in the product. (3) The organizations engaged in such activities (Defense Technical Information Center, 2017, p. 116).

Like defining the conceptualization of national and homeland security, the concept of intelligence initiatives is complex. Executive Order 12333 established six objectives within the responsibilities of the Intelligence Community:

1. Collection of information need by the president, the National Security Council, the Secretary of State, the Secretary of Defense, and other executives branch officials for the performance of their duties and responsibilities.

2. Production and dissemination of intelligence.

3. Collection of information concerning and the conduct of activities to protect against intelligence activities directed against the United States, international terrorist and/or narcotics activities, and hostile activities directed against the United States by foreign powers, organizations, persons, and their agents.

4. Special activities (defined as activities conducted in support of U.S. foreign policy objectives abroad which are planned and executed so that the role of the United States government is not apparent or acknowledged publicly and functions in support of such activities, but which are not intended to influence United States political processes, public opinion, policies, or media, and do include diplomatic activities or the collection and production of intelligence or related support functions).

5. Administrative and support activities within the United States and abroad necessary for the performance of authorized activities.

6. Such other intelligence activities as the president may direct from time to time (Executive Order 12333—United States Intelligence Activities, 1981, p. 200).

Military Intelligence Program (MIP) and National Intelligence Program (NIP)

MIP is a program that directly works with military service branches to conduct intelligence operations for planning and conducting strategic/tactical operations for the United States Armed Forces. In 2005, the Department of Defense merged *Joint Military Intelligence Program* and the *Tactical Intelligence and Related Activities*, which is now the MIP. The Under Secretary of Defense for Intelligence is responsible for all MIP operations and responsibilities. NIP is predicated on the National Security Act of 1947, which references all programs and assignments within the Intelligence Community established by the Director of National Intelligence and the president of the United States.

The *National Intelligence Program (NIP)*, which was known as the National Foreign Intelligence Program, was outlined by the NSA Act of 1947 and is responsible for all programs and undertakings with the IC as established by the Director of National Intelligence. The National Intelligence Program (NIP) is responsible for "providing funds for IC activities in six federal departments, the CIA, and the Office of the Director of National Intelligence" (Director of National Intelligence, 2016, p. 1). According to the Director of National Intelligence office, the program is responsible for nearly sixty billion dollars in discretionary funds to support national security goals and most essential capabilities. In doing so, factors include:

- Sustaining key investments to strengthen intelligence collection and critical operational capabilities supporting counterterrorism, counterintelligence, and counterproliferation.

- Protecting the IC's core mission areas and maintaining global coverage to remain vigilant against emerging threats.

- Promoting increased intelligence sharing and advancing IC integration through continued investment in enterprise-wide capabilities and use of cloud technology to facilitate greater efficiency and improve the safeguarding of information across the intelligence information environment.

- Identifying resources for strategic priorities, including advanced technology to improve strategic warning, evolved collection and exploitation capabilities, and increased resiliency.

- Supporting ongoing Overseas Contingency Operations while adjusting to the changing defense force posture as directed by the president.

- Reforms—achieves savings by reducing lower-priority programs (National Intelligence Program, 2016, p. 1).

Office of Strategic Services

The *Office of Strategic Services* (OSS) was a wartime intelligence agency that was established during World War II before the Central Intelligence Agency was brought to fruition. The OSS was designed to fulfill requirements of intelligence collection, provide support for allies, and fight the enemy during the war. The Joint Chiefs of Staff (JCS) were responsible for all OSS functions and coordinated espionage missions conducted by the United States Armed Forces. Before OSS, the U.S. did not have a structured intelligence organization, and a solid structure was still lacking during its inception. Its direct mission was to supervise and control espionage operatives during the Second War. Multiple departments, such as the Department of State and War Department, implemented ad hoc organizations to deal with intelligence and secret missions (i.e. the Committee of Secret Correspondence). During the Second War, President Franklin D. Roosevelt was apprehensive about American intelligence deficits and asked William J. Donovan, with Senior British military intelligence officer William Stephenson's recommendation, to devise an intelligence organization. Roosevelt knew the British had the *Secret Intelligence Service* and *Special Operation Executive (SOE)*. According to the National Park Service, William Donovan was at a football game when he was telephoned by the American government. He received notice that the Japanese had bombed Pearl Harbor, and immediately Congress declared war. President Roosevelt established the OSS and named Donovan as director. Donovan had a very impressive background as a decorated World War I veteran and businessman. As the director of the OSS, he was the first to succeed in establishing and maintaining a civilian-controlled agency during global wartime operations.

Roosevelt recognized that the service, state, and war departments worked independently on intelligence operations. Working separately posed great risks for the United States, as there were not any effective communications among the departments. He also knew increased tensions in Europe and Asia would eventually be dangerous for the United States. Donovan was tasked with evaluating global military positioning to determine American intelligence requirements. On July 11, 1941, Donovan developed the Memorandum of Establishment of Strategic Information, which formalized the *Coordination of Information (COI)*. The Americans coordinated with the British, and Donovan had responsibilities under the new office but did not secure an authoritative position. In addition, President Roosevelt wanted to implement modern ideas in reforming national intelligence plans, but political pressure prevented him from doing so. This arrangement made Americans hesitant because British involvement was significant in the process, such as intelligence agents training with the *British Security Coordination (BSC)* in Canada and various regions within the United States. Most intelligence was gathered from the United Kingdom, so it was easy for Donovan to develop a blueprint based on MI6 and SOE, which became the foundation for an amalgamated intelligence entity. The British were pivotal in providing equipment and supplies until American construction plans were established. On June 13, 1942, President Roosevelt executed a presidential military order for OSS to collect, gather, and analyze strategic information for conducting special operatives in congruence with the Joint Chiefs of Staff.

With British guidance and oversight, Donovan leased federally-owned land and built critical infrastructures in proximity to Washington, D.C. He acquired isolated areas, such as the *Chopawamsic Recreational Demonstration Area* (now *Prince William Forest Park*) and *Catoctin Mountain Park*, to conduct training and mission operations. Quickly, individuals were recruited as OSS agents and were chosen based on proficiencies and experience after passing numerous psychological and mental tests. Recruits were sent to the new site locations and given supplies and equipment for training. They received false identification documents, and their real identities were never disclosed.

During the war, the OSS managed numerous missions with specialized instruments. The equipment was unique to each mission to give the United States and its allies a competitive advantage. The organization's research and development department spent countless man-hours manufacturing weapons.

Air Force Intelligence

Air Force Intelligence (AFI) was first known as the United States Air Force Security Service (USAFSS) when it was established on October 20, 1948. Once the agency began cryptologic and communications security services, it was renamed the Air Force Intelligence Surveillance Reconnaissance Agency (AFISRA) as a field operating intelligence organization, headquartered in Arlington, Virginia. The agency's mission was to "provide intelligence, surveillance, and reconnaissance (ISR) products, applications, capabilities, and resources" under the newly established Department of the Air Force, which seceded from the United States Army (Martin, 2011, p. 552). AFRISA also provide cryptologic services for the National Security Agency and Central Security Service for all Air Force processes. Some prominent historical events of USAFSS involvement of successful missions was providing aid to the United Nations Command during the

Korean War. USAFSS personnel trained at Yale University to learn the Korean language and could effectively communicate with ground forces on the Korea Peninsula. During the Cold War, USAFSS personnel flew intelligence missions and established communications in Europe and during the Vietnam War, the agency created five special security offices in Vietnam and the Philippines to support threat warning missions. On September 29, 2014, AFRISA was restructured and became Twenty-Fifth Air Force to align with the Numbered Air Force (NAF) under the Air Combat Command division. Now, the agency's mission has expanded to support "airborne, space, and cyberspace senor operations and delivers decision advantage to enable commanders to achieve kinetic and non-kinetic effects on targets anywhere on the global in support of national, strategic, operational, and tactical elements" (Members of the IC, n.d., para. 1). At the highest level, the Air Force AF/A2 is the most Senior Intelligence Officer and is responsible for "functional management of all Air Force global integrated ISR capabilities, planning, programming, budgeting, training, education, readiness, and development of Air Force policies" (Member of the IC, n.d., para. 1).

Army Intelligence

The Military Intelligence Corps (MIC) is the intelligence branch of the U.S. Army. The primary mission of military intelligence in the United States Army is to provide timely, relevant, accurate, and synchronized intelligence and electronic warfare support to tactical, operational and strategic-level commanders (USA International Business Publications, 2007, p. 70). Their operations are not only for its service branch missions, but for other organizations within the IC. In 1863, the Bureau of Military Information was established for the Union Army during the Civil War and dissolved when the conflict ended. By 1885, the Army created the Military Intelligence Division (MID) and by the late mid-1900's, MID was designated as the Military Intelligence Service (MIS). MIS was a small intelligence entity, consisting of less than 30 personnel. By the end of the year, the organization had increased to nearly 350 officers and 1,000 enlisted soldiers and civilians. Two months before its transition, the U.S. Army Corps of Intelligence Police was established in response to missions during World War I and was later renamed the U.S. Army Counter Intelligence Corps. During the summer of 1942, former Director of Intelligence, Alfred McCormack, created a specialized unit under MIS: Communications Intelligence or COMINT. Three years later, the special unit was renamed to the Army Security Agency and responsible for national and tactical intelligence. By the late twentieth century, the Army Intelligence branch combined with the Army Security Agency and was known as the U.S. Army Intelligence and Security Command providing intelligence, surveillance, and electronic warfare operations. In the early 1970s, the United States Army Intelligence Center became the "Home of Military Intelligence" in Fort Huachuca, Arizona (The Army Intelligence Center is Established, 1 September 1954, n.d., para. 5). Eventually, in the late 1980s, MIC was established under the U.S. Army Regimental System. Like the Air Force, the Army's highest Senior Intelligence Officer is the G-2 responsible for the "policy formulation, planning, programming, budgeting, management, staff supervision, evaluation, and oversight for intelligence activities for the Department of the Army" (Member of the IC, n.d., para. 2).

Central Intelligence Agency

The *Central Intelligence Agency (CIA)* is the largest foreign intelligence agency in the United States. Created through the NSA of 1947, the CIA does not have law enforcement capabilities. The CIA's sole responsibility is "research, development, and deployment of high-leverage technology for intelligence purposes" (About CIA, 2006, para. 5). Additional responsibilities include:

- Creating special, multidisciplinary centers to address such high-priority issues such as nonproliferation, counterterrorism, counterintelligence, international organized crime and narcotics trafficking, environment, and arms control intelligence.

- Forging stronger partnerships between the several intelligence collection disciplines and all-source analysis.

- Taking an active part in Intelligence Community (IC) analytical efforts and producing all-source analysis on the full range of topics that affect national security.

- Contributing to the effectiveness of the overall IC by managing services of common concern in imagery analysis and open-source collection and participating in partnerships with other intelligence agencies in the areas of research and development and technical collection (About CI, 2006, para. 7).

The *Director of Central Intelligence (DCI)* serves as the "head of the United States Intelligence Community and acts as a principal adviser to the president for intelligence matters related to national security…and serves as the head of the Central Intelligence Agency" (2006, para. 1). DCI's responsibilities include:

- Collecting intelligence through human sources and by other appropriate means, except that he shall have no police, subpoena, or law enforcement powers or internal security functions;

- Correlating and evaluating intelligence related to the national security and providing appropriate dissemination of such intelligence;

- Providing overall direction for and coordination of the collection of national intelligence outside the United States through human sources by elements of the IC authorized to undertake such collection and in coordination with other departments, agencies, or elements of the United States government which are authorized to undertake such collection, ensuring that the most effective use is made of resources and that appropriate account is taken of the risks to the United States and those involved in such collection; and

- Performing such other functions and duties related to intelligence affecting the national security as the president or the Director of National Intelligence may direct (About CIA, 2006, para. 3).

In 1942, the Office of Strategic Services was created, as the need for intelligence services increased during World War II. OSS was responsible for clandestine operations, counterintelligence, espionage, and intelligence analysis. By 1945, OSS had dissolved and halted all intelligence operations, but some branches were distributed to other government agencies. During this era, President Harry S. Truman was responsible for restructuring intelligence concerns, resulting in the creation of the Central Intelligence Agency under the National Security Act of 1947.

The organizational structure of the CIA was critical during this time, and specific offices were transferred to enhance security and intelligence methodologies. The Office of Policy and Coordination and the Office of Special Operations were consolidated to form the Directorate of Plans. Also, the Directorate of Intelligence, the Directorate of Administration, and the Directorate of Research (later formed as the Directorate of Science and Technology) were created to perform administrative, intelligence, and analysis processes. In the late 1990s, the Directorate of Intelligence and Analysis was established and was considered a vital component of the organization with responsibilities of analyzing and collecting data to produce better intelligence documents.

Coast Guard Intelligence

Coast Guard Intelligence (CGI) is a military intelligence subsidiary of the U.S. Coast Guard and an element of the Central Security Service. CGI's inception was in 1915 under Article 304 of the Coast Guard's regulations, which appointed a Chief Intelligence Officer to head the agency. The Chief Intelligence Officer's responsibilities were outlined in Article 614, stating the CIO would be accountable for the "securing of information which is essential to the Coast Guard in carrying out its duties, for the dissemination of this information to responsible officers, operating units of the Coast Guard, the Treasury Department and other collaborating agencies, and the maintenance of adequate files and records of law enforcement activities" (The U.S. Coast Guard and OSS Maritime Operations During World War II, 2009, para. 5).

CGI was not well-known until the establishment of the Prohibition Act, which increased the agency's personnel. In 1930, the agency's headquarters were formulized due to the success CGI had during the prohibition era, and three years later, regional offices were established. CGI's focus was to support domestic intelligence and counterintelligence operations within the United States as well as hold accountability to its own personnel by conducting investigations on its own. Additionally, CGI investigated all potential recruits and merchant marines attached to naval and marine units while examining Coast Guard regulatory compliance with its processes and methods. Today, CGI has similar responsibilities, expanding its roles and relationships outside the agency to other intelligence agencies under the Department of Defense. In response to the September 11th attacks, CGI increased its missions in alien migration interdiction, counternarcotics, marine resource protection, maritime safety, port security, and search and rescue. According to the Director of National Intelligence, CGI has a diverse mission

Central Security Service is an agency within the Department of Defense and is integrated with the National Security Agency, specializing in cryptology, information assurance, and signals intelligence.

In 1919, the Eighteenth Amendment was ratified prohibiting the manufacturing, transporting, and sale of alcohol, known as the Prohibition Act.

and sets broad legal authorities, allowing the agency to fill a unique niche within the IC and because of its unique access, emphasis, and expertise in the maritime domain Coast Guard Intelligence can collect and report intelligence that only supports Coast Guard missions, but also support national objectives (Member of the IC, n.d., para. 4).

Defense Intelligence Agency

The Defense Intelligence Agency (DIA) is an external military intelligence agency within the Department of Defense. A member of the IC, DIA consists of civilian, military, and defense policymakers to provide military intelligence to warfighters as well as plan, manage, and execute intelligence operations during peacetime, crisis, and war (About DIA, n.d., para. 1). DIA falls under the jurisdiction of the Department of Defense and reports to the Undersecretary of Defense for Intelligence, who directly reports to the Secretary of Defense. Although DIA does not belong to any specific service department, all uniformed services work within organization with most of it employees being civilian and government contractors. DIA's primary focus is to anticipate capabilities and objectives of foreign governments and non-state actors (through military assistance) while providing support to other military intelligence agencies within the IC. Some responsibilities are the DIA are collecting and analyzing military-related economic, foreign political, geographical, industrial, and medical and health intelligence (George & Bruce, 2014, p. 30). The intelligence agency's operations span from the United States to overseas locations (including combat zones and American embassies) to collect and analyze human intelligence (HUMINT) operations, covert missions, and support military-diplomatic relations between the United States and foreign countries (Executive Order 12333, 1981). In addition, to HUMINT collection, DIA is the national manager of the measurement and signature intelligence (MASINT) and counterintelligence (CI) programs (2012–2017 Defense Intelligence Agency Strategy, 2017, p. 3).

Centralized on foreign military and defense-related matters, DIA will:

1. Provide strategic warning and integrated risk assessment
2. Plan and direct defense intelligence agencies for all-source analysis, collection management, intelligence, surveillance, and reconnaissance, HUMINT, CI, open-source intelligence (OSINT), MASINT, technical collection, and international engagement
3. Collect information through HUMINT, CI, OSINT, MASINT, and technical means
4. Process and exploit information collected through HUMINT, CI, OSINT, MASINT, and technical means
5. Produce all-source intelligence analysis from all available collection means
6. Integrate and disseminate defense intelligence products and data (2012–2017 Defense Intelligence Agency Strategy, 2017, p. 3).

A young agency, DIA was established under the order of President John F. Kennedy to support intelligence operations during the Cold War. The Director of DIA is generally the military highest ranking intelligence officer and heads the organization. The Director is nominated by the President with confirmation of the Senate and is the primary

Human intelligence (HUMINT) is intelligence gathered through human sources.

Measure and signature intelligence (MASINT) is the detection, tracking, identification of distinctive characteristics of vigorous target sources through intelligence gathering.

military intelligence officer to advises and reports to the Secretary of Defense and the Director of National Intelligence. The Director position also has joint responsibilities such as the Joint Functional Component Command for Intelligence, Surveillance, and Reconnaissance, which is a subsidiary of the U.S. Strategic Command, is a member of the Military Intelligence Board, and a key component of the Intelligence Community.

Department of Energy

The Department of Energy (DOE) is a federal government agency responsible for the nation's policies and initiatives on energy and the safe handling of nuclear materials. The United States' domestic energy production, energy conservation, energy-related research, nuclear weapons program, nuclear reactor production (for the U.S. Navy), and radioactive waste disposal programs are under the realm of DOE. Additionally, the Human Genome Project is initiative that was established within the agency. DOE is responsible for more than half the research in the physical sciences that any of the any other federal agency within the nation. The Secretary of Energy runs DOE and is appointed by the President with confirmation from the Senate.

The United States' first need for an agency was in 1942 during the inception of the Manhattan Project during World War II. After the war ended, U.S. Congress established the Atomic Energy Commission to "foster and control the peacetime development of atomic science and technology" (Buck, 1983, p. 1). On August 1, 1946, President Harry S. Truman signed the Atomic Energy Act (McMahon Act), which transferred the control of energy from the military to civilians, giving the control of all facilities and personnel who worked on the atomic bombing during the war. The act gave the Atomic Energy Commission unprecedented powers and authority over all nuclear science and technology fields. With such authority, there were strict protocols on the commission transferring technology between the United States and its allies and security partners. Transactions as such were prohibited Though the commission was praised for its involvement for establishing funding and resources for the nation's Ecosystem ecology, it received criticism for its lax regulations in several critical areas such as environmental protection, nuclear reactor safety, radiation protection protocol, and plant siting. The commission never recovered from the harsh criticism, resulting in its dissolution by Congress in 1974 under the Energy Reorganization Act of 1974. Under the reorganization, the Energy Research and Development Administration and the Nuclear Regulatory Commission. Three years later, President Jimmy Carter signed the Department of Energy Organization Act of 1977, establishing the Department of Energy.

DOE assumed the responsibilities of the Federal Energy Administration, Energy Research and Development Administration, the Federal Power Commission, and other agencies relevant to the agency's mission. Though the department is response for all energy and nuclear matters, it presented a key role within the Intelligence Community. In 1977, DOE's Office of Intelligence and Counterintelligence was established to support it intelligence gathering initiatives. The office protects "vital national security information and technologies, representing intellectual property of incalculable value" (About DOE, n.d., para. 1). The agency is responsible for intelligence and counterintelligence operations, including nearly 30 offices nationwide. Its mission is to "protect, enable, and represent the vast scientific brain trust resident in DOE's laboratories and plans" (Members of the IC, n.d., para. 6).

Department of Homeland Security

DHS is an executive cabinet of the American federal government and is responsible for protecting its citizens and the homeland. DHS is the third largest Cabinet department in the nation behind DoD and Veterans Affairs. All homeland security policy is coordinated through the White House and Homeland Security Council and coordinates with the departments of Energy, Health and Human Services, and Justice, as these agencies have significant responsibilities and homeland security initiatives.

The Human Genome Project was a global scientific research study to determine the progression of nucleotide base pairs that creates human DNA through ascertaining and diagramming of all genes of the human genome from an operative and physical position. The Department of Energy was heavily involved in the premature stages of the American-led initiative.

The Manhattan Project was a research and development project to produce the nation's first nuclear weapon.

The agency was established on November 25, 2002 under the Homeland Security Act 2002 and was instituted to amalgamate all federal agencies that involved homeland security initiatives into a single department. According to experts, the reorganization was the largest since the Cold War during the era of the National Security Act of 1947. The restructure established the Secretary of Defense role in military service departments, the CIA and NSC. After margining and establishing 22 federal agencies under DHS, Tom Ridge was named the first Secretary of DHS and agency officially opened the same day while the merged entities were officially categorized under DHS on March 1, 2003.

DHS works closely with the civilian realm to protect the United States and its borders. The mission of DHS is to ensure a "homeland that is safe, secure, and resilient against terrorism and other hazards" (Mission, n.d., Department of Homeland Security., para. 1). In addition, the department is accountable for preparing, preventing, and responding to domestic emergencies. In 2003, the United States Immigration and Naturalization Service became a subsidiary of the department and was streamlined to formulize the United States Immigration and Customs Enforcement, and Citizenship and Immigration services. The investigative aspects of both agencies created the Homeland Security Investigations division. Under DHS, United States Border Patrol and Customs Service and Plant Health Inspection Service merged to form the United States Customs and Border Protection agency, consisting of 22 federal agencies.

In 2007, the Office of Intelligence and Analysis under the Department of Homeland Security and is responsible for using information and intelligence from multiple sources to identify and assess current and future threats to the United States (Member of the IC, n.d., para. 7). The subsidiary of DHS is headed by the Under Secretary of Homeland Security for Intelligence and Analysis, who is accountable for increasing intelligence methods through collection and analysis throughout the department.

Department of State

The Department of State (or State Department) is a federal executive agency within the American government responsible for all foreign policy matters. The agency deals with international relations and negotiations agreements and treaties with foreign establishments and does so as a member of the United Nations. Created in 1789, the State Department is accountable for diplomatic operations on behalf of the United States abroad, and is also responsible for employing American foreign policy efforts, which is the depositary for more than 200 multilateral agreements. The mission of the State Department is to "advance the national interests of the United States and its people... and to shape and sustain a peaceful, prosperous, just, and democratic world and foster conditions for stability and progress for the benefit the American people and people everywhere" (Mission, n.d., U.S. Department of State, para. 6).

The Secretary of State heads the State Department, and like the SECDEF and Secretary of DHS, is nominated by the President and confirmed by the Senate. The Secretary of State is a cabinet position and is a member of the NSC. The position is the principal foreign-policy advisor and support all foreign activities for the federal government, including the *United States Agency for International Development (USAID)*, DHS, CIA, and Department of Commerce. In 1787, when the United States Constitution was drafted in Philadelphia and ratified by the original 13 colonies, the reformed body of law gave the President authority to conduct American foreign relations and establish policies and initiatives. The State Department consists of a civilian workforce that employs a significant amount of Foreign Service Officers and other diplomatic personnel to conduct operations overseas to analyze and report on economic, political, social, and visa matters. Employees of the State Department are also responsible for the needs and protection of American citizens who live abroad.

On July 21, 1789, the Department of Foreign Affairs was established by the House of Representatives and the Senate and President George Washington signed the legislation into law nearly a week later. This law was the first federal agency created under the new Constitution. The State Department's primary responsibilities were foreign policy and diplomacy, but expanded to management of the United States Census and Mint operations. On September 29, 1789, President Washington appointed Thomas Jefferson as the first Secretary of State.

The department's Bureau of Intelligence and Research was established in 1975, which is responsible for providing all-source intelligence to American diplomats and ambassadors. Initially, the bureau was founded as the Research and Analysis Branch under the Office of Strategic Services and was transferred to the Department of State after World War II. The agency provides timely, objective analysis of global developments as well as real-time insights from all-source intelligence (Member of the IC, n.d., para. 8). The Bureau of Intelligence and Research's priorities are:

- Expanding electronic dissemination of intelligence so that Department policy-makers can access intelligence quickly and securely from the desktop;

- Creating and maintaining an expert workforce through recruitment, training, and professional development in support of the national security mission;

- Tracking and analyzing issues that may undermine efforts to promote peace and security such as terrorism, the spread of WMD, and trafficking in humans and illicit drugs;

- Playing a key role in the IC to optimize intelligence collection and requirements so that current and future diplomatic information needs are met, resulting in enhanced intelligence support for policymakers;

- Increasing collaboration and information sharing on humanitarian issues through the interagency Humanitarian Information Unit;

- Serving as a leader in the USG for foreign public opinion surveys and polls that will help inform the USG's public diplomacy initiatives; and

- Providing all-source analyses and assessments that examine trends in governance, democracy, and human rights and assess domestic policies and leadership performance in countries of interest (D & CP—Bureau of Intelligence and Research, n.d., p. 173).

Because of the sensitivity of the bureau's operations, its personnel and budgetary information are classified. The Assistant Secretary of State for Intelligence and Research runs the Bureau of Intelligence and Research, who reports to the Secretary of State. The Assistant Secretary of State plays an integral role in ensuring the agency's intelligence missions are congruent with American foreign policy and that other agencies within the Intelligence Community effectively communicates the analysis to senior leaders and policymakers.

Department of the Treasury

The Department of the Treasury is a Cabinet-level agency within the federal government. In 1789, Congress created the agency to regulate the nation's revenue by producing currency, collecting taxes and paying the government's debts. The Department of the Treasury's mission is to "maintain a strong economy and create economic and job opportunities by promoting the conditions that enable economic growth and stability at home and abroad, strengthen national security by combating threats and protecting the integrity of the financial system, and manage the U.S. government's finances and resources effectively" (About DOT, 2016, para. 1). The organization consults on fiscal policy and manages federal finances by supervising the nation's banks to ensure accuracy and accountability. The Secretary of the Treasury runs the agency and is responsible for economic prosperity and financial security of the United States.

Alexander Hamilton, one of the Founding Fathers of the United States was the nation's first Secretary of the Treasury, as he was instrumental in interpreting the U.S. Constitution and considered one of the founders of the nation's financial system (Wright & Cowen, 2006). Appointed by George Washington, the first President of the United States, Hamilton was independently birth the United States' financial system and proved to be strong presence with the presidential administration. The Department of the Treasury is comprised of two major departments: The Departmental Offices and operating bureaus. Both parties are responsible for the agency's formulation of policy, management, and functions such as:

- Supervising thrift institutions
- Advising on domestic and international financial, monetary, economic, trade and tax policy
- Enforcing federal finance and tax laws
- Investigating and prosecuting tax evaders, counterfeiters, and forges (Duties and Functions of the U.S. Department of the Treasury, 2016, para. 4).

The department's Office of Intelligence and Analysis is relatively new, as it was established in 2004 under the Intelligence Authorization Act. The office plays an important in the mitigation of financing domestic and international terrorism. Its mission is built on the strong tradition of intelligence and national security at the Department of the Treasury (Terrorism and Financial Intelligence, 2012, para. 1). One of its core missions is to protect the financial integrity of the nation's asset through terrorism mitigation, supporting its mission by the following:

- Driving intelligence to meet the priorities of Treasury decision-makers and external customers
- Producing all-source assessments and other material to identify threats and vulnerabilities in licit and illicit networks that may be addressed by Treasury-led action
- Delivering timely, accurate, relevant intelligence to decision-makers
- Providing the security infrastructure necessary to safeguard the Treasury's national security information (Terrorism and Financial Intelligence, 2012, para. 2).

Finally, the Office of Intelligence and Analysis is accountable for the collection, analyzation, and distribution of intelligence/counterintelligence data that is congruent with treasury operations. It is part of the Terrorism and Financial Intelligence organization, which is focused on the deterrence of illegal financial schemes and financial terrorism. Both organizations work together to safeguard the nation's financial system against illicit use and combating rogue nations, terrorist facilitators, weapons of mass destruction proliferators, money launderers, drug kingpins, and other national security threats (Member of the IC, n.d., para. 9).

Drug Enforcement Administration

The Drug Enforcement Administration (DEA) a federal law enforcement agency, which falls under the Department of Justice. It is the leading agency for enforcing domestic drug laws and combating drug smuggling within the United States. DEA falls under the Controlled Substances Act (CSA), which President Richard Nixon passed in 1971 to regulate the distribution, importation, manufacture, and possession specific substances. Under CSA, the DEA shares contemporaneous jurisdiction the Department of Homeland Security, the Federal Bureau of Investigation, Immigration and Customs Enforcement, and U.S. Border Patrol. The agency's mission is to:

> Enforce the controlled substance laws and regulations of the United States and bring to the criminal and civil justice system of the United States, or any other competent jurisdiction, those organizations and principal members of organizations, involved in the growing, manufacture, or distribution of controlled substances appearing in or destined for illicit traffic in the United States, and to recommend and support non-enforcement programs aimed at reducing the availability of illicit controlled substances on the domestic and international markets (DEA Mission Statement, n.d., para. 1).

DEA's responsibilities include:

- Investigation and preparation for the prosecution of major violators of controlled substance laws operating at interstate and international levels.

- Investigation and preparation for prosecution of criminals and drug gangs who perpetrate violence in our communities and terrorize citizens through fear and intimidation.

- Management of a national drug intelligence program in cooperation with federal, state, local, and foreign officials to collect, analyze, and disseminate strategic and operational drug intelligence information.

- Seizure and forfeiture of assets derived from, traceable to, or intended to be used for illicit drug trafficking.

- Enforcement of the provisions of the Controlled Substances Act as they pertain to the manufacture, distribution, and dispensing of legally produced controlled substances.

- Coordination and cooperation with federal, state and local law enforcement officials on mutual drug enforcement efforts and enhancement of such efforts through exploitation of potential interstate and international investigations beyond local or limited federal jurisdictions and resources.

- Coordination and cooperation with federal, state, and local agencies, and with foreign governments, in programs designed to reduce the availability of illicit abuse-type drugs on the United States market through non-enforcement methods such as crop eradication, crop substitution, and training of foreign officials.

- Responsibility, under the policy guidance of the Secretary of State and U.S. Ambassadors, for all programs associated with drug law enforcement counterparts in foreign countries.

- Liaison with the United Nations, Interpol, and other organizations on matters relating to international drug control programs (DEA Mission Statement, n.d. para. 3).

Most importantly, DEA has sole responsibility for handling drug investigations within the United States and overseas.

On July 1, 1973, President Richard Nixon established DEA through the Reorganization Plan No. 2 of 1973, creating a law enforcement agency to enforce federal laws within the United States and control the government's drug activities. The agency was well-received by Congress because of the growing epidemic of drugs being imported from Central America during this time. The development of DEA merged the Bureau of Customs, the Bureau of Narcotics and Dangerous Drugs, the Customs Agency Service, the Office of Drug Abuse Law Enforcement, and other subsidiaries charged with protecting the United States from the drug widespread. DEA became disreputably popular in the mid-1990's when domestic terrorist and extremist, Timothy McVeigh bombed the Alfred P. Murrah Federal Building in Oklahoma City because it contained DEA offices, the Bureau of Alcohol and Tobacco, Tobacco, Firearms and Explosives (ATF), and the FBI. All offices were responsible for the raids (Waco Seige and Ruby Ridge) and McVeigh believed the raids were a violation of American citizens' rights. The bombing killed 168 and injured over 600 people, including two DEA agents (more about Timothy McVeigh and the Oklahoma City bombing can be found in chapter seven).

Since the inception of the DEA, intelligence has played a pivotal role within the agency's operations. Responsible for coordination with local, state, and federal (and foreign) law enforcement drug entities, DEA has been accountable for all collection, analysis, and distribution of intelligence gathered in drug operations. The agency's intelligence initiative is responsible for major drug investigations, strengthening ongoing ties and subsequent prosecutions, develops information that leads to seizures and arrests, and provides policymakers with drug trend information upon which programmatic decision can be based (Intelligence Topics at DEA, Intelligence Products: El Paso Intelligence Center, n.d., para. 1). In 2006, DEA formulized the Office of National Security Intelligence and facilitate full and appropriate intelligence coordination and information sharing with other the members of the U.S. Intelligence Community and homeland security elements (Member of the IC, n.d., para. 10). DEA's intelligence mission consists of the following:

- Collect and produce intelligence in support of the administrator and other federal, state, and local agencies
- Establish and maintain close working relationships with all agencies that produce or use narcotics intelligence
- Increase the efficiency in the reporting, analysis, storage, retrieval, and exchange of such information
- Undertake a continuing review of the narcotics intelligence effort to identify and correct deficiencies (Law Enforcement Intelligence: A Guide for State, Local, and Tribal Law Enforcement Agencies, n.d., p. 180).

Its missions are predicated on three categorized elements: tactical, investigative, and strategic.

- Tactical intelligence is evaluated information on which immediate enforcement action (i.e. arrests, seizures, and interdictions)

- Investigative intelligence provides analytical support to investigations and prosecutions to dismantle criminal organizations and gain resources
- Strategic intelligence focuses on the current picture of drug trafficking from cultivation to distribution that can be used for management decision making, resource deployment, and policy planning (The Drug Enforcement Administration's Use of Intelligence Analysis, 2008, p. 14).

As DEA's role has expanded, legislation has increased the agency's authority within the IC to fight the war on drugs. With distinctive realms of its responsibilities, DEA conducts high-level assessments that involve complex intelligence missions to provide senior leaders and policymakers with the most current drug and trafficking information. Such methods have claimed success in DEA's ability to deter major drug missions and dismantle large drug and trafficking organizations.

Federal Bureau of Investigation

Created in 1908 as the Bureau of Investigation (BOI), the Federal Bureau of Investigation (named changed in 1935) is the United States' federal intelligence and law enforcement agency. The FBI is a subcomponent of the Department of Justice and a member of the nation's intelligence community, which concurrently reports to the Attorney General of the United States and the Director of National Intelligence. The FBI is the nation's leading agency specializing in counterintelligence, counterterrorism operations, and criminal investigations. Its primary mission is to support other federal agencies in protecting national security, with federal law enforcement authority.

The agency has over 400 offices across the United States, and it has sixty offices throughout the world, serving U.S. consulate and embassy offices to coordinate with foreign security entities. The FBI has the authority to conduct international intelligence and clandestine operations, though coordination is usually required between the United States and foreign governments. The FBI headquarters is in Washington, D.C. at the J. Edgar Hoover Building.

The FBI's mission is to "protect the American people and uphold the Constitution of the United States" by:

- Protecting civil rights
- Combating transnational/national criminal organizations and enterprises
- Combating major white-collar crime
- Combating significant violent crime (FBI's Mission, n.d., para. 2).

According to the Department of Justice, the FBI's priorities are to:

- Protect the United States from terrorist attacks
- Protect the United States against foreign intelligence operations and espionage
- Protect the United States against cyber-based attacks and high-technology crimes

- Combat public corruption at all levels
- Protect civil rights
- Combat transnational and national criminal organizations and enterprises
- Combat major white-collar crime
- Combat significant violent crime
- Support federal, state, county, municipal, and international partners
- Upgrade technology to successfully perform the FBI's mission (Organization, Mission, and Function Manual: Federal Bureau of Investigation, n.d., para. 3).

The major functions of the FBI are to:

- Conduct professional investigations and authorized intelligence collection to identify and counter the threats posed by domestic and international terrorists and their supporters within the United States, and to pursue extraterritorial criminal investigations to bring the perpetrators of terrorist acts to justice. In furtherance of this function, the FBI designs, develops, and implements counterterrorism initiatives which enhance the FBI's ability to minimize the terrorist threat.
- Conduct counterintelligence activities and coordinate counterintelligence activities of other agencies in the intelligence community within the United States. (Executive Order 12333 includes international terrorist activities in its definition of counterintelligence.)
- Coordinate the efforts of U.S. government agencies and departments in protecting the nation's critical infrastructure by identifying and investigating criminal and terrorist group intrusions through physical and cyber-attacks.
- Investigate violations of the laws of the United States and collect evidence in cases in which the United States is or may be a party in interest, except in cases in which such responsibility is by statute or otherwise specifically assigned to another investigative agency.
- Locate and apprehend fugitives for violations of specified federal laws and, when so requested, state and local fugitives pursuant to federal statutory authority.
- Conduct professional investigations to identify, disrupt, and dismantle existing and emerging criminal enterprises whose activities affect the United States. Address international criminal organizations and terrorist groups which threaten the American people and their property through expanded international liaisons and through the conduct of extraterritorial investigations as mandated by laws and executive orders.
- Gather, analyze and assess information and intelligence of planned or committed criminal acts.
- Establish and implement quality outreach programs that will ensure FBI and community partnerships and sharing.
- Conduct personnel investigations requisite to the work of the Department of Justice and whenever required by statute or otherwise.

- Establish and conduct law enforcement training programs and conduct research to aid state and local law enforcement personnel. Participate in interagency law enforcement initiatives which address crime problems common to federal/state/local agencies.

- Develop new approaches, techniques, systems, equipment and devices to improve and strengthen law enforcement and assist in conducting state, local, and international law enforcement training programs.

- Provide timely and relevant criminal justice information and identification services concerning individuals, stolen property, criminal organizations and activities, crime statistics, and other law enforcement related data not only to the FBI but to qualified law enforcement, criminal justice, civilian, academic, employment, licensing, and firearms sales organizations.

- Operate the Federal Bureau of Investigation Laboratory not only to serve the FBI but also to provide, without cost, technical and scientific assistance, including expert testimony in federal or local courts, for all duly constituted law enforcement agencies, other organizational units of the Department of Justice, and other federal agencies, and to provide identification assistance in mass disasters and for other humanitarian purposes.

- Review and assess operations and work performance to ensure compliance with laws, rules, and regulations and to ensure efficiency, effectiveness, and economy of operations.

- Effectively and appropriately communicate and disclose information on the FBI mission, accomplishments, operations, and values to Congress, the media, and the public (Organization, Mission, and Function Manual: Federal Bureau of Investigation, n.d., para. 3).

Prior to the FBI, the *National Bureau of Criminal Identification* was established in 1896, which was a national agency charged with establishing a massive database to identify criminals. With the assassination of President William McKinley in 1901, President Theodore Roosevelt feared the United States would be viewed as anarchist and mandated additional authority to monitor them. When the Oregon land fraud scandal happened, President Roosevelt reiterated his demands to form an investigative service which would have its own special agents. At the president's request, Attorney General Charles Bonaparte organized the Bureau of Investigation.

On July 26, 1908, the Bureau of Investigation was created using Department of Justice expeditionary funds. According to Tim Weiner, author of *Enemies: A History of the FBI,* Attorney General Charles Bonaparte used the Department of Justice expense fund to hire 34 personnel to work for BOI (2012, p. 11). Stanley Finch was hired as BOI's first director. The new investigative agency's first task was enforcing the *Mann Act*, to mitigate prostitution within the United States. By 1932, the agency was renamed to the United States Bureau of Investigation and the following year, the Division of Investigation. By 1935, the investigation was recognized as a separate entity of the Department of Justice and was named the Federal Bureau of Investigation.

The FBI's most prestigious director was J. Edgar Hoover, who served a total of 45 years with BOI, DOI, and FBI. Over the years, his roles expanded with increased authority, as he was responsible for establishing the Scientific Crime Detection Laboratory (known as the FBI Laboratory). During his tenure, agents began investigating homicide and mitigating the violence of white supremacy and Neo-Nazi groups. Hoover was involved in high-profile and major investigations during his career, and with his longevity with the bureau, it was known that he made some controversial decisions. After his tenure and death, Congress passed legislation that FBI Directors would serve no more than ten years.

By the 1930s, the FBI was involved in wiretapping in attempts to capture bootleggers. Due to the conflict of wiretapping as a violation of the Fourth Amendment, Congress passed the *Communications Act of 1934,* which banned the FBI from wiretapping without approval, but bugging was considered legal. However, after *Nardone vs. United States*, Congress decided the evidence the FBI received through phone tapping was considered unacceptable. By 1967, Congress passed another act, *Omnibus Crime Control Act,* giving law enforcement the authority to receive warrants first and then tap phones during open investigations.

By the 1940s, national security became a crucial addition to the FBI's mission. Counter-espionage operations became a clandestine mission for the agency when it was evident that foreign spies were infiltrating and gathering information against the United States and its coalition forces. In the next two decades, the FBI would be heavily involved in investigating civil rights violations and organized crime, conducting counter-intelligence operations to disrupt rebellious and extremist groups within the United States. Hoover would have increasing tensions with civil rights leader and activist Martin Luther King, Jr., who would accuse the director of giving special treatment to white supremacy groups. Hoover publicly denied these claims.

In the 1980s, the FBI established special teams such as hostage rescue teams (HRT), Special Weapons and Tactics (SWAT), and the Computer Analysis and Response Team (CART) to respond to terrorist acts and violent crimes. Toward the end of the Cold War, over 300 special agents were reassigned because the threat of terrorism was mitigated, and they began more domestic missions, such as aiding with developing DNA testing and fingerprinting procedures. By the mid-1990s, the counterterrorism effort was increased again due to the substantial terrorist threats and attacks against the United States by domestic and international terrorists (i.e. 1993 World Trade Center bombing, the Oklahoma City bombing, and the Unabomber).

Not until the twenty-first century did the FBI significantly increase its counterterrorism tactics after the September 11 attacks. Robert Mueller was sworn in as the director of the FBI just weeks before the attacks and mandated a reorganization of all FBI critical infrastructure and operations. Director Mueller's leadership was pivotal as he made all federal crimes a top priority (FBI, 2015). Though Director Mueller's efforts were positive, the 9/11 Commission Report identified the CIA and FBI as responsible for the lack of intelligence reports and information sharing that could have potentially mitigated the attacks.

Because of the FBI's critical and sensitive operations, which makes it an integral part of federal law enforcement, its intelligence division has an expanded, authoritative role within the United States and coordinating offices abroad. In 2014, former FBI Director Jamey Comey created the FBI's intelligence branch to lead the integration of intelligence and operations within the organization (FBI: Intelligence Branch, n.d., para. 2). The Directorate of Intelligence was appointed to oversee the division's strategic outlook and provide to support to not only the FBI but other supporting agencies with the IC. The intelligence branch is responsible for the planning and direction, collection, processing and exploitation, analysis and production, and dissemination of all intelligence gathered to properly analyze for senior leaders and policymakers in making sound decisions of the United States homeland and national security objectives. The branch's method of intelligence gathering is dependent upon the following: electronic intelligence (ELINT), human intelligence (HUMINT), signals intelligence (SIGINT), imagery intelligence (IMINT), measure and signatures intelligence (MASINT), and open-source intelligence (OSINT).

Marine Corps Intelligence

The U.S. Marine Corps earliest history of intelligence operations dates to 1939 when the Commandant of the Marine Corps created M-2 Intelligence division. On April 21, 1939, the Commandant restructured organizations within the service branch, designating the letter "M" with numbers to represent the new structure offices. M-2 was the intelligence branch was established under the reorganization. It was not until the twenty-first century the Marine Corps established a permanent organization to represent its unique intelligence operations. On April 27, 2000, Commandant of the Marine Corps, General James L. Jones created the Marine Corps Intelligence. A subsidiary of the IC, the Marine Corps Intelligence is managed by the Director of Intelligence, who is responsible for division's budget, plans, policy, programming, and Marine Corps intelligence operations. The Director is also responsible for the oversight of the Marine Corps Intelligence Activity, which supports the Commandant of the Marine Corps. The intelligence division conducts its operations under counterintelligence (CI), geospatial intelligence (GEOINT), advanced geospatial intelligence, and human intelligence (HUMINT). The Marine Corps Intelligence agency develops strategy for the Marine Corps Intelligence, Surveillance and Reconnaissance program.

The U.S. Marine Corps has a unique mission when it comes to intelligence operations. It produces tactical and operational intelligence to support marines on the battlefield. The Marine Corps intelligence division consists of intelligence experts who represent its Commandant of the Marine Corps in the role of the Joint Chiefs of Staff position to discuss important matters with other officers of the Joint Chief Staff and the Chairman of the Joint Chiefs of Staff respectively (Headquarters Marine Corps: Intelligence Department, n.d., para. 1).

National Geospatial-Intelligence Agency

National Geospatial-Intelligence Agency (NGA) is a federal intelligence agency that falls under the Department of Defense and the Intelligence Community. NGA's mission is to "collect, analyze, and distribute geospatial intelligence (GEOINT) in support of national security" (National Geospatial-Intelligence Agency [NGA], n.d., para. 1). NGA's primary responsibilities are:

1. NGA delivers the strategic intelligence that allows the president and national policymakers to make crucial decisions on counterterrorism, weapons of mass destruction, global political crises and more.

2. NGA enables the warfighter to plan missions, gain battlefield superiority, precisely target the adversary, and protect our military forces.

3. NGA provides timely warnings to the warfighter and national decision makers by monitoring, analyzing and reporting imminent threats. Often, NGA has the only "eyes" focused on global hot spots and can give unique insight into these critical areas.

4. NGA protects the homeland by supporting counterterrorism, counternarcotics, and border and transportation security. NGA supports security planning for special events, such as presidential inaugurations, state visits by foreign leaders, international conferences and major public events (Olympics, Super Bowls, satellite launchings, etc.).

5. NGA ensures safety of navigation in the air and on the seas by maintaining the most current information and highest quality services for U.S. military forces and global transport networks.

6. NGA defends the nation against cyber threats by supporting other intelligence agencies with in-depth analysis of cyber networks.

7. NGA creates and maintains the geospatial foundation data, knowledge, and analysis that enable all other missions.

8. NGA assists humanitarian and disaster relief efforts by working directly with the lead federal agencies responding to fires, floods, earthquakes, landslides, hurricanes or other natural or manmade disasters (About NGA, n.d., para. 1).

The NGA Director is its top executive and is responsible for all operations within the organization. Imagery intelligence was a major component during WWII and was very important in obtaining photographs on the battlefield. Before NGA was established, the National Imagery and Mapping Agency (NIMA) was the leading organization in imagery for intelligence operations and had three primary responsibilities: corporate affairs, operations, and systems and technology. After NIMA's creation, the agency joined five additional imagery organizations:

- Central Imagery Office
- CIA's Office of Imagery Analysis
- DIA's Office of Imagery Analysis
- Defense Mapping Agency
- National Photographic Interpretation Center

With many offices responsible for imagery intelligence, NIMA eventually merged the concept of charts, environmental maps, and imagery to form geospatial intelligence. The organization was instrumental in undertaking domestic and international matters and played an important role in homeland security immediately after the September 11 attacks.

National Reconnaissance Office

The National Reconnaissance Office (NRO) is another federal agency that is a part of the Department of Defense and the Intelligence Community and is charged with "innovative overhead intelligence systems for national security" (National Reconnaissance Office [NRO], n.d., para. 2). The extended mission is to

> advance and shape the Intelligence Community's understanding of the discipline, practice, and history of national reconnaissance. The agency's objective is to ensure NRO leadership has the analytical framework and historical context to make effective policy and programmatic decisions. We [NRO] focus on social science and historical research, with a goal to enable the NRO to meet its mission objectives (Center for the study of national reconnaissance, n.d. para. 3).

Established on September 6, 1961, and considered one of the top five intelligence agencies in the United States, the NRO is responsible for coordinating CIA reconnaissance activities, and its primary function is to manage deployment, procurement, research and development, operation and imaging, ocean surveillance satellites, and signals intelligence. The agency's creation stemmed from the inefficient processes, bad management, and inadequate advancement of the United States Air Force's satellite reconnaissance program. The first program established was the Corona Program, which used film capsules dropped by satellites and recovered by American military aircraft. The program's first successful launch was the Discoverer XIII which produced the first images seen from space. According to the organization's website, the NRO's systems are responsible for:

- Monitoring the proliferation of weapons of mass destruction
- Tracking international terrorists, drug traffickers, and criminal organizations
- Developing highly accurate military targeting data and bomb damage assessments
- Supporting international peacekeeping and humanitarian relief operations
- Assessing the impact of natural disasters, such as earthquakes, tsunamis, floods, and fires (Center for the study of national reconnaissance, n.d., para. 3).

The Director of the NRO is responsible for all operations within the agency and reports to the Director of National Intelligence and the Secretary of Defense. The NRO Director also serves as the Assistant Secretary of the Air Force for Intelligence Space Technology. The NRO designs, builds, and operates reconnaissance satellites and provides satellite intelligence (SIGINT) to several federal agencies such as the Defense Intelligence Agency, Central Intelligence, the National Geospatial Agency, the National Security Agency, the Naval Research Laboratory, and United States Strategic Command. Additionally, the organization operates reconnaissance systems to conduct intelligence-related activities for national security objectives. The organization has operations throughout the world and is responsible for the collection and distribution of intelligence gathered from reconnaissance satellites.

344 I Homeland and National Security

National Security Agency/Central Security Service

The National Security Agency (NSA) is a federal intelligence agency that is a subsidiary of the Department of Defense and is under the purview of the Director of National Intelligence. Created on November 4, 1952 by President Harry S. Truman, the NSA is responsible for "global monitoring, collection, and processing of information and data for foreign intelligence and counterintelligence purposes: SIGINT" (Signal Intelligence Activities, n.d., para. 1). The organization's mission is leading the "U.S. government in cryptology that encompasses both signals intelligence (SIGINT) and information assurance products and services, and enables computer network operations to gain advantage for the nation and our allies under all circumstances" (Signal Intelligence Activities, n.d.., para. 1). NSA is also responsible for securing American communications network and information systems.

NSA's SIGINT mission is predicated on gathering intelligence on foreign countries, agencies, people, and international terrorists. SIGINT (signal intelligence) is derived from "electronic signals and systems used by foreign targets, such as communications systems, radars, and weapons systems. SIGINT provides a vital window for our nation into foreign adversaries' capabilities, actions, and intentions" (Signals Intelligence Activities, n.d., para. 1). The organization's scope of responsibility includes intercepting Internet and telephone communications on over one billion people throughout world to gather intelligence on foreign interests regarding economic development, government and politics, military progression, and terrorist activities.

The Central Security Service (CSS) is a federal intelligence agency that integrated with the National Security Agency in 1972. CSS and the NSA is the nation's cryptologic organization that coordinates, direct, and performs highly specialized activities to protect U.S. information systems and to produce foreign signals intelligence (Member of the IC, n.d., para. 15). After the end of World War II, the federal government restructured agencies that were no longer needed. The Army Security Agency (ASA) and the Naval Communications Intelligence Organization (NCIO) were the main agencies activated during the war, and when it ended, NCIO deactivated and became the Communications Support Activities division. ASA was the primary intelligence agency that specialized in signals intelligence (SIGINT). During this era, the U.S. Air Force had its own security service (U.S. Air Force Security Service), which specialized in communications intelligence (COMINT).

By 1949, the Armed Forces Security Agency was established and became the leading organization for the nation's COMINT and communications security (COMSEC). Because there were tensions between the service departments and the control of SIGINT operations, AFSA dissolved and President Harry S. Truman created the National Security Agency. CSS was developed to promote a full partnership with the National Security and Service Cryptologic Elements of the U.S. Armed Forces (Central Security Service, n.d., para. 2).

Navy Intelligence

The U.S. Navy's Office of Naval Intelligence (ONI) is the nation's older intelligence division within the IC. In 1882, ONI was created to enhance the Navy's modernization efforts in maritime intelligence. The office's mission to "gain and hold a decision information advantage over America's potential adversaries" (Our Mission, n.d., para. 1). ONI is responsible for the collection, analyzation, and production of maritime intelligence, which is distributed to primary operations, strategic, and tactical policymakers. The most senior intelligence division is accountable for supporting combat operations and providing critical information to meet the standards of the Department of Defense. The Navy's intelligence unit has a unique mission to "produce maritime intelligence on naval weapons and technology proliferation, transnational threats in civil maritime counter-proliferation, counter-narcotics and the global maritime environment, and other activities that directly support the U.S. Navy, joint warfighters, and national decision makers (Our Mission, n.d., para. 1).

U.S. CUSTOMS AND BORDER PROTECTION AND TRANSPORTATION SECURITY ADMINISTRATION

On March 1, 2003, the *U.S. Customs and Border Protection (CBP)* was established under the Department of Homeland Security and is considered the largest federal law enforcement agency within the agency. CBP's mission is to "safeguard America's borders thereby protecting the public from dangerous people and materials while en-hancing the nation's global economic competitiveness by enabling legitimate trade and travel" (About CBP. (n.d.)., n.d., para. 1). The organization has nearly 50,000 sworn federal agents and officers who safeguard the nation's borders. Though CBP is primarily charged with protecting the American borders, preventing terrorism, and detecting weapons of mass destruction, the agency is also accountable for preventing individuals from illegally entering the United States.

History

CBP superseded portions of the U.S. Customs Service (USCS) which also merged with the U.S. Immigration and Naturalization Service (now known as *Immigration and Customs Enforcement-ICE*), which was the reigning federal agency responsible for border security operations and collecting import tariffs on shipments into the United States. USCS dates to July 31, 1789, in the aftermath of the American Revolutionary War, when President George Washington enforced the *Tariff Act*, which sanctioned duties on imported goods. Weeks later, Congress formulized USCS and specified ports of entry to implement imported goods and service operations. In response to the

September 11 attacks, USCS dissolved, and CBP became the official federal agency of DHS on March 1, 2003, which includes the Animal and Plant Health Inspection Service and USCS (now ICE).

Responsibilities of CBP officers include:

- Implementing the CBP Canine Program
- Inspecting and examining cargo and passengers at 326 ports of entry within the United States, Bermuda, Canada, the Caribbean, Ireland, and the Middle East.
- Prevention of harmful and illegal agricultural diseases contaminating American farms and food supply (i.e. agroterrorism or bioterrorism)
- Prevention of weapons of mass destruction entering the United States by air or sea (i.e. drug trafficking, human trafficking, or unconventional weapons)
- Protecting American borders in cooperation with Canadian and Mexican alliances
- Regulating the agency's tariff laws and trade processes (i.e. the Container Security Initiative)

One of CBP's primary roles is to assess all passengers arriving to the United States by utilizing specific systems such as Advanced Passenger Information System, the Joint Terrorism Task Force, the Student Exchange Visitor System, and the United States Visitor and Immigration Status Indication Technology. There are low-threat systems that are specifically used for the United States' neighbors such as the Secure Electronic Network for Travelers Rapid Inspection program for Mexico and the Nexus program for Canada. Both countries have a bilateral coalition effort known as the *Free and Secure Trade* act which uses transponder technology and shipment information to process vehicles arriving at American borders. In addition, the agency works closely with the U.S. Food and Drug Administration to screen imported food shipments to detect agro-terrorism and bioterrorism operations.

Transportation Security Administration

Like the CBP, the Transportation Security Administration (TSA) was established in response to the September 11 attacks under the *Aviation and Transportation Security Act (ATSA)*. Enacted by President George W. Bush on November 19, 2001, the agency was endorsed by Representative Don Yong and Senator Ernest Hollings. During its inception, TSA was a subsidiary of the U.S. Department of Transportation but transferred to DHS on March 9, 2003. TSA is responsible for security of public transportation within the United States. TSA's mission is to "protect the nation's transportation systems to ensure freedom of movement for people and commerce" (Mission Transportation Security Administration, n.d., para. 1). The agency is primarily accountable for air travel and consists of TSA agents, Federal Air Marshals, and dog handler teams.

CRITICAL INFRASTRUCTURE, INDUSTRIAL, AND UTILITY FACILITIES

Critical infrastructure "provides the essential services that underpin American society and serve as the backbone of our nation's economy, health, and security" (Critical Infrastructure Security, n.d., para. 1). Sixteen vital critical infrastructures within the United States are considered significant physical and virtual systems that if compromised or destroyed could debilitate American national security objectives. These critical infrastructures formulate the economic, health, and safety securities of the United States, and it is imperative that awareness, education, modern technology, and training are used to protect all sectors. The *National Protections and Programs Directorate's Office of Infrastructure Protection* is responsible for the coordination and implementation of national security policies which directly affect management of risks to the nation's critical infrastructures.

The *Presidential Policy Directive 21: Critical Infrastructure Security Resilience* is a body of legislation responsible for "strengthening and maintaining secure, functioning, and resilient critical infrastructure" (DHS, 2016, para. 1). This framework superseded the *Homeland Security Presidential Directive 7: Critical Infrastructure Identification, Prioritization, and Protection* policy. The critical infrastructures of the United States are compartmentalized in sixteen sectors:

1. Chemical
2. Commercial facilities
3. Communications
4. Critical manufacturing
5. Dams
6. Defense industrial base
7. Emergency services
8. Energy
9. Financial services
10. Food and agriculture
11. Government facilities
12. Healthcare and public health
13. Information
14. Nuclear reactors, materials, and waste
15. Transportation
16. Water and wastewater

Chemical Sector is responsible for the management of dangerous chemicals.

Commercial Facilities Sector is comprised of a wide range of sites that attract large populations for business, entertainment, and travel.

Communication Sector is the largest communications system for American business, government, and private/public sectors.

Critical Manufacturing Sector is vital for sustaining American economic growth and permanence.

Dams Sector transports water control and retention services within the American hydroelectric system.

Defense Industrial Base Sector is the manufacturing compound that provides research and development, production, delivery, and maintenance of American military weapons systems.

Emergency Services Sector provides awareness, mitigation, and preparedness services to emergency management organizations on the local, state, and federal levels within the United States.

Energy Sector comprises the largest energy infrastructure of the United States.

Financial Services Sector is responsible for the financial aspects of local, state, and federal agencies of the United States.

Food and Agriculture Sector is the agency charged with America's food and agricultural industry, which is primarily privatized.

Government Facilities Sector covers local, state, and federal government agencies within the United States and abroad that are responsible for business, commercial, and recreational activities.

Healthcare and Public Health Sector involves all agencies within the United States that protect from manmade and natural disasters, outbreaks, and terrorist acts.

Information Technology Sector is America's hub for business, economic, education, government, public health, and security information in the areas of technology and innovation.

Nuclear Reactors, Materials, and Waste Sector is responsible for all American nuclear power accounts and electrical generation.

Transportation Systems Sector is America's primary agency for all modes of transportation.

Water and Wastewater Systems Sector is responsible for the safe consumption of water, preventing disease, and protecting the environment.

The key to utility security is:

- Cybersecurity
- Emergency preparedness procedures
- Executive orders
- Physical security of critical infrastructure
- Security laws and initiatives

RAILROAD AND PORT SECURITY

The United States has not had many attacks on the railroad system when compared to national disasters and terrorism. Because there have been rare instances of railroad attacks, security measures have been relaxed and insufficient. Even though there are security measures established, railroad systems are still highly vulnerable to attack. Therefore, increased security standards are required to mitigate future threats. This chapter will discuss major vulnerabilities across the national railroad system.

The national railroad system is under the *Federal Railroad Administration (FRA)*, which is a subsidiary of the *Department of Transportation (DoT)*. The FRA was established under the *Department of Transportation Act of 1966*, and its mission is to "enable the safe, reliable, and efficient movement of people and goods for a strong America, now, and in the future" (U.S. DOT Takes New Emergency Actions as Part of Comprehensive Strategy to Keep Crude Oil Shipments Safe, n.d., para. 1). It is one of the ten organizations within the Department of Transportation that deals with intermodal transportation and operates through the following departments:

- Chief Counsel
- Financial Management and Administration
- Public Engagement
- Railroad Policy and Development
- Safety

Port security refers to defense measures to protect maritime and port operations. The United States Coast Guard and the United States Customs and Border Protection agencies collaborate and are responsible for all port security operations within the United States. If needed, the FBI and local law enforcement agencies have responsibility to assist in collaborative efforts. Port security matters became heavily debated when P&O Ports, a British company, was sold to Dubai Ports World in 2006. The company included American assets, which led to speculation that the purchase would affect national security objectives. Dubai Ports World sold the American interests to the American International Group in 2006. The incident highlighted the need for American port security efforts, and President George W. Bush signed the Security and Accountability for Every Port Act (SAFE Port Act) into law on October 13, 2006.

Port security is a critical concept in national security because of possible terrorist attacks. The American **maritime system** is comprised of over 300 sea and river ports with nearly 4,000 cargo and passenger terminals. The world is dependent upon American commercial shipping as it's the most dependable and cost-effective system for transporting products in the world. Currently, the United States is responsible for twenty percent of the world's maritime business and trade. With such significant responsibility, terrorist attacks are highly probable, and any type of attack against the American port system can severely debilitate one of the United States' largest critical infrastructures, which can gravely impact national and global economies.

Possible Security Breaches

Vulnerability of the American port system can lead to possible security breaches in the container shipping industry. Increased volume in maritime traffic raises significant concern over cargo and passenger ships and possible pirate attacks. There are also concerns for the accountability for the transportation of products as cargo containers present the greatest security risks and vulnerabilities. According to J.F. Fritelli of *Port and Maritime Security: Background and Issues for Congress*, an estimated global inventory of over twelve million shipping containers creates a challenge when it comes to inspecting, securing, transporting, and tracking (2005). Creating a stabilized and effective port security process is very costly and time-consuming. For example, a large container ship can hold thousands of containers, making it very difficult to inspect all items without delaying or disrupting shipment schedules. Due to this, the United States physically inspects only two percent of the shipments that transport through Customs (Scanning and Imaging Shipping Containers Overseas: Costs and Alternatives, 2016).

Various security incidents can compromise port security methods such as the smuggling of weapons of mass destruction. Clark C. Abt, author of *The Economic Impact of Nuclear Terrorist Attacks on Freight Transport Systems in an Age of Seaport Vulnerability*, notes that a large-scale nuclear attack at a major seaport could possibly kill between 50,000 and one million people (2003). Nuclear attacks are an attractive terrorist strategy for adversaries, and all ports are susceptible to possible terrorist attacks. Security measures cannot significantly impact global shipping operations, therefore increasing national security threats. Because inspections of shipments create vulnerable scenarios, unpredictability is part of the threat if terrorists infiltrate containers. Factors involved in the possible infiltration of shipment containers include:

- Specific geographic/physical designs
- Hijackers
- Low percentage of inspections increases probability for the shipment of illegal products/weapons of mass destruction

The economic effect of a port attack would be astronomical, especially for the United States. Closure of major American ports could cost up to one billion dollars per day for the first week and exponentially increase subsequently (Fritelli, 2003). For example, when the International Longshore and Warehouse Union went on strike, resulting in twenty-nine port closures for ten days, statistics showed this incident cost the American economy over $19 million (Cohen, 2016). As mentioned, security inspections impact shipment schedules, and businesses cannot afford such delays, even with innovative methods such as the **just-in-time distribution model**, which is responsible for decreasing business logistic costs. Possible attacks on major ports could force alternative routes and overwhelmingly congested ports.

Security Responsibilities

The United States Coast Guard, the United States Customs and Border Protection (CBP), the *Maritime Administration (MARAD)*, and the Transportation Security Administration (TSA) are major agencies located at seaports. The Coast Guard's responsibilities include boarding, evaluating, and inspecting commercial ships approaching American waters to mitigate terrorist attacks. The agency is also charged with protecting naval ships that are docked at American ports. CBP is responsible for inspecting cargo arriving into U.S. ports. TSA is responsible for all modes of transportation, and, therefore, plays a supporting role to the Coast Guard and CBP. Finally, MARAD publishes the Maritime Security Reporters and national planning information on port security standards.

Although federal agencies play a significant role in port security, local and state governments are responsible for port regulations and initiatives. States have jurisdiction to advise and regulate laws that threaten state interests (Ports Primer: 3.2 Port Governance, n.d.). Some ports security standards are enforced by local law enforcement agencies. According to the United States Accounting Office (2002), there have been recommendations to consolidate federal agencies involved with port security. This consolidation has been projected to produce long-term benefits, but varying standards of funding, methods, and participation could challenge this proposition. Internal and external stakeholders are critical to providing cooperative tools in establishing initiatives, and cultural differences among agencies can be a valid consideration, as adjusting to standards of one agency may be deemed difficult. As mentioned, port security standards can be quite expensive and making large-scale improvements may require a significant amount of funding.

The September 11 attacks initiated new levels of maritime and port security standards. The Coast Guard initiated a process which enforced better methods for evaluating carrier and shipping information. In addition, CBP enacted the *Container Security Initiative and the Customs Trade Partnership against Terrorism*. The CSI was enacted to increase security for container cargo shipments to the United States, and CTPT is a security initiative that centralized security efforts with private companies against terrorism. In addition, President George W. Bush signed the *Maritime Transportation Security Act* on November 25, 2002 to acknowledge port and waterway security standards.

EMERGENCY OPERATIONS: GOVERNMENT AND PRIVATE SECTOR PLANNING

Government and business roles in homeland security date to the "federalist" times when the federal government played a key role after the American Revolutionary War. During this time, Congress sanctioned the deferment of federal bond payments in the aftermath of a disaster, which was a fire in New Hampshire. The federal government aided and provided emergency relief for the area, increasing close relationships among local, state, and federal governments, non-governmental organizations, and private/public sectors.

Government planning is the key to protecting national security. President Jimmy Carter increased awareness of government planning when he passed Presidential Policy Directive 58 towards the end of his presidential term. After President Carter left office, President Ronald Reagan revised the directives, creating his own in 1983, *National Security Decision Directive 77*. Portions of these directives are in effect to this day.

Government planning was established to sustain the constitutional government and ensured government entities are structured to recover from various operational challenges. Such standards are applicable for public and private sectors. It is important that **continuity planning** is consolidated with governments and corporations. Planning may be considered a process that integrates preparedness capabilities for emergency operations, recovery, and conducting operations following the aftermath of a disaster. The importance of federal government continuity planning is that essential activities should have little to no interruption (i.e. any emergency or logistics agencies that respond to the incident). These agencies are vital to sustaining government operations.

The current directive on continuity policy by President Obama (*Presidential Policy Direct 40, National Continuity Policy*) is not available to the public, so most presidential policies are predicated on President George W. Bush's 2007 *National Security Presidential Directive, NSPD 51, National Continuity Policy*, which is responsible for implementing processes for federal government continuity for emergency purposes. The unclassified portion of NSPD 51 was released on May 9, 2007, and the framework is to "maintain a comprehensive and effective continuity capability composed of continuity of operations and continuity of government programs to ensure the preservation of the nation's form of government under the constitution and the continuing performance of national essential functions under all conditions" (Fagel, 2012, p. 44). Even though there is not a revised NSPD, the White House established the *White House Continuity of Government Plan*, which is predicated on NSPD 51. This framework

> directs the geographic dispersion of leadership, staff, and infrastructure in order to maintain the functions of the United States Government in the event the nation's capital is incapacitated by a terrorist attack. The continuity plan is the strategy for the mass evacuation and relocation of every federal government agency including The White House and the military in response to an exceptional catastrophic event within the National Capital Region. Each agency is required to have a detailed Continuity of Operations Plan (COOP) in place (White House Continuity of Government Plan, 2017, para. 3).

There are eight critical responsibilities that the federal government is mandated to follow during a national crisis:

1. Ensure the continued functioning of government under the Constitution, including the functioning of three separate branches of government;
2. Provide leadership visible to the nation and the world and maintain the trust and confidence of the American people;
3. Defend the Constitution of the United States against all enemies, foreign and domestic, and preventing or interdicting attacks against the United States or its people, property, or interests;
4. Maintain and foster effective relationships with foreign nations;
5. Protect against threats to the homeland and bring to justice perpetrators of crimes or attacks against the United States or its people, property, or interests;
6. Provide rapid and effective responses to and recovery from the domestic consequence of an attack or other incident;
7. Protect and stabilize the nation's economy and ensure public confidence in its financial systems;
8. Provide for critical federal government services that address the national health, safety, and welfare needs of the United States (Policy Defense, 2007, 595).

Because of the unpredictability of operational challenges, NSPD 51 mandates that the framework be incorporated in all federal government policies.

In the directive, the president is responsible for ensuring government operations continue during disruption. The Assistant to the President for Homeland Security and Counterterrorism is appointed as the National Continuity Coordinator (NPC) and is responsible for the development and implementation of government continuity planning for all executive branch departments and subsidiaries. The Continuity Policy Coordination Committee was established to work with the NPC to ensure these tasks are accomplished.

The private sector is a very important part of emergency and government planning. America's business, education, industry, trading, and networking are predicated on working with emergency management agencies and government to ensure preparedness and mitigation of natural and manmade disasters. The evolution of private and public sectors progressed by the 1900s, and the government's role was in a limited capacity. After WWII and throughout the Cold War, such partnerships remained stable. During this time, American citizens were trained to assist during crises and to work closely with local governments to establish emergency management policies. At the time, the manufacturing industry within the United States was booming and established new demands for the corporate world.

Shared governance is a collaboration among the various levels of an organization that requires accountability and a clear decision-making process. For governments, leadership must make key decisions for the betterment of its entities. In the private sectors, organizations are responsible for planning and making decisions to earn trust from the stakeholders involved in their processes. Developing strategic goals should be a priority for all organizations involved, and such plans must shape the direction of how it will work in the decision-making process to accomplish mission objectives. Effective organizations have the following commonalities:

- They establish a board or committee for strategic mission objectives.
- They ensure establishment of multiple priorities.
- They analyze company metrics to identify and monitor important information.
- They certify funding is adequate for the organization's plan.

Strategic planning is the primary difference between government, public, and private business sectors. Effective organizations continue to pursue improvements and those who staff "strategic thinkers" increase their chances of producing innovative methods to improve their organizations.

SUMMARY

The Intelligence Community dates to the National Security Act of 1947, as the framework was the largest reorganization of military service department structure and intelligence entities in American history following WWII. Revised by President Reagan's Executive Order 12333, the IC's responsibilities are based on collecting and yielding domestic and foreign intelligence to assist with mitigating espionage, military planning, and protecting American national security. The sixteen intelligence agencies charged with these obligations have been successful in funding, promoting cooperation, and providing oversight, but proved to lack well-defined government and leadership structure.

This chapter also discusses the important of America's sixteen critical infrastructures and how risk and security vulnerability can negatively impact the country's systematic structure of innovation and technology. The railroad system is another major resource that lacks sufficient security to mitigate adversaries who are willing to destroy or disrupt national lines as well as all modes of transportation to cripple the flow of operations in the country. The United States Customs and Border Protection and the Coast Guard are responsible for the nation's ports, ensuring each are safe from acts of terrorism. Finally, relationships between the government and public and private sectors are key to protecting the homeland. As previously stated, government planning is vital to improving national security objectives, and collaborating with corporate America provides internal and external stakeholders with various methods of establishing policies to ensure shared governance and sophisticated decision-making processes to build a stronger nation.

CHAPTER 10 CASE STUDIES

Case Study 1
The Snowden Effect on National Security

One of the largest breaches of classified information occurred in 2013, not by a foreign terrorist, but by an American citizen. Edward Snowden, a former Central Intelligence Agency employee, obtained a position at the National Security Agency (NSA) to gain access to NSA's internal website, gather data, and copy thousands of classified documents that he later leaked to the public via the *Guardian* and the *Washington Post*. Upon discovery, Snowden was charged with espionage under the 1917 Espionage Act, which includes government property theft, willful communication of classified communications intelligence, and unauthorized communication of national defense information. Coined as "the Snowden Effect" in 2013 by media critic Jay Rosen, Snowden's revelations set in motion a series of events surrounding U.S. surveillance operations, including national debate about the expansion of the NSA's powers to spy both at home and abroad (Mazzetti & Schmidt, 2013).

It's believed that an estimated 15,000 or more Australian files, 58,000 British intelligence files, and 50,000 to 200,000 NSA files were released (Cameron & Maley, 2013). However, according to Army General Martin Dempsey, "the vast majority of the documents that Snowden...infiltrated from our highest levels of security...had nothing to do with exposing government oversight of domestic activities. The vast majority of those were related to our military capabilities, operations, tactics, techniques and procedures" (Capra, 2014). As an immediate consequence of the leaks, the intelligence community lost collection capability against foreign individuals or groups targeted for surveillance, such as al-Qaeda and other high value targets, who changed their tactics, techniques and procedures once they learned their vulnerabilities were known. Snowden's unauthorized disclosures had made it easier for terrorist groups to evade U.S. surveillance by changing their encryption methods, many switching to more secure communication methods, leaving less chance for interception (Aftergood, 2015).

Snowden also released information that jeopardized U.S. cyber-intelligence operations worldwide, specifically against China, one of the biggest hacking threats to U.S. government and business. The ex-NSA contractor claimed that there were more than 61,000 hacking operations, with hundreds directed at China and Hong Kong, further implying the existence of other ongoing activities in place to counter China's cyber warfare capabilities. His affirmation of operations against China gave the country "moral equivalence," allowing Chinese officials to use the Snowden revelations as a response when U.S. officials pressure China to end state-sponsored hacking (Bolton, 2013). Since cyber hacking has never been admitted by China (only accusations of others) and thus, not "confirmed," Chinese officials continuously use the Snowden situation to remind everyone that the moral balance is in China's favor, leaving little leverage for the U.S. (Bowe, 2015). Prior to Snowden's untimely disclosures, U.S. officials were preparing to publicly confront Chinese officials over the country's online economic warfare, demanding that the country rein in their cyber activities. With a little international pressure, the U.S. believed that the confrontation would help temper one of the biggest threats to the nation's economic security (Eichenwald, 2013). However, two days before the meeting, classified documents containing information about U.S. foreign cyber operations were released. While China does not limit its cyber hacking to the U.S., revelations about the U.S. surveillance of partner nations have divested the U.S. of an opportunity to join forces with other countries in condemning China (Eichenwald, 2013).

Director of National Intelligence James Clapper stated that the former NSA employee's leaks had created a "perfect storm," not only degrading the intelligence community's capabilities by forcing the U.S. to discontinue collecting intelligence on certain targets, putting the nation at greater risk, but also damaging relationships with foreign and corporate stakeholders and straining budget resources (Sink, 2014). U.S. officials hastily made efforts to mend relations with allies after news of American eavesdropping on diplomatic leaders, notably the German chancellor and Brazilian president's cell phones, came out, but it was too late. The image of the U.S. had been sullied by Snowden's revelations, especially in Europe and Latin America (Mazzetti & Schmidt, 2013). Several state visits were canceled, and negotiations over the Transatlantic Trade and Investment Partnership (T-TIP), a foreign policy priority for the U.S., were strained (Grover, 2016).

While Snowden's unauthorized leaks have done "significant and irreversible damage" to U.S. national security interests, they did generate debate about the intersection of national security and individual privacy (Ackerman & Rushe, 2013). On June 2, 2015, the U.S. Senate passed the USA Freedom Act, which restored with some modification several provisions of the Patriot Act that had expired the day before. For the first time, it also imposed limits on bulk phone data collection, requiring the NSA to obtain information about targeted individuals with permission from a federal court (Daimond, n.d.). The changes, widely seen as stemming from the disclosures, were designed to make the revised Patriot Act work better, while still protecting the privacy of the people (Kelly, 2015). Similarly, in Brazil, Snowden's revelations on U.S. spying activities helped lead Brazil to create its "Internet Constitution" that outlined the rights and duties of individuals, governments, and businesses to keep Internet freedom "open and decentralized" (Kelly, 2015).

Snowden's unauthorized and intentional disclosure of classified documents is still a divisive topic today. While his initial releases can be considered for the sake of the public, the second set of releases involved U.S. activities overseas, which did not have anything to do with U.S. citizens' privacy. Nonetheless, Snowden's actions forced the nation to finally address an important debate. Despite the importance of the debate, it was not worth the damage he generated because there was another way of doing it that did not involve risking U.S. national security.

Case Study 2
Chelsea Manning's Disclosure

Three years before Edward Snowden released classified information from NSA, the U.S. government suffered another leak of information. It was considered the most voluminous, indiscriminate unauthorized disclosure of classified information. Like the Snowden situation, the culprit was an insider threat—an Army soldier deployed in Iraq, disillusioned with U.S. foreign policy and its wars.

Private First Class Bradley Manning (now Chelsea Manning) was deployed as an intelligence analyst with the Second Brigade Combat Team, Tenth Mountain Division in Iraq (Nicks, 2012). While deployed, she grew increasingly frustrated with U.S. foreign policy, which eventually led to her trying to expose perceived wrongdoings of the U.S. military and diplomats. Manning had access to classified networks, where she downloaded more than 700,000 classified documents, including 470,000 battlefield reports from Iraq and Afghanistan, war-zone videos, and thousands of military chat logs and diplomatic cables (Bradley Manning leaks cause, 2013). She handed the material over to her acquaintances at Wikileaks, an international nonprofit anti-secrecy group that posted her disclosures. Manning was convicted of twenty offenses, including six Espionage Act violations, five theft counts, and a computer fraud charge. She was also initially charged with aiding the enemy, but the judge later acquitted her of that (Bradley Manning leak has had, 2013).

While a report written by the Department of Defense a year after the disclosures found that the leaks had no significant strategic impact on U.S. war efforts, it cautioned that the leaks had the potential to cause considerable damage to intelligence sources, informants, and the Afghan population as well as significant consequences for the lives of cooperative Afghans, Iraqis, and other sources since the material leaked cooperative locals by name (The Department of Defense secretly concludes, 2017).

As an immediate result of Manning's disclosures, U.S. officials had to scramble to protect sources and operations identified in some of the reports. Major General Michael Nagata, former deputy commander of the Office of Defense Representative to Pakistan, said that the leaks had affected his mission because local populaces were less inclined to cooperate with U.S. military (Childress, n.d.). Although combat operations are important to military operations, another mission they are charged with is the protection of the local populace. However, if the enemy knows which people in the village are cooperating with U.S. forces, those individuals are put at risk, which could cause some of them to stop helping U.S. forces (Jaffe & Partlow, 2010). Without the help of the local populace, U.S. soldiers and operations are at an increased risk of danger since they no longer have collaborative information about threats.

Furthermore, while it was discovered that much of the material released was un-classified, it contained sensitive information about the inner workings of U.S. diplomacy as well as unguarded assessments of foreign diplomats and exchanges by U.S. diplomats, including talks about U.S. intelligence and counterintelligence efforts, sanctions against Iraq, attempts to remove enriched uranium from Pakistan, and North Korea's involvement in Iran's weaponry program. The cables also contained quotes from various offices by name, expressing concerns they had not expressed in public. However, field reporting is meant to be candid and is often incomplete. Their reporting helps to add knowledge on a wide range of important issues, but it does not necessarily represent policy (Kessler, 2010).

Despite that, the release of the cables damaged diplomatic efforts and relationships with allies. Several ambassadors were recalled, expelled, or reassigned because of em-barrassing disclosures (York, 2017). Foreign officials became less inclined to talk freely with U.S. diplomats, knowing that what was said in secrecy may not remain private. It also made individuals and potential sources who thought about working with the U.S. government rethink their decision. With foreign officials unwilling to share information, the U.S. faced increased risk to national security (Childress, n.d.). Additionally, the U.S. was reliant on the goodwill of host nations to bring supplies into war zones. The U.S. diplomats' candidness and criticism of how that host nation responded to the situation created friction with these nations, which affected communications and negotiations (Army general, 2013).

Although the final report stated that Manning's unauthorized disclosures did not have a significant strategic impact on U.S. interests, it did have real and serious consequenc-es to U.S. operations and perception. More importantly, it affected information sharing and source recruitment, putting the U.S. at a higher risk of danger from enemy threats.

CHAPTER 10 PRACTICE PROBLEMS

1. What is the difference between the Department of Defense and the Department of Homeland Security?

2. Although the DHS is responsible for public safety, in recent years, most of the terrorist attacks/incidents have been foiled by other departments such as the FBI or CIA. With those departments and the National Guard, which serves as part of the first line of defense for the U.S., what value does the DHS provide?

3. Both DHS and DOJ have investigatory and law enforcement functions that are domestically focused. Would it make sense to incorporate them into one department?

4. The Department of Homeland Security has five core missions. Is it wise to concentrate all these missions into the one department?

5. Why isn't the U.S. Coast Guard part of the Department of Defense?

6. What is the most important aspect of emergency planning? Why?

7. Why should the private sector be considered as part of government and emergency planning?

8. How does the U.S. protect against terrorist attacks on a port?

9. The Transportation Security Administration (TSA) has made many changes to security procedures since the 9/11 attacks to help prevent future attacks. How successful are these preventative measures?

10. Why is possessing a robust maritime system important to national security?

CHAPTER 11

Emergency Operating Procedures: Preparedness and Mitigation

CBRNE weapons

Civil defense

Civil protection

Disaster management

Mitigation

Preparedness

Prevention

Preventative measures

Risk assessments

Vulnerability assessments

LEARNING OBJECTIVES

After reading this chapter, students will be able to:

- Understand the structure of CRBNE preventative measures for mitigation and prevention procedures for possible attacks against the United States

- Summarize mitigation and preparedness initiatives and policies for terrorist acts targeting the homeland

- Discuss emergency management organizations and community responsibilities for CBRNE incidents

- Analyze civil-government relationships and exercise-planning frameworks for emergency response

INTRODUCTION

In the aftermath of the September 11 attacks, emergency management operations have been a top priority, ensuring that the United States can respond to emergencies, natural disasters, and terrorist attacks. There are four elements of emergency management processes: preparedness, response, recovery, and mitigation. These elements describe how the United States addresses the needs of American citizens as well as how the government safeguards assets and critical infrastructures. Preparedness ensures the nation is ready for any type of emergency that might happen. Emergency Operation Plans are pivotal at every level of government, as well as in the private sector, to provide awareness and training and to educate local communities about what to do during an emergency.

Responding to emergency situations is pivotal to ensure that the American population is safe when a disaster or emergency happens. Emergency Operations Center are responsible for notifying experienced personnel representing each department to conduct emergency operations. Such personnel are instrumental in the decision-making process that determines how all emergency information will be relayed to the American public. Additionally, intergovernmental and private sector policies are established to address jurisdictional purview and how cities and/or states will provide support during disastrous events. The response element is very important because it continues the preparedness concept of ensuring communities have the resources necessary, and everyone is responsible for their safety obligations.

Disastrous events and emergency situations are inevitable, so when an event occurs, the recovery period is a pivotal time to ensure that further is damage is not completed and that individuals are safe. Resiliency is the key to restore communities after the storm. The Federal Emergency Management Agency is nation's largest emergency management agency and is responsible for "supporting American citizens and first responders to ensure that as a nation everyone works together to build, sustain, and improve the nation's capability to prepare for, protect against, respond to, recover from, and mitigate all hazards" (FEMA Mission, n.d., para. 1). FEMA works with all state agencies to support in times of crisis and provides disaster recovery teams to deliver assistance such as loans and grants.

Mitigation is one of the most strategic elements in emergency management operations to prevent future losses of people, resources, and critical infrastructures. The best measures to address mitigation are awareness and education within communities, allowing local governments to make decisions and establish policies on how to apply mitigation efforts to prevent losses. This chapter covers CRBNE preventative measures for mitigation and prevention procedures for possible attacks against the United States. The chapter also addresses how the nation will respond as well as mitigation and preparedness initiatives and policies for terrorist acts targeting the homeland. This chapter also discusses emergency management organizations and community responsibilities for CBRNE incidents and will also analyze civil-government relationships and exercise-planning frameworks for emergency response.

CBRNE PREVENTATIVE MEASURES

There has always been the possibility of a CBRNE attack (i.e. chemical, biological, radiological, nuclear, and other explosives) within the United States. The probability increased after the September 11 attacks. **Risk** and **vulnerability assessments** have shown public health is a major concern, and it is important for local, state, and federal governments to monitor such matters. The *Center for Disease Control (CDC)* is responsible for public health policies and initiatives to recognize the intentional propagation of CBRNE weapons. Public health frameworks include preparedness planning, detection and surveillance, analysis of emergency response, and communication systems. Awareness, education, research, and training are indicative of CBRNE **preventative measures** (measures taken to mitigate something from happening). Furthermore, having the appropriate professionals such emergency management, law enforcement, medical and public health specialists, and the military is critical to the success of improving preventative measures.

Mitigation and preventative measures are the primary elements in preventing CBRNE attacks. Mitigation is the power to reduce loss of life or diminishing the impact of any type of disaster. These elements are also important facets of the disaster management cycle. The two concepts are usually implemented if a disaster happens, but they are vital in the aftermath, as emergency management methodologies are based on reducing large-scale destruction of critical infrastructures, elimination of resources, and loss of life. **Preparedness** is the conceptualization of a readiness response to crises or any type of emergency occurrence. Awareness, education, and training are principal activities to increase preventative and mitigation initiatives to reduce security risk or lessen the impact of unpredictable disasters (i.e. natural disasters).

There are various options for local communities and the American public to prepare for possible CBRNE attacks. Such options involve specific methodologies to avoid direct contact with CBRNE weapons. Shelter-in-place is one of the most effective preventative measures to reduce exposure to, contamination from, and/or spread of CBRNE weapons. The following information on preventative measures about what to do before, during, and after CRBNE attacks can be found on the Ready.gov website, an official site for the Department of Homeland Security.

What You Should Do to Prepare for a Chemical Threat

- Build an emergency supply kit, which includes items like non-perishable food, water, a battery-powered or hand-crank radio, extra flashlights, and batteries. Also include:
  › A roll of duct tape and scissors.
  › Plastic for doors, windows, and vents for the room in which you will shelter in place. To save critical time during an emergency, pre-measure and cut the plastic sheeting for each opening.

U.S. Department of Homeland Security, "Chemical Emergencies," Ready.gov.

- Make a family emergency plan. Your family may not be together when disaster strikes, so it is important to know how you will contact one another, how you will get back together, and what you will do in case of an emergency.
  › Plan places where your family will meet, both within and outside of your immediate neighborhood.
  › It may be easier to make a long-distance phone call than to call across town, so an out-of-town contact may be in a better position to communicate among separated family members.
  › You may also want to inquire about emergency plans at places where your family spends time: work, daycare, and school. If no plans exist, consider volunteering to help create one.
  › Know your community's warning systems and disaster plans.
  › Notify caregivers and babysitters about your plan.
  › Make plans for your pets.
  › Choose an internal room to shelter, preferably one without windows and on the highest level.

What You Should Do in Case of a Chemical Attack

- Quickly try to define the impacted area or where the chemical is coming from, if possible.
- Take immediate action to get away.
- If the chemical is inside a building where you are, get out of the building without passing through the contaminated area, if possible.
- If you can't get out of the building or find clean air without passing through the area where you see signs of a chemical attack, it may be better to move as far away as possible and shelter in place.

If you are instructed to remain in your home or office building, you should:

- Close doors and windows and turn off all ventilation, including furnaces, air conditioners, vents, and fans.
- Seek shelter in an internal room and take your disaster supplies kit.
- Seal the room with duct tape and plastic sheeting.
- Listen to your radio for instructions from authorities.

If you are caught in or near a contaminated area, you should:

- Move away immediately in a direction upwind of the source.
- Find shelter as quickly as possible.

- If you are outside, quickly decide what is the fastest way to find clean air. Consider if you can get out of the area or if you should go inside the closest building and shelter in place.

After a Chemical Attack

Decontamination is needed within minutes of exposure to minimize health consequences. Do not leave the safety of a shelter to go outdoors to help others until authorities announce it is safe to do so. A person affected by a chemical agent requires immediate medical attention from a professional. If medical help is not immediately available, decontaminate yourself and assist in decontaminating others.

Decontamination guidelines are as follows:

- Use extreme caution when helping others who have been exposed to chemical agents.
- Remove all clothing and other items in contact with the body. Contaminated clothing normally removed over the head should be cut off to avoid contact with the eyes, nose and mouth. Put contaminated clothing and items into a plastic bag and seal it. Decontaminate hands using soap and water. Remove eyeglasses or contact lenses. Put glasses in a pan of household bleach to decontaminate them and then rinse and dry.
- Flush eyes with water.
- Gently wash face and hair with soap and water before thoroughly rinsing with water.
- Decontaminate other body areas likely to have been contaminated. Blot (do not swab or scrape) with a cloth soaked in soapy water and rinse with clear water.
- Change into uncontaminated clothes. Clothing stored in drawers or closets is likely to be uncontaminated.
- Proceed to a medical facility for screening and professional treatment (Chemical Emergencies, n.d.).

Before a Biological Threat

Unlike an explosion, a biological attack may or may not be immediately obvious. While it is possible that you will see signs of a biological attack, as was sometimes the case with the anthrax mailings, it is more likely that local health care workers will report a pattern of unusual illness, or a wave of sick people will seek emergency medical attention. You will probably learn of the danger through an emergency radio or TV broadcast or some other signal used in your community. You might get a telephone call, or emergency response workers may come to your door.

U.S. Department of Homeland Security, "Bioterrorism," Ready.gov.

The following are things you can do to protect yourself, your family, and your property from the effects of a biological threat:

- Build an emergency supply kit, which includes items like non-perishable food, water, a battery-powered or hand-crank radio, extra flashlights, and batteries.
- Make a family emergency plan. Your family may not be together when disaster strikes, so it is important to know how you will contact one another, how you will get back together, and what you will do in case of an emergency.
  › Plan places where your family will meet, both within and outside of your immediate neighborhood.
  › It may be easier to make a long-distance phone call than to call across town, so an out-of-town contact may be in a better position to communicate among separated family members.
  › You may also want to inquire about emergency plans at places where your family spends time: work, daycare, and school. If no plans exist, consider volunteering to help create one.
  › Know your community's warning systems and disaster plans.
  › Notify caregivers and babysitters about your plan.
  › Make plans for your pets.
- Check with your doctor to ensure all required or suggested immunizations are up to date. Children and older adults are particularly vulnerable to biological agents.
- Consider installing a High-Efficiency Particulate Air (HEPA) filter in your furnace return duct. These filters remove particles in the 0.3-micron to 10-micron range and will filter out most biological agents that may enter your house. If you do not have a central heating or cooling system, a stand-alone portable HEPA filter can be used.

Filtration in Buildings

Building owners and managers should determine the type and level of filtration in their structures and the level of protection it provides against biological agents. The National Institute of Occupational Safety and Health (NIOSH) provides technical guidance on this topic in the publication *Guidance for Filtration and Air-Cleaning Systems to Protect Building Environments from Airborne Chemical, Biological, or Radiological Attacks*. To obtain a copy, call 1-800-35NIOSH or visit the *National Institute for Occupational Safety and Health website* and request or download NIOSH Publication 2003–136.

Using High-Efficiency Particulate Air (HEPA) Filters

High-Efficiency Particulate Air (HEPA) filters are useful in biological attacks. If you have a central heating and cooling system in your home with a HEPA filter, leave it on if it is running or turn the fan on if it is not running. Moving the air in the house through the filter will help remove the agents from the air. If you have a portable HEPA filter, take it with you to the internal room where you are seeking shelter and turn it on.

If you are in an apartment or office building that has a modern central heating and cooling system, the system's filtration should provide a relatively safe level of protection from outside biological contaminants. HEPA filters will not filter chemical agents.

During a Biological Threat

The first evidence of an attack may be when you notice symptoms of the disease caused by exposure to an agent. Follow these guidelines during a biological threat:

- In the event of a biological attack, public health officials may not immediately be able to provide information on what you should do. It will take time to determine exactly what the illness is, how it should be treated, and who is in danger. However, you should watch TV, listen to the radio, or check the Internet for official news and information including signs and symptoms of the disease, areas in danger, if medications or vaccinations are being distributed, and where you should seek medical attention if you become ill.

- If you become aware of an unusual and suspicious substance, quickly get away.

- Protect yourself. Cover your mouth and nose with layers of fabric that can filter the air but still allow breathing. Examples include two to three layers of cotton such as a t-shirt, handkerchief or towel. Otherwise, several layers of tissue or paper towels may help.

- There may be times when you would want to consider wearing a face mask to reduce spreading germs if you are sick or to avoid encountering contagious germs if others around you are sick.

- If you have been exposed to a biological agent, remove and bag your clothes and personal items. Follow official instructions for disposal of contaminated items.

- Wash yourself with soap and water and put on clean clothes.

- Contact authorities and seek medical assistance. You may be advised to stay away from others, or you may be quarantined.

- If a family member becomes sick, it is important to be suspicious.

- Do not assume, however, that you should go to a hospital emergency room or that any illness is the result of the biological attack. Symptoms of many common illnesses may overlap.

- Use common sense, practice good hygiene and cleanliness to avoid spreading germs, and seek medical advice.

- Consider if you are in the group or area authorities believe to be in danger.

- If your symptoms match those described, and you are in the group considered at risk, immediately seek emergency medical attention.

- Follow instructions of doctors and other public health officials.

- If the disease is contagious, expect to receive medical evaluation and treatment. You may be advised to stay away from others, or you may be deliberately quarantined.

- For non-contagious diseases, expect to receive medical evaluation and treatment.
- In a declared biological emergency or developing epidemic, there may be reason to stay away from crowds where others may be infected.

Be prepared to improvise with what you have on hand to protect your nose, mouth, eyes and cuts in your skin. Anything that fits snugly over your nose and mouth, including any dense-weave cotton material, can help filter contaminants in an emergency. It is very important that most of the air you breathe comes through the mask or cloth, not around it. Do whatever you can to make the best fit possible for children. There are also a variety of face masks readily available in hardware stores that are rated based on how small a particle they can filter in an industrial setting. Simple cloth face masks can filter some of the airborne "junk" or germs you might breathe into your body but will probably not protect you from chemical gases.

Symptoms and Hygiene

If a family member develops any of the symptoms below, keep the person separated from others if possible, practice good hygiene and cleanliness to avoid spreading germs, and seek medical advice.

- A temperature of more than 100 degrees
- Nausea and vomiting
- Stomach ache
- Diarrhea
- Pale or flushed face
- Headache
- Cough
- Earache
- Thick discharge from nose
- Sore throat
- Rash or infection of the skin
- Red or pink eyes
- Loss of appetite
- Loss of energy or decreases in activity

Hygiene

If someone is sick, you should practice good hygiene and cleanliness to avoid spreading germs.

- Wash your hands with soap and water frequently.
- Do not share food or utensils.
- Cover your mouth and nose when coughing or sneezing.

- Consider having the sick person wear a face mask to avoid spreading germs.
- Plan to share health-related information with others, especially those who may need help understanding the situation and what specific actions to take.

After a Chemical Threat

In some situations, such as the case of the anthrax letters sent in 2001, people may be alerted to potential exposure. If this is the case, pay close attention to all official warnings and instructions on how to proceed. The delivery of medical services for a biological event may be handled differently to respond to increased demand. The basic public health procedures and medical protocols for handling exposure to biological agents are the same as for any infectious disease. It is important for you to pay attention to official instructions via radio, television, and emergency alert systems.

Antibiotics

While antibiotics are often an appropriate treatment for the diseases associated with biological weapons, the specific drug must match the illness to be effective. One antibiotic, for example, may be appropriate for treating anthrax exposure but is inappropriate for treating smallpox. All antibiotics can cause side effects including serious reactions. Speak with your health care provider in advance about what makes sense for your family. Visit the Center for Disease Control and Prevention website for a complete list of potential agents/diseases and appropriate treatments (Bioterrorism, n.d.).

RADIOLOGICAL DISPERSION DEVICE (RDD) EVENTS

There is no way of knowing how much warning time will be available before an attack by terrorists using a Radiological Dispersion Device (RDD), so being prepared in advance and knowing what to do and when is important.

Before a Radiological Dispersion Device (RDD) Event

To prepare for an RDD event, you should do the following:

- Build an emergency supply kit, which includes items like non-perishable food, water, a battery-powered or hand-crank radio, extra flashlights, and batteries. Also include:

U.S. Department of Homeland Security, "Radiological Dispersion Device," Ready.gov.

> › A roll of duct tape and scissors.

> › During periods of heightened threat increase your disaster supplies to be adequate for up to two weeks.

- Make a family emergency plan. Your family may not be together when disaster strikes, so it is important to know how you will contact one another, how you will get back together, and what you will do in case of an emergency.

  > › Plan places where your family will meet, both within and outside of your immediate neighborhood.

  > › It may be easier to make a long-distance phone call than to call across town, so an out-of-town contact may be in a better position to communicate among separated family members.

  > › You may also want to inquire about emergency plans at places where your family spends time: work, daycare, and school. If no plans exist, consider volunteering to help create one.

  > › Know your community's warning systems and disaster plans.

  > › Notify caregivers and babysitters about your plan.

  > › Make plans for your pets.

  > › Choose an internal room to shelter, preferably one without windows.

- Find out from officials if any public buildings in your community have been designated as fallout shelters. If none have been designated, make your own list of potential shelters near your home, workplace, and school. These places would include basements or the windowless center area of middle floors in high-rise buildings, as well as subways and tunnels.

- If you live in an apartment building or high-rise, talk to the manager about the safest place in the building for sheltering and about providing for building occupants until it is safe to go out.

Taking shelter during an RDD event is necessary. There are two kinds of shelters—blast and fallout. The following describes the two kinds of shelters:

- Blast shelters are specifically constructed to offer some protection against blast pressure, initial radiation, heat, and fire, but even a blast shelter cannot withstand a direct hit from a nuclear explosion.

- Fallout shelters do not need to be specially constructed for protecting against fallout. They can be any protected space, provided that the walls and roof are thick and dense enough to absorb the radiation given off by fallout particles.

During a Radiological Dispersion Device (RDD) Event

While the explosive blast will be immediately obvious, the presence of radiation will not be known until trained personnel with specialized equipment are on the scene. Whether you are indoors or outdoors, at home or at work, be extra cautious. It would be safer to assume radiological contamination has occurred, particularly in an urban setting or near other likely terrorist targets, and take the proper precautions. As with any radiation, you want to avoid or limit exposure. This is particularly true of inhaling radioactive dust that results from the explosion. As you seek shelter from any location (indoors or outdoors), if you see visual dust or other contaminants in the air, breathe though the cloth of your shirt or coat to limit exposure. If you manage to avoid breathing radioactive dust, your proximity to the radioactive particles may still result in some radiation exposure. If the explosion or radiological release occurs inside, get out immediately and seek safe shelter. Otherwise, if you are:

OUTDOORS	INDOORS
Seek shelter indoors immediately in the nearest undamaged building. If appropriate shelter is not available, cover your nose and mouth and move as rapidly as is safe upwind, away from the location of the explosive blast. Then, seek appropriate shelter as soon as possible. Listen for official instructions and follow directions.	If you have time, turn off ventilation and heating systems, close windows, vents, fireplace dampers, exhaust fans, and clothes dryer vents. Retrieve your disaster supplies kit and a battery-powered radio and take them to your shelter room. Seek shelter immediately, preferably underground or in an interior room of a building, placing as much distance and dense shielding as possible between you and the outdoors where the radioactive material may be. Seal windows and external doors that do not fit snugly with duct tape to reduce infiltration of radioactive particles. Plastic sheeting will not provide shielding from radioactivity nor from blast effects of a nearby explosion. Listen for official instructions and follow directions.

After a Radiological Dispersion Device (RDD) Event

After finding safe shelter, those who may have been exposed to radioactive material should decontaminate themselves. To do this, remove and bag your clothing (and isolate the bag away from you and others) and shower thoroughly with soap and water. Seek medical attention after officials indicate it is safe to leave shelter.

Contamination from an RDD event could affect a wide area, depending on the number of conventional explosives used, the quantity and type of radioactive material released, and meteorological conditions. Radiation dissipation rates vary, but radiation from an RDD will likely take longer to dissipate due to a potentially larger localized concentration of radioactive material.

Follow these additional guidelines after an RDD event:

- Continue listening to your radio or watch the television for instructions from local officials, whether you have evacuated or sheltered in place.

- Do not return to or visit an RDD incident location for any reason (Radiological Dispersion Device, n.d.).

MITIGATION AND PREPAREDNESS FOR TERRORIST ACTS

Terrorism threats are unpredictable, and everyone is potentially at risk, and that is why we must be alert always. The establishment of DHS was to ensure the federal government implements and executes homeland security initiatives to maintain national security. While the agency focuses on federal and state-wide efforts, local communities may not have sufficient resources to prepare for and mitigate potential terrorist acts. Some frameworks and initiatives to combat this issue have been recommended within local communities.

Counterterrorism strategies are the primary methodologies for combating terrorist acts within the United States. Since September 11, 2001, the country has avoided large-scale attacks by foreign terrorist organizations. Though mitigating future terrorist attacks is a main priority for all levels of government, that should not be the only focus, as it can pose a risk by neglecting other types of disasters that are more imminent. Local communities must be aware of the risks, as inexperienced or uneducated areas can be the most vulnerable to terrorist acts.

Past terrorist acts have proven that adversaries often target specific locations predicated on religious or sociopolitical ideologies, claiming responsibility in the aftermath. Terrorism is unpredictable, as terrorists tend to aim for innocent people, citizens, and children rather than military targets. According to Jibum Chung, author of "Counterterrorism and Emergency Management: Keeping a Proper Balance," "terrorists attack innocent civilians indiscriminately without prior notification, making it more difficult to prevent" (2010, para. 2).

The psychological effects of terrorist acts have been significant and long-term for victims and countries affected. Even though structural damage can be restored, the psychological aftermath has proven to damage communities and delay resiliency to move on and become a stronger community. Understanding the characteristics of innovative terrorism is the first step to finding solutions. Researcher Paul Slovic notes several characteristics to innovative terrorism (also called contemporary terrorism):

- Usually unknown
- Frightening

- Uncontrollable
- Involuntary
- Indiscriminately fatal (Slovic, 1987, p. 283).

As previously mentioned, counterterrorism is imperative, and the federal government should enforce preventative measures to avoid domestic and international terrorism. At the same time, there should be a sense of preparation, but without instilling fear in the nation. Nevertheless, terrorism is unpredictable, and security risks are realistic. American citizens should be aware of the consequences and aftermath of a potential attack. The Department of Homeland Security's website provides critical information on what to do to prevent terrorism.

Understanding Evolving and Emerging Threats

- Terrorist tactics continue to evolve, and we must keep pace. Terrorists seek sophisticated means of attack, including chemical, biological, radiological, nuclear and explosive weapons, and cyber-attacks. Threats may come from abroad or be homegrown.
- We must be vigilant against new types of terrorist recruitment as well by engaging communities at risk being targeted by terrorist recruiters.

Improving Terrorism Prevention

DHS efforts to prevent terrorism are centered on a risk-based, layered approach to security in passenger and cargo transportation systems and at borders and ports of entry. It includes new technologies to:

- Detect explosives and other weapons,
- Help protect critical infrastructure and cyber networks from attack, and
- Build information-sharing partnerships.

This work is done cooperatively with other federal, state, local, tribal, and territorial law enforcement as well as international partners (Preventing Terrorism Overview, n.d.).

Counter Violent Extremism

Violent extremist threats come from a range of groups and individuals, including domestic terrorists and homegrown violent extremists in the United States, as well as international terrorist groups like al-Qaeda and ISIL. Lone offenders or small groups may be radicalized to commit violence at home or attempt to travel overseas to become foreign fighters. The use of the Internet and social media to recruit and radicalize individuals to violence means that conventional approaches are unlikely to identify and disrupt all terrorist plots.

Here in the United States, acts perpetrated by violent extremists can have far-reaching consequences. Countering violent extremism (CVE) has therefore become a key focus of DHS's work to secure the homeland. CVE aims to address the root causes of violent extremism by providing resources to communities to build and sustain local prevention efforts and promote the use of counter-narratives to confront violent extremist messaging online. Building relationships based on trust with communities is essential to this effort (Terrorism Prevention Partnerships, n.d.).

CIVIL-GOVERNMENT RELATIONS AND EXERCISE PLANNING

Civil defense is the concept of non-combatants protecting citizens from military effects or natural disasters. Civil protection is a vital element of emergency management services, and its principles are based on prevention, mitigation, preparation, response, emergency evacuation, and recovery during the aftermath. The ideological principle of civil defense dates to the 1920s, and formal policies were implemented during the 1930s as nuclear weapons attacks became an international threat during this time.

The United States federal civil defense program existed under *Public Law 920*. The federal program was reformed in 1993 by Public Law 103–160, and a major reformation occurred the following year. Today sections are in *Title VI of the Robert T. Stafford Disaster Relief* and *Emergency Assistance Act*, *Public Law 100–107*. Since the beginning of the Cold War, civil defense has become a prominent focus due to modern concepts of consequence management, contingency planning, crisis management, emergency management, emergency services, and civil protection. Civil defense became a global matter, but ideological principles, functions, policies, and implementation were different among Western countries. The United States established the *Office of Civil Defense* in May 1941 to organize civil defense efforts. The office was a subsidiary of the Department of the Army, which existed until the *Civil Air Patrol (CAP)* was organized on December 1, 1941. CAP's primary mission was search and rescue during wartime contingencies until it was banned from combat duties through Public Law 79–476. Today, CAP's mission is search and rescue for downed aircraft, pilots, and aircrew. When the Department of the Air Force was formed, CAP became an auxiliary component. CAP also has a subsidiary, the *Coast Guard Auxiliary*, which has a similar responsibility.

Civil defense was a primary concern during the 1950s and 1960s when a nuclear attack seemed imminent. The United States and other NATO countries executed exercises during the period, as civil defense practices and missions were needed more than ever. In for the United States, nuclear weapons threats were at their height, and an imminent attack required a larger response for civil protection. Not until the Cold War era did civil defense become controversial. In 1950, the *National Security Resources Board* created a document called the Blue Book, which was the prototype for civil defense legislation.

For civil defense, some of the most noted efforts were the establishment of shelters. President John F. Kennedy was motivated to construct shelters throughout the United States. Such shelters would mitigate the radiological efforts of a nuclear war. In 1951, under the *Control of Electromagnetic Radiation*, primary stations would alert other stations throughout the network. A prominent study predicted that approximately 27 million citizens would be saved through civil defense awareness and education training when the United States Armed Forces performed a military exercise during the Cold War era. Again, controversial matters arose, as policymakers believed a ballistic missile defense system would be more beneficial than standing up a full-scale civil defense platform. Researchers believed the cost-benefit analysis conducted at the time proved this theory because of the inconsistent civil defense preparations with other NATO countries. Also, theorists believed a ballistic missile program was more cost-effective since a civil defense program was deemed too expensive. The lack of consistent civil defense efforts was in part because some Western countries did not believe the Soviet Union's nuclear threats were imminent. Meanwhile, the USSR had master plans of minimizing nuclear weapons striking on its own territory. Thus, the country considerably strengthened its civil defense tactics and was better prepared than the United States.

The decline of civil defense preparations was inevitable because most Western countries were conflicted by the theory of *Mutual Assured Destruction (MAD)*. Because of the issues with funding a large program based on the unpredictability of adversarial threats and natural disasters, Western countries believed that a full-scale defense program was too expensive. Also, some countries believed that a civil defense program would be largely ineffective program for a powerful nuclear weapon attack. Interest in a civil defense program waned as the program did not seem to be an important asset for emergency management programs. The United States ad-hoc civil defense programs (i.e. CAP) existed until such responsibilities were outlined under FEMA in 1979. In 2002, FEMA became a part of the Department of Homeland Security. Specific civil defense preparations for nuclear weapons transferred to all hazards outlined in the *Comprehensive Emergency Management*. After the September 11 attacks, the United States ideology of civil defense has been discussed under the realm of homeland security. Natural disasters and the development of modern threats have centralized focus on new forms of civil protection versus traditional civil defense methodologies.

Civil protection is different concept from civil defense and should be emphasized, as it is also a critical component of the preventative measures of emergency management procedures. Civil protection is an essential component to preparation for any type of disaster. Again, if the focus is predicated just on national security, it can pose a challenge for the civilian population, resulting in a more catastrophic scenario, especially if the population is not prepared. A concept of balance between mitigation against all disaster types and implementing proper emergency management procedures is necessary to ensure that the civilian population is prepared.

Because of many factors that create a challenge, the United States is at risk for environmental modifications such as climate change issues that can influence the nation. In addition, the United States faces the outbreak of new diseases, agroterrorism, ecoterrorism, and other manmade disasters that can pose a threat for not only the homeland but the civilian population. The American government must address society's concerns and formulate solutions that will work for the sustainment of the nation.

Emergency management concerns should be based on education, training, awareness, scientific evidence and research, and policymaking.

The National Response Plan (NRP) was enacted in 2004 in response to the costly disasters that happened in the United States (i.e. Hurricane Katrina). The United States experienced the most severe disaster in its history, and some communities were not prepared because local governments' situational awareness on preparedness, mitigation, and prevention was subpar. In addition, due to lack of communication between civilians and governments, assistance was delayed, resulting in a significant number of illnesses and deaths. At the time, experts believe that the NRP was not clearly interpreted and that was the reason for lack of training and inexperience.

SUMMARY

Understanding the appropriate emergency management procedures for natural and manmade attacks is crucial to the survival of American citizens and protection of the homeland. Preparedness and mitigation are the primary keys to invoking solid, innovative policies that are congruent to today's adversarial threats and security risks that are inevitable. The comprehensive review of CBRNE preventative measures is a very important component, as agent attacks are just as prevalent as traditional terrorism. The information provided from the Ready government website gives critical information and procedures for civil population, emergency management, and first responders during and after all CBRNE attacks to prevent exposure, contamination, and/or the spread of such pathogens.

Mitigation of and preparedness for terrorist acts are critical elements in preserving the American population and maintaining national security. As mentioned in this section, terrorism threats are unpredictable, and everyone is potentially at risk. DHS was established to ensure that the federal government implements and executes homeland security initiatives to protect national security. The federal government must sustain counterterrorism preventative measures to ensure another 9/11 does not happen on U.S. soil. Also, all levels of government and emergency management organization must work closely together to ensure all preventative measures and frameworks are relevant to today's threats (i.e. innovative terrorism).

Finally, identifying the relationships between the civil population and American government is vital to the success of implementing plans that have been mentioned throughout this textbook. Having American citizens involved with government plans is one of the facets of governing a stronger nation with highly skilled, trained, and cognizant people in addressing emergency management concerns and formulating solutions to anticipate incidents and be ready when they happen. Securing the homeland and protecting its people and resources has been emphasized throughout all chapters. Partnerships between the public and private sectors and the nation's international allies and security partners are keys to not only protecting the United States, but protecting the world.

CHAPTER 11 CASE STUDIES

Case Study 1
Science and Technology and CBRNE

In the aftermath of the Anthrax Attacks of 2001, U.S. officials quickly realized that the nation had no mechanisms in place or contingency plans prepared in the event of a non-traditional attack, leaving the U.S. vulnerable to threats from chemical, biological, radiological, and nuclear (CBRNE) agents. As demonstrated by the Anthrax Attack, officials worried that the effective dissemination of a lethal biological agent within a U.S. city could endanger the lives of hundreds of thousands of people and have economic, societal, and political consequences (Jenkins, 2012). Since terrorists had declared their intentions to acquire and use CBRNE agents as weapons to inflict sizeable destruction against the U.S., it became imperative that this security vulnerability be fixed (National strategy for homeland security, 2007). The DHS was charged with assessing the risks posed by CBRNE agents, identifying those that presented the highest risk, and developing necessary response plans and capabilities, including CBRNE threat and risk assessments to analyze the potential for adverse outcomes as a result of an attack with such agents (Jenkins, 2012).

Although several offices and agencies under DHS have responsibilities in the development of risk assessments, response plans, and capabilities, the Science and Technology (S&T) Directorate was charged with planning, organizing, and guiding the homeland security-related scientific, engineering, and technological resources of the nation and leveraging these resources into technical tools to protect the homeland, as well as serving the science and technological needs of the larger homeland security enterprise, including first responders and other entities responsible for disaster response (Williams, 2009). As such, they were responsible for the development of DHS's CBRNE risk assessments—the Terrorism Risk Assessment (TRAs) and Material Threat Assessments (MTAs) (Jenkins, 2012). Each TRA assesses the relative risks presented by multiple CBNE agents based on variable threats, vulnerabilities, and consequences, while each MTA assesses the threat posed by a given individual CRBN agent or class of agents and the potential number of human exposures in plausible, high-consequence scenarios (Jenkins, 2012). The MTAs are also used to determine which CBRNE agents pose a threat sufficient to affect national security. Project BioShield, signed into law by President George W. Bush as part of a broader strategy to defend the nation against the threat of weapons of mass destruction, describes specific ways in which MTAs may be used in efforts to procure certain medical countermeasures (Project BioShield, 2004). Project BioShield provides new tools to improve medical countermeasures, including accelerating research, development, and purchase and availability of effective medical countermeasures to protect the nation against a CBRNE attack (Medical countermeasures, 2016).

Over the past few years, the DHS has partnered with various research enterprises, including businesses, research institutes, universities, and government laboratories, as well as federal departments and agencies (National strategy for homeland security, 2007). The Homeland Security Act of 2002 authorizes DHS to draw on the expertise of all government laboratories, specifically the Department of Energy's National Laboratories to provide DHS with science, technology, and engineering expertise to support its research needs. The Act also directs DHS and DOE to enter cooperative agreements regarding DHS's use of the National Laboratories and authorizes the National Laboratories to accept work from DHS on an equal basis with DOE work. The Act also allows for the S&T Office for National Laboratories to coordinate S&T's use of the National Laboratories (National strategy for homeland security, 2007).

S&T, as the research and development branch of DHS, also has component liaisons staffed throughout to help with coordination efforts and reduce duplication. This is essential since S&T has control over less than one third of the federal homeland security-related research budget and has no authority over the other stakeholder in this strategic plan but is still responsible for developing and supporting a homeland security-related strategic plan for all agencies (Maurer, 2012). S&T also works closely with first responders to include the disciplines of emergency management, emergency medical services, fire, hazardous material, law enforcement, bomb squads, tactical operations/special weapons assault teams, and search and rescue to develop technologies that would be useful to them and address their needs regarding responding to emergency situations as well as public health consequences.

Furthermore, S&T manages CBRNE-specific capabilities that are designed to prevent, detect, or respond to CBRNE incidents to assess the extent to which these capabilities are informed by DHS's CBRNE risk assessments. The Chemical Security Analysis Center (CSAC) works to provide a scientific basis for understanding the risks posed by chemical threat agents and for attribution associated with their use in a terrorist attack. The National Bio-Forensic Analysis Center (NBFAC) is the lead federal facility for conducting and facilitating the technical forensic analysis and interpretation of materials recovered following a biological attack in support of the appropriate lead federal agency as well as conducting bio-forensic analysis of evidence from a bio-crime or terrorist attack to obtain a "biological fingerprint" to help investigators identify perpetrators and determine the origin and method of attack (Jenkins, 2012).

The S&T community is a critical stakeholder in addressing national security problems in a period when the sciences are converging, and national and international security threats are expanding significantly, from state-sponsored weapons programs to terrorism. The U.S. derives much of its strength from its advantage in S&T. Innovative research and development must continue to be encouraged to protect and defend against CBRNE threats confronting the homeland.

Case Study 2
Post 9/11 Counterterrorism Measures

The terrorist attack on September 11, 2001 was a catalyst within the U.S. government, leading to widespread changes in politics and policy, including the passing of new or modified anti-terrorism legislation as well as the establishment of the Department of Homeland Security (DHS). Efforts to protect communities from terrorism and other threats, while safeguarding the fundamental rights of Americans became a priority.

As the point organization in protecting the U.S. from terrorism, the DHS instituted several preventative counter-terrorism measures to include nationwide suspicious activity report and additional security screenings. New fusion centers operated as state and major urban area focal points for the receipt, analysis, gathering, and sharing of threat-related information, acting as the primary conduit between frontline personnel, state, and local leadership, and the rest of the Homeland Security Enterprise (Preventing terrorism and enhancing security, 2016). It relied on active involvement of state, local, tribal, and federal law enforcement agencies, as well as private sector entities to provide the input of raw information for intelligence analysis, operating on the premise that as the multitude of diverse information sources increased, more accurate and robust analysis could be disseminated as intelligence (Carter and Carter, 2009).

The DHS also established the Nationwide Suspicious Activity Reporting (SAR) Initiative (NSI), a joint collaborative effort by the DHS, the FBI, and state, local, tribal, and territorial law enforcement partners. It trained state and local law enforcement to recognize behaviors and indicators related to terrorism, crime, and other threats as well as established a standardized national capacity for gathering, documenting, processing, analyzing, and sharing SAR information (The nationwide SAR initiative, n.d.). The NSI was created in response to the 2007 National Strategy for Information Sharing (NSIS) mandate to establish a "unified process for reporting, tracking, and accessing SAR" in a manner that protects the privacy and civil liberties of the U.S. public (National strategy information sharing, 2007).

The U.S. also raised security levels at its borders and other points of entry into the country. Through the Recovery Act and annual appropriations, formalization of airport screening by the Transportation Security Agency (TSA) raised barriers to more weapons and explosives. New technologies were used to detect the next generation of threats, including advanced imaging technology units, explosive detection systems, explosives trace detection units, advanced technology x-ray systems, and bottled liquid scanners. Furthermore, the DHS required airlines flying to the U.S. to provide advance passengerInformation and passenger name record (PNR) data prior to departure to identify high-risk travelers and facilitate legitimate travel. During 2008 and 2009, PNR helped the United States identify individuals with potential ties to terrorism in more than 3,000 cases (Preventing terrorism and enhancing security, 2016). Similarly, U.S. Customs Service passed the Container Security Initiative which focused on the maritime threat to border security and global trade, ensuring all containers that pose a potential risk for terrorism are identified and inspected at foreign ports before they are placed on ships destined for the U.S. (CSI, 2014). The DHS also deployed radiation detection technologies to seaports, land border ports, and mail facilities around the world (Preventing terrorism and enhancing security, 2016).

In addition to the DHS' initiatives, the U.S. government also implemented several counterterrorism polices that gave federal investigators and intelligence agencies expanded tools, such as the PATRIOT ACT and the post-9/11 amendments to the Foreign Intelligence Surveillance Act, to conduct operations. Provisions under these policies made it easier to monitor individuals or search or seize property. Although it was illegal for the government to single out U.S. citizens based on race, ethnicity, or religion, investigators and officials pushed the boundary with "voluntary" interviews of Muslim and Arab Americans and immigrants. However, this did not necessarily work in their favor since countering terrorism tactics typically requires that the state win the battle for "hearts and minds" among bystander populations. By treating certain populations with suspicion, the state may be discouraging cooperation and even reinforcing terrorist narratives and recruitment efforts (Adams, Nordhaus, and Shellenberger, 2011).

The government also reorganized the Intelligence Community, creating the position of Director of National Intelligence (DNI) to serve as the president's chief intelligence advisor and the head of the Intelligence Community. The DNI was charged with coordination and integration of the sixteen agencies that make up the Intelligence Community and its operations. Additionally, as part of the Office of the Director of National Intelligence, the National Counterterrorism Center (NCTC) was set up to serve as a multi-agency center analyzing and integrating all intelligence pertaining to terrorism, including threats to U.S. interests at home and abroad (ODNI Home, n.d.).

Through these and other efforts, the U.S. has taken considerable effort to implement counterterrorism measures to prevent another 9/11 event. However, the U.S. should be cautioned to not grow complacent with these measures. The enemy is evolving and adapting new tactics, and the U.S. needs to stay ahead of them to keep the homeland safe.

CHAPTER 11 PRACTICE PROBLEMS

1. You and your family have just moved into a new house. You want to make sure that in the event of an emergency, your family knows what to do. What is your family emergency plan?

2. What are some indicators that a biological attack may have occurred?

3. There's been a terrorist attack on your building. In the chaos, people around you are panicking. You don't know what type of attack it was, but you felt a large blast. People are coughing. What should you do?

4. What are some things you want to look for when choosing a shelter?

5. What is the difference between civil defense and civil protection?

6. What role did the ballistic missile play in civil defense?

7. What is extremism and how do you counter it?

8. How effective was MAD as a civil defense strategy?

9. What are some steps that could be taken to better educate the American people on emergency management procedures?

10. What is the more dangerous attack, biological, chemical, or radiological? Why?

CHAPTER 12

Communication, Response, Recovery, and Technology

KEY TERMS

Applied research

Crisis management

Emergency management

Incident management

Modernization

Multilateral cooperation agreements

National Information Management System (NIMS)

National Response Framework (NRF)

Research and development

Risk management

Situational reports

LEARNING OBJECTIVES

After reading this chapter, students will be able to:

- Analyze crisis- and risk-management concepts and how the United States developed emergency management programs based on the inception of disasters from the twentieth century

- Discuss the National Incident Management System and its importance to the American emergency management program

- Examine the various responses through emergency management organization at federal, state, and local government levels

- Consider the challenges in the evolution of research and development through corporate and government research facilities

CRISIS AND RISK MANAGEMENT

Crisis management is how an organization handles unexpected events that are deemed harmful to an organization, its stakeholders, or the American public. The conceptualization of crisis management stems from natural and manmade disasters that occurred in the United States in the twentieth century. Due to the occurrence of large-scale environmental disasters in the 1980s, the federal government established initiatives and directives on how to handle crises and the aftermath of disasters. There are three commonalities to addressing crisis management:

1. The element of surprise, unpredictability of a crisis
2. Decision makers and leadership must react quickly, providing critical decisions in a short amount of time
3. The criticality of the threat toward the organization

Crisis management is a systematic concept which is predicated on roles, responsibilities, and the process related to a company's mission requirements. Such preventative measures include prevention, assessment, handling, and termination. The primary role of organizations is to ensure preparation, accurate and rapid response, sustain active lines of communication and reporting during the crisis, and provide procedures for termination in the aftermath.

Incident management involves various aspects of crisis-management concepts:

- Confrontation
- Cyber-attacks/cyber terrorism
- Malevolence
- Natural disasters
- Organizational misdeeds
- Rumors
- Terrorism/manmade disasters
- Workplace violence

Risk management is the concept of understanding risks and vulnerabilities by identifying, assessing, prioritizing, and establishing procedures to minimize hazards and manage the control and/or probability of disastrous events. The conceptualization of risk management is predicated on business and financial methodologies and how vulnerabilities will affect the operations of organizations. Security risk management is centralized on configurations, cultures, and practices that are indicative of security methods to support business objectives. Organizations implement specific risk-based approaches to highlight activities that determine the probability of risks and vulnerabilities, and produce the best outcome to mitigate such hazards.

Companies should develop security-management initiatives to detect risks to their employees, information, levels of risk tolerance, and resources. In addition, organizations are responsible for appropriate protections to reduce or remove risks within the workplace, and protect business and employee information by establishing cyber security methods. To understand and tolerate levels of risks, there are concepts based on organizational missions and objectives, resulting in processes that should be considered reasonable, transparent, and clear.

FEDERAL, STATE, AND LOCAL RESPONSE

The federal government is the highest level of authority within the United States and when crises are so severe that local and state governments together cannot find a means to aid, the request is escalated. FEMA is the federal organization that organizes the execution and implementation of the federal plan so states can work together to support local and tribal governments. Local governments do not work directly with the federal. Instead, state governments are the liaison for aiding from the federal level. The federal government is responsible for conducting joint *Preliminary Damage Assessments (PDAs)* with local and state governments to distinguish damage of agricultural facilities, critical infrastructures, private sector companies, and alleviate specific activities pre- and post-disasters.

The federal government approves and denies requests, which are specific processes. If federal requests are approved, the government appoints a *Federal Coordinating Officer (FCO)* to lead the *Emergency Response Team (ERT)* and is responsible for establishing the *Disaster Field Office (DCO)* to organize response and recovery efforts. The FCO works closely with the *State Coordinating Officer (SCO)* to address and respond to recovery procedures, and activates *Federal Response Plans (FRP)* to assess federal resources. The federal government also establishes an *Emergency Support Team (EST)* to monitor and observe mission operations and identify *Emergency Support Functions (ESF)* from Washington, DC.

Local governments can escalate requests to the state level when local resources are inadequate. The challenge is the state many have numerous local governments requesting aid simultaneously, causing delays or possible lack of assistance. State governments are registered agents when local jurisdictions need federal assistance. State governments are responsible for monitoring local jurisdictions situations. It also reviews and evaluates local government's situational reports, response procedures, and assistance requests. State governments activate their *State Emergency Operation Center* to determine state assistance availability and regulates if local emergency matters are beyond the scope of state and federal assistance. State governments also declare states of emergency to initiate a *State Disaster Preparedness Plan* and provide state assistance, resources, and initiate the process for requesting federal assistance. Requesting federal assistance includes an emergency declaration under the *Robert T. Stafford Disaster Relief and Emergency Resistance Act* and a specialized request for federal agencies for their own emergency management programs.

Most national disasters occur at the local level, and local governments are responsible for emergency management services. Citizens of the local area are those who suffer in the aftermath, and their local governments are responsible to aid. Local governments are accountable for funding, response and recovery efforts, and requesting assistance from state and federal governments. Also, local governments are responsible for providing first responders for emergency response services. They establish policies such as the *Emergency Operations Center* and *Comprehensive Emergency Management Plans* as guidelines for national emergency-readiness procedures. Emergency management professionals are charged with coordinating response objectives with citizens, private-sector companies, and medical-service providers. In times of imminent crises and disasters, the local government (state governor) notifies the State Emergency Agency on such situations and actively submits **situational reports** (SITREPs) on status updates, emerging threats, or nearing-aftermath events.

Local government involvement in emergency policies is vital to activating mutual aid compacts and **multilateral cooperation agreements** (binding or non-binding agreements between organizations, governments, or foreign entities, addressing legal policies to work together on how to handle interests, responsibilities, and rights of member states). The government also works with intergovernmental agencies, state, and federal departments to formulate response state of agreements. Such initiatives assert emergency plans for governments to authorize and utilize resources, disburse funds, and relinquish traditional bidding courses for goods and services. Finally, local governments (state governor) can request state of emergency management to provide state and/or federal assistance.

NATIONAL INCIDENT MANAGEMENT SYSTEM (NIMS)

In 2004, the Department of Homeland Security established **National Incident Management System (NIMS)**, which is an incident-management system utilized to coordinating responses between emergency management agencies within the federal government. NIMS was established as a large information-sharing tool for all forms of government and businesses to coordinate responses to national incidents. The emergency management mechanism is a component of the National Preparedness System and provides the fundamental standards for the *National Planning Frameworks*. NIMS' primary responsibility is managing national incidents by providing standardized procedures that requires efficient and effective coordination across the country. When NIMS is effectively utilized, businesses and communities provide a comprehensive approach to prospective hazards, threats, and vulnerabilities.

The **National Response Framework (NRF)** is a component of the National Strategy for Homeland Security (like National Security Strategy), which is the outline for all levels of domestic response to prepare for national disasters. The NRF works together with NIMS and the ICS to coordinate and prepare for disasters at all levels. On March 22, 2008, NRF replaced the *National Response Plan* to centralize policy on homeland security. While a companion source to NIMS, NRF policies are responsible for improving the nation's incident management system and response capabilities during disasters and other emergency-related matters. NIMS is the systematic tool for managing incidents, and NRF provides the overall infrastructure for national-level homeland security policies for incident-response matters. NIMS and NRF amalgamate all capabilities and resources necessary from various governments and organizations. Three categorical elements formulate NIMS:

- The Incident Command System
- The Multi-Agency Coordination System
- Public Information Systems

NIMS does not replace local and state-level incident-management systems. Instead, NIMS is the federal framework that local and state governments can use as a basis for their own emergency and preparedness policies. DHS states that NIMS is the leading structure to improve the capabilities of responders and emergency management teams. In times of distress and lack of resources, the federal government will intervene and provide resources, such as incident-management procedures and personnel to assist during times of disaster and/or conflict. At the same rate, the federal government recognizes the sovereignty of local and state governments and only intervenes in a "supportive" role to improve roles in crisis-management concerns.

NIMS is an important element, as it offers reliable national principles and methodologies to allow all levels of government and businesses to work together and prepare for disasters at all levels. Organizations that effectively utilize NIMS increase effective and rapid responses, mitigating further damage or destruction. In addition, organizations that implement NIMS into their standard operating procedures and concept of operations are likely prepared to respond to disasters on short notice and comprehend incident-management procedures. According to Federal Emergency Management Agency, five components are responsible for the incident management system:

- Communication and information management
- Command and management
- Ongoing management and maintenance
- Preparedness
- Resource management

The system is applicable NIMS to "federal, state, local and tribal governments, private-sector organizations, critical infrastructure, owners and operators, nongovernmental organizations with an active role in emergency management and incident response" (NIMS: Frequently Asked Questions, n.d., p. 1). This incident system has a preparedness mechanism called the NIMS Preparedness Component, which is considered a baseline for all incident management linked to all systematic approaches. Preparedness is the most significant concept in crisis and emergency-management fields. FEMA states preparedness is "essential for effective incident and emergency [preparedness] and involves engaging in a continuous cycle of planning, organizing training, equipping, exercising, evaluating, and taking correct action to achieve and maintain readiness to respond to emergencies" (FEMA, n.d., p. 1).

RESEARCH AND DEVELOPMENT

Research and development is the concept of linking corporate and government **modernization**. The conceptualization of innovation differs among countries and within internal governments and its private and public sectors. It is considered the first step to introducing a potential new product or service into a country's industry. Such activities begin with staffing of engineers and scientists who deal with **applied research** (discipline used to employ current scientific knowledge to develop better practical applications) in scientific or technological fields. The primary reasoning behind research and development is original creations and services are not intended to acquire immediate revenue. Instead, research and development projects are known to present larger risks and uncertain return of investment.

Research and development is the primary service of corporations and government. In an ever-changing world, companies must continue to innovate products and services. The purpose is to stay current of competition and continue technological change to appease the companies' customers. Not maintaining research and development initiatives, companies trust acquisitions, networking schemes, and strategic alliances, which can be challenging if marketing and research protocols are invested. Initiatives are implemented through companies, governments, or can be outsourced to research contracting agencies, state agencies, and universities. It is considered a long-term strategy in science and technology and is predicated on statistical data, which organizations use to announce competition, industry standards, and progression.

Many countries support scientific and technological research endeavors. The United States does so through government-funded agencies such as the Defense Advanced Research Projects Agency and the *National Science Foundation*, which focuses on engineering, science, and emerging technologies for military use. The American government runs its own research facilities because its involvement in research and development can provide specific resources and services that some research facilities within the private market may not support. For example, if new developments within research studies can be distributed and imitated at a lower cost, meaning individuals of the private sector can exploit or financially benefit from others, then the social return could possibly be higher than the private return to those who incur costs and generate risk. This will cause the market to fluctuate, which could lead to lack of investment on research and development initiatives, requiring a need for government involvement. There have been resolutions to mitigate lack of investment, but these have not been proven to be successful in strengthening intellectual property rights, but such rights have been known to fund investors' long-term economic benefits for their inventions or research discoveries. On the contrary, such rights could post restrictions on patenting new ideas, prohibiting future research and development initiatives that would be vital to commercial applications within American industry.

In the twenty-first century, research and development is predicated on global trends, competition, funding, public priorities, and technical assessments. The United States' funding on research and development has been consistent over the past few decades, which could possibly overshadow modern developments. The federal government's spending on research and development initiatives has lessened and the *Gross Domestic Product (GDP)* and private sector continued to increase since the twenty-first century. Also, research and development endeavors have focused on related trends, and government spending primarily supports science and technology. As the federal government continues to fund science and technological efforts, it is important Congress judiciously prioritize funding.

The United States remains the leading country in research and development, science, and innovation, but countries such as China and India are close behind as emerging economies. China has significantly increased its spending, although it is still less than the American GDP. At any rate, it is important for all participating countries to invest in research and development to globalize science and technology. The globalization of research and technology benefits all countries because it increases innovation around the world. As the leader of innovation, it is important for the United States to continue to play an active role in sustaining science and technology to increase globalization efforts. The American government should focus on bolstering research and scientific initiatives while the private sector supports applied research for domestic and international commercial purposes. Furthermore, the government should continue direct funding for government research facilities, providing grants to the private and public sectors (including universities) and awarding contracts to strengthen scientific research efforts. Experts have found such processes are more effective if they are based on long-term strategic investments. It is very important for the federal government to continue its efforts in research and development to enhance creation and innovation. Also, funding is the key to ensuring appropriate technical standards are drafted and implemented, and measures are taken to mitigate lack of investing.

SUMMARY

Crisis management is how an organization handles unexpected events that are deemed harmful to an organization, its stakeholders, or the American public. Risk management is the concept of understanding risks and vulnerabilities by identifying, assessing, prioritizing, and establishing procedures to minimize hazards and manage the control and/or probability of disastrous events. Having comprehensive plans ensures all federal, state, and local governments and businesses are prepared. Business and government sectors should understand the criticality of any kind of disaster and how it could impact customers, employees, and the American public. Natural and manmade disasters are unpredictable and inevitable, so having advanced procedures implemented such as a crisis plan and implementing a risk-management program will mitigate lack of preparedness, loss of life and damage to critical infrastructures. Imperative steps such as producing a plan, having a leader, transparency, maintaining effective communication, and keeping plans current is the gateway to prevention and mitigation.

Communication and effective emergency-management operations are key to mitigating risks. Additionally, communicating is an important resource for the emergency-management community to relay to the American public the importance of alerts and warnings of disasters. Having sufficient information can be a life-or-death situation. The United States has implemented important critical-incident management systems such as NIMS to coordinate all national incidents. In addition, such systems provide rapid response, so emergency management, first responders, and the nation's citizens can quickly prepare and counter risks and disasters. The threat of terrorism is real and has revolutionized the way the American government and federal emergency organizations respond. The ultimate solution for strengthening communication and emergency management initiatives is to find a balance to providing timely and accurate information to the American public.

Finally, research and development is the concept of linking corporate and government modernization. The conceptualization of innovation differs among countries and within internal governments and its private and public sectors. It is considered the first step to introducing a potential new product or service into a country's industry. Challenges rise as scientific research is costly and time consuming, as government and civilian facilities employ the best researchers to complete testing and experiments. Understanding the need for innovation and maintaining international partners to mandate effective research and development standards is an important element. Acknowledging these challenges and improving scientific and technological methodologies are the gateways to economic growth.

CHAPTER 12 CASE STUDIES

Case Study 1
Response to Active Shooter

In the last decade, the term "active shooter" has become a staple in U.S. emergency-management vocabulary. The nation has seen an increased frequency of individuals motivated by a range of ideological beliefs and individual factors engaging in terrible acts of mass violence, targeting innocent civilians in communities across the U.S. These perpetrators are known as active shooters, individuals actively engaged in killing or attempting to kill people in a confined and populated area. Active shooters are a serious threat due to the simplicity of attack and high impact, which can be achieved in a short amount of time (*Department of Homeland Security active shooter event*, n.d.). Most active shooter situations occur at locations that have limited security measures to protect members of the public. There is no pattern or method to their victim selection. In most instances, when confrontation with responding law enforcement becomes unavoidable, shooters will commit suicide by police or their own hand, or surrender. As active shooters have become the new reality, there has been a subsequent paradigm shift for law enforcement and first-responder training, incorporating lessons learned from each active shooter situation, such as the San Bernardino shooting and the Orlando Night Club shooting, to better prepare and prevent for future situations (Special analysis: The active shooter threat, 2012).

The San Bernardino shooting and attempted bombing targeted public health employees at a holiday event. Homegrown terrorists were responsible. Within minutes, fourteen people were killed and twenty-two injured in the center's conference room. The first police unit to respond arrived in four minutes following the initial 911 emergency call and executed Immediate Action Rapid Deployment (IARD) tactics, a rapid-response tactic where responding officers take immediate action to *confront* a threat (With mass shootings on the rise, 2016). Praised for their handling of the incident, law enforcement leaders in the San Bernardino shooting credited their response to active-shooter training they had received prior to the attack, as well as the rewritten policies, procedures, and practices that came about because of the Christopher Dorner attack, an ex-Los Angeles police department officer who was responsible for a string of shootings in 2013 (Christopher Dorner: Police under attack, 2014).

Following the Orlando Night Club shooting, criticism of law enforcement's delay to subdue the shooter led to changes in training and recognizing a hostage situation versus an active shooter situation. Unlike a hostage situation, "active shooters aim to inflict mass casualties as quickly as possible, usually in a matter of minutes." Due to the situation with the gunman holding hostages inside the club, the police responding to the attack followed protocols and best practice for hostage situations, not an active shooter (The police response to active shooter incidents, 2014). However, Omar Mateen, the self-radicalized perpetrator, was not interested in taking hostages. Proclaiming allegiance to the Islamic State terrorist group ISIS, he committed the worst act of terrorism on American soil since September 11, 2001, leaving fifty dead and many more injured (Alvarez & Perez-Pena, 2016).

Furthermore, recent active shooter incidents coupled with IED threats illustrate that some traditional practices need to be realigned and enhanced to improve the survivability of victims and the safety of first responders in an increasingly complicated threat environment. As demonstrated in San Bernardino and as threatened in Orlando, the increased presence of IEDs, suicide bombers, and taking of hostages suggests that greater emphasis must be placed on providing training for patrol officers arriving on the scene of a terrorist attack from domestic and foreign individuals and groups (First responder guide, 2015).

Active-shooter situations are unpredictable and evolve quickly, typically lasting ten to fifteen minutes. Although local and state law enforcement agencies are normally the first ones on the scene, the Federal Bureau of Investigation has played a significant role in supporting the response to every major incident in recent years, such as providing operations, behaviorally based threat assessment and threat-management services to help detect and prevent acts of targeted violence. The agency also provided training to recognize and disrupt potential active shooters who may be on a trajectory toward violence. The Investigative Assistance for Violent Crimes Act of 2012 authorized the U.S. attorney general to provide federal assistance during active-shooter incidents and mass killings in public places. For these events, the attorney general has delegated this responsibility to the FBI (Active shooter resources, 2016).

Furthermore, as a response to the Columbine High School shooting in 1999, the FBI partnered with the Department of Justice's Bureau of Justice Assistance and a training organization at Texas State University called Advanced Law Enforcement Rapid Response Training (ALERRT) to develop a training course designed to arm front-line defenders with appropriate skills and training to handle these dangerous situations, and safely and effectively end the violence immediately, rather than wait for a SWAT team to arrive (Advanced law enforcement rapid response training, 2008). Many state and local police departments have also adopted it as a standard for active-shooter response, ensuring law enforcement officers arriving on the scene understand how others are trained to respond (The police response to active shooter incidents, 2014).

In addition to ALERRT, the Department of Homeland Security, in partnership with the FBI, launched the Countering Violent Extremism (CVE) and Active Shooter (AS) Web Portal on the Homeland Security Information Network, which provides training resources covering numerous CVE and AS topics. The website includes information on outreach initiatives and subject matter experts as well as forums to provide feedback, share products, and ask questions. It also provides a forum for the exchange of information to all levels of law enforcement officers, federal employees affiliated with the criminal justice system or intelligence communities, military personnel, and government agencies associated with infrastructure protection of the United States (First responder, 2017).

Active-shooter situations, especially those that involve homegrown extremists, are becoming increasingly frequent with constantly evolving tactics. They do not fit into traditional law enforcement prevention-and-response paradigms, posing a threat to the U.S. and its people. Local law enforcement officers, particularly those assigned to routine patrol work, are the most important resource for identifying, preventing, and responding to the threat. Faced with this reality, it is imperative to continuously evaluate the threat environment and ensure that U.S. law enforcement officers are prepared to prevent or respond to the next attack (Straub, Zeunik, & Gorban, 2017).

Case Study 2
Congressional Budgeting Concerns for Terrorism

Intelligence appropriations are a significant part of the federal budget. Since the terrorist attack on September 11, 2001, U.S. intelligence spending has doubled, allowing intensive analytical expertise to be dedicated to determining terrorist groups' memberships, locations, and plans, as well as intelligence operations worldwide to be carried out. Despite the importance of this mission, the intelligence community is not exempt from the fiscal constraints of the government. With a responsibility to lower the excessive national debt, the U.S. government has imposed rounds of budget cuts for its programs and departments year after year.

However, indiscriminate cuts in defense spending that are budget-driven and not strategy-driven can be dangerous to the U.S. at home and abroad, as well as the nation's interests in the world. Former Director of National Intelligence James Clapper, Jr., warned that sequestration would require a seven percent cut, or roughly $4 billion, to the National Intelligence Program (NIP) budget, which would reduce global coverage and decrease human and technical intelligence collection (Erwin and Belasco, 2013). Intelligence spending is spread across the seventeen organizations comprising the intelligence community, but fiscal pressures will require intelligence officials to more clearly establish priorities and to make difficult choices between different intelligence collection platforms and agencies.

The current budgeting system does not budget for national security in a specific way. There is no clear-cut definition directing how national security plays into any of the sets of boundaries in the current budget process, to include executive branch agencies, appropriations subcommittees, or budget functions (Dale, Serafino, and Towell, 2013). However, if Congress requires boundaries for national security for the purposes of budgeting, it would require a significant paradigm shift as there currently is no shared understanding of the arenas and activities that contribute to national security. Furthermore, a comprehensive review would need to be conducted since other components that are not typically associated with national security such as energy, the environment, and the economy, would need to be incorporated into the overarching national security umbrella (Dale, Serafino, & Towell, 2013).

For fiscal year 2016, defense spending totaled $607 billion overall, encompassing all defense-related appropriations to include mandatory funding for retirement and pension payments and nuclear weapons spending at the Department of Energy (Gillan, 2016). Base discretionary funding—money that goes toward acquiring weapons systems, fund research, and keep bases open—ate through $522.9 billion for fiscal year 2016, leaving $49.7 billion for Overseas Contingency Operations (OCO). These funds are the part of the budget that goes to fighting wars and includes the air campaign against ISIS, U.S. military presence in Iraq and Afghanistan, and initiatives to assist with counterterrorism efforts in the Middle East and NATO Allies concerned about Russia (Gillan, 2016). However, since OCO funds have very little oversight and are not subject to sequestration, many critics liken OCO to the Pentagon's slush funds, arguing that the both OCO and the larger defense budget could be cut (Overseas contingency operations, n.d.).

However, if defense spending decreases, it will be critical for intelligence spending to remain static or increase as it will have to compensate and provide forewarning to a smaller, nimbler DoD. Since 9/11, the range and complexity of threats to the U.S. has grown to include not only state actors, but also non-state actors involved in activities such as terrorism, cyber-attacks, and drug trafficking. To fulfill the strategic needs of decision makers, the community must to some degree dedicate resources toward those threats. In comparison, while DoD must do contingency planning to address a diversity of threats, it does not necessarily need to dedicate resources toward each of them (Erwin & Belasco, 2013).

Despite the fiscal pressures of sequestration and inevitable budget cuts, it is critical for the United States' national and economic security that the nation has advanced solutions and a budget that allows it to stand against the challenges of the future.

CHAPTER 12 PRACTICE PROBLEMS

1. What are three commonalities to address crisis management?
2. What is the importance of research and development as they relate to homeland security?
3. What is the danger of not maintaining research and development initiatives?
4. What can the U.S. do to bolster research and scientific initiatives?
5. Conduct a risk management assessment on cyber-attacks/cyberterrorism against the Defense Intelligence Agency. Be sure to identify vulnerabilities and establish procedures to minimize hazards and manage the control and/or probability of disastrous events.

6. NRF policies are responsible for improving the nation's incident-management system and response capabilities during disasters and other emergency-related matters. Are there any policies that should be included in the NRF, but do not appear?

7. What is the relationship between NIMS, NRF and the NRP?

8. Is it necessary for the U.S. to have an incident-management system utilized for coordinating responses between emergency-management agencies within the federal government?

9. What can organizations do to reduce or remove risks within the workplace and protect business and employee information?

10. How does the National Response Framework relate to the State Disaster Preparedness Plan?

CHAPTER 13

Where National Security Meets Homeland Security

KEY TERMS

Congress

Democratic Party

Direct election

Executive branch

Foreign policy

House of Representatives

Independent

Judicial branch

Legislation

Legislative branch

Multilateral agreements

Republican Party

Senate

Separation of powers

Treaties

LEARNING OBJECTIVES

After reading this chapter, students will be able to:

- Discuss congressional roles and how a formal American assembly created one of the world's largest democratic governments

- Compare the nation's secretarial positions and responsibilities in homeland and national security

- Examine the history of the Department of Defense, Department of Homeland Security, and Department of State

- Understand American foreign policy affairs and how international treaty agreements affect national security objectives

INTRODUCTION

The chapter begins the debate on the where homeland security and national security meet. As this book is titled, *Homeland and National Security: Understanding America's Past to Protect the Future,* there are many concerns about the difference between homeland and national security that need to be addressed. This book began with the past conflicts (international and domestic) prior to the Declaration of Independence to show how America (when still the British colonies) handled tensions and conflicts with other countries and how specific strategic policies revolutionized American initiatives, foreign policy, and international relations. Prior to the September 11th, 2001, attacks, ambiguity on protecting the homeland was not issue, as most decisions and policies were dependent up national defense objectives. When President George W. Bush signed the Homeland Security Act of 2002, establishing another Cabinet-level department tasked with protecting the homeland with an emphasis on domestic strategies, this caused many challenges.

The Department of Defense and Department of Homeland Security clearly have overlapping responsibilities when it comes to protecting the United States from enemies, foreign and domestic. But the emphasis with DoD is utilizing the world's strongest and most advanced military forces to protect the nation from foreign adversaries and threats. The military is responsible for American freedom and protections while also focusing on internal threats at stateside military installations. DHS focuses on domestic and international terrorism within its borders as well as immigration, port security, economic security, and border security to ensure that threats do not invade on homeland soil.

The chapter will discuss the congressional roles and involvement on homeland and national security matters and how the Senate works with DoD and DHS to ensure policies are formulized, implemented, and executed. Understanding the roles of the Secretary of Defense, the Secretary of Homeland Security, and the National Security Advisor are covered in this chapter, as it outlines the roles on how homeland and national security issues are handled. Finally, the Department of State is acknowledged in this chapter to outline how foreign policy and international relations play an extension role on homeland and national security. To distinguish the nation's top homeland security concerns from national security, the *2014–2018 Fiscal Years Strategic Plan* established by former Secretary of Homeland Secretary Jeh Johnson is a critical part of the chapter, as it addresses how the nation address matters on protecting the homeland and the American public.

CONGRESSIONAL ROLES AND INVOLVEMENT

Congress is the dualistic legislature system of the American federal government, which consists of the **Senate** and the **House of Representatives**. Established on March 4, 1789, Congress convened in Washington, D.C., on Capitol Hill where Senators and representatives are now chosen through **direct election** by the people. The largest parties are Democratic and Republican with the third being **Independent**. Congress has 535

Figure 13.1 U.S. Capitol Hill building

voting members: 435 Representatives and 100 Senators. The House of Representatives has six non-voting members from U.S. Territories, each serve for two-year terms, representing their district. The congressional district is allocated to each state by its population, which is based on the decennial United States Census. Each state has two Senators who represent and serve, which are elected-at-large for six-year terms. The terms are staggered so every two years at least one-third of the Senate is qualified for election.

Congress was initially known as the *First Continental Congress* when representatives from 12 of the 13 original British colonies in North America gathered to make decisions. It was the *Second Continental Congress* that adopted the *Declaration of Independence*, creating the new America in 1776. By 1781, the Articles of Confederation established the *Congress of the Confederation*, which was a unicameral legislature among the states and each one had the authority to veto many decisions made within the body of government. At the time, Congress had executive rights but not governmental authority and as a result federal judiciary standards were confined to the jurisdiction within the courts of law. Also, there were not any law on the enforcement of laws, the regulation of commerce, taxes, and tariffs.

The lack of power within Congress resulted in the *Convention of 1787*, which recommended the committee revise the Constitution to a bicameral legislature. Small states opposed, in its place, wanting equal representation across the government. Instead, the Great Compromise of 1787 was established where representatives were chosen by state population and Senators represented state governments. This compromise created the federal infrastructure of the state and national governments. The **executive**, **judicial**, and **legislative** branches produced divided portions of authority within the American government. The **separation of powers** prevents abuse of powers and are checks and balances within the House of Representatives and the Senate.

During the formative era (1780's—1820's), federalists and anti-federalists fought for power within Congress in the early stages of government when political partners were contemplated. Because both sides could not agree to a party, some activists joined the *Anti-Administration Party* that Thomas Jefferson and James Madison created. Consequently, the *First Party of the United States* was known as the *Jeffersonian*

Democratic Party. Thomas Jefferson's presidency was highlighted a peaceful transition involving congressional parties during this era.

The partisan era (1830s-1900s) showed the development and power between the political parties. The American Civil War was pivotal in ending slavery and strengthening the country under federal authority, but at the same time, states' rights were significantly weakened. During this time, lobbying increased as well as birth rates and immigration. The *Progressive Era* showed powers and strength in leadership with the House of Representatives and the Senate. On the contrary, this was a time for reform policies and those who opposed disrupted operations, corrupting policies within Congress. The Senate became very powerful and it was decided twelve men would control the House. The Speaker of the House became the most powerful position in Congress.

During the committee era (1910s-1960s) the authority of some Congressional members increased, enabling both parties to serve longer terms with constant re-election. The position of Chairman (of various committees) was very influential during this time, as Congress established important policies that were predicated on public opinion; however, some negative effects were considered that undermined authority of state governments. Regulating the economy became an important Supreme Court matter where congressional powers could constitute the commerce closure. Also during this time, most New Deal policies were established during the Great Depression of the 1930s. The **Democratic Party** controlled both houses of Congress and the Republican Party formed the Conservative coalition, which was an unofficial congressional affiliation that amalgamated the conservative majority of the Republican Party and the Southern conservatives of the Democratic Party. The Democrats controlled most of Congress during this era but struggled with authority in the aftermath of WWII.

The contemporary era (1970s to present) was a rather dormant Congress during this period, but the Watergate scandal revived judicial procedures, provoking policies that were responsible for mitigating presidential conspiracies and alleged misconduct. The scandal significantly reformed relationships between the branches of government, increased lobbying, partisanship, and most importantly the inception of Political Action Campaigns (PACs). PACs became a major influence in the contemporary era as the donations not only helped candidates get elected, but the donations increased to millions, which involved local business and professionals. In the twentieth century, the news media became a major factor in congressional issues and was the center of most of the backlash. According to Sheila Coronal, author of *Corruption and Watchdog Role of the News Media* from Harvard University, the media undermined the power and authority of political powers and the sensationalism was responsible for the negative side of congressional matters (n.d).

NATIONAL SECURITY ADVISOR AND SECRETARIES OF DEPARTMENT AND HOMELAND DEFENSE

Known as the *Assistant to the President for National Security Affairs*, the National Security Advisor is the senior aide to the Executive Office of the President of the White House. The National Security Advisor is the chief advisor and is appointed by the President. It is a special position that does not require confirmation by the Senate. The advisory role is an executive member of the President's cabinet and is part of the National Security Council. The role of the National Security Advisor has been dependent upon the presidential administration. Furthermore, the role is predicated on the management and style of the president as well as the qualities and experience of the individual appointed. The advisor serves in the best interest of the President based on national security policies. The advisor's office is situated in the White House near the *Office of the President,* and during crisis events, is located near the Situation Room.

The position of National Security Advisor was established under the *National Security Council* of the National Security Act of 1947 (indirectly) after the Cold War. The importance of the position is that the advisor coordinates defense, foreign affairs, international economic policy, and intelligence; and was a large reorganization that established the Central Intelligence Agency and the Department of Defense. Since the appointment of the first advisor in 1953, the position has significantly changed, especially with responsibilities in the National Security Council. Robert Cutler was the first National Security Advisor under President Dwight D. Eisenhower where the position did not change for decades. It was not until President Richard Nixon's era where Henry Kissinger emphasized the importance of the advisory position, which controlled the flow of information to the president and updating him on national security and foreign policy matters throughout the day. In 1987, Gen. Colin Powell became the first African-American National Security Advisor under President Ronald Reagan, and Dr. Condoleeza Rice became the first female to hold the position in 2001 under President George W. Bush.

Secretary of Defense

The *Secretary of Defense (SECDEF)* heads the Department of Defense (DoD) and is an Executive officer in the American federal government. SECDEF is considered the "Chief Executive Officer" of DoD headquarters, the Pentagon, in the Arlington, Virginia. The SECDEF is responsible for the United States Armed Forces, federal civilian employees, and government contractors. The position is appointed by the President of the United Sates and confirmed by the Senate.

The War Department, headed by the Secretary of War, was created by Congress in 1789. Proposals were made based on the aftermath of WWII, which resulted in the National Security Act of 1947 to negotiate between the Army and Navy, centralizing and decentralizing preferences of how the departments should be operated. The congressional act merged the Department of War and the Department of the Navy, which formalized the Secretary of Defense position. In addition, the congressional act separated the Army Air Forces, becoming the Department of the Army and the Department of the Air Force. During this time, each service had quasi-cabinet status, but James V. Forrestal (the first appointed Secretary of Defense) believed it was too difficult to exercise authority over service departments with limited powers. Therefore, Congress amended the National Security Act of 1947 two years later and consolidated the national defense structure to mitigate inter-service tensions and have service secretaries report to the Secretary of Defense. The National Military Establishment was renamed the Department of Defense and it became an executive department under the presidential cabinet. The amended act also established the Deputy Secretary of Defense position, making it the

Figure 13.2 Flag of the Secretary of Defense

number-two position within the Department of Defense headquarters. Except for NSA Act of 1947, the Goldwater-Nichols Department of Defense Reorganization Act of 1986 was the second largest revision of statutory framework regarding national security and military infrastructure.

According to the United States Code Title 10 113, SECDEF is a statutory office and has the "authority, control, and direction over the Department of Defense, which is further designated by the same statute as the principal assistant to the President in all matter relating to the Department of Defense" (Cornell University, n.d., para. 1). Because there should be civilian control of the military, an individual should not be appointed in the position within seven years after the relief from active duty as a commissioned officer from a branch of service (McInnis, 2017). In 2017, Congress faced this issue when President Donald Trump nominated retired General James Mattis, who had only transitioned from the Marine Corps in May 2013. A waiver was also required in the past for those who were nominated for the SECDEF position and did not fully complete the seven-year requirement. For example, former Army Chief of Staff, George Marshall was retired from the Army only five years when he was selected as SECDEF under the President Harry S. Truman's administration.

SECDEF manages the command and control for administrative and operational responsibilities of the President for the service departments. This also includes the United States Coast Guard during period of conflict, when control is transferred to DoD. The President and SECDEF are the only two positions that can authorize the operational control of forces between the service departments and the combatant commands.

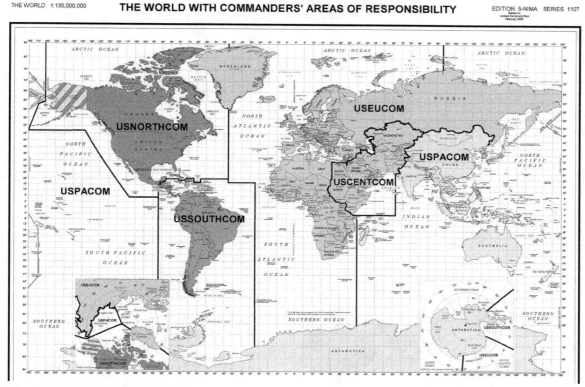

Figure 13.3 Unified Combatant Commands

As the head of the Pentagon, SECDEF is the primary witness for congressional committees and has oversight responsibilities for DoD. The Senate Armed Forces Committee (SASC) and the House Armed Services Committee (HASC) along with the Senate Appropriations (SAC) Committee and the House Appropriation Committee (HAC) are congressional committees that authorize many programs with DoD. In addition, the Senate Select Committee on Intelligence and the House Permanent Select Committee on Intelligence have principal oversight on DoD intelligence programs. SECDEF is a statutory member of the National Security Council and is authorized to act as the convening authority in military justice system for General-Courts Martial, Special-Courts Martial, and Summary-Courts Martial.

Secretary of Homeland Security

The *Secretary of Homeland Security* is the leader of the Department of Homeland Security (DHS). DHS is the nation's third largest agency within the federal government, which is responsible for its citizens and the homeland. Like SECDEF, the Secretary of Homeland Security is a member of the President's cabinet and is a part of the National Security Council. The position was established under the Homeland Security Act of 2002 in response to the September 11, 2001 attacks. On January 24, 2003, President George W. Bush appointed former Pennsylvania Governor Tom Ridge as the first Secretary of Homeland Security. Before DHS was established, the Assistant to the President for the Office of Homeland Security was formulized directly following 9/11.

Figure 13.4 Secretary of Homeland Security Flag

The Secretary of Homeland Security is responsible for nearly 230,000 U.S. government employees and 22 federal agencies that protect America's borders. Furthermore, the Secretary is accountable for "counterterrorism, aviation security, cyber security, border security, port security, maritime security, administration and enforcement of our immigration laws, protection of our national borders, protection of critical infrastructure, detection and protection against chemical, biological, and nuclear threats to the homeland, and response to disasters" (n.d., para. 1).

DEPARTMENT OF DEFENSE (DOD) AND DEPARTMENT OF HOMELAND SECURITY (DHS)

The Department of Defense is the oldest and largest federal agency within the United States. Also, the nation's largest employer, DoD is responsible for over 1.3 million United States Armed Forces, 826,000 national guardsmen and reservists, and 742,000 civilian personnel. DoD headquarters, the Pentagon, is in one of the world's largest office buildings in Arlington, Virginia. The mission of DoD is to provide "military forces needed to deter war and protect the security of country and to support the overall mission of the Department of Defense by providing official, timely and accurate information about defense policies, organizations, functions, and operations" (About the Department of Defense (DoD). Mission, n.d., para. 10). The Secretary of Defense runs the DoD and consists of the following departments:

- Department of the Air Force
- Department of the Army
- Department of the Navy (includes Marine Corps)
- Defense Intelligence Agency (DIA)
- National Security Agency (NSA)
- National Geospatial-Intelligence Agency (NGA)
- National Reconnaissance Organization (NRO)
- Defense Advanced Research Projects Agency (DARPA)
- Defense Logistics Agency (DLA)
- Missile Defense Agency (MDA)
- Defense Threat Reduction Agency (DTRA)
- Defense Security Service (DSS)
- Pentagon Force Protection Agency
- National Defense University

DoD also includes Defense Agencies such as:

- Armed Forces Radiobiology Research Institute
- Department of Defense Education Activity (DoDEA)
- Defense Commissary Agency
- Defense Contract Audit Agency
- Defense Contract Management Agency
- Defense Finance and Accounting Service
- Defense Information Systems Agency
- Defense Legal Services Agency
- Defense Security Cooperation Agency
- Defense Technical Information Center

DHS is an executive cabinet of the American federal government and is responsible for protecting its citizens and the homeland. DHS is the third largest Cabinet department in the nation behind DoD and Veterans Affairs. All homeland security policy is coordinated through the White House and Homeland Security Council and coordinates with the departments of Energy, Health and Human Services, and Justice, as these agencies have significant responsibilities and homeland security initiatives.

The agency was established on November 25, 2002 under the Homeland Security Act 2002 and was instituted to amalgamate all federal agencies that involved homeland security initiatives into a single department. According to experts, the reorganization was the largest since the Cold War during the era of the National Security Act of 1947. The restructure established the Secretary of Defense role in military service departments, the CIA and NSC. After margining and establishing 22 federal agencies under DHS, Tom Ridge was named the first Secretary of DHS and agency officially opened the same day while the merged entities were officially categorized under DHS on March 1, 2003.

DHS works closely with the civilian realm to protect the United States and its borders. The mission of DHS is to ensure a "homeland that is safe, secure, and resilient against terrorism and other hazards" (Mission, n.d., Department of Homeland Security., para. 1). In addition, the department is accountable for preparing, preventing, and responding to domestic emergencies. In 2003, the United States Immigration and Naturalization Service became a subsidiary of the department and was streamlined to formulize the United States Immigration and Customs Enforcement, and Citizenship and Immigration services. The investigative aspects of both agencies created the Homeland Security Investigations division. Under DHS, United States Border Patrol and Customs Service and Plant Health Inspection Service merged to form the United States Customs and Border Protection agency, consisting of 22 federal agencies.

DEPARTMENT OF STATE (DOS) AND FOREIGN DIPLOMACY

The Department of State (or State Department) is a federal executive agency within the American government responsible for all foreign policy matters. The agency deals with international relations and negotiations agreements and treaties with foreign establishments and does so as a member of the United Nations. Created in 1789, the State Department is accountable for diplomatic operations on behalf of the United States abroad, and is also responsible for employing American foreign policy efforts, which is the depositary for more than 200 **multilateral agreements** (agreement with two or more countries). The mission of the State Department is to "advance the national interests of the United States and its people … and to shape and sustain a peaceful, prosperous, just, and democratic world and foster conditions for stability and progress for the benefit the American people and people everywhere" (Mission, n.d., U.S. Department of State, para. 6).

The Secretary of State heads the State Department, and like the SECDEF and Secretary of DHS, is nominated by the President and confirmed by the Senate. The Secretary of State is a cabinet position and is a member of the NSC. The position is the principal foreign-policy advisor and support all foreign activities for the federal government, including the *United States Agency for International Development (USAID)*, DHS, CIA, and Department of Commerce. In 1787, when the United States Constitution was drafted in Philadelphia and

Figure 13.5 Department of State Seal

ratified by the original 13 colonies, the reformed body of law gave the President authority to conduct American foreign relations and establish policies and initiatives. The State Department consists of a civilian workforce that employs a significant amount of Foreign Service Officers and other diplomatic personnel to conduct operations overseas to analyze and report on economic, political, social, and visa matters. Employees of the State Department are also responsible for the needs and protection of American citizens who live abroad.

On July 21, 1789, the Department of Foreign Affairs was established by the House of Representatives and the Senate and President George Washington signed the legislation into law nearly a week later. This law was the first federal agency created under the new Constitution. The State Department's primary responsibilities were foreign policy and diplomacy, but expanded to management of the United States Census and Mint operations. On September 29, 1789, President Washington appointed Thomas Jefferson as the first Secretary of State.

Foreign Policy

American **foreign policy** is indicative of the goals forwarded by the Department of State, which are to "create a more secure, democratic, and prosperous world for the benefit of the American people and in the international community" (Mission, n.d., para. 1). Furthermore, the House of Representatives established the United States House Committee on Foreign Affairs (also known as the House Foreign Affairs Committee), which has authority over all legislation that involves American foreign policy matters. The President is responsible for negotiations with foreign policy affairs and **treaties** (agreements with foreign entities) with foreign countries, along with the confirmation of the Senate (treaties are passed if two-thirds of the Senate approve). The Secretary of State is the principal advisor on all foreign diplomacy and policy matters. Additionally, the President appoints the Secretary of State and all American ambassadors with confirmation of the Senate. Even though State Department has the authority to conduct foreign policy matters, Congress sanctions commerce operations with foreign countries.

Foreign policy was a vital concern after the American Revolutionary War, WWI, WWII, and the Cold War. All conflicts heavily affected national security, as the United States rose to be the global superpower and international relationships were crucial to not only the dominant standing, but to ensure economic stability, promote peace, and guarantee security around the world. Precedent events within the history of the United States have paved the way for foreign policy. For example, President George Washington's farewell address was crucial to emphasizing foreign policy affairs because it lead to establishment of policies for the Federalist Party. After the end of the War of 1812, the United States formed an alliance with France, and it would not be until the twentieth century that a treaty was signed (the North Atlantic Treaty). Except for the War of 1812 and the Spanish-American War, the United States had diplomatic relations with foreign countries and expanded foreign trade. For instance, the Louisiana Purchase in 1803 extended America's geographical range; Spain ceded Florida in 1819, and the Texas annexation in 1845 increased the United States' geographic area. The Civil War was also a significant event which reshaped foreign policy. Finally, the United States purchased Alaska from

Russia in 1867, Puerto Rico became an American territory after the Spanish-American war in 1898, and Hawaii became a territory in 1900—symbolizing imperialism and the evolution of foreign affairs.

Legal ramifications for foreign affairs and treaties include:

- **Congressional executive agreements**—established by the President of the United States. Congress is the legislative body that makes such agreements binding after they are signed by the President.
- **Sole executive agreements**—the President is the only individual to sign and bind such agreements.
- **Treaties**—are multilateral agreements with foreign countries that are predicated on the Treaty clause of the United States Constitution.

In addition to agreements, the United States is a member of foreign alliances that are responsible for protecting global security, maintaining peace, protecting humanity, and promoting globalization. The nation is one of the founding members of the United Nations, which is an intergovernmental organization to strengthen international relationships and maintain international order. The United States is a member of the following organizations for economic development and governmental matters:

- Asia-Pacific Economic Cooperation
- Group of Seven
- International Monetary Fund
- North American Free Trade Agreement
- Organization of American States
- Organization for Security and Co-Operation in Europe
- World Bank Group
- World Customs Organization
- World Trade Organization

Multilateral Agreements

The United States formulized one of the largest treaties in the Pacific: *The Trust of the Pacific Islands*, which was a United Nations trust territory agreement within Micronesia (the agreement dissolved in 1986). As a result, the Northern Mariana Islands became a U.S. territory and the other islands such as Micronesia, the Marshall Islands, and Palau became independent nations. All countries signed the *Compact of Free Association* agreement that authorized the United States unlimited military access if the nation provides financial aid, manages military foreign policy matters, and offers defense protection. Such agreements give these countries' citizens the opportunity to live in the United States with their families in return for free trade. Because of becoming members of every agreement could possibly destabilize other agreements the United

States has with other countries, there is not maximum participation with all international agreements. For example, Frederick. S. Northedge, author of *The League of Nations*, expressed the United States is not actively involved with agreements associated with highly developed countries (1986). Participation in such agreements could jeopardize the nation's sovereignty, causing maltreatment of American citizens.

HOMELAND SECURITY STRATEGY GOALS

Like the President's National Security Strategy to protect national security, the Secretary of Homeland Security has strategic goals to protect American citizens and the homeland. Under the department's leaderships, there are strategic goals and objectives that all organizations within DHS are mandated to implement and execute. According to the agency's website there are "long-term strategic goals, which articulate statement of what the agency wants to achieve to advance itsf mission and address relevant national problems, needs, challenges, and opportunities" (Mission, n.d., Department of Homeland Security, para. 2). DHS's mission is the department will:

- Prevent terrorism and enhance security
- Secure and manage our borders
- Enforce and administer our immigration laws
- Safeguard and secure cyberspace
- Strengthen national preparedness and resilience (Mission, n.d., Department of Homeland Security, para. 1).

The following are the five strategic goals that have been implemented by DHS and how all the organizations under its umbrella will handle matters that are considered detrimental and a threat against homeland security. In *2014–2018 Fiscal Years Strategic Plan,* former Secretary of Homeland Security, Jeh Johnson, outlines how the Department of Homeland Security matters.

Mission 1: Prevent Terrorism and Enhance Security

Preventing terrorism is the cornerstone of homeland security. Within this mission, we focus on the goals of preventing terrorist attacks; preventing and protecting against the unauthorized acquisition or use of chemical, biological, radiological, and nuclear materials and capabilities; and reducing risk to the nation's most critical infrastructure, key leaders, and events. The 2014 Quadrennial Homeland Security Review described a

Selection from U.S. Department of Homeland Security, Fiscal Years 2014-2018 Strategic Plan, pp. 14-39. 2014.

more integrated, networked approach to counterterrorism and community engagement efforts. To improve overall Departmental unity of effort, we will work with our partners to identify, investigate, and interdict threats as early as possible; expand risk-based security; focus on countering violent extremism and preventing complex mass-casualty attacks; reduce vulnerabilities by denying resources and targets; and uncover patterns and faint signals through enhanced data integration and analysis. DHS shares the responsibility to prevent terrorist attacks with several federal departments and agencies, including the departments of State, Justice, and Defense, and the Office of the Director of National Intelligence; as well as with state, local, tribal, territorial, and private-sector partners. DHS further collaborates with foreign partners on security issues of concern.

Mission Priorities

The following Mission Priorities represent the highest priority efforts for the Department of Homeland Security within Mission 1. While the Department will continue to work on all of the mission goals and objectives laid out in the 2014 Quadrennial Homeland Security Review and the 2014–2018 Strategic Plan, the following are the top areas of focus in terms of investment, strategic and operational planning, and stakeholder engagement; and will be addressed through actions undertaken in one or more of the following DHS foundational activities: Joint Requirements Council, joint operational plans and operations, enhanced budget and investment processes, and focused strategic and analytic efforts.

- Prevent terrorist's travel into the United States by enhancing information sharing, international cooperation, and risk-based targeting, including by focusing on foreign fighters.
- Strengthen aviation security by implementing risk-based mitigation strategies.
- Prevent the hostile use of nuclear materials against the homeland by deterring or preventing adversaries from smuggling nuclear weapons and materials, and enhancing the ability to detect nuclear weapons and materials out of regulatory control.
- Protect key leaders, facilities, and National Special Security Events by deterring, minimizing, and responding to identified vulnerabilities and threats against the President, Vice President, other protected individuals, the White House Complex, and other sites.

Goal 1.1: Prevent Terrorist Attacks

The Department remains vigilant to new and evolving threats to protect the nation from a terrorist attack. Although the U.S. Government's counterterrorism efforts have degraded the ability of al-Qa'ida's senior leadership in Afghanistan and Pakistan to centrally plan and execute sophisticated external attacks, since 2009 we have seen the rise of al-Qa'ida affiliates, such as al-Qa'ida in the Arabian Peninsula and the al-Nusrah Front in Syria. These groups have made attempts to export terrorism to our nation. Additionally, we face the threat of domestic-based "lone offenders" and those who are inspired by violent extremist ideologies to radicalize and commit acts of terrorism against Americans and the nation. These threats come in multiple forms and, because of the nature of independent actors, may be hardest to detect. We will pursue the following strategies to prevent terrorist attacks: Analyze, fuse, and disseminate terrorism information by sharing information with, and utilizing threat analysis alongside, stakeholders across the homeland security enterprise.

We remain committed to integrating critical data sources, such as those for biometric data, by consolidating or federating screening and vetting operations. We will continually increase and integrate domain awareness capabilities, as well as improve our ability to fully utilize vast amounts of intelligence and other information—the so-called "big data" challenge—while rigorously protecting privacy and civil rights and civil liberties. We will deter and disrupt operations by leveraging the intelligence, information sharing, technological, operational, and policy-making elements within DHS to facilitate a cohesive and coordinated operational response. We will develop intelligence sources and leverage research and analysis to identify and illustrate the tactics, behaviors, and indicators potentially associated with violent extremism as well as factors that may influence violent extremism, and jointly develop with federal, state, local, tribal, and territorial partners training for frontline law enforcement officers on behaviors that may be telling regarding violent extremist activity. We will strengthen transportation security by using a multi-layered risk-based approach to detect malicious actors and dangerous items at various entry and exit points in the travel and trade system. We will also improve coordination with foreign governments and stakeholders to expand pre-departure screening and enhance transportation security operations among willing partners to mitigate risks from overseas. We will counter violent extremism by:

- Supporting community-based problem-solving and integration efforts, as well as local law enforcement programs
- Working with our partners to share information with frontline law enforcement partners, communities, families, and the private sector about how violent extremists are using the Internet and how to protect themselves and their communities.

Goal 1.2: Prevent and Protect Against the Unauthorized Acquisition or Use of Chemical, Biological, Radiological, and Nuclear Materials and Capabilities

Chemical, biological, radiological, and nuclear threats are enduring areas of concern. The consequences of these attacks are potentially high even though the likelihood of their occurrence is relatively low. Small-scale chemical attacks are expected to remain more likely because the relative lack of specialized skills and knowledge required to conduct such attacks. However, nuclear terrorism and bioterrorism pose the most strategically significant risk because of their potential consequences. Although the difficulty of stealing a nuclear weapon or fabricating one from stolen or diverted weapons materials reduces the likelihood of this type of attack, the extremely high consequences of an improvised nuclear device attack make it an ongoing top homeland security risk.

We will pursue the following strategies to prevent and protect against the unauthorized acquisition or use of chemical, biological, radiological, and nuclear materials and capabilities: Anticipate chemical, biological, radiological, and nuclear emerging threats by identifying and understanding potentially dangerous actors, technologies, and materials; and prioritizing research and development activities including:

- analyses of alternative technology options
- assessments of complex issues such as the relative risk of different chemical, biological, radiological, and nuclear threats
- experimentation and operational test and evaluation of technologies proposed for acquisition
- detailed technical characterization of potential biological threat organisms;
- the creation of a consensus of standards that enable cost-effective progress across many fields
- the determination of nuclear material characteristics through nuclear forensics techniques. Identify and interdict unlawful acquisition and movement of chemical, biological, radiological, and nuclear precursors and materials by leveraging investigative and enforcement assets towards domestic and international movement of these materials and by engaging in information sharing with all stakeholders to monitor and control this technology. Detect, locate, and prevent the hostile use of chemical, biological, radiological, and nuclear materials and weapons by
- combining authorities and assets with other departments and agencies
- building the U.S. Government's global nuclear detection capability through the Global Nuclear Detection Architecture, a framework for detecting (through technical and non-technical means), analyzing, and reporting on nuclear and other radioactive materials that are out of regulatory control
- advancing nuclear forensics capabilities to close nuclear smuggling networks, promote global nuclear security, and deter would-be nation-state terrorist facilitators from transferring nuclear materials to terrorists
- providing unimpeachable forensic data for use by law enforcement authorities in the investigation and prosecution of crimes involving biological agents;
- regulating high-risk chemical facilities to ensure that they take proper steps to mitigate risks; and
- preventing the occurrence of significant biological incidents, where possible, but, when unable to prevent, stopping them from overwhelming the capacity of our state, local, tribal, and territorial partners to manage and respond. To this last point, DHS will deploy technologies that enable early detection of biological agents prior to the onset of symptoms, pursue more rapid responder capabilities, and increase the capacity and effectiveness of local public health, medical, and emergency services.

Goal 1.3: Reduce Risk to the Nation's Critical Infrastructure, Key Leadership, and Events

DHS has national leadership responsibility for enhancing security to the Nation's critical infrastructure and protecting key leaders, facilities, and National Special Security Events. DHS reduces risk across a wide portfolio of activities, including the agriculture and food sector, the travel and trade system, and the financial services sector. These systems are vulnerable to criminal exploitation and both physical and cyber-attacks. DHS also maintains constant guard over key leaders and during high-profile events, reducing the possibility that these events could be exploited by criminal or terrorist actors. We will pursue the following strategies to reduce risk to the nation's critical infrastructure, key leadership, and events. Enhanced security for the Nation's critical infrastructure from terrorism and criminal activity will be achieved by:

- identifying critical infrastructure and related vulnerabilities;
- developing and deploying a scalable assessment methodology depending on the level of threat and the nature of the target;
- inserting and/or developing appropriate technologies;
- tracking protective measures of our partners across the homeland security enterprise;
- conducting investigations that maximize disruption of criminal enterprises that pose the greatest risk to the United States. We will also enhance the nation's ability to counter improvised explosive devices (IEDs) by coordinating whole community efforts to prevent, protect against, respond to, and mitigate terrorist and criminal use of explosives. Protect key leaders, facilities, and National Special Security Events by:
  › working with partners across the homeland security enterprise to coordinate intelligence, information sharing, security, and response resources;
  › protecting the President, the Vice President, visiting heads of state, major-party Presidential candidates, and other designated protectees;
  › protecting federal facilities, employees, and visitors; and
  › assessing risk and coordinating support to partners during major special events across the nation through the Special Events Assessment Rating.

Mission 2: Secure and Manage Our Borders

Secure, well-managed borders must not only protect the United States against threats from abroad, they must also safeguard and expedite the flow of lawful trade and travel. Achieving this end requires that we focus on three interrelated goals: 1) secure U.S. air, land, and sea borders and approaches; 2) safeguard and expedite lawful trade and travel; and 3) disrupt and dismantle transnational criminal organizations and other illicit actors.

The 2014 Quadrennial Homeland Security Review defined a risk segmentation approach to managing the flows of people and goods: minimize disruption to and facilitate safe and secure inbound and outbound legal flows of people and goods; prioritize efforts to counter illicit finance, and further increase transnational criminal organization perception of risk through targeted interdiction and other activities, while continuing to increase efficiencies in operations; and counter terrorist travel into the United States, terrorism against international travel and trade systems, and the export of sensitive goods and technology.

Building on that work, the U.S. Southern Border and Approaches Campaign Planning Effort (2014), one of the first management imperatives from the Unity of Effort Initiative, articulates four mutually supporting key areas of effort for securing the southern border and approaches: 1) segment and expedite flows of people and goods at ports of entry; 2) strengthen the security and resilience of the global supply chain and the international travel system; 3) combat transnational organized crime and terrorism; and 4) prevent flows of illegal people and goods between ports of entry.

Mission Priorities

The following Mission Priorities represent the highest priority efforts for the Department of Homeland Security within Mission 2. While the Department will continue to work on all of the mission goals and objectives laid out in the 2014 Quadrennial Homeland Security Review and the 2014–2018 Strategic Plan, these are the top areas of focus in terms of investment, strategic and operational planning, and stakeholder engagement, and will be addressed through actions undertaken in one or more of the following DHS foundational activities: Joint Requirements Council, joint operational plans and operations, enhanced budget and investment processes, and focused strategic and analytic efforts.

- Secure the U.S. Southern Border and approaches by implementing a strategic framework.
- Combat transnational organized crime by countering illicit finance and further integrating elements of the layered defense.

Goal 2.1: Secure U.S. Air, Land, and Sea Border and Approaches

Flows of people and goods around the world have expanded dramatically in recent years. DHS employs a range of strategies to improve upon border security, as well as to exclude terrorist threats, drug traffickers, and other threats to national security, economic security, and public safety. DHS and our partners ensure transit via legal pathways; identify and remove people and goods attempting to travel illegally; and ensure the safety and integrity of these flows of people and goods by safeguarding the conveyances, nodes, and pathways that make up the travel and trade system.

DHS relies on a combination of people, technology, assets (e.g., surface and aviation platforms), and infrastructure (e.g., roads, fences) across DHS operating components to enable situational awareness and secure the border. Given the inherently transnational nature of securing our borders, DHS also continues to build international partnerships to enhance our ability to identify threats or hazards before they emerge in the United States. We will pursue the following strategies to secure U.S. air, land, and sea border and approaches: Prevent illegal import and entry by employing a layered, risk-based approach to screen, identify, and intercept threats at points of departure and at U.S. ports of entry.

Using a variety of intelligence, automated tools, and information collected in advance of arrival for passengers and cargo at air, land, and seaports, DHS screens, identifies, and intercepts threats at points of departure before they reach our borders. In the approaches to the United States, DHS maintains domain awareness efforts to establish and maintain a common operating picture of people, vehicles, aircraft, and marine vessels approaching our borders, as well as interdiction capabilities to achieve a law enforcement resolution. Prevent illegal export and exit through a risk-based strategy to inspect people, cargo, and conveyances departing the United States through all airports, seaports, land border crossings, and international mail/courier facilities. Using this information, law enforcement organizations such as Immigration and Customs Enforcement will investigate illegal exports and exit.

Goal 2.2: Safeguard and Expedite Lawful Trade and Travel

The clear majority of people and goods entering and exiting the United States represent lawful trade and travel. Lawful trade and travel provides enormous economic benefits to our society, evident by a substantial increase in the number of tourists and business travelers and in the value of U.S. exports and imports between 2005 and 2012, and underscored by projections for continued growth at an average of six percent annually through 2030. DHS and our partners work to secure and expedite these flows of people and goods, as they are a main driver of U.S. economic prosperity. We will pursue the following strategies to safeguard and expedite lawful trade and travel: Safeguard key nodes, conveyances, and pathways by establishing and enforcing security standards and plans that maintain or restore infrastructure capabilities to be resilient from attacks and natural disasters; this includes facilities at ports of entry, modes of transportation, and pathways. Manage the risk of people and goods in transit by employing a risk-segmentation approach that identifies low-risk and high-risk people and goods moving within legal channels as far from the homeland as possible, and then expediting low-risk, lawful movement to and through the United States. Maximize compliance with U.S. trade laws and promote U.S. economic security and competitiveness by: 1) working with international partners, such as the International Maritime Organization, the International Civil Aviation Organization, and INTERPOL, to create global standards for security and resilience of the global trade and travel system and 2) conducting cargo recognition programs to reduce redundancies for industry while maintaining a commensurate level of security.

Goal 2.3: Disrupt and Dismantle Transnational Criminal Organizations and Other Illicit Actors

Transnational criminal organizations are increasing in strength and capability. They rely on revenues generated through the sale of illegal drugs and counterfeit goods, human trafficking and smuggling, and other criminal activities. They are also gaining strength by taking advantage of the same innovations in management and supply chain structures that are propelling multinational corporations. We will pursue the following strategies to disrupt and dismantle transnational criminal organizations and other illicit actors: Identify, investigate, disrupt, and dismantle TCOs by: 1) targeting illicit financing activities that transnational criminal organizations depend on, such as money laundering, and increasing outbound inspection to deter practices such as cash smuggling; and 2) creating a deterrent effect from injecting the greatest amount of uncertainty and concern into criminal decision-making by swiftly shifting assets, presence, technology, and tools, further targeting and focusing interdiction activities, and emphasizing strategic communications that project the effectiveness of homeland security capabilities. Disrupt illicit actors, activities, and pathways by using intelligence to target and interdict illicit people and goods through a rapid response workforce as well as surveillance and enforcement assets to detect, identify, monitor, track, and interdict targets of interest, and board vessels.

Mission 3: Enforce and Administer Our Immigration Laws

Immigration is essential to our identity as a nation of immigrants. Most American families have an immigration story—some recent, some more distant. Many immigrants have taken on great risks to work and contribute to America's prosperity or were provided refuge after facing persecution abroad. Americans are extremely proud of this tradition. Smart and effective enforcement and administration of our immigration laws remains a core homeland security mission. The following priorities from the 2014 Quadrennial Homeland Security Review inform the strategic approach in this mission area: 1) Building a stronger, smarter border enforcement system; 2) Achieving smart and effective interior enforcement; 3) Creating a twenty-first century legal immigration system; 4) Facilitating reunions for long-separated families; 5) Creating an earned path to citizenship; and 6) Enhancing management and organization to develop a responsive immigration system.

Mission Priorities

The following Mission Priorities represent the highest priority efforts for the Department of Homeland Security within Mission 3. While the Department will continue to work on all of the mission goals and objectives laid out in the 2014 Quadrennial Homeland Security Review and the 2014–2018 Strategic Plan, these are the top areas of focus in terms of investment, strategic and operational planning, and stakeholder engagement, and will be addressed through actions undertaken in one or more of the following DHS foundational activities: Joint Requirements Council, joint operational plans and operations, enhanced budget and investment processes, and focused strategic and analytic efforts.

- Strengthen the immigration benefits system by transforming procedures for the adjudication of applications, strengthening anti-fraud measures, and expanding best practices and supporting capabilities.

- Strengthen and focus DHS interior enforcement activities by providing clear guidelines with respect to the arrest, detention, and removal of priority individuals, namely national-security, public-safety, and border-security threats.

We will pursue the following strategies to strengthen and effectively administer the immigration system: Promote lawful immigration by uniting families, providing refuge, fostering economic opportunity, and promoting citizenship. We will also work to better assist high-skilled immigrants, streamline the processing of immigrant visas to encourage businesses to grow in the United States, and develop innovative programs to enable immigrants to reach their potential in the United States. Effectively administer the immigration services system by:

- Providing effective customer-oriented immigration benefit and information services at home and abroad
- Making all information needed to make immigration decisions available to appropriate agencies electronically and in real-time, including active individual case files and biometric information
- Ensuring that only eligible applicants receive immigration benefits through expanded use of biometrics, a strengthening of screening processes, improvements to fraud detection, increases in legal staffing to ensure due process, and enhancements of interagency information sharing. Promote the integration of lawful immigrants in American society by enhancing educational resources and promoting opportunities to increase understanding of U.S. civic principles and the rights, responsibilities, and importance of citizenship, and supporting comprehensive immigration reform that provides an earned pathway to citizenship.

Goal 3.1: Strengthen and Effectively Administer the Immigration System

At the center of any good immigration system must be a structure able to rapidly respond to regulatory changes and the flow of demand around the world while at the same time safeguarding security. We are constantly seeking ways to better administer benefits and use technology to make information more accessible and secure.

Mission 4: Safeguard and Secure Cyberspace

Each day, the United States faces a myriad of threats in cyberspace, from the theft of trade secrets, credit-card data, and other sensitive information through cyber intrusions to denial-of-service attacks against Internet websites and attempted intrusions of U.S. critical infrastructure. DHS works closely with government and private-sector partners to strengthen cyber security capabilities, investigate cybercrime, and share actionable information to ensure a secure and resilient cyberspace that protects privacy and civil rights and civil liberties by design, supports innovation and economic growth, and supports public health and safety. The 2014 Quadrennial Homeland Security Review outlines four strategic priorities to safeguard and secure cyberspace:

- Strengthen the security and resilience of critical Infrastructure against cyber-attacks and other hazards
- Secure the federal civilian government information technology enterprise
- Advance cyber law enforcement, incident response, and reporting capabilities
- Strengthen the cyber ecosystem.

Goal 4.1 Strengthen the Security and Resilience of Critical Infrastructure Against Cyber-Attacks and Other Hazards

The concept of critical infrastructure as discrete, physical assets has become outdated as everything becomes linked to cyberspace. This "cyber-physical convergence" has changed the risks to critical infrastructure in sectors ranging from energy and transportation to agriculture and healthcare. DHS coordinates with its private-sector partners as well as with state, local, tribal, and territorial governments to share information and intelligence regarding cyber threats and vulnerabilities, foster development of trustworthy products and services, and encourage the adoption of best-in-class cyber security practices.

We will pursue the following strategies to strengthen the security and resilience of critical infrastructure against cyber-attacks and other hazards: Enhance the exchange of information and intelligence on risks to critical infrastructure and develop real-time situational awareness capabilities that ensure machine and human interpretation and visualization by increasing the volume, timeliness and quality of cyber threat reporting shared with the private sector and state, local, tribal, and territorial partners, and enabling the National Cybersecurity and Communications Integration Center (to receive information at "machine speed") by enabling networks to be more self-healing, using mathematics and analytics to mimic restorative processes that occur biologically. Partner with critical infrastructure owners and operators to ensure the delivery of essential services and functions by building effective partnerships to set a national focus and determine collective actions, aiding local and regional partners, and leveraging incentives to advance security and resilience, as described in the National Infrastructure Protection Plan: Partnering for Security and Resilience. Identify and understand interdependencies and cascading impacts among critical systems by leveraging regional risk assessment programs, organization-specific assessment, asset and network-specific assessment, and cross-sector risk assessments. Collaborate with agencies and the private sector to identify and develop effective cyber security policies and best practices through voluntary collaboration with private-sector owners and operators (including their partner associations, vendors, and others) and government entity counterparts. Reduce vulnerabilities and promote resilient critical infrastructure design by identifying and promoting opportunities that build security and resilience into critical infrastructure as it is being developed and updated, rather than focusing solely on mitigating vulnerabilities present within existing critical infrastructure.

Goal 4.2 Secure the Federal Civilian Government Information Technology Enterprise

The Federal Government provides essential services and information on which many Americans rely. Not only must the government protect its own networks, it must serve as a role model to others in implementing security services. DHS itself plays a leading role in securing federal civilian networks, allowing the Federal Government to do its business securely. DHS partners with agencies to deploy products such as the EINSTEIN set of capabilities that provide perimeter network-based intrusion detection and prevention. We will pursue the following strategies to secure the federal civilian government information technology enterprise: Coordinate government purchasing of cyber technology to enhance cost-effectiveness by using strategically sourced tools and services such as the Continuous Diagnostics and Mitigation program.

Equip civilian government networks with innovative cyber security tools, information, and protections by supporting research and development and making the innovations from research and development available not only to the Federal Government but widely available across the public and private spheres. Ensure government-wide policy and standards are consistently and effectively implemented and measured by promoting the adoption of enterprise-wide policy and best practices and working with interagency partners to develop government-wide requirements that can bring the full strength of the market to bear on existing and emergent vulnerabilities.

Goal 4.3: Advance Cyber Law Enforcement, Incident Response, and Reporting Capabilities

Online criminal activity threatens the Internet's safe and secure use. Law enforcement performs an essential role in achieving our Nation's cyber security objectives by detecting, investigating, and preventing a wide range of cybercrimes, from theft and fraud to child exploitation, and apprehending and prosecuting those responsible. In addition to criminal prosecution, there is a need to rapidly detect and respond to incidents, including through the development of quarantine and mitigation strategies, as well as to quickly share incident information so that others may protect themselves. Safeguarding and securing cyberspace requires close coordination among federal law enforcement entities, network security experts, state, local, tribal, and territorial officials, and private sector stakeholders. We will pursue the following strategies to advance cyber law enforcement, incident response, and reporting capabilities: Respond to and assist in the recovery from cyber incidents by managing incident response activities through the National Cybersecurity and Communications Integration Center and fostering enhanced collaboration between law enforcement and network security officials to pre-plan responses to cyber incidents. Deter, disrupt, and investigate cybercrime by 1) increasing the quantity and impact of cybercrime investigations; 2) partnering with other agencies to conduct high-profile criminal investigations, prioritize the recruitment and training of technical experts, and develop standardized methods; and 3) strengthening law enforcement agencies' ability to detect, investigate, and arrest those that make illicit use of cyberspace.

Goal 4.4 Strengthen the Cyber Ecosystem

Our entire society, from government and law enforcement to the private sector and members of the public, must work collaboratively to improve our network defense. Ensuring a healthy cyber ecosystem will require collaborative communities, innovative and agile security solutions, standardized and consistent processes to share information and best practices, sound policies and plans, meaningful protection of privacy, civil rights, and civil liberties, and development of a skilled workforce to ensure those policies and plans are implemented as intended. We will pursue the following strategies to strengthen the cyber ecosystem: Drive innovative and cost-effective security products, services, and solutions throughout the cyber ecosystem by working with domestic and international partners across the public and private spheres, and across the science and policy communities to identify promising technology, policy and standards that enable robust, trust-based, automated sharing of cyber security information and collective action to limit the spread of incidents and minimize consequences. Conduct and transition research and development, enabling trustworthy cyber infrastructure by supporting initiatives to develop promising new security technologies and techniques including:

- security automation techniques to facilitate real-time incident response;
- interoperability to support security cooperation across sectors; and
- privacy-enhancing authentication to enable better system protection.

Develop skilled cyber security professionals by promoting cyber security knowledge and innovation, developing Department-wide human capital strategies, policies, and programs intended to enhance the DHS cyber workforce, and working with public and private sector partners to increase the pipeline of highly qualified homeland security professionals through academic and federal training programs. Enhance public awareness and promote cyber security best practices by promoting National Cybersecurity Awareness Month and the "Stop. Think. Connect. ™" campaign, which raise awareness through collaborative outreach efforts and distributing materials, resources, and tips to promote cyber security. Advance international engagement to promote capacity building, international standards, and cooperation by working to establish and deepen relationships with foreign computer incident response teams both bilaterally and through participation in operationally focused multilateral fora, such as the Forum for Incident Response and Security Teams.

Mission 5: Strengthen National Preparedness and Resilience

Despite ongoing vigilance and efforts to protect the United States and its citizens, major accidents, disruptions, and natural disasters, as well as deliberate attacks, will occur. The challenge is to build the capacity of American society to be resilient in the face of disruptions, disasters, and other crises. Our goals in this mission require us to:

- enhance national preparedness

- mitigate hazards and vulnerabilities
- ensure effective emergency response
- enable rapid recovery

The 2014 Quadrennial Homeland Security Review reaffirms the Whole Community approach to national preparedness and resilience, which calls for the investment of everyone—not just the government—in preparedness efforts. Whole Community is a means by which emergency managers, organizational and community leaders, government officials, private- and nonprofit sectors, faith-based and disability organizations, and the public can collectively understand and assess the needs of their respective communities as well as determine the best ways to organize and strengthen their assets, capacities, and interests.

Mission Priorities

The following Mission Priorities represent the highest priority efforts for the Department of Homeland Security within Mission 5. While the Department will continue to work on all of the mission goals and objectives laid out in the 2014 Quadrennial Homeland Security Review and the 2014–2018 Strategic Plan, these are the top areas of focus in terms of investment, strategic and operational planning, and stakeholder engagement, and will be addressed through actions undertaken in one or more of the following DHS foundational activities: Joint Requirements Council, joint operational plans and operations, enhanced budget and investment processes, and focused strategic and analytic efforts.

- Prepare the Nation for those threats and hazards that pose the greatest risk to the security of the Nation by building and sustaining capabilities to achieve the National Preparedness Goal.
- Ensure effective, unified incident response operations

Goal 5.1: Enhance National Preparedness

National preparedness underpins all efforts to safeguard and secure the Nation against those threats and hazards that pose the greatest risk. Presidential Policy Directive 8 calls for a National Preparedness Goal, which is "[a] secure and resilient Nation with the capabilities required across the Whole Community to prevent, protect against, mitigate, respond to, and recover from the threats and hazards that pose the greatest risk." We will pursue the following strategies to enhance national preparedness: Empower individuals and communities to strengthen and sustain their own preparedness by engaging public and community organizations through programs such as "America's Preparathon!" to build a collective understanding of their risks, the resources available to assist their preparations, and their roles and responsibilities in the event of a disaster. Build and sustain core capabilities nationally to prevent, protect against, mitigate, respond to, and recover from all hazards by conducting such activities as:

- Fostering capability development by providing tools and technical assistance;
- Providing planning and reach-back expertise;

- Using grant programs such as the State Homeland Security Grant Program and the Urban Area Security Initiative (which collectively provide funds to state, local, tribal, territorial, and regional government and port, transit, and nonprofit entities); and

- Promoting the use of the National Planning Frameworks. These activities support the Department's intent to build and sustain a national integrated network of capabilities across all levels of government and to promote the involvement of the Whole Community in the Nation's preparedness efforts. Assist federal entities in the establishment of effective continuity programs that are regularly updated, exercised, and improved by administering the National Exercise Program, the cornerstone of a collective effort to test, improve, and assess national preparedness.

Goal 5.2: Mitigate Hazards and Vulnerabilities

DHS is uniquely positioned not only to support communities during a disaster, but also to enable partners to take steps that will decrease risk and mitigate future hazards before a disaster strikes. While risk cannot be eliminated, DHS can influence and support more positive outcomes in reducing risks. National risk management emphasizes focusing on those actions and interventions that reduce the greatest amount of strategic risk to the Nation. We will pursue the following strategies to mitigate hazards and vulnerabilities: Promote public and private sector awareness and understanding of community-specific risks by providing credible and actionable data and tools to support risk-informed decision-making, incentivizing and facilitating investments to manage current and future risk. Reduce vulnerability through standards, regulation, resilient design, effective mitigation, and disaster-risk reduction measures by encouraging appropriate land use and adoption of building codes, while also applying engineering and planning practices in conjunction with advanced technology tools. Prevent maritime incidents by establishing, and ensuring compliance with standards and regulations by licensing U.S. mariners, conducting and sharing findings of casualty investigations, and providing grants and support for government and non-government boating safety efforts.

Goal 5.3: Ensure Effective Emergency Response

DHS, primarily through the Federal Emergency Management Agency (FEMA) on land and the U.S. Coast Guard at sea, acts as the federal coordinator during disaster response, supporting state, local, tribal, territorial, and regional governments while working closely with nongovernmental organizations and the private sector to help leverage the resources they can bring to bear. We will pursue the following strategies to ensure effective emergency response:

Provide timely and accurate information to individuals and communities to support public safety and inform appropriate actions by the public before, during, and after emergencies. Conduct effective, unified incident response operations by following the National Response Framework, Second Edition; maximizing interagency coordination, information sharing, and preparation; and implementing initiatives to ensure a stable, flexible, and fully qualified disaster workforce. Provide timely and appropriate disaster assistance through "survivor-centric" programs that support, streamline, and simplify the delivery of services for individuals and communities. DHS will strengthen capabilities and operationalize resource-sharing opportunities to achieve the greatest potential to change outcomes on the ground in catastrophic disasters. Ensure effective emergency communications through the provision of technical communications capabilities enabling security, situational awareness, and operational decision-making to manage emergencies under all circumstances.

Goal 5.4: Enable Rapid Recovery

DHS plays a key role in facilitating recovery following a disaster by supplementing communities' recovery core capabilities; promoting infrastructure-resilience guidelines and use of standards; and encouraging the development of continuity plans for communities, government entities, and private-sector organizations. The devastating effects of recent disasters have highlighted the need to reform our national approach to long-term recovery. Communities devastated by a disaster, particularly large-scale events such as Hurricane Sandy, face complex and difficult challenges including restoring economic viability, rebuilding infrastructure and public services, and establishing resilience against future hazards. We will pursue the following strategies to enable rapid recovery: Ensure continuity and restoration of essential services and functions by: 1) supplementing communities' recovery core capabilities; 2) encouraging the development of continuity plans for communities, government entities, and private-sector organizations; and 3) working to ensure continuity and rapid restoration of essential services. Support and enable communities to rebuild stronger, smarter, and safer by following the National Disaster Recovery Framework and implementing programs that: 1) fund authorized federal disaster support activities; 2) support eligible reconstruction projects and disaster survivors; 3) provide subject matter experts to assist in planning and coordinating rebuilding efforts; and 4) focus on how best to restore, redevelop, and revitalize the health, social, economic, natural, and environmental fabric of the community and build a more-resilient nation.

SUMMARY

Where national security meets homeland security is one of the important chapters of this textbook, with the understanding that national and homeland security are two different concepts that contribute to protecting the U.S., while acknowledging that overlapping impressions of both identify an outlet for combating threats. Congressional roles and involvement led to the inception of one of the world's largest democratic governments and how political parties were established, organized, and regulate public policies. The Democratic and Republican parties were formulized after years of multiple governance regulations that were congruent with the behaviors, political stances, and support of numerous presidential administrations.

The positions of the National Security Advisor, Secretary of Defense, Secretary of Homeland Security, Secretary of State were discussed in this chapter to show the single responsibilities that are vital to federal agencies that are accountable for protecting the homeland domestically and internationally while establishing foreign policy matters to cooperate with international countries and set standards for American agencies. Each position has its own mission, but all executive positions are the principal advisor from their respective agencies to ultimately to protect American citizens, its resources, and the homeland.

Finally, examining the nation's largest federal agencies gives a glimpse of how the United States has the most innovative, technically advanced, and methodical democratic processes to deter the adversary and be an autonomous example of the world to ensure global security and continue globalization efforts. With over three million employees working in these departments, the United States has the world's best employees that are highly skilled and trained to continue efforts on protecting American citizens, resources, and the homeland. To sustain these efforts, it is imperative to improve educational standards, sustain research and development strengths, and sustain innovative methods along with strengthening foreign relationships with the nation's allies and security partners.

CHAPTER 13 CASE STUDIES

Case Study 1
The Secretary of Defense

Since the establishment of the Department of Defense when the National Security Act of 1947 was signed into law, there has been 26 Secretaries of Defense. The Secretary of Defense (SECDEF) is the chief executive officer and head of the Department of Defense, which is the United States' largest federal government agency. With such a prestigious position, SEDEF is only second in power of running the United States next to the President, and is a Cabinet member as well as a member of the National Security Council. The position is comparable to foreign countries' Ministers of Defense. SECDEF is nominated by the President and confirmed by the Senate.

The Secretary of Defense has the "authority, direction, and control over the Department of Defense and is further designated by the same statute as the principal assistant to the President in all matters relating to the Department of Defense" (Cornell University, n.d., para. 1). SECEF is also a "Commander-in-Chief" to the nation's Armed Forces, having responsibility for over 2 million active duty, reserve, and guard personnel. Because there must be civilian control over the military, only civilian personnel are chosen. If a retired or veteran military member is nominated, he or she must not be "within seven years after relief from active duty as a commissioned officer of a regular component of an armed force" (Cornell University, n.d., para. 1). The Secretary of Defense's primary role is the chief principal advisor to the President on all defense matters and is the chain of command for operational and administrative methodologies for all branches of service.

Since 1947, the roles, responsibilities, power, and authority have changed throughout many policies that fought for the Secretary of Defense to have a stake in the U.S.

military and protecting the homeland from foreign threats. SECDEF is accountable for making keen decisions on national defense policies and strategies so the President can have informed decisions on the current threats and how to handle them. Because SECDEF has the highest authority for the nation and its defense, should there be more authoritative decisions within the White House? Should SECDEF have the authority to declare war on foreign adversaries who threaten or attack the nation? Should SECDEF be the spokesperson (instead of the President) for all decisions that affects national defense?

Case Study 2
The Secretary of Homeland Security

The Secretary of Homeland Security is the top civilian executive for the third-largest federal government agency in the United States: The Department of Homeland Security. The Secretary's responsibilities are protecting America from domestic and international terrorism as well as how the nation will respond to natural disasters. Like the Secretary of Defense, the Secretary of Homeland Security is a Cabinet member and the National Security Council. The Office of the Secretary of Homeland Security "oversees DHS's efforts to counter terrorism and enhance security, secure and manage our borders while facilitating trade and travel, enforce and administer our immigration laws, safeguard and secure cyberspace, build resilience to disasters, and provide essential support for national and economic security—in coordination with federal, state, local, international, and private sectors" (U.S. Department of Homeland Security [DHS], n.d., para. 1).

When President George W. Bush signed the Homeland Security Act 2002, the Department of Homeland was created along with Secretary of Homeland Security position in response to the September 11th, 2001, attacks (DHS, 2002). The September 11th attacks was responsible for the largest reorganization since the National Security Act of 1947, following World War II (U.S. Senate Committee on Homeland Security and Governmental Affairs, n.d). DHS was instrumental in transferring homeland security-related agencies from other cabinet departments to its new entity to streamline processes, provide continuity, and increase accountability. The U.S. Coast Guard, the Federal Protective Service, U.S. Customs and Border Protection, U.S. Immigration and Customs Enforcement, the Secret Service, and the Federal Emergency Management Agency were top federal agencies that immediately transferred to DHS.

Since the inception of DHS, the Secretary of Homeland Security responsibilities have increased with 22 federal agencies and making homeland security policies to address America's top homeland security concerns. It is evident that homeland and national security objectives overlap, knowing both concepts are protecting the American people, the homeland, critical infrastructures, and other resources. However, there are difference missions, objectives, and policies on how both homeland and national security are handled. Are there any challenges with having homeland and national security objectives overlap? Should more objectives and strategic plans overlap? Why or why not? Is there any conflict with having two large agencies charged with protecting the homeland from an international and domestic perspective?

CHAPTER 13 PRACTICE PROBLEMS

1. What caused the formulization of a legislative body to govern the United States?

2. Explain the differences between the Democratic, Independent, and Republican parties and what ideologies existed, which was a need for separate political parties. Please be specific.

3. What is the purpose of the separation of powers?

4. What policy increased the responsibility of the Secretary of Defense and how did this affect DoD and U.S. military infrastructure?

5. Please explain differences between the roles of the National Security Advisor and the Secretary of Defense. What are some similar responsibilities?

6. Besides creating DHS, what was the purpose of the Homeland Security Act of 2002?

7. Are there any conflicts of interest between DoD and DHS initiatives? Why or why not?

8. What is the difference between foreign policy and foreign diplomacy?

9. What would be the consequence if the United States did not participate in international relation matters and did not establish multilateral agreements with foreign entities?

10. What are the differences between and overlapping responsibilities of DoD and DHS?

CHAPTER 14

The Future of National and Homeland Security

KEY TERMS

Artificial Intelligence (AI)

Counterintelligence

Cyber espionage

Cyber hacking

Internet of Things (IoT)

Orbital weaponry

Proliferation

Risk management

Security risk management

Transnational Organized Crime (ToC)

Weapons of mass destruction (WMDs)

LEARNING OBJECTIVES

After reading this chapter, students will be able to:

- Discuss the debate on the future of national and homeland security objectives in the twenty-first century
- Understand the evolution of security/risk management and top national security concerns
- Assess the United States' role in combating illicit occurrences and how to further promote globalization
- Evaluate America's position on sustaining global roles and maintaining relationships with coalition forces

THE DEBATE

As the evolution of global terrorism continues, government officials engage in debate on decision making over national security concerns. Currently, the nation's national security concerns are outlined in President Obama's 2015 *National Security Strategy (NSS)* and have yet to be updated by the new administration, which took over the White House in 2017. Scholars and experts suggest national security concerns remain the same, but it remains important to review threats and vulnerabilities that could impact the homeland and Americans. Economic strength and security are the foundation to national security objectives and affect the nation's alliances, coalition forces, and security partners.

As long-term wars ended in Afghanistan and Iraq, the United States and other Western countries faced the most dangerous and wealthiest terrorist organization in the world: ISIS. The group has controlled large portions of Iraq and Syria for more than a decade, and the demise of its operations is a major priority for the United States. Furthermore, ISIS has conducted highly skilled and strategic operations throughout the world, expanding violent extremism to a new high and expanding innovative forms of terrorism. In addition to traditional terrorism, agro-terrorism, bioterrorism, and cyber-terrorism have climbed the ladder of top national security concerns and pose major threats to global security. The debate is not necessarily identifying such concerns but having American leaders (civilian and military) agree on the order of importance and formulate short-term and long-term strategies, decision making, and implementation. As the global and dominant force, the United States must lead the world in the fight against global terrorism, enforce international security and peace, and urge universal laws to advance national security objectives, promote globalization, and most importantly, protect American citizens.

SECURITY RISKS AND ASSESSMENTS

Security risk management is the "identification, assessment and prioritization or risks followed by coordinated and economical application of resources to minimize, monitor, and control the probability and/or impact of unforeseen events" (Australian Government, 2016, para. 1). This is a thorough definition of what defines traditional risk matters in business, but can this same definition apply to risk management within security standards? The definition clearly identifies specific concepts that can apply to security management objectives and how to resolve these matters within federal agencies. As previously mentioned, definitions are the precursor to identify specific needs, but understanding the lexicon is the key to decision making. Understanding security management concepts is critical to managing risk to protect the American homeland.

Former Dept. of Homeland Security Secretary Janet Napolitano established an initiative for *Integrated Risk Management (IRM)* for DHS in May 2010. This risk-management model was established to effectively manage risks and vulnerabilities through the department alongside other federal, state, local, nongovernment organization (NGOs), private companies, and other external stakeholders that are invested into homeland security objectives for the United States. DHS is the primary agency responsible for identifying risks, threats, and vulnerabilities and implementing IRM to manage such concepts to protect the United States from "diverse and complex sets of hazards, including acts of terrorism, national and manmade disasters, pandemics, cyber attacks, and transnational crime" (DHS, 2011, para. 1).

The homeland security realm is very complex and predicated on primary national objectives. Understanding security risk management is important to providing safety and security measures along with establishing resilience to mitigate manmade and natural disasters. DHS is responsible for leading the nation in managing and understanding risk-management standards by utilizing innovative systems to handle dynamic functions for national security. Undertaking this matter is key to technological advancement for battling the nation's top security concerns as well as controlling the evolution of non-nation states' threats and the development of our alliances and security partners. Security risk management is based on:

- Identifying American security risks
- Approaches to risk management
- Decision making
- Homeland security principles
- Risk management applications and models
- Risk management processes
- Values

It is important to identify the security risks of the twenty-first century. The relevance of security risks to the United States will continue to expand as adversaries revolutionize their methods. America faces probable and realistic dangers, especially after the September 11 attacks in 2001, which increased modifications of how the federal government conducts business in the organizational and political structure. The main priorities are protecting the United States, its people, and its resources with the urgency of securing borders. After the 9/11 attacks, President George W. Bush passed legislation for the Office of Homeland Security and appointed its first secretarial position to run its operations in the White House. Soon President Bush established the Department of Homeland Security, a cabinet-level agency, responsible for all homeland security matters while creating accountability that mandated such responsibilities. On November 24, 2002, DHS was created and was the largest departmental reorganization since the National Security Act of 1947 restructured all service departments and intelligence agencies.

TOP NATIONAL SECURITY CONCERNS

Top national security concerns remain the same from President Obama's 2015 National Security Strategy and Director of National of Intelligence Daniel R. Coats 2017 *Statement for the Record: Worldwide Threat Assessment of the U.S. Intelligence Community.* As of 2017, these national security concerns remain a top priority. It is important that coalition forces agree which objectives are a high priority and how to mitigate such threats.

Global Threats

- Cyber threat
- Emerging and disruptive technologies
- Terrorism
- Weapons of mass destruction and proliferation
- Space and counter-space
- Counterintelligence
- Transnational organized crime
- Economics and natural resources
- Human security

Regional Threats

- East Asia
- Russia and Eurasia
- Europe
- Middle East and North Africa
- South Asia
- Sub-Saharan Africa
- Latin America and the Caribbean

Cyber Security and Technology

Chapter seven covered in-depth knowledge of cyber security measures to protect the United States from cyberterrorism. This section will discuss how modernization is the key to understanding information technology and how the Intelligence Community can use information sharing to make a significant impact on mitigating cyber threats. Federal agencies and the nation's military have developed innovative devices and increased technological advancements to deter threats that may affect American systems, resulting in major threats and vulnerabilities to critical infrastructures and U.S. government structures. Certain vulnerabilities such as smart devices can affect the nation's electrical grid system, energy program, and public transportation, destroying data privacy and integrity or continuity of services, also known as the **Internet of Things (IoT)**. This section will discuss all avenues of cyber concerns for the United States and how threats should be mitigated by the federal government.

Artificial Intelligence (AI) is the theoretical concept of developing computer systems to perform human responsibilities. For example, the United States is the lead country and one of fifty that are conducting computer science experiments concerning AI mechanisms that imitate human cognitive behavior, learning, and problem-solving functions. The concern with AI experiments is the fear of using robotic machines to perform militant duties in combat zones. Because many countries are investing millions of dollars into research, there is a possibility of hyper-intelligence functions that would allow militaries to use "artificial soldiers" to provide military duties. In addition, increased research can lead to cyber attacks because specific experiments can lead to major accidents, liability concerns, and the generation of advanced forms of weapons of mass destruction.

In the innovative world of electronics and smart data, companies heavily rely on technology to complete many operations and responsibilities. Even though the United States is leading in research, international countries are growing, and are dependent on, AI for decision-making procedures, which can increase global threats and vulnerabilities. Fabricated information, miscalculations, and unforeseen systems have caused substantial instabilities within the stock market because companies relied on financial software programs for trading. Furthermore, AI mechanisms are highly susceptible to manipulation and illusive tactics that would be especially dangerous if national networks and systems were affected.

International countries are increasing their research methods at a rapid pace and are openly purchasing American research along with collecting data from social media sites to develop their own work. Foreign data science developed through U.S.-supplied information produces susceptibility for the nation's original research programs that have been easily accessible through unclassified publications. Such processes will continue and increase over the next decade until international countries can produce systems and technology at affordable prices, causing this process to expand throughout the world. For example, *Augmented Reality (AR)* and *Virtual Reality (VR)* programs have been developed predicated on computer-generated images to view the real world through a multi-factorial view. Corresponding technology shows that AR and VR systems sell at a competitive price point and will increase over the next few years because mechanisms have first-rate communication apparatuses, decreasing the need for human interaction.

Technology like AI, AR, and VR are powerful inventions that significantly decrease the need for humans to complete tasks. Along with brilliant experiments comes the need for research facilities to emphasize veracity and implement policies that specifically deter the manipulation of data that comprises integrity. Sacrificing reliability to produce technology negatively impacts the decision-making process and mitigates the validity of networks and systems. Manipulation can cause disastrous affects to physical infrastructure and other critical facilities. Director Coats testified that continuing the research and production of AI through expansion of IoT can intensify the effects of these systems (2017). Protecting information and resources is crucial to sustaining networks and systems within the United States. Based on Director Clapper's testimony, protecting information resources includes the following:

- Identity
- Integrity
- Infrastructure
- Interoperability
- Restraint
- Accountability (Clapper, 2016, pp. 2–3).

The United States' main adversaries involving cyber hacking and cyber terrorism are China and Russia. As the second superpower, China continues to create tensions by successfully conducting cyber espionage operations against the United States and its allies (i.e. attacks on corporate infrastructure and IP hijacking in 2010 and the U.S. Office of Personnel Management hack in 2015). As a result, the United States is charged with monitoring China's compliance to prevent future cyber attacks against American networks and systems. In the interim, there is belief that China has attempted hacking activity against the United States, but rumors have not been verified as to the country's or its allies' involvement, nor whether China has committed such actions for profit. Intelligence suggests China's capital, Beijing, will continue to aim at the United States and its allies for cyber espionage purposes, but the bilateral agreement between the two countries has significantly decreased the attacks (i.e., the 2015 Chinese-US Cyber Agreements).

Russia has implemented **cyber hackings** (or cyber crime) against the United States and remains a significant threat toward the American government. The Russian government has developed a technologically advanced cyber offensive and over the past few years, has increased its offensive measures in an aggressive manner. Its methods were evident during the 2016 American presidential election when the FBI reported one of the computer systems owned by the Democratic National Committee had been hacked by a Russian cyber espionage team known as the Dukes, a group connected to the Russian government. The same hackers were responsible for hacking into federal unclassified systems of the White House, State Department, and the Joint Chiefs of Staff, which was one of the first indicators of Russia's attempt to influence a presidential election. Based on evidence, Russia initially conducted its hack as an information-gathering operation, which turned into a vendetta to affect Hillary Clinton's campaign and strengthen Donald Trump's position. In addition to the United States, Russia has executed large-scale cyber attacks in Eurasia and Europe, damaging critical infrastructure and interrupting networks by posing as third parties. Like China, Russia will continue cyber operations to gather information on the United States and its allies to benefit Russian political and military objectives.

In addition, research and evidence suggests Iran and North Korea are cyber hackers, targeting the United States and its allies. Iran's capital, Tehran, is known to conduct **cyber espionage** (using advanced technical, Internet, and virtual methods to spy on other countries) operations and has targeted the United States and security partners to support its counteroffensive strategies and security interests (i.e. 2013 U.S. hack and

2014 network intrusion of an American casino). North Korea is known for the infamous hack of Sony Pictures Entertainment in which hacker group Guardians of Peace released sensitive employee information, including information on their families, e-mails, salaries, and unreleased films.

Finally, criminals and terrorists are known for relying on the Internet and social media to cement platforms on their ideologies, political agendas, propaganda, and recruitment. More sophisticated than ever, criminals are creating advanced cyber programs to support illegal activities. The last innovative software, ransomware, is used to block users from accessing their own data through deception and encryption and has been expended to disrupt medical institutions. Terrorist organizations such as Hamas, Hezbollah, and ISIS use the Internet and social media to further terrorist goals. In 2015, ISIS was responsible for the release of personal information on U.S. military personnel and a hit list as a threat to instill fear in military families and the American public.

Genome Editing

Genome editing, or genetic engineering to change the DNA of cells or organisms, is one of the most significant developing research fields within the United States and continues to increase, with the emphasis on agricultural, biological, environmental, health, and medical matters. Because of the challenges in establishing fair policies and initiatives on genome editing, the continued development can possibly be delayed, as applications are likely to accrue ethical and regulatory concerns. Finally, among the top security concerns on the American government list is the continued research and development of next-generation semiconductors. According to author Michael Siyang Li in "Keeping Up with Moore's Law" in the *Dartmouth Undergraduate Journal of Science*, when semiconductors were established, the integrated circuits significantly decreased the space between transistors and developed efficiency for computer and power systems (2013).

The following section is President Barack Obama's 2015 National Security Strategy, and the top national security concerns are explained in depth as to why these elements are concerns and how the United States will deal with them.

2015 NATIONAL SECURITY STRATEGY: PRESIDENT BARACK OBAMA

The United States government has no greater responsibility than protecting the American people, yet our obligations do not end at our borders. We embrace our responsibilities for underwriting international security because it serves our interests, upholds our commitments to allies and partners, and addresses threats that are truly global. There is no substitute for American leadership whether in the face of aggression, in the cause of universal values, or in the service of a more secure America. Fulfilling our responsibilities depends on a strong defense and secure homeland. It also requires a global security posture in which our unique capabilities are employed within diverse international coalitions and in support of local partners. Such a shift is possible after a period of prolonged combat. Six years ago, there were roughly 180,000 U.S. troops in Iraq and Afghanistan. Today, there are fewer than 15,000. This transition has dramatically reduced U.S. casualties and allows us to realign our forces and resources to meet an evolving set of threats while securing our strategic objectives. In so doing, we will prioritize collective action to meet the persistent threat posed by terrorism today, especially from al-Qa'ida, ISIL, and their affiliates. In addition to acting decisively to defeat direct threats, we will focus on building the capacity of others to prevent the causes and consequences of conflict to include countering extreme and dangerous ideologies. Keeping nuclear materials from terrorists and preventing the proliferation of nuclear weapons remains a high priority, as does mobilizing the international community to meet the urgent challenges posed by climate change and infectious disease. Collective action is needed to assure access to the shared spaces—cyber, space, air, and oceans—where the dangerous behaviors of some threaten us all. Our allies will remain central to all these efforts. The North Atlantic Treaty Organization (NATO) is the world's preeminent multilateral alliance, reinforced by the historic close ties we have with the United Kingdom, France, Germany, Italy, and Canada. NATO is stronger and more cohesive than at any point in its history, especially due to contributions of the Nordic countries and newer members like Poland and the Baltic countries. Our alliances in Asia underwrite security and enable prosperity throughout Asia and the Pacific. We will continue to modernize these essential bilateral alliances while enhancing the security ties among our allies. Japan, South Korea, and Australia, as well as our close partner in New Zealand, remain the model for interoperability while we reinvigorate our ties to the Philippines and preserve our ties to Thailand. And our allies and partners in other regions, including our security partnership and people-to-people ties with Israel, are essential to advancing our interests.

Strengthen Our National Defense

A strong military is the bedrock of our national security. During over a decade of war, the all-volunteer force has answered our nation's call. To maintain our military edge and readiness, we will continue to insist on reforms and necessary investment in our military

The White House, "National Security Strategy." 2015.

forces and their families. Our military will remain ready to deter and defeat threats to the homeland, including against missile, cyber, and terrorist attacks, while mitigating the effects of potential attacks and natural disasters. Our military is postured globally to protect our citizens and interests, preserve regional stability, render humanitarian assistance and disaster relief, and build the capacity of our partners to join with us in meeting security challenges.

U.S. forces will continue to defend the homeland, conduct global counterterrorism operations, assure allies, and deter aggression through forward presence and engagement. If deterrence fails, U.S. forces will be ready to project power globally to defeat and deny aggression in multiple theaters. As we modernize, we will apply the lessons of past draw-downs. Although our military will be smaller, it must remain dominant in every domain. With the Congress, we must end sequestration and enact critical reforms to build a versatile and responsive force prepared for a more diverse set of contingencies. We will protect our investment in foundational capabilities like the nuclear deterrent, and we will grow our investment in crucial capabilities like cyber and space intelligence and surveillance, and reconnaissance. We will safeguard our science and technology base to keep our edge in the capabilities needed to prevail against any adversary. Above all, we will take care of our people.

We will recruit and retain the best talent while developing leaders committed to an ethical and expert profession of arms. We will honor our sacred trust with veterans and the families and communities that support them, making sure those who have served have the benefits, education, and opportunities they have earned. We will be principled and selective in the use of force. The use of force should not be our first choice, but it will sometimes be the necessary choice. The United States will use military force, unilaterally if necessary, when our enduring interests demand it: when our people are threatened, when our livelihoods are at stake, and when the security of our allies is in danger. In these circumstances, we prefer to act with allies and partners. The threshold for military action is higher when our interests are not directly threatened. In such cases, we will seek to mobilize allies and partners to share the burden and achieve lasting outcomes. In all cases, the decision to use force must reflect a clear mandate and feasible objectives, and we must ensure our actions are effective, just, and consistent with the rule of law. It should be based on a serious appreciation for the risk to our mission, our global responsibilities, and the opportunity costs at home and abroad. Whenever and wherever we use force, we will do so in a way that reflects our values and strengthens our legitimacy.

Reinforce Homeland Security

Our homeland is more secure. But, we must continue to learn and adapt to evolving threats and hazards. We are better able to guard against terrorism—the core responsibility of homeland security—as well as illicit networks and other threats and hazards due to improved information sharing, aviation and border security, and international cooperation. We have emphasized community-based efforts and local law enforcement programs to counter homegrown violent extremism and protect vulnerable individuals from extremist ideologies that could lead them to join conflicts overseas or carry out attacks here at home. Through risk-based approaches, we have countered terrorism and transnational organized crime in ways that enhance commerce, travel, and tourism and, most fundamentally, preserve our civil liberties. We are more responsive and resilient when prevention fails or disaster strikes as witnessed with the Boston Marathon bombings and Hurricane Sandy. The essential services that underpin American society must remain secure and functioning in the face of diverse threats and hazards. Therefore, we take a Whole of Community approach, bringing together all elements of our society—individuals, local communities, the private- and nonprofit sectors, faith-based organizations, and all levels of government—to make sure America is resilient in the face of adversity.

We are working with the owners and operators of our Nation's critical cyber and physical infrastructure across every sector—financial, energy, transportation, health, information technology, and more—to decrease vulnerabilities and increase resilience. We are partnering with states and local communities to better plan for, absorb, recover from, and adapt to adverse events brought about by the compounding effects of climate change. We will also continue to enhance pandemic preparedness at home and address the threat arising from new drug-resistant microbes and biological agents.

Combat the Persistent Threat of Terrorism

The threat of catastrophic attacks against our homeland by terrorists has diminished but persists. An array of terrorist threats has gained traction in areas of instability, limited opportunity, and broken governance. Our adversaries are not confined to a distinct country or region. Instead, they range from South Asia through the Middle East and into Africa. They include globally oriented groups like al-Qa'ida and its affiliates, as well as a growing number of regionally focused and globally connected groups—many with an al-Qa'ida pedigree like ISIL, which could pose a threat to the homeland. We have drawn from the experience of the last decade and put in place substantial changes to our efforts to combat terrorism, while preserving and strengthening important tools that have been developed since 9/11. Specifically, we shifted away from a model of fighting costly, large-scale ground wars in Iraq and Afghanistan in which the United States—particularly our military—bore an enormous burden. Instead, we are now pursuing a more sustainable approach that prioritizes targeted counterterrorism operations, collective action with responsible partners, and increased efforts to prevent the growth of violent extremism and radicalization that drives increased threats. Our leadership will remain essential to disrupting the unprecedented flow of foreign terrorist fighters to and from conflict zones. We will work to address the underlying conditions that can help foster violent extremism such as poverty, inequality, and repression. This means supporting alternatives to extremist messaging and greater economic opportunities for women and disaffected youth. We will help build the capacity of the most vulnerable states and communities to defeat terrorists locally. Working with Congress, we will train and equip local partners and provide operational support to gain ground against terrorist groups. This will include efforts to better fuse and share information and technology as well as to support more inclusive and accountable governance. In all our efforts, we aim to draw a stark contrast between what we stand for and the heinous deeds of terrorists.

We reject the lie that America and its allies are at war with Islam. We will continue to act lawfully. Outside of areas of active hostilities, we endeavor to detain, interrogate, and prosecute terrorists through law enforcement. However, when there is a continuing, imminent threat, and when capture or other actions to disrupt the threat are not feasible, we will not hesitate to take decisive action. We will always do so legally, discriminately, proportionally, and bound by strict accountability and strong oversight. The United States—not our adversaries—will define the nature and scope of this struggle, lest it define us.

Our counterterrorism approach is at work with several states, including Somalia, Afghanistan and Iraq. In Afghanistan, we have ended our combat mission and transitioned to a dramatically smaller force focused on the goal of a sovereign and stable partner in Afghanistan that is not a haven for international terrorists. This has been made possible by the extraordinary sacrifices of our U.S. military, civilians throughout the interagency, and our international partners. They delivered justice to Osama bin Laden and significantly degraded al-Qa'ida's core leadership. They helped increase life expectancy, access to education, and opportunities for women and girls. Going forward, we will work with partners to carry out a limited counterterrorism mission against the remnants of core al-Qa'ida and maintain our support to the Afghan National Security Forces (ANSF). We are working with NATO and our other partners to train, advise, and assist the ANSF as a new government takes responsibility for the security and well-being of Afghanistan's citizens. We will continue to help improve governance that expands opportunity for all Afghans, including women and girls.

We will also work with the countries of the region, including Pakistan, to mitigate the threat from terrorism and to support a viable peace and reconciliation process to end the violence in Afghanistan and improve regional stability. We have undertaken a comprehensive effort to degrade and ultimately defeat ISIL. We will continue to support Iraq as it seeks to free itself from sectarian conflict and the scourge of extremists. Our support is tied to the government's willingness to govern effectively and inclusively and to ensure ISIL cannot sustain a haven on Iraqi territory. This requires professional and accountable Iraqi Security Forces that can overcome sectarian divides and protect all Iraqi citizens. It also requires international support, which is why we are leading an unprecedented international coalition to work with the Iraqi government and strengthen its military to regain sovereignty. Joined by our allies and partners, including multiple countries in the region, we employed our unique military capabilities to arrest ISIL's advance and to degrade their capabilities in both Iraq and Syria. At the same time, we are working with our partners to train and equip a moderate Syrian opposition to provide a counterweight to the terrorists and the brutality of the Assad regime. Yet, the only lasting solution to Syria's civil war remains political—an inclusive political transition that responds to the legitimate aspirations of all Syrian citizens.

Build Capacity to Prevent Conflict

We will strengthen U.S. and international capacity to prevent conflict among and within states. In the realm of inter-state conflict, Russia's violation of Ukraine's sovereignty and territorial integrity—as well as its belligerent stance toward other neighboring countries—endangers international norms that have largely been taken for granted since the end of the Cold War. Meanwhile, North Korean provocation and tensions in the East and South China seas are reminders of the risks of escalation.

American diplomacy and leadership, backed by a strong military, remain essential to deterring future acts of inter-state aggression and provocation by reaffirming our security commitments to allies and partners, investing in their capabilities to withstand coercion, imposing costs on those who threaten their neighbors or violate fundamental international norms, and embedding our actions within wider regional strategies. Within states, the nexus of weak governance and widespread grievance allows extremism to take root, violent non-state actors to rise, and conflict to overtake state structures. To meet these challenges, we will continue to work with partners and through multilateral organizations to address the root causes of conflict before they erupt, and to contain and resolve them when they do. We prefer to partner with those fragile states that have a genuine political commitment to establishing legitimate governance and providing for their people. The focus of our efforts will be on proven areas of need and impact, such as inclusive politics, enabling effective and equitable service delivery, reforming security and rule of law sectors, combating corruption and organized crime, and promoting economic opportunity, particularly among youth and women. We will continue to lead the effort to ensure women serve as mediators of conflict and in peace-building efforts, and they are protected from gender-based violence. We will continue to bolster the capacity of the U.N. and regional organizations to help resolve disputes, build resilience to crises and shocks, strengthen governance, end extreme poverty, and increase prosperity, so that fragile states can provide for the basic needs of their citizens and can avoid being vulnerable hosts for extremism and terrorism. We will meet our financial commitments to the U.N., press for reforms to strengthen peacekeeping, and encourage more contributions from advanced militaries. We will strengthen the operational capacity of regional organizations like the African Union (AU) and broaden the ranks of capable troop-contributing countries, including through the African Peacekeeping Rapid Response Partnership, which will help African countries rapidly deploy to emerging crises.

Prevent the Spread and Use of Weapons of Mass Destruction

No threat poses as grave a danger to our security and well-being as the potential use of nuclear weapons and materials by irresponsible states or terrorists. We therefore seek the peace and security of a world without nuclear weapons. If nuclear weapons exist, the United States must invest the resources necessary to maintain—without testing—a safe, secure, and effective nuclear deterrent that preserves strategic stability. However, reducing the threat requires us to constantly reinforce the basic bargain of the Nuclear Non-Proliferation Treaty, which commits nuclear weapons states to reduce their stockpiles while non-nuclear weapons states remain committed to using nuclear energy only for peaceful purposes.

For our part, we are reducing the role and number of nuclear weapons through New START and our own strategy. We will continue to push for the entry into force of important multilateral agreements like the Comprehensive Nuclear Test-Ban Treaty and the various regional nuclear weapons-free zone protocols, as well as the creation of a Fissile Material Cut-Off Treaty. Vigilance is required to stop countries and non-state actors from developing or acquiring nuclear, chemical, or biological weapons, or the materials to build them. The Nuclear Security Summit process has catalyzed a global effort to lock down vulnerable nuclear materials and institutionalize nuclear security best practices. Our commitment to the denuclearization of the Korean peninsula is rooted in the profound risks posed by North Korean weapons development and proliferation. Our efforts to remove and destroy chemical weapons in Libya and Syria reflect our leadership in implementation and progress toward universalization of the Chemical Weapons Convention. We have made clear Iran must meet its international obligations and demonstrate its nuclear program is entirely peaceful. Our sanctions regime has demonstrated that the international community can—and will—hold accountable those nations that do not meet their obligations, while also opening a space for a diplomatic resolution. Having reached a first step arrangement that stops the progress of Iran's nuclear program in exchange for limited relief, our preference is to achieve a comprehensive and verifiable deal that assures Iran's nuclear program is solely for peaceful purposes. This is the best way to advance our interests, strengthen the global nonproliferation regime, and enable Iran to access peaceful nuclear energy. However, we retain all options to achieve the objective of preventing Iran from producing a nuclear weapon.

Confront Climate Change

Climate change is an urgent and growing threat to our national security, contributing to increased natural disasters, refugee flows, and conflicts over basic resources like food and water. The present-day effects of climate change are being felt from the Arctic to the Midwest. Increased sea levels and storm surges threaten coastal regions, infrastructure, and property. In turn, the global economy suffers, compounding the growing costs of preparing and restoring infrastructure. America is leading efforts at home and with the international community to confront this challenge. Over the past six years, U.S. emissions have declined by a larger total magnitude than those of any other country. Through our Climate Action Plan and related executive actions, we will go further with a goal of reducing greenhouse gas emissions by 26 to 28 percent of 2005 levels by 2025. Working with U.S. states and private utilities, we will set the first-ever standards to cut the amount of carbon pollution our power plants emit into the air. We are also working to strengthen resilience and address vulnerabilities to climate impacts. These domestic efforts contribute to our international leadership. Building on the progress made in Copenhagen and in ensuing negotiations, we are working toward an ambitious new global climate change agreement to shape standards for prevention, preparedness, and response over the next decade. As the world's two largest emitters, the United States and China reached a landmark agreement to take significant action to reduce carbon pollution. The substantial contribution we have pledged to the Green Climate Fund will help the most vulnerable developing nations deal with climate change, reduce their carbon pollution, and invest in clean energy. More than 100 countries have joined with us to reduce greenhouse gases under the Montreal Protocol—the same agreement the world used successfully to phase out ozone-depleting chemicals. We are partnering with African entrepreneurs to launch clean energy projects and helping farmers practice climate-smart agriculture and plant more durable crops. We are also driving collective action to reduce methane emissions from pipelines and to launch a free trade agreement for environmental goods.

Ensure Access to Shared Spaces

The world is connected by shared spaces—cyber, space, air, and oceans—that enable the free flow of people, goods, services, and ideas. They are the arteries of the global economy and civil society, and access is at risk due to increased competition and provocative behaviors. Therefore, we will continue to promote rules for responsible behavior while making sure we have the capabilities to assure access to these shared spaces.

As the birthplace of the Internet, the United States has a special responsibility to lead a networked world. Prosperity and security increasingly depend on an open, interoperable, secure, and reliable Internet. Our economy, safety, and health are linked through a networked infrastructure that is targeted by malicious government, criminal, and individual actors who try to avoid attribution. Drawing on the voluntary cyber security framework, we are securing Federal networks and working with the private sector, civil society, and other stakeholders to strengthen the security and resilience of U.S. critical infrastructure will continue to work with the Congress to pursue a legislative framework that ensures high standards. We will defend ourselves, consistent with U.S. and international law, against cyber attacks and impose costs on malicious cyber actors, including through prosecution of illegal cyber activity. We will assist other countries to develop laws that enable strong action against threats that originate from their infrastructure. Globally, cyber security requires that long-standing norms of international behavior—to include protection of intellectual property, online freedom, and respect for civilian infrastructure—be upheld, and the Internet be managed as a shared responsibility between states and the private sector with civil society and Internet users as key stakeholders.

Space Security

Space systems allow the world to navigate and communicate with confidence to save lives, conduct commerce, and better understand humanity, our planet, and the depths of the universe. As countries increasingly derive benefits from space, we must together to deal with threats posed by those who may wish to deny the peaceful use of outer space. We are expanding our international space cooperation activities in all sectors, promoting transparency and confidence-building measures such as an International Code of Conduct on Outer Space Activities, and expanding partnerships with the private sector in support of missions and capabilities previously claimed by governments alone. We will also develop technologies and tactics to deter and defeat efforts to attack our space systems; enable indications, warning, and attributions of such attacks; and enhance the resiliency of critical U.S. space capabilities.

Air and Maritime Security

The United States has an enduring interest in freedom of navigation and overflight as well as the safety and sustainability of the air and maritime environments. We will therefore maintain the capability to ensure the free flow of commerce, to respond quickly to those in need, and to deter those who might contemplate aggression. We insist on safe and responsible behaviors in the sky and at sea. We reject illegal and aggressive claims to airspace and in the maritime domain and condemn deliberate attacks on commercial passenger traffic. On territorial disputes, particularly in Asia, we denounce coercion and assertive behaviors that threaten escalation. We encourage open channels of dialogue to resolve disputes peacefully in accordance with international law. We also support the early conclusion of an effective code of conduct for the South China Sea between China and the Association of Southeast Asian States (ASEAN). America's ability to press for the observance of established customary international law reflected in the U.N. Convention on the Law of the Sea will be enhanced if the Senate provides its advice and consent—the ongoing failure to ratify this Treaty undermines our national interest in a rules-based international order. Finally, we seek to build on the unprecedented international cooperation of the last few years, especially in the Arctic as well as in combating piracy off the Horn of Africa and drug smuggling in the Caribbean Sea and across Southeast Asia.

Increase Global Health Security

The spread of infectious diseases constitutes a growing risk. The Ebola epidemic in West Africa highlights the danger of a raging virus. The spread of new microbes or viruses, the rise and spread of drug-resistant viruses, and the deliberate release of pathogens all represent threats that are exacerbated by the globalization of travel, food production and supply, and medical products. Despite important scientific, technological, and organizational accomplishments, most countries have not yet achieved international core competencies for health security, and many lack sufficient capacity to prevent, detect, or respond to disease outbreaks. America is the world leader in fighting pandemics, including HIV/AIDS, and in improving global health security. At home, we are strengthening our ability to prevent outbreaks and ensure sufficient capacity to respond rapidly and manage biological incidents. As an exemplar of a modern and responsive public health system, we will accelerate our work with partners through the Global Health Security Agenda in pursuit of a world that is safer and more secure from infectious disease. We will save lives by strengthening regulatory frameworks for food safety and developing a global system to prevent avoidable epidemics, detect and report disease outbreaks in real time, and respond more rapidly and effectively. Finally, we will continue to lead efforts to combat the rise of antibiotic resistant bacteria.

Prosperity

Our economy is the largest, most open, and innovative in the world. Our leadership has also helped usher in a new era of unparalleled global prosperity. Sustaining our leadership depends on shaping an emerging global economic order that continues to reflect our interests and values. Despite its success, our rules-based system is now competing against alternative, less-open models. Moreover, the American consumer cannot sustain global demand—growth must be more balanced. To meet this challenge, we must be strategic in the use of our economic strength to set new rules of the road, strengthen our partnerships, and promote inclusive development. Through our trade and investment policies, we will shape globalization so that it is working for American workers. By leveraging our improved economic and energy position, we will strengthen the global financial system and advance high-standard trade deals. We will ensure tomorrow's global trading system is consistent with our interests and values by seeking to establish and enforce rules through international institutions and regional initiatives and by addressing emerging challenges, such as state-owned enterprises and digital protectionism. U.S. markets and educational opportunities will help the next generation of global entrepreneurs sustain momentum in growing a global middle class. To prevent conflict and promote human dignity, we will also pursue policies that eradicate extreme poverty and reduce inequality.

Put Our Economy to Work

The American economy is an engine for global economic growth and a source of stability for the international system. In addition to being a key measure of power and influence, it underwrites our military strength and diplomatic influence. A strong economy, combined with a prominent U.S. presence in the global financial system, creates opportunities to advance our security. To ensure our economic competitiveness, we are investing in a new foundation for sustained economic growth that creates good jobs and rising incomes. Because knowledge is the currency of today's global economy, we must keep expanding access to early childhood and affordable higher education. The further acceleration of our manufacturing revolution will create the next generation of high technology manufacturing jobs. Immigration reform that combines smart and effective enforcement of the law with a pathway to citizenship for those who earn it remains an imperative. We will deliver quality, affordable healthcare to more and more Americans. We will also support job creation, strengthen the middle class, and spur economic growth by opening markets and leveling the playing field for American workers and businesses abroad. Jobs will also grow as we expand our work with trading partners to eliminate barriers to the full deployment of U.S. innovation in the digital space. These efforts are complemented by more modern and reliable infrastructure that ensures safety and enables growth. In addition to the positive benefits of trade and commerce, a strong and well-regulated economy positions the United States to lead international efforts to promote financial transparency and prevent the global financial system from being abused by transnational criminal and terrorist organizations to engage in, or launder the proceeds of illegal activity. We will continue to work within the Financial Action Task

Force, the G-20, and other fora to enlist all nations in the fight to protect the integrity of the global financial system.

Advance Our Energy Security

The United States is now the world leader in oil and gas production. America's energy revival is not only good for growth, it offers new buffers against the coercive use of energy by some and new opportunities for helping others transition to low-carbon economies. American oil production has increased dramatically, impacting global markets. Imports have decreased substantially, reducing the funds we send overseas. Consumption has declined, reducing our vulnerability to global supply disruption and price shocks. However, we still have a significant stake in the energy security of our allies in Europe and elsewhere. Seismic shifts in supply and demand are underway across the globe. Increasing global access to reliable and affordable energy is one of the most powerful ways to support social and economic development and to help build new markets for U.S. technology and investment. The challenges faced by Ukrainian and European dependence on Russian energy supplies puts a spotlight on the need for an expanded view of energy security that recognizes the collective needs of the United States, our allies, and trading partners as well as the importance of competitive energy markets. Therefore, we must promote diversification of energy fuels, sources, and routes, as well as encourage indigenous sources of energy supply. Greater energy security and independence within the Americas is central to these efforts. We will also stay engaged with global suppliers and our partners to reduce the potential for energy-related conflict in places like the Arctic and Asia. Our energy security will be further enhanced by living up to commitments made in the Rome Declaration and through our all-of-the-above energy strategy for a low-carbon world. We will continue to develop American fossil resources while becoming a more efficient country that develops cleaner, alternative fuels and vehicles. We are demonstrating that America can and will lead the global economy while reducing our emissions.

Lead in Science, Technology, and Innovation

Scientific discovery and technological innovation empower American leadership with a competitive edge that secures our military advantage, propels our economy, and improves the human condition. Sustaining that edge requires robust Federal investments in basic and applied research. We must also strengthen science, technology, engineering, and mathematics (STEM) education to produce tomorrow's discoverers, inventors, entrepreneurs, and high-skills workforce. Our commitment remains strong to preparation and compensation for STEM teachers, broadband connectivity and high-tech educational tools for schools, programs that inspire and provide opportunities for girls and underrepresented minorities, and support for innovation in STEM teaching and inclusion in higher education. We will also keep our edge by opening our national labs to more commercial partnerships while tapping research and development in the private sector, including a wide range of start-ups and firms at the leading edge of America's innovation economy.

Shape the Global Economic Order

We have recovered from the global economic crisis, but much remains to be done to shape the emerging economic order to avoid future crises. We have responsibilities at home to continue to improve our banking practices and forge ahead with regulatory reform, even as we press others to align with our robust standards. In addition to securing our immediate economic interests, we must drive the inclusive economic growth that creates demand for American exports. We will protect the free movement of information and work to prevent the risky behavior that led to the recent crisis, while addressing resurgent economic forces, from state capitalism to market-distorting free-riding. American leadership is central to strengthening global finance rules and making sure they are consistent and transparent. We will work with the G-20 to reinforce the core architecture of the international financial and economic system, including the World Trade Organization, to ensure it is positioned to foster both stability and growth. We remain committed to governance reforms for these same institutions, including the World Bank and the International Monetary Fund, to make them more effective and representative. In so doing, we seek to ensure institutions reinforce, rather than undermine, an effective global financial system. We believe trade agreements have economic and strategic benefits for the United States. We will therefore work with the Congress to achieve bipartisan renewal of Trade Promotion Authority and to advance a trade agenda that brings jobs to our shores, increases standards of living, strengthens our partners and allies, and promotes stability in critical regions. The United States has one of the most open economies in the world. Our tariffs are low, and we do not use regulation to discriminate against foreign goods. The same is not true throughout the world, which is why our trade agenda is focused on lowering tariffs on American products, breaking down barriers to our goods and services, and setting higher standards to level the playing field for American workers and firms. Through the Trans-Pacific Partnership (TPP) and Transatlantic Trade and Investment Partnership (T-TIP), we are setting the world's highest standards for labor rights and environmental protection, while removing barriers to U.S. exports and putting the United States at the center of a free trade zone covering two-thirds of the global economy. Our goal is to use this position, along with our highly skilled workforce, strong rule of law, and abundant supply of affordable energy, to make America the production platform of choice and the premier investment destination. In addition to these major regional agreements, we will work to achieve groundbreaking agreements to liberalize trade in services, information technology, and environmental goods—areas where the United States is a global leader in innovation. And we will make it easier for businesses of all sizes to expand their reach by improving supply chains and regulatory cooperation. All countries will benefit when we open markets further, extend and enhance tools such as the African Growth and Opportunity Act (AGOA), and reduce inefficiencies in the global trading system through trade facilitation improvements. And through our development initiatives—such as Power Africa, Trade Africa, Feed the Future, and the Open Government Partnership—we will continue to work closely with governments, the private sector, and civil society to foster inclusive economic growth, reduce corruption, and build capacity at the local level. Investment in critical infrastructure and security will facilitate trade among countries, especially for developing and emerging economies.

End Extreme Poverty

We have an historic opportunity to end extreme poverty within a generation and put our societies on a path of shared and sustained prosperity. In so doing, we will foster export markets for U.S. businesses, improve investment opportunities, and decrease the need for costly military interventions. Growth in the global economy has lifted hundreds of millions out of extreme poverty. We have already made significant progress guided in part through global consensus and mobilization around the Millennium Development Goals. The world cut the percentage of people living in extreme poverty in half between 1990 and 2010. In that period, nearly 800 million people rose above the international poverty line. By 2012, childhood mortality decreased almost 50 percent since 1990. Twenty-nine countries registered as low income in 2000 have today achieved middle-income status, and private capital and domestic resources far outstrip donor assistance as the primary means for financing development. Trends in economic growth also signal what is possible; sub-Saharan Africa has averaged an aggregate annual growth rate of more than five percent for the past decade despite the disruptions of the world financial crisis. We are now working with many partners to put ending extreme poverty at the center of a new global sustainable development agenda that will mobilize action for the next fifteen years. We will press for transformative investments in areas like women's equality and empowerment, education, sustainable energy, and governance. We will use trade and investment to harness job-rich economic growth. We will concentrate on the clear need for country ownership and political commitment and reinforce the linkage between social and economic development. We will lead the effort to marshal diverse resources and broad coalitions to advance the imperative of accountable, democratic governance. We will use our leadership to promote a model of financing that leverages billions in investment from the private sector and draws on America's scientific, technological, and entrepreneurial strengths to take to scale proven solutions in partnership with governments, business, and civil society. And we will leverage our leadership in promoting food security, enhancing resilience, modernizing rural agriculture, reducing the vulnerability of the poor, and eliminating preventable child and maternal deaths as we drive progress toward an AIDS-free generation.

Values

To lead effectively in a world experiencing significant political change, the United States must live our values at home while promoting universal values abroad. From the Middle East to Ukraine to Southeast Asia to the Americas, citizens are more empowered in seeking greater freedoms and accountable institutions. But these demands have often produced an equal and opposite reaction from backers of discredited authoritarian orders, resulting in crackdowns and conflict. Many of the threats to our security in recent years arose from efforts by authoritarian states to oppose democratic forces—from the crisis caused by Russian aggression in Ukraine to the rise of ISIL within the Syrian civil war. By the same token, many of our greatest opportunities stem from advances for liberty and rule of law—from sub-Saharan Africa to Eastern Europe to Burma. Defending democracy and human rights is related to every enduring national interest. It aligns us with the aspirations of ordinary people throughout the world. We know from our own history people must lead their own struggles for freedom if those struggles are to succeed. But America is also uniquely situated—and routinely expected—to support peaceful democratic change. We will continue mobilizing international support to strengthen and expand global norms of human rights. We will support women, youth, civil society, journalists, and entrepreneurs as drivers of change. We will continue to insist that governments uphold their human rights obligations, speak out against repression wherever it occurs, and work to prevent, and, if necessary, respond to mass atrocities. Our closest allies in these efforts will be, as they always have, other democratic states. But, even where our strategic interests require us to engage governments that do not share all our values, we will continue to speak out clearly for human rights and human dignity in our public and private diplomacy. Any support we might provide will be balanced with an awareness of the costs of repressive policies for our own security interests and the democratic values by which we live. Because our human rights advocacy will be most effective when we work in concert with a wide range of partners, we are building coalitions with civil society, religious leaders, businesses, other governments, and international organizations. We will also work to ensure people enjoy the same rights—and security—online as they are entitled to enjoy offline by opposing efforts to restrict information and punish speech.

Live Our Values

Our values are a source of strength and security, and our ability to promote our values abroad is directly tied to our willingness to abide by them at home. In recent years, questions about America's post-9/11 security policies have often been exploited by our adversaries, while testing our commitment to civil liberties and the rule of law at home. For the sake of our security and our leadership in the world, it is essential we hold ourselves to the highest possible standard, even as we do what is necessary to secure our people. To that end, we strengthened our commitment against torture and have prohibited so-called enhanced interrogation techniques that were contrary to American values, while implementing stronger safeguards for the humane treatment of detainees. We have transferred many detainees from Guantanamo Bay, and we are working with the Congress to remove the remaining restrictions on detainee transfers so that we can finally close it. Where prosecution is an option, we will bring terrorists to justice through both civilian and, when appropriate, reformed military commission proceedings that incorporate fundamental due process and other protections essential to the effective administration of justice. Our vital intelligence activities are also being reformed to preserve the capabilities needed to secure our interests while continuing to respect privacy and curb the potential for abuse. We are increasing transparency so the public can be confident our surveillance activities are consistent with the rule of law and governed by effective oversight. We have not and will not collect signals intelligence to suppress criticism or dissent or to afford a competitive advantage to U.S. companies. Safeguards currently in place governing how we retain and share intelligence are being extended to protect personal information, regardless of nationality.

Advance Equality

American values are reflective of the universal values we champion all around the world—including the freedoms of speech, worship, and peaceful assembly; the ability to choose leaders democratically; and the right to due process and equal administration of justice. We will be a champion for communities that are too frequently vulnerable to violence, abuse, and neglect—such as ethnic and religious minorities; people with disabilities; lesbian, gay, bisexual, and transgender (LGBT) individuals; displaced persons; and migrant workers. Recognizing that no society will succeed if it does not draw on the potential of all its people, we are pressing for the political and economic participation of women and girls—who are too often denied their inalienable rights and face substantial barriers to opportunity in too many places. Our efforts include helping girls everywhere get the education they need to participate fully in the economy and realize their potential. We are focused on reducing the scourge of violence against women around the globe by providing support for affected populations and enhancing efforts to improve judicial systems so perpetrators are held accountable.

Support Emerging Democracies

The United States will concentrate attention and resources to help countries consolidate their gains and move toward more democratic and representative systems of governance. Our focus is on supporting countries that are moving in the right direction—whether it is the peaceful transitions of power we see in sub-Saharan Africa; the movement toward constitutional democracy in Tunisia; or the opening taking place in Burma. In each instance, we are creating incentives for positive reform and disincentives for backsliding. The road from demanding rights in the square to building institutions that guarantee them is long and hard. In the last quarter century, parts of Eastern Europe, Latin America, Africa, and East Asia have consolidated transitions to democracy, but not without setbacks. The popular uprisings that began in the Arab world took place in a region with weaker democratic traditions, powerful authoritarian elites, sectarian tensions, and active violent extremist elements, so it is not surprising setbacks have thus far outnumbered triumphs. Yet, change is inevitable in the Middle East and North Africa, as it is in all places where the illusion of stability is artificially maintained by silencing dissent but the direction of that change is not predetermined. We will therefore continue to look for ways to support the success and ease the difficulties of democratic transitions through responsible assistance, investment and trade, and by supporting political, economic, and security reforms. We will continue to push for reforms in authoritarian countries not currently undergoing wholesale transitions.

Good governance is also predicated on strengthening the state-society relationship. When citizens have a voice in the decision-making that affects them, governments make better decisions and citizens are better able to participate, innovate, and contribute. The corrosive effects of corruption must be overcome. While information sharing allows us to identify corrupt officials more easily, globalization has also made it easier for corrupt officials to hide the proceeds of corruption abroad, increasing the need for strong and consistent implementation of the international standards on combating illicit finance. The United States is leading the way in promoting adherence to standards of accountable and transparent governance, including through initiatives like the Open Government Partnership. We will utilize a broad range of tools to recover assets stolen by corrupt officials and make it harder for criminals to hide, launder, and benefit from illegal proceeds. Our leadership toward governance that is more open, responsible, and accountable makes clear that democracy can deliver better government and development for ordinary people.

Empower Civil Society and Young Leaders

Democracy depends on more than elections, or even government institutions. Through civil society, citizens come together to hold their leaders accountable and address challenges. Civil society organizations often drive innovations and develop new ideas and approaches to solve social, economic, and political problems that governments can apply on a larger scale. Moreover, by giving people peaceful avenues to advance their interests and express their convictions, a free and flourishing civil society contributes to stability and helps to counter violent extremism. Still, civil society and individual activists face challenges in many parts of the world. As technology empowers individuals and nongovernmental groups to mobilize around a wide array of issues—from countering corruption and advancing the rule of law to environmental activism—political elites in authoritarian states, and even in some with more democratic traditions, are acting to restrict space for civil society. Restrictions are often seen through new laws and regulations that deny groups the foreign funding they depend on to operate, that criminalize groups of people like the LGBT community, or deny political-opposition groups the freedom to assemble in peaceful protest. The United States is countering this trend by providing direct support for civil society and by advocating rollback of laws and regulations that undermine citizens' rights. We are also supporting technologies that expand access to information, enable freedom of expression, and connect civil society groups in this fight around the world. More than fifty percent of the world's people are under thirty years old. Many struggle to make a life in countries with broken governance. We are taking the initiative to build relationships with the world's young people, identifying future leaders in government, business, and civil society and connecting them to one another and to the skills they need to thrive. We have established new programs of exchange among young Americans and young people from Africa to Southeast Asia, building off the successes of the International Visitor and Young African Leaders initiatives. We are fostering increased education exchanges in our hemisphere. And we are catalyzing economic growth and innovation within societies by lifting and promoting entrepreneurship.

Prevent Mass Atrocities

The mass killing of civilians is an affront to our common humanity and a threat to our common security. It destabilizes countries and regions, pushes refugees across borders, and creates grievances that extremists exploit. We have a strong interest in leading an international response to genocide and mass atrocities when they arise, recognizing options are more extensive and less costly when we act preventively before situations reach crisis proportions. We know the risk of mass atrocities escalates when citizens are denied basic rights and freedoms, are unable to hold accountable the institutions of government, or face unrelenting poverty and conflict. We affirm our support for the international consensus that governments have the responsibility to protect civilians from mass atrocities and that this responsibility passes to the broader international community when those governments manifestly fail to protect their populations. We will work with the international community to prevent and call to account those responsible for the worst human rights abuses, including through support to the International Criminal Court, consistent with U.S. law and our commitment to protecting our personnel. Moreover, we will continue to mobilize allies and partners to strengthen our collective efforts to prevent and respond to mass atrocities using all our instruments of national power.

International Order

We have an opportunity—and obligation—to lead the way in reinforcing, shaping, and where appropriate, creating the rules, norms, and institutions that are the foundation for peace, security, prosperity, and the protection of human rights in the twenty first century. The modern-day international system currently relies heavily on an international legal architecture, economic and political institutions, as well as alliances and partnerships the United States and other like-minded nations established after World War II. Sustained by robust American leadership, this system has served us well for 70 years, facilitating international cooperation, sharing burden and accountability. It carried us through the Cold War and ushered in a wave of democratization. It reduced barriers to trade, expanded free markets, and enabled advances in human dignity and prosperity. But, the system has never been perfect, and aspects of it are increasingly challenged.

We have seen too many cases where a failure to marshal the will and resources for collective action has led to inaction. The U.N. and other multilateral institutions are stressed by, among other things, resource demands, competing imperatives among member states, and the need for reform across a range of policy and administrative areas. Despite these undeniable strains, the clear majority of states do not want to replace the system we have. Rather, they look to America for the leadership needed to both fortify it and help it evolve to meet the wide range of challenges described throughout this strategy. The United States will continue to make the development of sustainable solutions in these areas a foreign policy priority and devote diplomatic and other resources accordingly. We will continue to embrace the post-World War II legal architecture—from the U.N. Charter to the multilateral treaties that govern the conduct of war, respect for human rights, nonproliferation, and many other topics of global concern—as essential to the ordering of a just and peaceful world, where nations live peacefully within their borders, and all men and women can reach their potential. We will lead by example in fulfilling our responsibilities within this architecture, demonstrating to the world it is possible to protect security consistent with robust values. We will work vigorously both within the U.N. and other multilateral institutions, and with member states, to strengthen and modernize capacities—from peacekeeping to humanitarian relief—so they endure to provide protection, stability, and support for future generations. At the same time, we will exact an appropriate cost on transgressors. Targeted economic sanctions remain an effective tool for imposing costs on those irresponsible actors whose military aggression, illicit proliferation, or unprovoked violence threaten both international rules and norms and the peace they were designed to preserve. We will pursue multilateral sanctions, including through the U.N., whenever possible, but will act alone, if necessary. Our sanctions will continue to be carefully designed and tailored to achieve clear aims while minimizing any unintended consequences for other economic actors, the global economy, and civilian populations. In many cases, our use of targeted sanctions and other coercive measures are meant not only to uphold international norms, but to deter severe threats to stability and order at the regional level. We are not allowing the transgressors to define our regional strategies based on the immediate threats they present. Rather, we are advancing a longer-term affirmative agenda in each of the regions, which prioritizes reinvigorating alliances with long-standing friends; making investments in new partnerships with emerging democratic powers with whom our interests are increasingly aligned; and continuing to support the development of capable, inclusive regional institutions to help enforce common international rules.

Advance Our Rebalance to Asia and the Pacific

The United States has been and will remain a Pacific power. Over the next five years, nearly half of all growth outside the United States is expected to come from Asia. That said, the security dynamics of the region—including contested maritime territorial claims and a provocative North Korea—risk escalation and conflict. American leadership will remain essential to shaping the region's long-term trajectory to enhance stability and security, facilitate trade and commerce through an open and transparent system, and ensure respect for universal rights and freedoms. To realize this vision, we are diversifying our security relationships in Asia as well as our defense posture and presence. We are modernizing our alliances with Japan, South Korea, Australia, and the Philippines, and enhancing the interactions among them to ensure they are fully capable of responding to regional and global challenges. We are committed to strengthening regional institutions such as ASEAN, the East Asia Summit, and Asia-Pacific Economic Cooperation to reinforce shared rules and norms, forge collective responses to shared challenges, and help ensure peaceful resolution of disputes. We are also working with our Asian partners to promote more open and transparent economies and regional support for international economic norms that are vital to maintaining it as an engine for global economic growth. The TPP is central to this effort. As we have done since World War II, the United States will continue to support the advance of security, development, and democracy in Asia and the Pacific. This is an important focus of the deepening partnerships we are building in Southeast Asia including with Vietnam, Indonesia, and Malaysia.

We will uphold our treaty obligations to South Korea, Japan, the Philippines, and Thailand, while encouraging the latter to return quickly to democracy. We will support the people of Burma to deepen and sustain reforms, including democratic consolidation and national reconciliation. The United States welcomes the rise of a stable, peaceful, and prosperous China. We seek to develop a constructive relationship with China that delivers benefits for our two peoples and promotes security and prosperity in Asia and around the world. We seek cooperation on shared regional and global challenges such as climate change, public health, economic growth, and the denuclearization of the Korean Peninsula. While there will be competition, we reject the inevitability of confrontation. At the same time, we will manage competition from a position of strength while insisting that China uphold international rules and norms on issues ranging from maritime security to trade and human rights. We will closely monitor China's military modernization and expanding presence in Asia, while seeking ways to reduce the risk of misunderstanding or miscalculation.

On cyber security, we will take necessary actions to protect our businesses and defend our networks against cyber theft of trade secrets for commercial gain whether by private actors or the Chinese government. In South Asia, we continue to strengthen our strategic and economic partnership with India. As the world's largest democracies, we share inherent values and mutual interests that form the cornerstone of our cooperation, particularly in the areas of security, energy, and the environment. We support India's role as a regional provider of security and its expanded participation in critical regional institutions. We see a strategic convergence with India's Act East policy and our continued implementation of the rebalance to Asia and the Pacific. At the same time, we will continue to work with both India and Pakistan to promote strategic stability, combat terrorism, and advance regional economic integration in South and Central Asia.

Strengthen Our Enduring Alliance with Europe

The United States maintains a profound commitment to a Europe that is free, whole, and at peace. A strong Europe is our indispensable partner for tackling global security challenges, promoting prosperity, and upholding international norms. Our work with Europe leverages our strong and historic bilateral relationships throughout the continent. We will steadfastly support the aspirations of countries in the Balkans and Eastern Europe toward European and Euro-Atlantic integration, continue to transform our relationship with Turkey, and enhance ties with countries in the Caucasus while encouraging resolution of regional conflict. NATO is the strongest alliance the world has ever known and is the hub of an expanding global security network. Our Article 5 commitment to the collective defense of all NATO Members is ironclad, as is our commitment to ensuring the Alliance remains ready and capable for crisis response and cooperative security. We will continue to deepen our relationship with the European Union (EU), which has helped to promote peace and prosperity across the region, and deepen NATO-EU ties to enhance transatlantic security.

To build on the millions of jobs supported by transatlantic trade, we support a pro-growth agenda in Europe to strengthen and broaden the region's recovery, and we seek an ambitious T-TIP to boost exports, support jobs, and raise global standards for trade. Russia's aggression in Ukraine makes clear that European security and the international rules and norms against territorial aggression cannot be taken for granted. In response, we have led an international effort to support the Ukrainian people as they choose their own future and develop their democracy and economy. We are reassuring our allies by backing our security commitments and increasing responsiveness through training and exercises, as well as a dynamic presence in Central and Eastern Europe to deter further Russian aggression. This will include working with Europe to improve its energy security in both the short and long term. We will support partners such as Georgia, Moldova, and Ukraine so they can better work alongside the United States and NATO, as well as provide for their own defense. And we will continue to impose significant costs on Russia through sanctions and other means while countering Moscow's deceptive propaganda with the unvarnished truth. We will deter Russian aggression, remain alert to its strategic capabilities, and help our allies and partners resist Russian coercion over the long term, if necessary. At the same time, we will keep the door open to greater collaboration with Russia in areas of common interests, should it choose a different path—a path of peaceful cooperation that respects the sovereignty and democratic development of neighboring states.

Seek Stability and Peace in the Middle East and North Africa

In the Middle East, we will dismantle terrorist networks that threaten our people, confront external aggression against our allies and partners, ensure the free flow of energy from the region to the world, and prevent the development, proliferation, or use of weapons of mass destruction. At the same time, we remain committed to a vision of the Middle East that is peaceful and prosperous, where democracy takes root and human rights are upheld. Sadly, this is not the case today, and nowhere is the violence more tragic and destabilizing than in the sectarian conflict from Beirut to Baghdad, which has given rise to new terrorist groups such as ISIL.

Resolving these connected conflicts and enabling long-term stability in the region requires more than the use and presence of American military forces. For one, it requires partners who can defend themselves. We are therefore investing in the ability of Israel, Jordan, and our Gulf partners to deter aggression while maintaining our unwavering commitment to Israel's security, including its Qualitative Military Edge. We are working with the Iraqi government to resolve Sunni grievances through more inclusive and responsive governance. With our partners in the region and around the world, we are leading a comprehensive counterterrorism strategy to degrade and ultimately defeat ISIL. At the same time, we will continue to pursue a lasting political solution to the devastating conflict in Syria. Stability and peace in the Middle East and North Africa also requires reducing the underlying causes of conflict. America will therefore continue to work with allies and partners toward a comprehensive agreement with Iran that resolves the world's concerns with the Iranian nuclear program. We remain committed to ending the Israeli-Palestinian conflict through a two-state solution that ensures Israel's security and Palestine's viability. We will support efforts to deescalate sectarian tensions and violence between Shi'a and Sunni communities throughout the region. We will help countries in transition make political and economic reforms and build state capacity to maintain security, law and order, and respect for universal rights. In this respect, we seek a stable Yemen that undertakes difficult structural reforms and confronts an active threat from al-Qa'ida and other rebels. We will work with Tunisia to further progress on building democratic institutions and strengthening its economy. We will work with the U.N. and our Arab and European partners to help stabilize Libya and reduce the threat posed by lawless militias and extremists. And we will maintain strategic cooperation with Egypt to enable it to respond to shared security threats, while broadening our partnership and encouraging progress toward restoration of democratic institutions.

Invest in Africa's Future

Africa is rising. Many countries in Africa are making steady progress in growing their economies, improving democratic governance and rule of law, and supporting human rights and basic freedoms. Urbanization and a burgeoning youth population are changing the region's demographics, and young people are increasingly making their voices heard. But there are still many countries where the transition to democracy is uneven and slow with some leaders clinging to power. Corruption is endemic and public health systems are broken in too many places. And too many governments are responding to the expansion of civil society and free press by passing laws and adopting policies that erode that progress. Ongoing conflicts in Sudan, South Sudan, the Democratic Republic of the Congo, and the Central African Republic, as well as violent extremists fighting governments in Somalia, Nigeria, and across the Sahel, all pose threats to innocent civilians, regional stability, and our national security.

For decades, American engagement with Africa was defined by aid to help Africans reduce insecurity, famine, and disease. In contrast, the partnerships we are forging today, and will expand in the coming years, aim to build upon the aspirations of Africans. Through our Power Africa Initiative, we aim to double access to power in sub-Saharan Africa. We will increase trade and business ties, generating export-driven growth through initiatives like Trade Africa and AGOA. We will continue to support U.S. companies to deepen investment in what can be the world's next major center of global growth, including through the Doing Business in Africa campaign. Moreover, we are investing in tomorrow's leaders—the young entrepreneurs, innovators, civic leaders, and public servants who will shape the continent's future. We are strengthening civilian and military institutions through our Security Governance Initiative, and working to advance human rights and eliminate corruption. We are deepening our security partnerships with African countries and institutions, exemplified by our partnerships with the U.N. and AU in Mali and Somalia. Such efforts will help to resolve conflicts, strengthen African peacekeeping capacity, and counter transnational security threats while respecting human rights and the rule of law. Our investment in nutrition and agricultural capacity will continue, reducing hunger through initiatives such as Feed the Future. We will keep working with partners to reduce deaths from Ebola, HIV/AIDS, malaria, and tuberculosis across Africa through such initiatives as the President's Emergency Plan for AIDS Relief and the Global Health Security Agenda. The Ebola epidemic in 2014 serves as a stark reminder of the threat posed by infectious disease and the imperative of global collective action to meet it. American leadership has proven essential to bringing to bear the international community to contain recent crises while building public health capacity to prevent future ones.

Deepen Economic and Security Cooperation in the Americas

We will continue to advance a Western Hemisphere that is prosperous, secure, democratic, and plays a greater global role. In the region the number of people in the middle class has surpassed the number of people living in poverty for the first time in history, and the hemisphere is increasingly important to global energy supplies. These gains, however, are put at risk by weak institutions, high crime rates, powerful organized crime groups, an illicit drug trade, lingering economic disparity, and inadequate education and health systems. To meet these challenges, we are working with Canada and Mexico to enhance our collective economic competitiveness while advancing prosperity in our hemisphere. With Chile, Peru, Mexico, and Canada, we are setting new global trade standards as we grow a strong contingent of countries in the Americas that favor open trading systems to include TPP. We seek to advance our economic partnership with Brazil, as it works to preserve gains in reducing poverty and deliver the higher standards of public services expected by the middle class. We are also championing a strong and effective inter-American human rights and rule of law system. We are expanding our collaboration across the Americas to support democratic consolidation and increase public-private partnerships in education, sustainable development, access to electricity, climate resilience, and countering transnational organized crime. Such collaboration is especially important in vulnerable countries like Guatemala, El Salvador, and Honduras, where government institutions are threatened by criminal syndicates. Migration surges involving unaccompanied children across our southern border is one major consequence of weak institutions and violence. American leadership, in partnership with these countries and with the support of their neighbors, remains essential to arresting the backward slide and to creating steady improvements in economic growth and democratic governance.

Likewise, we remain committed to helping rebuild Haiti and to put it and our other Caribbean neighbors on a path to sustainable development. We will support the resolution of longstanding regional conflicts, particularly Colombia's conclusion of a peace accord with the Revolutionary Armed Forces of Colombia. Overall, we have deepened our strategic partnership with Colombia, which is a key contributor to international peace and security. Equally, we stand by the citizens of countries where the full exercise of democracy is at risk, such as Venezuela. Though a few countries in the region remain trapped in old ideological debates, we will keep working with all governments that are interested in cooperating with us in practical ways to reinforce the principles enumerated in the Inter-American Democratic Charter. As part of our effort to promote a fully democratic hemisphere, we will advance our new opening to Cuba in a way that most effectively promotes the ability of the Cuban people to determine their future freely (Obama, National Security Strategy, 2015, pp. 7–28).

Terrorism

There have been trepidations of traditional terrorism for many decades, but it was not until the United States experienced the largest attack in history on homeland soil when al-Qaeda executed 9/11, changing America forever. Terrorist organizations are more sophisticated and technologically advanced, causing global terrorism to remain a diverse and polygonal concern for the United States, its allies, and security partners for implementing strategies on how to mitigate it. Groups and violent extremists remain the primary threat in their areas of comfort and will also push limits to commit attacks outside their regional areas. On America's radar are Sunni extremists who are linked to Iran, which is a state sponsor of terrorism and supports Hezbollah violent operations in the Middle East. In addition, conflicts within Iraq, Syria, and Yemen have influenced global security and will continue to be a threat for the United States and its security partners. Domestic extremism has been an ever-growing threat, primarily homegrown violent extremists, and will continue to increase due to perceived cost effectiveness and unpredictability. Small groups of terrorists or even "lone wolves" pose an even greater than large terrorist organizations.

Weapons of Mass Destruction and Proliferation

As mentioned in chapter eight, **weapons of mass destruction** and **proliferation** are very important elements in protecting American national security, if necessary against the adversary. The United States and cooperating international communities acknowledge the use of chemical, biological, radiological, or nuclear devices an affront to global security and violations against humanity. The use of WMDs is so dangerous that the international community established global initiatives and efforts on deterrence. Initiatives such as multilateral agreements, global laws and architecture, and treaties were aimed preventing the proliferation of WMDs, which is a major concern with non-nation states. Important legislative acts like the International Security Program and the Project on Nuclear Issues Program are responsible for timely analysis and research on refuting the expansion of WMDs. WMDs can eliminate a large population in a short time frame, and the international treaties imposed will assist in reducing the proliferation and/or execution of these weapons. However, non-nation states do not support international frameworks and will continue to seek or develop illicit weapons, which poses a great threat to national security.

Space and Counter-space

The space industry continues to expand as countries are developing and expanding space-enabled capabilities. Specific global trends influence and bring awareness, increasing the availability of technology, providing private-sector investments, and providing partnerships for operations and production. Both commercial and government entities have access to space information, which is pivotal for global satellite and navigation systems.

Intelligence and military operations are critical to space and counter-space operations. Powerful countries are dedicated to improving intelligence collection, missile warning, information sharing, and military communications systems to increase situational awareness and tactical weapons targeting. For example, Russia anticipates expanding its imagery constellation program and will attempt to double its satellite system in orbit by 2025. Space warfare is another program important to America because superpowers China and Russia threaten the United States military advantage in terms of civil defense and commercial space systems. Such countries are considering attacks against satellite systems as a strategy for warfare doctrine. Both countries will continue to execute offense tactics against the United States to reduce effectiveness in the satellite program system.

Counter-space Weapons

Space weapons are weaponry used in space warfare, which are used to attack space systems and/or targets on Earth from space or to disable missiles traveling through space. Some of these weapons were first developed during the Cold War between the United States and the Soviet Union when the countries were competing to become the first to dominate space efforts. Anti-satellite weapons were developed to interdict air-to-space and surface-to-space missiles by the United States, Russia, and China.

On March 23, 1983, President Ronald Reagan proposed the Strategic Defense Initiative, a research program formulized to launch defensive systems to destroy adversarial intercontinental ballistic missiles (ICBMs). Brilliant Pebbles, "a system of spaced-based missile interceptors," was designed to use high-velocity projectiles as kinetic warheads (Baucom, 2004, p. 143). However, the program was not deemed successful, as no mechanisms were developed for actual deployment. Not until early in the twenty-first century did the military test lasers mounted on Boing 747 aircraft to destroy missiles, but the practices ceased because of constant airborne operations near possible launch sites.

Orbital weaponry is a weapon in orbit around an astronomic object (i.e. the moon or planets). As of early 2017, there are not any orbital weapons, but there are various surveillance systems to observe other countries' progression. The United States and Russia developed most of the orbital weaponry systems during the Cold War, and in addition, Nazi Germany attempted development during WWII (see Sun Gun). The continued expansion of orbital weapons was halted by the *Outer Space* and *SALT* treaties. Both covenants banned the development of weapons of mass destruction targeting astronomical objects. The *Space Preservation Treaty*, enacted in 1967, banned the placement of any form of weaponry in space. This includes the existence of kinetic bombardment systems, which do not violate space treaties. Kinetic bombardment or "orbital bombardment" involves space weapons targeting objects in outer space.

Counterintelligence

Espionage is an older, strategic tactic used during times of conflict to collect intelligence for competitive advantage. Spies are increasing to steal America's secrets. Espionage is no longer just a tool used to collect data and sell to foreign countries. Instead, the mode of clandestine operations is to exploit sociopolitical propaganda, especially enemies against the United States and Western cultures. Stealing American secrets can be positive for adversaries because sensitive information can boost other economies. Since the early 1900s, the FBI has been responsible for reducing espionage and other surveillance tactics against the United States. The agency's counterintelligence division was responsible for "neutralizing national security threats from foreign intelligence offices and was the principal organization for exposing, preventing, investigating intelligence on U.S. soil" (n.d., para. 3). The FBI's goals on counterintelligence were deemed critical to the agency's mission:

- Protect the secrets of the U.S. Intelligence Community, using intelligence to focus investigative efforts, and collaborating with our government partners to reduce the risk of espionage and insider threats.
- Protect the nation's critical assets, like advanced technologies and sensitive information in the defense, intelligence, economic, financial, public health, and science and technology sectors.
- Counter the activities of foreign spies. Through proactive investigations, the Bureau identifies who they are and stops what they're doing.
- Keep weapons of mass destruction from falling into the wrong hands, and use intelligence to drive the FBI's investigative efforts to keep threats from becoming reality (n.d., para. 4).

Transnational Organized Crime

Transnational organized crime (TOC) is an illicit operation, which coordinates missions across national borders by individuals or groups who are involved in illegal business operations. Such individuals or groups use methodical corruption strategies and violence to execute their operations. The following are examples of TOC:

- Cybercrime/cyberterrorism
- Drug smuggling
- Human smuggling
- Human trafficking
- Money laundering
- Transporting weapons of mass destruction
- Terrorism
- Weapons smuggling

TOC dates to before WWI when cooperating countries formulized international policies, but the strategy was not successful. In the early 1900s, there were challenges with policy agency autonomy from political actions to survive as bureaucratic professionals. The *First International Criminal Police Congress* convened in Monaco where criminal justice professionals from nearly thirty countries met to discuss arrest methods, international crime records extradition procedures, and identification practices. The Congress was deemed promising, but dissolved with the outbreak of WWI.

By 1923, a second Congress was established with the intention of only "fighting against the common of humankind: the ordinary criminal" (Deflem, 2000). Three years later, the 15 founding members (excluding the United States) proposed each country develop a centralized policy structure. By the early 1940s, Nazi Germany took cover under ICPC, which caused the organization to dissolve again. After the end of WWII, Belgium was one of the leading countries to revive the organization known as Interpol. In 1971, the United Nations accepted Interpol as an intergovernmental organization, which at the time faced major challenges with global drug trafficking. The same year, President Richard Nixon declared the War on Drugs. The issues raised security concerns and posed a critical compromise to the health and safety of Americans.

TOC negatively impacts global democratic governance, disrupts free markets, the development of stable societies, and decreases global assets. TOC and terrorist organizations threaten global security, which can cause instability within governments, and provokes the control of the countries affected. The world's largest most highly industrialized and trading partners are responsible for the highest markets for illegal products and services. There have been many efforts on mitigating TOC, but according to the White House, statistical data has not been reported to determine if solutions have impacted prevention rates. TOC requires effective investigative techniques and professional methods. According to Bruce G. Ohr, author of *Effective Methods to Combat Transnational*, there are three primary techniques to combat TOC:

- Confidential informants
- Electronic surveillance
- Undercover operations

As the superpower, many countries look to the United States on leading and innovating solutions to the war on TOC. In 2010, the White House emphasized the need to heighten security measures to combat transnational organized crime. Excerpts from President Obama's 2010 National Security Strategy state:

Combating transnational criminal and trafficking networks requires a multidimensional strategy that safeguards citizens, breaks the financial strength of criminal and terrorist networks, disrupts illicit trafficking networks, defeats transnational criminal organizations, fights government corruption, strengthens the rule of law, bolsters judicial systems, and improves transparency. While these are major challenges, the United States will be able to devise and execute a collective strategy with other nations facing the same threats (2010, para. 1).

By 2011, the White House released the *Strategy to Combat Transnational Organized Crime*, which was established to "build, balance, and integrate the tools of American power to combat transnational organized crime and related threats to national security—and to urge our foreign partners to do the same" (The White House, 2011, para. 1). This framework ensured five facets of policies objectives that aligned with the 2010 NSS:

1. Protect Americans and our partners from the harm, violence, and exploitation of transnational criminal networks.

2. Help partner countries strengthen governance and transparency, break the corruptive power of transnational criminal networks, and sever state-crime alliances.

3. Break the economic power of transnational criminal networks and protect strategic markets and the U.S. financial system from TOC penetration and abuse.

4. Defeat transnational criminal networks that pose the greatest threat to national security, by targeting their infrastructures, depriving them of their enabling means, and preventing the criminal facilitation of terrorist activities.

5. Build international consensus, multilateral cooperation, and public-private partnerships to defeat transnational organized crime (The White House, n.d., paras. 1–5).

Economic and Natural Resources

The global economy remains in a passive, yet stabilized position, as statistics showed that the international global domestic product (GDP) remained steady during the past couple of years. Data showed from the International Monetary Fund (IMF) that the GDP improved only from four-tenths of a percent from 2016 to 2017 (2016). Behind the United States, China's rapidly emerging economy has proven to be an accomplishment in promoting globalization, but the increasing interest rates based on the boost could potentially pose security risks for full recovery. However, the significant funding loaned to the country could prove to decline its rising economic platform, which could significantly impact the global economic flow. The projected outlook for growing economies has prospered because of the stabilization of service prices and amplified capital flows. Continued global growth is predicated on the United States' performance, in addition with its allies, who can support the growth of emerging countries. Although some European countries remain stabilized, it plays safe with low interest rates and budgetary policies.

The prices of goods and services have had a negative impact on the plateaued global economic progression. China and India have proved to be successful, as countries such as Venezuela have suffered oil price declines, an unstable economy, and excess government spending. The economies of Saudi Arabia and other Persian Gulf countries continue to flourish as oil prices increase annually, but deficits have caused budget cuts in mandatory spending areas. Oil prices have also been deemed stagnant, which have challenged the attempt to improve resources and expand innovative undertakings to promote globalization. The American government projected the development on new projects will more than like be underway in the next five years, but long-term plans have been halted until the global economy improves.

Human Security

Environmental challenges and climate change has proven to affect humanity. Risks such as global pollution have proven to not only create health concerns, but increase global waste and adversely affect the atmosphere. Agriculture, energy levels, forest burning, rapid industrialization, and urbanization have also contributed to environmental damage. In addition, such concerns have increased climate-change concerns, as pollution drastically affects temperatures of the global climate. According to the World Health Organization (WHO), an estimated ninety-two percent of the world's population lives in areas where WHO air quality standards are not met (2014). Low-income regions experience poor air- and water-quality standards, creating protests and tensions throughout the world. Global biodiversity is declining due to these conditions. With environmental challenges, the global population is declining at a rapid extinction rate.

Health standards are declining due to poor environmental standards. In addition, diseases remain a primary factor in increasing death rates round the world. Zika virus has increased in the Western culture, and though it is not considered deadly, it is considered responsible for birth defects of pregnant females who become infected. Bacterial diseases and viruses continue to contribute to increasing death rates, which is significantly surpassing the development of new medicine to mitigate the diseases. Also, drug-resistant diseases are rapidly increasing, which poses an epidemic, as there currently no cure or treatment. The materialization of austere global public health emergencies is impossible to avoid and can pose health and security risks.

The number of refugees has exponentially increased over the past few years, significantly impacting America and its allies. According to the *United Nations High Commissioner for Refugees Global Trends Report: World at War*, the number of people forcibly removed from their countries is at the highest levels (2015). Third World countries expect the United States and other participating countries to support global displacement due to conflicts and natural disasters. Former Director of National Intelligence Dan Coats testified to the Senate that global displacement is predicated on:

1. Primary drivers of global displacement include conflicts, such as those in Afghanistan, Somalia, South Sudan, and Syria; weak border controls, such as in Libya, which broadened a route from Africa to Europe; relatively easy and affordable access to routes and information; endemic violence, such as in parts of Burundi, Central America, Nigeria, and Pakistan; and persecution, such as in Burma and Eritrea.

2. The UN estimated that 65.3 million persons had been forcibly displaced worldwide at the end of 2015, including approximately 21.3 million refugees, 40.8 million IDPs, and 3.2 million asylum seekers. Refugees displaced for five or more years are more likely to remain in their host communities than to return home, according to academic research.

3. In 2016, thousands of Syrian, Somali, Sudanese, and Afghan refugees who had fled their countries in preceding years were returned to their countries of origin, which are still undergoing intense conflict. These returnees are now internally displaced in areas still in conflict (Coats, 2017, p. 13).

AMERICA'S INTERNAL WAR ON SUSTAINING GLOBAL ROLES AND COALITION RELATIONS

For the United States to effectively lead the world in economic, political and social change, the nation must set the standard by living the values instilled from its forefathers. Because of how democracy promotes equality, fairness, and freedom, America must have standards on empowerment to maintain these privileges. Considering Western culture objectives, such opportunities are not supported or accepted, causing adversaries to discredit global leadership, governments, and initiatives. Many global conflicts that the United States has experienced were due to authoritarian extremists, non-states, and terrorism, which does not recognize democratic governance, causing aggression and promoting sociopolitical agendas and violent extremism. However, some countries in the same regions appreciate and envision international opportunities by implementing and supporting the concept of the universal law of mankind.

Because of many conflicts in promoting democracy around the world, the primary concern is defining democratic initiatives and protecting human rights for not only the United States but every country. Understanding that each country must overcome its own challenges to succeed, the United States has become the leading country to implement democratic change. To lead such initiatives, the nation should sustain international support and strengthen relationships with its allies, coalition forces, and security partners. The evolution of democratic change is to break the stereotypical mold and stigmas which have kept the United States from completely moving forward. Improving educational standards for following generations, mandating the equality of women in the workforce, maintaining integrity in national journalism, and supporting private- and public-sector businesses are primary concerns to driving change within the United States and setting the standard. In addition, the American government should continue to defend global standards on democracy, human rights responsibilities, deter terrorism and transnational crime, and prevent mass atrocities.

The United States' closest allies are those that epitomize democratic governance concepts and have similar strategic interests and values to strengthen the campaign on international security and promote globalization. In addition to working with alliances, America should continue to publicly express support for diplomacy and human rights and balance a broad awareness on funding these efforts. To do so, the United States must continue to work with its allies and security partners in those regions to strengthen ties with cooperating businesses, governments, leaders, and organizations.

American values are the backbone of security and strength and promoting such characteristics directly affects the nation's ability to sustain those efforts. The aftermath of 9/11 posed vulnerabilities in which adversaries exploited the United States security policies, challenging the obligations of preserving civil liberties and laws mandated by the federal government. The United States must hold the highest standards to protect the American public. The United States should focus on resources to assist its allies and promote democratic governance throughout the world. Nations, along with co-operating governments, must be steadfast with the evolution of egalitarian practice due to uprisings that began in the Arab region. Countries with weakened democratic governance are susceptible to violent extremist and criminal activity and the possibility of coups. In this instance, the United States is charged with formulating solutions to establish economic, political, and security reforms, along with ensuring developments that are successfully executed in strict governments undergoing major transitions. Tolerable governance is centered on strengthening a society and state relationships. When citizens have a voice in decision-making efforts, policymaking and judgments on governmental issues significantly increase, creating an environment for contribution, innovation, and participation.

Corruption and violence are primary challenges in establishing global democracy. Post-9/11, the United States developed fusion centers and the concept of intelligence-led policing to increase information-sharing among federal agencies not only to mitigate crime and terrorism, but to target corrupt officials in a better fashion. With promoting globalization, international corruption has become prominent, making some operations difficult to complete. The platform allows corrupted leaders to hide illegal assets and weapons, which makes international money laundering and other illicit financial operations easier to execute and more challenging to detect. As the superpower, the United States is the leading country for the **Open Government Partnership (OGP)**, which is a multilateral agreement focused on security commitments from governments to "promote democracy, empower citizens, fight corruption, and harness new technologies to strengthen governance" (2017, para. 1). By following standards of OGP, operations the United States can salvage stolen assets and hold corrupt offices accountable for illegal actions. American leadership is critical and shows transparency, which enhances government processes.

Maintaining global democratic standards is not only the responsibility of government leaders, but the public. As mentioned earlier, citizens are essential to the decision-making process and assist leaders in making better informed policy-making decisions. For instance, the public-at-large can provide innovative ideas and methodologies to solve economic, political, and social challenges that governments may not be able to solve and that can be implemented from a larger platform. Providing citizens the opportunity to express their interests and concerns results in emerging countries being able to maintain stability to counter violent extremism and terrorism.

However, civilization can promote challenges, and technology is one of the most powerful mechanisms to exacerbate the concern. Furthermore, technology makes it easier for corruption and radical activism, which increases restriction for civil societies in non-democratic states. America is opposing this challenge by enacting new laws and regulatory policies that prevent international funding to any organization that marginalizes and oppresses people within the LGBT community or suppresses political opposition and the rights for individuals to assemble in respectful and diplomatic protests. Also, the nation can do so by aiding international civil societies and advocating the reform of laws and initiatives that demoralize citizen and human rights. Finally, the United States supports the expansion of technology to access information, support civil liberties, and unite with other countries to fight the war for global peace and security.

Ensuring global peace and security is indicative of the work of younger generations. According to the 2015 National Security Strategy, President Obama said, "more than fifty percent of the world's population is under thirty years old" (p. 21). With such a youthful world, it is imperative to prepare future generations to avoid fractured governance. Countries should engage the world's young people and recognize potential leaders in business, civil society, and governments and afford them opportunities to thrive and continue the progress for peace and security. For example, the United States established new initiatives and programs such as exchange programs for young Americans to build relationships and learn international policies from Africa to Southeast Asia, known as the *International Visit and Young African Leader Initiatives*. With this program, the nation bolsters global education initiatives, enhances international growth and modernization within civil societies, and increases globalization efforts.

With promoting globalization and bolstering international relationships comes the revelation that mass atrocities could be taking place in previously closed societies. Large-scale attacks and murders of civilians demoralize universal laws of humanity and damage our security efforts. Furthermore, it disrupts the United States, it alliances, and security partners' stratagem for global progression and undermines all efforts for global peace and security.

Moreover, global regions with weakened democratic governments are heavily affected, forcing refugees to leave their homelands, which creates massive grievance and chaos. Extremists use such tactics to exploit these challenges, making it easier to infiltrate and control regions for their ideological, religious, propaganda, or sociopolitical views. With innovation and technological advancement, the United States has an interest in leading the global response to apartheid, genocide, and other mass killings. Additionally, the nation is keen on finding cost-effective and innovative solutions to mitigate atrocities before they arise.

Understanding the reasoning for heinous crimes is the key to readiness operations to prevent them. Lack of action exacerbates these situations when citizens are denied fundamental rights and opportunities. Countries must protect citizens from crime, fear, poverty, and violence. The international movement to prevent mass killings includes all alliances and security partners that will use all instruments of global power to ensure mobilization and establish solid relationships in this effort.

Sustaining International Order

The international system is dependent upon global legal architecture, economic matters, political institutions, and partnerships that were established in the twentieth century. This system has been maintained by American powers since 1945, facilitating accountability, global cooperation, and information-sharing challenges. In addition, this mechanism has survived through the Cold War into the era of heavily promoting democratic governance, which has lessened obstacles for international trade, expanded free markets, and enabled human dignity and prosperity. Even though it has been the only system, there are still challenges where neglect of implementation has caused inactivity. For instance, there has been a need for international reform of antiquated policies and multilateral agreements, and the responsibility falls on the shoulders of the United Nations. Reforms needed have been debated, as many UN member nations do not believe in the need for an innovative system. Instead, these states depend on America's leadership to meet the needs of the ever-evolving global order.

As the leading nation, the United States will continue global progression with resolutions to implement foreign policy and stay dedicated to diplomatic initiatives. Also, the country must embrace and recognize policies such as human rights, multilateral agreements, proliferation, and other important topics that concern improving global efforts. By doing so, the United States works closely with the UN, its alliances, other multifaceted establishments, member states, and security partners to innovate and strengthen global capabilities to provide protection, stability, and assistance. An aggressive strategy for sustaining these requirements requires posing economic sanctions on rogue countries or actors who are acting aggressively, promoting unlawful proliferation, or promoting or participating in violent extremism. The United States and supporting countries must continue sanctions whenever deemed necessary. Such sanctions will be reviewed and analyzed to accomplish goals while diminishing penalties for other challenges, the global economy, and populations.

Another important factor in sustaining global roles is rebalancing within Asia and the Pacific. A global shift raises security concerns, especially with maritime territorial claims, conflict, and terrorist acts. America is responsible for shaping Asia's long-term sustainability to enable commerce operations, improve security, maintain stability, and implement the Open Government Partnership initiative. The United States will diversify its defense posture, maintain its presence, and mandate security objectives within Asia. The United States and its alliances are responsible to sustain and strengthen relations. All Asian countries should modernize efforts and enhance interactions to guarantee full capabilities of responding to global and regional challenges. Multilateral agreements such as *Associate of Southeast Asian Nations (ASEAN)*, the *East Asia Summit*, and the *Asia-Pacific Economic Cooperation* were enacted to reinforce law, improve regulatory standards, resolve challenges, and restore peace. In addition, these agreements will continue to bolster advanced security efforts and establish development and better democracy within Asia and the Pacific.

SUMMARY

The future of the United States is unpredictable. This chapter emphasized the amalgamation of national and homeland security initiatives to emphasize the complex issues that threaten the nation. Such framework dates to how America became its own country, winning the American Revolutionary War after decades of disagreement with the British Parliament. Establishing its own governance and body of law, our Founding Fathers realized the need for national security, as foreign countries threatened the homeland, and frameworks for national defense had not been established. The debate is the concern over the future of homeland and security objectives for the United States. Because adversarial threats are rapidly increasing, America must formulate long-term and short-term solutions to ensure another 9/11-style attack does not ever touch the homeland again. To do so, the United States and its allies are charged with strengthening international relationships and focusing on the primary concerns of the world, including the top security issues that plague global security and the environment.

Security risk management is another facet of homeland and national security, which includes assessment, identification, and prioritization of risks and managing specific economic and security applications of resources to control and/or mitigate the possibility of incidents. This chapter discussed the top national security concerns based on testimony from professional experts such as the former Director of National Intelligence to emphasize that to improve the world, it is necessary to prevent illicit transnational crime, address environmental and health concerns, coordinate with international members on climate change, protect universal laws and humanity, and promote globalization.

Finally, evaluating America's internal war is as important as monitoring global terrorism. The United States faces an increase in domestic extremism/terrorism, homegrown terrorists, and lone wolves, all of which are distracting to the objectives of deterring international adversaries and solely focusing on national issues. In addition, internal conflicts within in the United States not only destabilize the nation's economy but affect the safety of the American public, crippling the dominant standing within the world and increasing security risks. The nation must work on unifying a divided country and must concentrate on the backdoor operations of the global enemies who want to remove the United States as the superpower and control the world with their political, religious, and sociopolitical agendas. Understanding the global roles of America and its allies, coalition forces, and security partners is vital to strengthening relationships and improving global security. Protecting the homeland and understanding national security objectives is the key to America's sustainability of dominance, power, and security.

CHAPTER 14 CASE STUDIES

Case Study 1
National Security vs. Homeland Security: America's Internal War

Since the attacks on September 11, 2001, the United States has put itself in a better position to protect its citizens and homeland from another large-scale attack. However, emerging threats and innovative terrorist acts still exist from adversaries that keep America vigilant of vulnerabilities. Addressing America's top national security concerns and how those matters will be resolved in pivotal in keeping the homeland safe. The Trump administration has yet to produce the latest National Security Strategy, but top security concerns from President Barack Obama are still legitimate factors that are believed to be aligned with President Trump's vision on how to protect national security. The 2015 National Security Strategy outlines what America needs to do to protect its citizens, critical infrastructure, resources, and the homeland:

Security

- Strengthen Our National Defense
- Reinforce Homeland Security
- Combat the Persistent Threat of Terrorism
- Build Capacity to Prevent Conflict
- Prevent the Spread and Use of Weapons of Mass Destruction
- Confront Climate Change
- Assure Access to Shared Spaces
- Increase Global Health Security

Prosperity

- Put Our Economy to Work

- Advance Our Energy Security
- Lead in Science, Technology, and Innovation
- Shape the Global Economic Order
- End Extreme Poverty

Values

- Live Our Values
- Advance Equality
- Support Emerging Democracies
- Empower Civil Society and Young Leaders
- Prevent Mass Atrocities

International Order

- Advance Our Rebalance to Asia and the Pacific
- Strengthen Our Enduring Alliance with Europe
- Seek Stability and Peace in the Middle East and North Africa
- Invest in Africa's Future
- Deepen Economic and Security Cooperation in the Americas (National Security Strategy [NSS], 2015, Table of Contents).

All facets of what President Obama's NSS outlines are matters that are still relevant for the next decade and beyond. However, there are constant changes within the country plus global instability, unpredictability, and internal chaos. Additional needs must be addressed because there is no national security without homeland security objectives. Homeland security concerns are just as important as domestic problems that should be identified. America's internal problems may affect its "superpower" position in the world, create tensions with allies and security partners, and most importantly destabilize the environment for the American citizens. The United States is the most progressive country in the world, but greater concerns that stem from more than 200 years of history may prevent the country from moving forward, distracting from major concerns and threats. According to David Inserra, Policy Analyst, Homeland Security and Cyber Policy at the Douglas and Sarah Allison Center for Foreign Policy, the top five priorities for homeland security are:

1. Enforcement of Immigration Law
2. The United States Coast Guard
3. Federal Emergency Management Agency
4. Refugee and Visa Setting
5. Department of Homeland Security Oversight Reform (2016, paras. 1–5).

Inserra's concerns are like those of the U.S. Senate Committee on Homeland Security and Governmental Affairs. The committee addressed these main concerns: **immigration; border and port security; and biological, chemical, and nuclear security** (n.d., paras.

2–3). While these concerns are valid, some critical problems have higher levels of concerns, and if they are not mitigated by the Secretary of Homeland Security and the President of the United States, the world will watch America crumble.

1. Agroterrorism and Bioterrorism
2. Domestic Extremism
3. Lone Wolves and Homegrown Terrorists
4. International Terrorism
5. White Supremacy
6. Police Brutality and Unjustified Killings
7. Political Extremism (Chouraeshkenazi, 2017).

How do national and homeland security concerns overlap? Also, if homeland security matters are not addressed, how does this affect the lives of American citizens and the nation's stance as the strongest and most advanced country in the world? America is fighting an internal war with its own people, politicians, and law enforcement. If this continues, the adversary will make its move.

Case Study 2
Did Russia Hack into the Democratic National Committee Systems?

For more than 200 years the two superpowers have had a unique, complex diplomatic relationship, competing for economic and political influence throughout the world, which has been faced with many challenges ("Two Hundred Years," para. 1). In the beginning, the United States and Russia (then the Soviet Union) had managed to have a professional and business relationship. When Russia sold Alaska to the United States in the mid-1800s, the transaction identified both countries' joint relationship and support during the American Civil War. Not until the early 1900s did relationships between the two countries became tense. Nonetheless, there was not any direct conflict or aggression towards either country (hence the Cold War), and both countries continued to communicate and negotiate government dealings. No matter how much tensions intensified, the two countries demonstrated the importance of the stability of the world, especially during World War I when the two countries had a common enemy. The distrust began when the Soviet Union failed to follow agreements and treaties with Western allies, and the relationship has not been the same. Fast forward to the twenty-first century, the relationship between the United States and Russia is considered more "dangerous today than it has been at any point since the end of the Cold War" (Maidment, 2017, para. 1).

Tensions have increased since the United States imposed sanctions on Russia. On July 27, 2017, "the U.S. Senate's vote expanded sanctions against Russia due to interference in the U.S. presidential elections" (Smeltz & Wojtowicz, 2017, para. 1). Because of the sanctions, the Russian government "confiscated two U.S. diplomatic properties in Russia and ordered Washington to cut its diplomatic and technical staff" (Smeltz & Wojtowicz, 2017, para. 1). The accusations began with suspicion that Russia was involved in the presidential election voting, which began in September 2015 when the FBI contacted the Democratic National Committee (DNC) alleging that one of their computer systems may have been compromised by Russian hackers. IT experts ran scans and did not find anything, so they failed to report this leadership. Two months later, the FBI contacted DNC to inform them that one of their systems was transmitting information to Russia.

In spring 2016, Hillary Clinton's campaign manager received a phishing email posed as a Google email alert, notifying that a user tried to access her account. A link prompted John Podesta to change his password. Suspicious, Podesta contacted a staffer to determine if the email was valid. Instead of the staffer replying that the email was "illegitimate," it was written that it was "legitimate," and Podesta changed his password. After his password was changed, hackers had access to his emails ("2016 Presidential Campaign Hacking Fast Facts," 2017, para. 3). In June 2016, Donald Trump, Jr., received an email from Russian singer Emin Agalarov suggesting that he had official documents that could incriminate presidential candidate Hillary Clinton. The email also entailed that the Russian government was willing to assist with helping Donald Trump win the election and would offer information to discredit Clinton. Trump, Jr., said, "If it's what you say, I love it—especially later in the summer" (CNN, 2017, para. 4).

Agalarov contacted Donald Trump, Jr., again about meeting in person with a Russian government attorney that was arriving in the United States (New York) to discuss Trump's campaign at the Trump Tower. On June 9, 2016, Trump, Jr., his brother-in-law, and Paul Manafort meet with Russian attorney, Natalia Veselnitskaya, but it is uncertain what was discussed. On June 14, 2016, the *Washington Post* reported that Russian hackers accessed DNC computer systems and stole oppositional research on Donald Trump, but the Kremlin denied the accusations. On June 15, 2016, DNC's hired computer firm found that two Russian hacking groups, "Cozy Bear" and "Fancy Bear," were linked to Russian intelligence. Another hacker, "Guccifer 2.0" claimed responsibility for the attacks and stated it was an isolated incident that was not linked to the Russian government.

By the end of July 2016, more than 20,000 emails from the DNC were published by WikiLeaks, which provoked the FBI to begin an investigation. On September 1, 2016, Russian President Vladimir Putin made a statement that the Russian government was not involved in the DNC hacking. However, ranking members of the Senate cited intelligence proving the Russians were trying to interfere with the presidential elections. Nearly 60,000 emails were stolen and leaked to the public. On October 7, 2016, the Department of Homeland Security and the Office of National Intelligence made a public statement saying that they were sure the Russian government was involved based on past Russian attacks against the U.S. government. The intent was to persuade voters to vote for Donald Trump with the intent of negatively impacting Hillary Clinton's campaign.

More information by the end of the year was made public. The DNC's late response to reporting the hacks lead to a complete infiltration of its computer networks, and DC Leaks and Guccifer 2.0 were linked to Russia. As a result, President Obama issued sanctions against Russia for its participation in the hacking. When sanctions were issued, six Russian individuals were addressed and nearly forty Russian diplomats were ordered to leave the United States within three days of the sanctions. Reports from the Office of National Intelligence found that the computer systems for voting were not actually breached, but the Russian government was involved, alleging President Putin ordering "Pro-Trump Propaganda" on the night of the election with the hash tag "#DemcoracyRIP" (CNN, 2017, para. 14).

On January 17, 2017, former FBI Director James Comey announced the FBI was considering the connection with Russia and members from Trump's campaign. After Director Comey testified before the Senate, President Trump fired him. Again, President Putin claimed that the Russian government was not involved in the hackings. On June 5, 2017, Leigh Winner, an NSA employee, was arrested and charged with "transmitting classified information" when an investigative website published reports that the Russian government had organized a phishing attack on computers at an American voting machine company, which compromised one email account and affected computer systems in at least twenty-one states (CNN, 2017, para. 17).

The back and forth between the actual involvement of the Russian government hacking into American computer systems has been continuing for more than two years. Congress is close to obtaining all information on whether members of Trump's campaign (and family members), in fact, did conspire with Russia, as well as the level of President Putin and his government's involvement to rig the election and to heavily influence American citizens to vote for Trump rather than Hillary Clinton. How does this scandal impact American homeland and national security? How does this affect American foreign policy and how the nation moves forward with foreign entities? Additionally, when the president of the United States becomes involved with (or aware of) foreign interference, what should be the consequences for his presidency and administration?

CHAPTER 14 PRACTICE PROBLEMS

1. How do long-term wars in Afghanistan and Iraq affect the future of American homeland security initiatives? What about national security objectives?

2. What is the importance of security risk management? How did the Integrated Risk Management plan influence security risk management initiatives?

3. Why is artificial intelligence a top cyber-security concern, and how does it affect American national and homeland security?

4. Is cyber terrorism more of a concern than traditional terrorism in the twenty-first century? Why or why not? Please be specific.

5. Because weapons of mass destruction are considered unconventional weapons, should the United Nations sanction all countries that currently have such weapons in their possession, especially nuclear weapons? What would be the consequences? How would sanctions affect international security and globalization?

6. How does the American space program protect national security and the homeland?

7. What is the difference between international terrorism and transnational organized crime? Are there any similarities? Please be specific.

8. What would be the economic, political, and social consequences if the United States were no longer a superpower? How would this change the international and security platform?

9. Please explain the international system and how it affects the United States economic and security platforms.

10. What are some initiatives on climate change? How is the United States working with other countries to address the matter?

Glossary

Abolitionist—an individual who opposes slavery.

Abortion extremism—radical acts and extreme violence by individuals and/or groups who oppose abortion.

Absolute monarchy—type of government where the monarch has absolute authority over its citizens and country.

Aggression—hostile and/or violent behavior with the alacrity to attack or confront the adversary.

Agroterrorism—terrorist acts through the act of use of biological and chemical weaponry to destroy a country's agricultural system.

Air Superiority (or air dominance)—where a nation state has complete control of airspace over opposing forces or adversarial threats.

Allocations—the process of distributing expenditures.

American diaspora—U.S. citizens who live outside of the United States.

Anarchist extremism—belief that society should not have a structured society or governmental system.

Applied research—discipline used to employ current scientific knowledge to develop better practical applications.

Appropriation—the sum of money allocated for a specific purpose.

Articles of Confederation—an agreement among the thirteen colonies that served as the original Constitution before it was replaced by the United States Constitution at the Constitutional Convention.

Artificial Intelligence (AI)—the theoretical concept of developing computer systems to perform human responsibilities.

Articles of War—frameworks established to regulate how a nation conducts its military operations.

Atomic bomb—a weapon of mass destruction and explosive device that is created through fission, fusion, or both; a nuclear weapon.

Australia, New Zealand, United States (ANZUS) Treaty—a security agreement among the countries to assist with military matters in the Pacific region.

Bay of Pigs Invasion—a failed U.S. military attempt to invade Cuba with Cuban refugees sponsored by CIA partisan initiatives in April 1961.

Berlin Airlift—the largest blockade crisis during the Cold War. The Soviet Union blocked Western allies, denying access to the Berlin section that was under Western control. Thus, Western allies performed an airlift to get supplies to West Berlin citizens.

Bill of Rights—the first ten amendments of the United States Constitution.

Biological warfare—the use of biological weapons with the intent to kill a large population in an act of war or retaliation.

Biological weapons—biological toxins or infectious agents used with the intention to kill humans, animals, and agriculture during conflict.

Bioterrorism—a denial weapon, bio agents can target single individuals up to an entire large population with little detection or distraction. Because bio weapons can be developed or maintained by nation states and rogue nations, the distribution and use of them are illegal.

Blockade—an action of blocking a location to prevent imports or exports from entering or leaving the premises.

Capitalism—an economic mechanism in which private sector companies make profit through means of production and not associated with the government.

Central Intelligence Agency—an intelligence agency under the United States federal government charged with gathering, processing, and analyzing national security information internationally to foster national security.

Chain of Command—a hierarchy of authority, usually within the United States Military. Also the order of authority within an organization.

Chairman of the Joint Chiefs of Staff—the highest-ranking senior military officer in the United States Armed Forces who is charged with consulting the president, Secretary of Defense, the National Security Council, and the Homeland Security Council on all military matters.

Chemical warfare—the use of chemical weapons with the intent to kill a large population in an act of war or retaliation.

Civil defense—is the concept of non-combatants protecting citizens from military effects or natural disasters.

Civil protection—a different concept from civil defense and should be emphasized as it is also a critical component of the preventative measures of emergency management procedures.

Coercive power—the ability to influence decision making by enforcing punishment or some type of action if an individual does not follow instructions.

Cold War—a political and military tension after World War II between the Western and Eastern powers which lasted over forty years.

Colonialism—political and economic control of a country.

Combatants—individuals, especially military personnel, who are actively engaged in combat during a war.

Combatant Commanders—commanders who are appointed over unified or specified commands.

Common law—English customs and laws adopted by the United States.

Communism—an economic, political, and social system where means of production does not exist, the government controls all private property, and there is not any hierarchy of social status, funding, or governance.

Congress—the legislative body of the United States of America.

Conference report—the final legislation negotiated between the House of Representatives and the Senate from the conference committee.

Conflict spectrum—a range of military events to which experts refer when hypothesizing conflict by alliances and adversaries on the effectiveness, methods, forces, sophistication, and level and challenge/difficulty.

Consequence management—emergency management and safety operations to rebuild government and civilian services in response to a crisis following the aftermath of an incident involving weapons of mass destruction.

Containment—a geopolitical strategy to mitigate expansion of the country.

Continental Congress—a group of delegates from the thirteen American colonies that was appointed as the governing body of the United States during the American Revolutionary War.

Contingency planning—a plan formulated to help risk-management programs to mitigate catastrophic events. These plans are commonly used by governments and the military.

Continuing resolution—an appropriation bill that allocates money for specific federal government agencies and programs.

Continuity of government—procedures permitting a government to continue vital operations in the wake of a disastrous event.

Conventional Constitution of 1787—a convention by five statesmen to discuss the revisions of the Articles of Confederation, which established the United States Constitution.

Conventional weapons—historical and traditional weapons used in conflict.

Counterproliferation—military operatives to prevent the spread of nuclear weapons.

Covert operations—a concealed operation to mask the identity of those involved and the responsibilities.

Crisis management—how an organization handles unexpected events that are deemed harmful to an organization, its stakeholders, or the American public.

Critical infrastructure—essential services that underpin American society and serve as the backbone of our nation's economy, health, and security.

Cuban Missile Crisis—the conflict between the United States and the Soviet Union concerning Soviet secret ballistic missile arrangement in Cuba.

Cyberespionage—using advanced technical, Internet, and virtual methods to spy on other countries.

Cyber hackings—cybercrimes.

Cybersecurity—protection against theft, damage, or sabotage to computer or hardware programs and the disruption of system networks.

Cyberterrorism—any premeditated politically motivated attack against computer programs and network systems, data, or information which results in violence against non-combatant targets by subnational groups or clandestine agents.

Declaration of Independence—declaration by the Second Continental Congress stating the thirteen American colonies were free from British rule.

Defense Pact—is a military armistice among alliances where parties make a pact to defend each other.

Defense policy—a facet of initiatives predicated on international security and military strategies.

Democracy—a system of government in which citizens select members of state through elections.

Democratic Party—one of the two major parties in the United States government.

Denial weapons—non-lethal, directed-energy, counter-personal systems with an extended range greater than currently fielded non-lethal weapons.

Department of the Air Force—one of three military service departments within the Department of Defense. The United States Air Force is responsible for aerial warfare and is the largest and most advanced air force in the world.

Department of the Army—one of three military service departments within the Department of Defense. The Army is responsible for all land-based operatives and is the largest military force in the United States.

Department of Defense (DoD)—the largest federal government agency within the United States that is responsible for overseeing and organizing subordinate agencies concerned with national security and United States Armed Forces.

Department of the Navy—the naval warfare branch of the United States Military including the Marine Corps. The United States Navy is largest navy in the world.

Department of War—part of the United States Cabinet department that was responsible for the Army and Navy Departments. Because of the National Security Act of 1947, the named was changed to the Department of Defense.

Direct action—criminal activity designed to cause economic loss or to destroy victims' operations or property.

Director of Central Intelligence—a former position as the Chief Executive Officer of the Central Intelligence Agency. The position was renamed the Director of National Intelligence on April 21, 2005.

Discretionary spending—the process of government spending through an appropriations bill.

Domestic terrorism—see homegrown terrorism.

Emergency management—the management of resources and responsibilities by first responders, emergency management professionals, and governments to deal with preparedness, response, and recovery in the before, during, and after an emergency.

Emancipation—free from the control of slavery.

Emancipation Proclamation—legislation which freed all slaves in the Confederate states and was justified through a wartime operation.

Emergency responders—firefighters, military, paramedics, law enforcement, transportation and logistics, and other emergency management professionals who respond to emergencies.

Enhanced Defense Cooperation Agreement—an agreement to boost the relationship between the United States and the Philippines that was initially formed over sixty years ago. EDCA allows the United States to establish transient military installations and ground forces for deployment.

Electronic intelligence (ELINT)—gathering intelligence using electronic sensors.

Executive branch—a federal branch of United States government that is responsible for employing and supporting laws and regulations established by the legislatives and judicial branches.

Executive orders—orders issued by the president of the United States that are announced to federal agencies within the American government for adherence and awareness. Such orders are predicated on the U.S. Constitution.

Expatriates—individuals who do not live in their native country.

Expert power—the capability to influence those based on experience and knowledge.

Fallout—when a nuclear explosion produces radiative materials, sending out rays of nuclear radiation.

Fatwa—religious decision of Islamic law made by one of Islamic authority.

Federalists—individuals who support federalism and/or were members of the Federalist Party.

Federalist Party—the first political party in the United States from the late 1790s to the early 1800s. The political party mandated strong national government ideologies which promoted economic stability and bolstered relations with Europe.

First Balkan War—a war in which the Balkan League defeated the Ottoman Empire, which lasted from October 1912 to May 1913.

First responders—please see emergency responders.

Force structure—ensuring military organizations are prepared through combat readiness planning by determining how military personnel, resources, weapons, operations, and doctrine are relevant during conflict.

Foreign diplomacy—the concept of maintaining positive relationships between foreign governments.

Foreign policy—policies and strategies on how a country deals with foreign countries.

Feudalism—a specific social system during the Middle Ages in which land was held for a fee between a lord and vassal.

Fusion centers—information sharing centers between two or more agencies, primarily military, intelligence, and law enforcement, to detect, prevent, examine, and respond to criminal and terrorist events.

Germ theory—the concept of germs being produced by microorganisms.

Global dominance—a country or state dominating on an international level based on national power.

Globalization—the process of interacting with investments, trading, people, companies, cultures, and governments of different countries.

Goldwater-Nichols Act of 1986—an act signed by President Ronald Reagan and named after Senator Barry Goldwater and Representative William Flynt Nichols that was considered the largest reorganization policy for the command structure of the United States Military since the National Security Act of 1947. The legislation was passed to improve interoperability within the Department of Defense and military components.

Gulf War—(codename Operation Desert Shield) war lasting from August 2, 1990 to January 17, 1991 that led to a military buildup in Saudi Arabia against the United States and its allies versus Iraq in response to Iraq's invasion of Kuwait.

Governance—the act of governing.

Government planning—planning to sustain the constitutional government and ensure that government entities are structured to recover from various operational challenges.

Great Depression—a severe economic depression that happened during the 1930s in the Western industrialized world.

Greco-Turkish War of 1919—a war fought between Greece and the Turkish National Movement, which resulted in the Turkish War of Independence.

Homeland Security Council—an executive committee under the Executive Office of the president that consults on homeland security matters.

Homeland security—the concept of protecting the American land by coordinating emergency management efforts to detect, respond, prepare, investigate, and mitigate terrorist attacks and other large-scale disasters.

Homegrown terrorism—terrorist acts committed by citizens or permanent residents of their country without influence from international terrorist organizations to instill fear in the population or government to express ideological, political, or religious objectives.

House of Representatives—one of the two chambers of United States Congress that is responsible for the legislative branch.

Ideologies—system of beliefs and principles.

Imperialism—the practice of extending economic and political powers of a nation.

Insurrection—a violent rebellion against a government.

Intelligence—information collected from specific agencies to be analyzed, produced, and distributed based on government requirements and responsibilities.

Inter-American Treaty of Republic Assistance or Rio Treaty—an agreement that was signed on September 2, 1947 by most of the countries in North and South America. If any country faced aggression or threats from outside, it would be considered an attack against all under the Pan-American arrangement.

International terrorism—terrorist acts that are dangerous and violent in nature against the United States, its citizens, and resources by a foreign individual(s) and/or terrorist organizations.

Internet of Things (IoT)—certain vulnerabilities (such as smart devices) that can affect the nation's electrical grid system, energy program, and public transportation, destroying data privacy and integrity or the continuity of services.

Islamic extremism—radical form of Islam that opposes democracy, Western civilization, and the universal law of mutual equality and respect for different faiths and ideologies.

Islamic State of Iraq and the Levant (ISIL)—a jihadist terrorist organization that follows the Wahhabi doctrine derived from Sunni Islam.

Jihad—the spiritual struggle against enemies of Islam.

Joint Chiefs of Staff—a group of appointed senior military officials who are advisers to the president, Secretary of Defense, the Homeland Security Council, and National Security Council on all military matters.

Judiciary branch—a federal branch of United States government that is responsible for interpreting laws and overseeing justice.

Just-in-time distribution model—strategies used to increase efficiency within an organization and decrease waste by using only what is needed in the production phase.

Just-war theory—the explanation as to how and why wars are fought.

Korean Armistice Agreement—the armistice agreement between North and South Korea that ended the Korean War in 1953.

Left-wing extremism—extremists who are focused on revolutionary socialism and believe they can accomplish such goals by involving themselves in the American government and political system.

Legislative branch—part of the federal branch of United States government that is responsible for writing and passing laws.

Legitimate power—the ability to obtain power through a position or office held at an authoritative level within an agency.

Liberalism—the concept of having liberal views.

Loyalists—American patriots who were loyal to the British during the American Revolutionary War.

Lone wolves—individuals who commit terrorist acts and other expressions of violence to accomplish economic, political, or religious goals.

Mandatory spending—legislation enacted by the federal government to set aside funding for specific programs dictated by the government authority.

Manifest Destiny—a notion that settlers within the United States were meant to expand democratic establishments across North America.

Maritime system—the American maritime system comprised of over 300 sea and river ports with nearly 4,000 cargo and passenger terminals.

Martial law—the suspension of ordinary law through military action.

Mass assured destruction—military doctrine and national security frameworks detailing a full-scale nuclear weapons attack by two more oppositions that would obliterate both the attacker and defender.

Militia extremists—a faction of radicals who conduct militant operations to protect a country.

Mitigation—the power to reduce loss of life or diminish the impact of any type of disaster.

Mujahideen—one engaged in jihad.

Multilateral cooperation agreements—binding or non-binding agreements between organizations, governments, or foreign entities, addressing legal policies to work together to handle interests, responsibilities, and rights of member states.

Narcoterrorism—drug trafficking organizations that use terrorist tactics to advance illegal operations.

National Military Establishment—initial name of the United States Department of Defense prior to the National Security Act of 1947.

NATO Treaty—treaty signed on April 4, 1949, establishing the North Atlantic Treaty Organization.

National Incident Management System (NIMS)—an incident-management system utilized to coordinate responses between emergency management agencies within the federal government.

National Military Strategy—a military strategy issued by the Chairman of the Joint Chiefs of Staff that summaries the strategic operations of the United States Armed Forces.

National Response Framework (NRF)—a component of the National Strategy for Homeland Security (like National Security Strategy), which is the outline for all levels of domestic response to prepare for national disasters.

National Security Act of 1947—the United States largest reorganization of foreign policy and military establishment of the federal government.

National Security Agency—a federally funded intelligence agency accountable for the international monitoring, collection, and processing of signals intelligence (SIGINT).

National Security Strategy—a policy prepared by the executive branch and signed by the president that summarizes top national security concerns and outlines how the government will address those matters.

Noncombatants—civilians and/or military personnel who are not considered combatants or engaged in conflict.

Noncombatant immunity—civilians or service members who are not engaged in armed conflict or are immune from combative operations.

Nonproliferation—the inhibition of spreading nuclear weapons.

Non-state actors—individuals and/or groups that are politically involved but are not considered a coalition force or ally to any country or nation state.

Nuclear warfare—the use of nuclear weapons with the intent to kill a large population and destroy infrastructures to incapacitate a country in an act of war or retaliation.

Nuclear weapon—see atomic bomb.

Orbital weaponry—a weapon in orbit around an astronomic object.

Open Government Partnership (OGP)—a multilateral agreement focused on security commitments from governments to promote democracy, empower citizens, fight corruption, and harness new technologies to strengthen governance.

Operation Inherent Resolve—executed on August 21, 2016, an American military operation codenamed for the combat operation against ISIL in Iraq and in Syria.

Operation MONGOOSE—a clandestine operation led by the Central Intelligence Agency to overthrow the Communist regime under Fidel Castro's reign, which was approved by President John F. Kennedy on November 30, 1961.

OPLAN (Operational Plan)—a comprehensive policy that cover strategies for joint military operations.

Ottoman Empire—an empire established in the thirteenth century by Turkish leader and Ottoman founder Osman Gazi.

Permissive Action Links—security mechanisms to prevent unauthorized detonation of nuclear weapons.

Policy of Deliberate Ambiguity—states a country can deliberately be ambiguous on specific aspects of foreign policy, particularly if a country has WMDs.

Policymakers—senior executive military, civilian officials, and politicians, in high-risk political and government positions who make effective and complex decisions, especially in government.

Political asylum—protections granted by a country to a foreigner who has left his/her native land as a political refugee.

Port security—defense measures to protect maritime and port operations.

Power projection—the capability of a country to apply elements of national power, including economic, political, and military factors, and how such factors can be effectively and precipitously used to respond to and deter crises as well as improve regional stability and security.

Preparedness—the conceptualization of a response to crises or any type of emergency.

Presidential Accountability Act—legislation passed by Congress to ensure the president or vice president does involvement himself/herself or participate in any venture that may affect his/her personal financial interests.

President of the United States—the head of state and government for the United States and the Commander-in-Chief for the United States Armed Forces.

Preventative measures—measures taken to mitigate possible situations.

Primogeniture laws—the right of succession belonging to the first-born child, a common-law matter.

Proliferation—a rapid increase in numbers, particularly referring to nuclear weapons.

Public policy—courses of action, financial processes, regulatory concerns, and system of laws to implement government policies that affects a population.

Radicalism—extreme beliefs or ideologies of those who seek political, religious, or societal reform.

Reconnaissance—military observation to observe adversarial activity or determine strategic movement.

Redemption movement—those who support the American conspiracy theory that believes the federal government deserted the gold standard program and used citizens as collateral to borrow money from other countries.

Referent power—indicative of interpersonal relationships in which individuals support others within an agency.

Representative government—a specific social system during the Middle Ages in which land was held for a fee between a lord and vassal.

Republicanism—a sociopolitical system in which citizens are under a republic with popular sovereignty.

Republican Party—referred to as Grand Old Party, one of the two major political parties in United States government.

Republic of South Korea—signed on October 1, 1953, the agreement between the United States and South Korea to provide mutual aid if either country faced aggression from adversarial threats. As with the Japanese treaty, the United States established permanent military bases in South Korea.

Research and development—the idea of linking corporate and government modernization.

Reward power—the ability to influence a person (or persons) by providing incentives within an organization.

Right-wing extremism—those whose ideologies are predicated on racial supremacy and are anti-government, anti-regulatory, anti-Catholic, and anti-Semitic.

Risk assessment—the process of examining potential risks in specific activities.

Risk management—the concept of understanding risks and vulnerabilities by identifying, assessing and prioritizing them and establishing procedures to minimize hazards and manage the probability of disastrous events.

Rogue nation (rogue state)—states that are accused of breaking international law and pose a threat to other nation states.

Satellite states—countries that were autonomous but are now politically and economically controlled by another country.

Secretary of Defense—a senior defense official and head of the Department of Defense.

Security—the mitigation of danger and/or threats.

Security risk management—the identification, assessment and prioritization of risks followed by coordinated application of resources to minimize, monitor, and control the probability and/or impact of unforeseen events.

Senate—one of the two chambers in the upper assembly of United States Congress.

Signals intelligence (SIGINT)—the act of gathering intelligence through communications between people or electronic signals (electronic intelligence—ELINT).

Situational reports (SITREPs)—reports that include status updates on emerging threats or nearing aftermath events.

Socialism—a political system in which the government controls private property and natural resources and citizens live in entitlement. What is manufactured is shared by those contributed to its production.

Southeast Asia Treaty Organization (SEATO)—a former international security agreement to provide defense in the Southeast Asian region.

Sovereign citizen extremism—radical citizens who do not recognize societal structures or political or government systems.

Special interest terrorism—terrorism which is focused on political change and structure.

State of emergency—when a government suspends normal daily and working operations in the event of a natural disaster or emergency.

Status quo ante bellum—existing before the war.

Third World—the underdevelopment of a country.

Threat modeling—processes to identify who are motivated and the motivation behind system and network attacks.

Transnational organized crime (TOC)—an illicit operation which coordinates missions across national borders by individuals or groups who are involved in illegal business operations.

Treaty of Mutual Cooperation and Security—an agreement between the United States and Japan to maintain peace in East Asia and for both countries to react to threats against each other, requiring the United States to have a permanent presence in Japan.

Treaty on the Non-Proliferation of Nuclear Weapons (or NPT)—an international agreement in which five nation states agree to mitigate the extent of nuclear weapons and technology, support peace of nuclear energy, and assist with global nuclear disarmament.

Trench warfare—a type of military warfare in which both parties create trenches as a defense.

Truman Doctrine—American foreign policy established to mitigate Soviet geopolitical theologies during the Cold War.

Unconventional warfare—combat operations that are conducted by enemies through guerilla (or insurgency) tactics and/or subversion.

Unconventional weapons—asymmetrical weaponry not considered weapons of mass destruction or any ordnance that is classified as non-conventional weapons.

Unified Combatant Commands—nine combatant commands established to provide effective control of U.S. Armed Forces during peace and contingency operations; a command within the Department of Defense that is comprised of military departments to provide effective command and control missions of the United States Armed Forces.

United Nations—a transnational agency that promotes global cooperation among supporting nation states.

United States Armed Forces—the federal United States Military that is comprised of the Air Force, Army, Navy, Marine Corps, and Coast Guard.

United States Coast Guard—one of the seven uniformed services under the United States Armed Forces. Its mission is performing maritime law enforcement with jurisdiction in domestic and international waters.

United States Constitution—the supreme law and national framework of the United States government.

Union of Soviet Socialist Republics (USSR)—regulated by the Community Party, was a political state of subordinate Soviet countries within Eurasia that existed from 1922–1991.

Vulnerability assessment—the process of examining potential vulnerabilities in specific activities.

Weapons of mass destruction (WMD)—biological, chemical, nuclear, or radiological agents that are used to cause pervasive destruction and death.

Western civilization—the modern culture of Europe and North America.

White supremacy—extremists who seek national dominance and believe they are the superior race.

World War I—an international war that began in Europe between Western allies against Germany and Austria-Hungary. More than 70 million military forces were mobilized making it one of the largest wars in history. The war lasted from July 28, 1914 to November 11, 1918.

World War II—an international war that was a result of WWI between Allies (United States, China, Soviet Union, and Great Britain) and Axis nations (Germany, Japan, and Italy). The war lasted from September 1, 1939 to September 2, 1945.

Yield—the measure of power distributed and the sum amount of energy released in an explosion.

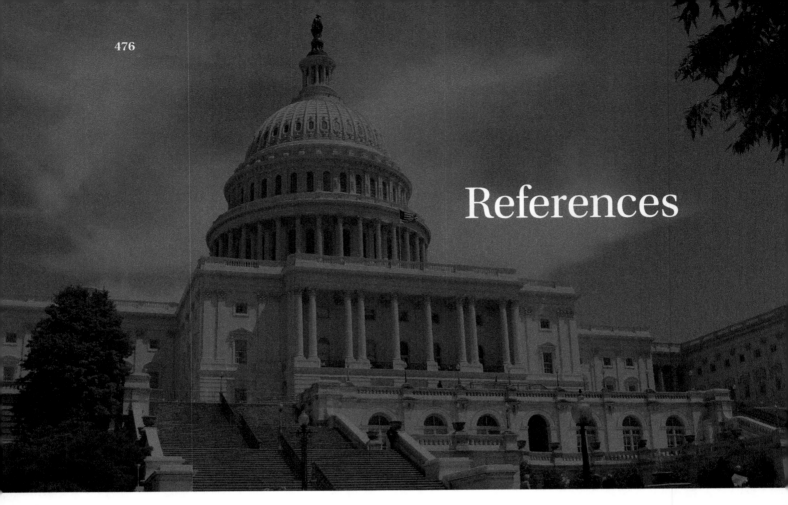

476

References

9/11 attacks. (2010). *History.com*. Retrieved June 29, 2017, from http://www.history.com/topics/9-11-attacks.

9/11 Commission. (2011). History.com. Retrieved June 17, 2017, from http://www.history.com/topics/9-11-commission.

The 9/11 Commission Report. (2014). National Commission on Terrorist Attacks Upon the United States. Retrieved June 29, 2017 from http://govinfo.library.unt.edu/911/report/911Report_Exec.htm.

10 U.S. Code 113—Secretary of Defense. (n.d.). *Legal Information Institute.* Cornell University. Retrieved from https://www.law.cornell.edu/uscode/text/10/113

10 U.S. Code 164—Commanders of Combatant Commands: Assignment; Powers and Duties. *Government Accountability Office.* Retrieved from https://www.gpo.gov/fdsys/granule/USCODE-2010-title10/USCODE-2010-title10-subtitleA-partl-chap6-sec164 (accessed on 9 December 2017).

18 U.S. Code 113B—Terrorism. (2010). *Government Printing Office.* Retrieved from http://eur-lex.europa.eu/legal-content/EN/TXT/?uri=celex%3A32017L0541 (accessed on 12 December 2017).

18 U.S. Code 2331—definitions. (n.d.). *Legal Information Institute.* Cornell University. Retrieved from https://www.law.cornell.edu/uscode/text/18/2331

2012–2017 Defense Intelligence Agency Strategy. (2017). *Defense Intelligence Agency.* Retrieved from https://www.hsdl.org/?view&did=683174 (accessed on 15 December 2017).

2014 Laws with DHS Impacts. (n.d.). *Department of Homeland Security*. Retrieved from https://www.dhs.gov/2014-laws-dhs-impacts (accessed on 18 December 2017).

2016 Presidential campaign hacking fast facts. (2017). CNN. Retrieved from http://www.cnn.com/2016/12/26/us/2016-presidential-campaign-hacking-fast-facts/index.html (accessed on 13 August 2017).

Aberbach, M. & Aberbach, D. (2000). *Abstract. In: The Roman-Jewish Wars and Hebrew Cultural Nationalism.* Palgrave Macmillan: London. p. 1.

A brief history of the Office of Strategic Services: America's first intelligence agency. (2014). *Imminent Threat Solutions.* Retrieved from http://www.itstactical.com/centcom/history-centcom/a-brief-history-of-the-office-of-strategic-services-americas-first-intelligence-agency/

Allison, G. (2010). U.S. National Interests. *Harvard University.* Retrieved from https://portals.jhuapl.edu/media/RethinkingSeminars/021810/Allison_ppt.pdf (accessed on 7 December 2017).

A look back. (2008). Central Intelligence Agency. Retrieved on June 14, 2017 from https://www.cia.gov/news-information/featured-story-archive/2008-featured-story-archive/national-security-act-of-1947.html

A look back: Intelligence and the committee of secret correspondence. (n.d.). Central Intelligence Agency. Retrieved from https://www.cia.gov/news-information/featured-story-archive/2011-featured-story-archive/intelligence-and-the-committee-of-secret-correspondence.html

About CIA. (n.d.) Central Intelligence Agency. Retrieved from https://www.cia.gov/about-cia

About CBP. (n.d.). U.S. Customs and Border Protection. Retrieved from https://www.cbp.gov/about

About DOE. (n.d.). *Office of Intelligence and Counterintelligence.* Retrieved from https://energy.gov/intelligence/office-intelligence-and-counterintelligence (accessed on 15 December 2017).

About DIA. (n.d.). *Defense Intelligence Agency.* Retrieved from http://www.dia.mil/About/ (accessed on 15 December 2017).

About NGA. (n.d.). National Geospatial-Intelligence Agency. Retrieved from https://www.nga.mil/About/Pages/Default.aspx (accessed on 11 August 2017).

About the Department of Defense (DoD). Mission. (n.d.) U.S. Department of Defense. Retrieved from http://www.defense.gov/About-DoD

About DOT. (2016). *U.S. Department of the Treasury.* Retrieved from https://www.treasury.gov/about/role-of-treasury/Pages/default.aspx (accessed on 15 December 2017).

Abt, Clark C. (2003) The economic impact of nuclear terrorist attacks on freight transport systems in an age of seaport vulnerability. *Abt Associates.* Retrieved from http://www.abtassociates.com/reports/es-economic_impact_of_nuclear_terrorist_attacks.pdf (accessed 16 June 2017).

Abu Mohammad al-Julani. (2017). *Middle East Journal.* Retrieved from https://middleeastwarjournalweb.wordpress.com/2017/04/20/abu-mohammad-al-julani/ (accessed on 17 August 2017).

Abubakar, A.A. (2017). Three years later, nearly 200 Nigerian schoolgirls still missing. *USA Today.* Retrieved from https://www.usatoday.com/story/news/world/2017/04/13/chibok-nigeria-girls-still-missing-boko-haram/100319108/ (accessed on 15 August 2017).

Ackerman, S. and Rushe, D. (2013). NSA director: Edward Snowden has caused irreversible damage to U.S. *The Guardian.* Retrieved June 22, 2017 from https://www.theguardian.com/world/2013/jun/23/nsa-director-snowden-hong-kong.

Active denial system FAQs. (n.d.) U.S. Department of Defense. Retrieved from http://jnlwp.defense.gov/About/Frequently-Asked-Questions/Active-Denial-System-FAQs/ (accessed 6 May 2017).

Active shooter resources. (2016). FBI. Retrieved June 27, 2017, from https://www.fbi.gov/about/partnerships/office-of-partner-engagement/active-shooter-resources.

Adams, N., Nordhaus, T., and Shellenberger, M. (2011). Counterterrorism since 9/11: Evaluating the efficacy of controversial tactics. [Scholarly project]. *The Breakthrough Organization.* Retrieved June 26, 2017 from https://thebreakthrough.org/images/pdfs/CCT_Report_revised-3-31-11a.pdf.

Adeyemi, Ph.D., A. E. (2015). *Terrorism and Transnational Security Threats in West Africa: A Global Perspective.* Xilbris Corporation: Bloomington, IN.

The Administration. The White House. (n.d.). National Security Council. Retrieved on June 17, 2017 from https://obamawhitehouse.archives.gov/administration/eop/nsc/.

Advanced law enforcement rapid response training (ALERRT) and train-the-trainer. (2008). PoliceOne.com. Retrieved June 27, 2017, from https://www.policeone.com/active-shooter/articles/1672495-Advanced-Law-Enforcement-Rapid-Response-Training-ALERRT-and-Train-the-Trainer/.

Aftergood, S. (2015). Leaks damaged U.S. intelligence, official says. Federation of American Scientists. Retrieved June 22, 2017 from https://fas.org/blogs/secrecy/2015/02/leaks-damaged/.

Agroterrorism: Threats to America's economy and food supply. (February 16, 2012). FBI. Retrieved June 30, 2017 from https://leb.fbi.gov/2012/february/agroterrorism-threats-to-americas-economy-and-food-supply.

Agroterrorism: What is the threat and what can be done about it? (Rep. No. RB7565OSD). (2003). Rand Corportation. Retrieved June 30, 2017 from http://www.rand.org/pubs/research_briefs/RB7565/index1.html.

Airfield Development and Activities Behind the Lines. (n.d.). *U.S. Marine Corps.* Retrieved from http://www.marines.mil/Portals/59/Publications/History%20of%20the%20U.S.%20Marine%20Corps%20in%20WWII%20Vol%20IV%20-%20Western%20Pacific%20Operations%20%20PCN%2019000262700_4.pdf (accessed on 12 December 2017).

Allison, G.T. and Blackwill, R. (2010). *America's national interests: A report from the commission on America's national interests.* Cambridge, MA: Belfer Center for Science and International Affairs, Harvard University.

Alvarez, L. and Perez-Pena, R. (2016, June 12). Orlando gunman attacks gay nightclub, leaving 50 dead. *New York Times.* Retrieved June 27, 2017 from http://incidentreviews.org/wp-content/uploads/2014/05/Police-Under-Attack.pdf.

Ambient (outdoor) air quality and health. (2016). World Health Organization. Retrieved from http://www.who.int/mediacentre/factsheets/fs313/en/ (accessed 17 June 2017).

American expanding. (n.d.) *U.S. History: A New Nation Emerging.* University of North Texas. Retrieved from http://web3.unt.edu/cdl/course_projects/HIST2610/content/03_Unit_Three/12_lesson_twelve/00_unit_three_lesson_twelve.htm

American Revolution history. (2009). AE Network. Retrieved June 19, 2017, from http://www.history.com/topics/american-revolution/american-revolution-history.

American Revolution to World War II: Secret writing. (n.d.). Federation of American Scientists. Retrieved from https://fas.org/irp/ops/ci/docs/ci1/ch1c.htm (accessed on 9 December 2017).

Anastacio, O. LCDR. (2004). Battle damage repair at sea. *Faceplate: United States Navy.* Retrieved from http://www.navsea.navy.mil/Portals/103/Documents/SUPSALV/faceplate/April%202004.pdf

Anderson, T.A. (1983). Bomb kills 28 at U.S. embassy. *Syracuse Herald Journal.* Retrieved from https://newspaperarchive.com/us/massachusetts/lowell/lowell-sun/1983/04-24/page-55?tag=terry+anderson+us+embassy&rtserp=tags/us-embassy?pf=terry&pl=anderson&page=3/

Animal liberation front. (2007). *Wikipedia.* Retrieved from http://www.animalliberationfront.com/ALFront/Premise_History/ALF_Wikipedia.htm

Ansari, A. (2016). State Department ups reward for ISIS leader to $25 million. *CNN.* Retrieved from http://www.cnn.com/2016/12/17/politics/state-department-isis-al-baghdadi-reward/index.html (accessed on 15 August 2017).

Anthrax. (2014). CDC. Anthrax. Retrieved June 21, 2017 from https://www.cdc.gov/anthrax/bioterrorism/threat.html.

Anti-Money Laundering/Counter Terrorist Financing. (n.d.). *U.S. Department of State.* Retrieved from https://www.state.gov/j/inl/c/crime/c44634.htm (accessed on 17 December 2017).

The arms trade treaty. (n.d.) United Nations. Retrieved from https://unoda-web.s3.amazonaws.com/wp-content/uploads/2013/06/English7.pdf (accessed 8 August 2017).

Army general: Manning's leaks hurt relationship with Afghan. (2013). CBS.com. Retrieved on June 25, 2017 from http://www.cbsnews.com/news/army-general-mannings-leaks-hurt-relationships-with-afghans/

The Army Intelligence Center is Established, 1 September 1954. (n.d.). *U.S. Army.* Retrieved from https://www.army.mil/article/110383/the_army_intelligence_center_is_established_1_september_1954 (accessed on 15 December 2017).

Arneson, R.J. (2006). Just warfare theory and noncombatant immunity. *Cornell International Law Journal, (39)*3. Article 9.

Arquilla, J. (2013). Last war standing. *Foreign Policy.* Retrieved from http://foreignpolicy.com/2013/08/13/last-war-standing/ (accessed 23 March 2017).

Arquilla, J. and Ronfeldt, D. (n.d.) A new epoch—and spectrum—of conflict. Rand.org. Retrieved from https://www.rand.org/content/dam/rand/pubs/monograph_reports/MR880/MR880.ch1.pdf

Attack at Pearl Harbor, 1941. (1997). *EyeWitness to History.com.* Retrieved June 28, 2017 from http://www.eyewitnesstohistory.com/pearl.htm

Aulard, A. (1922). *Modern France: A companion to French studies.* New York: Cambridge Press. p. 115.

Baldwin, D.A. (1997). The Concept of Security. *Review of International Studies.* Retrieved from http://www.princeton.edu/~dbaldwin/selected%20articles/Baldwin%20(1997)%20The%20Concept%20of%20Security.pdf

Basu, R. (2012). *International Politics: Concepts, Theories and Issues.* Sage Publications, Inc: Thousand Oaks, CA. p. 385.

Battles of Lexington and Concord. (2009). AE Network. Retrieved June 19, 2017 from http://www.history.com/topics/american-revolution/battles-of-lexington-and-concord.

Baucom, D.R. (2004) The rise and fall of brilliant pebbles. *Missile Defense Agency.* Retrieved from http://highfrontier.org/oldarchive/Archive/hf/The%20Rise%20and%20Fall%20of%20Brilliant%20Pebbles%20-Baucom.pdf (accessed 17 June 2017).

The Bay of Pigs invasion and its aftermath, April 1961-October 1962. (n.d.). The Office of the Historian. Retrieved from https://history.state.gov/milestones/1961-1968/bay-of-pigs

Bea, K., Krouse, W., Morgan, D., Morrisey, W., and Redhead, C.S. (2003). Emergency preparedness and response directorate of the Department of Homeland Security. *CRS Report for Congress: Congressional Research Service.* Retrieved from https://fas.org/sgp/crs/RS21367.pdf

Bean, H. (2009). Exploring the relationship between homeland security information sharing and Local emergency preparedness. *Homeland Security Affairs. (5)*5. Retrieved from https://www.hsaj.org/articles/104 (accessed on 18 December 2017).

Belasco, A. and Towell, P. (2013). Government shutdown: Operations of the Department of Defense during a lapse in appropriations. (Rep. No. R41745). Retrieved June 18, 2017 from Congressional Research Service website: https://fas.org/sgp/crs/natsec/R41745.pdf.

Benedict Arnold. (2009). History.com. Accessed June 19, 2017. http://www.history.com/topics/american-revolution/benedict-arnold.

Bergen, P.L. September 11 attacks. (April 5, 2017). *Encyclopedia Britannica.* Retrieved June 29, 2017 from https://www.britannica.com/event/September-11-attacks.

Bergen, P.L. (2006). The Osama bin Laden I know. New York City: NY. Simon and Schuster. p. 370.

Berkowitz, M. and Bock, P.G. (1965). *American national security.* New York: Free Press.

Berkowitz, M. and Bock, P.G. (1996). The emerging field of national security. *World Politics, (19)*124.

Best, S., and Nocella, II, A.J. (2006). *Igniting a revolution: Voices in defense of the Earth.* Oakland, CA: AK Press.

Bertrand, N. (2015). We're getting to know just how different ISIS is from al-Qaeda. *Business Insider.* Retrieved from http://www.businessinsider.com/difference-between-isis-and-al-qaeda-2015-5 (accessed on 18 December 2017).

Bidgoli, H. (2004). *The Internet encyclopedia, volume 1.* Hoboken, NJ: John Wiley & Sons.

The biological weapons conventions. (2017). United Nations Office for Disarmament Affairs. Retrieved from https://www.un.org/disarmament/wmd/bio/ (accessed 6 May 2017).

Bioterrorism. (n.d.). *Department of Homeland Security.* Retrieved from https://www.ready.gov/Bioterrorism (accessed on 12 December 2017).

Blake, A. Islamic state hacker sentenced for sssisting terrorist group with "kill list." (2016). *The Washington Times.* Retrieved from http://www.washingtontimes.com/news/2016/sep/24/ardit-ferizi-hacker-who-aided-islamic-state-senten/ (accessed 23 March 2017).

Blakeley, R. (2012). State violence as state terrorism. *The Ashgate Research Companion to Political Violence.* Ashgate: London. pp. 63–78. Retrieved from https://kar.kent.ac.uk/24178/1/State%20Violence%20as%20state%20terrorism%20%5B ashgate%20final%5D.pdf (accessed on 6 September 2017).

Boko Harams leaders designated as terrorists by US. (2012). *BBC News.* Retrieved from http://www.bbc.com/news/world-africa-18542030 (accessed on 15 August 2017).

Boko Haram threatens U.S. in video. (2013) *CNN.* Retrieved from https://www.youtube.com/watch?v=s6flerfasbk (accessed on 15 August 2017).

Bolonkin, A. (2008). Cheap method for shielding a city from rocket and nuclear warhead impacts. Arxiv.org. Retrieved from https://arxiv.org/pdf/0801.1694.pdf (accessed on 10 August 2017).

Bolton, J. (2013). Edward Snowden's leaks are a grave threat to U.S. national security. *The Guardian*. Retrieved June 22, 2017 from https://www.theguardian.com/commentisfree/2013/jun/18/edward-snowden-leaks-grave-threat.

The bombing of Hiroshima and Nagasaki. (2009). History.com. Retrieved on June 20, 2017 from http://www.history.com/topics/world-war-ii/bombing-of-hiroshima-and-nagasaki.

Booth, K. & Dunne, T. (2002). Worlds in collision: Terror and the Future of global order. New Hampshire: Palgrave Macmillan. p. 128.

Boren Awards for International Study. (2016). Boren Awards. Retrieved from http://www.boren-awards.org/national_security.html

Bowe, A. (2015). Cybersecurity: We need a Chinese Snowden. *The Diplomat*. Retrieved June 22, 2017 from http://thediplomat.com/2015/07/cybersecurity-we-need-a-chinese-snowden/.

Bowers, S.R., and Parke, S.M. (2009). Identification of transnational threats. *Liberty University: Helms School of Government*. Retrieved from http://digitalcommons.liberty.edu/cgi/viewcontent.cgi?article=1080&context=gov_fac_pubs

Bradford, J.C. (1985). Command under sail: Makers of the American naval tradition, 1775–1850. Annapolis, MD: United States Naval Institute.

Bradley Manning leak has had chilling effect on U.S. foreign policy, court hears. (2013). *The Guardian*. Retrieved on June 24, 2017 from https://www.theguardian.com/world/2013/aug/05/bradley-manning-leak-foreign-policy-sentencing.

Bradley Manning leaks cause "horror and disbelief" at State Department. (2013). *The Guardian*. Retrieved on June 25, 2017 from https://www.theguardian.com/world/2013/aug/01/bradley-manning-wikileaks-state-department.

Brooks, R. (2005). Failed states, or the state as failure? *The University of Chicago Law Review, 72*(4), 1159–1196. Retrieved from http://www.jstor.org/stable/4495527 (Retrieved on 5 September 2017).

Brush, P. (2002). What Bush knew before Sept. 11. CBS News. Retrieved June 18, 2017 from http://www.cbsnews.com/news/what-bush-knew-before-sept-11/.

Bucci, S., Inserra, D., Lesser, J., Mayer, M., Spencer, J., Slattery, B., and Tubb, K. (2013), After Hurricane Sandy: Time to learn and implement the lessons in preparedness, response, and resilience. *The Heritage Foundation*. http://w. ww.heritage.org/homeland-security/report/after-hurricane-sandy-time-learn-and-implement-the-lessons-preparedness#_ftnref33.

Buck, A. (1983). The Atomic Energy Commission. *U.S. Department of Energy: Office of Management, Office of the Executive Secretariat, Office of History and Heritage Resources*. Retrieved from https://energy.gov/sites/prod/files/AEC%20History.pdf (accessed on 15 December 2017).

Bucknell III, H. (1972). *Energy and the national defense*. Lexington, KY: University of Kentucky.

Bullock, J.A., Haddow, G.D., Coppola, D.P., and Yeletaysi, S. (2009). *Introduction to homeland security*. 4th ed. Oxford, UK: Butterworth-Heinemann.

Bundy, M. (1962). National security action memorandum 181. The White House, Washington, DC.

Burke, B. T. (2017). Understanding, assessing, and responding to terrorism: Protecting critical infrastructure and personnel. Hoboken, NJ: John Wiley and Sons. p. 23.

Burwell, S.M. (2013). Impacts and costs of the government shutdown. [Web log post]. Retrieved June 18, 2017 from https://obamawhitehouse.archives.gov/blog/2013/11/07/impacts-and-costs-government-shutdown.

Bush, G. (2007). National strategy for homeland security. President of the United States. Retrieved from https://www.dhs.gov/xlibrary/assets/nat_strat_homelandsecurity_2007.pdf

Byman, D.L. (2015). Comparing al-Qaeda and ISIS: Different goals, different target. *Brooking Institute*. Retrieved from https://www.brookings.edu/testimonies/comparing-al-qaeda-and-isis-different-goals-different-targets/ (accessed on 18 December 2017).

Byrne, M. (2013). Sandy response shows how FEMA has changed. *Emergency Management*. Retrieved from http://www.govtech.com/em/disaster/Sandy-Response-Shows-How-FEMA-has-Changed.html.

Cameron, S. and Maley, P. (2013). Edward Snowden stole up to 20,000 Aussie files. *The Australian*. Retrieved June 20, 2017 from http://www.theaustralian.com.au/national-affairs/policy/edward-snowden-stole-up-to-20000-aussie-files/story-fn59nm2j-1226775491490.

Cappon, L.J., ed. (1988). *Adams-Jefferson letters.* Chapel Hill, NC: University of North Carolina Press.

Capra, T. (2014). Snowden leaks could cost military billions: Pentagon. NBC News. Retrieved June 20, 2017 from http://www.nbcnews.com/news/investigations/snowden-leaks-could-cost-military-billions-pentagon-n46426.

Carlin, D. (2013). The American peril [audio blog post]. Retrieved June 19, 2017 from http://www.dancarlin.com/portfolio/hh-49-the-american-peril/.

Carter, D. and Carter, J. (2009). *The intelligence fusion process for state, local and tribal law enforcement* (11th ed., Vol. 36). Retrieved June 26, 2017, from http://journals.sagepub.com/doi/pdf/10.1177/0093854809345674.

Cavendish, M. (2011). Horrific Invasion. Tarrytown, NY: Marshall Cavendish Corporation. p. 93.

Center for the study of national reconnaissance. (n.d.). National Reconnaissance Office. Retrieved from http://www.nro.gov/history/index.html (accessed on 11 August 2017).

Chalmers, D. (2010). Essay: The Klu Klux Klan. *Southern Poverty Law Center.* Retrieved from https://www.splcenter.org/fighting-hate/intelligence-report/2010/essay-ku-klux-klan (accessed on 26 September 2017).

Chang, L. and Kornbluh, P. (1992). *The Cuban Missile Crisis, 1962.* The National Security Archive: George Washington University. New York: The Press.

Change of mandate. (2015). Federal Bureau of Investigation. Retrieved from https://web.archive.org/web/20150106195636/http://www2.fbi.gov/libref/historic/history/changeman.htm (accessed on 14 August 2017).

Chari, C. (2008). *War, peace, and hegemony in a globalized world: The changing balance of power in the twenty-first century.* New York: Routledge.

Charles, B. S. (2014). ISIS. Are they using Bitcoins to fund criminal activities? *Security Intelligence.* Retrieved from https://securityintelligence.com/isis-are-they-using-bitcoins-to-fund-criminal-activities/ (accessed on 17 December 2017).

Chemical Emergencies. (n.d.). *Department of Homeland Security.* Retrieved from https://www.ready.gov/chemical (accessed on 12 December 2017).

Childress, S. Just how damaging were Manning's WikiLeaks? PBS. Retrieved on June 25, 2017 from http://www.pbs.org/wgbh/frontline/article/just-how-damaging-were-mannings-wikileaks/.

Christopher Dorner: Police under attack: Southern California law enforcement response to the attacks. (2014). Police Foundation. Retrieved June 27, 2017 from http://incidentreviews.org/wp-content/uploads/2014/05/Police-Under-Attack.pdf.

Chung, J. (2013). Counter-terrorism and emergency management: Keeping a proper balance. *Brookings.* Retrieved from https://www.brookings.edu/opinions/counter-terrorism-and-emergency-management-keeping-a-proper-balance/ (accessed 18 June 2017).

Chouraeshkenazi, M. (2018). *Homeland & National Security: Understanding America's Past to Protect The Future.* Cognella Academic Publishing, Inc: San Diego, CA.

Clark, J. (2008). What's mutual assured destruction? HowStuffWorks.com. Retrieved on 14 June, 2017 from http://people.howstuffworks.com/mutual-assured-destruction.htm.

Cohen, I.S. and Tuttle, A.C. (1972). *National security affairs: A syllabus.* National Strategy Information Center. New Jersey: Seton Hall University Press.

Cohen, S. (2006). Boom boxes: Containers and terrorism. *Protecting the Nation's Seaports: Balancing and Cost.* Retrieved from http://www.ppic.org/content/pubs/report

The Cold War. (n.d.) John F. Kennedy Presidential Library and Museum. Retrieved from https://www.jfklibrary.org/JFK/JFK-in-History/The-Cold-War.aspx

The Commission Report. (2004). National Commission on Terrorist Attacks Upon the United States. Retrieved from http://govinfo.library.unt.edu/911/report/911Report.pdf

Conroy, s. (2007). Judge: Sudan liable for USS bombing. *CBS News.* Retrieved from https://www.cbsnews.com/news/judge-sudan-liable-for-uss-cole-bombing/ (accessed on 12 December 2017).

Consolidated United Nations Security Council sanctions list. (n.d.). United Nations Security Council. Retrieved from https://www.un.org/sc/suborg/en/sanctions/un-sc-consolidated-list (accessed on 16 August 2017).

The convention on certain conventional weapons. (n.d.) United Nations. Retrieved from https://www.un.org/disarmament/geneva/ccw/ (accessed on 8 August 2017).

Convention (II) with respect to the laws and customs of war on land (Hague, II) (29 Jul 1899). (n.d.) The Organisation for the Prohibition of Chemical Weapons. Retrieved from https://www.opcw.org/chemical-weapons-convention/related-international-agreements/chemical-warfare-and-chemical-weapons/hague-convention-of-1899/

Conventional weapons. (2017). United Nations Regional Centre for Peace and Disarmament in Asia and the Pacific. Retrieved from http://unrcpd.org/conventional-weapons/ (accessed on August 8, 2017).

Conyers, A.K.L. (2015). *Cyberwarfare sourcebook*. Raleigh, NC: Lulu. p. 54.

Cornell University. 10 U.S. Code 113—Secretary of Defense. Retrieved from https://www.law.cornell.edu/uscode/text/10/113 (accessed on 13 August 2017).

Cornell University. (n.d.). U.S. Code: Title 10—Armed Forces. *Legal Information Institute.* Retrieved from https://www.law.cornell.edu/uscode/text/10 (accessed on 13 August 2017).

Coronel, S. (n.d.) Corruption and the watchdog role of the news media. Harvard University. Retrieved from https://www.hks.harvard.edu/fs/pnorris/Acrobat/WorldBankReport/Chapter%205%20Coronel.pdf (accessed 18 June 2017).

Corti, D. and Swain, A. (2009). War on drugs and war on terror: Case of Afghanistan. *Peace and Conflict Review*. Retrieved June 30, 2017 from http://www.review.upeace.org/pdf.cfm?articulo=86&ejemplar=17.

Cottey, A. (2016). Security in the 21st century. United Kingdom: Palgrave Macmillan. p. 7.

Counterintelligence. (n.d.) Federal Bureau of Investigation. Retrieved from https://www.fbi.gov/investigate/counterintelligence

Country reports on terrorism 2005 statistical annex. (2005). National Counterterrorism Center. Retrieved from https://www.state.gov/documents/organization/65489.pdf

Critical infrastructure. (2016). U.S. Department of Homeland Security. Retrieved from https://www.dhs.gov/what-critical-infrastructure

Critical infrastructure sectors. (2016). U.S. Department of Homeland Security. Retrieved from https://www.dhs.gov/critical-infrastructure-sectors

Critical Infrastructure Security. (n.d.). *Department of Homeland Security.* Retrieved from https://www.dhs.gov/topic/critical-infrastructure-security (accessed on 12 December 2017).

CSI: Container security initiative. (2014). U.S. Customs and Border Patrol. Retrieved June 26, 2017, from https://www.cbp.gov/border-security/ports-entry/cargo-security/csi/csi-brief

Central Security Service. (n.d.). *National Security Agency.* Retrieved from Central Security Service (accessed on 16 December 2017).

The Cuban Missile Crisis timeline. (n.d.). The History of Cuba. Retrieved from http://www.history-ofcuba.com/history/Crisis/crisis2.htm

The Culper gang. (n.d.). *Spy Letters of the American Revolution*. Retrieved June 19, 2017 from http://clements.umich.edu/exhibits/online/spies/stories-networks-3.html.

The Culper spy ring. (2010). *History.com*. Retrieved June 19, 2017, from http://www.history.com/topics/american-revolution/culper-spy-ring.

Current Developments in Monetary and Financial Law. (2005). *International Monetary Fund.* p. 244.

Currie, C. (2015). FEMA has made progress since hurricanes Katrina and Sandy, but challenges remain. *United States Government Accountability Office*. Retrieved from http://www.gao.gov/assets/680/673279.pdf.

Currie, L. (2013). *Through the eyes of the pack*. Washington, DC: Library of Congress.

Cyber-attacks eclipsing terrorism as gravest domestic threat—FBI. (2013). Guardian. Retrieved from https://www.theguardian.com/world/2013/nov/14/cyber-attacks-terrorism-domestic-threat-fbi (accessed 23 March 2017).

Cyberspace overview. (2016). U.S. Department of Homeland Security. Retrieved from https://www.dhs.gov/cybersecurity-overview

Daimond, J. (n.d.). NSA surveillance bill passes after weeks-long showdown. CNN. Retrieved June 12, 2015 from http://www.cnn.com/2015/06/02/politics/senate-usa-freedom-act-vote-patriot-act-nsa/

Dale, C., Serafino, N., and Towell, P. (2013). A unified national security budget? Issues for Congress (Rep. No. R42997). Retrieved June 28, 2017, from Congressional Research Service website: https://fas.org/sgp/crs/natsec/R42997.pdf.

"Day of infamy" speech. p. 1. (1941). National Archives, Washington, DC.

DEA Mission Statement. (n.d.). *Drug Enforcement Agency.* Retrieved from https://www.dea.gov/about/mission.shtml (accessed on 16 December 2017).

D & CP—Bureau of Intelligence and Research. (n.d.). *Federation of American Scientists.* p. 173. Retrieved from https://fas.org/irp/agency/inr/fy2009just.pdf (accessed on 15 December 2017).

Declaration of Independence. (n.d.) Maurer School of Law, Indiana University. Retrieved from http://www.law.indiana.edu/uslawdocs/declaration.html

Declaration of Independence: A transcription. (n.d.). *America's Founding Documents.* National Archives. Retrieved from https://www.archives.gov/founding-docs/declaration-transcript

Defending our nation. Securing the future. (n.d.). National Security Agency. Retrieved from https://www.nsa.gov/

Defense Technical Information Center. (2017). DoD Dictionary of Military and Associated Terms. Retrieved from http://www.dtic.mil/doctrine/new_pubs/dictionary.pdf (accessed on 19 September 2017).

Definition of terrorism in U.S. Code. (n.d.). Federal Bureau of Investigation. Retrieved from https://www.fbi.gov/investigate/terrorism

Deflem, M. (2000). Bureaucratization and social control: Historical foundations of international police cooperation. *Law & Society Review.* pp. 739–778. Retrieved from https://www.jstor.org/stable/3115142?seq=1#page_scan_tab_contents (accessed 17 June 2017).

Delogu, J.C. (2014). Tocqueville. *University of Michigan.* Retrieved from https://quod.lib.umich.edu/o/ohp/12538666.0001.001/1:4/—tocqueville-and-democracy-in-the-internet-age?rgn=div1;view=fulltext (accessed 7 December 2017).

Denning, D. (1999). *Information Warfare and Security.* New York: ACM Press.

Department of Defense dictionary of military and associated terms. (2017). Defense Information Technical Center. Retrieved from http://www.dtic.mil/doctrine/new_pubs/dictionary.pdf

Department of Defense focus on Asia-Pacific rebalance. (n.d.). U.S Department of Defense. Retrieved from https://www.defense.gov/News/Special-Reports/0415_Asia-Pacific-Rebalance (accessed on 24 June 2017).

The Department of Defense secretly concludes Chelsea Manning's intelligence leaks did not harm national security. (2017). *The Week.* Retrieved June 24, 2017 from http://theweek.com/speedreads/707075/department-defense-secretly-concluded-chelsea-mannings-intelligence-leaks-did-not-harm-national-security

Department of Homeland Security active shooter event: Quick reference guide [Pamphlet]. (n.d.). Washington DC: Department of Homeland Security. Retrieved on June 27, 2017, from https://www.dhs.gov/sites/default/files/publications/active_shooter_pamphlet_508.pdf

Department six-point agenda. (n.d.). U.S. Department of Homeland Security. Retrieved from https://www.dhs.gov/department-six-point-agenda

Dionisi, D. J. (2005). American Hiroshima: The reasons why and a call to strengthen America's democracy. Victoria, Canada: Trafford Publishing. p. 65.

Directive (EU) 2017/541 of the European Parliament and of the Council. (2017). *European Union.* Retrieved from https://www.un.org/press/en/2004/sc8214.doc.htm (accessed on 12 December 2017).

Dr. Edward Bancroft. (n.d.). Federation of American Scientists. Retrieved from https://fas.org/irp/ops/ci/docs/ci1/ch1c.htm

Dodd, B. (n.d.). The nexus between drugs and terrorism. *U.S. Drug Enforcement Administration: Counter-Narcoterrorism Operations Center Special Operations Division.* p. 1. Retrieved from http://www.dtic.mil/ndia/2010/homeland/Dodd.pdf (accessed 25 March 2017).

Domestic terrorism: Anarchist extremism: A primer. (2010). Federal Bureau of Investigation. Retrieved from https://archives.fbi.gov/archives/news/stories/2010/november/anarchist_111610/anarchist_111610

Domino theory. (2009). History.com. Retrieved on June 15, 2017 from http://www.history.com/topics/cold-war/domino-theory.

The Drug Enforcement Administration's Use of Intelligence Analysts. (2008). *U.S. Department of Justice.* p. 14. Retrieved from https://oig.justice.gov/reports/DEA/a0823/final.pdf (accessed on 16 December 2017).

Dunford, J. (2015). National military strategy. *Joint Chiefs of Staff.* Retrieved from http://www.jcs.mil/Portals/36/Documents/Publications/2015_National_Military_Strategy.pdf

Dunlap, J. (1778). Containing proceedings from January 1, 1776 to January 1, 1777. *Journals of Congress.* Vol. 2. York, PA: York-Town Publishing.

Eggen, D. (2006). 9/11 panel suspected deception by Pentagon. *Washington Post.* Retrieved June 18, 2017 from http://www.washingtonpost.com/wp-dyn/content/article/2006/08/01/AR2006080101300.html?sub=AR.

Egyptian Islamic Jihad: Narrative Summary. (n.d.). *Stanford University.* Retrieved from http://web.stanford.edu/group/mappingmilitants/cgi-bin/groups/view/401 (accessed on 18 December 2017).

Eichenwald, K. (2013). How Edward Snowden escalated cyber war with China. *Newsweek.* Retrieved June 22, 2017 from http://www.newsweek.com/how-edward-snowden-escalated-cyber-war-1461

Elder, D.A. (1979). The historical background of common article 3 of the Geneva Convention of 1949. School of Law, Case Western Reserve University. Retrieved from http://scholarlycommons.law.case.edu/cgi/viewcontent.cgi?article=1940&context=jil

Elliot, A. and Hsu, E. L. (2016). *The consequences of global disasters.* New York: Routledge.

European Union. (2002). Council framework decision of 13 June 2002 on combating terrorism. *The Council of the European Union.* Retrieved from http://eur-lex.europa.eu/legal-content/EN/TXT/?uri=uriserv:OJ.L_.2002.164.01.0003.01.ENG (accessed on 19 September 2017).

Erwin, M.C. and Belasco, A. (2013). Intelligence spending and appropriations: Issues for Congress (Rep. No. R42061). Retrieved June 28, 2017 from Congressional Research Service website: https://fas.org/sgp/crs/intel/R42061.pdf.

Estimated cost of post-9/11 wars: 225,000 lives, up to $4 trillion. *Brown University.* Retrieved from https://news.brown.edu/articles/2011/06/warcosts (accessed on 14 December 2017).

Ex-9/11 panel chief denies secret White House ties, (2008, January 30). ABC News.

Executive Order 12333—United States Intelligence Activities. (1981). *National Archives.* Retrieved from https://www.archives.gov/federal-register/codification/executive-order/12333.html (accessed on 12 December 2017).

Executive Order 1233—United States Intelligence Activities. (1981). *Central Intelligence Agency.* Retrieved from https://www.cia.gov/about-cia/eo12333.html (15 December 2017).

Exhibit no. 23 (Hart inquiry). (Rep. No. 067712). (1941). Retrieved June 28, 2017 from http://www.ibiblio.org/pha/pha/hart/xha-023.html.

Fact sheet: Strategy to combat transnational organized crime. (2011). The White House. Retrieved from https://obamawhitehouse.archives.gov/the-press-office/2011/07/25/fact-sheet-strategy-combat-transnational-organized-crime (accessed on 17 June 2017).

Fagel, M.J. (2012). *Principles of emergency management: Hazard specific issues and mitigation strategies.* New York: CRC Press, Taylor and Francis Group.

Farah, D. (1993, December 3). Escobar killed in Medellin. *Washington Post.* Retrieved June 30, 2017 from https://www.washingtonpost.com/archive/politics/1993/12/03/escobar-killed-in-medellin/36339ba2-8021-4942-8c7a-00604b95070a/?utm_term=.fd2dc4417627.

FBI: Cyber-attacks surpassing terrorism as major domestic threats. (2013). Reuters. Retrieved from https://www.rt.com/usa/fbi-cyber-attack-threat-739/ (accessed 23 March 2017).

FBI: Intelligence Branch. (n.d.). *Federal Bureau of Investigation.* Retrieved from https://www.fbi.gov/about/leadership-and-structure/intelligence-branch (accessed on 16 December 2017).

Federal Bureau of Investigation. (2002). Terrorism 2002–2005. Retrieved from https://www.fbi.gov/stats-services/publications/terrorism-2002–2005 (accessed on 19 September 2017).

Federal Law Enforcement Intelligence: A Guide for State, Local, and Tribal Law Enforcement. (n.d.). *Federal of American Scientists.* Retrieved from https://fas.org/irp/agency/doj/lei/chap11.pdf (accessed on 16 December 2017).

FEMA: Evidence of fraud in Hurricane Sandy reports. (2015). *60 Minutes*. CBS. http://www.cbsnews.com/news/fema-evidence-of-fraud-in-hurricane-sandy-reports/

Ferdinando, L. (2016). Carter proposes updates to Goldwater-Nichols Act. Department of Defense. Retrieved from http://www.defense.gov/News/Article/Article/713930/carter-proposes-updates-to-goldwater-nichols-act

Fisher, M. (2016). Straightforward answers to basic questions about Syria's war. *New York Times*. Retrieved from https://www.nytimes.com/2016/09/19/world/middleeast/syria-civil-war-bashar-al-assad-refugees-islamic-state.html (accessed on 18 December 2017).

First inaugural address. (2008). *The Avalon Project at Yale Law School.* Yale University. Retrieved from http://avalon.law.yale.edu/19th_century/jefinau1.asp

First responder. (2017). Department of Homeland Security. Retrieved June 27, 2017 from https://www.dhs.gov/first-responder.

First responder guide for improving survivability in improvised explosive device and/or active shooter incidents. (2015). USA, Department of Homeland Security, Office of Health Affairs. Retrieved June 27, 2017 from https://www.dhs.gov/sites/default/files/publications/First%20Responder%20Guidance%20June%202015%20FINAL%202.pdf.

Food prices and spending. (2014). Economics Research Service, U.S. Department of Agriculture. Retrieved from https://www.ers.usda.gov/data-products/ag-and-food-statistics-charting-the-essentials/food-prices-and-spending/

Ford, P. L. (1899). Letter to P.S. du Ponte de Nemours—The writings of Thomas Jefferson.

Foreign terrorist organizations. (n.d.). U.S. Department of State. Retrieved from https://www.state.gov/j/ct/rls/other/des/123085.htm

Franks, B. and Wilson, M. (2010). *Anarchism and moral philosophy*. New York: Palgrave Macmillan, St. Martin's Press.

French and Indian War/Seven Years' War, 1754–63. (n.d.). Office of the Historian. Retrieved from https://history.state.gov/milestones/1750-1775/french-indian-war

Freudenburg, W.R., Gramling, R., et al. (2009). *Catastrophe in the making*. Washington, DC: Island Press.

Frittelli, J.F. (2005). Port and maritime security: Background and issues for Congress. Congressional Research Service. Retrieved from https://fas.org/sgp/crs/homesec/RL31733.pdf

Frittelli, J.F. (2003). *Port and maritime security: Background and issues.* New York: Novinka Books.

From George Washington to Major Benjamin Tallmadge, 24 September 1779. (1779. National Archives. Retrieved from https://fas.org/irp/ops/ci/docs/ci1/ch1c.htm (accessed on 9 December 2017).

From Title 50-War and National Defense. (n.d.). Chapter 34—National Emergencies. *The U.S. House of Representatives.* Retrieved from http://uscode.house.gov/view.xhtml?path=/prelim@title50/chapter34&edition=prelim (accessed on 9 December 2017).

Fursenko, A. and Naftali, T. (1997). *One hell of a gamble: Khrushchev, Castro, and Kennedy 1958–1964.* New York: W.W. Norton & Company, Inc.

Garamone, J. (2016). Carter: DoD will rebuild, sustain its nuclear deterrence enterprise. Defense.gov. Retrieved from http://www.defense.gov/News/Article/Article/956050/carter-dod-will-rebuild-sustain-its-nuclear-deterrence-enterprise

Garthoff, R.L. (1989). *Reflections on the Cuban Missile Crisis: Revised to include new revelations from Soviet and Cuban sources*. Washington, DC: The Brookings Institution.

Gates, Robert M. (2008). National Defense Strategy. Department of Defense. Retrieved from http://archive.defense.gov/pubs/2008NationalDefenseStrategy.pdf

General DHS Laws. (n.d.). *Department of Homeland Security.* Retrieved from https://www.dhs.gov/key-dhs-laws (accessed on 18 December 2017).

George, R. Z. & Bruce, J.B. (2014). Analyzing intelligence national security practitioners' perspectives. 2nd ed. Washington, DC: Georgetown University. p. 30.

Ghosh, P. (2016). *International relations*. 4th ed. New Delhi, India: PHI Learning Private Limited.

Gillin, J. (2016). Less than ten percent of defense budget is for fighting terrorism, Sanders says. Retrieved June 28, 2017 from http://www.politifact.com/truth-o-meter/statements/2016/jan/18/bernie-s/less-10-percent-defense-budget-fighting-terrorism-/

Gilson, D. (2003). A conflicted land: Rebellions, wars, and insurgencies in the Philippines. WGBH Educational Foundation. Retrieved June 16, 2017, from http://www.pbs.org/frontlineworld/stories/philippines/tl01.html.

Goldfein, D. (2013). Operations in chemical, biological, radiological, and nuclear environments. *Joint Publication 3–11*. Retrieved from http://www.dtic.mil/doctrine/new_pubs/jp3_11.pdf (accessed on 8 August 2017).

Goodwin, J. (2005). Inside Able Danger: The secret birth, extraordinary life and untimely death of a U.S. military intelligence program. *GSN Magazine*. Retrieved June 17, 2017 from http://www.gsnmagazine.com/sep_05/shaffer_interview.html.

Gormley, K. (2016). *The Presidents and the Constitution: A Living History.* New York: NY. NYU Press. p. 27.

Government Accountability Office. (2010). Title 18 of United States Code 113B. Retrieved from https://www.gpo.gov/fdsys/pkg/USCODE-2009-title18/pdf/USCODE-2009-title18.pdf (accessed on 19 September 2017).

Grabianowski. E. (2005). How FEMA works. *HowStuffWorks.com*. Retrieved June 10, 2017 from http://people.howstuffworks.com/fema.htm

Grant, M. (1916). *The passing of the great race.* New York: Charles Scribner and Sons.

Green, M. (2016). How 9/11 changed America: Four major lasting impacts (with lesson plan). KQED News. Retrieved June 29, 2017 from https://ww2.kqed.org/lowdown/2014/09/10/13-years-later-four-major-lasting-impacts-of-911/

Greenemeier, L. (2008, September 19). Seven years later: Electrons unlocked post-9/11 anthrax mail mystery. *Scientific American*. Retrieved June 21, 2017 from https://www.scientificamerican.com/article/sandia-anthrax-mailing-investigation/

Grover, S. (2016). Snowden's global impact: Visual timeline. Retrieved June 22, 2017 from http://www.whoishostingthis.com/blog/2015/05/20/snowdens-global-impact/

Hagan, K.J. and Skinner, E. (n.d.). Nuclear strategy and diplomacy—The futile strategy of atomic monopoly. In *Encyclopedia of the New American Nation*. Retrieved June 20, 2017 from http://www.americanforeignrelations.com/E-N/Nuclear-Strategy-and-Diplomacy-The-futile-strategy-of-atomic-monopoly.html

Hamilton, A. (1788). Concerning the militia. *The Federalist No. 29*. Retrieved from https://www.congress.gov/resources/display/content/The+Federalist+Papers#TheFederalistPapers-29

Handel, M.J. (2003). *The sociology of organizations: Classic, contemporary, and critical readings.* Thousand Oaks, CA: Sage Publishing, Inc.

Harris, D.B. and Bailey, L.H. (2014). *The Democratic Party: Documents Decoded*. Santa Barbara, CA: Library of Congress.

Hay'at tahrir al-sham (formerly Jabhat al-nursa). (2017). Stanford University. Retrieved from http://web.stanford.edu/group/mappingmilitants/cgi-bin/groups/view/493 (accessed on 15 August 2017).

Hayden, C. (2014). NSC Staff, the Name is Back! So Long, NSS. *The White House.* Retrieved from https://obamawhitehouse.archives.gov/blog/2014/02/10/nsc-staff-name-back-so-long-nss (accessed on 9 December 2017).

Headquarters Marine Corps: Intelligence Department. (n.d.). *U.S. Marine Corps.* Retrieved from http://www.hqmc.marines.mil/intelligence (accessed 16 December 2017).

Herrick, N.Q. (2009). *After Patrick Henry: A second American Revolution.* Portland, OR: Black Rose Books.

Hibberd, J. (2002). Tramped-up eco-terrorism. An arsonist's tale. *The New York Times*. Retrieved from http://www.nytimes.com/2002/02/12/us/trumped-up-eco-terrorism-an-arsonist-s-tale.html

Higgins, J.J. (2017). Articles: Understanding narco-terrorism. Retrieved June 30, 2017 from http://www.americanthinker.com/articles/2017/06/understanding_narcoterrorism.html.

History of National Security Council 1947–1997. (n.d.). *The White House.* Retrieved from https://georgewbush-whitehouse.archives.gov/nsc/history.html (accessed on 9 December 2017).

The history of Pennsylvania's early capitols. (n.d.). Pennsylvania Capital Preservation Committee. Retrieved from http://cpc.state.pa.us/history/the-history-of-pennsylvanias-early-capitols.cfm

Hittle, J.D. (1947). The Marine Corps and the National Security Act. Marine Corps Association and Foundation. Retrieved on June 17, 2017 from https://www.mca-marines.org/gazette/marine-corps-and-national-security-act

HLS 101—Weapons of mass destruction. (n.d.). Eastern Kentucky University. Retrieved from http://hlsonline.eku.edu/hls-101-weapons-mass-destruction-wmd

Hoffman, B. (1998). *Inside Terrorism.* New York: Columbia University Press. p. 34.

Hoffman, B. (2006). *Inside Terrorism.* New York: Columbia University Press. pp. 2–3.

Hoffman, B. (1988). Recent trends and future prospects of terrorism in the United States. *Defense Technical Information Center.* Retrieved from http://www.dtic.mil/dtic/tr/fulltext/u2/a220301.pdf (accessed on 26 September 2017).

Holmes, J.L. (n.d.). Ramp up physical security. *United States Army Logistics University.* Retrieved from http://www.alu.army.mil/alog/issues/JulAug01/MS690.htm

Homeland Security. (n.d.) U.S. Senate Committee on Homeland Security and Governmental Affairs. Retrieved from https://www.hsgac.senate.gov/issues/homeland-security (accessed on 13 August 2017).

Homeland Security Act of 2002. Public Law 107–296. (2002). 107th Congress. Retrieved from https://www.dhs.gov/xlibrary/assets/hr_5005_enr.pdf

Homeland Security Act of 2002. (2002). U.S. Department of Homeland Security. Retrieved from https://www.dhs.gov/homeland-security-act-2002 (accessed on 13 August 2017).

Homeland Security Information Network—Law Enforcement. (n.d.). *Department of Homeland Security.* Retrieved from https://www.dhs.gov/law-enforcement (accessed on 18 December 2017).

Homeland Security Presidential Directive 51. (2007). *Policy Defense.* Retrieved from http://policy.defense.gov/portals/11/Documents/hdasa/references/HSPD-20.pdf

Homeland Security. (n.d.) U.S. Senate Committee on Homeland Security and Governmental Affairs. Retrieved from https://www.hsgac.senate.gov/issues/homeland-security (accessed on 13 August 2017).

Hooker, Jr. R.D. (2016). The NSC Staff: New choices for a new administration. *INSS Strategic Institute for National Strategic Studies.* National Defense University. p. 3. Retrieved from http://ndupress.ndu.edu/Portals/68/Documents/strat-monograph/The-NSC-Staff.pdf?ver=2016-11-15-154433-837 (accessed on 9 December 2017).

Hosenball, M. (2013, October 1). U.S. spy agencies face big layoffs in government shutdown. *Reuters.* Retrieved June 18, 2017 from http://in.reuters.com/article/usa-fiscal-spies-idINL1N0HR11P20131001.

Huddleston, S. (2010). Hasan sought gun with "high magazine capacity." *My San Antonio.* Retrieved from http://blog.mysanantonio.com/military/2010/10/hasan-sought-gun-with-high-magazine-capacity/

Human rights, harm reduction key to drug policy, UN rights chief says. (2009). *UN News Centre.* United Nations. Retrieved from http://www.un.org/apps/news/story.asp?NewsID=30135#.WOHALRLyub8 (accessed 2 April 2017).

Hurricane Katrina. (2009). *History.com.* Retrieved June 17, 2017 from http://www.history.com/topics/hurricane-katrina

Hurricane Katrina: 2005. (2005). National Hurricane Center. Retrieved from http://www.nhc.noaa.gov/outreach/history/

Hurricane Sandy: Atlantic Ocean. (2013). NASA. Retrieved from https://www.nasa.gov/mission_pages/hurricanes/archives/2012/h2012_Sandy.html

Hutchinson, A. (2002). International drug and trafficking and terrorism. *U.S. Department of State.* Retrieved from https://2001-2009.state.gov/p/inl/rls/rm/9239.htm (accessed on 25 March 2017).

In Congress, July 4, 1776, the unanimous declaration of the thirteen United States of America. (1987). University of Chicago. Retrieved from http://press-pubs.uchicago.edu/founders/print_documents/v1ch1s5.html

Ignatius, D. (2012). Al-Qaeda affiliate playing larger role in Syria rebellion. *The Washington Post.* Retrieved from https://www.washingtonpost.com/blogs/post-partisan/post/al-qaeda-affiliate-playing-larger-role-in-syria-rebellion/2012/11/30/203d06f4-3b2e-11e2-9258-ac-7c78d5c680_blog.html?utm_term=.2942e834df9e (accessed on 18 December 2017).

Inserra, D. (2016). "Top Five Priorities for Homeland Security in 2016." *The Heritage Foundation.* Retrieved from http://www.heritage.org/homeland-security/report/top-5-priorities-homeland-security-2016 (accessed on 13 August 2017).

Insinna, V. (2012). Hurricane Sandy puts new National Guard command mechanism to work. *National Defense.*

Islamic Terrorism from 1945 to the rise of ISIS. (2017). *Constitutional Rights Foundation.* Retrieved from http://www.crf-usa.org/america-responds-to-terrorism/islamist-terrorism-from-1945-to-the-death-of-osama-bin-laden.html (accessed on 18 December 2017).

Intelligence Topics at DEA, Intelligence Products: El Paso Intelligence Center. (n.d.). *Drug Enforcement Agency.* Retrieved from https://www.dea.gov/ops/intel.shtml (accessed 16 December 2017).

Intelligence in the war of independence. (1975). Central Intelligence Agency. Historical Intelligence Collection: Central Reference Service DD/I. Retrieved from https://www.fordlibrarymuseum.gov/library/document/0067/1563276.pdf

(Intelligence Reform and Terrorism Prevention Act of 2004. (2004). *Office of the Legislative Counsel: U.S. House of Representatives.* Retrieved from https://legcounsel.house.gov/Comps/Intelligence%20Reform%20And%20Terrorism%20Prevention%20Act%20Of%202004.pdf (accessed on 18 December 2017).

Intelligence techniques. (n.d.). Central Intelligence Agency. Retrieved from https://www.cia.gov/library/publications/intelligence-history/intelligence/intelltech.html

International Diaspora Engagement Alliance. (n.d.). U.S. Department of State. Retrieved from https://www.state.gov/s/partnerships/diaspora/ (accessed 6 August 2017).

Introduction to CBO. (n.d.) Congressional Budget Office. Retrieved from https://www.cbo.gov/about/overview

ISIL-linked hacker pleads to providing material support. (2016). U.S. Department of Justice. Retrieved from https://www.justice.gov/opa/pr/isil-linked-hacker-pleads-guilty-providing-material-support (accessed 23 March 2017).

ISIL-linked Kosovo hacker sentenced to 20 years in prison. (2016). Office of Public Affairs, U.S. Department of Justice. Retrieved from https://www.justice.gov/opa/pr/isil-linked-kosovo-hacker-sentenced-20-years-prison (accessed 23 March 2017).

Jacobson, M. & Royer, H. (2010). Aftershocks: The impact of clinic violence on abortion services. *RAND Corporation.* Retrieved from http://users.nber.org/~jacobson/JacobsonRoyer6.2.10.pdf (accessed on 28 September 2017).

Jaffe, G. and J. Partlow. (2010, July 30). Mullen says leak put troops and Afghans in danger; WikiLeaks documents include names of informants helping U.S. *The Washington Post.* Retrieved on June 25, 2017 from http://pqasb.pqarchiver.com/washingtonpost/access/2095259091.html?FMT=ABS&FMTS=ABS:FT&date=Jul+30%2C+2010&author=Greg+Jaffe%3BJoshua+Partlow&pub=The+Washington+Post&edition=&startpage=A.4

James F. Byrnes. (2017). Atomic Heritage Foundation. Retrieved June 20, 2017 from http://www.atomicheritage.org/profile/james-f-byrnes

Janes, D. and Houen, A. (2014). *Martyrdom and terrorism: Pre-modern to contemporary perspectives.* New York: Oxford University Press.

Jarboe, J.F. (2002). Before the House Resources Committee, Subcommittee on Forests and Forest Health, Washington DC. *Federal Bureau of Investigation.* Retrieved from https://archives.fbi.gov/archives/news/testimony/the-threat-of-eco-terrorism

Jedburgs. (n.d.). *Office of Strategic Services.* Retrieved June 19, 2017 from http://www.soc.mil/OSS/jedburghs.html

Jenkins, B. (1980). The study of terrorism: Definitional problems. *Rand Corporation.* Retrieved from https://www.rand.org/content/dam/rand/pubs/papers/2006/P6563.pdf (accessed on 6 September 2017).

Jenkins, W.O. (2012). Chemical, biological, radiological, and nuclear risk assessments DHS: Should establish more specific guidance for their use. Retrieved June 26, 2017, from United States Government Accountability Office website: http://www.gao.gov/assets/590/587674.pdf.

Johnson, J. (2014). Fiscal years 2014–2018 strategic plan. *Department of Homeland Security.* Retrieved from https://www.dhs.gov/sites/default/files/publications/FY14-18%20Strategic%20Plan.PDF (accessed on 13 August 2017).

Johnson, J. O. (2015). Remarks by Secretary of Homeland Security Jeh Johnson on "The Realities of Homeland Security" as Part of the Landon Lectures Series on Public Issues. *Department of Homeland Security.* Retrieve from https://www.dhs.gov/news/2015/05/27/remarks-sec-retary-homeland-security-jeh-charles-johnson-"-new-realities-homeland (accessed on 12 December 2017).

Joint Inquiry into Intelligence Community Activities Before and After the Terrorist Attacks of September 11, 2002. (2001). *Government Publishing Office.* p. 7, 355. Retrieved from https://www.gpo.gov/fdsys/pkg/CRPT-107hrpt792/pdf/CRPT-107hrpt792.pdf (accessed on 18 December 2017).

Jones, S.G. (2012). Hunting in the shadows: The pursuit of the Al-Qaida since 9/11. New York: W.W. Norton & Company, Inc.

Joshi, S.R. (2007). Microbes: Redefined personality. *Department of Biotechnology and Bioinformatics North Eastern Hill University Shillong.* New Delhi, India: APH Publishing Corporation.

Joyce, P. (2015). The Congressional Budget Office at middle age. University of Maryland School of Public Policy. Retrieved from https://www.brookings.edu/wp-content/uploads/2016/06/PJ_WorkingPaper9_Feb11_Final.pdf

Judge finds Sudan is liable in Cole case. (2007). *New York Times.* Retrieved from http://query.nytimes.com/gst/fullpage.html?res=9D02E5DC1E31F936A25750C0A96198B63

Justice Department and FBI announce formal conclusion of investigation into 2001 anthrax attacks. (2010). Retrieved June 21, 2017, from https://www.justice.gov/opa/pr/justice-de-partment-and-fbi-announce-formal-conclusion-investigation-2001-anthrax-attacks.

Kaijankoski, A. (2015). Cybersecurity information sharing between public-private sector agencies. Naval Postgraduate School: Monterey, California. Retrieved from http://www.dtic.mil/dtic/tr/fulltext/u2/a620766.pdf

Kaplan, E. (2006). Tracking down terrorist financing. *Council on Foreign Relations.* Retrieved from https://www.cfr.org/backgrounder/tracking-down-terrorist-financing (accessed on 14 December 2017).

Kaplan, M. (1957). *System and process in international politics.* New York: Wiley.

Keating, J.E. (2010). What's the difference between combat and noncombat troops? *Foreign Policy.* Retrieved from http://foreignpolicy.com/2010/08/03/whats-the-difference-between-combat-and-noncombat-troops/ (accessed on 5 August 2017).

Kelly, E. (2015, June 2). Senate approves USA Freedom Act. USA Today. Retrieved June 22, 2017 from https://www.usatoday.com/story/news/politics/2015/06/02/patriot-act-usa-freedom-act-senate-vote/28345747/.

Kennedy Library observes fortieth anniversary of Missile Crisis. (1962). *Prologue Magazine. (34)*3, National Archives.

Kessler, G. (2010, November 29). WikiLeaks' unveiling of secret State Department cables exposes U.S. diplomacy. *Washington Post.* Retrieved on June 25, 2017 from http://www.washingtonpost.com/wp-dyn/content/article/2010/11/28/AR2010112802395.html?sid=ST2010112802494.

Klekowski von Koppenfels, A. (2015). *American abroad: A disillusioned diaspora?* Migration Policy Institute. Retrieved from http://www.migrationpolicy.org/article/americans-abroad-disil-lusioned-diaspora (accessed on 6 August 2017).

Knorr, K. (1973). National security studies: Scope and structure of the field. Frank K. Trager and Philip S. Kroenberg & Trager, F. N. eds. (1986). *National Security and American Society: Theory, Process, and Policy.* Lawrence, Kansas: University Press of Kansas.

Knott, S.F. (1996). *Secret and sanctioned: Covert operations and the American presidency.* New York: University Oxford Press. p.35.

Kochman, B. (2015). Former NYC teacher who admitted to selling weapons to likely terrorists gets 15 years behind bars. *NY Daily News.* Retrieved from http://www.nydailynews.com/new-york/ex-teacher-15-years-selling-weapons-terrorists-article-1.2424815 (accessed on 17 December 2017).

Koehler, D. (2015). The radical online: Individual radicalization processes and the role of the inter-net. *Journal for Deradicalization: Simon Fraser University.* Retrieved from http://journals.sfu.ca/jd/index.php/jd/article/viewFile/8/8

Kohls, R. (1984). The values Americans live by. The Washington International Center. Retrieved from http://www1.cmc.edu/pages/faculty/alee/extra/American_values.html

Kuipers, B. (2004). How to defeat terrorism. University of Texas at Austin. Retrieved from http://www.cs.utexas.edu/users/kuipers/opinions/defeating-terrorism.html

Kuipers, D. (1989). Arizona: Earth's first last roundup. *Spin*. pp. 33–38.

Laqueur, W. (2003). No end to war: Terrorism in the twenty-first century. Continuum: New York.

Laqueur, W. (1986). Reflection on terrorism. *Foreign Affairs*. Retrieved from https://www.foreignaffairs.com/articles/1986-09-01/reflections-terrorism (accessed on 6 September 2017).

Lazar, A. (2013). Government shutdown has domino effect on defense industry. *ABC News*. Retrieved June 18, 2017 from http://abcnews.go.com/blogs/politics/2013/10/government-shutdown-has-domino-effect-on-defense-industry/

Lead Inspector General for overseas contingency operations: Operation Inherent Resolve. (2015). U.S. Department of State. Retrieved from https://oig.state.gov/system/files/oir_quarterly_december_2015_-_a2.pdf (accessed on 15 August 2017).

Leadership. (n.d.). U.S. Department of Homeland Security. Retrieved from https://www.dhs.gov/leadership

Leffler, M.P. (1990). National security. *Journal of American History. (77)*145.

Legal brief: Life unworthy of life. (n.d.). University of Michigan. Retrieved from http://holocaust.umd.umich.edu/lul/Readings/Reading%2011B.pdf (accessed on 15 August 2017).

Lewis, B. (2002). *The Assassins: A Radical Sect in Islam*. Weidenfeld & Nicolson: London. p. 169.

Lewis, H. (1992). The age of enlightenment. *The European Dream of Progress and Enlightenment*. Retrieved from http://history-world.org/age_of_enlightenment.htm

Lewis, J.E. (2004). Before the Senate Judiciary Committee: Washington D.C. Federal Bureau of Investigation. Retrieved from https://archives.fbi.gov/archives/news/testimony/animal-rights-extremism-and- ecoterrorism

Lieu, T. (2017). Trump removes Steve Bannon from National Security Council. *United States Representative Ted Lieu Representing California's 33rd District*. Retrieved from https://lieu.house.gov/media-center/in-the-news/trump-removes-steve-bannon-national-security-council-post (accessed on 9 December 2017).

Lippman, W. (1943). *U.S. foreign policy: Shield of the republic*. London: Hamish Hamilton.

Lister, T., Sanchez, R., Bixler, M. O'Key, S., Hogenmiller, and Tawfeeq, M. (2016). ISIS goes global: 143 attacks in 29 countries have killed 2,043. *CNN News*. Retrieved from http://www.cnn.com/2015/12/17/world/mapping-isis-attacks-around-the-world/

Logan, J. T. (2001). The American Revolution—The French and Indian War. *The American Revolution*. Retrieved June 19, 2017 from http://theamericanrevolution.org/EventDetail.aspx?event=4.

Ludden, J. (2006). 1965 immigration law changed face of America. NPR. Retrieved from http://www.npr.org/templates/story/story.php?storyId=5391395

MacNab, J.J. (2014). Context matters: The Clive Bundy standoff—part 3. *Forbes*. Retrieved from https://www.forbes.com/sites/jjmacnab/2014/05/06/context-matters-the-cliven-bundy-standoff-part-3/#7b65bec65993

Madison, J. (2008). The alleged danger from the powers of the union to state governments considered the independent journal. *The Federalist*. Retrieved from http://avalon.law.yale.edu/18th_century/fed45.asp

Maga, T. (2003). *Eyewitness history: The 1960's*. New York: InfoBase Publishing.

Magee, J.J. (2013). *Indictment: For the murder of John F. Kennedy*. Bloomington, IN: Author House.

Maidment, J. (2017). Relationship between Russia and U.S. most dangerous since Cold War, says former UK Ambassador to Moscow. *The Telegraph*. Retrieved from http://www.telegraph.co.uk/news/2017/07/07/relationship-russia-us-dangerous-since-cold-war-says-former/ (accessed on 13 August 2017).

The Maine explodes. (n.d.) *History.com*. Retrieved on June 17, 2017 from http://www.history.com/this-day-in-history/the-maine-explodes

Maritime Force Protection Command to activate Oct. 1. (2004). *United States Navy.* Commander, Fleet Forces Command Public Affairs. Retrieved from http://www.navy.mil/submit/display.asp?story_id=15309

Martin, G. (ed.). (2011). *The SAGE encyclopedia of terrorism.* Thousand Oaks, CA: SAGE Publications. 2nd ed. p. 552.

Matthews, D. (2013, February 20). The sequester: Absolutely everything you could possibly need to know in one FAQ. *Washington Post.* Retrieved June 18, 2017 from https://www.washingtonpost.com/news/wonk/wp/2013/02/20/the-sequester-absolutely-everything-you-could-possibly-need-to-know-in-one-faq/?utm_term=.81b9d26ee6c7

Matusitz, J. (2005). Cyberterrorism. *American Foreign Policy Interests. (2).*

Maurer, D.C. (2012). Department of Homeland Security oversight and coordination of research and development should be strengthened. Retrieved June 26, 2017, from United States Government Accountability Office website: http://www.gao.gov/assets/650/648152.pdf

Mazzetti, M. (2007, December 22). 9/11 panel study finds that C.I.A. withheld tapes. *New York Times.* Retrieved June 17, 2017 from http://www.nytimes.com/2007/12/22/washington/22intel.html

Mazzetti, M. and Schmidt, M.S. (2013, December 14). Officials say U.S. may never know the extent of Snowden's leaks. *New York Times.* Retrieved June 22, 2017 from http://www.nytimes.com/2013/12/15/us/officials-say-us-may-never-know-extent-of-snowdens-leaks.html?smid=tw-share

McCants, W. (2015). The believer: How an introvert with a passion for religion and soccer became Abu Bakr al-Baghdadi: Leader of the Islamic State. *Brookings Institute.* Retrieved from http://csweb.brookings.edu/content/research/essays/2015/thebeliever.html (accessed on 15 August 2017).

McCaul, M.T. (2012). A line in the sand: Countering crime, violence and terror at the southwest border. *United States House Committee on Homeland Security Subcommittee on Oversight, Investigations, and Management.* 112th Congress, Second Session. Retrieved from https://homeland.house.gov/files/11-15-12-Line-in-the-Sand.pdf (accessed 2 April 2017).

McGeehan, P. (2013). Displaced by Hurricane Sandy, and living in limbo. *The New York Times.* Retrieved March 24, 2014.

McInnis, K.J. (2017). Statutory restrictions on the position of Secretary of Defense: Issues for Congress. *Congressional Research Service.* Retrieved from https://fas.org/sgp/crs/natsec/R44725.pdf (accessed 18 June 2017).

Measures to Eliminate Terrorism. (1994). *United Nations: General Assembly.* Retrieved from http://www.marines.mil/Portals/59/Publications/History%20of%20the%20U.S.%20Marine%20Corps%20in%20WWII%20Vol%20IV%20-%20Western%20Pacific%20Operations%20%20PCN%2019000262700_4.pdf (accessed on 12 December 2017).

Measuring and Understanding the Impact of Terrorism. (2015). *Global Terrorism Index.* Retrieved from http://economicsandpeace.org/wp-content/uploads/2015/11/Global-Terrorism-Index-2015.pdf (accessed on 18 December 2017).

Measuring and understanding the impact of terrorism. (2015). *Global Terrorism Index.* Retrieved from http://economicsandpeace.org/wp-content/uploads/2015/11/Global-Terrorism-Index-2015.pdf (accessed on 15 August 2017).

Medical countermeasures. (2016). Retrieved June 26, 2017, from https://www.medicalcountermeasures.gov/barda/cbrn/project-bioshield-overview/

Melillo, M.R. (n.d.). Outfitting a big-war military with small-war capabilities. Strategic Studies Institute, *U.S. Army War College.* (n.d.). Retrieved from http://strategicstudiesinstitute.army.mil/pubs/parameters/articles/06autumn/melillo.pdf

Members of the IC. (n.d.). Office of the Director of National Intelligence. Retrieved from https://www.dni.gov/index.php/what-we-do/members-of-the-ic (accessed on 9 December 2017).

Membership of the Biological Weapons Convention. (n.d.). United Nations Office at Geneva. Retrieved from http://www.unog.ch/80256EE600585943/(httpPages)/7BE6CBBEA0477B52C12571860035FD5C?OpenDocument

Michael, L. and Herbeck, D. (2002). *American terrorist. Timothy McVeigh and the Oklahoma City bombing.* New York: First Avon Books. p. 234.

Michael, M. (2004). Bin Laden, in statement to U.S. people, says he ordered Sept. 11 attacks. *San Diego Union Tribune.* Retrieved from http://legacy.sandiegouniontribune.com/news/nation/terror/20041029-1423-binladentape.html

Michaels, J. (2013, October 1). Government shutdown has impact on military bases. *USA Today.* Retrieved June 18, 2017 from https://www.usatoday.com/story/news/politics/2013/10/01/bragg-hagel-obama-shutdown/2903915/

Milestones: 1750–1775: French and Indian War. (n.d.). Office of the Historian, Bureau of Public Affairs, United States Department of State. Retrieved June 19, 2017 from https://history.state.gov/milestones/1750-1775/french-indian-war

Milestones: 1750–1775: Parliamentary taxation. (n.d.). Office of the Historian, Bureau of Public Affairs, United States Department of State. Retrieved June 19, 2017, from https://history.state.gov/milestones/1750-1775/parliamentary-taxation.

Milestones: 1776–1783: Continental Congress. (n.d.). Office of the Historian, Bureau of Public Affairs, United States Department of State. Retrieved June 19, 2017 from https://history.state.gov/milestones/1776-1783/continental-congress

Milestones: 1776–1783: Declaration of Independence. (n.d.). Office of the Historian, Bureau of Public Affairs, United States Department of State. Retrieved June 19, 2017, from https://history.state.gov/milestones/1776-1783/declaration

Milestones: 1776–1783: Secret committee. (n.d.). Office of the Historian, Bureau of Public Affairs, United States Department of State. Retrieved June 19, 2017, from https://history.state.gov/milestones/1776-1783/secret-committee

Milestones: 1866–1898: Spanish American War. (n.d.). Office of the Historian, Public Affairs, United States Department of State. Retrieved June 17, 2017 from https://history.state.gov/milestones/1866-1898/spanish-american-war

Milestones: 1945–1952: Atomic diplomacy. (n.d.) Office of the Historian, Public Affairs. United States Department of State. Retrieved on June 13, 2017 from https://history.state.gov/milestones/1945-1952/atomic.

Milestones: 1945–1952: Berlin Airlift. (n.d.). Office of the Historian, Public Affairs. United States Department of State. Retrieved on June 13, 2017 from https://history.state.gov/milestones/1945-1952/berlin-airlift.

Milestones: 1945–1952: National Security Act. (n.d.). Office of the Historian, Public Affairs. United States Department of State. Retrieved on June 16, 2017 from https://history.state.gov/milestones/1945-1952/national-security-act

Milestones: 1945–1952: The Marshall Plan. (n.d.) Office of the Historian, Public Affairs. United States Department of State. Retrieved on June 13, 2017 from https://history.state.gov/milestones/1945-1952/marshall-plan

Militia extremists. (n.d.). Federal Bureau of Investigation. Retrieved from https://cve.fbi.gov/whatare/?state=domestic

Miller, E.S. (2007). *War Plan Orange: The U.S. Strategy to Defeat Japan, 1897–1945.* Annapolis, MD: Naval Institute Press.

Mills, C.W. (1956). *The power elite.* New York: Oxford University.

Mission. (n.d.). Department of Homeland Security. Retrieved from https://www.performance.gov/agency/department-homeland-security#stgob (accessed on 13 August 2017).

Mission. (n.d.). U.S. Department of Homeland Security. Retrieved from https://www.dhs.gov/our-mission

Mission. (n.d.). U.S. Department of State. Retrieved from https://www.state.gov/s/d/rm/rls/dosstrat/2004/23503.htm (accessed on 18 June 2017).

Mission. (n.d.). Federal Bureau of Investigation. Retrieved from https://www.fbi.gov/about/mission (accessed on 14 August 2017).

Mission. (n.d.). Federal Emergency Management Agency. Retrieved from https://www.fema.gov/about-agency (accessed on 11 August 2017).

Mission. (n.d.). Federal Railroad Administration. Retrieved from https://www.fra.dot.gov/Page/P0002

Mission. (n.d.). National Security Agency. Retrieved from https://www.nsa.gov/about/mission-strategy/ (accessed on 11 August 2017).

Mission. (n.d.). Transportation Security Administration. Retrieved from https://www.tsa.gov/about/tsa-mission (accessed 16 June 2017).

Mission. (n.d.). U.S. Department of Defense. Retrieved from https://www.defense.gov/About/ (accessed on 16 June 2017).

Mission. (n.d.). U.S. Department of State. Retrieved from https://diplomacy.state.gov/discoverdiplomacy/diplomacy101/issues/170606.htm

Mitchell, C., Carelton, D., Lopez, G., & Stohl, M. (1986). *State Terrorism: Issues of Concept of Measurement.* Greenwood Press, Inc: New York. p. 5.

Mohr, G.A, Edwin, F., & Richard, S. (2015). *World War 3: When and how it will end?* Australia: Australian Self-Publishing Group. p. 159

Mohr, H. and Weiss, M. (2016). Records: Orlando gunman talked about violence as early as 3rd grade. *The Orange County Register.* Retrieved from http://www.ocregister.com/articles/mateen-719674-school-high.html

Monke, J. (2004). Agroterrorism: Threat and preparedness. *Congressional Research Service.* Retrieved from https://fas.org/irp/crs/RL32521.pdf

Mooy, K.D. (2003). The wisdom of Thomas Jefferson. *Philosophy Library.* New York: Kensington Publishing Corporation. p. 114.

Mossholder, K.W., Bennett, N., Kemery, E.R., and Wesolowski, M.A. (1998). Relationships between bases of power and work reactions. The mediation role of procedure justice. *Journal of Management, 24*(4). 533–552.

Mroue, B. (2013). Hezbollah chief says group is fighting in Syria. *San Diego Tribune.* Retrieved from http://www.sandiegouniontribune.com/sdut-hezbollah-chief-says-group-is-fighting-in-syria-2013may25-story.html (accessed on 16 August 2017).

Murder of U.S. national outside the United States; Conspiracy to murder U.S. nationals outside the United States; Attack on a federal facility resulting in death. (2008). Federal Bureau of Investigation. Retrieved from https://web.archive.org/web/20080103044553/http://www.fbi.gov/wanted/topten/fugitives/laden.htm (accessed on 16 August 2017).

Nancy Morgan Hart (1735–1830). (n.d.) National Women's History Museum. Retrieved from https://www.nwhm.org/education-resources/biography/biographies/nancy-morgan-hart/

Nathan, M.D., Greenblatt, J.A., Jacobson, K., Lauter, D.M., Freeman, S.M., Lewy, G.S., Friedman, D., Segal, O., Pitcavage, M., and Hill, C. (2016). Tattered robes: The state of the Klu Klux Klan in the United States. *Anti-Defamation League.* Retrieved from https://www.adl.org/sites/default/files/documents/assets/pdf/combating-hate/tattered-robes-state-of-kkk-2016.pdf

Nathanson, P. (2013). Voices from the field: FBI agent accounts of the real consequences of budget cuts (Rep.). FBI. Retrieved June 18, 2017 from FBI Agents Association website: https://c.ymcdn.com/sites/fbiaa.site-ym.com/resource/resmgr/docs/voices_from_the_field_-_fbia.pdf

National Abortion Federation. (2017). Violence statistics and history. Retrieved from https://prochoice.org/education-and-advocacy/violence/violence-statistics-and-history/ (accessed on 28 September 2017).

The National Commission on Terrorist Attacks Upon the United States. (2004). *The 9/11 Report: The National Commission on Terrorist Attacks Upon the United States.* New York: NY. St. Martin's Paperbacks. p. 592.

National Continuity Policy. (2007). National Security Presidential Directive 51. Retrieved from https://fas.org/irp/offdocs/nspd/nspd-51.htm

National Intelligence Program. (2016). Director of National Intelligence. Retrieved from https://www.dni.gov/files/documents/FY%202016%20NIP%20Fact%20Sheet.pdf (accessed 11 August 2017).

The National Security Act of 1947. (n.d.) The Office of the Historian. Retrieved from https://history.state.gov/milestones/1945-1952/national-security-act

National Security Council. (n.d.). The White House. Retrieved from https://www.whitehouse.gov/administration/eop/nsc

National strategy for homeland security. (2007). United States, Homeland Security Council, White House. Retrieved June 26, 2017, from https://www.dhs.gov/xlibrary/assets/nat_strat_homelandsecurity_2007.pdf

National strategy information sharing. (2007). United States, Executive Office, White House. Retrieved June 26, 2017, from https://fas.org/sgp/library/infoshare.pdf

The nationwide SAR initiative. (n.d.). Retrieved June 26, 2017, from https://nsi.ncirc.gov/

National Terrorist Financing Risk Assessment. (2015). *U.S. Department of the Treasury.* p. 15. Retrieved from https://www.treasury.gov/resource-center/terrorist-illicit-finance/Documents/National%20Terrorist%20Financing%20Risk%20Assessment%20-%2006-12-2015.pdf (accessed on 17 December 2017).

NATO's military concept for defence against terrorism. (2016). Internal Military Staff. North Atlantic Treaty Organization. Retrieved from http://www.nato.int/cps/en/natohq/topics_69482.htm

The naval quarantine of Cuba, 1962. (2015). Naval History and Heritage Command. Retrieved from https://www.history.navy.mil/research/library/online-reading-room/title-list-alphabetically/n/the-naval-quarantine-of-cuba.html

Naylor, B. (2012). Lessons from Katrina boost FEMA's Sandy response. *NPR.* Retrieved from http://www.npr.org/2012/11/03/164224394/lessons-from-katrina-boost-femas-sandy-response

Nicks, D. (2012). *Private: Bradley Manning, Wikileaks, and the biggest exposure of official secrets in American history.* Chicago, IL: Chicago Review Press.

NIMS: Frequently asked questions. (n.d.). *Department of Homeland Security.* Retrieved from https://www.fema.gov/national-incident-management-system (accessed on 16 December 2017).

NIMS: Frequently asked questions. (n.d.). Federal Emergency Management Agency. Retrieved from https://www.fema.gov/pdf/emergency/nims/nimsfaqs.pdf (13 June 2017).

North Atlantic Treaty Organization (NATO), 1949. (n.d.). The Office of the Historian. Retrieved from https://history.state.gov/milestones/1945-1952/nato

Northedge, F.S. (1986). *The League of Nations: Its life and times, 1920–1946.* New York: Holmes and Meier.

Nossiter, A. (2010). Lonely trek to radicalism for terror suspect. *The New York Times.* Retrieved from http://www.nytimes.com/2010/01/17/world/africa/17abdulmutallab.html?hp

Nuclear blast. (n.d.). Ready. Retrieved from https://www.ready.gov/nuclear-blast

Nurick, L. (1945). The distinction between combatant and noncombatant in the law of war. *The American Journal of International Law, 39*(4). 680–697. doi:10.2307/2193409

Nye, J.S. and Lynn-Jones, S.M. (1988). International security studies: A report of a conference on the state of the field. *International Security, (12)*5–27.

Obama, B. (2015). National security strategy, 2015. The White House. Retrieved from https://www.whitehouse.gov/sites/default/files/docs/2015_national_security_strategy.pdf (accessed on 9 December 2017).

ODNI Home. (n.d.). Retrieved June 26, 2017, from https://www.dni.gov/index.php/nctc-who-we-are/history

Office of Management and Budget. President Donald J. Trump. (n.d.). The White House. Retrieved from https://www.whitehouse.gov/omb

Office of the secretary. (n.d.) U.S. Department of Homeland Security. Retrieved from https://www.dhs.gov/office-secretary (accessed on 13 August 2017).

The Office for State and Local Law Enforcement. (n.d.). *Department of Homeland Security.* Retrieved https://www.dhs.gov/office-state-and-local-law-enforcement (accessed on 18 December 2017).

Office of Strategic Services. (n.d.). *Dictionary of American History.* Retrieved June 19, 2017 from http://www.encyclopedia.com/history/dictionaries-thesauruses-pictures-and-press-releases/office-strategic-services.

Office of Strategic Services. Catoctin Mountain Park, Prince William Forest Park. (n.d.) National Park Service. Retrieved from https://www.nps.gov/articles/office-of-strategic-services.htm

Ogren, J.G. and Langevin, J.R. (1999). Responding to the threat of cyberterrorism through information assurance. Naval Postgraduate School: Monterey, California. Retrieved from http://www.dtic.mil/dtic/tr/fulltext/u2/a366792.pdf (accessed 23 March 2017).

Ohr, B.G. (2015). Effective methods to combat transnational organized crime in criminal justice process. *United Nations Asia and Far East Institute.* Retrieved from http://www.unafei.or.jp/english/pdf/PDF_rms/no58/58-05.pdf (accessed 17 June 2017).

Olson, D. (2012). Agroterrorism: Threat to America's economy and food supply. *FBI Law Enforcement Bulletin*. Retrieved from https://leb.fbi.gov/2012/february/agroterrorism-threats-to-americas-economy-and-food-supply

Operation Enduring Freedom. (2005). *National Defense Research Institute.* Rand Corporation. Retrieved from file:///Users/Dr.Mo/Downloads/RAND_RB9148.pdf (accessed on 6 August 2017).

Operation Enduring Freedom fast facts. (2016). CNN. Retrieved from http://www.cnn.com/2013/10/28/world/operation-enduring-freedom-fast- facts/index.html (accessed on 6 August 2017).

Operation Freedom's Sentinel Qualifies for Campaign Medal. (2015). *Department of Defense.* Retrieved from https://www.defense.gov/News/Article/Article/604135/operation-freedoms-sentinel-qualifies-for-campaign-medal/ (accessed on 14 December 2017).

Operation Inherent Resolve. (n.d.) U.S. Department of Defense. Retrieved from http://www.defense.gov/News/Special-Reports/0814_Inherent-Resolve

Operation Just Cause: The invasion of Panama, December 1989. (n.d.). United States Army. Retrieved from https://www.army.mil/article/14302/operation-just-cause-the-invasion-of-panama-december-1989

Opinion: Pelosi targets transportation. (2004). *The Journal of Commerce Online.* Retrieved from http://www.joc.com/opinion-pelosi-targets-transportation_20040120.html

Oppenheimer, J.R. (2011). Now I am become death, the destroyer of worlds. Realexpo. Video retrieved from https://www.youtube.com/watch?v=_LmxlptS3cw

Organization and staffing. (n.d.). Congressional Budget Office. Retrieved from https://www.cbo.gov/about/organization-and-staffing

Organization, mission, and function manual: Federal Bureau of Investigation. (n.d.) Department of Justice. Retrieved from https://www.justice.gov/jmd/organization-mission-and-functions-manual-federal-bureau-investigation (accessed on 14 August 2017).

OSS primer—operational groups. (n.d.). *Office of Strategic Services.* Retrieved June 19, 2017, from http://www.soc.mil/OSS/operational-groups.html

Ostrovsky, A. (2015). ISIS and Hamas: The double standard. *Huffington Post.* Retrieved from https://www.huffingtonpost.com/arsen-ostrovsky/isis-and-hamas-the-double_b_5695734.html (accessed on 18 December 2017).

Otton, S. (1983). *The secret six: John Brown and the abolitionist movement.* Murphys, CA: Uncommon Books.

Our Mission. (n.d.). *Office of Naval Intelligence.* Retrieved from http://www.oni.navy.mil/Our_Mission/ (accessed on 17 December 2017).

Overseas contingency operations: The Pentagon slush fund. (n.d.). National Priorities. Retrieved June 28, 2017 from https://www.nationalpriorities.org/campaigns/overseas-contingency-operations/

Overview. (n.d.). National Preparedness Divison. Retrieved from https://www.fema.gov/national-preparedness-directorate

Overview of response to Hurricane Sandy-Nor'Easter and recommendations for improvement. (2013). *U.S. Department of Energy.* Retrieved from https://energy.gov/sites/prod/files/2013/05/f0/DOE_Overview_Response-Sandy-Noreaster_Final.pdf

Overview of the law enforcement strategy to combat international organized crime. (2008). U.S. Department of Justice. Retrieved from https://www.justice.gov/sites/default/files/criminal-icitap/legacy/2015/04/23/04-23-08combat-intl-crime-overview.pdf

Pablo Escobar. (2016). A&E Network. Retrieved June 30, 2017 from https://www.biography.com/people/pablo-escobar-9542497

Pagliery, J. (2015). Inside the $2 billion ISIS war machine. *CNN Money.* Retrieved from http://money.cnn.com/2015/12/06/news/isis-funding/index.html (accessed on 17 December 2017).

Pakistan to demand Taliban give up Bin Laden as Iran seals Afghan border. (2001). Fox News. Retrieved from http://www.foxnews.com/story/2001/09/16/pakistan-to-demand-taliban-give-up-bin-laden-as-iran-seals-afghan-border.html

Paquette, J. & Miller, C. (2006). The National Security Council. *Harvard Model Congress Europe.* Harvard Unviersity. Retrieved from http://www.hcs.harvard.edu/~hmce/files/downloads/National%20Security%20Council%20Guide.pdf (accessed on 9 December 2017).

Pate, R. (2004). The anthrax attacks, 9/11, & war: The anthrax mystery: Solved. Anthrax Attacks. Retrieved June 21, 2017 from http://www.anthraxattacks.net/2009/07/the-anthrax -mystery-solved/#more-737

Pearl Harbor. (2009). *History.com*. Retrieved June 28, 2017 from http://www.history.com/topics/ world-war-ii/pearl-harbor

Pearl Harbor attack. (2017). *Encyclopedia Britannica*. Retrieved June 28, 2017, from https:// www.britannica.com/event/Pearl-Harbor-attack.

Pearl Harbor attack. (n.d.). *United States History*. Retrieved June 28, 2017 from http://www. u-s-history.com/pages/h1649.html.

Perlroth, N. and Sanger, D. E. (2013). Cyberattacks seem meant to destroy, not just disrupt. *The New York Times*. Retrieved from http://www.nytimes.com/2013/03/29/technology/ corporate-cyberattackers-possibly-state-backed-now-seek-to-destroy-data.html (accessed 26 March 2017).

Perry, W.J. (2005). *Worst weapons in worst hands: U.S. inaction on the nuclear terror threat since 9/11, and a path of action*. Washington, DC: The National Security Advisory Group.

Personal Core Values. (n.d.). National Reconnaissance Office. Retrieved from http://www.nro.gov/ about/nro/mission.html (accessed on 11 August 2017).

Philippine American War. (n.d.). University of Hawaii. Retrieved from http://opmanong.ssc.hawaii. edu/filipino/PAWLinks.html#Benevolent (accessed on 6 August 2017).

The Philippine-American War, 1899–1902. (n.d.). Office of the Historian. Retrieved from https:// history.state.gov/milestones/1899-1913/war

Philpott, D. (2015). Understanding the department of homeland security. Lanham, MD: Bernan Press. p. 279.

Plaza, V. (2015). *American mass murders*. Raleigh, NC: Lulu.com Publishing.

Plummer, B. (2013, September 30). Absolutely everything you need to know about how the government shutdown will work. *Washington Post*. Retrieved June 18, 2017 from https:// www.washingtonpost.com/news/wonk/wp/2013/09/30/absolutely-everything-you-need-to- know-about-how-the-government-shutdown-will-work/?utm_term=.1366e754bfda

The police response to active shooter incidents. (2014). Police Executive Research Forum. Retrieved June 27, 2017 from http://www.policeforum.org/assets/docs/Critical_Issues_Series/the%20 police%20response%20to%20active%20shooter%20incidents%202014.pdf

Post-Katrina Emergency Management Reform Act. (n.d.). Federal Emergency Management Agency. Retrieved https://emilms.fema.gov/IS230c/FEM0101200.htm (accessed 7 August 2017).

Preamble. (n.d.). Cornell University. Retrieved from https://www.law.cornell.edu/constitution/ preamble

Preface. (2004). National Commission on Terrorist Attacks Upon the United States. Retrieved from http://govinfo.library.unt.edu/911/report/911Report_Pref.htm

President establishes Office of Homeland Security: Summary of the President's Executive Order: The Office of the Homeland Security and the Homeland Security Council. (2001). *The Avalon Project: Documents in Law, History, and Diplomacy*. Yale University. Retrieved from http:// avalon.law.yale.edu/sept11/president_038.asp

Presidential Memorandum Organization of the National Security Council and Homeland Security. (2017). *Office of the Press Secretary*. Retrieved from https://www.whitehouse.gov/the-press- office/2017/01/28/presidential-memorandum-organization-national-security-council-and (accessed on 9 December 2017).

Preventing terrorism and enhancing security. (2016). Department of Homeland Security. Retrieved June 26, 2017, from https://www.dhs.gov/preventing-terrorism-and-enhancing-security. February 9, 2016.

Preventing Terrorism Overview. (n.d.). *Department of Homeland Security*. Retrieved from https:// www.dhs.gov/topic/preventing-terrorism-overview (accessed on 12 December 2017).

Profile: Sayed Hassan Nasrallah. (2016). Al Jazeera. Retrieved from http://www.aljazeera.com/ archive/2006/04/2008410115816863222.html (accessed 16 August 2017).

Ports Primer: 3.2 Port Governance. (n.d.). *Environmental Protection Agency*. Retrieved from https://www.epa.gov/ports-initiative/ports-primer-32-port-governance (accessed on 12 December 2017).

Project BioShield. (2004). White House. Retrieved June 26, 2017, from https://georgew-bush-whitehouse.archives.gov/infocus/bioshield/

Quadrennial Homeland Security Review Report: A Strategic Framework for a Secure Homeland. (2010). *Department of Homeland Security.* Retrieved from https://www.dhs.gov/xlibrary/assets/qhsr_report.pdf (access 10 December 2017).

Quintero, C.E. (2014). A typology of homegrown terrorists. California State University San Bernardino: CSUSB Scholar Works. pp. 3–5. Retrieved from http://scholarworks.lib.csusb.edu/cgi/viewcontent.cgi?article=1113&context=etd

Radiological Dispersion Device. (n.d.). *Department of Homeland Security.* Retrieved from https://www.ready.gov/radiological-dispersion-device (accessed on 12 December 2017).

Rangel, C.B. (1988). Legalize drugs? Not on your life. *The New York Times.* Retrieved from http://www.nytimes.com/1988/05/17/opinion/legalize-drugs-not-on-your-life.html

Raw, L. (2011). *Exploring Turkish culture: Essays, Interviews, and Reviews.* England: Cambridge Scholars. p. 301.

Raza, M. (2009). *Confronting Terrorism.* India: Penguin India. p. 28.

Reed, J. and Lubold, G. (2013). Exclusive: Air Force grounds fighter jets as shutdown takes hold. *Foreign Policy.* Retrieved June 18, 2017 from http://foreignpolicy.com/2013/10/02/exclusive-air-force-grounds-fighter-jets-as-shutdown-takes-hold/

Reischauer, R.D. (1993). CBO testimony: Joint Committee on the Organization of Congress of the United States. *Congressional Budget Office.* Retrieved from https://www.cbo.gov/sites/default/files/103rd-congress-1993-1994/reports/1993_06_10_mission.pdf

The response to Hurricane Katrina. (2012). *International Risk Governance Council.* http://www.irgc.org/wp-content/uploads/2012/04/Hurricane_Katrina_full_case_study_web.pdf

Returning from Iraq and Afghanistan: Preliminary assessment of readjustment needs of veterans, service members, and their families. (2010). The National Academies of Sciences, Engineering, and Medicine. The National Academies Press. Retrieved from https://www.nap.edu/read/12812/chapter/4 (accessed on 5 August 2017).

Richardson, L. (2006). What terrorist want. *New York Times.* Retrieved from http://www.nytimes.com/2006/09/10/books/chapters/0910-1st-rich.html?pagewanted=all&_r=0 (accessed on 19 September 2017).

Risk management fundamentals. (2011). U.S. Department of Homeland Security. Retrieved from https://www.dhs.gov/xlibrary/assets/rma-risk-management-fundamentals.pdf

Roberts, J. (2002). Kissinger to head 9–11 Commission. CBS News. Retrieved June 17, 2017 from http://www.cbsnews.com/news/kissinger-to-head-9-11-commission/

Robertson, C. (2015, May 23). Decade after Katrina pointing finger more firmly at Army Corps. *New York Times.* Retrieved October 31, 2015.

Rogers, J.D. (2008). Development of the New Orleans flood protection system prior to Hurricane Katrina. *Journal of Geotechnical and Geoenvironmental Engineering.* DOI: 10.1061/ASCE1090-02412008134:5602. p. 608.

Roggio, B. (2017). State offers $10 million for leader of "the Syria branch of Al Qaeda." *Long War Journal.* Retrieved from http://www.longwarjourna.org/archives/2017/05/state-offers-10-million-for-leader-of-the-syria-branch-of-al-qaeda.php (accessed on 15 August 2017).

The Role of State and Local Law Enforcement Agencies in Homeland Security: Revisiting Community-Oriented Policy. (n.d.). *Sam Houston State University.* Retrieved from http://www.cjcenter.org/trcpi/doc/articles/oce.pdf (accessed on 18 December 2017).

Rooney, B. (2011). Who gets Bin Laden's $25 million bounty? *CNN Money.* Retrieved from http://money.cnn.com/2011/05/02/news/osama_bin_laden_reward/index.htm (16 August 2017).

Roychoudhury, H. (2013). *My journey and sovereign United Bengal.* India: Partridge Publishing.

Russell, J. and Cohn, R. (n.d.). *Departments of the Continental Army.* Moscow: Bookvika Publishing.

Russo, J. *The American diaspora.* (n.d.). Petersen International Underwriters. Retrieved from https://www.piu.org/communicators/the-american-diaspora (accessed 6 August 2017).

Sarkesian, S.C., Williams, J.A., and Cimbala, S.J. (2013). *U.S. National: Policymakers, processes, and policies.* 5th ed. Boulder, CO: Lynne Reinner Publishers, Inc.

Saul, B. (2008). Defining terrorism to protect human rights. *Sydney Legal Law of Studies Research Paper.* Retrieved from https://papers.ssrn.com/sol3/papers.cfm?abstract_id=1292059 (accessed on 19 September 2017).

Scanning and imaging shipping containers overseas: Costs and alternatives. (2016). Congressional Budget Office. Retrieved from http://www.joc.com/opinion-pelosi-targets-transportation_20040120.html (accessed 16 June 2017).

Scharre, P. (2012). Spectrum of what? *Military Review.* Retrieved from http://usacac.army.mil/CAC2/MilitaryReview/Archives/English/MilitaryReview_20121231_art012.pdf

Schmid, A.P. and Jongman, A.J. (2005). Political terrorism: A guide to actors, authors, concepts, data bases, theories, and literature. Center for International Affairs, Harvard University. 2nd ed. Piscataway, NJ: Transactions Publishers.

Schmid, A. & Jongman, A. J. (1988). Political terrorism: A new guide to actors, authors, Concepts, data bases, theories, & literature. New York: Routledge, New York. p. 28.

Schmitt, G.R. (2007). Agroterrorism—Why we're not ready: A look at the role of law enforcement. *National Institute of Justice,* (257). Retrieved June 30, 2017 from https://nij.gov/journals/257/pages/agroterrorism.aspx

Schultz, R., Godson, R., and Greenwood, T. (1993). A recent forum on security in arms control. *Security Studies for the 1990s.*

Schwartau, W. (1994). *Information warfare: Chaos on the electronic superhighway.* New York: Thunder's Mouth Press.

Schwartz, B.E. (2015). *Right of boom: The aftermath of nuclear terrorism.* New York: The Overlook Press, Peter Mayer Publishers, Inc., 2015.

Schweller, R.L. (2014). *Maxwell's demon and the golden apple: Global discord in the new millennium.* Baltimore, MD: Johns Hopkins University Press.

Scott, O. (1979). The secret six: John Brown and the abolitionist movement. New York: First Printing. p. 3.

Secret committee of correspondence/Committee of Foreign Affairs, 1775–1777. (n.d.). Office of the Historian. Retrieved from https://history.state.gov/milestones/1776-1783/secret-committee

Secret journals of the acts of proceedings. (1820). Vol. 1, p. 34. U.S. Congress. Retrieved from https://archive.org/stream/secretjournalsof2unit/secretjournalsof2unit_djvu.txt (accessed on 16 June 2017).

Secret methods and techniques. (n.d.). *Spy Letters of the American Revolution: From the Collections of the Clements Library.* University of Michigan. Retrieved from http://clements.umich.edu/exhibits/online/spies/index-methods.html

Security Council Acts Unanimously to Adopt Resolution Strongly Condemning Terrorism as one of the Most Serious Threats to Peace. (2004). *United Nations.* Retrieved from https://www.un.org/press/en/2004/sc8214.doc.htm (accessed on 12 December 2017).

Security. (2016). Oxford University Press. Retrieved from https://en.oxforddictionaries.com/definition/security

Security of Homeland Security. (n.d.). U.S. Homeland Security. Retrieved from https://www.dhs.gov/secretary

Security Risk Management. (2016). Australian Government. Retrieved from https://www.protectivesecurity.gov.au/governance/security-risk-management/Pages/Security-risk-management.aspx

Semple, K. (2006). Saddam Hussein is sentenced to death. *New York Times.* Retrieved from http://www.nytimes.com/2006/11/05/world/middleeast/05cnd-saddam.html?mcubz=1 (accessed on 16 August 2017).

Senate Report, 2006: 14–2.

September 11, 2001: Background and timeline of the attacks. (2016). CNN. Retrieved June 29, 2017 from http://www.cnn.com/2013/07/27/us/september-11-anniversary-fast-facts/index.html

Shah, A. (2005). Hurricane Katrina. *Global Issues.* Retrieved from http://www.globalissues.org/article/564/hurricane-katrina

Shane, S. and Lipton, E. (2009). Passengers' quick action halted attack. *New York Times.* Retrieved from http://www.nytimes.com/2009/12/27/us/27plane.html?pagewanted=all&_r=0

Signals Intelligence Activities. (n.d.). *Central Intelligence Agency.* Retrieved from https://www.cia.gov/library/reports/Policy-and-Procedures-for-CIA-Signals-Intelligence-Activities.pdf (accessed on 12 December 2017).

Signals intelligence. (n.d.) National Security Agency. Retrieved from https://www.nsa.gov/what-we-do/signals-intelligence/ (accessed on 11 August 2017).

Silke, A. (2004). *Research on Terrorism: Trends, Achievements, and Failures*: Frank Cass: New York. p. 2.

Singer, P.W. (2012). The cyber terror bogeyman. *Brookings Institution*. Retrieved from https://www.brookings.edu/articles/the-cyber-terror-bogeyman/

Sink, J. (2014). Intelligence chief says Snowden leaks created "perfect storm." *The Hill*. Retrieved April 11, 2015 from http://thehill.com/policy/technology/218155-intelligence-chief-says-snowden-leaks-created-perfect-storm.

Sirohi, M.N. (2015). *Cyber terrorism and information warfare*. Delhi, India: Alpha Editions.

Siyang Li, M. (2013). Keeping up with Moore's Law. *Dartmouth Undergraduate Journal of Science*. 15th ed.

Slovic, P. (1987). Perception of risk. *Science. (236)*4799, p. 283.

Smeltz, D. and Wojtowicz, L. (2017). American opinion on US-Russia relations: From bad to worse. *The Chicago Council on Global Affairs.* Retrieved from https://www.thechicagocouncil.org/publication/american-opinion-us-russia-relations-bad-worse (accessed on 13 August 2017).

Smith, M. (2013). CNN explains: Sequestration. *CNN*. Retrieved June 18, 2017 from http://www.cnn.com/2013/02/06/politics/cnn-explains-sequestration/index.html.

Smollett, T.G. (1796). *The critical review: Or, annals of literature*. London: A. Hamilton, Falcon-Court, Fleet-Street.

Smoke, R. (1975). National security affairs. *Handbook of Political Science, Vol. 8: International Politics, (8)*259.

Snow, D.M. (1998). *National security: Defense policy in a changed international order*. 4th ed. New York: St. Martin's Press.

Solomon, E. (2006). 9/11: Truth, lies and conspiracy interview: Lee Hamilton. CBC News, Canada. Retrieved June 17, 2017 from https://web.archive.org/web/20070108233707/http://www.cbc.ca/sunday/911hamilton.html#top

Southern Poverty Law Center. (n.d.). Klu Klux Klan. Retrieved from https://www.splcenter.org/fighting-hate/extremist-files/ideology/ku-klux-klan (accessed 26 September 2017).

Sovereign citizens. (n.d.). The Law Society of British Columbia. Retrieved from https://www.lawsociety.bc.ca/page.cfm?cid=2627

Sovereign citizens' movement. (n.d.). Southern Poverty Law Center. Retrieved from https://www.splcenter.org/fighting-hate/extremist-files/ideology/sovereign-citizens-movement

Spanish American War. (2010). *History.com*. Retrieved on June 17, 2017 from http://www.history.com/topics/spanish-american-war

Special analysis: The active shooter threat. (2012). *MSA Worldview*. Retrieved June 27, 2017, from https://www.msasecurity.net/hs-fs/hub/91068/file-15973733-pdf/docs/msa_special_analysis_-_active_shooter_threat_8.20.12.pdf.

Spying and espionage. (2017). MountVernon.org. Retrieved June 19, 2017 from http://www.mountvernon.org/george-washington/the-revolutionary-war/spying-and-espionage/

Stanchak, J.E. (2007). Cloak and dagger army: The OSS. *America in WWII*. Retrieved June 19, 2017 from http://www.americainwwii.com/articles/cloak-and-dagger-army-the-oss/.

State and Major Urban Area Fusion Centers. (n.d.). *Department of Homeland Security.* Retrieved from https://www.dhs.gov/state-and-major-urban-area-fusion-centers (accessed on 18 December 2017).

State of New Jersey Office of Homeland Security & Preparedness. (2017). Anti-abortion extremists. *Offices of Governor Chris Christie & Lieutenant Governor Kim Guadagno*. Retrieved from https://www.njhomelandsecurity.gov/analysis/anti-abortion-extremists (accessed on 28 September 2017).

Statistical abstract of the United States: 2004–2005. (2004). U.S. Bureau of Statistics.

Stone, L. (2015). Why Americans are going abroad: When citizenship globalizes, governance changes. *In a State of Migration*. Retrieved from https://medium.com/migration-issues/why-are-americans-leaving-75fe530ce49d (accessed 6 August 2017).

The storm after the storm. (2015). *60 Minutes*. CBS. Retrieved April 6, 2015.

Strategic Air Command (SAC). (2014). In *Encyclopedia Britannica*. Retrieved June 20, 2017, from https://www.britannica.com/topic/Strategic-Air-Command-United-States-Air-Force

Strategy to combat transnational organized crime. (n.d.). The White House. Retrieved from https://obamawhitehouse.archives.gov/administration/eop/nsc/transnational-crime/strategy (accessed on 17 June 2017).

Strategy to combat transnational organized crime: Introduction. (2010). The White House. Retrieved from https://obamawhitehouse.archives.gov/administration/eop/nsc/transnational-crime/introduction (accessed 17 June 2017).

Straub, F., Zeunik, J., and Gorban, B. (2017). Lessons learned from the police response to the San Bernardino and Orlando terrorist attacks. *CTC Sentintel, 10*(5). Retrieved June 27, 2017 from https://ctc.usma.edu/posts/lessons-learned-from-the-police-response-to-the-san-bernardino-and-orlando-terrorist-attacks

Subcommittees. (n.d.). U.S. House of Representatives Committee on Appropriations. Retrieved from http://appropriations.house.gov/subcommittees/

Sullivan, J. O. (1845). Annexation. *The United States Magazine and Democratic Review,* Vol. 17. New York, NY: pp. 5–6, 9–10. Retrieved from https://pdcrodas.webs.ull.es/anglo/OSullivanAnnexation.pdf (accessed 7 December 2017).

Subchapter IV—Accountability and Reporting Requirements of the President. (n.d.). *Legal Information Institute.* Cornell University. Retrieved from https://www.law.cornell.edu/uscode/text/50/chapter-34/subchapter-IV (accessed on 8 December 2017).

Sword of the Lord. (n.d.). Army of God. Retrieved from https://www.armyofgod.com/

Tafoya, W.L. (2011). Cyber terror. Federal Bureau of Investigation. Retrieved from https://leb.fbi.gov/2011/november/cyber-terror

Talmon, J.L. (1952). *The origins of totalitarian democracy.* 2nd ed. New York: Praeger.

Taylor, J.M. (1989). *General Maxwell Taylor: The sword and the pen.* New York: Doubleday.

Taylor, M.D. (1976). *Precarious security.* New York: Norton.

Terrorism Act 2000. (2000). *United Kingdom Government.* Retrieved from https://www.legislation.gov.uk/ukpga/2000/11/section/1 (accessed on 12 December 2017).

Terror attack over, 147 dead at Kenya University. (2015). *USA Today.* Retrieved from https://www.usatoday.com/story/news/world/2015/04/02/kenya-university-attack/70815094/ (accessed on 18 December 2017).

Terrorism 2002/2005. (2002). *Federal Bureau of Investigation.* Retrieved from https://www.fbi.gov/stats-services/publications/terrorism-2002–2005 (accessed on 12 December 2017).

Terrorism and Funding Intelligence (2012). *U.S. Department of the Treasury.* Retrieved from https://www.treasury.gov/about/organizational-structure/offices/Pages/Office-of-Intelligence-Analysis.aspx (accessed on 15 December 2017).

Terrorism Funding. (n.d.). *Security Council Counter-Terrorism Committee: United Nations.* Retrieved from https://www.un.org/sc/ctc/focus-areas/financing-of-terrorism/ (accessed on 15 December 2015).

Terrorism. (2017). *Defense Technical Information Center.* Retrieved from http://www.dtic.mil/doctrine/dod_dictionary/data/t/7591.html (accessed on 12 December 2017).

Terrorism. (n.d.). U.S. Department of Defense. Retrieved from http://www.dtic.mil/doctrine/dod_dictionary/?zoom_query=terrorism&zoom_sort= 0&zoom_per_page=10&zoom_and=1

Terrorism FAQs. News and Information. (2013). Central Intelligence Agency. Retrieved from https://www.cia.gov/news-information/cia-the-war-on-terrorism/terrorism-faqs.html

Terrorism Prevention Partnerships. (n.d.). *Department of Homeland Security.* Retrieved from https://www.dhs.gov/terrorism-prevention-partnerships# (accessed on 12 December 2017).

Thony, J.F. (n.d.). Money laundering and terrorism financing: An overview. *International Money Fund.* Retrieved from https://www.imf.org/external/np/leg/sem/2002/cdmfl/eng/thony.pdf (accessed on 14 December 2017).

Tomson, C. (2016). ISIS is on the verge of capturing Ar-Rutbah City in surprise offensive. *Al-Masadar News*. Retrieved from https://www.almasdarnews.com/article/isis-verge-capturing-ar-rutbah-city-surprise-offensive/

Toothman, J. (2010). What was the impact of the Age of Enlightenment? HowStuffWorks.com. Retrieved June 19, 2017 from, http://history.howstuffworks.com/historical-events/impact-age-of-enlightenment.htm

Transcript: Bin Laden video excerpts. (2001). BBC News. Retrieved from http://news.bbc.co.uk/2/hi/middle_east/1729882.stm

Trueman, C.N. (2015). The nuclear arms race. historylearningsite.co.uk. Retrieved on Aug. 16, 2016 from http://www.historylearningsite.co.uk/modern-world-history-1918-to-1980/the-cold-war/the-nuclear-arms-race/

The Truman Doctrine, 1947. (n.d.). The Office of the Historian. Retrieved from https://history.state.gov/milestones/1945-1952/truman-doctrine

Truman signs the National Security Act. (2009). History.com. AE Network. Retrieved on June 17, 2017 from http://www.history.com/this-day-in-history/truman-signs-the-national-security-act

Turner, M.A. (2005). Historical dictionary of the United States Intelligence. Lanham, MD. Scarecrow Press. p. 136.

Two hundred years of U.S.-Russia relations. (n.d.). U.S. Department of State. Retrieved from https://www.state.gov/p/eur/ci/rs/200years/ (accessed on 13 August 2017).

Tyler, B.C. (2014). Setauket spy ring story. Emmaclark.com. Accessed June 19, 2017. http://spyring.emmaclark.org/SetauketSpyRingStory.pdf

Ullman, R.H. (1983). Redefining security. *International Security*. Cambridge, MA: MIT Press. *(8)*1.

USA International Business Publications. (2007). *U.S. Military Intelligence Handbook*. p. 70.

The United States Air Force. (n.d.). *Encyclopedia Britannica*. Retrieved June 19, 2017 from https://www.britannica.com/topic/The-United-States-Air-Force#ref253459

United States Court of Appeals for the Second Circuit. (2003). United States vs. Ramzi Ahmed Yosef, Eyad Ismoil. Retrieved from http://news.findlaw.com/cnn/docs/terrorism/usyousef40403opn.pdf (accessed on 12 December 2017).

United States Military Intelligence Handbook: Volume 1 strategic linformation, procedures, and developments. (2011). Washington, DC: Global Investment Center.

U.S. Agriculture trade data update. (2006). Economic Research Service, U.S. Department of Agriculture. Retrieved from http://www.ers.usda.gov/ Data/FATUS/MonthlySummary.htm

The U.S. Coast Guard and OSS Maritime Operations During World War II. (2009). *Central Intelligence Agency.* Retrieved from https://www.cia.gov/library/center-for-the-study-of-intelligence/csi-publications/csi-studies/studies/vol-52-no-4/guardian-spies.html (accessed on 15 December 2017).

U.S. collective defense arrangements. (n.d.). U.S. Department of State. Retrieved from http://www.state.gov/s/l/treaty/collectivedefense/

U.S. Department of Defense. (n.d.). Secretary of defense. Retrieved from https://www.defense.gov/Leaders/Secretary-of-Defense/ (accessed on 13 August 2017).

U.S. DOT Takes New Emergency Actions as Part of Comprehensive Strategy to Keep Crude Oil Shipments Safe. (2014). *U.S. Department of Transportation.* Retrieved from https://www.fra.dot.gov/eLib/Details/L05223 (accessed on 12 December 2017).

U.S. National Interests. (1962). Excerpt from statement by Soviet Ambassador Valerian A. Zorin to U.N. Security Council. Retrieved from https://www.mtholyoke.edu/acad/intrel/zorin2.htm (accessed on 7 December 2017).

Veneman, A. (2003). Statement by Secretary Veneman submitted for the record to the Gilmore Commission. U. S. Department of Agriculture. Retrieved from https://www.rand.org/content/dam/rand/www/external/nsrd/terrpanel/USDAStatementSept2003.pdf

Viereck, P. (2006). *Conservative thinkers: From John Adams to Winston Churchill.* New Brunswick, NJ: Transaction Publishers.

Walker, D.M. (2004). 9/11 Commission Report: Reorganization, transformation, and information sharing. Government Accountability Office. Retrieved from http://www.gao.gov/assets/120/111208.pdf (accessed on 16 August 2017).

Wallace, W.M. (2017). American Revolution in *Encyclopædia Britannica*, Retrieved June 19, 2017 from https://www.britannica.com/event/American-Revolution

Walt, Stephen M. (1991). The renaissance of security studies. *International Studies Quarterly, (35)*, 211–239.

Wanted: Information that brings justice. Abukar Shekau up to $7 million reward. (2013). U.S. Department of State. Retrieved from https://rewardsforjustice.net/english/abubakar_shekau.html (accessed on 15 August 2017).

Watson, D. (2002). Before the Senate Select Committee on Intelligence: Washington, DC. Federal Bureau of Investigation. Retrieved from https://archives.fbi.gov/archives/news/testimony/the-terrorist-threat-confronting- the-united-states

Weeks, W.E. (1996). *Building the continental empire: American expansion from the Revolution to the Civil War.* Chicago, IL: Ivan R. Dee Publisher.

Weicker, L. (2011). *Remembering 9/11 and anthrax: Public health's vital role in national defense: Summary of the investigation into the anthrax attacks* (Rep.). Trust for America's Health. Retrieved June 21, 2017 from http://healthyamericans.org/assets/files/TFAH911Anthrax10YrAnnvFINAL.pdf

Weiner, T. (2012). *Enemies: A history of the FBI.* New York: Random House Publishing.

Weldes, J. (1999). *Constructing national interests: The United States and the Cuban Missile Crisis.* Minneapolis: University of Minnesota Press.

Wenger, A. (2000). *Living with Peril: Eisenhower, Kennedy, and Nuclear Weapons.* Maryland: Rowan & Littlefield. p. 278.

What is Greenpeace's mission? (2009). *Greenpeace International.* Retrieved from http://www.greenpeace.org/international/en/about/faq_old/questions-about-greenpeace-in/

What is the open government partnership? (2017). Open Government Partnership. Retrieved from https://www.opengovpartnership.org/about/about-ogp

White House Continuity of Government Plan. (2017). *The White House,* Retrieved from https://whitehouse.gov1.info/continuity-plan/ (accessed on 12 December 2017).

White, M.J. (1996). *The Cuban Missile Crisis.* London: MacMillan Press Ltd.

Whittaker, A.G., Brown, S.A., Smith, F.C., and McKune, E. (2011). The national security policy process: The National Security Council and Interagency System. University of Virginia. Retrieved from http://www.virginia.edu/cnsl/pdf/national-security-policy-process-2011.pdf

Whittaker, D.J. (2003). *The terrorism reader.* 2nd ed. London and New York: Routlege Taylor and Francis Group.

Wilkinson, P. (1992). *International Terrorism: New Risks to World Order. Dilemmas of World Politics: International Issues in a Changing World.* Clarenden Press: London. pp. 228–229.

William J. Donovan. (2017). *Encyclopedia Britannica.* Retrieved June 19, 2017 from https://www.britannica.com/biography/William-J-Donovan

Williams, C.L., et al. (2009). Department of Homeland Security science and technology directorate: Developing technology to protect America.". National Academy of Public Administration. Retrieved June 26, 2017, from http://www.napawash.org/wp-content/uploads/2009/09-10.pdf

Williams, L.K., Koch, M.T., and Smith, J.M. (2012). The political consequences of terrorism: Terror events, casualties, and government duration. *International Studies Perspectives.* pp. 1–19. Retrieved from http://faculty.missouri.edu/williamslaro/Williams,%20Koch%20and%20Smith%202012.pdf

Williamson, M. (2009). *Terrorism, war and international law: The legality of the use of force against Afghanistan in 2001.* New York: Routledge Publishing.

Williamson, M. (2009). *Terrorism, War and International Law: The Legality of the Use of Force against Afghanistan in 2001.* New York: Routledge Publishing, p. 166.

Wilson, G. and Saetren, W. (2016). Quite possibly the dumbest military concept ever: A limited nuclear war. *The National Interest.* Retrieved from http://nationalinterest.org/blog/the-buzz/quite-possibly-the-dumbest-military- concept-ever-limited-16394 (accessed on 10 August 2017).

Wikenheiser, F.J. (1975). *The United States military in the Cuban Missile Crisis* (Doctoral dissertation). Retrieved from PDX Scholar. (Accession number 2386).

Windrem, R. and Limjoco, V. (2008). 9/11 Commission controversy. [Web log post]. MSNBC. Retrieved June 17, 2017 from https://web.archive.org/web/20080407223205/http://deep-background.msnbc.msn.com/archive/2008/01/30/624314.aspx

With mass shootings on the rise, police are updating their active shooter training and response tactics. (2016). Retrieved June 27, 2017, from https://www.missionmanager.com/with-mass-shootings-on-the-rise-law-enforcement-agencies-are-updating-their-active-shooter-training-and-response-tactics-based-on-lessons-learned/

Wolfers, A. (1973). *In American defense and détente.* New York: Dodd, Mead.

Wolfers, A. (1952). National security as an ambiguous symbol. *Political Science Quarterly*, *67*(4).

World economic and financial surveys: World economic outlook subdued demands and symptoms and remedies. (2016). *International Monetary Fund*. Retrieved from https://www.imf.org/external/pubs/ft/weo/2016/02/pdf/text.pdf

Worldwide displacements hit all-time high as war and persecution increase. (2015). United Nations High Commissioner for Refugees. Retrieved from http://www.unhcr.org/en-us/news/latest/2015/6/558193896/worldwide-displacement-hits-all-time-high-war-persecution-increase.html (accessed 17 June 2017).

Wright, R. E. & Cowen, D. J. (2006). Financing founding fathers: The men who made America rich. *University of Chicago*. Retrieved from http://www.press.uchicago.edu/Misc/Chicago/910687.html (accessed on 15 December 2017).

Wright, R.K. (2016). The Continental Army. Center of Military History, United States Army, Washington, DC.

Wyler, G. (2011). The Mexican drug cartels are a national security issue. *Business Insider*. Retrieved June 30, 2017 from http://www.businessinsider.com/why-the-us-needs-to-stop-fighting-the-drug-war-and-start-fighting-the-cartels-2011-6

Yagami, K. (2009) Bombing Hiroshima and Nagasaki: Gar Alperovitz and his critics. *Southeast Review of Asian Studies, 31*, 301–307. Retrieved on June 20, 2017 from http://www.uky.edu/Centers/Asia/SECAAS/Seras/2009/25_Yagami_2009.pdf

Yarger, R.H. and Barber, G.F. eds. (1997). The U.S. Army War College methodology for determining interests and levels of intensity. Retrieved from http://www.au.af.mil/au/awc/awcgate/army-usawc/natinte.htm

Yen, H. (2006, February 3) Ties between White House, Sept. 11 Chief. *USA Today*. Retrieved June 17, 2017 from http://usatoday30.usatoday.com/news/washington/2008-02-03-2749617369_x.htm

York, C. (2017). How Chelsea Manning's leaks changed the world and showed the brutal reality of war. *Huffington Post UK*. Retrieved on June 25, 2017 from https://www.msn.com/en-gb/news/world/how-chelsea-mannings-leaks-changed-the-world-and-showed-the-brutal-reality-of-war/ar-AAm0lp9

Yukl, G.A. (2012). *Leadership in organizations*. 8th ed. Pearson Education: Upper Saddle River, NJ.

Zalman, A. (2014, June 19). Narcoterrorism. ThoughtCo.Com Retrieved June 30, 2017 from https://www.thoughtco.com/definition-of-narcoterrorism-3209253

Zelin, A.Y. (2014). Abu Bakr al-Baghdadi: Islamic state's driving force. *BBC News*. Retrieved from http://www.bbc.com/news/world-middle-east-28560449 (accessed on 15 August 2017).

Index

A

32nd Marine Amphibious Unit, 175
624th Operations Center, 259
9/11, 183
9/11 Commission Report, 123, 278
688th Cyberspace Wing, 259
689th Combat Communications Wing, 259
67th Cyberspace Wing, 259
Abbas Mossauwi, 243
Abd al-Rahim al-Nishin, 182
Abdul Rahmah, 177
Abigail Adams, 9
Abolitionism, 20, 97
Abolitionist, 20, 169
Abortion extremism, 213
Abraham Lincoln, 19, 21, 96
Absolute monarchy, 10
Abu Ali al-Harithi, 182
Abu Nidal Organization, 175
Abu Sayyaf, 144
Adolf Hitler, 30, 99, 237, 238
Agadir Crisis – 1911, 27
Age of Enlightenment, 227
Aggression, 134, 192, 426, 437
Agroterrorism, 255, 267
Ahmed Ajaj, 177
Air Force Cyber Command (AFCC), 259
Air Force Intelligence, 123, 323

Alex P. Schmid, 171, 200
Alfred McCormack, 324
Allied Powers, 27, 28, 32
Allison Incident, 172
al-Nusra Front, 212
Al-Qaeda, 143, 184, 186
Al-Qaeda in the Arabian Peninsula (AQAP), 235
Al-Shabaab, 207, 211
Al Udeid Air Base, 181
Amal Movement, 243
American Airlines, 184, 194
American Civil War, 19, 94, 96, 459
American Diaspora, 142, 145
American Revolutionary War, 4, 10, 37, 343, 399, 456
Anarchism, 204, 220, 224
Anarchist extremism, 213, 220
Andrew Jackson, 17, 20, 97
Anglo-German Naval Arms Race 1898-1912, 27
Anglo-Russian Entente – 1907, 27
Animal Liberation Front, 215, 267
Animal rights, 213, 215, 267
Antietam, 20, 97
Antiterrorism and Force Protection Warfare
        Center, 183
Anwar al-Awalaki, 234, 235
Arab Socialist Ba'ath Party, 239
Archduke Ferdinand, 27
Ardit Ferizi, 261
Armed Islamic Group, 207

Army Intelligence, 123, 324
Army of God, 214
Articles of Confederation, 8, 39, 43, 88, 148, 391
Aryan race, 227
Ashton B. Carter, xi, 65, 292
Assassination of Franz Ferdinand 1914, 27
Atomic bomb, 32, 101, 302
Autodefensas Unidas de Columbia (AUC), 263
Axis Powers, 29, 80, 238, 313
Ayman al-Zawahiri, 184, 208, 240, 241

B

Bachir Gemayel, 175
Backdoor, 260, 456
Baghdad-based Ba'ath Party, 239
Balkan Wars – 1912–1913, 27
Barack Obama, 94, 127, 457
Battle at Harper's Ferry, 20, 97, 204
Battle of Concord, 4, 38, 108, 179
Battle of Dogger Bank, 28
Battle of Jutland, 28
Battle of Lexington, 38, 108
Battle of Manila Bay, 22
Battle of Midway, 32, 100
Battle of Tanneberg, 28
Battle of the Bulge, 32, 101
Battle of Valmy, 15
Battle of Yorktown, 4, 39, 103
Bay of Pigs Invasion, 34, 55, 56
Benjamin Franklin, 5, 14, 109
Berlin Wall, 35, 36
Bill of Rights, 8, 463
Boko Haram, 207, 209, 210
Bosnian Crisis – 1908–1909, 27
Boston Marathon Bombing, 246, 428
Bottom-Up Review (BUR), 156
Brian Michael Jenkins, 171
Bruce Hoffman, 171, 198, 199
Bull Run, 20
Bundy Standoff, 222

C

Camille Desmoulins, 12
Catholic Church, 13
Central Intelligence Agency, 49, 54, 91, 325
Central Powers, 27, 29
Central Security Service, 323, 326, 342
Chancellorsville, 20, 97
Chemical Stockpile Emergency Preparedness Program, 155
Chief Intelligence Officer, 154, 326
Chinese Communist Party, 35
Chouraeshkenazi, xxiv, 202, 459
Christian, 175, 214
Christian Patriot, 226
Civil defense, 61, 160, 370
Civil Rights Movement, 20, 97, 227, 229
Clickjacking, 260
Coast Guard Intelligence, 123, 326

Cold War, xv, 30, 32, 324, 327, 370
Colonialism, 21, 40
Combatants, 138, 139
Common laws, 225
Communications intelligence (COMINT), 342
Communists Party of Peru, 263
Complex coordinated, 258
Comprehensive Emergency Management Plans, 159, 380
Computer Fraud and Abuse Act, 262
Confederate of the United States, 21
Confederates, 20, 97
Confederate States of America, 19, 96, 227
Congressional Act of 1803, 156
Consequence management, 160
Containment, 33
Continental Army, 4, 39, 102, 103
Continental Congress, 101, 105, 109, 391
Contingency planning, 160, 370
Continuity of government, 187, 350
Covert operations, 109, 111, 216, 298
Crisis management, 160, 276, 370, 378
Critical Infrastructure Information Act of 2002, 149, 275
Cuban Missile Crisis, 34, 52, 56
Cuban Revolutionary War, 22
Cybersecurity, 150, 259, 410
Cyber Security Enhancement of Act of 2002, 149, 275
Cyberterrorism, 256, 257

D

Dahwah, 211
Dan Herbeck, 179
Death Penalty of 1996, 180
Declaration of Independence, 4, 5, 391
Democracy, 3, 65, 101, 439, 440
Democratic Republic, 17, 445
Democratic Societies, 14
Denial of service corruption, 260
Department of Energy, 123, 328, 329
Department of Homeland Security, xxii, 67, 149, 166, 170, 390
Department of Justice, 119, 122, 213
Department of Transportation, 344, 347
Department Six-point Agenda, 153, 154
Direct action, 216
Directory, 12
Disaster Relief Act of 1974, 156
Domestic extremism, 191, 446, 458
Domestic Nuclear Detection Office (DNDO), 155
Domestic terrorism, 76, 169
Drug Enforcement Agency (DEA), 332
Drug Tobacco Firearms (DTF), 246, 334
Dubai Ports World Controversy, 154
Dzhokhar Tsarnaev, 246, 248

E

Earth First!, 218
Earth Liberation Front, 216, 267

Eastern bloc, 32, 239
Eavesdropping, 260, 353
Egypt, 28, 205, 241, 444
Egyptian Islamic (Jihad), 206, 241
Ejercito Liberacio Nacional (ELN), 263
Elain Duke, 152
Electronic intelligence (ELINT), 339
Elijah Parish Lovejoy, 169
Emancipation Proclamation, 21, 98
Emergency management, xxiii, 148, 149, 150, 155, 156, 160
Emergency Preparedness and Response Directorate (EPRD), 150, 275
Emergency responders, 157
Emergency Services Sector (ESS), 157
Emergency Services Sector-Specific Plan, 158
Emiliano Zapata, 26
Enforcement Acts, 228
Entente Cordiale – 1904, 27
Environmental extremism, 213
European Union, 35, 201, 244
Executive branch, 8, 76, 284, 351
Executive Order 12127, 156
Exon-Florio Amendment, 154
Expatriates, 12, 142, 145
Expeditionary Mobile Diving and Salvage Forces, 183
Explorer I, 33
Explosive Ordnance Disposal, 183
Eyad Ismoil, 177, 206

F

Fahd Mohammed Ahmed al-Quso, 182
Fatwa, 184
Federal Bureau of Investigations, 149
Federalist Party, 14, 17, 399
Federal Protective Services, 149, 274
Felix Diaz, 26
Feudalism, 11
Fidel Castro, 55, 56, 61
Final Solution, 31, 100
First Battle of Bull Run, 97
First Battle of the Marne, 28
First Moroccan Crisis 1905–1906, 27
First Party System, 14
First responders, 157, 159, 162, 165, 166, 190, 258, 295
Flight 11, 184, 194
Flight 77, 184, 194
Flight 175, 184
Force structure, 124, 125, 135, 136, 137, 138
Foreign diplomacy, 92, 110, 135, 137, 399
Foreign policy, 399, 400, 416, 418
Fort Hood Shooting, 233
Franco-Russian Alliance 1914, 27
Franklin D. Roosevelt, 88, 172, 174, 322
French and Indian War, 3, 37
French Revolution, 6, 10, 11, 12
Fuerzas Armadas Revolucionas de Columbia (FARC), 263
Fumimaro Konoe, 173
Fusion centers, 190, 212

G

George Meade, 21, 98
Georges Danton, 12
George Washington, 10, 14, 17, 39, 102, 330, 331, 343
George W. Bush, 64, 143, 148, 149, 162, 187, 188, 277, 278, 282, 393, 395, 417
German idealism, 224, 225
German-Soviet Nonaggression Pact, 30, 31, 99
Gettysburg, 20, 21, 97, 98
Global Information Grid, 259
Global War on Terrorism, 139, 187, 194, 212, 235
Governance, 134, 137, 144, 145, 148
Government Accountability Office, 279, 280
Greenpeace, 215, 217
Guillermo Endara, 24

H

Hajj, 251
Hamas, 207, 211, 245, 263, 264, 425
Hardesty Avengers, 215
Hassan Nasrallah, 208, 210, 243
Hate crime, 187, 252
Henry Laurens, 5
Hezbollah, 208, 210, 425, 446
Hiroshima, 29, 74, 295
Homegrown terrorism, 229
Homeland Security, 197, 270, 274, 275, 276, 281, 329, 345
Homeland Security Act of 2002, 107, 149, 162, 373, 390
Homeland Security Investigations, 149, 274
House Un-American Activities Committee, 34
Hugo Chavez, 264
Human Genome Project, 328, 329
Human intelligence (HUMINT), 116, 328, 339
Hurricane Katrina, 162, 163, 164, 280

I

Idealism, 221, 225
Ideologies, 205, 213, 218, 226, 228, 229, 231, 232, 237
Imagery intelligence (IMINT), 339
Imam, 234, 235, 243
Imperialism, 3, 19, 24, 39, 41, 230, 264, 400
Imperial Japanese Navy Air Service, 172
Insurrection, 24
International Cybercrime Reporting and Cooperation Act, 262
International terrorism, 199, 205, 212, 229, 231
Internet, 212, 232, 250, 252, 256, 257, 258, 261, 265
Iraqi Ba'ath Party, 239
Ironclad Oath, 228
ISIS/ISIL, 208
Islamic extremism, 226, 251, 293
Islamic fundamentalism, 206, 207, 208, 245
Islamic Jihadism, 208, 235, 241, 245
Islamic Jihad Organization, 174

Islamic movement, 207, 246
Islamic State, 207, 208, 210, 211, 212, 241, 242, 244, 245, 251, 255
Israel, 206, 210, 211, 234, 243, 251
Israel Defense Forces, 210
Israeli-Lebanese Ceasefire Understanding, 243
Italo-Turkish War – 1911-1912, 27

J

Jacobins, 12, 204, 225
Jaish-e-Muhammad, 208
Jamal Ahmad al Badawl, 182
James Forrestal, 44, 91
Janet Napolitano, 152, 155, 420
Japanese Invasion of Manchuria, 172
Jay's Treaty, 15
Jefferson Republic Party, 15
Jeh Johnson, 152, 390, 401
Jihad, 174, 184, 194, 206
Jihadi, 232, 235, 244
John Adams, 5, 9, 15, 223
John F. Kennedy, 47, 55, 78, 93, 161, 327
John Jay, 5, 111, 113
John Kelly, 152
John Moore Allison, 172
John Wilkes Booth, 21, 98
Jones Act, 24
Joseph Grew, 173
Judicial branch, 8, 76
July Crisis 1914, 27
Junaid Hussain, 261
Just-war theory, 140

K

Kansas-Nebraska, 20, 97
Khalid Sheikh Mohammed, 184, 185, 194
Khobar Towers Bombing, 180
Kimberly Munley, 233
King Louis XVI, 11, 12
Klu Klux Klan, 205, 227, 228
Kurdistan Worker's Party, 211

L

Lackland Air Force Base, 259
League of Nations, 29, 30, 99, 401
Lebanese Civil War, 174, 176, 243
Lebanon, 174, 175, 176, 180, 186, 187
Left-wing extremism, 230
Legislative Assembly, 12
Legislative branch, 8, 76, 283, 391
Lend-Lease Act, 31, 100
Liberalism, 6, 10, 16, 222
London bombings, 206
Lone wolves, 213, 232, 233, 265
Lou Michael, 214, 425
Luis Terrazas, 26
Lushkar-e-Taiba, 208

M

Maastrict Treaty, 35
Mahmud Abouhalima, 206
Major Command (MAJCOM), 259
Majuhideen, 184
Manifest Destiny, 18, 19
Manual Antonio Noriega, 24
Margarette Gillespie, 185
Marine Corps Intelligence, 320, 339
Maritime Force Protection Command, 183
Mark Todd, 233
Marquis Condorcet, 13
Martial law, 22, 105
Martin Van Buren, 18
Marwan al-Shehhi, 185
Maximilien de Robespierre, 12
Maxwell Thurman, 25
Measure and signature intelligence (MASINT), 328
Menachem Begin, 175
MI5, 235
Michael Chertoff, 151, 153
Middle East, 176, 186, 187, 194
Military Intelligence Corps, 320, 324
Military Intelligence Section 5, 235
Military Intelligence Service, 324
Military Operations on Urbanized Terrain, 25
Militia extremism, 213, 222
Model Treaty, 14
Modern radicalism, 224
Mohamed Atta, 185, 278
Mohammad Salameh, 177, 206
Mohammed Atef, 184
Moner Mohammad Abu Salha, 255
Multinational Force in Lebanon, 174
Mumbai bombings, 206
Muslim, 207, 209, 210, 234

N

Nagasaki, 295, 303, 306, 308, 314
Narcoterrorism, 263, 264, 265, 266
National Aeronautics and Space Administration, 33
National Assembly, 11, 12, 240
National Convention, 12, 204, 225
National Counterterrorism Center, 171, 279, 282, 375
National Infrastructure Protection Plan (NIPP), 158
Nationalism, 13, 28, 204, 211
National Liberation Front, 205, 263
National Security Act of 1947, 274, 319, 321, 326, 329, 351
National Security Agency, 320, 323, 341, 342, 352
National September 11 Memorial and Museum, 187
National Socialist, 30, 99, 237
Naturalization Act of 1790, 227
Naval Coastal Warfare, 183
Nazi Party, 30, 99, 237, 238
Nidal Ayyad, 177, 206
Nidal Malik Hasan, 233, 234
Nigerian military forces, 209
Noncombatant immunity, 140

Noncombatants, 134, 138, 139, 140, 141
Non-state actors, 135, 137, 198, 199, 430
Noor Salman, 254
Nordicism, 227
North Atlantic Treaty Organization (NATO), 69, 171, 426

O

Office of Intelligence and Analysis, 153, 154,
    320, 329, 332
Office of Policy, 153, 154, 326
Office of Special Investigations, 181
Oklahoma City Bombing, 178, 180, 205
Omar Mateen, 252, 385
Open-source intelligence (OSINT), 327, 339
Operation Accountability, 243
Operation Barbarossa, 31, 100
Operation Enduring Freedom, 139, 143, 144
Operation Grapes of Wrath, 243
Operation Iraqi Freedom, 89, 139, 186
Operation Just Cause, 24, 25
Operation Nimrod Dancer, 25
Operation Peace for Galilee, 175
Operation Southern Watch, 180
Osama bin Laden, 182, 184, 185, 186, 193
Ottoman Empire, 27, 28, 30, 47

P

Pablo Escobar, 263, 265, 266
Palestine, 186, 211
Palestine Liberation Organization, 175
Panamanian Defense Forces, 24
Pancho Villa, 26, 27
Paramilitary, 55, 117, 118, 210, 221
Pascual Orozco, 26
Pearl Harbor, 31, 35, 100, 114, 172
Pentagon, xiv, 51, 92, 183, 206, 278, 396
Pentagon Memorial, 187
People for Ethical Treatment of Animals (PETA), 215
Phalange, 175
Philippine-American War, 23, 24, 41
Philosophical radicals, 199
Phineas Priesthood, 214, 215
Phishing, 260, 460
Plan de Guadalupe, 27
Policymakers, 88, 123, 134, 154, 187
Policy of Attraction, 24
Political asylum, 177, 247, 248
Political reverence, 8
Populism, 224, 225
Porfirio Diaz, 25
Posee Comitatus, 221
Postdam Declaration, 32, 314
Post-Katrina Emergency Management Reform Act of
    2006, 155, 280
Power projection, 72, 135
Prescript, 228
Presidential Reorganization Plan No. 3 of 1978, 156
President Jimmy Carter, 156, 162, 328, 349
Primogeniture laws, 7

Prohibition Act, 326
Protecting Cyberspace as a National Asset Act of 2010,
    262
Public policy, x, xxiv, 136

Q

Quadrennial Homeland Security Review (QHSR), 155

R

Radical ideology, 10, 223
Radicalism, 219, 222, 223, 224, 231
Radiological Preparedness Program, 155
Ramzi Ahmed Yousef, 177
Ramzi bin al-Shibh, 185
Random Access Measures, 182
Reagan Doctrine, 35
Reconcentration Policy, 22
Redemption movement, 226
Reign of Terror, 12, 204
Representative government, 11, 26, 37
Republicanism, 7
Revolutionary Armed Forces, 263, 446
Right-wing extremism, 230
Robert G. Doumar, 182
Robert T. Stafford Disaster Relief and Emergency
    Resistance Act, 159, 379
Ruby Ridge Siege, 222
Russian Revolution, 28, 238
Russo-Finnish War, 31, 100

S

Saddam Hussein, 239, 240
SAFE Port Act of 2006, 154, 283, 347
Salafist jihadist, 211, 212
San Bernardino shootings, 252
Satellite states, 32, 80
Sea Shepherd Conservation Society, 217
Second Battle of Bull Run, 20, 97
Second Battle of the Marne, 29
Second Stage Review, 153
Secretary of Homeland Security, 107, 137, 149, 151,
    166, 390, 395, 401
Senate Foreign Relations Committee, 176
Senate Intelligence Committee, 181, 188
Seven Years' War, 3, 14, 94, 95, 127
Shari'a Law, 207, 208
Sheikh Omar Abdel Rahman, 177
Shining Path, Partido Comunista, 263
Signals intelligence (SIGINT), 339, 342, 469
Sitora Yusufiy, 254
Situational reports, 159, 379, 380
Slavery, 6, 7, 96, 392
Social engineering, 260
Socialism, 55, 211, 237
Social law, 7
Son of Malta, 228
Sovereign citizen extremism, 213, 225

Soviet-Afghan War, 184
Spanish-American War, 19, 21, 399
Special interest terrorism, 230, 231
Spoofing, 260
Sputnik, 33, 80, 315
State Disaster Preparedness, 159, 379
State Emergency Operation Center, 159, 379
State of emergency, 156, 159, 380
Strategic Arms Limitation Treaty, 34, 35
Syrian Civil War, 212, 248, 437
Syrian Social National Party, 175

T

Taliban, 143, 195, 209
Tamerlan Tsarnaev, 247
Tampering, 260
Teller Amendment, 22
Tennis Court Oath, 11
Ten Years' War, 22
Terrorism, 23, 24, 73, 83, 169, 170
Terry Nichols, 178, 179
Th3Dir3ctory, 261
The Coalition to Save the Preserves, 215, 219
The Invasion of Panama, 24
The Jefferson Era, 15
The Mexican Revolution, 25
The Oklahoma City Bombing, 123, 178, 222
The Robert T. Stafford Disaster Relief and Emergency
    Assistance Act (Public Law 100–707), 156, 160,
    370, 379
The San Bernardino Shootings, 252
The White House, 82, 93, 275, 285, 289, 291, 329, 350
Thomas Jefferson, 109, 110, 223, 330, 391, 399
Threat modeling, 262
Timothy McVeigh, 178, 179, 195, 334
Title 22 of the United States Code, Section 2656,
    170, 171
Title VI of the Robert T. Stafford Disaster Relief and
    Emergency Assistance Act, Public Law 100–
    107, 160, 370
Tom Ridge, 148, 151, 319, 329, 395, 398
Treaty of Alliance, 14
Treaty of Amity, 14
Treaty of Guadalupe Hidalgo, 25
Treaty of Paris, 3, 5, 7, 14, 23, 40, 41
Trench warfare, 27
Tripartite Pact, 173
Triple Alliance 1882, 27
Twelfth Amendment, 15
Twelfth Battle of the Isonzo River, 28
Twenty-Fourth Air Force, 259

U

Ulysses Grant, 21, 98
Umar Farouk Abdulmutallab, 235
U.N. Commission on Narcotic Drugs, 264
Underwear Bomber, 235, 236
Uniformed Services University of Health Sciences, 234
United Airlines, 184, 194, 290

United Self-Defense of Columbia, 263
United States Code 1030, 262
United States Foreign Intelligence Surveillance Court,
    188
United States Strategic Command (USSTRATCOM),
    108, 259
USA PATRIOT Act, 187, 271, 293
U.S. Constitution, 37, 107, 136, 331
U.S. Department of Defense, 306
U.S. Department of Homeland Security, 417
U.S. Department of State, 263, 306, 330, 398
U.S. Naval Special Warfare Development Group, 209
U.S. Navy Seals, 209
USS Cole bombing, 181, 182, 242
USS Maine, 22, 40
USS Missouri, 32, 101
USS Panay, 172
USS Stark, 181

V

Valeriano Weyler, 22
Versailles Treaty, 29
Vicksburg, 20, 21, 97, 98
Victim Allocation Clarification Act of 1997, 180
Victoriano Huerta, 26
Vulnerabilities, 66, 67, 134, 180, 181

W

Waco Siege, 179
Wahhabi organization, 208
Walter Reed Army Medical Center, 234
Western bloc, 32, 239, 240
Western Civilization, 10, 13, 185, 212, 221,
    226, 250, 265
Whigs, 18, 222
Whiskey Rebellion, 15
White supremacy, 122, 226, 227, 228, 458
William Henry Harrison, 18
Willis Tower, 177
Women's Movement, 9
World Trade Center, 65, 123, 176, 177, 183, 187, 193,
    194, 195
World War I, 297, 299, 324, 459
World War II, 29, 322, 325, 326, 328, 330, 342

Z

Ziad Jarrah, 185

Figure Credits

Fig. 0.1: Source: https://commons.wikimedia.org/wiki/File:Ash_Carter_DOD_Secretary_Portrait.jpg.

Fig. 2.1: Source: https://commons.wikimedia.org/wiki/File:Flickr_-_USCapitol_-_Signing_of_the_Constitution.jpg.

Fig. 2.2: Source: https://commons.wikimedia.org/wiki/File:Harry_S._Truman_-_NARA_-_530677_(cropped2).jpg.

Fig. 2.3: Source: https://commons.wikimedia.org/wiki/File:Helicopters_of_the_170th_and_the_189th_Helicopter_Assault_Companies,_await_the_leading_of_troops_at_Polei_Kleng,_in..._-_NARA_-_531458.tif.

Fig. 2.4: Source: https://commons.wikimedia.org/wiki/File:Reichsparteitag_1935.jpg.

Fig. 2.5: Source: https://commons.wikimedia.org/wiki/File:Photograph_of_President_Truman_at_his_desk_in_the_Oval_Office,_signing_the_National_Security_Act_Amendments_of_1949..._-_NARA_-_200168.tif.

Fig. 2.6: Source: https://commons.wikimedia.org/wiki/File:Vice_President-elect_Alben_W._Barkley_shakes_hands_with_James_V._Forrestal,_with_others_looking_on._-_NARA_-_199940.tif.

Fig. 2.7: Source: https://commons.wikimedia.org/wiki/File:US_Navy_051128-N-2383B-013_An_aerial_view_of_the_headquarters_of_the_United_States_Department_of_Defense_located_between_the_Potomac_River_and_Arlington_National_Cemetery.jpg.

Fig. 2.8: Source: https://commons.wikimedia.org/wiki/File:EXCOMM_meeting,_Cuban_Missile_Crisis,_29_October_1962.jpg.

Fig. 3.1a: Source: https://commons.wikimedia.org/wiki/File:Congressman_William_F._Nichols_Official_Portrait,_1986.jpg.

Fig. 3.1b: Source: https://commons.wikimedia.org/wiki/File:Secretary_Adams_and_Barry_Goldwater.jpg.

Fig. 3.2: Source: https://commons.wikimedia.org/wiki/File:General_George_Washington_at_Trenton_by_John_Trumbull.jpeg.

Fig. 4.1: Adapted from: Stanford University, "Conceptual Framework for State Analysis," https://web.stanford.edu/group/ncpi/unspecified/assessment_states/framework.html. Copyright © 2003 by National Center for Postsecondary Improvement.

Fig. 4.2: Source: https://commons.wikimedia.org/wiki/File:Naturalization_Ceremony_(27691778085).jpg.

Fig. 5.1: Source: https://commons.wikimedia.org/wiki/File:DHS_S_W.png.

Fig. 5.2: Source: https://commons.wikimedia.org/wiki/File:Immigration_and_Customs_Enforcement_(US)_badge_-_Special_Agent.jpg.

Fig. 5.3: Source: https://commons.wikimedia.org/wiki/File:Tom_Ridge.jpg.

Fig. 5.4: Source: https://commons.wikimedia.org/wiki/File:Michael_Chertoff,_official_DHS_photo_portrait,_2007.jpg.

Fig. 5.5: Source: https://commons.wikimedia.org/wiki/File:Janet_Napolitano_official_portrait.jpg.

Fig. 5.6: Source: https://commons.wikimedia.org/wiki/File:Jeh_Johnson_official_DHS_portrait.jpg.

Fig. 5.7: Source: https://commons.wikimedia.org/wiki/File:John_Kelly_official_DHS_portrait.jpg.

Fig. 5.8: Source: https://commons.wikimedia.org/wiki/File:Elaine_Duke_official_photo.jpg.

Fig. 5.9: Source: https://www.publicsafety.gc.ca/cnt/rsrcs/pblctns/mrgnc-mngmnt-pnnng/index-en.aspx#figure_1.

Fig. 6.1: Source: https://commons.wikimedia.org/wiki/File:Photograph_of_a_small_boat_rescuing_a_seaman_from_the_burning_USS_West_Virginia_in_Pearl_Harbor_-_NARA_-_306532.jpg.

Fig. 6.2: Source: https://commons.wikimedia.org/wiki/File:Fdr_delivers_speech.jpg.

Fig. 6.3: Source: https://commons.wikimedia.org/wiki/File:BombenanschlagUS-BotschaftBeirut.jpg.

Fig. 6.4: Source: https://commons.wikimedia.org/wiki/File:FEMA_-_1547_-_Photograph_by_FEMA_News_Photo_taken_on_04-26-1995_in_Oklahoma.jpg.

Fig. 6.5: Source: https://commons.wikimedia.org/wiki/File:The_front_of_Bldg._131.JPG.

Fig. 6.6: Source: https://commons.wikimedia.org/wiki/File:USS_Cole_(DDG-67)_Departs.jpg.

Fig. 6.7: Source: https://commons.wikimedia.org/wiki/File:September_17_2001_Ground_Zero_02.jpg.

Fig. 7.1: Source: https://commons.wikimedia.org/wiki/File:Army_mil-55717-2009-11-11-091126.jpg.